Compendium on the Diaconate:

A Resource for the Formation, Ministry, and Life of Permanent Deacons

Edited by Enzo Petrolino

Libreria Editrice Vaticana

United States Conference of Catholic Bishops

Washington, DC

The editor thanks Fr. Edmondo Caruana for his collaboration in preparing this work.

Title of the Italian: *Enchiridion sul Diaconato: Le Fonti e i Documenti Ufficiali della Chiesa.* LEV, 2009.

First printing, May 2015

ISBN 978-1-60137-503-2

Contents

Acronymns and Abbreviations xi

Note on Translation xiii

Introduction 1

The Biblical-Patristic Roots of the Diaconate 9

Chapter I: The Scriptural Sources 15

Chapter II: The Patristic Sources 23

A. The Fathers of the Church from the First and Second Centuries .. 23

Clement of Rome (ca. 96) 23
Ignatius of Antioch (70–107) 24
Polycarp of Smyrna (ca. 69–155) 30
Hermas (ca. 140) 31
Justin (ca. 100–ca. 165) 32
Irenaeus of Lyons (ca. 130–ca. 202) 33

B. The Fathers of the Third Century: The School of Alexandria 35

Clement of Alexandria (ca. 150–ca. 215) 35
Origen (185–254) 36
Dionysius of Alexandria (190–265) 41
Firmilian of Caesarea (died ca. 268) 42

C. The Latin Fathers from the Third Century 44

Tertullian (ca. 150–ca. 220) 44
Passion of Perpetua and Felicity (ca. 203) 45

Cyprian of Carthage (ca. 210–ca. 258) ... 45
Commodian (ca. Third–Fifth Century) ... 47
Fabian (?–250) ... 48
Cornelius of Rome (?–253) ... 49

D. Eastern Fathers of the Fourth Century ... 50

Eusebius of Caesarea (ca. 265–ca. 340) ... 50
Pseudo-Athanasius ... 51
Cyril of Jerusalem (ca. 315–386) ... 52
Cyril and John of Jerusalem (? 315) ... 53
John Chrysostom (ca. 344/354–ca. 398/407) ... 55
Theodore of Mopsuestia (ca. 350–428) ... 58
Theodoret of Cyrus (ca. 393–ca. 457) ... 59
Pseudo-Dionysius (The Areopagite) ... 60
Egeria ... 67

E. The Cappadocian Fathers ... 70

Gregory of Nazianzus (330–390) ... 70
Gregory of Nyssa (ca. 332–394) ... 72
Basil (ca. 329–379) ... 73

F. The Latin Fathers of the Fourth Century ... 74

Passion of Euplius the Deacon (304) ... 74
Ambrose (339–397) ... 76
Jerome (ca. 347–419) ... 77
Pseudo-Jerome ... 78
Augustine (354–430) ... 78
Maximus of Turin (ca. 350–423) ... 82
Leo the Great (?–461) ... 84

G. Canonical-Liturgical Literature ... 86

Didache (First Century) ... 86
Didascalia of the Apostles (Third Century) ... 87
Apostolic Tradition (ca. 215) ... 93
Ecclesiastical Canons of the Same Holy Apostles (Third Century) ... 96
Testamentum Domini ... 98

H. The Apocrypha 102

Pseudo-Clementines (Third Century) 102
Revelation of Paul (Fourth Century) 104
I. Ordination Prayers of the Third Century 105

Chapter III: The Diaconate in the Councils of the Fourth Century 108

Council of Elvira (Spain, 306–309) 108
Council of Arles (Provence, 314) 109
Ecumenical Council of Nicaea (Bithynia, Asia Minor, 325) 109

Chapter IV: The Diaconate in the Documents of the Council of Trent and of Vatican II 110

Council of Trent 110

Council of Trent (Session 23: July 15, 1563) 110

Second Vatican Council 111

The Diaconate in the Debates of the Council 112
The Diaconate in the Documents of Vatican II 122

Chapter V: The Diaconate in the Pontifical Magisterium 130

Leo XIII 130
Pius XII 131
John XXIII 132
Paul VI 132
John Paul II 153
Benedict XVI 193

Chapter VI: The Diaconate in the Documents of the Holy See ... 205

Congregation for Catholic Education (for Seminaries and Educational Institutions) ... 205

Circular Letter on the Diaconate ... 205

***Codex Iuris Canonici* (*Code of Canon Law*)** ... 209

***Catechism of the Catholic Church* (2nd edition)** ... 211

Pontifical Council for the Promotion of Christian Unity ... 213

Directory for the Application of Principles and Norms on Ecumenism ... 213

Congregation for Divine Worship and the Discipline of the Sacraments ... 217

Circular Letter (*June 6, 1997*) ... 217

Congregation for Catholic Education ... 219

Pontifical Work for Ecclesiastical Vocations ... 219

Congregation for Catholic Education, Congregation for the Clergy 221

Basic Norms for the Formation of Permanent Deacons ... 222

Directory for the Ministry and Life of Permanent Deacons ... 222

Congregation for Catholic Education ... 230

Ratio Fundamentalis Institutionis Diaconorum Permanentium (Basic Norms for the Formation of Permanent Deacons) ... 230

Congregation for the Clergy ... 263

Directorium pro Ministerio et Vita Diaconorum Permanentium (Directory for the Ministry and Life of Permanent Deacons) ... 263

Congregation for the Clergy 309

Instruction *The Priest, Pastor, and Leader of the Parish Community* 309

International Theological Commission 312

From the *Diakonia* of Christ to the *Diakonia* of the Apostles* 312

Congregation for Bishops 408

Apostolorum Successores (Directory for the Pastoral Ministry of Bishops) 408

Congregation for Divine Worship and the Discipline of the SacramentS 416

Instruction *Redemptionis Sacramentum* (On Certain Matters to be Observed or to be Avoided Regarding the Most Holy Eucharist) 416

VII International Congress for the Pastoral Care of Circus and Traveling Show People 421

Synod of Bishops, XII Ordinary General Assembly 422

Instrumentum Laboris The Word of God in the Life and Mission of the Church 422

Appendix: National Directory for the Formation, Ministry, and Life of Permanent Deacons in the United States 425

ACRONYMNS AND ABBREVIATIONS

Bibliographical Sources

AAS: *Acta Apostolicae Sedis*, (Vatican City, 1909)

ASS: *Acta Sanctae Sedis*, (Rome, 1865-1908)

CA: *Constitutiones Apostolorum*

CCE: *Catechismus Catholicae Ecclesiae*

CSCO: *Corpus Scriptorum Christianorum Orientalium*

CSEL: *Corpus Scriptorum Ecclesiasticorum Latinorum* (Vienna, 1866)

DA: *Didascalia Apostolorum*

DS: Denzinger-Schönmetzer, *Enchiridion Symbolorum, Definitionum et Declarationum de Rebus Fidei et Morum*

EV: *Enchidirion Vaticanum*, vol 1-10, (Bologna: Edizioni Dehoniane Bologna [EDB], 1976)

Insegnamenti: *Insegnamenti* of Paul VI, VIII-XVI, (Vatican City: LEV)

PG: *Patrologiae Cursus Completus,* Part II, Greek and Oriental series (*Patrologia Graeco-Latina*), ed. Jacques-Paul Migne, 1857-1886

PL: *Patrologiae Cursus Completus*, Part I, Latin series (*Patrologia Latina*), ed. Jacques-Paul Migne, 1844-1855

S[AE]: Veronese Sacramentary, Sahidic Version, Ethiopian

SCh: Sources Chrétiennes (Paris, 1942)

Documents of the Second Vatican Council

AA: Decree *Apostolicam Actuositatem*

AG: Decree *Ad Gentes*

CD: Decree *Christus Dominus*

DV: Dogmatic Constitution *Dei Verbum*

GS: Pastoral Constitution *Gaudium et Spes*

LG: Dogmatic Constitution *Lumen Gentium*

OE: Decree *Orientalium Ecclesiarum*

PO: Decree *Presbyterorum Ordinis*

SC: Constitution *Sacrosanctum Concilium*

UR: Decree *Unitatis Redintegratio*

Documents of the Holy See

AP: Paul VI, Apostolic Letter, Moto Proprio *Ad Pascendum*

CCC: Catechism of the Catholic Church

CIC: *Codex Iuris Canonici*

PDV: *Pastores Dabo Vobis*

SDO: *Sacrum Diaconatus Ordinem* Paul VI, Apostolic Letter

NOTE ON TRANSLATION

This edition of the Italian compendium, *Enchiridion sul Diaconato*, makes use of various English texts. The introduction by Enzo Petrolino and shorter introductory notes that precede scholarly work have been newly translated from the original Italian. Translations of theological and ancient historical texts are from sources in the public domain. The translations of many patristic texts are taken from a 38-volume collection of writings of the early Church Fathers in the public domain: *Ante-Nicene Fathers*, edited by Alexander Roberts, and *Nicene and Post-Nicene Fathers*, Series 1 and Series 2, edited by Philip Schaff. In some cases, parenthetical terms included in the Italian compendium were added to the English translation. For example, New Testament quotations contain Greek terms related to the diaconate in parentheses.

When text was unavailable in the public domain or inaccessible in English for other reasons, a new translation of the Italian text has been provided, retaining italics and Italian citations; the translation is noted in a bracketed footnote. More recent texts from the Holy See that are available in English are reprinted here with permission.

Shorter excerpts from scholarly sources generally do not include the original footnotes; this is in keeping with the style in the Italian compendium. Longer texts that are printed in full—such as the International Theological Commission text—contain the original footnotes.

In some instances, capitalization has been modernized or modified slightly. Titles are generally capitalized according to the American norm. In text from the public domain, words not customarily capitalized (e.g., "priest," "deacon," "bishop," and pronouns referring to God) may now appear in lowercase, while others (e.g., "Apostles," "Catholic") may now appear capitalized. Original italics from the Italian compendium and from English source texts were preserved whenever possible. Section titles from patristic sources frequently retain the title given in the Italian compendium, rather than the section title from the English source text.

Introduction

The goal of this volume is to offer a collection of fundamental texts for understanding the roots of the diaconate, understanding its ministerial specificity and its potential for development in today's world as well as the Church's pastoral care. The scriptural and patristic sources, documents of the councils and of the Holy See, and the Pontifical Magisterium until Pope Benedict XVI point out the long, gradual course of diaconal ministry up to our time, highlight its most significant steps, and open the way to reflection, research, and depth of understanding.

In these last years there has arisen a growing theological-pastoral interest in *ministerial service* and *ministries* in the Church, with a particular emphasis on the *diaconal ministry*. Such interest has found its most thorough examination in conciliar and post-conciliar reflection that today has led to renewed attention toward the role deacons have in the Church.

In the whole ministerial Church, the Council affirms, "That divine mission, entrusted by Christ to the apostles, will last until the end of the world. . . . Thus, as St. Irenaeus testifies, through those who were appointed bishops by the apostles, and through their successors down in our own time, the Apostolic Tradition is manifested and preserved throughout the world. With their helpers, the priests and deacons, bishops have therefore taken up the service of the community."[1] And then it adds: "Thus the divinely established ecclesiastical ministry is exercised on different levels by those who from antiquity have been called bishops, priests and deacons."[2] The Church, therefore, is herself *ministry, service, diaconia*; and in her the essence of *ordained* ministry of the diaconate consists in not being at the service of one aspect or of one particular sector of the Church's mission and community but of the whole ensemble that its energy and vitality characterizes. Vatican II, a prevalently pastoral Council, with its ecclesiology of communion centered on *Lumen Gentium*, establishes unmistakably that

1 Cf. Second Vatican Ecumenical Council, Dogmatic Constitution on the Church, *Lumen Gentium* (LG), no. 20.

2 LG, no. 28.

diaconal ministry[3] should be reborn in the Church as a proper ministry and not only as a stage for candidates to the priesthood. The conciliar document treats the diaconate in the context of chapter 3 (no. 29), where it talks about the *hierarchical constitution of the Church*, establishing that such a ministry can be conferred on both celibate and married men. The placement of the diaconate within Orders is emphasized with reference to the *laying on of hands* and to *sacramental grace*, which underscores—even if prudently—the *sacramentality* of the diaconate. In any case, this indication emerges from the whole of the written conciliar proceedings, which does see the placement of the diaconate as within Orders, as a true part—even if in an *inferior degree*—of the *sacred ministries.* The expression "inferior" used in *Lumen Gentium* reflects a current terminology consecrated by use and by law at that time. Subsequent research has preferred expressions that favor the specificity of the various ministries rather than the superiority or inferiority of the degree. In the Constitution, terms are used that clearly express the three traditional degrees of hierarchical Orders: *Episcopate, Presbyterate,* and *Diaconate.* The three-part articulation of the Sacrament of Orders is affirmed time and again in *Lumen Gentium.* The conciliar text, speaking about the service of the bishops,[4] affirms that it is exercised with the help of priests and of deacons. Again it underlines that the "ecclesial ministry" of divine institution from ancient times has been exercised through the various orders: bishops, priests.[5]

It is the successive and important affirmation of the conciliar Constitution that deacons receive the laying on of hands *not for the priesthood but for service,*[6] inasmuch as, *sustained by sacramental grace in the ministry of the liturgy, of preaching and of charity, they serve the People of God in communion with the*

3 Cf. LG, no. 29.

4 Cf. LG, no. 28.

5 Cf. LG, no. 28.

6 The expression is taken from the *Apostolic Tradition* compiled by Hippolytus in 235 BC. In the preface to the ordination rite he says that the deacon receives "the laying on of hands of the bishop alone, because the deacon is ordained not to priesthood but to the service of the bishop." The conciliar document, then, excludes the deacon being at the service of the bishop as stated in the *Apostolic Tradition*, unless Hippolytus' text be interpreted according to the suggestion of J. Colson (*La fonction diaconal aux origines de l'église*, Desclée 1960, 99. He says that "*the deacon is not ordained to the priestly function of the bishop, but to his diaconal function. . . . He in fact does not participate in the counsel of the priests, but administers and points out to the bishop what is necessary, nor does he receive the common Spirit in which all presbyters participate, but that which is conferred to him by the power of the bishop. Only for this does the bishop ordain the deacon.*" According to the author, therefore, the deacon is not ordained to the service of the bishop but to carry out one of the ministerial dimensions of the bishop, which is that of *serving* the Church.

bishop and his priests; such an assertion confirms on the one hand the whole tradition that excludes the diaconate from priestly functions and, on the other, places the ministry of deacons as "intermediary between that of the bishop and that of priests with the rest of the People of God." Consequently, the formula *sustained by sacramental grace* states how the deacon is made capable for his functions thanks to a sacramental virtue. The conciliar text then lists the three fundamental functions, even giving their specific applications.

The *Dogmatic Constitution on the Church* contains another particularly interesting reference to the diaconate. In chapter 5,[7] in the context of the universal call to holiness, it is said that the deacons' striving for a life of holiness derives above all from their specific participation in the *supreme mission and grace of the High Priest.* The Council has thus identified the "peculiarity" of the deacon in his "service" to the "mysteries of Christ and of the Church."

In other conciliar texts[8] we find reference to the diaconate as well, especially in *Ad Gentes* (*Decree on the Church's Missionary Activity*). This text understands the supernatural sensitivity expressed by the Council in reference to "sacramental grace," inserting the permanent ministry of the deacon within the plurality of the ministries called forth by the Spirit of God in his People, confirming and reinforcing a service that is in fact already exercised. In the context of the chapter that deals with the structure of the local Church, the document[9] lists the various *truly diaconal* ministries: from the prophetical one of the Word, to the pastoral and charitable-social. In order, however, to carry out such a ministry in a fruitful way, the decree on missions underlines the importance of the laying on of hands, which puts the deacon in a tighter relationship with the altar. In this "visible" relationship of the deacon with the liturgical ministry we can see clearly how the essential dimension of the deacon should be: it is in service to

7 Cf. LG, no. 41.

8 We found mentions of the diaconate in other conciliar texts also (cf. CD, no. 15; DV, no. 25; SC, nos. 35, 68). The deacon is again placed in communion with the bishop and his priest and with his ministry is made an instrument of solid communion of the Hierarchy with the rest of the People of God. The Council has furthermore called attention to the concern and continuous contact that the deacons must have for and with the Scriptures, preparing them for other ministries of the Word. Precisely for this reason they are called to "direct" the celebrations of the Word of God as a guide. *Sacrosanctum Concilium* contains another point where it is remembered that the deacon is an ordinary minister of Baptism.

9 Cf. Second Vatican Ecumenical Council, Decree on the Church's Missionary Activity, *Ad Gentes* (AG), no. 16, in *Enchiridion Vaticanum, I Documenti Ufficiali del Concilio Vaticano II (1962-65)*, Dehoniane, Bologna 1979, no 16.

the liturgy and in particular to that of the Eucharist that he finds the lifeblood for his ministry and not simply one of the many activities linked to it.

A global interpretation of the ecclesiology of Vatican II leads to a clearer explanation of the steps for diaconate. Founded on "mystery" and "sacrament," it emphasizes the vision of the Church as communion, community, and communication. The very conciliar texts on the diaconate substantially express this reality, placing this ministry in the root of the mystery of the Church's communion and in its sacramental reality. This reflection will give birth to consequence that will be made more explicit further on, when we speak concretely about the exercise of the diaconal duties.

A new season for the diaconate begins with the Council, and a vital and laborious journey starts on two fronts: on the one hand, the normative deepening of understanding on the part of the Holy See and of the episcopal conferences, and on the other the awareness of the communities that open themselves, even if slowly, to welcoming this ministry.

With regard to the conciliar texts, the pontifical document *Sacrum Diaconatus Ordinem*[10] takes up the duties indicated within it, bringing to them some innovation. Among the functions of the diaconate is added that of *guide of scattered communities.* Such a perspective, as we shall see, will open new, not-yet fully explored horizons for parish communities. Furthermore, it gives directives on the formation of "young" or "adult" candidates, marking out the minimum age for ordination: twenty-five years for single men, thirty for married men. The remaining issues concerning the restoration of the diaconate are delegated to the episcopal conference of the various countries.

In the intervening period between the Ecumenical Council and the *Motu Proprio*, Pope Paul VI makes two pronouncements on the diaconate.[11] In both discourses there is above all the exhortation to put the conciliar provisions into practice in order to further understand the deacon's mission, whether single or married, and at the same time to offer candidates an adequate formation. At the

10 Paul VI, *Sacrum Diaconatus Ordinem* (June 18, 1967) in *Enchiridion Vaticanum, I Documenti Ufficiali del Concilio Vaticano II (1962-65),* Dehoniane (Bologna, 1979). The document, after a preface referring to number 29 of LG and to number 16 of AG, is subdivided into eight chapters: I. The Competencies of Bishops Surrounding Permanent Diaconate; II. Young Deacons; III. Deacons of Mature Age; IV. Incardination and Support of Deacons; V. Duties and Deacons; VI. Spiritual Life and Responsibilities of Deacons; VII. The Diaconate Among Religious; VIII. Discipline in the Ordination of Deacons.

11 One to the members of the First International Congress on the Diaconate (October 25, 1965) and the other to those of the Study Commission for the Permanent Diaconate (February 24, 1967).

same time the pope urges the restoration of the diaconate in the Latin Church to take place in charity, in such a way that the presence of the deacon might enrich not only the ministerial order but also the community at large. The way in which Paul VI sees the presence of the deacon, united with meekness and affection to his own bishop, is highly significant. It also underlines the spirit of service that should characterize the deacon himself, who "is defined precisely by service and, in service, finds his configuration to Christ who, as Matthew says (20:28), 'came not to be served, but to serve.'" This is truly a duty of great force, because through the deacon the sign of the Church's duty finds its expression: placing oneself at the service of the world. The profile of the diaconal ministry is even better delineated in the document *Apostolic Letter Establishing Some Norms Concerning the Sacred Order of Deacons* (*Ad Pascendum*).[12] Here Paul VI reiterates that the deacon is "a driving force for the Church's service or *diakonia* toward the local Christian communities, and . . . a sign or sacrament of the Lord Christ himself."

Although John Paul II made no explicit document on the diaconate, we can certainly refer widely to some of the pope's discourses given during encounters with deacons. Of special significance are those directed to deacons from Italy and from the United States.[13]

Among the many aspects highlighted by the pope, one that carries particular weight is the affirmation that the deacon is the *sacramentalized* service of the Church. Precisely because of this we cannot deal with it as just one among many ministries, but rather, as Pope Paul VI was saying, this ministry should truly be a "moving force" for the *diakonia* of the Church. Considering the profound spiritual nature of this *diakonia*, it is possible to better understand the relationship between the three ministerial areas of the deacon as minister of the Word, of the liturgy, and of charity. John Paul II also speaks of a "special witness" that deacons are called to give in society, precisely because their *secular occupation* allows access to the temporal sphere in a special way that is normally not available to other members of the clergy. In the same way, the married deacon offers a considerable contribution to the transformation of family life through the grace of the double sacramentality that marks his ministry. It is also especially significant

12 Paul VI, *Ad Pascendum* (August 15, 1972), in *Enchiridion Vaticanum, I Documenti Ufficiali del Concilio Vaticano II (1971-73)* (Dehoniane: Bologna, 1979).

13 Discourse held by John Paul II for the episcopal delegates for the permanent diaconate and for the deacons promoted to the Episcopal Commission for the Clergy, of the Italian Bishop's Conference, Rome, March 15, 1985; Discourse held for U.S. deacons on September 19, 1987.

that there is emphasis on the involvement of the wife of a deacon in her husband's public ministry in the Church, carried out through *the enrichment and deepening of sacrificial love between husband and wife.*

Reference to the ordination rite, then, binds the deacon to a spiritual formation that will last his whole life, in such a way that there be growth and perseverance in his service that will truly edify the people of God.

The pope dealt with the theme of the diaconate systematically in a short series of Wednesday catecheses.[14] On the occasion of the Plenary Assembly of the Congregation for the Clergy, which examined an *Instrumentum laboris* with the intention of preparing a document concerning the life and ministry of permanent deacons similar to that for priests, John Paul II held a discourse[15] that constitutes an important contribution to shaping the diaconal ministry. With his starting point as conciliar doctrine—which later found its juridical expression in the *Code of Canon Law*—the pope openly hopes for an attentive theological investigation and a prudent pastoral direction in the light of acquired experience, having the New Evangelization on the horizon at the threshold of the third millennium. The pope sums up all that can refer to the life and ministry of deacons in a single word: *faithfulness.* That means *faithfulness to the Catholic Tradition* given witness to by the *lex orandi; faithfulness to the Magisterium; faithfulness to undertaking re-evangelization.*

All of this requires a challenging promotion in every environment of the Church for "*a sincere respect for the theological, liturgical, canonical, and theological identity proper to the sacrament conferred on deacons.*"

Leading with this affirmation, the pope offers some seeds of reflection, keeping in mind the present situation of deacons in the Universal Church.

In the first place, with the Sacrament of Orders, the deacon receives a special "configuration to Christ Servant, Head and Shepherd of the Church" through the laying on of hands of the bishop and the specific prayer of consecration.

The deacon thus is no longer a layman nor can be "reduced" to the lay state in the strict sense. He was ordained specifically for this: for the *exercise of a ministry proper to him* that requires a *spiritual availability of complete dedication.* That means that there are no "part-time" deacons, inasmuch as they are "ministers of

14 The pope held these catecheses on October 6, 13, and 20 of 1993 (*L'Osservatore Romano*, October 7, 14, and 21 of 1993, 4).

15 Cf. John Paul II, discourse held on November 30, 1995, on the occasion of the Plenary Assembly of the Congregation for the Clergy, in *L'Osservatore Romano*, CXXXV (1995), a77, 5.

the Church" to full effect. Diaconate is not a *profession*, but a *mission*! It is in this light and from this perspective that the problems still existing and not few in number are being examined, linked to the need to make involvement in church service compatible with other obligations (*family, professional, social, etc.*).

To carry out his mission in a full, authentic way, the deacon must necessarily have a *profound interior life* through an intense life of prayer that unites him to Christ and allows him to reconcile the exercise of his ministerial activities with other professional, family, and social duties.

While keeping their own identity and specific juridical value, two documents are brought into consideration and complement each other by reason of their logical continuity: the *Basic Norms for the Formation of Permanent Deacons* and the *Directory for the Ministry and Life of Permanent Deacons*, promulgated respectively by the Congregation for the Clergy and by the Congregation for Catholic Education.

The documents respond to the urgency noticed on many fronts to clarify and regulate the diversity of existing experiences, both on the level of discernment or of preparation, and on the level of ministerial updating and of permanent formation.

Such a demand has also been motivated by the fact that, following the restoration of the diaconate desired by Vatican II, in many ecclesiastical regions there is a veritable "*explosion*" of diaconal vocations,[16] a sign of the enthusiasm and hope that it has stirred.

Finally, the text of the document of the International Theological Commission (ITC), *From the Diakonia of Christ to the Diakonia of the Apostles*, constitutes a significant expression of the theological reflection on the diaconate and represents a considerable contribution to acquiring a more mature awareness of the diaconal ministry in the post-conciliar Church. In continuity with Tradition and with the fruits maturing from Vatican II to the present, the document enters into dialogue with the today of our history and opens up to further understanding and research.

---

16 It suffices to read the currently available statistical data: from a total of 25,122 deacons in 1998, North America alone accounted for a little more than half, or rather 12,801 (50.9 percent), while Europe had 7,864 (31.3 percent); for the industrialized nations of the northern hemisphere that represents a total of 20,665 deacons (82.2 percent). The remaining 17.8 percent is divided thus: South America, 2,370 (9.4 percent); Central America and the Antilles, 1,387 (5.5 percent); Africa, 307 (1.22 percent); Asia, 219 (0.87 percent). Oceania closes the list with 174 deacons, 0.69 percent of the total.

Surely this document's publication is further proof that the restoration of the diaconate is one of the most beautiful gifts that the Spirit has made to the Church with the Second Vatican Council. Just as in the first centuries of the Church, it is now undergoing a marvelous revival. In reality, it is at present the only vocation seeing growth.

The challenge we are being given today is for a continued depth of theological-pastoral understanding aimed at promoting specific conditions of comprehension and of growth so that this vocation may be ever more an authentic expression of *communality* and of *diakonia* in the Church and of the Church.

The diaconate is an "ecclesial event" that is carried out with prophetic courage but also with the required discernment and depth of understanding, all within the framework of an authentic renewal of the whole life of the Church. It is a fascinating journey that brings with it the joyous labor of planting; an ever new journey, possible and certainly fertile, if the efforts of all converge to make that communion, which in the Church is the most authentic fruit of the presence of the Spirit, grow.

Enzo Petrolino

The Biblical-Patristic Roots of the Diaconate

1. The Biblical Sources of the Diaconate

The biblical sources, while confirming as certain the ministerial presence of deacons and of other collaborators starting with Paul (see Phil 1:1), do not give us exact information on the precise duties they performed or on the effective role they played in the heart of the local community in the work of evangelization, of formation, or of liturgical celebrations (cf. Ti 1:5-9; 2 Tm 2:24-26; 1 Pt 5:1-3; 2 Cor 1:24). We only know that deacons were considered ministers of a local church, with responsibilities of governing that were not well defined, placed next to the presbyter-bishops, as companions in the work of evangelization and associated with filling in the role left behind by the Apostles (cf. 1 Thes 3:2; Col 1:7). We can form a vague idea through the indications of the various collaborators that Paul makes mention of in his letters: something a little more precise. The instructions given by Paul to Timothy give us a glimpse into their function (1 Tm 3:8-13) and into the criteria of discernment to follow for their suitability for candidacy to the ordained deaconhood.

In the first Christian communities the *diakonía* was not always considered an ethical imperative but the fruit of the conformation to Christ that the Spirit was operating in the believers. In this context we can grasp the sense of that "diaconal" climate that had rather quickly led the Jerusalemite community to institute the "Seven" for the "service of the tables," as is related by Luke (cf. Acts 6:1-6), to collaborate in the daily *diakonía* on behalf of the Greek-speaking poor. This passage, recalled in the diaconal ordination prayer and by magisterial documents, is presented by a strong ecclesial tradition as the historical place of the institution of deacons. From an exegetical point of view this identification is, in reality, very controversial.[1] Still, the Lucan account is enlightening as it reveals the Christian anthropology that inspires and sustains the "diaconal sense" of the origins, almost as if caught in the very act of its emergence and of its institutional formation.

It is right in the Eucharistic celebration of the Palestinian communities that it seems best to place the nascent theology of New Testament *diakonía.* It elaborates various forms of service as a debt of justice toward the unmerited love poured out by God in our hearts that is given in witness to our fellow man and to the poor (cf. Acts 11:27-30). Thus the diaconate is the actual sharing of that attitude of service given witness to by Christ who made himself obedient to the point of being bread broken and wine poured.

2. The Biblical-Theological Meaning of *Diakonía*

If the New Testament books do not offer exhaustive information on the actual duties of deacons and their role in the Church, they do give us many significant

1 Cf. G. Bella, *Il diaconato permanente alle origini della Chiesa*, in "Seminarium" no. 4 (2008), 649-686.

The first thing that strikes us is that Luke, even while writing in a time when the "deacons" already existed as an institution in the Church (cf. Phil 1:1), does not at all use such a term to designate the "seven" nor the corresponding "*diakonía*" to express their specific service. In fact, "*diakonía*" can equally mean either the charitable duty on behalf of the widows of the Greek-speaking community (v. 2), or the duty of "preaching" (*diakonía tou lógou*: v. 4), which the Apostles hold especially bound with their mission. This fluctuation in terms seems to mean, according to many exegetes, that for St. Luke, those famous "seven," whose names he even lists for us, do not correspond to what would later be true and proper "deacons" as a ministerial body in the Church.

In reality it seems that the first person to see true and proper "deacons" in the "seven," in the sense of ordained ministers for the service of charity, was St. Irenaeus around AD 180. The other ancient writers, while speaking frequently about deacons, do not link them to the "seven" presented in the Acts of the Apostles. For a bibliography on this subject, see the commentary by G. Schneider, *Die Apostolgeschichte*, 1. Teil (Herders Theologischer Kommentar zum N.T.) (Freiburg-Basel-Wien, 1980), 417-419.

indications about the nature and meaning of diaconate,[2] a term that takes on several meanings in Scripture:[3]

- Service rendered on behalf of others, individually or collectively
- Charitable service of collections for the poor
- Above all, the missionary and prophetic ministry of the Word, or of the Gospel, which is also the ministry of the new covenant (2 Cor 3:6) and the glorious *diakonía* of the spirit (2 Cor 3:8), for reconciliation with God in Christ
- And, finally, it even expresses the different forms of apostolic ministry, indicating all forms of service in the community (1 Cor 12:5)

Christian *diakonía* thus assumes a double meaning: it can indicate a disciple's special way of being in his relationship with the brothers and sisters and to "outsiders" and, at the same time, the work and duties of those who carry out a service within the community. Since the sub-apostolic period, these duties seem to be structured into three large ministerial dimensions: the *diakonía* of the Word, the *diakonía* of Communion, and the liturgical-charitable *diakonía*.

In Scripture, then, *diakonía* and diaconal sentiment, service and *kénosis*, act of worship and agapic activity all draw on each other, revealing, with the self-annihilation of God in Christ, a historical sign of the *diakonía* of the disciple who continues, in time, the salvific action of the Lord toward the marginalized and the poor.

Thus, alongside the common *diakonía* of every baptized person, as fruit of that sanctification brought about by the Spirit of Christ, we find the specific and sacramental one of the minister.

---

2 In Scripture, the frequent use of the lexical group *diakonéo* recurs thirty-six times in the New Testament: twenty-one in the synoptic Gospels and Acts, eight in the Pauline corpus, three in John and in 1 Peter, and one time in Hebrews. From the original meaning of serving at the table or for the poor (Mt 22:13; Mk 1:31; Lk 12:37, 17:8, 22:26ff.; Jn 2:5, 9, 12:2) or for procuring food (Mt 4:11; Lk 10:40; Acts 6:2), it later means any form of assistance given to a hungry or thirsty person, to someone in need of lodging, to the naked, the sick, or the imprisoned (Mt 25:42-44), to finally meaning an attitude of openness, of welcome, or of availability to one's brother first and to the poor and needy after—actions proper to one who, imitating the very behavior of the Master, takes on a service-oriented attitude for others (Mk 1:13, 15:41; Mt 27:55; Lk 8:3; Acts 6:1; Rom 12:7; Phil 13; 1 Pt 4:11).

3 The noun recurs thirty-three times: twenty-two in the Pauline Letters, eight in Acts, one in Lk 10:40; Heb 1:14; and Rev 2:19.

3. The Patristic *Traditio* on the Diaconate

After the Apostolic Fathers the diaconate is much more richly documented and given witness to as regards the sacramental nature of its ecclesial function, its presence and spread in the different churches of the first centuries, the human and spiritual qualities demanded of deacons, their actual duties within and outside the communities, the rites and prayers of ordination, their ecclesiastical and family status, as well as some thorny questions arising from their activity, which, while generous and proactive was at times judged to be in their self-interest and invasive, to the point that it was considered challenging to or conflicting with the other degrees of ordination.

Within this framework we learn how deacons, always present in all of the communities from their foundations, were believed to derive from the Apostolic Tradition itself, being established from the beginning according to various customs of commitment and testimony within and outside the Church. The *Shepherd of Hermas*, for example, considers the help lent to those in need to be a *diakonía* conferred on all disciples, but at the same time holding that bishops and deacons have a special responsibility in carrying out charitable service.

In the following centuries, already from the time of the pre-Constantinian church, the duties and tasks assigned to deacons continue increasing, diversifying according to various ecclesial and social contexts. We know that they are helping the bishops with preaching and with distributing the Eucharist, accompanying them on journeys and serving them as secretaries and messengers. Their collaboration with the *diakonía* of worship and charity gradually increased until becoming institutionalized, becoming a defined form of liturgical and assisting *diakonía* and, in many cases, one could say, of true social service. They are specifically requested to be "the eye, the ear, the mouth and the heart of the bishop" in the local church, being called to know the all of the faithful personally, especially the neediest and most marginalized. In particular, they are to take care of orphans and widows, bringing their needs to the thoughtful attention of the bishop and the community.

Among the main charitable tasks entrusted to deacons, there is indeed no lack of true public assistance work. Here are some of these binding tasks:

- Caring for the sick and the elderly at home
- Assisting widows and orphans, foreigners and the needy

- The responsibility of visiting and comforting persecuted brethren in prison
- The pious duty of undertaker to wash, anoint, and bury the dead
- Availability to host outsiders who offered certain guarantees
- The obligation of aiding the unfortunate and needy on the streets
- The duty of combing the shore after storms to search for possible shipwreck victims to either help or bury

In conclusion, what defines the diaconal ministries in the theological thought of the Fathers is anchored firmly to apostolic witness and is founded on the differing intensity that distinguishes the role of ministers in relation to the one Lord operating in the Eucharist.

CHAPTER I

The Scriptural Sources

The Old Testament Texts

For as much as the Old Testament knows what it means to serve, and contains in Leviticus 19:18 the commandment of love; and, more generally, for as much as Israel as well as the entire East were familiar with works of mercy, *diakonéo* never appears in the LXX.[1] *Diákonos* is found only seven times in the sense of *servant of the court* (for example, Est 1:10) or even in the sense of *aid to an avenger*. *Diakonía* is found only in two irrelevant passages (Est 6:3, 5). Instead we find the word groups of *douléuo*, *latréuo*, or *leitourgéo* in the context of worship.

Leviticus

"Take no revenge and cherish no grudge against your own people. You shall love your neighbor as yourself. I am the Lord" (19:18).

Esther

"On the seventh day, when the king was merry with wine, he instructed Mehuman, Biztha, Harbona, Bigtha, Abagtha, Zethar, and Carkas, the seven eunuchs who attended King Ahasuerus" (1:10).

"The king asked, 'What was done to honor and exalt Mordecai for this?' The king's attendants replied, 'Nothing was done for him.'

"The king's attendants answered him, 'Haman is waiting in the court.' The king said, 'Let him come in'" (6:3, 5).

1 [Septuagint]

Proverbs

"A well educated son will be wise, but the foolish one will be in need of a *diákonos*" (10:4a).[2]

The New Testament Texts

"The first pertinent and fundamental piece of information in the New Testament is that the word *diakonein* indicates the very mission of Christ as servant (Mk 10:45 & parr.; cf. Mt 12:18; Acts 4:30; Phil 2:6-11). This word or its derivatives also indicate the exercise of service on the part of his disciples (Mk 10:43 ff.; Mt 20:26 ff., 23:11; Lk 8:3; Rom 15:25), services of various types in the Church, above all the apostolic service of preaching the Gospel, and other charismatic gifts. The terms *diakonein* and *diakonos* are very generic in the language of the New Testament. The *diakonos* can mean the servant at table (for example, Jn 2:5, 9), the servant of the Lord (Mt 22:13; Jn 12:26; Mk 9:35; 10:43; Mt 20:26, 23:11), the servant of a spiritual power (2 Cor 11:15; Eph 3:7; Col 1:23; Gal 2:17; Rom 15:8; 2 Cor 3:6), the servant of the Gospel, of Christ, of God (2 Cor 11:23). Pagan authorities are also at the service of God (Rom 13:4), and deacons are the servants of the Church (Col 1:25; 1 Cor 3:5). In the case where the deacon belongs to one of the Churches, the Vulgate does not employ the term *minister*, but preserves the Greek word as *diaconus*. This shows rightly that Acts 6:1-6 is not a question of the institution of the diaconate. "Diaconate" and "apostolate" are sometimes synonymous, as in Acts 1:17-25 where, on the occasion of Matthias's addition to the eleven Apostles, Peter defines the apostolate as "part of our ministry" (v. 17: *ton klēron tēs diakonias kai apostolēs*, which is translated by the *Traduction Oecuménique de la Bible* [TOB]): "the service of the apostolate"). This text from Acts also quotes Psalms 109:8: "May another take his office (*tēn episkopēn*)." The question arises: *diakonia*, *apostolē*, *episkopē*, are they or are they not equivalent? According to the opinion of M.J. Schmitt and J. Colson, the "apostolate" is "a redactional clause correcting 'diakonias.'" Acts 6:1-6 describes the institution of the "Seven" "for the service of the tables." Luke gives us the reason, indicating tension within the community: "The Hellenists complained (*egeneto goggysmos*) against the Hebrews because their widows were

2 [Translation of the Italian text, which uses the LXX version of Proverbs 10:4a.]

being neglected in the daily distribution" (Acts 6:1). It is not known whether the widows of the "Hellenists" belonged fully to the community, given the strict respect for ritual purity. Did the Apostles perhaps wish to send to the countryside the oppositional "Hellenists" of Jerusalem, who were causing increasing provocations with their preaching in the synagogue? Perhaps this was the reason the Apostles chose the Seven, a number corresponding to the number of magistrates of the provincial communities connected to a synagogue? Yet, at the same time, with act of laying on of hands, they wanted to preserve the unity of the Spirit and avoid a rupture. The commentators on Acts do not explain the meaning of such a laying on of the Apostles' hands. It is probable that the Apostles had designated the Seven to be at the head of the "Hellenists" (baptized, Greek-speaking Jews) to carry out the same responsibility as the presbyters among the Christian "Jews." The reason given for the designation of the chosen Seven (the grumbling among the Hellenists) is in contradiction with their activity as described subsequently in Luke. We hear nothing of table service. In regard to the Seven, Luke speaks only of the activity of Stephen and Philip; or, more precisely, of Stephen's discourse in the synagogue of Jerusalem and of his martyrdom, and of the apostolate in Samaria of Philip, who even baptized. And the others? In the Churches entrusted to the apostolic care of St. Paul, the deacons appear next to the *episkopoi* exercising a ministry that is both subordinate and coordinate to theirs (Phil 1:1; 1 Tm 3:1-13). In the apostolic writings there is already mention of deacons with the bishop or of the bishop with presbyters. On the other hand, rarely do the historical sources cite the three together: bishop, presbyter, and deacon (cf. International Theological Commission [ITC], "Data from the New Testament" in "*From the Diakonia of Christ to the Diakonia of the Apostles,*" Chap. II, 1-2).[3]

The Gospel of Matthew

"Then the devil left him and, behold, angels came and ministered (*diakónoun*) to him" (4:11).

"But it shall not be so among you. Rather, whoever wishes to be great among you shall be your servant; whoever wishes to be first among you shall be

3 [In this section, all instances of Greek in parentheses, including in the New Testament quotes, are retained from the Italian compendium.]

your slave. Just so, the Son of Man did not come to be served but to serve and to give his life as a ransom for many" (20:26-28).

"The greatest among you must be your servant (*diákonos*)" (23:11).

"Then they will answer and say, 'Lord, when did we see you hungry or thirsty or a stranger or naked or ill or in prison, and not minister (*diekonésamen*) to your needs?' He will answer them, 'Amen, I say to you, what you did not do for one of these least ones, you did not do for me'" (25:44-45).

The Gospel of Mark

"Then he sat down, called the Twelve, and said to them, 'If anyone wishes to be first, he shall be the last of all and the servant of all'" (9:35).

"But it shall not be so among you. Rather, whoever wishes to be great among you will be your servant (*diákonos*); whoever wishes to be first among you will be the slave (*doulos*) of all. For the Son of Man did not come to be served (*diakonethénai*) but to serve (*diakonésai*) and to give his life as a ransom for many" (10:43-45).

The Gospel of Luke

"Accompanying him were the Twelve and some women who had been cured of evil spirits and infirmities, Mary, called Magdalene, from whom seven demons had gone out, Joanna, the wife of Herod's steward Chuza, Susanna, and many others who provided (*diekónoun*) for them out of their resources" (8:1-3).

"Blessed are those servants whom the master finds vigilant on his arrival. Amen, I say to you, he will gird himself, have them recline at table, and proceed to wait on (*diakonései*) them" (12:37).

"Then an argument broke out among them about which of them should be regarded as the greatest. He said to them, "The kings of the Gentiles lord it over them and those in authority over them are addressed as 'Benefactors'; but among you it shall not be so. Rather, let the greatest among you be as the youngest, and the leader as the servant (*diakonón*). For who is greater: the one seated at table or the one who serves (*diakonón*)? Is it not the one seated at table? I am among you as the one who serves (*diakonón*)" (22:24-27).

The Gospel of John

"Whoever serves (*diakoné*) me must follow me, and where I am, there also will my servant (*diákonos*) be. The Father will honor whoever serves (*diakoné*) me" (12:26).

"So when he had washed their feet [and] put his garments back on and reclined at table again, he said to them, 'Do you realize what I have done for you? You call me "teacher" and "master," and rightly so, for indeed I am. If I, therefore, the master and teacher, have washed your feet, you ought to wash one another's feet. I have given you a model to follow, so that as I have done for you, you should also do'" (13:12-15).

Acts of the Apostles

"At that time, as the number of disciples continued to grow, the Hellenists complained against the Hebrews because their widows were being neglected in the daily distribution (*diakonia*). So the Twelve called together the community of the disciples and said, 'It is not right for us to neglect the word of God to serve (*diakonéin*) at table. Brothers, select from among you seven reputable men, filled with the Spirit and wisdom, whom we shall appoint to this task, whereas we shall devote ourselves to prayer and to the ministry (*diakonia*) of the word.' The proposal was acceptable to the whole community, so they chose Stephen, a man filled with faith and the holy Spirit, also Philip, Prochorus, Nicanor, Timon, Parmenas, and Nicholas of Antioch, a convert to Judaism. They presented these men to the apostles who prayed and laid hands on them" (6:1-6).

"Yet I consider life of no importance to me, if only I may finish my course and the ministry (*diakonian*) that I received from the Lord Jesus, to bear witness to the gospel of God's grace" (20:24).

"He greeted them, then proceeded to tell them in detail what God had accomplished among the Gentiles through his ministry (*diakonias*)" (21:19).

Letter to the Romans

"Now I am speaking to you Gentiles. Inasmuch then as I am the apostle to the Gentiles, I glory in my ministry (*diakonian*)" (11:13).

"Welcome one another, then, as Christ welcomed you, for the glory of God. For I say that Christ became a minister (*diákonon*) of the circumcised to show God's truthfulness, to confirm the promises to the patriarchs" (15:7-8).

"I commend to you Phoebe our sister, who is [also] a minister (*diákonon*) of the church at Cenchreae" (16:1).

First Letter to the Corinthians

"There are different kinds of spiritual gifts but the same Spirit; there are different forms of service (*diakonión*) but the same Lord" (12:4-5).

"I urge you, brothers—you know that the household of Stephanas is the firstfruits of Achaia and that they have devoted themselves to the service of the holy ones" (16:15).

Second Letter to the Corinthians

"You are our letter, written (*diakonethéisa*) on our hearts, known and read by all, shown to be a letter of Christ administered by us, written not in ink but by the Spirit of the living God, not on tablets of stone but on tablets that are hearts of flesh" (3:2-3).

"Not that of ourselves we are qualified to take credit for anything as coming from us; rather, our qualification comes from God, who has indeed qualified us as ministers (*diakónous*) of a new covenant, not of letter but of spirit; for the letter brings death, but the Spirit gives life. Now if the ministry (*diakonia*) of death, carved in letters on stone, was so glorious that the Israelites could not look intently at the face of Moses because of its glory that was going to fade, how much more will the ministry (*diakonia*) of the Spirit be glorious? For if the ministry (*diakonia*) of condemnation was glorious, the ministry (*diakonia*) of righteousness will abound much more in glory" (3:5-9).

"Therefore, since we have this ministry (*diakonian*) through the mercy shown us, we are not discouraged" (4:1).

"And all this is from God, who has reconciled us to himself through Christ and given us the ministry (*diakonian*) of reconciliation" (5:18).

"We cause no one to stumble in anything, in order that no fault may be found with our ministry (*diakonia*); on the contrary, in everything we commend ourselves as ministers (*diakonoi*) of God, through much endurance, in afflictions, hardships, constraints" (6:3-4).

"For according to their means, I can testify, and beyond their means, spontaneously, they begged us insistently for the favor of taking part in the service (*diakonias*) to the holy ones, and this, not as we expected, but they gave themselves first to the Lord and to us through the will of God" (8:3-5).

"For the administration of this public service (*diakonia*) is not only supplying the needs of the holy ones but is also overflowing in many acts of thanksgiving to God. Through the evidence of this service (*diakonias*), you are glorifying God for your obedient confession of the gospel of Christ and the generosity of your contribution to them and to all others" (9:12-13).

Letter to the Philippians

"Paul and Timothy, slaves of Christ Jesus, to all the holy ones in Christ Jesus who are in Philippi, with the overseers and ministers (*diákonois*)" (1:1).

Letter to the Ephesians

"Of this I became a minister (*diákonos*) by the gift of God's grace that was granted me in accord with the exercise of his power" (3:7).

"And he gave some as apostles, others as prophets, others as evangelists, others as pastors and teachers, to equip the holy ones for the work of ministry (*érgon diakonias*), for building up the body of Christ, until we all attain to the unity of faith and knowledge of the Son of God, to mature manhood, to the extent of the full stature of Christ" (4:11-13).

Letter to the Colossians

"Epaphras our beloved fellow slave, who is a trustworthy minister (*diákonos*) of Christ on your behalf" (1:7).

"Provided that you persevere in the faith, firmly grounded, stable, and not shifting from the hope of the gospel that you heard, which has been preached to every creature under heaven, of which I, Paul, am a minister (*diákonos*)" (1:23).

"And tell Archippus, 'See that you fulfill the ministry (*diakonian*) that you received in the Lord'" (4:17).

First Letter to Timothy

"Similarly, deacons (*diakónous*) must be dignified, not deceitful, not addicted to drink, not greedy for sordid gain, holding fast to the mystery of the faith with a clear conscience. Moreover, they should be tested first; then, if there is nothing against them, let them serve as deacons (*diakonéisthosan*). Women, similarly, should be dignified, not slanderers, but temperate and faithful in everything. Deacons (*diákonoi*) may be married only once and must manage their children and their households well. Thus those who serve well as deacons (*oi kalós diaikonésantes*), gain good standing and much confidence in their faith in Christ Jesus" (3:8-13).

"If you will give these instructions to the brothers, you will be a good minister (*diákonos*) of Christ Jesus, nourished on the words of the faith and of the sound teaching you have followed" (4:6).

Second Letter to Timothy

"May the Lord grant him to find mercy from the Lord on that day. And you know very well the services he [Onesiphorus] rendered (*ósa diekónesen*) in Ephesus" (1:18).

"But you, be self-possessed in all circumstances; put up with hardship; perform the work of an evangelist; fulfill your ministry (*diakonian*)" (4:5).

"Luke is the only one with me. Get Mark and bring him with you, for he is helpful to me in the ministry (*diakonian*)" (4:11).

Letter to the Hebrews

"For God is not unjust so as to overlook your work and the love you have demonstrated for his name by having served and continuing to serve (*diakonésantes . . . kaidiadonoúntes*) the holy ones" (6:10).

First Letter of Peter

"As each one has received a gift, use it to serve (*diakonoúntes*) one another as good stewards of God's varied grace. Whoever preaches, let it be with the words of God; whoever serves (*diakonéi*), let it be with the strength that God supplies, so that in all things God may be glorified through Jesus Christ, to whom belong glory and dominion forever and ever. Amen" (4:10-11).

CHAPTER II

The Patristic Sources

A. The Fathers of the Church from the First and Second Centuries

Clement of Rome (ca. 96)

Attributed to the name of Clement, who, according to tradition, was the fourth bishop of Rome, is a letter (composed around 96) addressed from the Church of Rome to the Church of Corinth to resolve some internal problems in the latter community. The letter is the first writing of the so-called "Apostolic Fathers," a designation that comprises a series of Christian authors and works written between the end of the first and the beginning of the second centuries. The letter was rather widespread in the ancient Church and was translated into several languages. It is an important document for understanding the life of the Roman Church and its relationship with the other Churches at the end of the first century.

Letter to the Corinthians

Apostolic Institution of the Bishops and Deacons

"XLII. The Apostles have preached to us from the Lord Jesus Christ; Jesus Christ [has done so] from God. Christ therefore was sent forth by God, and the Apostles by Christ. Both of these appointments, then, were made in an orderly way, according to the will of God. Having therefore received their orders, and being fully assured by the Resurrection of our Lord Jesus Christ, and established in the Word of God, with full assurance of the Holy Ghost, they [the Apostles] went forth proclaiming that the Kingdom of God was at hand. And thus preaching through countries and cities, they appointed the first-fruits [of their labors], having first proved them by the Spirit to be bishops and deacons of those who should afterwards believe. Nor was this any new thing, since indeed many ages before it was written concerning bishops and deacons. For thus saith the Scripture in a certain place, 'I will appoint their bishops in righteousness, and their deacons in faith' (Is 60:17)."

Ignatius of Antioch (70–107)

Ignatius, bishop of Antioch of Syria, was arrested and brought to Rome at an uncertain date, in the first decades of the second century (the traditional date of his martyrdom in 107 seems dubious). During the voyage he traversed Asia Minor and wrote some letters to the Churches of that region and to the Church of Rome. He knew Polycarp and spent some time with him in Smyrna. It is uncertain whether or when he arrived in Rome and underwent martyrdom. We have seven of letters of his that are of great interest in questions of theology (against Christological heresies), church organization (ministries), and the spirituality of martyrdom (letter to the Romans). He is one of the "Apostolic Fathers."

Letter to the Ephesians

Obedience to the Bishop and Presbyters

"II. As to my fellow-servant Burrhus, your deacon in regard to God and blessed in all things, I beg that he may continue longer, both for your honor and that of your bishop. And Crocus also, worthy both of God and you, whom I have received as the manifestation of your love, hath in all things refreshed me, as the Father of our Lord Jesus Christ shall also refresh him; together with Onesimus, and Burrhus, and Euplus, and Fronto, by means of whom, I have, as to love, beheld all of you. May I always have joy of you, if indeed I be worthy of it. It is therefore befitting that you should in every way glorify Jesus Christ, who hath glorified you, that by a unanimous obedience 'ye may be perfectly joined together in the same mind, and in the same judgment, and may all speak the same thing concerning the same thing,' and that, being subject to the bishop and the presbytery, ye may in all respects be sanctified."

Letter to the Christians of Magnesia

Harmony

"VI. Since therefore I have, in the persons before mentioned, beheld the whole multitude of you in faith and love, I exhort you to study to do all things with a divine harmony, while your bishop presides in the place of God, and your presbyters in the place of the assembly of the Apostles, along with your deacons, who are most dear to me, and are entrusted with the ministry of Jesus Christ, who was with the Father before the beginning of time, and in the end was revealed. Do ye all then, imitating the same divine conduct, pay respect to one another, and let no one look upon his neighbor after the flesh, but do ye continually love each other in Jesus Christ. Let nothing exist among you that may divide you; but be ye united with your bishop, and those that preside over you, as a type and evidence of your immortality."

Firm in the Precepts of the Lord and of the Apostles

"XIII. Study, therefore, to be established in the doctrines of the Lord and the Apostles, that so all things, whatsoever ye do, may prosper both in the flesh and spirit; in faith and love; in the Son, and in the Father, and in the Spirit; in the beginning and in the end; with your most admirable bishop, and the well-compacted spiritual crown of your presbytery, and the deacons who are according to God. Be ye subject to the bishop, and to one another, as Jesus Christ to the Father, according to the flesh, and the Apostles to Christ, and to the Father, and to the Spirit; that so there may be a union both fleshly and spiritual."

Letter to the Trallians

Submissive to the Bishop as to Jesus Christ

"II. For, since ye are subject to the bishop as to Jesus Christ, ye appear to me to live not after the manner of men, but according to Jesus Christ, who died for us, in order, by believing in his Death, ye may escape from death. It is therefore necessary that, as ye indeed do, so without the bishop ye should do nothing, but should also be subject to the presbytery, as to the apostle of Jesus Christ, who is our hope, in whom, if we live, we shall [at last] be found. It is fitting also that the deacons, as being [the ministers] of the mysteries of Jesus Christ, should in every respect be pleasing to all. For they are not ministers of meat and drink, but servants of the Church of God. They are bound, therefore, to avoid all grounds of accusation [against them], as they would do fire."

Without the Deacons, the Presbyters, and the Bishop, There Is No Church

"III. In like manner, let all reverence the deacons as an appointment of Jesus Christ, and the bishop as Jesus Christ, who is the Son of the Father, and the presbyters as the sanhedrim of God, and assembly of the Apostles. Apart from these, there is no Church. Concerning all this, I am persuaded that ye are of the same opinion. For I have received the manifestation of your love, and still have it with me, in your bishop, whose very appearance is highly instructive, and his meekness of itself a power; whom I imagine even the ungodly must reverence, seeing they are also pleased that I do not spare myself. But shall I, when permitted to write on this point, reach such a height of self-esteem, that though being a condemned man, I should issue commands to you as if I were an apostle?"

Within the Sanctuary

"VII. Be on your guard, therefore, against such persons. And this will be the case with you if you are not puffed up, and continue in intimate union with Jesus Christ our God, and the bishop, and the enactments of the Apostles. He that is within the altar is pure, but he that is without is not pure; that is, he who does anything apart from the bishop, and presbytery, and deacons, such a man is not pure in his conscience."

Letter to the Philadelphians

Greeting

"Ignatius, who is also called Theophorus, to the Church of God the Father, and our Lord Jesus Christ, which is at Philadelphia, in Asia, which has obtained mercy, and is established in the harmony of God, and rejoiceth unceasingly in the Passion of our Lord, and is filled with all mercy through his Resurrection;

which I salute in the Blood of Jesus Christ, who is our eternal and enduring joy, especially if [men] are in unity with the bishop, the presbyters, and the deacons, who have been appointed according to the mind of Jesus Christ, whom he has established in security, after his own will, and by his Holy Spirit."

The Flesh of Christ Is One

"IV. Take ye heed, then, to have but one Eucharist. For there is one Flesh of our Lord Jesus Christ, and one cup to [show forth] the unity of his Blood; one altar; as there is one bishop, along with the presbytery and deacons, my fellow-servants: that so, whatsoever ye do, ye may do it according to [the will of] God."

Guard the Flesh as a Temple of God

"VII. For though some would have deceived me according to the flesh, yet my spirit is not deceived; for I have received it from God. For it knows both whence it comes and whither it goes, and detects the secrets [of the heart]. For when I was among you, I cried, I spoke with a loud voice—the word is not mine, but God's—Give heed to the bishop, and to the presbytery and deacons. But if ye suspect that I spake thus, as having learned beforehand the division caused by some among you, He is my witness, for whose sake I am in bonds, that I learned nothing of it from the mouth of any man. But the Spirit made an announcement to me, saying as follows: Do nothing without the bishop; keep your bodies as the temples of God; love unity; avoid divisions; be ye followers of Paul, and of the rest of the Apostles, even as they also were of Christ."

The Peace of the Church of Antioch in Syria

"X. Since, according to your prayers, and the compassion which ye feel in Christ Jesus, it is reported to me that the Church which is at Antioch in Syria possesses peace, it will become you, as a Church of God, to elect a deacon to act as the ambassador of God [for you] to [the brethren there], that he may rejoice along with them when they are met together, and glorify the name [of God]. Blessed is he in Jesus Christ, who shall be deemed worthy of such a ministry; and ye too shall be glorified. And if ye are willing, it is not beyond your power to do this, for the sake of God; as also the nearest Churches have sent, in some cases bishops, and in others presbyters and deacons."

Farewell

"XI. Now, as to Philo the deacon, of Cilicia, a man of reputation, who still ministers to me in the word of God, along with Rheus Agathopus, an elect man, who has followed me from Syria, not regarding his life—these bear witness in your behalf; and I myself give thanks to God for you, that ye have received them, even as the Lord you. But may those that dishonored them be forgiven through the grace of Jesus Christ! The love of the brethren at Troas salutes you; whence also I write to you by Burrhus, who was sent along with me by the Ephesians and Smyrnaeans, to show their respect. May the Lord Jesus Christ honor them, in whom they hope, in flesh, and soul, and faith, and love, and concord! Fare ye well in Christ Jesus, our common hope."

Letter to the Smyrnaeans

Following the Bishop and the Clergy

"VIII. See that ye all follow the bishop, even as Jesus Christ does the Father, and the presbytery as ye would the Apostles; and reverence the deacons, as being the institution of God. Let no man do anything connected with the Church without the bishop. Let that be deemed a proper Eucharist, which is [administered] either by the bishop, or by one to whom he has entrusted it. Wherever the bishop shall appear, there let the multitude [of the people] also be; even as, wherever Jesus Christ is, there is the Catholic Church. It is not lawful without the bishop either to baptize or to celebrate a love-feast; but whatsoever he shall approve of, that is also pleasing to God, so that everything that is done may be secure and valid."

My Soul and My Chains

"X. Ye have done well in receiving Philo and Rheus Agathopus as servants of Christ our God, who have followed me for the sake of God, and who give thanks to the Lord in your behalf, because ye have in every way refreshed them.

None of these things shall be lost to you. May my spirit be for you, and my bonds, which ye have not despised or been ashamed of; nor shall Jesus Christ, our perfect hope, be ashamed of you."

Farewell

"XII. The love of the brethren at Troas salutes you; whence also I write to you by Burrhus, whom ye sent with me, together with the Ephesians, your brethren, and who has in all things refreshed me. And I would that all may imitate him, as being a pattern of a minister of God. Grace will reward him in all things. I salute your most worthy bishop, and your very venerable presbytery, and your deacons, my fellow-servants, and all of you individually, as well as generally, in the name of Jesus Christ, and in his Flesh and Blood, in his Passion and Resurrection, both corporeal and spiritual, in union with God and you. Grace, mercy, peace, and patience, be with you forevermore!"

Letter to Polycarp

Let No One Be a Deserter

"VI. Give ye heed to the bishop, that God also may give heed to you. My soul be for theirs that are submissive to the bishop, to the presbyters, and to the deacons, and may my portion be along with them in God! Labor together with one another; strive in company together; run together; suffer together; sleep together; and awake together, as the stewards, and associates, and servants of God. Please ye him under whom ye fight, and from whom ye receive your wages. Let none of you be found a deserter. Let your Baptism endure as your arms; your faith as your helmet; your love as your spear; your patience as a complete panoply. Let your works be the charge assigned to you, that ye may receive a worthy recompense. Be long-suffering, therefore, with one another, in meekness, as God is toward you. May I have joy of you for ever!"

Polycarp of Smyrna (ca. 69–155)

According to a tradition attested to by Irenaeus, Polycarp was a disciple of John. This does not, however, seem to mean the Apostle, but rather a presbyter of the same name. Ignatius of Antioch wrote him a letter, and a letter of Polycarp to the Philippians has been handed down to us. He traveled to Rome between 155 and 160 to discuss the problem of the Easter date with Pope Anicetus. Polycarp met his martyrdom in the persecution that hit Smyrna: the contested date of his martyrdom, burned at the stake, is placed between 156 and 167. The account of his martyrdom is contained in a letter sent soon after his death from the bishop of the Church of Smyrna to that of Philomelium: it is the first Christian text to use the title of "martyr" to designate a Christian who died for the faith.

Letter to the Philippians

Duties of Deacons, Young Men, and Virgins

"V. Knowing, then, that 'God is not mocked,' we ought to walk worthy of his commandment and glory. In like manner should the deacons be blameless before the face of his righteousness, as being the servants of God and Christ, and not of men. They must not be slanderers, double-tongued, or lovers of money, but temperate in all things, compassionate, industrious, walking according to the truth of the Lord, who was the servant of all. If we please him in this present world, we shall receive also the future world, according as he has promised to us that he will raise us again from the dead, and that if we live worthily of him, 'we shall also reign together with him,' provided only we believe. In like manner, let the young men also be blameless in all things, being especially careful to preserve purity, and keeping themselves in, as with a bridle, from every kind of evil. For it is well that they should be cut off from the lusts that are in the world, since 'every lust warreth against the spirit;' and 'neither fornicators, nor effeminate, nor abusers of themselves with mankind, shall inherit the Kingdom of God,' nor those who do things inconsistent and unbecoming. Wherefore, it is needful to abstain from all these things, being subject to the presbyters and deacons, as unto God and Christ. The virgins also must walk in a blameless and pure conscience."

Hermas (ca. 140)

Hermas is the author of the Shepherd, a work which, more than any other, transports us into the living heart of the Christian community in the first half of the second century. The community is expanding and not all of its members are affected by the same fervor. The main subject of the Shepherd *is penance connected to moral reform. Hermas sets himself up against the rigorists who denied the efficacy of penance for the forgiveness of sins committed after Baptism. On the other hand, he also opposes the laxists, insisting that penance is necessary and cannot be left aside. The expository procedure is not a linear narration but rather a continuous dialogue between the author and the personifications of the Church. The work is divided into five visions, twelve precepts, and ten allegorical similes.*

The Shepherd

Third Vision

The Stones of the Tower and Penance at an Opportune Time

"V. Hear now with regard to the stones which are in the building. Those square white stones which fitted exactly into each other, are Apostles, bishops, teachers, and deacons, who have lived in godly purity, and have acted as bishops and teachers and deacons chastely and reverently to the elect of God. Some of them have fallen asleep, and some still remain alive. And they have always agreed with each other, and been at peace among themselves, and listened to each other. On account of this, they join exactly into the building of the tower."

Ninth Similitude

The Believers of the Ninth Mountain

"XXVI. And they who believed from the ninth mountain, which was deserted, and had in it creeping things and wild beasts which destroy men, were the following: they who had the stains as servants, who discharged their duty ill, and who plundered widows and orphans of their livelihood, and gained possessions for themselves from the ministry, which they had received. If, therefore, they remain under the dominion of the same desire, they are dead, and there is no hope of life for them; but if they repent, and finish their ministry in a holy manner, they shall be able to live."

Justin (ca. 100–ca. 165)

Philosopher and martyr, Justin was originally from what is now modern day Nablus (Samaria). After seeking the truth in several philosophical schools, he converted to Christianity. Having gone to Rome, he there wrote his works and met death under the prefect Rusticus. As a first-level representative of the first Christian apologetics, his thought is important for the way it seeks to make Greek philosophy meet Christianity. Of the several works that he wrote, the only works that remain to us are the two Apologies *addressed to Emperor Antoninus Pius and the* Dialogue with Trypho. *This latter is the oldest apology known to us, directed to the Jewish world. In the first* Apology *he makes rebuttals for the accusations against Christians and critiques the pagan religion. Above all, however, he reveals the cardinal tenets of the Christian faith, with important information on the liturgy. It is placed around the years 150-155.*

First Apology: Administration of the Sacraments

"LXV. And when the president has given thanks, and all the people have expressed their assent, those who are called by us deacons give to each of those present to partake of the bread and wine mixed with water over which the thanksgiving was pronounced, and to those who are absent they carry away a portion."

First Apology: On the Day Called "the Sun's Day"

"LXVII. Then we all rise together and pray, and, as we before said, when our prayer is ended, bread and wine and water are brought, and the president in like manner offers prayers and thanksgivings, according to his ability, and the people assent, saying Amen; and there is a distribution to each, and a participation of that over which thanks have been given [1915] and to those who are absent a portion is sent by the deacons."

Irenaeus of Lyons (ca. 130–ca. 202)

Irenaeus, even if only in passing, speaks of the presence of deacons (1,13,5: "One of our deacons . . ."), though without specifying their duties. What is certain, however, is that the bishop of Lyons considered the diaconate to be of apostolic institution and can be traced back to the "seven" spoken of in Acts 6:1-6 (1,26,3); he calls Stephen in particular the "first deacon" (3,12,10; 4,15,1).

Furthermore, he traces the Nicolaitans of Revelation 2:6 to Nicholas, "one of the seven first ordained to the diaconate by the apostles" *(1,26,3). Just as the Twelve had a traitor, so even the Seven had one who defected.*

Against Heresies

The Testimony of Stephen

"III, 12, 10. And still further, Stephen, who was chosen the first deacon by the Apostles, and who, of all men, was the first to follow the footsteps of the martyrdom of the Lord, being the first that was slain for confessing Christ, speaking boldly among the people, and teaching them, says: 'The God of glory appeared to our father Abraham . . . and said to him, Get thee out of thy country, and from thy kindred, and come into the land which I shall show thee . . . and he removed him into this land, wherein ye now dwell. And he gave him none inheritance in it, no, not so much as to set his foot on; yet he promised that he would give it to him for a possession, and to his seed after him. . . . And God spake on this wise, That his seed should sojourn in a strange land, and should be brought into bondage, and should be evil-entreated four hundred years; and the nation whom they shall serve will I judge, says the Lord. And after that shall they come forth, and serve me in this place. And he gave him the covenant of circumcision: and so [Abraham] begat Isaac.' And the rest of his words announce the same God, who was with Joseph and with the patriarchs, and who spake with Moses."

"IV, 15, 1. They (the Jews) had therefore a law, a course of discipline, and a prophecy of future things. For God at the first, indeed, warning them by means of natural precepts, which from the beginning he had implanted in mankind, that is, by means of the Decalogue (which, if any one does not observe, he has no salvation), did then demand nothing more of them. As Moses says in Deuteronomy, 'These are all the words which the Lord spake to the whole assembly of the sons of Israel on the mount, and he added no more; and he wrote them on two tables of stone, and gave them to me.' For this reason [he did so], that they who are willing to follow him might keep these commandments. But when they turned themselves to make a calf, and had gone back in their minds to Egypt, desiring to be slaves instead of free-men, they were placed for the future in a state of servitude suited to their wish—[a slavery] which did not indeed cut them off from God, but subjected them to the yoke of bondage; as Ezekiel the prophet, when stating the reasons for the giving of such a law, declares: 'And their eyes were after the desire of their heart; and I gave them statutes that were not good, and judgments in which they shall not live.' Luke also has recorded that Stephen, who was the first elected into the diaconate by the Apostles, and who was the first slain for the testimony of Christ, spoke regarding Moses as follows: 'This man did indeed receive the commandments of the living God to give to us, whom your fathers would not obey, but thrust [him from them], and in their hearts turned back again into Egypt, saying unto Aaron, Make us gods to go before us; for we do not know what has happened to [this] Moses, who led us from the land of Egypt. And they made a calf in those days, and offered sacrifices to the idol, and were rejoicing in the works of their own hands. But God turned, and gave them up to worship the hosts of heaven; as it is written in the book of the prophets: O ye house of Israel, have ye offered to me sacrifices and oblations for forty years in the wilderness? And ye took up the tabernacle of Moloch, and the star of the god Remphan, figures which ye made to worship them;' pointing out plainly, that the law being such, was not given to them by another God, but that, adapted to their condition of servitude, [it originated] from the very same [God as we worship]. Wherefore also he says to Moses in Exodus: 'I will send forth my angel before thee; for I will not go up with thee, because thou art a stiff-necked people.'"

B. THE FATHERS OF THE THIRD CENTURY: THE SCHOOL OF ALEXANDRIA

Clement of Alexandria (ca. 150–ca. 215)

Clement of Alexandria (died before 215), completed his studies in Athens, southern Italy, and the East (perhaps Antioch). Afterwards, he settled in Alexandria, where he had Pantenus as a teacher. Soon afterwards, perhaps due to misunderstandings with Bishop Demetrius, he had to leave the city and move to Jerusalem, where Alexander was bishop. The presence of Clement in Jerusalem is attested to by a letter from Alexander himself to the Church of Antioch: "I send you this letter, my esteemed brethren."

Referring to a work (lost) by Clement on the subject of Easter, Eusebius mentions the former's intention of putting the traditions heard "from the ancient presbyters" into writing.

From this we can deduce that the "presbyters" had a teaching duty, while the deacons rendered more practical, assistive forms of service.

In a passage from the Pedagogue, *Clement mentions a project of commenting on scriptural references concerning* presbyters, bishops, deacons, and widows, *but we do not know if he followed through on his plan.*

In the passage cited from the Stromata, *Clement makes a clear distinction between the three degrees of church hierarchy in an ascending order (deacons, presbyters, and bishops). These can be understood as a reflection of the angelic hierarchy, as well as the degrees of glory that will mark the definitive eschatological growth of perfect disciples.*

Stromata

True Presbyters and True Deacons

"VI, 13. Those, then, also now, who have exercised themselves in the Lord's commandments and lived perfectly and gnostically according to the Gospel, may be enrolled in the chosen body of the Apostles. Such an one [sic] is in reality a presbyter of the Church and a true minister (deacon) of the will of God if he does and teaches what is the Lord's; not as being ordained by men, nor regarded righteous because a presbyter, but enrolled in the presbyterate because righteous. And although here upon earth he be not honored with the chief seat, he will sit down on the four-and-twenty thrones, judging the people, as John says in the Apocalypse."

Origen (185–254)

In contrast to Clement, Origen touched on the theme of ministers on an extraordinarily large number of occasions, especially in homilies and biblical commentaries. This is not, however, an explicit reflection, just as his work generally lacks an explicit reflection on the Church, but is rather a collection of observations on the lives of various Christian communities.

The image of the Church that arises from Origen's writings does not differ substantially from that available in other third-century sources. It is the People of God, gathered under the care of shepherds and teachers, meaning the bishop, with the presbyters and deacons. This trilogy is an already well-established structure, which Origen never calls into question. Between deacons, presbyters, and bishops there is a difference of degree. Following an already common usage, Origen draws a parallel between the deacons *and the* Levites, *the* presbyters *and the* priests *of the Old Testament, and the* bishop *and the* high priest.

These ecclesiastical orders represent the "dignities," endowed with power and authority, but that are exercised in a way that is not worldly, but evangelical. Here Origen develops a whole spirituality of service, which has Christ as its proper model.

The triple hierarchy, if united in dignity, is also united in responsibility. All that is said principally *about the bishop is applied in a certain measure even to the presbyters and to the deacons as the bishop's collaborators.*

Homily on Jeremiah

It Is Not the Office That Saves

"There are some among the clergy who do not live in a way in which they draw benefit from it, nor do honor to the clergy. It is for this reason, say the commentators, that it is written: *Their office shall not be to their benefit.*

"What is indeed of use is not the fact of sitting in the presbytery, but of living in a way worthy of that position, as the word demands. The word, in fact, asks both you and us to live in a holy manner; yet, if the saying is true that *The greater shall be examined in a greater manner*, then it must be asked of me more than the deacon, of the deacon more than the layman, and even more so from the man to whom church authority has been entrusted over us all.

"Listen to what is said by the Apostle, to whom great things had been entrusted: everyone should consider us as servants of Christ and as distributers of God's mysteries. Now, what you require of a steward is that he be a trustworthy person. And so rare it is to find a trustworthy, honest steward that Jesus, who knows everything before it takes place, says: Who, then, is the trustworthy, wise servant, whom his master will put in charge of his household, to give the grain ration to his servants at the allotted time? He then admonishes some stewards saying: If the wicked servant begins to say, 'My master delays in coming,'and begins to strike his fellow servants and the housemaids, to eat, and to drink to a stupor, the master of that servant will come on a day he does not expect and at an hour he does not know, and will slice him in two, meting out to him the lot of the infidels (11, 3)."[1]

Commentary on Matthew

The Monogamy of Ordained Ministers

"XIV, 22. But, while dealing with the passage, I would say that we will be able perhaps now to understand and clearly set forth a question which is hard to grasp and see into, with regard to the legislation of the Apostle concerning ecclesiastical matters; for Paul wishes not one of those of the church, who has attained to any eminence beyond the many, as is attained in the administration of the sacraments, to make trial of a second marriage. For laying down the law in regard to bishops in the first Epistle to Timothy, he says, 'If a man seeketh the office of a bishop, he desireth a good work. The bishop, therefore, must be without reproach, the husband of one wife, temperate, sober-minded,' etc.; and, in regard to deacons, 'Let the deacons,' he says, 'be the husbands of one wife, ruling their children and their own houses well,' etc. Yea, and also when appointing

1 [Translation of the Italian text.]

widows, he says, 'Let there be no one as a widow under threescore years old, having been the wife of one man;' and after this, he says the things superadded, as being second or third in importance to this. And, in the Epistle to Titus, 'For this cause,' he says, 'I left thee in Crete that thou shouldst set in order the things that were wanting, and appoint elders in every city as I gave thee charge. If anyone is blameless, the husband of one wife, having children, that believe'—of course—and so on.

"Now, when we saw that some who have been married twice may be much better than those who have been married once, we were perplexed why Paul does not at all permit those who have been twice married to be appointed to ecclesiastical dignities; for also it seemed to me that such a thing was worthy of examination, as it was possible that a man, who had been unfortunate in two marriages, and had lost his second wife while he was yet young, might have lived for the rest of his years up to old age in the greatest self-control and chastity."

Unworthy Bishops, Presbyters, and Deacons

"What [the Gospel] says about the *dove sellers* [in the Temple] can also be applied, I believe, to those who hand the Church over to bishops, presbyters, and deacons, who are eager for gain, despotic, ignorant, and without fear of the Lord.... In God's Church, there should indeed be nothing other than *prayer*. That is to say that every holy work that brings God's approving presence is considered prayer before God and makes *praying without ceasing* a possibility.

"You, on the other hand, you disgraceful people with your wickedness have transformed the *house of prayer* into a *den of thieves*. Nor is it difficult in many places to find renowned churches whose conditions have deteriorated so much over time, that the public assembly gathered in Christ's name no longer differs in any way from a *den of thieves*. To them it could be said: *Because of you my name is ever blasphemed among the nations*.

"Rather than the *money changers*, whose money *tables* were *overturned* by the Lord, it is the deacons who do not administer the Church's money well; they have it always on hand, yet do not dispense it rightly; on the contrary, they hoard said wealth and money until they become rich with what is given for the poor (16, 22)."[2]

2 [Ibid.]

They Say and Do Not Do

"Let us say that the [Gospel] saying: *Do everything that they tell you, but do not follow what they do*, beyond its literal interpretation, tries to point out that, in the Church, there are some who have the capacity to teach marvelous things with their speech and to expound on it rightly, but do not want to behave according to what they say. Therefore, it is necessary to listen to their teaching, but not necessary to imitate their behavior.

"And very often, these are the same people who *love places of honor at banquets, greetings in the squares, and hearing the people call them 'rabbi'* or some other equivalent title; like those who, for example, want to hear themselves called 'bishop' or 'presbyter,' or 'deacon.' Each of these, even if they are called so by another person, should at least show God their own awareness of not wanting to be called by that name, which really belongs to another. 'Bishop,' in fact, is really the Lord Jesus, and 'presbyters' are [really] Abraham, Isaac, and Jacob, which is clear for those who in Genesis consider what is written of their descendants; or even those others who were held worthy of this name, as the Apostles were. 'Deacons,' then, are [really] the seven archangels of God, at the service of whom the seven deacons of Acts were ordained (10)."[3]

Careerism

"What, then, must be said of those who *love places of honor at banquets, the first seats in the assembly*, the first *greetings in the squares, and hearing the people call them 'rabbi'*? Clearly such deviations at that time were not only found—nor are they found now—just among the scribes and Pharisees; even in the Church of Christ we find not only those who accept invitations to banquets and to the private tables of those that throw them, but even those that *love* to have the *first places* and to be seen in society, especially to be made deacons; and not of the sort that Scripture speaks of, but of the sort that *devour the houses of widows with the excuse of making long prayers, and for this they shall receive grave condemnation*. And those that wish to be deacons in this manner consequently have their sights set on getting the visible *first seats* of those that are called presbyters. If only everybody would hear this saying, but most especially the deacons, presbyters, and bishops, especially those that think it is not written: *he who exalts*

3 [Ibid.]

himself shall be made humble. It follows that, by not knowing the rest of the saying: *he who humbles himself shall be exalted,* they are not listening to the one that has said: *Learn from me, for I am meek and humble of heart.* In fact, they are swollen with pride, and for this reason *they fall into condemnation of the devil.* They do not seek to avoid such a condemnation with humility, while they should remember the saying of Wisdom that goes: *The greater you are, so much the more must you humble yourself, and you will find favor with God.* The Lord has been the first to put this into practice: as great as he had been, so much the more did he humble himself (12)."[4]

Commentary on the Letter to the Romans

Doing Honor to One's Own Ministry

"Paul says that *as he is an apostle to the nations, he will do honor to his ministry*: and what is more worthy than to do honor to the ministry which each person has received from God's Providence? He who exercises his own ministry well and gains merit and does honor to it; on the contrary, he who carries it out unworthily and carelessly dishonors his own ministry and makes a mockery of it to everyone.

"For example, in the ministry of the Church, *the deacon who serves well,* says [Paul], *gains for himself a degree of honor and much openness in the faith of Jesus Christ.* If, on the other hand, he does not carry out his ministry well—and is therefore not as the Apostle describes, namely *serious, not duplicitous of speech, not given over to much wine, nor greedy for dishonest gain, but possessing the mystery of faith in a pure conscience*—he not only does not acquire *a degree of honor,* but a severe punishment for having violated the divine ministry (8, 10)."[5]

4 [Ibid.]
5 [Ibid.]

Dispute with Heraclides

Lex Orandi and Lex Credendi

"We must pay attention to these teachings, because a great commotion has arisen out of them in the Church. Often they ask by letter that we give our signatures, that the bishop also sign or even that those who are held in suspicion sign; not only this, but that it be done in the presence of all the people, so that there may no longer be disagreement or controversy with regard to it.

"The offertory prayer is always made to the Almighty Father through Jesus Christ as the one who relates his divinity back to the Father. I am not [saying that] there should be two offerings, but [only one] to God through God. Is my proposal to respect these agreements when we pray somehow bold? And if this were not to happen, *you will have no human respect, nor will you allow yourself to be frightened by the figure of the powerful.* This man is a bishop, and he sets himself above everyone else? If he does not do this, namely if he does not observe these agreements, he gives rise to new disputes. Whether he be bishop or presbyter, he is no longer bishop, no longer presbyter, and not even laity: he is no longer laity nor participates in the assembly. If it seems just to you, let these agreements be made effective (4, 17–5, 7)."[6]

Dionysius of Alexandria (190–265)

Called the Great, Dionysius was bishop of Alexandria from 247 to 264. "His episcopate was but a series of trials and calamities." Before this responsibility, he was already a presbyter of the Alexandrian Church, taking care especially of the catechetical school, which he took over from Heracles who had become bishop in 232 or 233. During the persecutions of Decius (249–251) and of Valerian (257–258), Dionysius went into exile and was forced into house arrest.

He had something to offer in all of the doctrinal and disciplinary disputes of the time: the question of the lapsi, *the Baptism of heretics, Trinitarian doctrine, and Millenarianism. He wrote a great number of letters and several treatises, yet there are only fragments of these left to us.*

6 [Ibid.]

Letter to Domitius and Didymus

Courageous Presbyters and Deacons

"II, I, 2-3. Gaius and Peter and myself have been separated from our other brethren and shut up alone in a desert and sterile place in Libya, at a distance of three days' journey from Paraetonium. . . . And they concealed themselves in the city [*of Alexandria*], and secretly visited the brethren. I refer to the presbyters Maximus, Dioscorus, Demetrius, and Lucius. For Faustinus and Aquila, who are persons of greater prominence in the world, are wandering about in Egypt. I specify also the deacons who survived those who died in the sickness, namely, Faustus, Eusebius, and Chaeremon. And of Eusebius, I speak as one whom the Lord strengthened from the beginning and qualified for the task of discharging energetically the services due to the confessors who are in prison, and of executing the perilous office of dressing out and burying the bodies of those perfected and blessed martyrs. For even up to the present day, the governor does not cease to put to death, in a cruel manner, as I have already said, some of those who are brought before him; while he wears others out by torture and wastes others away with imprisonment and bonds, commanding also that no one shall approach them and making strict scrutiny lest anyone should be seen to do so. And nevertheless God imparts relief to the oppressed by the tender kindness and earnestness of the brethren."

Firmilian of Caesarea (died ca. 268)

Bishop of Caesarea, seat of Cappadocia, from 230 to ca. 268. Firmilian was in the forefront of the Eastern episcopate of his time.

Letter to Cyprian

The Singular Case of a Female Minister

"LXXIV, 10. But I wish to relate to you *some facts* concerning a circumstance which occurred among us, pertaining to this very matter. About two-and-twenty years ago, in the times after the Emperor Alexander, there happened in these parts many struggles and difficulties, either in general to all men, or privately to Christians. Moreover, there were many and frequent earthquakes, so that many places were overthrown throughout Cappadocia and Pontus; even certain cities, dragged into the abyss, were swallowed up by the opening of the gaping earth. So that from this also a severe persecution arose against us of the Christian name; and this arose suddenly after the long peace of the previous age, and with its unusual evils was made more terrible for the disturbance of our people. Serenianus was then governor in our province, a bitter and terrible persecutor. But the faithful being set in this state of disturbance, and fleeing hither and thither for fear of the persecution, and leaving their country and passing over into other regions—for there was an opportunity of passing over, for the reason that that persecution was not over the whole world, but was local—there arose among us suddenly a certain woman, who in a state of ecstasy announced herself as a prophetess, and acted as if filled with the Holy Ghost. And she was so moved by the impetus of the principal demons, that for a long time she made anxious and deceived the brotherhood, accomplishing certain wonderful and portentous things, and promised that she would cause the earth to be shaken. Not that the power of the demon was so great that he could prevail to shake the earth, or to disturb the elements; but that sometimes a wicked spirit, prescient, and perceiving that there will be an earthquake, pretends that he will do what he sees will happen. By these lies and boastings, he had so subdued the minds of individuals that they obeyed him and followed whithersoever he commanded and led. He would also make that woman walk in the keen winter with bare feet over frozen snow, and not be troubled or hurt in any degree by that walking. Moreover, she would say that she was hurrying to Judea and to Jerusalem, feigning as if she had come thence. Here also she deceived one of the presbyters, a countryman, and another, a deacon, so that they had intercourse with that same woman, which was shortly afterwards detected (in Cyprian, *Letters*)."

C. THE LATIN FATHERS FROM THE THIRD CENTURY

Tertullian (ca. 150–ca. 220)

Tertullian was born of pagan parents in Carthage around the middle of the second century. He completed his studies in rhetoric and law in the traditional schools, learning Greek. After practicing as a lawyer, first in Africa and then in Rome, he returned to his native city and converted to Christianity, probably around 195.

On Baptism

Ordinary and Extraordinary Ministers of Baptism

"XVII. For concluding our brief subject, it remains to put you in mind also of the due observance of giving and receiving Baptism. Of giving it, the chief priest (who is the bishop) has the right: in the next place, the presbyters and deacons, yet not without the bishop's authority, on account of the honor of the Church, which being preserved, peace is preserved."

Prescription Against the Heretics

On the Disorder of Ministries Among the Heretics

"III. For to the Son of God alone was it reserved to persevere to the last without sin. But what if a bishop, if a deacon, if a widow, if a virgin, if a doctor, if even a martyr, have fallen from the rule?"

"XLI. And so it comes to pass that today one man is their bishop, tomorrow another; today he is a deacon who tomorrow is a reader; today he is a presbyter who tomorrow is a layman. For even on laymen do they impose the functions of priesthood."

Passion of Perpetua and Felicity (ca. 203)

The Passion of Perpetua and Felicity is the recounting of the arrest, imprisonment, and execution of five young catechumens together with their catechist, Saturnus, who was instructing them in the faith. They belonged to the Church of Carthage.

In the Passion, there is mention made of deacons who took care of the brothers in prison, for which reason they are called "blessed."

Passion

"3, 7. Then Tertius and Pomponius, blessed deacons who were caring for us (*nobis ministrabant*) agreed [with the prison guards] on the compensation for getting us transferred in just a few hours to a less harsh section of the prison, where we were able to be a little more comfortable."[7]

Cyprian of Carthage (ca. 210–ca. 258)

Tascius Caecilius Cyprianus "by God's judgment and with the favor of the people was elected to priestly office and to the episcopal degree while yet a neophyte and, as far as is known, still young." In fact, shortly after receiving Baptism, he was accepted to the priesthood and acceded quite quickly to the episcopate, something that was quite outside the norm as is noted in his own biography.

His conversion had caused a radical change of life for him, especially due to the course he set in his priesthood: leaving his profession as a rhetorician, Cyprian, who had come from an aristocratic family, had distributed almost all of his large inheritance to the poor and had taken up an ascetic life, drawing the sympathy of the Christian community. This explains his episcopal election occurring to such popular clamor, something that did not fail to cause drawn-out opposition from a segment of the clergy. He died a martyr of the Catholic faith on September 14, 258, during the persecution of Valerian, who had given the order that "the bishops, presbyters and deacons be executed immediately." Cyprian's ancient biographer records that he was the first bishop of Roman Africa to receive the glory of martyrdom.

7 [Translation of the Italian text.]

For Cyprian, on the one hand there are the plebs, *the Christian people, who consist of various categories: widows, virgins, catechumens, and penitents. On the other, there are the* clerus, *or the ministers of the Church who, at that time, already existed in a rather complex, hierarchical structure. At the summit is the* bishop, *followed by the* presbyters *and by the* deacons. *Added to this classic trilogy are the* lectors, *the* subdeacons, *the* acolytes, *and the* exorcists. *As of yet there is no practice of a true and proper* iter, *though we do see Cyprian mentioning a period of "lectorate" before being admitted to the diaconate or presbyterate. In any case, the lectors and acolytes form part of the clergy and therefore live on the support of the Church, to whose service they must dedicate themselves full time, leaving behind all worldly occupations. For this reason, their choice must be a careful one.*

The deacons *are always named after the presbyters in Cyprian's letter headings. Following an ancient tradition that goes back to Acts 6:1-6, Cyprian affirms that they are of apostolic institution, at the service of the episcopate and of the Church.*

They help the bishop and priests in liturgical actions (Baptism and Eucharist) and in the Reconciliation of penitents. At the same time, deacons care for the administration of the church funds and charitable activity. Their number must certainly have been limited, as in Rome.

Cyprian never mentions a rite of ordination to the diaconate or presbyterate, but we also know how scarce any mentions in this regard are, even for episcopal ordinations. In any case, his conception of ordinatio *is much more juridical than sacramental. It encompasses the whole process of installation of a minister. For Cyprian, what makes an* ordinatio *valid, authentic, and legitimate is not only the correctness of the sacramental rite, but also the observance of all those passages that guarantee the ministers grafting onto the sanctifying power of the Church.*

Epistles

Submission of Deacons to Bishops

"LXIV, 1. I and my colleagues [*the bishops*] who were present with me were deeply and grievously distressed, dearest brother, on reading your letter in which you complained of your deacon, that, forgetful of your priestly station, and unmindful of his own office and ministry, he had provoked you by his insults and injuries. And you indeed have acted worthily, and with your accustomed humility toward us, in rather complaining of him to us; although you have power, according to the vigor of the episcopate and the authority of your See, whereby you might be justified on him at once, assured that all we your colleagues would regard it as a matter of satisfaction, whatever you should do by your priestly power in respect of an insolent deacon.

"LXIV, 3. But deacons ought to remember that the Lord chose apostles, that is, bishops and overseers; while apostles appointed for themselves deacons, after the ascent of the Lord into heaven, as ministers of their episcopacy and of the Church. But if we may dare anything against God who makes bishops, deacons may also dare against us by whom they are made; and therefore it behooves the deacon of whom you write to repent of his audacity, and to acknowledge the honor of the priest, and to satisfy the bishop set over him with full humility. For these things are the beginnings of heretics and the origins and endeavors of evil-minded schismatics—to please themselves, and with swelling haughtiness to despise him who is set over them. Thus they depart from the Church—thus a profane altar is set up outside—thus they rebel against the peace of Christ and the appointment and the unity of God. But if, further, he shall harass and provoke you with his insults, you must exercise against him the power of your dignity, by either deposing him or excommunicating him. For if the Apostle Paul, writing to Timothy, said, 'Let no man despise thy youth,' how much rather must it be said by your colleagues to you, 'Let no man despise thy age'? And since you have written, that one has associated himself with that same deacon of yours and is a partaker of his pride and boldness, you may either restrain or excommunicate him also and any others that may appear of a like disposition and act against God's priest. Unless, as we exhort and advise, they should rather perceive that they have sinned and make satisfaction and suffer us to keep our own purpose; for we rather ask and desire to overcome the reproaches and injuries of individuals by clemency and patience, than to punish them by our priestly power."

Commodian (ca. Third–Fifth Century)

"Commodian is perhaps the most enigmatic as well as problematic poet of Christian antiquity. There is no other paleo-Christian writer whose chronology, homeland, and even cultural environment has been so disputed, leading to such divergent

conclusions." Scholars are divided on its placement in either in the third or the fifth century. Today, however, the clear majority believe it to be from the third century.

The acrostic dedicated to the deacons *(LXVIII) is an exhortation without any particular references to concrete situations. Commodian alludes to the double office of the deacon, the administrative and the liturgical. The invitation to deacons to be submissive to the shepherds, i.e., to the bishops (v. 8), again confirms the close bond between these two ministries.*

Instructions

To the Deacons

"LXVIII. Exercise the mystery of Christ, O deacons, with purity; therefore, O ministers, do the commands of your Master; do not play the person of a righteous judge; strengthen your office by all things, as learned men, looking upwards, always devoted to the Supreme God. Render the faithful sacred ministries of the altar to God, prepared in divine matters to set an example; yourselves incline your head to the pastors, so shall it come to pass that ye may be approved of Christ."

Fabian (?–250)

The bishop of Rome, Fabian was elected in the year 236. During his fourteen years of episcopate, he took care of the organization and administration of the Roman Church. He divided the city into seven wards, each one entrusted to a deacon. He also gave further structure to the degrees of Orders, as it appears in a letter from his successor, Cornelius. He died on January 20, 250. It was only after about fourteen months of sede vacante *that Cornelius was finally elected in March of 251. During that time, it was the clergy—presbyters and deacons—who assured the continuation of ecclesial life. We know that during this period, the Roman clergy maintained a certain epistolary activity with the other Churches. We have evidence of six letters, of which one was addressed to Cyprian.*

In these letters, there is, above all, a clear awareness of the Roman Church's role within wider Christendom.

In the present passage, there is mention of the subdeacon, Crementius, who belonged to the Carthaginian clergy and acted as a courier between Africa and Rome. Subdiaconus, *from a linguistic point of view, is a hybrid. Cyprian, for his part, would always write* hypodiaconus. *The subdeacons, along with the deacons and acolytes, were often bearers of correspondence between the Churches.*

Epistles of Cyprian

The Good Shepherd Gives His Life for His Sheep

"II, 1. We have been informed by Crementius the sub-deacon, who came to us from you, that the blessed father Cyprian has for a certain reason withdrawn; 'in doing which he acted quite rightly, because he is a person of eminence, and because a conflict is impending,' which God has allowed in the world, for the sake of cooperating with his servants in their struggle against the adversary, and was, moreover, willing that this conflict should show to angels and to men that the victor shall be crowned, while the vanquished shall in himself receive the doom which has been made manifest to us. Since, moreover, it devolves upon us who appear to be placed on high, in the place of a shepherd, to keep watch over the flock."

Cornelius of Rome (?–253)

The presbyter Cornelius was made bishop of Rome in March of 251, after fourteen months of sede vacante *because of the Decian persecution. To his credit, his whole life was spent at the service of the Church, throughout the various degrees of Orders. He entered into the ministry as a celibate, and so was probably rather young. His brief episcopate (251–253) was marked by the grave schism of Novatian, also a presbyter of the Roman Church, a character notable for his education and theological capacity.*

Cornelius is extremely important for the information he offers about the clergy in Rome during his day. The order of the various degrees would remain unvaried in Rome (at least in theory) until the reform of the Second Vatican Council. In descending order, therefore, we find: bishops, presbyters, deacons, subdeacons, acolytes, exorcists, lectors, *and* doorkeepers. *This does not, however, mean that there was already a rigidly fixed clerical* cursus.

Also interesting are the figures that Cornelius gives: the number of deacons (and subdeacons) appears limited to seven in reference to the "Seven" of Acts 6.

Epistles

The Irregular Ordination of Novatian

"10. One of these bishops shortly after came back to the church, lamenting and confessing his transgression. And we communed with him as with a layman, all the people present interceding for him. And we ordained successors of the other bishops, and sent them to the places where they were.

"11. This avenger of the Gospel then did not know that there should be one bishop in a Catholic church; yet he was not ignorant (for how could he be?) that in it there were forty-six presbyters, seven deacons, seven sub-deacons, forty-two acolytes, fifty-two exorcists, readers, and janitors, and over fifteen hundred widows and persons in distress, all of whom the grace and kindness of the Master nourish (*Letter to Fabius of Antioch*, in Eusebius, *Church History*, Book VI, XLIII)."

D. EASTERN FATHERS OF THE FOURTH CENTURY

Eusebius of Caesarea (ca. 265–ca. 340)

Eusebius was probably born in Caesarea of Palestine, the city of which he later became bishop. Imprisoned during the persecution of Diocletian, he was later able to return to Palestine following the 311 Edict of Constantine, which made Christian worship permissible. His fame is mainly linked to the "Church History," a work precious for the knowledge it gives us on the origins of Christianity, yet its text also contains exegetical, dogmatic, and apologetic works.

The text that follows deals with a conflict between Pope Cornelius and the priest Novatian (called Novatus by Eusebius) in Rome around 250. It provides us with interesting information on the structure of the Roman Church in the third century and the role of the deacons.

Church History

News About Cornelius and Novatian

"Book VI, XLIII, 2. There upon a very large synod assembled at Rome, of bishops in number sixty, and a great many more presbyters and deacons. . . . 3. There have reached us epistles of Cornelius, bishop of Rome, to Fabius, of the Church at Antioch, which show what was done at the synod at Rome, and what seemed best to all those in Italy and Africa and the regions thereabout. . . . 5. Cornelius informs Fabius what sort of a man Novatus was, in the following words: . . . 16. Shortly after he says again: 'In the time of persecution, through cowardice and love of life, he denied that he was a presbyter. For when he was requested and entreated by the deacons to come out of the chamber in which he had imprisoned himself and give aid to the brethren as far as was lawful and possible for a presbyter to assist those of the brethren who were in danger and needed help, he paid so little respect to the entreaties of the deacons that he went away and departed in anger. For he said that he no longer desired to be a presbyter, as he was an admirer of another philosophy.'"

Pseudo-Athanasius

Under the name of the great bishop of Alexandria, Athanasius circulated a work titled De Trinitate. *The work was attributed to Didymus of Alexandria, but today it is held to be from an environment influenced by Cappadocian theology, perhaps from Constantinople.*

De Trinitate

"Bishops, presbyters, and deacons are consubstantial" (1, 27).[8]

Cyril of Jerusalem (ca. 315–386)

Born around 315 in Jerusalem or its outskirts, Cyril received an excellent literary formation; this was the foundation of his ecclesiastical education, centered on the study of the Bible. Ordained a presbyter by Bishop Maximus, he was ordained bishop in 348 by Acacius, metropolitan of Caesarea of Palestine, when Maximus either died or was deposed. Acacius was a philo-Arian, convinced that he had an ally in Cyril. For this reason he was suspected of having obtained his episcopal nomination after making concessions to Arianism.

In the course of about twenty years, Cyril knew three exiles. The first was in 357 after being deposed by a synod in Jerusalem. This was followed by a second exile in 360 by the hand of Acacius. Finally, he endured a third and longer exile (eleven years) in 367 by the initiative of the philo-Arian emperor Valens. It was only in 378, after the emperor's death, that Cyril was able to take definitive possession of his see, bringing unity and peace back among his faithful.

Twenty-four famous catecheses of his, which he presented as bishop around 350, have been preserved for us. The last five (19-23), are the so-called "mystagogical" catecheses. He died in Jerusalem on March 18, 386.

Baptismal Catechesis

The first deacons and particularly Stephen were filled with the Holy Spirit.

"XVII, 24. And it was not in the Twelve Apostles only that the grace of the Holy Spirit wrought, but also in the first-born children of this once barren Church, I mean the seven Deacons; for these also were chosen, as it is written, being 'full of the Holy Ghost and of wisdom.' Of whom Stephen, rightly so named, the first fruits of the Martyrs, a man 'full of faith and of the Holy Ghost, wrought great wonders and miracles among the people,' and vanquished those

8 [Translation of the Italian text.]

who disputed him; 'for they were not able to resist the wisdom and the Spirit by which he spake.' But when he was maliciously accused and brought to the judgment hall, he was radiant with angelic brightness; for 'all they who sat in the council, looking steadfastly on him, saw his face, as it had been the face of an angel.' And having by his wise defense confuted the Jews, those 'stiffnecked men, uncircumcised in heart and ears, ever resisting the Holy Ghost,' he beheld 'the heavens opened,' and saw 'the Son of Man standing on the right hand of God.' He saw him, not by his own power, but, as the Divine Scripture says, 'being full of the Holy Ghost, he looked up steadfastly into heaven, and saw the glory of God, and Jesus standing on the right hand of God.'"

Philip, one of the Seven, was an instrument of the Spirit.

"XVII, 25. In this power of the Holy Ghost, Philip, also in the Name of Christ, at one time in the city of Samaria drove away the unclean spirits, 'crying out with a loud voice,' and healed the palsied and the lame, and brought to Christ great multitudes of them that believe. To whom Peter and John came down, and with prayer and the laying on of hands, imparted the fellowship of the Holy Ghost, from which Simon Magus alone was declared an alien, and that justly. And at another time Philip was called by the angel of the Lord in the way, for the sake of that most godly Ethiopian, the eunuch, and heard distinctly the Spirit himself saying, 'Go near, and join thyself to this chariot.' He instructed the eunuch and baptized him, and so having sent into Ethiopia a herald of Christ, according as it is written, 'Ethiopia shall soon stretch out her hand unto God,' he was caught away by the angel and preached the Gospel in the cities in succession."

Cyril and John of Jerusalem (? 315)

Born around 315 in Jerusalem or its outskirts, Cyril received an excellent literary formation; this was the foundation of his ecclesiastical education, centered on the study of the Bible. Ordained a presbyter by Bishop Maximus, he was ordained bishop in 348 by Acacius, metropolitan of Caesarea of Palestine, when Maximus either died or was deposed. Acacius was a philo-Arian, convinced that he had an ally in Cyril. For this reason he was suspected of having obtained his episcopal nomination after making concessions to Arianism. The Eastern bishops officially recognize Cyril's absolute orthodoxy, the legitimacy of his episcopal ordination, and the merits of his pastoral service, which ended with his death in 387.

Of the last five Catecheses *attributed to Cyril of Jerusalem, called* "mystagogical," *his successor, John of Jerusalem (386–417), is considered the true author. They deal with the sacraments normally received on Easter.*

Mystagogical Catechesis

The Offertory: The Washing of Hands

"XXIII, 2. Ye have seen then the deacon who gives to the priest water to wash, and to the presbyters who stand round God's altar. He gave it not at all because of bodily defilement; it is not that; for we did not enter the Church at first with defiled bodies. But the washing of hands is a symbol that ye ought to be pure from all sinful and unlawful deeds; for since the hands are a symbol of action, by washing them, it is evident we represent the purity and blamelessness of our conduct. Didst thou not hear the blessed David opening this very mystery, and saying, 'I will wash my hands in innocency, and so will compass thine altar, O Lord'? The washing therefore of hands is a symbol of immunity from sin."

The Offertory: The Kiss of Peace

"XXIII, 3. Then the deacon cries aloud, 'Receive ye one another; and let us kiss one another.' Think not that this kiss is of the same character with those given in public by common friends. It is not such: but this kiss blends souls one with another, and courts entire forgiveness for them. The kiss therefore is the sign that our souls are mingled together and banish all remembrance of wrongs. For this cause, Christ said, 'If thou art offering thy gift at the altar, and there rememberest that thy brother hath aught against thee, leave there thy gift upon the altar, and go thy way; first be reconciled to thy brother, and then come and offer thy gift.' The kiss therefore is reconciliation, and for this reason holy: as the blessed Paul somewhere cried, saying, 'Greet ye one another with a holy kiss'; and Peter, 'with a kiss of charity.'"

John Chrysostom (ca. 344/354–ca. 398/407)

In the Antiochean Church, it is the thought of John Chrysostom that is most prevalent on deacons. According to him, the seven deacons spoken of in the Acts of the Apostles were ordained neither deacons nor presbyters in the actual sense of the terms, and the laying on of hands that they received was only for a narrowly defined purpose, responding to the need of the moment: the service of the tables.

Homily on the Acts of the Apostles

"XIV. But what sort of rank these (deacons) bore, and what sort of office (*cheirotonía*) they received, this is what we need to learn. Was it that (ordination) of deacons? And yet this is not the case in the Churches. But is it to the presbyters that the management belongs? And yet at present there was no bishop, but the Apostles only. Whence I think it clearly and manifestily follows, that neither deacons nor presbyters is their designation: but it was for this particular purpose that they were ordained (i.e., for serving the tables)."[9]

Homily on the First Letter to Timothy

The Gifts That a Candidate to the Diaconate Must Possess

"XI. Discoursing of bishops, and having described their character, and the qualities which they ought to possess, and having passed over the order of presbyters, he proceeds to that of deacons. The reason of this omission was, that between presbyters and bishops there was no great difference. Both had undertaken the office of teachers and presidents in the Church, and what he has said concerning bishops is applicable to presbyters. For they are only superior in having the power of ordination and seem to have no other advantage over presbyters.

"'Likewise the Deacons.' That is, they should have the same qualities as bishops. And what are these same? To be blameless, sober, hospitable, patient, not brawlers, not covetous. And that he means this when he says 'likewise,' is evident from what he says in addition, 'grave, not double-tongued'; that is, not

9 [Words in parentheses are from the Italian text.]

hollow or deceitful. For nothing so debases a man as deceit, nothing is so pernicious in the Church as insincerity. 'Not given to much wine, not greedy of filthy lucre; holding the mystery of the faith in a pure conscience.' Thus he explains what he means by 'blameless.' And here he requires, though in other words, that he be 'not a novice,' where he says, 'Let these also first be proved,' where the conjunction 'also' is added, as connecting this with what had been said before of bishops, for nothing intervenes between. And there is the same reason for the 'not a novice' in that case. For would it not be absurd that when a newly purchased slave is not entrusted with anything in a house till he has by long trial given proofs of his character, yet that one should enter into the Church of God from a state of heathenism and be at once placed in a station of preeminence? (1 Tm 3:8-10)."

It Was Announced to the Pagans, Believed in the World

"XI. He was heard of and believed in through all parts of the world, as the prophet foreshowed, saying, 'Their sound is gone out into all the world' (Ps 19:4). Think not that these things are mere words, for they are not, but full of hidden realities. 'Received up into glory.' He ascended upon clouds. 'This Jesus,' it is said, 'who is taken up from you, shall so come in like manner as ye have seen him go into heaven' (Acts 1:11).

"The discretion of the blessed Paul is observable. When he would exhort the deacons to avoid excess in wine, he does not say, 'Be not drunken,' but 'not' even 'given to much wine.' A proper caution; for if those who served in the Temple did not taste wine at all, much more should not these. For wine produces disorder of mind, and where it does not cause drunkenness, it destroys the energies and relaxes the firmness of the soul.

"The dispensation in our behalf he calls a 'mystery,' and well may it be so called, since it is not manifest to all, nay, it was not manifest to the angels, for how could it, when it was 'made known by the Church'? (Eph 3:10). Therefore he says, 'without controversy great is the mystery.'"

On the Priesthood

Priestly Dignity

"III, 4. And very naturally so: for neither man, nor angel, nor archangel, nor any other created power, but the Paraclete himself instituted this vocation and persuaded men while still abiding in the flesh to represent the ministry of angels."

On the Obscurity of Prophecies[10]

"Do you want to learn just how great the power of the prayer made in the Church is? Once Peter was held prisoner and was bound by many chains: 'a prayer rose continuously from the Church for him,' and it suddenly freed him from prison. What, then, could be more powerful than this prayer which came to his aid from the columns and towers of the Church? Peter and Paul, in fact, were towers and columns of the Church; well, one's mouth was opened, and the other's chains were broken. In order to demonstrate the double force of prayer on the basis not only of what happened then, but also on what takes place on an everyday basis, let us call to mind the very prayer made by the people. Certainly, if someone in the crowd were to order any one of you to pray on your own for the bishop's salvation, each one of you would refuse, that being a burden far beyond your strength. But all of you together, listening to the deacon ordering it, saying: 'Let us pray for the bishop, for his health in old age, for his protection, that he may correctly expound on the word of truth for those who are here and for those everywhere,' you do not refuse to follow the order, but raise your prayer with zeal, aware of the strength of your assembly. Those who have been initiated into the divine mysteries know what I say; in fact, this is not yet granted to the prayer of catechumens, for they have not yet arrived at this

10 5, 14-15. τοῦ διακόνου . . . λέγοντος. On this type of ecclesial prayer, led by the deacon, cf. *Apost. Const.* VIII, 10; ed. F. X. Funk, vol. I, Paderbonae 1906, 488-492, especially 489-490. On the Syrian liturgy in the fourth cent., cf. *Liturgies eastern and western being the texts original or translated of the principal liturgies of the Church*, ed. F. E. Brightman, vol. I, Oxford 1896, 9 ff. On the Antiochean liturgy according to the writings of Chrysostom, see F. Probst, *Liturgie des vierten Jahrhunderts und deren Reform*, Münster i. W. 1896, 9 ff.; on the prayer of the faithful, 171 ff. Regarding the function of deacons, it should be remembered that Chrysostom, in the commentary to Rom 8:26, seeing in this Pauline passage reference to the gift of prayer, notes that such a charism was only granted to some so that they might ask God for what was useful for the whole Church and adds that a symbol of this charismatic person is the deacon who prays for the people; in Rom 14:7; *Patrologia Graeco-Latina* (PG) 60, 533.

familiarity in speech. You, on the other hand, are encouraged by the one who has been made responsible for these, to make supplications for the world, for the Church spread to the ends of the earth, for all of the bishops that govern it; and you obey with commitment, giving witness with deeds to how great the power is of that prayer which the people in church raise with one heart."[11]

Theodore of Mopsuestia (ca. 350–428)

Theodore of Mopsuestia was bishop of Mopsuestia (corresponding to the modern-day village of Yakapinar in Turkey) from 392 to 428. He is also known as Theodore of Antioch, after his birthplace. He is the best known among the representatives of the school of Antiochian hermeneutics.

One reference to deacons is contained in the First Letter to Timothy: "Similarly, deacons must be dignified, not deceitful, not addicted to drink, not greedy for sordid gain, holding fast to the mystery of the faith with a clear conscience. Moreover, they should be tested first; then, if there is nothing against them, let them serve as deacons. Women, similarly, should be dignified, not slanderers, but temperate and faithful in everything. Deacons may be married only once and must manage their children and their households well. Thus those who serve well as deacons gain good standing and much confidence in their faith in Christ Jesus" (3:8-13).

Commentary on the Epistles of St. Paul

"This, then, stands as a prohibition and recommends that one may only be chosen for the episcopate if throughout his life he has given witness to integrity, or of demonstrating acts of extreme virtue, or proving with penitence of having gone from evil to goodness.

"Many still seek this out as the best custom, and they interpret it to mean this: married to only one wife, and happily so, since in those days there were many who had two legitimate wives, which seemed licit according to the law of Moses. Many, even if they had only one legitimate wife, and not being content with her, had relations with others or with their handmaidens, or very often

11 [Translation of the Italian text.]

cavorted with whomever should be willing, as even happens today with women who do not aspire to good behavior.

"Therefore, this is what Paul asks for: chosen for the episcopate is he who, united to only one wife, has lived with her prudently, being bound to her, and it is only with her that he has abandoned himself to natural passion. Yet, should he lose his first wife and marry a second lawfully, and live with her in the same way, let the episcopacy not be denied him, as Paul prescribes without a doubt" (cf. *Patrologia Graeco-Latina* (PG) 66,939 BC).[12]

Theodoret of Cyrus (ca. 393–ca. 457)

Theodoret, bishop of Cyrus and theologian, was born in Antioch around 393. From the time he was little, he was educated for an ecclesiastical, theological career, having studied the writings of Diodorus of Tarsus, St. John Chrysostom, and Theodore of Mopsuestia. In 423, he was named bishop of Cyrus in Syria.

From 430 on, Theodoret was involved in the Christological controversy between Nestorius and Cyril of Alexandria, aligning himself against the latter in the Council of Ephesus in 431, in which he demanded Cyril's deposition and excommunication. In 436, he wrote his Anatrope *(Confutation) against Cyril, in which he reaffirmed the duality of Christ's nature and accused Cyril of mixing the Christ's two natures in such a way as to form a single divine nature.*

Commentary on the Epistles of St. Paul

"Therefore, since in that time those who practiced chastity were not easy to find, he commanded that those who were married and had temperance were to be ordained.

"To me, then, it seems that they rightly indicated the man who had been married to only one wife.

"At one time, in fact, both Greeks and Jews had the practice of being joined in marriage to two, three, or even several wives. Truth be told, even now, some have relationships with concubines and harlots, even though the imperial laws prohibit marrying two wives simultaneously. They said, therefore, that

12 [Ibid.]

according to the divine Apostle, he who lives modestly with one wife is worthy of being ordained" (cf. PG 82,653A).[13]

The Same Principle Is Valid Even for Bishops

"Let deacons be married to only one wife: this should be interpreted in the same way as before. [Let it be] they who direct their own children and homes. And let these rules be also for those who are called bishops. Those who have indeed administered well shall gain a high degree for themselves, and much trustworthiness in the faith that is in Christ Jesus.

"'Similarly the women,' understanding the deaconesses. [Let them be] serious and not slandering; sober and loyal to all. All that he established for the men, [he established] also for the women. Just as he said 'honest deacons,' so also honest women; and just as he commanded the men not to be liars, so [did he command] the women not to be slanderers; and just as he established that the men not be given over to much wine, so also did he command that the women be sober" (cf. PG 82,856A).[14]

Pseudo-Dionysius (The Areopagite)

A body of writings known as the Corpus Areopagiticum *is attributed to Pseudo-Dionysius the Areopagite, the author of mysterious identity mentioned in Acts 17:34. Among these works,* The Church Hierarchy *holds a prominent place. Comprising seven chapters, the work illustrates the sacred order of the Church, corresponding to the angelic order. It describes and allegorically interprets the liturgical functions of the entrance of a new follower of the Christian religion (chapter 2), of the Mass and Sacrament of the Eucharist (chapter 3), of the consecration of the holy oils (chapter 4), and of the various funeral rites (chapter 7), then most especially examines the hierarchical structure of the Church as an image of the heavenly one. The tangible head of the church hierarchy is the bishop, who transmits initiation to the lower orders; but the true head of each hierarchy, heavenly or human, is God. The church hierarchy occupies an intermediate place between the heavenly one and the "legal" one of the Old Testament: like the heavenly one, it carries out*

13 [Ibid.]
14 [Ibid.]

the three functions of purification, illumination, and initiation, and is composed of three orders of initiators (bishops, priests, deacons) and of three orders of the initiated (the purified, the illuminated, the elect).

The Church Hierarchy

The Sacrament of Illumination

"Once the catechumen has completed this, he is ordered again three times to recite his profession of faith, and after he has recited it again three times, he prays, blesses him, and places his hands upon him. After the deacons have completely undressed him, the priests bring the sacred oil of unction. Then the bishop, after beginning to anoint him by making the sign of the cross on him three times, entrusts him to the priests so that they may continue to anoint his whole body and goes himself to the godmother [lit. "mother of adoption"]. He sanctifies his water with holy invocations and, having consecrated it with three cruciform infusions of the holy oil and with the same number of holy aspersions, intones the sacred chant that celebrates the font about the inspiration of prophets possessed by God, and he orders that the man be brought to him. A priest then pronounces the name of the man being baptized as well as his sponsor's in a loud voice on the basis of the registration that has taken place; the catechumen then is led by the priest to the baptismal water and is drawn in by the hand of the bishop" (Chap. II: "The Sacred Rites of Illumination").[15]

The Sacrament of the Eucharist or Communion

"Once the sacred prayer has been recited at the divine altar, the bishop commences incensing and, starting from the altar, proceeds along the perimeter of the holy enclosure. After returning to the divine altar, he begins to intone the sacred chant of the psalms; all of the ecclesiastical orders participate with him in this sacred, sung recitation. Soon after, the deacons perform the readings of sacred scriptural texts. After that, the catechumens and even those who are yet possessed by the devil and those who have repented leave the sacred enclosure, within which those who are worthy of laying eyes on the divine realities and

15 [Ibid.]

of communion with them remain. Some deacons stand at the closed doors of the temple, while others carry out some other function proper to their rank; those within the diaconal order who greatly excel instead place the bread and the "chalice of benediction" on the divine altar side-by-side with the priests after the whole assembly of the Church has sung the profession of the Catholic faith. The divine bishop then finishes reciting the sacred prayer and announces the holy peace to all, after which everyone embraces each other, and the mystical, solemn reading of the sacred lists takes place. The bishop and the priests wash their hands with water. The bishop then remains standing at the center of the divine altar, with only the best deacons standing around him together with the priests. After the holy, divine works have been commemorated, the bishop undertakes the most divine acts and shows what he has commemorated, making use of the symbols sacredly present. Once he has shown the gifts of these divine acts, he takes Communion himself in a holy manner and invites the others to do the same. After making the divine Communion and offering it to the others, he concludes the celebration with a sacred thanksgiving. While the crowd of those present is limited to penetrating only the meaning of the sacred symbols, he himself, under the guidance of the divine Spirit according to his hierarchical position, is elevated into a blessed and spiritual contemplation and into the purity of his state, similar to God toward the holy principles of the rite" (Chap. III: "The Sacred Rites of the Eucharist").[16]

The Spiritual Meaning

"I further believe, rather, I am very sure—that the most pure, distinctive, hierarchical criteria should have one thing present: the ones that are shaken even more than these inferior classes by the most horrid agitations are all of those who behave as wicked demons. In their extreme and wicked stupidity, on the one hand they refuse the true realities, the goods whose possession has no end and whose enjoyment is eternal, while on the other hand, they seek what is material, rich in many passions and changeable, pleasures that are corruptible and corrupting, unstable well-being consisting in external things, not real but only apparent, and they act accordingly. It is these last ones whom, before all others, the deacon must not allow when the separation is ordered. They are not permitted to participate in a sacred function other than 'hearing' the oracular

16 [Ibid.]

teaching that would have him turn toward a better life" (Chap. III: "The Sacred Rites of the Eucharist").[17]

The Sacrament of Orders

"On the one hand, in the celebrations that he performs, he illustrates the divine workings through the most holy symbols, making it possible to contemplate the sacramental rites and for those who approach them to take part in them; on the other hand, he directs those who desire to reach the knowledge of the sacred rites contemplated to the bishop. Therefore, the order of ministers, which purifies and separates dissimilarities, makes pure those who wish to approach the sacraments before leading them to the rites celebrated by the priests, freeing them of any hindering condition and making them able to contemplate the sacred rites and to take part in them. For this reason, on the occasion of their holy, divine birth, the deacons undress the postulant of his old clothing, remove his footwear, make him turn west in a sign of renunciation, and then lead him east. They order the postulants to completely cast away all of the clothing of their former life and, showing them the darkness, teach them how to be led to the light after renouncing the darkness. The order of deacons is a purifying one: it elevates those who have been purified toward the resplendent sacred rites of the priests, purifies those not yet initiated, brings them toward the birth to new life through the purifying illuminations and oracular teachings, and furthermore removes the impious from the sacred celebration, avoiding any confusion. This is why the hierarchical law places them close to the holy doors, alluding to the admission of completely purified aspirants to the holy ceremonies. Thanks to their purifying power, it grants them the possibility of approaching the ceremonies to contemplate them in a holy manner and to take part in them, and it welcomes them once they are without stain.

"It has been shown, then, how the order of bishops is the bringer of perfection and of initiation, just as that of priests is illuminating and leads to the light, and just as that of deacons is purifying and a worker of distinctions. It is clear, however, that the order of bishops does not only know how to initiate, but also to illuminate and purify, and that the power of priests reenters, along with the knowledge relating to illumination, that relating to purification as well. In effect, not only are the lower orders not able to jump toward the higher ones,

17 [Ibid.]

but they do not even have permission to attempt such a deception; the more divine powers, on the contrary, besides possessing the knowledge of their own powers, possess also that subordinate to their perfection.

"The bishop who approaches episcopal ordination, both knees bent before the divine altar, has on his head the oracular books handed down from God and the hand of the ordaining bishop; remaining in this position, he is ordained by the bishop who imparts ordination through most holy prayers. The priest, for his part, with both knees bent before the divine altar, has on his head the right hand of the ordaining bishop; in this position, he is sanctified by the bishop who ordains him through sanctifying prayers. The deacon, finally, bending one knee before the divine altar, has on his head the right hand of the bishop who ordains him, and is ordained by him through prayers proper to the ordination of deacons. On each of the ordinandi the ordaining bishop imprints the sign of the cross as a seal; and for each there is the sacred proclamation and embrace of ordination: all of the priests present and the ordaining bishop embrace the one who is ordained into one of the aforementioned priestly orders" (Chap. V: "The Sacrament of Orders").[18]

Spiritual Meaning

"In their priestly ordinations, the priests and deacons both have the approach to the divine altar, the genuflection, the laying on of hands by the bishop, the impression with the sign of the cross, the official proclamation, and the embrace proper to ordination in common. Instead, for the bishop, the distinctive element is represented by the laying on of the book of oracles on his head, which does not pertain to the lower orders; for priests, there is the kneeling, not prescribed for the diaconal ordination. The latter, in fact, as has been said, bend only one knee.

"On the other hand, bending both knees is reserved for priests as a distinctive sign with respect to the diaconal order, which bends only one and is ordained on the basis of gesture corresponding to his hierarchical degree.

"The genuflection indicates the approach he has submitted to: he who does the drawing submits to God him who draws near in a holy manner. But since, as we have said many times, the three orders of initiators with their three most holy initiations and their three most holy powers come before the three orders

18 [Ibid.]

of initiates and, under the guidance of the divine scales, perform the saving drawing-near of the latter, the diaconal order, being only purifying, are rightly limited to drawing the purified to the divine altar and entrusting them to it; thus the purified intelligences are consecrated transcendentally. The priests instead bend both knees insofar as those whom they draw are not only purified, but have even been ritually initiated by their resplendent liturgical rites for the condition and contemplative faculty proper to their already pure life, an indication of their elevation. The bishop, finally, when he bends both of his knees having on his head the book of oracles handed down by God, in conformity with his hierarchical rank, leads those who have been purified by the diaconal power and enlightened by the priestly power for the knowledge—in proportion to their capacity—of the sacred realities that they have contemplated, and through this he orders those who approach the full consecration proper to each" (Chap. V: "The Sacrament of Orders").[19]

The Initiates

"These are the priestly orders, their duties, their powers, their acts, and their ordinations. We must now illustrate the triad formed by the orders of initiates.

"Let us say, then, that the hosts of the purified are represented by all those who are held far from the sacred celebrations and liturgical rites that we have already recorded: one is still formed by the life-nurturing teaching of the deacons in view of their birth to life; another is called back to the holy life that they abandoned, by means of good oracles that work out their conversion; another, after letting themselves be frightened like cowards by scarily adverse situations, receives courage from the strengthening oracles; another is led from lower actions to holier ones; another, although already having been led, does not yet possess the most pure spotlessness of the most divine, stable state. These are the hosts purified by the life-nurturing action and purifying power of the deacons. The deacons make them perfect with their sacred powers so that, after being completely purified, they can be led to the illuminating contemplation of the splendid liturgical rites and to participation in them" (Chap. VI: "The Initiates").[20]

---

19 [Ibid.]
20 [Ibid.]

Spiritual Meaning

"Let us conclude then saying that the effects of the holy, sacramental rites are represented by purification, illumination, and perfection; that the order that purifies is that of the deacons; the order that illuminates is that of the priests; and the order that perfects is that of the bishops similar to God; that the purified class is that which cannot take part in holy contemplation and Communion, insofar as they are subject to purification; that the contemplative class is that of the holy people; and that the most perfect class is that of the monks similar to the One. In this way, indeed, our hierarchy—well-structured in a holy manner in the orders handed down by God—turns out to be similar to the celestial hierarchy and maintains those characteristics of it that imitate God and are similar to him in as much as is possible to mankind" (Chap. VI: "The Initiates").[21]

The Rite Regarding Those Who Have Died in a Holy Manner

"If the deceased had been part of the order of pure monks or of the holy people, the bishop has him placed inside of the venerable sanctuary in front of the entrance reserved for priests and then recites the prayer of thanksgiving to God. Following this, the deacons, having read the true promises concerning our holy resurrection contained in the divine oracles, piously intone the corresponding and equivalent chants and oracular psalms. The first among the deacons dismisses the catechumens and proclaims the names of the formerly deceased saints, making an analogous proclamation for the recently deceased one, and exhorts all to implore God for a blessed death in Christ. The divine bishop approaches and then recites over the deceased the most holy prayer, after which he embraces the deceased, as do all of those present after him. Once all have embraced him, the bishop pours the oil over the deceased and, after the holy prayer for all has been recited, has his body placed in a venerable seat in company with the other bodies of the same order" (Chap. VII: "The Rites Regarding the Deceased").[22]

---

21 [Ibid.]
22 [Ibid.]

Egeria

The work known as the Itinerarium Egeriae *is closely connected to the flow of pilgrims that took on the journey to the Holy Land in the fourth century. It is an account of a pilgrimage undertaken by a woman at the end of the fourth century. In the first section, there are descriptions of the visit to Sinai in the footsteps of the Exodus, of the ascent of Mount Nebo, and of journeys to Carneas and in Mesopotamia, with the return to Constantinople and the visit to St. Thecla's place of martyrdom. In the second part, the liturgy in Jerusalem is detailed, with the presence of deacons.*

Pilgrimage to the Holy Land

In Jerusalem and on Mount Nebo

"Wherefore setting out from Jerusalem and journeying with holy men, with a priest and deacons from Jerusalem and with certain brothers, that is monks, we came to that spot on the Jordan where the children of Israel had crossed when holy Joshua, the son of Nun, had led them over Jordan, as it is written in the book of Joshua, the son of Nun. The place where the children of Reuben and of Gad and the half tribe of Manasseh had made an altar was shown us a little higher up on that side of the riverbank where Jericho is" ("Visit to the Jordan Valley").

The Liturgy in Jerusalem—Daily Liturgy

"And from that hour to daybreak hymns are said and psalms are sung responsively (*responduntur*), and antiphons in like manner; and prayer is made after each of the hymns. For priests, deacons, and monks in twos or threes take it in turn every day to say prayers after each of the hymns or antiphons. But when day breaks, they begin to say the Matin hymns. Thereupon the bishop arrives with the clergy, and immediately enters into the cave, and from within the rails (*cancelli*), he first says a prayer for all.

"Now the light is not introduced from without, but it is brought forth from within the cave, that is from within the rails, where a lamp is always burning day and night, and the vesper psalms and antiphons are said, lasting for a considerable time. Then the bishop is summoned, and he comes and takes a raised seat, and likewise the priests sit in their proper places, and hymns and antiphons are said. And when all these have been recited according to custom, the bishop rises and stands before the rails, that is, before the cave, and one of the deacons makes the customary commemoration of individuals one by one. And as the deacon pronounces each name, the many little boys who are always standing by answer with countless voices: *Kyrie eleyson*, or as we say: *Miserere Domine*. And when the deacon has finished all that he has to say, first the bishop says a prayer and prays for all, then they all pray, both the faithful and catechumens together. Again the deacon raises his voice, bidding each catechumen to bow his head where he stands, and the bishop stands and says the blessing over the catechumens. Again prayer is made, and again the deacon raises his voice and bids the faithful, each where he stands, to bow the head, and the bishop likewise blesses the faithful. Thus the dismissal takes place at the Anastasis, and, one by one, all draw near to the bishop's hand" ("Jerusalem: Daily Offices").

The Sunday Liturgy

"But on the seventh day, that is on the Lord's Day, the whole multitude assembles before cockcrow, in as great numbers as the place can hold, as at Easter, in the basilica which is near the Anastasis, but outside the doors, where lights are hanging for the purpose. And for fear that they should not be there at cockcrow, they come beforehand and sit down there. Hymns as well as antiphons are said, and prayers are made between the several hymns and antiphons, for at the vigils there are always both priests and deacons ready there for the assembling of the multitude, the custom being that the holy places are not opened before cockcrow. Now as soon as the first cock has crowed, the bishop arrives and enters the cave at the Anastasis; all the doors are opened, and the whole multitude enters the Anastasis, where countless lights are already burning. And when the people have entered, one of the priests says a psalm to which all respond, and afterwards prayer is made; then one of the deacons says a psalm, and prayer is again made; a third psalm is said by one of the clergy, and prayer is made for the third time, and there is a commemoration of all. . . . And forthwith the bishop betakes himself to his house, and from that hour all the monks return to the Anastasis, where psalms and antiphons, with prayer after each psalm or antiphon, are said until daylight; the priests and deacons also keep watch in turn daily at the Anastasis with the people, but of the laypeople, whether men or women, those who are so minded remain in the place until daybreak, and those who are not return to their houses and betake themselves to sleep.

"And after the people, the bishop enters and goes at once within the rails of the cave of the martyrium. Thanks are first given to God, then prayer is made for all, after which the deacon bids all bow their heads where they stand, and the bishop standing within the inner rails blesses them and goes out, each one drawing near to his hand as he makes his exit" ("Jerusalem: Sunday Offices").

Holy Week

"Accordingly, at the seventh hour, all the people go up to the Mount of Olives, that is, to Eleona, and the bishop with them, to the church, where hymns and antiphons suitable to the day and to the place are said, and lessons in like manner. And when the ninth hour approaches, they go up with hymns to the Imbomon, that is, to the place whence the Lord ascended into heaven, and there they sit down, for all the people are always bidden to sit when the bishop is present; the deacons alone always stand. Hymns and antiphons suitable to the day and to the place are said, interspersed with lections and prayers.

"After this, when the dismissal at the cross has been made, that is, before the sun rises, they all go at once with fervor to Sion, to pray at the column at which the Lord was scourged. And returning thence, they sit for awhile in their houses, and presently all are ready. Then a chair is placed for the bishop in Golgotha behind the cross, which is now standing; the bishop duly takes his seat in the chair, and a table covered with a linen cloth is placed before him; the deacons stand around the table, and a silver-gilt casket is brought in, which is the holy wood of the Cross. The casket is opened and (the wood) is taken out, and both the wood of the Cross and the title are placed upon the table. Now, when it has been put upon the table, the bishop, as he sits, holds the extremities of the sacred wood firmly in his hands, while the deacons who stand around guard it. It is guarded thus because the custom is that the people, both faithful and catechumens, come one by one and, bowing down at the table, kiss the sacred wood and pass through. And because, I know not when, some one is said to have bitten off and stolen a portion of the sacred wood, it is thus guarded by the deacons who stand around, lest anyone approaching should venture to do so again. And as all the people pass by one by one, all bowing themselves, they touch the Cross and the title, first with their foreheads and then with their eyes; then they kiss the Cross and pass through, but none lays his hand upon it to touch it. When they have kissed the Cross and have passed through, a deacon stands holding the ring of Solomon and the horn from which the kings were anointed; they kiss the horn also and gaze at the ring . . . all the people are passing through up to the sixth hour, entering by one door and going out by another; for this is done in the same place where, on the preceding day, that is, on the fifth weekday, the oblation [*i.e., the Eucharist*] was offered" ("Jerusalem: Holy Week and the Festivals at Easter").

E. THE CAPPADOCIAN FATHERS

Gregory of Nazianzus (330–390)

Of all the different expressions used by the Nazianzen to designate the hierarchical degrees, we found one in particular that could bring us to a truer portrayal of the deacon: "not far from the same Spirit."

Orations and Letters

"See the assembly of the presbyters, honored for years and wisdom, the fair order of the deacons, who are not far from the same Spirit, the good conduct of the readers, the people's eagerness for teaching" (Oration 42, 11 [SCh 384, 74]).

In another text of the farewell oration to the episcopal see of Constantinople, Nazianzen goes through a list starting with the apostles:

"Farewell, ye Apostles . . . . Farewell, my throne, envied and perilous height; farewell assembly of high priests, honored by the dignity and age of its priests, and all ye others ministers of God round the holy table, drawing nigh to the God who draws nigh to you" (Oration 62, 26 [SCh 384, 110]).

In Letter 98, Gregory of Nazianzus directly names the deacon in charge of the chapel of martyrs with the title of priest. Gregory intervenes with the city administrators supporting the deacon Theotecnos so that he will not have to pay taxes unjustly. In this context, Theotecnos is called deacon, poor, stranger, charitable, venerable for his way of life, and also priest and pastor of the sanctuary of martyrs:

"You want to make my brother Theotecnos pay taxes on works he performs. What is there to say in the first place, or what is most important to say among all the just reasons in his defense? That he is a deacon, or needy, or a stranger, or that he has more relationships with others than with us, or that he is venerable for his way of life, being priest of the martyrs and living with them?" (Ep. 98).[23]

The deacon possesses the Holy Spirit, whom he has received with the laying on of hands. But in what measure? In the Oration full of exultation for the end of paganism, Gregory of Nazianzus remembers the importance of worthily performed sacrifice and puts "the dignity of deacons" in the forefront. We can take note here that Gregory uses the word σεμνότης *to indicate the dignity of deacons rather than the term* ἀξίωμα, *which is used both by the Cappadocians and by the canons of the Synods to indicate the dignity of bishops.*

It is important to see how the word σεμνότης *is sometimes translated with the meaning of "sacred character":*

"No more shall they turn their wicked sight upon our holy edifices. They will not dirty the altars that owe their name to purity and to unbloody sacrifice. They will no longer profane the inaccessible places of our temples with godless altars. They will not steal nor contaminate the offerings, combining greed with impiety, nor will they bring offense upon the gray hairs of the priests, the dignity of the deacons, the modesty of the virgins, . . . no longer, having fabricated a hoard of pestilence, shall they delight in curses against bishops, priests, or even against prophets, apostles, and even against Christ himself" (Or. 5, 29 [SCh 309, 352]).[24]

The situation of the deacon Glycerius, however, is very different. He is no longer a messenger, but involved in serving an old priest at the church of Venosa. Gregory of Nazianzus presents the deacon this way:

"This Glycerius, who is now so arrogant and demands respect from you, was ordained by us as a deacon of the church of Venosa, whether to serve the priest, or to care for church work. In fact, this man, even if he is strange in other regards, in practical things at least is not without his talents. However, barely was he ordained than he neglected his work to such a degree that it was as if he had never even been ordained."[25]

Up to this point, we can understand what the scope of deacon Glycerius' ordination was. He, however, shirks his duty and begins to carry out an activity

23 [Translation of the Italian text.]
24 [Ibid.]
25 [Ibid.]

that puts the church community at risk, creating a good amount of disorder. The Nazianzene continues:

"Having gathered some unfortunate young women according to his judgment and volition, he began to take lead of their group, which partly flocked to him spontaneously . . . partly reluctantly. He gave himself the name and dress of a patriarch and suddenly began to behave arrogantly, coming to such not from some reasonable cause or spirit of piety, but gaining from it a means of living as would anyone else from any other activity. He just about sent the whole Church into ruin, disrespecting his priest, a man venerated for his conduct and piety, disrespecting the dear bishop and even us as worthy of no heed, and filling the city and all the clergy continuously with upheaval and disorder" (Ep. 246 [G. II, 135-137]).[26]

Gregory of Nazianzen asks Basil to help intervene in the situation. If the deacon returns to wisdom and reasonable moderation, things will go smoothly; otherwise, he will cease from his ministry and fall from his rank.

Gregory of Nyssa (ca. 332–394)

Gregory of Nyssa offers few references to the activities undertaken by deacons. The details he gives from the funeral of his sister Macrina show their presence with the bishops and presbyters. Let us take a closer look at the performance of this rite: the bishop Araxius, present at the funeral "with the entire complement of his priests . . . summoned to him all present who shared with him in the priesthood, that the body might be borne by them."

De Vita S. Macrinae

"I got under the bed and called Araxius to the other side; two other distinguished priests took the hinder part of the bed. Then I went forward, slowly as was to be expected, our progress being but gradual. For the people thronged round the bed and all were insatiable to see that holy sight, so that it was not easy for us to complete our journey. On either side, we were flanked by a considerable number of deacons and servants, escorting the bier in order, all holding

26 [Ibid.]

wax tapers. The whole thing resembled a mystic procession, and from beginning to end, the voices blended in singing psalms, for example, the 'Hymn of the Three Children'" [994B; SC 178, 250; PG 46, 993B].

Basil (ca. 329–379)

Basil makes reference to deacons in one of his letters, even if in the context of clearly administrative matters.

Epistles

"The immediate object of my entreaty is as follows. By the old census, the clergy of God, presbyters and deacons, were left exempt. The recent registrars, however, without any authority from your lordship, have enrolled them, except that in some cases a few were granted immunity on the score of age (Letter 104 [Court. 11, 5; PG 32, 509])."

In De Spiritu Sancto, *he takes up the words that the Apostle Paul addressed to the Romans and affirms that "we are all members one of the other, having different charisms according to that grace of God which has been given to us." During the ordination rite, the Holy Spirit is received through the laying on of hands.*

In the Epistles to Anphilochius (Epistles 118-199), he highlights that it is through the laying on of hands that the chárisma *of the Spirit, conferring the power of baptizing and ordaining, is imparted:*

De Spiritu Sancto

"In fact, those who first distanced themselves had received the ordination of the Fathers, and immediately following the laying on of their hands, they possessed the spiritual gift (χάρισμα). Those who were rejected, however, once they became laymen, had neither the faculty of baptizing nor ordaining, since they could no longer communicate to others the grace of the Holy Spirit from which they had fallen away" (26, 61 [SC 17, 468]).[27]

27 [Ibid.]

F. THE LATIN FATHERS OF THE FOURTH CENTURY

Passion of Euplius the Deacon (304)

The Passion of St. Euplius is a hagiographical document that comes down to us in a brief Latin text compiled on the basis of the verbal account of the arrest, from Euplius' first confession, and from the interrogations immediately between his tortures. The martyr was a deacon of Catania and sacrificed his life in 304. The main cause of accusation against Euplius is possession of the Gospels, forbidden by an imperial edict.

"In Sicily, in the year 304, under the ninth consulate of Diocletian and the eighth of Maximian, on the 12th of August, in the city of Catania, Euplius, a deacon, was brought to the governor's audience-chamber, and attending on the outside of the curtain, cried out, 'I am a Christian, and shall rejoice to die for the name of Jesus Christ.' The governor, Calvisianus, who was of consular dignity, heard him and ordered that he who had made that outcry should be brought in and presented before him. Euplius went in with the book of the Gospel in his hand. One of Calvisianus' friends, named Maximus, said, 'You ought not to keep such writings, contrary to the edicts of the emperors.' Calvisianus said to Euplius, 'Where had you those writings? Did you bring them from your own house?' Euplius replied that he had no house, but that he was seized with the book about him. The judge bid him read something in it. The martyr opened it and read the following verses, 'Blessed are they that are persecuted for righteousness' sake; for theirs is the Kingdom of Heaven.'

"And again, 'If any man will come after me, let him deny himself, and take up his cross and follow me.'

"The judge asked what that meant. The martyr answered, 'It is the law of my Lord, which hath been delivered to me.' Calvisianus said, 'By whom?' Euplius answered, 'By Jesus Christ, the Son of the living God.' Calvisianus then pronounced, 'Since his confession makes his disobedience manifest, let him be delivered up to the executioners and examined on the rack.' This was immediately done. Whilst they were tormenting him, Calvisianus asked him whether he persisted in his former declaration. Euplius, making the sign of the cross on his forehead with the hand that he had at liberty, said, 'What I formerly said I now declare again, that I am a Christian and read the Holy Scriptures.' Calvisianus ordered him to be hoisted on the rack and more cruelly tormented. The martyr said, whilst undergoing torture, 'I thank thee, O Lord Jesus Christ, that I suffer for thy sake: save me, I beseech thee.' Calvisianus said, 'Lay aside thy folly; adore our gods, and thou shalt be set at liberty.' Euplius answered, 'I adore Jesus Christ; I detest the devils. Do what you please, add new torments, for I am a Christian. I have long desired to be in the condition in which I now am.'

"After the executioners had tormented him a long time, Calvisianus bade them desist and said: 'Wretch, adore the gods; worship Mars, Apollo, and Aesculapius.' Euplius replied, 'I adore the Father, Son, and Holy Ghost. I worship the Holy Trinity, beside whom there is no God.' Calvisianus said, 'Sacrifice, if you would be delivered.' Euplius answered, 'I sacrifice myself now to Jesus Christ, my God. All your efforts to move me are to no purpose. I am a Christian.' Then Calvisianus gave orders for increasing his torments.

"Whilst the executioners were exerting their utmost in torturing him, Euplius prayed thus: 'I thank thee, my God; Jesus Christ, succor me. It is for thy name's sake that I endure these agonies.' This he repeated several times. When his strength failed him, his lips were seen still to move, the martyr continuing to pray inaudibly when he could not speak.

"Then Calvisianus went behind the curtain and dictated the sentence of death. Coming out with the tablet in his hand, he read, 'Euplius, a Christian, despising the edicts of the emperors, blaspheming the gods, and not repenting, is condemned to death by the sword. Lead him away.'

"Then the Gospel was hung about his neck, and the herald went before him, as he was conducted to execution, crying, 'Euplius, a Christian, the foe of the gods and of the emperors.'

"But Euplius, full of joy, cried incessantly, 'Thanks be to Christ, my God.' And when he has come to the place, he again gave thanks, submitted his throat to the executioner, and was decapitated. Then the Christians took up his body, embalmed it with spices, and buried it" (*Lives of the Saints*, Sabine Baring-Gould, 116-118).

Ambrose (339–397)

Aurelius Ambrosius, member of two important Roman senatorial families (the Aurelian family on his mother's side, the Symmachus family on his father's), was born in 339 in Trier, Germany, where his father was praetorian prefect for Gaul. Being destined for an administrative career, he frequented the best schools in Rome.

After five years as magistrate in Smyrna, he was sent in 370 to Milan as governor of northern Italy. In 374, upon the death of the Arian bishop Auxentius of Milan, Ambrose was acclaimed bishop even though he had not yet even received Baptism. Within the course of a week, he was baptized and consecrated.

Ambrose found himself in conflict with the religious politics of Theodosius I. With the Edict of Thessalonica in 380, Christianity was proclaimed the state religion. In 381, the Council of Aquileia proclaimed its stance against Arianism. In 390, Ambrose excommunicated the emperor, and in 391, Theodosius, with a series of decrees, prohibited pagan worship. He died in Milan in 397.

Ambrose speaks eloquently about the martyrdom of the deacon Lawrence in the De Officiis *(chap. XLI, 214-216), in the passage that follows; likewise do St. Maximus of Turin, St. Peter Chrysologus, and St. Leo the Great.*

De Officiis

"XLI, 214. And let us not pass by St. Lawrence, who, seeing Xystus [Sixtus] his bishop led to martyrdom, began to weep, not at his sufferings but at the fact that he himself was to remain behind. With these words he began to address him: 'Whither, father, goest thou without thy son? Whither, holy priest, art thou hastening without thy deacon? Never wast thou wont to offer sacrifice without an attendant. What are thou displeased at in me, my father? Hast thou found me unworthy? Prove, then, whether thou hast chosen a fitting servant. To him to whom thou hast entrusted the consecration of the Savior's blood, to whom thou hast granted fellowship in partaking of the Sacraments, to him dost thou refuse a part in thy death? Beware lest thy good judgment be endangered, whilst thy fortitude receives its praise. The rejection of a pupil is the loss of the teacher; or how is it that noble and illustrious men gain the victory in the contests of their scholars rather than in their own? Abraham offered his son; Peter sent Stephen on before him! Do thou, father, show forth thy courage in thy son.

Offer me whom thou hast trained, that thou, confident in thy choice of me, mayest reach the crown in worthy company.'

"215. Then Xystus said: 'I leave thee not nor forsake thee. Greater struggles yet await thee. We as old men have to undergo an easier fight; a more glorious triumph over the tyrant awaits thee, a young man. Soon shalt thou come. Cease weeping; after three days, thou shalt follow me. This interval must come between the priest and his Levite. It was not for thee to conquer under the eye of thy master, as though thou neededst a helper. Why dost thou seek to share in my death? I leave to thee its full inheritance. Why dost thou need my presence? Let the weak disciples go before their master; let the brave follow him, that they may conquer without him. For they no longer need his guidance. So Elijah left Elisha. To thee I entrust the full succession to my own courage.'

"216. However, after three days, he was placed upon the gridiron by the tyrant whom he mocked and was burnt. He said: 'The flesh is roasted, turn it and eat.' So by the courage of his mind, he overcame the power of fire."

Jerome (ca. 347–419)

The greatest exegete of the ancient West was born in Stridon of Dalmatia. He studied in Rome, where he was baptized. He then went to Trier to the imperial court, but was attracted to monastic ideals. He then went to Syria, where he took up the ascetic life and immersed himself in further studies of Greek and Hebrew.

In Rome, he was at the service of Pope Damasus, but upon the latter's death, he left for Bethlehem, where he remained until his death. Here he was involved in the controversy arising at the end of the fourth century surrounding Origen, whom he had previously held in admiration. From his vastly prolific output, most notable is his Latin translation of the Old Testament, done directly from the Hebrew text and not on the Greek version on which his predecessors had based theirs. Also still in existence are several of his polemical works and an ample amount of letters.

Letters

"I am told that some one has been mad enough to put deacons before presbyters, that is, before bishops. . . . Must not a mere server of tables and of widows be insane to set himself up arrogantly over men through whose prayers the Body and Blood of Christ are produced? . . . But you will say, how comes it then that at Rome a presbyter is only ordained on the recommendation of a deacon?" (Letter CXLVI, to the presbyter Evangelus).

Pseudo-Jerome

Presented here is a passage from the work used also by Isidore of Seville (c. 560-636) in his De Ecclesiasticis Officiis.

Letter 12: De Septem Ordinibus Ecclesiae

"Let the deacons not stray from the temple of the Lord. . . . They are the altar of Christ. . . . Without the deacon, the priest has neither name for origin nor function" (cf. PL 30, 153).[28]

Augustine (354–430)

Augustine, of Berber ethnicity, yet brought up completely within Greco-Roman culture, was born in Tagaste on November 13, 354. Tagaste, now Souk-Ahras in Algeria, lies about sixty miles from Hippo. His family, while very respected, was not wealthy; and his father Patricius, one of the city's curiales (municipal councilors), was a pagan.

From his parents, Augustine received two opposing worldviews, and he often experienced the conflict between them. His mother, venerated as a saint by the Church, would have a large role in her son's life and upbringing. Augustine thus received a Christian education and was inscribed among the catechumens. Once, when he was very ill, he asked for Baptism; once the danger had suddenly passed,

28 [Translation of the Italian text.]

however, he decided to postpone reception of the sacrament, following a rather widespread practice of the day. But the religious crisis of this great soul would not be resolved until he was in Italy, thanks to the influence of Ambrose.

Sermon 304

This sermon was given on the Solemnity of the martyr Lawrence. The deacon is the minister of Christ's Blood. The mystery of the Lord's Supper.

"The Roman Church commends this day to us, the day of triumph for Blessed Lawrence, on which he trod on a world that grumbled threats against him, and spurned it as it tried to seduce him; in either case he was victorious against the devil that provoked his persecution. All of Rome, in fact, is witness to how glorious, how rich in virtue was the crown of the martyr Lawrence, woven with merits like the most diverse of flowers in a garland. In that Church, as you have often heard, he carried out the office of deacon. There he was a minister of the Blood of Christ; there, for the name of Christ, he poured out his own. He approached the Mighty One's table with wisdom, that table which Solomon's proverbs were telling us about just now, saying: *When you sit to dine at the table of the mighty, consider well what you are served and stretch out your hand, aware that you, too, should prepare a similar meal.* The blessed Apostle John explains the mystery of this supper clearly, saying: *Just as Christ has given his life for us, so must we, too, give our lives for our brothers.* Brethren, St. Lawrence understood it, understood it and practiced it; precisely what he partook of at that table, he also prepared. He loved Christ in his life, imitated him in his death (1.1).[29]

Sermon 314, On the *Dies Natalis* of Stephen

"Yesterday we celebrated the Birth of the Lord; today we celebrate the birth of his servant; but, while on the Birth of the Lord, we celebrate the day on which he deigned to be born, on the birth of the servant, we celebrate the day on which he received the crown. We have celebrated the Birth of the Lord, on which he received the garment of our flesh; we celebrate the birth of the servant, on which the latter left his fleshly garment. We have celebrated the Birth of the Lord, on

29 [Ibid.]

which he made himself similar to us; we celebrate the birth of the servant, on which the latter left to be at Christ's side" (1). [30]

Sermon 318

Augustine gave Sermon 318 in 425 on the occasion of the deposition of the relics of the protomartyr deacon.

It can happen that a member of the faithful falls ill; behold, present there is the Tempter. In exchange for a cure, he vows an illicit sacrifice, a reprehensible, sacrilegious amulet, a wicked incantation, a magic rite, saying: *That person and that other one were in worse danger than yourself and that is how they were freed; you need to make such arrangements if you want to live; you will die if you do not do it.* Take note whether that is not the same as 'you will die if you do not deny Christ.' . . . You have found the meaning of fighting: gain for yourself a true victory. You are in bed, and you are in an amphitheater; you find yourself lying down, and you are committed to fight. Persevere in the faith; and, while you are wearing yourself out, you are victorious. This, dearly beloved, is why you have no little comfort: a place of prayer. Let the martyr Stephen be venerated in this place, but, in his honor, let the one who crowned Stephen be adored" (1-3).[31]

Sermon 329, De Stephano Martyre

Sermon Given in Memory of St. Stephen the Deacon

"Read the Greek text and you will find the deacon. What is rendered in Latin as 'minister' is 'deacon' in Greek. For he is truly deacon in Greek, minister in Latin; just as 'martyr' in Greek is 'witness' in Latin; 'apostle' in Greek, 'envoy' in Latin. But we are accustomed by now to using Greek terms in place of the Latin ones. In fact, many Gospel texts read thus: 'where I am, there also is my deacon'" (VI, II).[32]

30 [Ibid.]
31 [Ibid.]
32 [Ibid.]

De Catechizandis Rudibus

This is surely the most well-known and appreciated synthesis of the Christian faith composed in the first centuries of the Church's life. Augustine responds to the crucial question, posed by the deacon Deogratias, of how to begin catechizing someone who desires to become a Christian without possessing theological tools and without familiarity with the traditions of the faith.

On the Catechizing of the Uninstructed

"I, 1. You have requested me, brother Deogratias, to send you in writing something which might be of service to you in the matter of catechizing the uninstructed. For you have informed me that in Carthage, where you hold the position of a deacon, persons who have to be taught the Christian faith from its very rudiments, are frequently brought to you by reason of your enjoying the reputation of possessing a rich gift in catechizing. This is due at once to an intimate acquaintance with the faith and to an attractive method of discourse. But you almost always find yourself in a difficulty as to the manner in which a suitable declaration is to be made of the precise doctrine, the belief of which constitutes us Christians, regarding the point at which our statement of the same ought to commence, and the limit to which it should be allowed to proceed. And with respect to the question whether, when our narration is concluded, we ought to make use of any kind of exhortation or simply specify those precepts in the observance of which the person to whom we are discoursing may know the Christian life and profession to be maintained. At the same time, you have made the confession and complaint that it has often befallen you that, in the course of a lengthened and languid address, you have become profitless and distasteful even to yourself, not to speak of the learner, whom you have been endeavoring to instruct by your utterance, and the other parties who have been present as hearers; and that you have been constrained by these straits to put upon me the constraint of that love which I owe to you, so that I may not feel it a burdensome thing among all my engagements to write you something on this subject."

Maximus of Turin (ca. 350–423)

Maximus was born in an uncertain village in northern Italy in the second half of the fourth century and was called to head the new cathedral of Julia Augusta Taurinorum barely erected by his teacher St. Eusebius of Vercelli. The priest Gennadius of Marseille, a Christian historian, in his work De Viris Illustribus, *presents Maximus as having profound knowledge of Sacred Scripture, a refined preacher, and author of several precious works that merited his consideration as one of the minor fathers of the Universal Church. He took part in the Synod of Milan in 451, appearing as one of the signers of a letter sent on that occasion to Pope Leo the Great. He was also present at the Council of Rome in 465. In a document of this Council, Maximus' signature immediately follows that of Pope Hilary, and since precedence in signing was determined by age, we can suppose that he was already quite aged and died not long after. Many historians, however, place his death much earlier, usually around 423.*

Sermon 4—The Birth of St. Lawrence into Heaven

"1. I believe that you know of the martyrdom of the Blessed martyr Lawrence, whose birth into heaven we celebrate today; and I have no doubt that your love can comprehend how atrocious were the torments that he endured in persecution. So great was the glory of his martyrdom that with his torments he enlightened the whole world. It is certain that Lawrence enlightened the world with that fire with which he himself was burned, and he warmed the hearts of all Christians with the flames he endured. Who, in fact, before such an example, would not want to burn for Christ with Lawrence to be able to receive the crown of Christ with Lawrence? Who would not wish to undergo Lawrence's fire for one hour, in order not to endure the eternal fire of Gehenna? From the example of blessed Lawrence, then, we are encouraged to martyrdom, enflamed for the faith, warmed up to devotion. Even if we lack the flames of the persecutor, we still do not lack the flame of faith. It is true, we do not burn for Christ in body, but we burn in our affection; the persecutor does not submit me to fire, but fire is given to me in my desire for the Savior. That a fire of the Lord exists, we read in the Gospel, since the Lord himself says: *Do you not know that I have come to bring fire to the earth? And how I desire that it were yet burning!* Blazing from such a fire, Emmaus and Cleopas said: *Were our hearts not burning within us along the way while the Lord Jesus was explaining the Scriptures?* Even blessed Lawrence, burning from such a fire, did not feel the searing of the flames; and while he burned with desire for Christ, he burned not from his persecutor's torments. As long as the ardor of faith was raging in him, the flame of his punishment cooled. Blessed Lawrence was indeed suffering from the blaze that devoured his body, but the divine ardor or the Savior kept extinguishing the material ardor of the tyrant. On the one hand, he is inflamed by the love of Christ, but on the other, he was tormented by the flame of the persecutor. Even if his members were in fact reduced to ash, still his courage in the faith was not reduced at all: he endures the damage of his flesh, but acquires the prize of salvation.

"2. It is true, brethren, blessed Lawrence was not laid low with a quick and easy martyrdom. The one who is decapitated dies at once; the one thrown into the flames of a furnace is freed in one fell swoop. Instead, he was tormented in a devious, drawn-out torture, such that death—inevitable in his punishment—did not intervene to give it an end. It is told that the punishment inflicted by that most cruel persecutor was like this: with a heap of burning coals, stretched out on an iron grill, he was scorched over a slow flame, in such a way that it would not kill him with its searing heat but rather torment him by burning him slowly; in fact, when the persecutor saw that one side had burned, he exposed his other side to roast as well. We read that the most blessed young men, Ananiah, Azariah, and Mishael, shut up by the king in a burning furnace, passed through the flames of their martyrdom and trod the scorching fire with their feet. Blessed Lawrence should then be placed even ahead of them with no lesser glory. The former passed right through the flames of their martyrdom, while the latter lies in the fire of his punishment; the first trod the flames with the soles of their feet, yet the second one quenches them with the devoted offer of his sides. The first, I say again, standing upright in their punishment, lifted their hands in adoration to the Lord, while the second, instead, stretched out in suffering, prays to the Lord with his whole body.

"3. Yet again blessed Lawrence, once his sides were burnt, was turned on his back and his kidneys were charred by the fire, so that the prophecy of the psalms that speak of Lawrence himself would be fulfilled: *Put me to the test, Oh Lord, and try me: burn my kidneys and my heart.* Burn, it says, my sides and my heart. He is surely asking to be burned by a double-natured fire. In fact, if it only meant to speak of worldly fire, it would have sufficed to offer only his sides to the flames; the heart, rather, is consumed by none other than the flame of Christ, as Emmaus and Cleopas said: *Did our heart not burn?* This is why he asks for a double fire, to show his devotion, so that he will face the fight and show that in him the love of Christ is more powerful than the punishment of the tyrant. Let us then honor blessed Lawrence, brethren, while he conquers the persecutor's flames with his faith, and teaches us to overcome the blaze of Gehenna with the fire of faith and, through Christ's love, not to fear the day of judgment."[33]

Leo the Great (?–461)

Leo was born in Tuscany at an unknown date. The first certain historical testimonies about Leo speak of him as a deacon of the Roman Church under Pope Celestine I (422-423). Leo's pontificate, like that of St. Gregory I, was the most significant and important of Christian antiquity. It took place in a period when the Church was experiencing the greatest obstacles to its progress due to the rapid disintegration of the Western Empire, while the East was gravely shaken by dogmatic controversies. This great pope, meanwhile, with shrewd, long-term vision and a powerful hand, guided the destiny of the Roman and Universal Church. On the doctrinal level, Leo's battle in defense of a Christological theology that affirmed both Christ's true humanity (against Nestorius) and his true divinity (against Eutychus), was ratified by the Council of Chaledon (451): "Peter has spoken through Leo's mouth," exclaimed the Fathers. It is interesting to note the very particular style of this writer and orator, who, while belonging to such a battered, unrestful age, knew how to express himself with admirable calm and harmony. He died in 461.

Sermon 85: On the Feast of St. Lawrence, Martyr

"1. Whilst the height of all virtues, dearly beloved, and the fullness of all righteousness is born of that love, wherewith God and one's neighbor is loved, surely in none is this love found more conspicuous and brighter than in the blessed martyrs; who are as near to our Lord Jesus, who died for all men, in the imitation of his love, as in the likeness of their suffering. For, although that love,

33 [Ibid.]

wherewith the Lord has redeemed us, cannot be equaled by any man's kindness, because it is one thing that a man who is doomed to die one day should die for a righteous man, and another that One who is free from the debt of sin should lay down his life for the wicked: yet the martyrs also have done great service to all men, in that the Lord, who gave them boldness, has used it to show that the penalty of death and the pain of the cross need not be terrible to any of his followers, but might be imitated by many of them. If therefore no good man is good for himself alone, and no wise man's wisdom befriends himself only, and the nature of true virtue is such that it leads many away from the dark error on which its light is shed, no model is more useful in teaching God's people than that of the martyrs. Eloquence may make intercession easy, reasoning may effectually persuade; but yet examples are stronger than words, and there is more teaching in practice than in precept.

"2. And how gloriously strong in this most excellent manner of doctrine the blessed martyr Laurentius is, by whose sufferings today is marked, even his persecutors were able to feel, when they found that his wondrous courage, born principally of love for Christ, not only did not yield itself, but also strengthened others by the example of his endurance. For when the fury of the Gentile potentates was raging against Christ's most chosen members and attacked those especially who were of priestly rank, the wicked persecutor's wrath was vented on Laurentius the deacon, who was preeminent not only in the performance of the sacred rites, but also in the management of the church's property, promising himself double spoil from one man's capture: for if he forced him to surrender the sacred treasures, he would also drive him out of the pale of true religion. And so this man, so greedy of money and such a foe to the truth, arms himself with double weapon: with avarice to plunder the gold; with impiety to carry off Christ. He demands of the guileless guardian of the sanctuary that the church wealth on which his greedy mind was set should be brought to him. But the holy deacon showed him where he had them stored, by pointing to the many troops of poor saints, in the feeding and clothing of whom he had a store of riches which he could not lose, and which were the more entirely safe that the money had been spent on so holy a cause.

"3. The baffled plunderer, therefore, frets, and blazing out into hatred of a religion, which had put riches to such a use, determines to pillage a still greater treasure by carrying off that sacred deposit, wherewith he was enriched, as he could find no solid hoard of money in his possession. He orders Laurentius to renounce Christ and prepares to ply the deacon's stout courage with frightful tortures: and, when the first elicit nothing, fiercer follow. His limbs, torn and mangled by many cutting blows, are commanded to be broiled upon the fire in an iron framework, which was of itself already hot enough to burn him, and on which his limbs were turned from time to time, to make the torment fiercer and the death more lingering.

"4. Thou gainest nothing, thou prevailest nothing, O savage cruelty. His mortal frame is released from thy devices, and, when Laurentius departs to heaven, thou art vanquished. The flame of Christ's love could not be overcome by thy flames, and the fire which burnt outside was less keen than that which blazed within. Thou didst but serve the martyr in thy rage, O persecutor: thou didst but swell the reward in adding to the pain. For what did thy cunning devise, which did not redound to the conqueror's glory, when even the instruments of torture were counted as part of the triumph? Let us rejoice, then, dearly beloved, with spiritual joy and make our boast over the happy end of this illustrious man in the Lord, Who is "wonderful in his saints," in whom he has given us a support and an example, and has so spread abroad his glory throughout the world, that, from the rising of the sun to its going down, the brightness of his deacon's light doth shine, and Rome is become as famous in Laurentius as Jerusalem was ennobled by Stephen. By his prayer and intercession, we trust at all times to be assisted; that, because all, as the Apostle says, "who wish to live holily in Christ, suffer persecutions," we may be strengthened with the spirit of love and be fortified to overcome all temptations by the perseverance of steadfast faith. Through our Lord Jesus Christ, etc."

G. CANONICAL-LITURGICAL LITERATURE

Didache (First Century)

This ancient Christian writing—dating as a whole back to the end of the first century—is a compilation of various writings, gathered for the edification of an ill-defined community. This work, containing strong traces of Jewish concepts, includes a moral teaching (the doctrine of the "two ways"), a series of liturgical traditions of extreme interest for their antiquity, and a disciplinary section that describes how the Christian mission was organized, making it possible for the work's origin to be traced to Syria.

"XV, 1. Appoint, therefore, for yourselves, bishops and deacons worthy of the Lord, men meek, and not lovers of money, and truthful and proved; for they also render to you the service of prophets and teachers."

Didascalia of the Apostles (Third Century)

The Didascalia of the Apostles *is an important document of Eastern Syrian Christianity from the third century. Aside from a very small fragment, the original Greek has been lost. Fortunately there is a full Syriac version from the fourth to fifth centuries, now legible in an adequate critical edition. In order to reach the original Greek, another important reference point is the* Apostolic Constitutions. *The author of this liturgical-disciplinary work of the second half of the fourth century used the* Didascalia *itself for Books 1-6. Given the rather liberal usage of such a source, however, recourse to the text of the* Constitutions *is not always possible.*

The Didascalia *is presented as a pseudepigraphical work inasmuch as it uses literary fiction to make the Twelve Apostles speak directly, gathered in Jerusalem on the occasion reported by Acts 15. They would prolong that assembly—having present "James, bishop of Jerusalem, brother of the Lord according to the flesh, together with his presbyters, deacons, and the whole Church"—and they would promulgate this document, namely the* Didascalia, *in order to make a stance against the pseudo-Apostles and their false doctrines. Evidently, here the third-century author projects the ministerial structure of his own time, i.e., the triple hierarchy of* bishop-presbyter-deacon, *onto the Church's origins. This pseudepigraphical framework is only the work of the final redactor, who very likely used even older material. In fact, we see that throughout the text, the triple ministerial structure never appears with that typical order that we find in Ignatius of Antioch's letters. What most strikes us in the* Didascalia *is the scant attention given the role of the* presbyters, *while the* bishop-deacon *pair is pushed clearly into the foreground. The necessity of the* deaconess *is also expressly affirmed, as well as the already traditional presence of the group of institutional widows. Of the other minor orders, there is almost no mention.*

The central figure of the bishop occupies central place in the Didascalia.

He is aided by the deacons, who are his close collaborators, directly in his service as his secretaries. They are like the eyes and ears of the bishop, his heart and soul. Therefore, between the bishop and deacons, there should be full accord, which will flow back out as peace onto the Church.

The deacons' duty is to visit those in need and to keep the bishop informed about them. If the bishop represents God the Father in the community, the deacon is the figure of Christ; and following the example of Christ "Servant," who washed the feet of his disciples, even the deacons must be ready to give their lives for their brothers and sisters.

The liturgical role of the deacon is barely mentioned: he assists the bishop during the Eucharistic offering and maintains discipline in the assembly. Here we see a deacon designated to watch the entrance of the assembly hall, a responsibility that will later be conferred upon the "doorkeepers." In II, 44, 1, we find the oldest diaconal admonition ever known. Concerning the number of deacons, it is only said that it should be proportionate to the number of the faithful so that their needs can be looked after in a timely fashion.

The same pastoral motive justifies the need for the deaconesses. The Didascalia *speaks of them repeatedly, as if it were trying to promote this institution, pointing out its usefulness, even its necessity. In the iconic-sacred vision typical of Syrian Christianity, if the bishop stands for God the Father, the deacons and deaconesses respectively represent Christ and the Holy Spirit. Even if the text doesn't state it, the underlying idea here seems to be that the Son and the Holy Spirit are the "hands" of the Father. In fact, according to the* Didascalia, *the deacons are like hands for the bishop. The ministry of the deaconesses is seen as very opportune in the rite of the pre-baptismal anointing of women themselves, in the catechesis of newly baptized women, and in visiting the female sick, where it is permitted to place hands on them.*

The New Priesthood

"Chap. IX, ii, 26. But the priests and Levites now are the presbyters and deacons, and the orphans and widows: but the Levite and high priest is the bishop. He is minister of the word and mediator; but to you a teacher, and your father after God, who begot you through the water. This is your chief and your leader, and he is your mighty king. He rules in the place of the Almighty: but let him be honored by you as God, for the bishop sits for you in the place of God Almighty. But the deacon stands in the place of Christ; and do you love him. And the deaconess shall be honored by you in the place of the Holy Spirit; and the presbyters shall be to you in the likeness of the Apostles."

How to Honor the Widows and the Ministers

"Chap. IX, ii, 28. [And again, if anyone gives bounties to widows, let him send her the rather who is in want.] But let the portion of the pastor be separated and set apart for him according to rule at the suppers or the bounties, even though he be not present, in honor of Almighty God. But how much (soever) is given to one of the widows, let the double be given to each of the deacons in honor of Christ, (but) twice twofold to the leader for the glory of the Almighty. But if anyone wishes to honor the presbyters also, let him give them a double (portion), as to the deacons; for they ought to be honored as the Apostles, and as the counsellors of the bishop, and as the crown of the Church; for they are the moderators and councillors of the Church. But if there be also a lector, let him too receive with the presbyters. To every order, therefore, let everyone of the laity pay the honor which is befitting him, with gifts and presents and with the respect due to his worldly condition."

The Dignity of Deacons and Bishops

"Chap. IX, ii, 28-31. But let them have very free access to the deacons, and let them not be troubling the head at all times, but making known what they require through the ministers, that is, through the deacons. For neither can any man approach the Lord God Almighty except through Christ. All things therefore that they desire to do, let them make known to the bishop through the deacons, and then do them.

"Do you therefore esteem the bishop as the mouth of God. For if Aaron, because he interpreted to Pharaoh the words which were given through Moses, was called a prophet, as the Lord said to Moses: *Behold, I have given thee as a god to pharaoh and Aaron thy brother shall be to thee a prophet*, why then should not you also reckon them as prophets, who are for you the mediators of the word, and worship them as God? But for us now, Aaron is the deacon, and Moses is the bishop. Now if Moses was called a god by the Lord, let the bishop also be honored by you as God, and the deacon as a prophet. Wherefore, for the honor of the bishop, make known to him all things that you do, and let them be performed through him. And if thou know of one who is in much distress, and the bishop know not of him, do thou inform him; and without him do not, to his discredit, anything, lest thou bring a reproach upon him as one who neglects the poor. For he who sets abroad an evil report against the bishop, whether by word or by deed, sins against God Almighty. And again, if any man speaks evil of a deacon, whether by word or deed, he offends against Christ. Wherefore in the Law also it is written: *Thou shalt not revile thy gods; and thou shalt not speak evil of a prince of thy people.* Now let no man think that the Lord speaks (here) of idols of stone; but he calls 'gods' those who preside over you."

Exhortation to Unity Among Bishops and Deacons

"Chap. XI, ii, 44. Strive therefore, O bishops, together with the deacons, to be right with the Lord; for the Lord has said: *If ye will be right with me, I also will be right with you; and if ye will walk perversely with me, I also will walk perversely with you, saith the Lord of Hosts.* Be *right* therefore, that you may deserve to receive praise of the Lord, and not blame (from him who is) of the contrary part.

"Let the bishops and the deacons, then, be of one mind; and do shepherd the people diligently with one accord. For you ought both to be one body, father and son; for you are in the likeness of the Lordship. And let the deacon make known all things to the bishop, even as Christ to his Father. But what things he can, let the deacon order, and all the rest let the bishop judge. Yet let the deacon be the hearing of the bishop, and his mouth and his heart and his soul; for when you are both of one mind, through your agreement, there will be peace also in the Church."

The Order in Assemblies: Role of the Deacons

"Chap. XII, ii, 57. But of the deacons let one stand always by the oblations of the Eucharist; and let another stand without by the door and observe them that come in; and afterwards, when you offer, let them minister together in the Church. And if anyone be found sitting out of his place, let the deacon who is within reprove him and make him to rise up and sit in a place that is meet [proper] for him. For our Lord likened the Church to a fold; for as we see the dumb animals, oxen and sheep and goats, lie down and rise up, and feed and chew the cud, according to their families, and none of them separate itself from its kind; and (see) the wild beasts also severally range with their like upon the mountains: so likewise in the Church ought those who are young to sit apart, if there be room, and if not to stand up; and those who are advanced in years to sit apart. And let the children stand on one side, or let their fathers and mothers take them to them; and let them stand up. And let the young girls also sit apart; but if there be no room, let them stand up behind the women. And let the young women who are married and have children stand apart, and the aged women and widows sit apart. And let the deacon see that each of them on entering goes to his place, that no one may sit out of his place. And let the deacon also see that no one whispers, or falls asleep, or laughs, or makes signs. For so it should be, that with decency and decorum they watch in the Church, with ears attentive to the Word of the Lord."

The Conduct of Widows

"Chap. XV, iii, 8. But if you obey not the mind of the bishops and deacons, they indeed will be quit of your offenses, but you shall render an account of all that you do of your own will, whether men or women."

The Ministry of Deaconesses

"Chap. XVI, iii, 12. Wherefore, O bishop, appoint thee workers of righteousness as helpers who may cooperate with thee unto salvation. Those that please thee out of all the people thou shalt choose and appoint as deacons: a man for the performance of the most things that are required, but a woman for the ministry of women. For there are houses whither thou canst not send a deacon to the women, on account of the heathen, but mayest send a deaconess. Also, because in many other matters, the office of a woman deacon is required. In the first place, when women go down into the water, those who go down into the water ought to be anointed by a deaconess with the oil of anointing; and where there is no woman at hand, and especially no deaconess, he who baptizes must of necessity anoint her who is being baptized. But where there is a woman, and especially a deaconess, it is not fitting that women should be seen by men: but with the imposition of hand do thou anoint the head only. As of old the priests and kings were anointed in Israel, do thou in like manner, with the imposition of hand, anoint the head of those who receive Baptism, whether of men or of women; and afterwards—whether thou thyself baptize, or thou command the deacons or presbyters to baptize—let a woman deacon, as we have already said, anoint the women. But let a man pronounce over them the invocation of the divine Names in the water. And when she who is being baptized has come up from the water, let the deaconess receive her, and teach and instruct her how the seal of Baptism ought to be (kept) unbroken in purity and holiness. For this cause we say that the ministry of a woman deacon is especially needful and important. For our Lord and Savior also was ministered unto by women ministers, *Mary Magdalene, and Mary the daughter of James and mother of Jose, and the mother of the sons of Zebedee*, with other women beside. And thou also hast need of the ministry of a deaconess for many things; for a deaconess is required to go into the houses of the heathen where there are believing women, and to visit those who are sick, and to minister to them in that of which they have need, and to bathe those who have begun to recover from sickness."

Spirituality of the Deacons

"Chap. XVI, iii, 13. And let the deacons imitate the bishops in their conversation: nay, let them even be laboring more than he. And let them *not love filthy lucre*; but let them be diligent in the ministry. And in proportion to the number of the congregation of the people of the Church, so let the deacons be, that they may be able to take knowledge (of each) severally and refresh all; so that for the aged women who are infirm, and for brethren and sisters who are in sickness—for every one they may provide the ministry which is proper for him.

"But let a woman rather be devoted to the ministry of women, and a male deacon to the ministry of men. And let him be ready to obey and to submit himself to the command of the bishop. And let him labor and toil in every place whither he is sent to minister or to speak of some matter to anyone. For it behooves each one to know his office and to be diligent in executing it. And be you (bishop and deacon) of one counsel and of one purpose, and one soul dwelling in two bodies. And know what the ministry is, according as our Lord and Savior said in the Gospel: *Whoso among you desireth to be chief, let him be your servant: even as the Son of Man came not to be ministered unto, but to minister, and to give his life as a ransom for many.* So ought you the deacons also to do, if it fall to you to lay down your life for your brethren in the ministry which is due to them. For neither did our Lord and Savior himself disdain (to be) ministering to us, as it is written in Isaiah: *To justify the righteous, who hath performed well a service for many.* If then the Lord of heaven and earth *performed a service* for us, and bore and endured everything for us, how much more ought we to do the like for our brethren, that we may imitate him. For we are imitators of him, and hold the place of Christ. And again in the Gospel you find it written how our Lord *girded a linen cloth about his loins and cast water into a washbasin,* while we reclined (at supper), and drew nigh *and washed the feet of* us all *and wiped them with the cloth.* Now this he did that he might show us (an example of) charity and brotherly love, that we also should do in like manner one to another. If then our Lord did thus, will you, O deacons, hesitate to do the like for them that are sick and infirm, you who are workmen of the truth, and bear the likeness of Christ? Do you therefore minister with love, and neither murmur nor hesitate; otherwise you will have ministered as it were for men's sake and not for the sake of God, and you will receive your reward according to your ministry in the day of judgment. It is required of you deacons therefore that you visit all who are in need and inform the bishop of those who are in distress; and you shall be his soul and his mind; and in all things, you shall be taking trouble and be obedient to him."

Apostolic Tradition (ca. 215)

Among the various collections of ancient Church organization, the Apostolic Tradition, *attributed to Hippolytus of Rome and composed around 215, carries very particular importance. It in fact appears to have directly or indirectly influenced all the other collections, whether translations or liberal adaptations. How the identification of such a work by Hippolytus was arrived at is too long to treat here in depth. The reconstituted text of the* Apostolic Tradition, *though, is no more than a sort of archetype with regard to the successive translations and elaborations. That such an archetype substantially coincides with Hippolytus' work is only a supposition. In fact, the text presents numerous difficulties which could not be explained under the hypothesis of a single author, but that are understandable when considering successive interventions and manipulations. In any case, keeping these reservations in mind, it is still true that we have a document of exceptional value for liturgical history. This is especially true for the ecclesial ministries.*

Chapters 2-14 deal precisely with those in the Church who have a particular responsibility or state. They are listed in the following order: bishops, presbyters, *deacons, confessors of the faith, widows, lectors, virgins, subdeacons, and finally those who have received the gift of healing. For the first time in the patristic literature that has come down to us, the ministries are defined by reciprocal relationships: we see the accurately emphasized distinction between those ministries conferred through the laying on of hands (*cheirotonein = *"to ordain") and prayer by the bishop, with a view to divine service (*leitourgía*), and the "instituted" (*kathistánai*) ministries without the laying on of hands, as for widows (chapter 10), or conferred simply by "nomination," as for subdeacons (chapter 13). There is also still a trace of particular charisms, whose authenticity is judged by the deeds (chapter 14).*

To the ordained ministers belong the bishop in first place, then the presbyters, and finally the deacons.

The deacon is in the bishop's service, but does not participate in the priesthood. In fact, he alone presents the oblation (for the Eucharist) to the bishop, but does not place his hands over them with the bishop during the Eucharistic Prayer. The deacons do not form part of the priest's council, but have administrative duties; moreover, they should regularly meet with the bishop and make known to him the sick to be visited.

The unity and collaboration of these three ministries appear clearly in the sacramental rites above all else. The administration of Baptism is normally conferred by the bishop, aided by the presbyters and deacons: the bishop blesses the oils, places his hands on the one to be baptized, and makes the triple interrogation; in addition, he carries out the rite of chrismation after Baptism (chapter 21); the presbyters have the baptismal candidate make the renunciation of Satan, then anoint him with the oil of exorcism and the consecrated oil, before and after the triple immersion respectively; they can also administer Baptism in the absence of the bishop. The deacons hold the oil vials and help the baptismal candidates in the immersion (chapter 21). Even for the Eucharist, it is the bishop who presides, surrounded by the presbyters and helped by the deacons. These present the Eucharistic gifts to the bishop (chapters 4 and 21), aid the presbyters in the breaking of the bread (chapter 22) and in giving Communion to the faithful, holding the various chalices (chapter 21).

Ordination of a Deacon

"But the deacon, when he is ordained, is chosen according to those things that were said above, the bishop alone in like manner laying his hands upon him, as we have prescribed. When the deacon is ordained, this is the reason why the bishop alone shall lay his hands upon him: he is not ordained to the priesthood but to serve the bishop and to carry out the bishop's commands. He does not take part in the council of the clergy; he is to attend to his own duties and to make known to the bishop such things as are needful. He does not receive that Spirit that is possessed by the presbytery, in which the presbyters share; he receives only what is confided in him under the bishop's authority.

"For this cause the bishop alone shall make a deacon. But on a presbyter, however, the presbyters shall lay their hands because of the common and like Spirit of the clergy. Yet the presbyter has only the power to receive; but he has no power to give. For this reason a presbyter does not ordain the clergy; but at the ordination of a presbyter, he seals while the bishop ordains.

Over a deacon, then, he shall say as follows:

"O God, who has created all things and hast ordered them by thy Word,
the Father of our Lord Jesus Christ,
whom thou didst send to minister thy will
and to manifest to us thy desire;
grant [the] Holy Spirit of grace and care and diligence
to this thy servant,
whom thou hast chosen to serve the Church
and to offer in thy holy sanctuary
the gifts that are offered to thee by thine appointed high priests,
so that serving without blame
and with a pure heart
he may be counted worthy of this exalted office,
by thy goodwill, praising thee continually.
Through thy servant Jesus Christ,
Through whom be to thee glory and honor,
with [the] Holy Spirit,
in the holy Church,
both now and always and world without end. Amen."

The Deacons Should See the Bishop Consistently

Visits to the Sick

"Each of the deacons, with the subdeacons, shall be alert on the bishop's behalf, for the bishop must be informed if any are sick so that, if he pleases, he may visit them; for a sick man is greatly comforted when the high priest is mindful of him" (30).

Deacons and Catechizing Presbyters

"Let the deacons and the presbyters assemble daily at the place which the bishop may appoint; let the deacons [in particular] never fail to assemble unless prevented by sickness. When all have met, they shall instruct those who are in the church, and then, after prayer, each shall go to his appointed duties" (33).

Ecclesiastical Canons of the Same Holy Apostles (Third Century)

While the text of the Didascalia *is rather verbose, that of the* Ecclesiastical Canons of the Same Holy Apostles *is very brief and lacks any reference to geographical or historical situations.*

For the first section, that of moral character (4-14), the author used a previous document, the Doctrina Apostolorum *or* On the Two Ways, *known to us from the* Didache, *from the* Letter of Barnabas, *and from an ancient Latin version which places the name of an Apostle at the head of each paragraph, not without some additions and omissions.*

Of special interest are chapters 15-21, regarding ministries, which were already announced in the introduction. In the introductory paragraph, we find the following list: bishops, presbyters, deacons, lectors, widows. It is taken up again in chapters 15-21, the only variation being that lectors are placed before deacons.

In chapter 20, the deacons seem to have a very important place in the community, to the point that they have authority to exclude the arrogant. In chapter 22, deacons seem instead to have the sole charge of properly distributing the common funds (the collection), and in exchange for good service they are promised a promotion to the office of pastor (= bishop). It is surprising that they are attributed no liturgical role.

Chapters 24-28 are also interesting in that they contain a small discussion amongst the apostles on the ministry of women. Not everything in this text is clear—the focus of the discussion, however, is quite clear: the question of a female diakonia *with regards to the Eucharist is brought up explicitly. The answer is in the negative, based on two reasons: (1) at the moment of its institution at the Last Supper, Jesus did not allow the women to stand with the Apostles; (2) women themselves admit that this was fair, based on a saying* (ágraphon) *of Jesus. James closes the discussion, affirming that, while women do have an attendant ministry, it is only with regards to the female gender.*

The type of ministerial organization provided for by the document fits well into the context of the third century, and more so into the first half of the second: there is no mention of lesser ministries, such as the subdeacon, acolyte, exorcist, and porter, all of which were found in Rome by 251.

As for the place of origin, we can believe it to be Egypt (given the importance given to presbyters in addition to deacons).

Institution and Qualities of Deacons

"Matthew said: 'Let three deacons be instituted. It is written: *Every question will be decided on the word of two or three witnesses. Let them be put to the test* in every type of service, have a good reputation in the community, be married only once, have brought up their children well, be sober, temperate, calm; let them not be gossips, *duplicitous in speech*, quick to anger—*indeed, anger is the wise man's undoing*; let them have no favoritism toward the rich, nor oppress the needy; *let them not be given over to wine*, and let them be ready to serve. Let them know how to encourage hidden works, putting pressure on the more wealthy brothers to open their hands. Let they themselves be generous and know how to share; let them be demanding with *those who behave in a disorderly fashion*, admonishing some, exhorting others, and taking yet others to task. Let them be resolute in keeping the haughty far away, aware that those who are belligerent, disrespectful, or offensive are opposed to Christ'" (20, 1-3).[34]

34 [Translation of the Italian text.]

On Deacons

"Andrew said: 'Deacons, being workers of good deeds, will go around everywhere day and night, neither despising the poor man nor having regard for the rich; they will recognize who is in need and shall not exclude him from the distribution. They will put pressure on those who have means in order that they may amass for themselves a treasure of good deeds, considering the words of our Master: *You have seen me hungry and have not fed me.* Indeed, those who carry out their office as deacons well and without grumbling will gain that of pastor'" (22, 1-2).[35]

Testamentum Domini

"Testament or words that our Lord Jesus Christ risen from the dead spoke to his Apostles, written by Clement of Rome, disciple of Peter, in eight books."

This is the title of the appendix to the Syriac Peshitta Bible, *known as the* Clementine Octateuch. *Only the first two books of the* Octateuch, *however, contain this apocryphal testament of Jesus. The title did not permit the work to be placed among other more well-known texts such as the* Didache of the Apostles, *the* Apostolic Tradition, *the* Didascalia, *or the* Apostolic Constitutions.

The work exists in Syriac, Coptic, Arabic, and in the Ethiopian language Ge'ez, all under various titles. If the Testamentum *and the* Traditio *are compared as a whole, one can undoubtedly notice that the* Testamentum *follows the* Traditio *closely from chapter 20 onward.*

The main theme of the Testamentum *is the structure and ordering of the entire Church. An introduction of fourteen brief chapters, original and without parallel in the* Traditio, *presents the Lord in conversation with the Apostles, while he prophetically announces to them what the life of the disciples will be. In chapters 15 and 16, the apostles and pious women question the Lord on the responsibilities and ministries to establish in the Church that they are about to propagate. It is important here to take note of the women's intervention in order to understand the role played by widows and deaconesses in the primitive Church. In chapter 17, the Lord answers the disciples' question on the Church regulation for ordination and the institution of the one who presides over the Church. A part of the things*

35 [Ibid.]

that Jesus will reveal is reserved only for ministers; the rest is communicated to the whole Church, but not to anyone on the outside. In reality, the following chapters do not distinguish between what is reserved for ministers and what is for the whole Church, since all the ordinations are done in public with the people's participation, Only the "arcanum" in dealings with infidels seems to be practiced really. Chapter 19 is the last of the chapters proper to the Testamentum, *since chapter 20 corresponds to book 1 of the* Traditio. *In chapter 19, it is explained, through the Lords mouth, what the arrangement of a church building should be like. One merit of chapter 19 is that it informs us of the place that each category of ministers, faithful, and catechumens occupies in the Church. From chapter 20 to 47, the end of the first book of the Syriac* Testamentum, *the author deals with various functions or Church ministries, for the bishop, the presbyter, the deacon, the confessor, the subdeacon, the lector, and the virgins.*

Choosing the Deacon

"The deacon should be of good conduct; pure, if chosen for his ascetic life; but, if married, let him be so only once. He should not bother himself with worldly affairs nor with art, and should have neither riches nor children. If he is married and has children, his children as well should be of such conduct as to be able to serve the Church" (chap. 33).[36]

The Ministry of the Deacon

"Above all, the ministry of the deacon will be that of making known or announcing what the bishop commands. He is the counselor of the whole clergy and is seen as a symbol of the Church. He cares for the sick and for foreigners, helps the widows, is father to the orphans, and visits the homes of the poor to see if anyone is in need, sick, or in misery. He even visits the catechumens at home to encourage those who hesitate, and to instruct the ignorant. He clothes the deceased and buries foreigners; he takes responsibility of those who have left their homeland or have been exiled; he makes the situation of those who are in need of help known to the Church. But let him not be bothersome to the bishop: only on Sunday will he give an account of everything.

36 [Ibid.]

"At the time of the gathering, we will go all about the church making sure no one there is haughty, careless, or given to chatter or gossip. Looking at everyone, he will reprehend anyone deserving punishment and escort them out; but if any of these ask to be allowed Communion, let it be permitted as a consolation. If anyone should persist in his lapse or unruly behavior, the deacon will make it known to the bishop, and the guilty person will be removed for seven days, after which he will be called back lest he be lost. If upon his return he persists and remains in his sin, he will be dismissed until the day he shall have truly repented, come to his senses, and begged to be allowed back in.

"If the deacon lives in a city near the sea, let him comb the shore to see if there is any shipwreck victim, clothe him, and bury him. In like manner, he shall inquire at the inns whether there are any sick, poor, or dead and tell the Church to do what is necessary. He shall wash the paralytic and the infirm to alleviate their suffering. He will obtain what each needs by means of the Church" (chap. 34).

At the end, chapter 34 gives us an overall accounting of the ministers of the Church: twelve priests, seven deacons, fourteen subdeacons, thirteen widows "having precedence."

It is clear that one lone person could not carry out all the duties proper to the deacon: the text confirms that there was more than one deacon. The subdeacons acted as true coadjutors of the deacon.

Chapter 35 begins with a beautiful definition of the deacon:

"In everything, the deacon shall be 'the eye of the Church'; he shall strive to be for the people a model of true piety" (chap. 35).

The rest of the chapter contains the formula of the deacon's proclamation or admonition; it is the text of a litany still in use by the Ethiopians that recalls what is known as the synapse of peace among the Byzantines. It is preceded by some admonitions similar to those preceding the anaphora, with the end of excluding the catechumens and unworthy persons. Among these admonitions is a type of "Sursum corda." All of this places the prayer of the faithful at the level of the Eucharistic anaphora. This synapse is given outside the context of any celebration, yet was certainly a part of it, given that it presupposes the prayer of the bishop or priest, as well as that of the kneeling faithful. In book 8 of the Apostolic Constitutions, *a similar litany is found for Vespers, Matins, and at the Mass. The synapse of the* Testamentum *is simpler than that of the* Constitutions *and seems even more ancient. In the supplication for the various categories of the members of the Church, we again get a comprehensive view of its composition:*

"Let us pray for the bishop, that our Lord will give him length of days in the faith, so that he will spread well the word of truth and remain pure and blameless at the head of the Church.

"Let us pray for the presbyterate, that the Lord may not take the spirit of priesthood from it and will grant it diligence and piety to the end.

"Let us pray for the deacons, that the Lord will grant it to them to complete a perfect course, to carry out all the works of holiness, and will remember their efforts and charity.

"Let us pray for the 'aged people,' that the Lord will hear their supplication, keep their hearts in the grace of the Spirit, and help them in their work.

"Let us pray for the subdeacons, the lectors, the deaconesses, that the Lord will grant them to receive recompense for their patience" (chap. 35).

The litany continues praying for the laity, for the catechumens, for the empire, for the princes, for the whole world, for those at sea and for travelers, for the persecuted, the dead, sinners, and for all present.

It has been pointed out that the prayer for the persecuted proves the dating of our document to be very ancient, prior to the peace of the Church, but it should not be forgotten that this document, written in Syriac, could be referring to other persecutions outside of the Roman Empire, that of the Persians, for example.

Chapter 36 describes in detail the deacon's functions at the church doors during the Eucharist:

"He should recognize the people entering in order to keep out the simply curious. He will not allow the latecomers, in order to avoid creating a disturbance for those praying; but, once the praise has finished, they will be admitted, and the deacon will propose praying for the latecomers. That, with the first thing, will serve as a lesson for the negligent and the lazy" (chap. 36).

Another of the deacon's functions, described in chapter 37, is that of judging certain sins and making decisions about people to admit to Communion or, in opposite manner, to prevent their entry into the church, even if they repent of their sin.

"The deacon has responsibility over those who do penance, bringing them to the bishop or priest to instruct them" (chap. 37).

The Testamentum *anticipates a Church in which the deacon exercises the function of judge over the moral life of the faithful; a Church where there is official penance, but where the bishop and priest intervene only to enlighten and instruct the penitents. The ordination prayer for the bishop recognized his apostolic function of dissolving all bonds, but the* Testamentum *does not anticipate the rite of absolution.*

The chapter closes with this recommendation:

"If the deacon cannot fulfill his duty, let him at least dedicate himself to prayer and look to supplication, meditation, charity, to the Way, to suffering as his work; let him have the fear [of God] before his eyes and be called a child of the light" (chap. 37).

Chapter 38 is consecrated to the deacon's ordination:

"He is ordained by the bishop alone, given that he is not ordained for priesthood, but only to serve the bishop and the Church" (chap. 38).

In the prayer of ordination it is asked that:

"The deacon may receive from God the attentiveness, the sweetness, the strength, the virtue of pleasing him. The Lord must make of him a loyal and blameless servant, meek, a friend of orphans, of pious people and of widows, fervent and a lover of goodness" (chap. 38).

In this prayer, one phrase, the only one that alludes to a liturgical function of the deacon at the altar, creates some difficulty of interpretation:

"Enlighten, Lord, the one you have chosen and selected to serve your Church and to offer in the holiness of your sanctuary what is offered to you for the heredity of the princes of your priesthood" (chap. 38).

This translation leads us to believe that it was the deacon who made the offering. In the Traditio, *the parallel text says that the deacon presents the offering to the celebrant. The same idea is in chapter 10 of the second book of the* Testamentum.[37]

H. THE APOCRYPHA

Pseudo-Clementines (Third Century)

The Pseudo-Clementines *are a group of writings composed of* The Letter of Peter to James, The Solemn Endeavor (*Diamartyria*), The Letter of Clement to James, Homilies, and Recognitions. *Numerous hypotheses have been formulated about the origin and composition of these writings. In their current form, they would be from the fourth century. Still, scholars are in agreement in considering one writing*

37 [Quotes in this section are a translation of the Italian text.]

to be the fundamental source of the Pseudo-Clementines. *Such a writing should be able to be dated around the first half of the second century.*

One particularity of these writings is the total absence of language dealing with worship or priesthood when applied to ministers of the Church and their duties. The deacons *are called "eyes of the bishop" because they have to inform him of those members of the community who are in spiritual danger or even illness.*

Mentioned after the deacons are the catechists, while there is not any mention made of lectors or of subdeacons. This fact may indicate great antiquity.

Letter of Clement to James

The Deacons, Eyes of the Bishop

"Moreover let the deacons of the Church, going about with intelligence, be as eyes to the bishop, carefully inquiring into the doings of each member of the Church, *ascertaining* who is about to sin, in order that, being arrested with admonition by the president, he may haply not accomplish the sin. Let them check the disorderly, that they may not desist from assembling to hear the discourses, so that they may be able to counteract by the word of truth those anxieties that fall upon the heart from every side, by means of worldly casualites and evil communications; for if they long remain fallow, they become fuel for the fire. And let them learn who are suffering under bodily disease, and let them bring them to the notice of the multitude who do not know of them, that they may visit them and supply their wants according to the judgment of the president. Yea, though they do this without his knowledge, they do nothing amiss. These things, then, and things like to these, let the deacons attend to" (chap. 12).

Allegory of the Church as a Ship

"For the whole business of the Church is like unto a great ship, bearing through a violent storm men, who are of many places and who desire to inhabit the city of the good kingdom. Let, therefore, God be your shipmaster; and let the pilot be likened to Christ, the mate to the bishop, and the sailors to the deacons, the midshipmen to the catechists, the multitude of the brethren to the passengers, the world to the sea; the foul winds to temptations, persecutions, and dangers; and all manner of afflictions to the waves; the land winds and their squalls to the discourses of deceivers and false prophets; the promontories and rugged rocks to the judges in high places, threatening terrible things; the meetings of two seas, and the wild places, to unreasonable men and those who doubt of the promises of truth. Let hypocrites be regarded as like to pirates. Moreover, account the strong whirlpool, and the Tartarean Charybdis, and murderous wrecks, and deadly founderings, to be nought but sins. In order, therefore, that, sailing with a fair wind, you may safely reach the haven of the hoped-for city, pray so as to be heard. But prayers become audible by good deeds.

"Let therefore the passengers remain quiet, sitting in their own places, lest by disorder they occasion rolling or careening. Let the midshipmen give heed to the fare. Let the deacons neglect nothing with which they are entrusted; let the presbyters, like sailors, studiously arrange what is needful for each one. Let the bishop, as the mate, wakefully ponder the words of the pilot alone. Let Christ, even the Savior, be loved as the pilot, and alone believed in the matters of which he speaks; and let all pray to God for a prosperous voyage" (chap.14; 15).

Homilies

The Support of the Bishop

"In the same manner, then, honor the presbyter catechists, the good deacons, the widows of exemplary life, the orphans [that are] like the Church's children. But even when there is need of some resource to face a need, contribute all together. Have sentiments of religious respect for one another, not being ashamed of supporting any thing whatsoever for your salvation" (Homily 3, 71).[1]

Revelation of Paul (Fourth Century)

During the era of Emperor Theodosius (379-395), a work was published presenting itself as an apocalypse written by St. Paul, but remaining hidden in the foundations of a house in Tarsus, the apostle's birthplace, and miraculously rediscovered by the devout resident of the house. This text served as an archetype. Taking inspiration from the autobiographical account of Paul's rapture to the third heaven (2 Cor

1 [Translation of the Italian text.]

12:1-5), the author imagines the apostle describing not only the Kingdom of the blessed in Paradise (19-30), but also the torments of the damned in hell (31-44). Of all of these, one particular mention is made of the ministers of the Church. They are named in order: presbyter, bishop, deacon, and lector. This list probably reflects the original one, even if the mention of the lector is lacking in the Greek copy. It should be especially noted that these four ministries are the same ones presented in the Ecclesiastical Canons of the Apostles *(193-196). The fact that the presbyter is named before the bishop does not mean the former's preeminence. What is said of the bishop shows clearly that he is the most important figure. A plausible explanation of the order followed here can be found if we place the author in a Syriac area, where the bishop-deacon pairing appears very close. With the purpose of keeping these two ministries close, if the author did not want to put the presbyter after the deacon, it was necessary to place him before the bishop.*

Torments of an Unworthy Deacon

"And I looked, and saw in the middle of the river another man up to the navel, having his hands all bloody, and worms were coming up through his mouth. And I asked the angel: Who is this, my lord? And he said to me: This whom thou seest was a deacon, who ate the offerings and fornicated, and did not do what is right before God. For this reason he undergoes uninterrupted suffering."[2]

The Greek text is more sparse: "This whom thou seest was a deacon, who ate and drank, and ministered (*diekónei*) to God." *The Syriac text is more wordy:* "This one was a deacon, who ate the offering out of turn, out of greediness for bread, and did not accomplish for even one day what was good in God's sight, for he even committed adultery. For this reason, no mercy is given him, and even his torment is without mercy" (36-37).[3]

I. Ordination Prayers of the Third Century

The laying on of hands in the third century constitutes the distinctive sign of the ordination ritual of major orders.

2 ["[T]he offerings . . . suffering" is a translation of the Italian text.]
3 [Translation of the Italian text.]

Apostolic Constitutions

"Grant him to fulfill satisfactorily the service that has been entrusted to him, in a pleasant manner, with neither deviation nor blame nor reproach, to be held worthy of a higher rank, with the mediation of your Christ" (VIII 18, 3).[4]

Veronese Sacramentary, Diaconal Ordination, Version L

"The deacon, then, when he is ordained, should be chosen according to those things stated before, similarly with only the bishop laying on hands, just as we have described."

"Let us pray . . . that (he) may keep the gifts favorable for those of the consecration granted . . . to those that you deign to call to the ministry of deacon, grant that they may be able to fulfill the ministry of the holy altar [ordering] to serve your name in the three degrees of ministry and with worthy successes from the lower degree may they merit by your grace to receive better things."[5]

Veronese Sacramentary, Diaconal Ordination, Sahidic Version, Ethiopian S[AE]

"The bishop will then institute (*kathistasthai*) the deacon that has been chosen, according to what was stated before."[6]

Sacramentary of Serapion, IV century, Prayer of Diaconal Ordination

"O Father of the Only Begotten, who have sent your Son and ordained the things on earth that you have given to the Church canons and orders for the benefit and salvation of your flock, you who have chosen bishops and priests and deacons for the service of your Catholic Church, you who have chosen seven deacons through your Only Begotten and have granted it your Spirit:

4 [Ibid.]
5 [Ibid.]
6 [Ibid.]

ordain this deacon for your holy, Catholic Church and place in him the Spirit of knowledge and discernment, so that he may serve among your holy people in a pure, immaculate way in this ministry through your Only Begotten Jesus Christ, through whom you have glory and power, in the Holy Spirit both now and unto ages of ages, Amen."[7]

7 [Ibid.]

CHAPTER III

The Diaconate in the Councils of the Fourth Century

"Besides the fact of the diaconate's existence in all of the Churches from the beginning of the second century onward and of its character as an ecclesiastical order, at the beginning, deacons carry out the same role everywhere, even though the emphases placed on different aspects of their endeavors are distributed differently in the various regions. The diaconate reaches a stable point during the fourth century. In the synodal and conciliar directives pertinent to such a period, the diaconate is considered an essential element of the local Church's hierarchy. In the Synod of Elvira (ca. 306-309), its prevalently administrative aspect in the Church is most especially emphasized. Paradoxically, while it places certain limits on the deacons' liturgical commitments, this same Synod attributes to them the possibility of giving absolution of sins in urgent cases. Such a tendency to encroach upon the field of the priests' competence, also made visible in the pretense of presiding over the Eucharist (even as an extraordinary minister), is rejected by the Synod of Arles (314) and above all by the Council of Nicaea (325, c. 18)" (cf. International Theological Commission (ITC), "*From the Diakonia of Christ to the Diakonia of the Apostles*," Chap. 3).

Council of Elvira *(Spain, 306–309)*

"Canon 32. The presbyter, and the deacon if the priest commands it, should give Communion to one excommunicated and in life-threatening danger."

"Canon 33. It has been decided absolutely to prohibit bishops, presbyters, and deacons, and all the members of the clergy placed in ministry, from marriage and the procreation of children; he who does so, let him be excluded from the clergy."[8]

8 [Translation of the Italian text.]

Council of Arles *(Provence, 314)*

"Canon 14. Insofar as the deacons are concerned, we have learned that in many places they celebrate the Eucharist; it has been decided that under no circumstance should that occur."[9]

Ecumenical Council of Nicaea *(Bithynia, Asia Minor, 325)*

"XVIII. That deacons should not give the Eucharist to presbyters; nor should they take a place before them.

"This great and holy council has come to know that in other places and cities, deacons give Communion to presbyters; such a thing is permitted by neither the sacred canons nor by custom: that is, that those who do not have the power to consecrate should give the Body of Christ to those who can offer it. It has also learned the following: that some deacons even receive the Eucharist before the bishops. Let all such be banned, and let the deacons remain within their proper limits, considering that these are ministers of the bishop and inferior to presbyters. Let them then receive the Eucharist, as is commanded, after the priests and from the hand of the bishop or of the priest. Nor is it licit for deacons to sit in the midst of the presbyters; that is, in fact, contrary to both the sacred canons and orders. If, then, anyone should refuse to obey, even after these proscriptions, let him be suspended from the diaconate."[10]

9 [Ibid.]
10 [Ibid.]

CHAPTER IV

The Diaconate in the Documents of the Council of Trent and of Vatican II

COUNCIL OF TRENT

The Council of Trent wanted to define Orders dogmatically as a sacrament; the sense of its doctrinal affirmations leaves no doubt in that regard. Still, it is not clear in what measure the sacramentality of the diaconate should be considered included in this dogmatic definition.

It is in the general theology of the Sacrament of Orders that Tridentine references to Orders, of which it makes explicit mention, should be inserted.

According to Trent, deacons are directly mentioned in the New Testament, even though it is not stated that they were instituted directly by Christ the Savior. In accordance with the way the other orders are considered, the diaconate is also conceived of as an aid for exercising "dignius et maiore cum veneratione ministerium tam sancti sacerdotii" *and for serving the priesthood* "ex officio" *(it is not said to be* "ad ministerium episcopi"*); furthermore, it appears to be a step for attaining priesthood (there is no explicit mention of a permanent diaconate).*

Council of Trent *(Session 23: July 15, 1563)*

Chapter 2

And whereas the ministry of so holy a priesthood is a divine thing; to the end that it might be exercised in a more worthy manner, and with greater veneration, it was suitable that, in the most well-ordered settlement of the Church, there should be several and diverse orders of ministers, to minister to the priesthood, by virtue of their office; orders so distributed as that those already marked with the clerical tonsure should ascend through the lesser to the greater orders. For the Sacred Scriptures make open mention not only of priests, but also of deacons; and teach, in words the most weighty, what things are especially to be attended to in the ordination thereof; and, from the very beginning of the Church, the names of the following Orders, and the ministrations proper to each one of them, are known to have been in use; to wit those of subdeacon, acolyte, exorcist, lector, and door-keeper; though these were not of equal rank: for the subdeaconship is classed amongst the greater orders by the Fathers and sacred Councils, wherein also we very often read of the other inferior orders.

Chapter 17

That the functions of Holy Orders, from the deacon to the janitor, which functions have been laudably received in the Church from the times of the Apostles, and which have been for some time interrupted in very many places, may be again brought into use in accordance with the sacred canons; and that they may not be traduced by heretics as useless; the holy Synod, burning with the desire of restoring the pristine usage, ordains that, for the future, such functions shall not be exercised but by those who are actually in the said orders; and it exhorts in the Lord all and each of the prelates of the churches, and commands them, that it be their care to restore the said functions, as far as it can be conveniently done, in the cathedral, collegiate, and parochial churches of their dioceses, where the number of the people and the revenues of the Church can support it; and, to those who exercise those functions, they shall assign salaries out of some part of the revenues of any simple benefices, or those of the fabric of the Church, if the funds allow of it, or out of the revenues of both together, of which stipends they may, if negligent, be mulcted in a part, or be wholly deprived thereof, according to the judgment of the Ordinary. And if there should not be unmarried clerics at hand to exercise the functions of the four minor orders, their place may be supplied by married clerics of approved life; provided they have not been twice married, be competent to discharge the said duties, and wear the tonsure and the clerical dress in church.

SECOND VATICAN COUNCIL

With Vatican II, after the Council of Trent's unfulfilled decision to restore the diaconate, the Latin Church reinstitutes the diaconate as a permanent degree of the hierarchy. Of fundamental relevance was the fact that the conciliar assembly, in October of 1963, gave an affirmative answer to one of the five proposals for the renewal of ecclesiastical life that dealt explicitly with the diaconate.

Vatican II, a predominantly pastoral council, with its ecclesiology of communion centered on Lumen Gentium, *establishes unequivocally that the diaconal ministry should be reborn in the Church as a proper ministry and not only as a stage for candidates to the presbyterate.*

The Diaconate in the Debates of the Council

Offered here are some of the interventions made in the Council hall by the Council Fathers, and the suggestions to the initial text of the De Ecclesia *delivered on November 23, 1962. Number 29 of the dogmatic constitution* Lumen Gentium *had a rather long and troubled process.*

Despite the appraisals of the document De Ecclesia *by the Council Fathers, the text was the object of much criticism and was completely rewritten.*

The Interventions of Cardinals J. L. Suenens and J. Döpfner

On October 30, 1963, "five issues" of importance were left to the vote of the Council Fathers with the purpose of plotting a secure direction for explaining doctrine on the episcopate and diaconate: "The Fathers are invited to declare whether they desire the outline to be drawn up in such a way as to say:

1. That episcopal consecration constitutes the highest degree of Orders;
2. That every legitimately consecrated bishop, in communion with the other bishops and with the pope, who is the head and principle of their unity, is a member of the body of bishops;
3. That the body or college of bishops succeeds the college of Apostles in its mission of evangelization, of sanctification, and of governance, and that the Body in union with its head, the Roman Pontiff, and never without this head (whose primatial right remains intact and complete over all pastors and faithful), possesses the plenary and supreme power over the Universal Church;
4. That this authority belongs by divine right to the same college of bishops united to its head."

The fifth issue poses the problem of the opportunity for restoring the diaconate as a separate, permanent degree of sacred orders, according to the necessity of the Church in different countries.

The context, then, in which the restoration of the diaconate is proposed, is highly significant, and the discussion that developed over the question saw numerous theologians engaged in profound debate.

It is to be kept in mind that the list of issues did not at all have a simple approbation or refusal of a determined formula as its objective; it was rather meant to allow the Theological Commission to learn the opinion prevalent among the bishops, and with a sufficient amount of certainty. Applying the conciliar regulation, the Commission would study all of the Fathers' proposals in depth in order to present a revised, adapted text to the Congregation's approval.

On the fifth question in particular, the result of the October 23, 1963, scrutiny was the following:

Number of votes: 2,120; Placet: 1,588; Non placet: 525; Blank ballots: 7.[11]

The Discourse of Cardinal Suenens

I wish to speak in favor of the establishment of a permanent diaconate.

Those who have opposed—it does not seem to me that they have kept in mind that such a question concerns the very constitution of the Church.

We should not begin from a certain natural realism, but rather *from a supernatural realism*, founded on a living faith in the sacramentality of the diaconate.

I would not like to insist on the subjects discussed until now, such as the interpretation of the pericope on the election of Stephen and the other six (Acts 6:3-6).

Furthermore, some points have been made certain and arise clearly from the New Testament, from the writings of the first Apostolic Fathers (especially Clement of Rome and Ignatius of Antioch), from the continuous tradition thereafter, and from the liturgical books of both East and West:

1. From the times of the apostolic and subapostolic Church, some charisms of sacred ministry were attributed to a determined degree of the priesthood according to a particular, constant process.

11 [The *Interventions of Cardinals J.L. Suenens and J. Döpfner* section is a translation of the Italian text.]

2. This degree seems to have been instituted especially to provide a direct help for the bishop, in particular

    a. To care for the poor and assure good order in the community
    b. To take on the responsibility of preparation, so to speak: both communitary (especially through charity among the brethren) and liturgical, *in the breaking of the bread* (Acts 2:42, 4:32-35; Heb 13:16), of the local Church in order to establish it as a true religious community.

If there is anyone who does not see the specifically sacred and necessarily liturgical essence of this responsibility—could it not be a question of not understanding how the Church is, which is founded on the sacraments and even on the charisms conferred by the Sacrament of Holy Orders?

The argument opposed to the restoration of the diaconate is not a valid one when it is said that these responsibilities proposed for deacons could be entrusted to laypeople.

It is not a question of attributing the exterior responsibilities in any way to any layperson whatsoever (for example, presiding at prayer gatherings, teaching catechism, heading social works). Such duties should be attributed only to someone who, in an objective, adequate way, has the necessary graces to care for them, so that supernatural efficacy will not lessen in bringing about a true community. Otherwise, the Church cannot be a true supernatural society, the true Mystical Body of Christ, built upon the structure of its ministries and on the grace foreseen by God.

Such gifts and graces, with which simple laypeople can be endowed inasmuch as they have been renewed by the Sacraments of Baptism and Confirmation and revived by an authentic supernatural spirit, are not enough.

Furthermore, other gifts have been given that are more apt for accomplishing community service with greater efficacy: it is important not to neglect them.

The Christian community has the right to make use of such gifts existing in the Church's patrimony.

Relying solidly on these theological foundations, let us take a look at how matters in various parts of the globe truly present themselves.

We have heard echoes of opposition.

But the objections directed at the diaconate's establishment, even if they might be of considerable proportion concerning some regions and in very determined circumstances, are not valid everywhere nor in every time.

For this reason it is not the present Council's place to resolve the question in general, nor to declare the diaconate more or less necessary in the entire Church.

All that the Council should do is more or less explicitly provide for the possibility of such a stable charge, not for the whole Church, but only for those regions where the legitimate pastors, with the consensus of the competent authority, value this practically necessary restoration, in order to avoid the Church's decline and allow for its expansion and development.

This, then, is what has been brought before our consciences, Venerable Fathers: not to close the door with purely negative decisions to every possibility of the restoration of this sacred order, a means provided by God, utilized by the Church for several centuries, and today *extremely necessary for the Church's renewal.*

According to the divine economy, the bishop receives the fullness and height of sacred ministry from God at the same time as he welcomes the mission of constituting all of the supernatural communities necessary for his people.

For this reason the bishop has the faculty of conferring upon other ministers a participation in his powers, a participation adapted to the structure of his people and to the circumstances of places and times.

In practice, the necessity of the diaconate is particularly urgent in two instances:

1. In the first place, when there is a very small community forced more and more to live *in diaspora*, meaning almost removed from any other Christian nucleus because of differences in confession, distances to cover, or political circumstances
2. In second place, when there are enormous multitudes of people, especially in the outskirts of cities, where a certain sense of Church as family should be created

Such, then, are the circumstances in which the Church is offered a chance to affirm itself as really and fully missionary, and to therefore allow for different solutions for different regions, notwithstanding the fact that all remain within the limits of their Constitution.

In such a case I would say: let the salvation of the people be the supreme law.

What we have said so far responds to the major objection made to the text of our outline, that is, fear that granting the diaconate to married men does not respect the law of *consecrated celibacy*, and at the same time that the number of priestly vocations will diminish.

And yet, if the diaconate is a gift, if it is a grace, and if legitimate pastors deem it convenient and appropriate to draw upon this patrimony of grace, then the establishment of the diaconate will not be able to diminish the measure of Christ's fullness in the Christian community, but should rather increase it.

One can very clearly see the value and witness of ecclesiastical celibacy according to the ancient and venerable practice of the Latin Church.

The diaconate, however, with the conditions for which it is not subject to the law of celibacy being well defined, does not go against this practice. Facing the negative consequences that some fear to such a degree that they do not hope for notable advantages, I would say:

1. There is no evident reason why the number of priestly vocations should decrease: this is an *a priori* affirmation. On the contrary, it can easily increase in the communities that will have been better united and prepared by deacons and whose life is more efficaciously nourished by the latter's charisms.
2. Priestly vocations themselves would become more sincere and more authentic and would be even better tested.
3. Perfect chastity *for the Kingdom of Heaven* would shine like never before and would offer a full witness.

In order to arrive at a practical conclusion, I would like to ask that it be placed under the deliberations of the Fathers with the following vote: "*Wherever the establishment of the permanent diaconate seems convenient to the episcopal conference, they are free to introduce it.*"[12]

The Discourse of Cardinal Döpfner

Most eminent presiders, venerable Fathers, on what is written about deacons in the outline *De Ecclesia* (page 26, lines 28-41), let me make the following

12 [The *Discourse of Cardinal Suenens* section is a translation of the Italian text.]

observations: I recommend insistently that this text, at least in its essence, be preserved as it is.

The reasons that guide me are the following:

1. Our outline, dealing with the Church's hierarchical constitution, can in no way silence the order of diaconate; for the tripartite nature of the hierarchy, consisting in order of the episcopate, presbyterate, and diaconate, is of divine right and is proper to the essence of the Church's constitution. At the very least there should be no wonder that the subject of diaconate as a permanent order, just like the presbyterate, is being brought up. And yet the diaconate cannot be proposed as if it were a mere step for gaining a higher title, just as the presbyterate cannot be considered a mere step to the episcopate. Such a consideration, indeed, offers neither a correct nor, in one way at least, a complete idea of the diaconate, nor does it correspond to the Church's doctrine as it has been proposed up to now.

2. This text presenting the possibility of the permanent diaconate teaches precisely those principles that even to this day have been contained in Church doctrine, especially in the decrees of the Council of Trent. In fact, that Council (a) teaches the necessity of the sacraments in general, which is necessary to be applied to the order of diaconate as well so that no one will doubt that it is a sacrament just as the order of episcopate, and (b) it furthermore requires that the ministries of the diaconate (as well as those of the other orders) be carried out only by those who have in fact been instituted in said order, so that such a sacrament will not be ridiculed by heretics as idle (Session 23, c. 17). Therefore, our text surely does not exceed what has been held with certainty in Catholic doctrine up to now. Rather, it poses the question even more cautiously and almost more restrictedly than did the Council of Trent. In fact, it deals merely with the possibility of the permanent diaconate and, in a more defined manner with respect to the Council of Trent, it recognizes that the necessity or usefulness of the permanent diaconate is conditioned and depends not only on the dogmatic argument but also on reasons of practicality, discipline, and positive influence that can all differ according to times and places. And yet, please note: we are

not discussing the institution of the permanent diaconate solely on the basis of its tradition or antiquity. It is certainly not for the mere fact of its existence in antiquity that we are recommending it for our times as well. It is absolutely true that being more ancient does not always mean being better. Still, if we reflect carefully on the reasons and under what conditions it existed in antiquity, it really becomes legitimate—perhaps even necessary in order to meet pastoral needs in the changed reality of our conditions—to examine in detail the way we can penetrate deeper into the essence of the diaconate and whether or not the restoration of the permanent diaconate can be recommended in our own times.

3. The outline's text does not actually give disciplinary or canonical provisions but only dogmatic foundations for such a provision, legitimate in a dogmatic outline even while it often happens elsewhere. Thus, in the first place, such a text corresponds to the pastoral disposition that, as we all know, is the theme of our Council. The possibility and faculty for a future pastoral development is being opened without already being compromised. In fact, there is no way in which our text hinders the state of the diaconate from remaining as it is in those regions where there are none nor does there seem to be a need for any. On the other hand, the lack of priests that already exists for the future in many regions of the world is such that the provident Council should now take care of this shortage, at least in part, by predisposing statutes for the possibility of the diaconate's restoration: it can aid daily Eucharistic life even with the lack of priests; it can more easily provide for the validity of matrimonies and the unity of Christian communities; charitable activity can be carried out in the measure that the administration of profane matters pertains even to the hierarchy as such. This is all intended for those regions where the shortage of priests would recommend the permanent diaconate's restoration in view of such ends. It is fitting for the provident shepherds of the Church to look toward the future, a future that, I dare say, is already beginning to manifest. Many prelates of the Church testify that the diaconate's restoration in many places of the world is considered absolutely necessary or of great benefit (see the testimonies of Rahner-Vorgrimler, *Diaconatus in Christo*,

Freiburg, 1962). If this is not true elsewhere, let these other regions not be hindered in the tasks that pastoral concern demands of them.

4. In the outline's text, nothing is compromised about the way to propose the future decision about the reintroduction of the permanent diaconate. Expressions such as "where the Church . . . shall have established to proceed" or "in which case the decision falls to those who have authority in the Church" do not mean other than that, in the case that there is judged to be some true necessity, the decision falls exclusively to the competent authority. This necessarily implies that nothing can happen without the order or statute or at the least the confirmation of the Holy See—if it is so decided in the episcopal conferences in different regions.

5. It cannot be said that great works (like seminaries, etc.) are needed to restore the diaconate. Where the demand for such a restoration occurs and is chosen, there is no reason to create and introduce new duties (*munera*) into the Church that do not already exist. There is reason, rather, that those men who, finding themselves already exercising such duties, and already educated and prepared by the Church, should receive the sacramental grace to exercise it more worthily and more perfectly—the grace, I must say, that is present in this sacramental Order and has still not been conferred on them. Let no new duties be created where there is no need, but let those that do exist be crowned by sacramental ordination appropriate for them according to the nature of this sacrament.

6. One final thing. We must still look into the question of whether our outline's text exposes the sacred law of celibacy for the presbyterate to danger. To such a question we must answer thus: in no case will the number of those who are truly apt for priesthood diminish. It is difficult to think that a man who would turn to the diaconate over the priesthood because of marriage would be apt for the priesthood.

   Certainly, this danger should not be denied, and could become reality if anyone who requested admission to the permanent diaconate were admitted indiscriminately. Therefore, when norms for the permanent diaconate's restoration must be proposed, it will be necessary to be very careful that the path to the diaconate be open to those and only to those who have a vocation to perform the duties proper to the deacon. Surely, the permanent diaconate must not be considered, so to speak, as a second-class priesthood reserved for those who would like to undertake the presbyterate but who do not believe they can be bothered with, or want to, or are capable of handling the obligations attached to the presbyterate. The permanent diaconate can be instituted only for those who perform it from the beginning and truly want to perform the ministry's duties (such as high-level catechists, men dedicated to the Church's social or charitable work, or even laymen who perform their own profession and who, if well prepared, could perform such duties due to the lack of priests). In reality, everywhere in the Church, and especially in certain areas (especially in the missions), such permanent duties exist and are performed generally by married men at the service of the Church hierarchy. Nor, up to this very moment, has this fact done any damage to celibacy. Why deny them all the sacramental grace that is present in and of itself? Certainly, the law of celibacy is to be kept holy, yet it should not and cannot be an obstacle to a well-founded, dogmatic development that is perhaps well-fitting to the need of our times. Therefore, I conclude: it is certain that several questions that still need clarifying concerning the restoration of the permanent diaconate should yet be carefully examined in the future. At present, however, only the path toward such an examination needs to be opened with this outline. Let the text, then, remain as it is. That is all.[13]

Suggestions of the German and Austrian bishops for the Outline De Ecclesia—*February, 1963 [Acta Syn. I/IV P. 627]*

With sacramental ordination, albeit in the lowest degree, even those named deacons are called to the ministry of bishop. Even if they are not priests and, for this reason, according to Apostolic Tradition, expressly cannot perform priestly acts, they still truly belong to the sacred hierarchy, dedicate themselves to the sacred sacrifice, are the extraordinary ministers of solemn Baptism and of the

13 [The *Discourse of Cardinal Döpfner* section is a translation of the Italian text.]

Eucharist, and can perform the various duties proper to the hierarchy, such as that of charity, of preaching, of assistance, as it is attributed to them by competent authority in the Church according to the diversity of times and places.

Admitting that, in today's Church, the diaconate is considered mostly as a step from which one rises to priesthood, still this practice has not always been in force nor is it observed everywhere. Moreover, in the future, the diaconate as a proper, permanent degree of the hierarchy will be able to be exercised when the Church deems to use it for the necessity of caring for souls, either in certain regions or in all of them. In this case, it falls to the ministers of the Church to discern whether such deacons are to be bound by the sacred law of celibacy or not.[14]

Intervention by Msgr. J.C. Maure (Bolivia)

The diaconate, according to common doctrine, imprints a permanent, indelible character on the soul. The best priests and bishops are without a doubt those who live according to their diaconal grace and character and who desire no more than to serve the lowest degree. For this reason we should want legislation in the Western Church to be renewed in such a way that the desire to rise to priesthood should in no way be the condition for receiving the order of diaconate. Thus the same legislation and institution that protects and elevates the humble deacon will be the continuous admonition for the higher degrees so that they may outdo the deacons in humility, insofar as that can be possible.

If the Council's task is still to confute the errors that encroach upon and tarnish the Church's beauty in the eyes of some, then truthfully this has positive efficacy most especially against the very frustrating error of those who consider the degrees of priesthood as a career for human glory.

The diaconate should be restored so that the Church will acquire and express a clearer conscience concerning its condition, appearing before all as Christ's handmaiden, very lovingly following and witnessing to the humility of the servant of God.[15]

---

14 [The *Suggestions of the German and Austrian Bishops* section is a translation of the Italian text.]

15 [The *Intervention by Msgr. J.C. Maure* section is a translation of the Italian text.]

The Diaconate in the Documents of Vatican II

Sacrosanctum Concilium (Constitution on the Sacred Liturgy)

Bible, Preaching, and Liturgical Catechesis

35. That the intimate connection between words and rites may be apparent in the liturgy:

1. In sacred celebrations there is to be more reading from holy Scripture, and it is to be more varied and suitable.
2. Since the sermon is part of the liturgical service, the preferred place for it is to be indicated even in the rubrics, as far as the nature of the rite will allow; and the ministry of preaching is to be fulfilled with exactitude and fidelity. The sermon, moreover, should draw its content mainly from scriptural and liturgical sources. Its character should be that of a proclamation of God's wonderful works in the history of salvation, that is, the mystery of Christ, which is ever made present and active within us, especially in the celebration of the liturgy.
3. Instruction which is more explicitly liturgical should also be imparted in a variety of ways; if necessary, short directives to be spoken by the priest or proper minister should be provided within the rites themselves. But they should occur only at the more suitable moments, and be in prescribed words or their equivalent.
4. Bible services should be encouraged, especially on the vigils of the more solemn feasts, on some weekdays in Advent and Lent, and on Sundays and feast days. They are particularly to be commended in places where no priest is available; when this is so, a deacon or some other person authorized by the bishop should preside over the celebration.

The Other Sacraments and the Sacramentals

68. The baptismal rite should contain adaptations, to be used at the discretion of the local ordinary, for occasions when a very large number are to be baptized together. Moreover, a shorter rite is to be drawn up, especially for mission lands,

for use by catechists, but also by the faithful in general when there is danger of death, and neither priest nor deacon is available.

The Divine Office

86. Priests engaged in the sacred pastoral ministry will offer the praises of the hours with fervor to the extent that they vividly realize that they must heed St. Paul's exhortation: "Pray without ceasing" (1 Thes 5:17). For only the Lord can give fruitfulness and increase to the works in which they are engaged. "Without me," He said, "you can do nothing" (Jn 15:5). That is why the apostles, appointing deacons, said: "We will devote ourselves to prayer and to the ministry of the word" (Acts 6:4).

Lumen Gentium (Dogmatic Constitution on the Church)

This document, the most solemn of the whole Council, begins with the words "Lumen gentium" *(light of the nations). The first chapter speaks of the mystery of the Church that "by her relationship with Christ, . . . is a kind of sacrament of intimate union with God, and of the unity of all mankind" (no. 1). After this first chapter outlining the relationship of the Church with God, Father, Son, and Holy Spirit, the second chapter presents the Church as the People of God, formed by Baptism and whose Head is Christ, journeying throughout history and destined to unite all men. This chapter reminds us of the bonds between the Church and non-Catholic Christians, its relations with non-Christians, and affirms the missionary character of the People of God.*

The Constitution then presents the members of the People of God: the hierarchy (bishops, priests, and deacons) and the laity. The third chapter, on the hierarchy, affirms the collegial nature of the episcopate (the bishops as successors of the Apostles, around the pope as Successor of Peter, their head, have received from Christ the responsibility for the Universal Church) and decides that the local episcopates can restore the diaconate as a permanent Order, conferring this Order on married men. The fourth chapter, on the laity, shows their participation in the life and mission of the Church (worship, announcing the Gospel, orienting life and activity of all humanity toward Christ).

The Hierarchical Structure of the Church, with Special Reference to the Episcopate

20. That divine mission, entrusted by Christ to the apostles, will last until the end of the world (Mt 28:20), since the gospel which was to be handed down by them is for all time the source of all life for the Church. For this reason the apostles took care to appoint successors in this hierarchically structured society.

For they not only had helpers in their ministry, but also, in order that the mission assigned to them might continue after their death, they passed on to their immediate cooperators, as a kind of testament, the duty of perfecting and consolidating the work begun by themselves, charging them to attend to the whole flock in which the Holy Spirit placed them to shepherd the Church of God (cf. Acts 20:28). They therefore appointed such men, and authorized the arrangement that, when these men should have died, other approved men would take up their ministry.

Among those various ministries which, as tradition witnesses, were exercised in the Church from the earliest times, the chief place belongs to the office of those who, appointed to the episcopate in a sequence running back to the beginning, are the ones who pass on the apostolic seed. Thus, as St. Irenaeus testifies, through those who were appointed bishops by the apostles, and through their successors down to our own time, the Apostolic Tradition is manifested and preserved throughout the world.

With their helpers, the priests and deacons, bishops have therefore taken up the service of the community, presiding in place of God over the flock whose shepherds they are, as teachers of doctrine, priests of sacred worship, and officers of good order. Just as the role that the Lord gave individually to Peter, the first among the apostles, is permanent and was meant to be transmitted to his successors, so also the apostles' office of nurturing the Church is permanent, and was meant to be exercised without interruption by the sacred order of bishops. Therefore, this sacred Synod teaches that by divine institution bishops have succeeded to the place of the apostles as shepherds of the Church, and that he who hears them, hears Christ, while he who rejects them, rejects Christ and Him who sent Christ (cf. Lk 10:16).

28. Christ, whom the Father sanctified and sent into the world (Jn 10:36) has, through His apostles, made their successors, the bishops, partakers of His consecration and His mission. These in their turn have legitimately handed on to different individuals in the Church various degrees of participation in this

ministry. Thus the divinely established ecclesiastical ministry is exercised on different levels by those who from antiquity have been called bishops, priests, and deacons.

29. At a lower level of the hierarchy are deacons, upon whom hands are imposed "not unto the priesthood, but unto a ministry of service." For strengthened by sacramental grace, in communion with the bishop and his group of priests, they serve the People of God in the ministry of the liturgy, of the word, and of charity. It is the duty of the deacon, to the extent that he has been authorized by competent authority, to administer baptism solemnly, to be custodian and dispenser of the Eucharist, to assist at and bless marriages in the name of the Church, to bring Viaticum to the dying, to read the sacred Scripture to the faithful, to instruct and exhort the people, to preside at the worship and prayer of the faithful, to administer sacramentals, and to officiate at funeral and burial services. Dedicated to duties of charity and of administration, let deacons be mindful of the admonition of Blessed Polycarp: "Be merciful, diligent, walking according to the truth of the Lord, who became the servant of all."

These duties, so very necessary for the life of the Church, can in many areas be fulfilled only with difficulty according to the prevailing discipline of the Latin Church. For this reason, the diaconate can in the future be restored as a proper and permanent rank of the hierarchy. It pertains to the competent territorial bodies of bishops, of one kind or another, to decide, with the approval of the Supreme Pontiff, whether and where it is opportune for such deacons to be appointed for the care of souls. With the consent of the Roman Pontiff, this diaconate will be able to be conferred upon men of more mature age, even upon those living in the married state. It may also be conferred upon suitable young men. For them, however, the law of celibacy must remain intact.

The Call of the Whole Church to Holiness

41. In the various types and duties of life, one and the same holiness is cultivated by all who are moved by the Spirit of God, and who obey the voice of the Father, worshiping God the Father in spirit and in truth. These souls follow the poor Christ, the humble and cross-bearing Christ, in order to be made worthy of being partakers in His glory. Every person should walk unhesitatingly according to his own personal gifts and duties in the path of a living faith which arouses hopes and works through charity.

In the first place, the shepherds of Christ's flock ought to carry out their ministry with holiness, eagerness, humility, and courage, in imitation of the eternal High Priest, the Shepherd and Guardian of our souls. They will thereby make this ministry the principal means of their own sanctification. Those chosen for the fullness of the priesthood are gifted with sacramental grace enabling them to exercise a perfect role of pastoral charity through prayer, sacrifice, and preaching, as through every form of a bishop's care and service. They are enabled to lay down their life for their sheep fearlessly, and, made a model for their flock (cf. 1 Pt 5:3), can lead the Church to ever-increasing holiness through their own example.

Thanks to Christ, the eternal and sole Mediator, priests share in the grace of the bishop's rank and form his spiritual crown. Like bishops, priests should grow in love for God and neighbor through the daily exercise of their duty. They should preserve the bond of priestly fraternity, abound in every spiritual good, and give living evidence of God to all men. Let their heroes be those priests who have lived during the course of the centuries, often in lowly and hidden service, and have left behind them a bright pattern of holiness. Their praise lives on in the Church.

A priest's task is to pray and offer sacrifice for his own people and indeed the entire People of God, realizing what he does and reproducing in himself the holiness of the things he handles. Let him not be undone by his apostolic cares, dangers, and toils, but rather led by them to higher sanctity. His activities should be fed and fostered by a wealth of meditation, to the delight of the whole Church of God. All priests, especially those who are called diocesan in view of the particular title of their ordination, should bear in mind how much their sanctity profits from loyal attachment to the bishop and generous collaboration with him.

In their own special way, ministers of lesser rank also share in the mission and grace of the supreme priest. First among these are deacons. Since they are servants of the mysteries of Christ and the Church, they should keep themselves free from every fault, be pleasing to God, and be a source of all goodness in the sight of men (cf. 1 Tm 3:8-10, 12-13).

Dei Verbum (Dogmatic Constitution on Divine Revelation)

Sacred Scripture in the Life of the Church

25. Therefore, all the clergy must hold fast to the sacred Scriptures through diligent sacred reading and careful study, especially the priests of Christ and others, such as deacons and catechists, who are legitimately active in the ministry of the word. This cultivation of Scripture is required lest any of them become "an empty preacher of the word of God outwardly, who is not a listener to it inwardly" since they must share the abundant wealth of the divine word with the faithful committed to them, especially in the sacred liturgy. This sacred Synod earnestly and specifically urges all the Christian faithful, too, especially religious, to learn by frequent reading of the divine Scriptures the "excelling knowledge of Jesus Christ" (Phil 3:8). "For ignorance of the Scriptures is ignorance of Christ." Therefore, they should gladly put themselves in touch with the sacred text itself, whether it be through the liturgy, rich in the divine word, or through devotional reading, or through instructions suitable for the purpose and other aids which, in our time, are commendably available everywhere, thanks to the approval and active support of the shepherds of the Church. And let them remember that prayer should accompany the reading of sacred Scripture, so that God and man may talk together; for "we speak to Him when we pray; we hear Him when we read the divine sayings."

It devolves on sacred bishops, "who have the apostolic teaching," to give the faithful entrusted to them suitable instruction in the right use of the divine books, especially the New Testament and above all the Gospels, through translations of the sacred texts. Such versions are to be provided with necessary and fully adequate explanations so that the sons of the Church can safely and profitably grow familiar with the sacred Scriptures and be penetrated with their spirit.

Furthermore, editions of the sacred Scriptures, provided with suitable comments, should be prepared also for the use of non-Christians and adapted to their situation. Both pastors of souls and Christians generally should see to the wise distribution of these in one way or another.

Christus Dominus (Decree on the Bishops' Pastoral Office in the Church)

Bishops and Their Particular Churches or Dioceses

15. In fulfilling their duty to sanctify, bishops should be mindful that they have been taken from among men and appointed their representatives before God in order to offer gifts and sacrifices for sins. Bishops enjoy the fullness of the sacrament of orders, and all priests as well as deacons are dependent upon them in the exercise of authority. For the "presbyters" are prudent fellow workers of the episcopal order and are themselves consecrated as true priests of the New Testament, just as deacons are ordained for service and minister to the People of God in communion with the bishop and his presbytery. Therefore bishops are the principal dispensers of the mysteries of God, just as they are the governors, promoters, and guardians of the entire liturgical life in the church committed to them.

Orientalium Ecclesiarum (Decree on Eastern Catholic Churches)

Rules Concerning the Sacraments

17. In order that the ancient discipline of the sacrament of orders may flourish again in the Eastern Churches, this sacred Synod ardently desires that where it has fallen into disuse the office of the permanent diaconate be restored. The legislative authority of each individual church should decide about the subdiaconate and the minor orders, including their rights and obligations.

Ad Gentes (Decree on the Missionary Activity of the Church)

Forming the Christian Community

15. Now, if the Church is to be planted and the Christian community grow, various ministries are needed. These are raised up by divine vocation from the midst of the faithful, and are to be carefully fostered and cultivated by all. Among these are the offices of priests, deacons, and catechists, as well as Catholic action.

By their prayers and by their active labors, religious men and women play an indispensable role too in rooting and strengthening the kingdom of Christ in souls, and in causing it to expand.

16. With great joy the Church gives thanks for the priceless gift of the priestly calling which God has granted to so many youthful members of those peoples recently converted to Christ. For the Church is more firmly rooted in any given sector of the human family when the various groupings of the faithful draw from their own members ministers of salvation in the orders of bishop, priest, and deacon. As these come to serve their brethren, the new Churches gradually acquire a diocesan structure equipped with its own clergy.

Where Episcopal Conferences deem it opportune, the order of the diaconate should be restored as a permanent state of life, according to the norms of the Constitution on the Church. For there are men who are actually carrying out the functions of the deacon's office, either by preaching the word of God as catechists, or by presiding over scattered Christian communities in the name of the pastor and the bishop, or by practicing charity in social or relief work. It will be helpful to strengthen them by that imposition of hands which has come down from the apostles, and to bind them more closely to the altar. Thus they can carry out their ministry more effectively because of the sacramental grace of the diaconate.

CHAPTER V

The Diaconate in the Pontifical Magisterium

Leo XIII

Encyclical *Rerum Novarum* (*On Capital and Labor*)

May 15, 1891

The Beneficence of the Church and the Deacons

29. The Church, moreover, intervenes directly on behalf of the poor, by setting on foot and maintaining many associations that she knows to be efficient for the relief of poverty. Herein, again, she has always succeeded so well as to have even extorted the praise of her enemies. Such was the ardor of brotherly love among the earliest Christians that numbers of those who were in better circumstances despoiled themselves of their possessions in order to relieve their brethren; whence "neither was there any one needy among them." To the order of deacons, instituted in that very intent, was committed by the Apostles the charge of the daily doles; and the Apostle Paul, though burdened with the solicitude of all the Churches, hesitated not to undertake laborious journeys in order to carry the alms of the faithful to the poorer Christians. Tertullian calls these contributions, given voluntarily by Christians in their assemblies, deposits of piety because, to cite his own words, they were employed "in feeding the needy, in burying them, in support of youths and maidens destitute of means and deprived of their parents, in the care of the aged, and the relief of the shipwrecked."

30. Thus, by degrees, came into existence the patrimony that the Church has guarded with religious care as the inheritance of the poor. Nay, in order to spare them the shame of begging, the Church has provided aid for the needy. The

common Mother of rich and poor has aroused everywhere the heroism of charity and has established congregations of religious and many other useful institutions for help and mercy, so that hardly any kind of suffering could exist that was not afforded relief. At the present day, many there are who, like the heathen of old, seek to blame and condemn the Church for such eminent charity. They would substitute in its stead a system of relief organized by the state. But no human expedience will ever make up for the devotedness and self-sacrifice of Christian charity. Charity, as a virtue, pertains to the Church; for virtue it is not, unless it be drawn from the Most Sacred Heart of Jesus Christ; and whosoever turns his back on the Church cannot be near to Christ.

Pius XII

Speech to the Participants of the Second World Congress of the Apostolate of the Laity, Rome

October 5, 1957

We have not yet spoken of the ordinations preceding the presbyterate and that, in the praxis of today's Church, are conferred only as a preparation for priestly ordination. The duties relative to the minor orders have long been carried out by the laity.

We know that at the present time some are thinking of introducing an order of deacon understood as an ecclesiastical function independent of the priesthood.

The idea, at least today, is not yet ripe; should it become so in the future, nothing that we have said would change except the fact that this diaconate would be placed with the priesthood in the distinctions indicated by us.[1]

1 [Translation of the Italian text.]

John XXIII

Encyclical Letter *Mater et Magistra* (*On Christianity and Social Progress*)

May 15, 1961

Deacons and the Torch of Charity

6. Small wonder, then, that the Catholic Church, in imitation of Christ and in fulfillment of his commandment, relies not merely upon her teaching to hold aloft the torch of charity, but also upon her own widespread example. This has been her course now for nigh on two thousand years, from the early ministrations of her deacons right down to the present time. It is a charity that combines the precepts and practice of mutual love. It holds fast to the twofold aspect of Christ's command to give, and summarizes the whole of the Church's social teaching and activity.

Paul VI

Speech at the Audience Given to Participants in the Congress of the Diaconate

October 25, 1965

Venerable Brothers and dear Sons,

We are happy to have you in our house and give you welcome. Under your presiders, Cardinals Giulio Döpfner, Raúl Silva Henríquez, and Franjo Šeper, since last Friday, you have worked in an international study session with zealous pastors and illustrious theologians reflecting on what "the deacon in today's Church and world" could and should be.

You face a concern of the Second Ecumenical Vatican Council that we have made our own, solemnly promulgating the *Lumen Gentium* (*Dogmatic*

Constitution of the Church). This work, after listing the deacon's functions and illustrating how they are "highly necessary for the life of the Church," affirms that the "diaconate can be restored in the future as its own, permanent degree in the hierarchy."

You are therefore gathered here to expound on the Council's teaching on the diaconate, reflecting at the same time on what the formation and mission of the deacon could be, whether celibate or married, according to the exigencies of differing situations in different countries.

Who does not see the great importance that the *diakonia* in our Christian communities can have, whether in announcing the Word of God or in administering the Sacraments and practicing charity? All of this speaks to the responsibility with which the pastors in charge should choose the new deacons and, at the same time, to the care they should take for their spiritual, doctrinal, and pastoral formation. For if many differing ways of life can be legitimately anticipated, as the case may be, it is quite certain that only the pious, zealous deacon nourished by the Gospel can offer bishops and priests the fraternal aid that they hope to receive for the greater good of God's people entrusted to their care.

Venerable Brethren and dear Children, may it be the will of Almighty God to make your work, for the greater glory and spread of his Reign, fruitful by his graces. It is not without a providential inspiration of the Holy Spirit that the Council has wished to restore the ancient diaconate at the service of God's people. This is the hour to set these conciliar dispositions into motion. May Stephen the first deacon, the martyr Lawrence, and all the holy deacons of the Church watch from heaven over those who prepare to enter the sacred order of the diaconate; and may the Lord bless all who answer his call, following their example, to serve God's people. This is our dearest prayer. And with great love, we grant you, as a pledge of the abundance of the divine graces, our special apostolic blessing.[2]

2 [Ibid.]

Speech to the Members of the Study Committee for the Permanent Diaconate

February 24, 1967

Venerable Brothers!

We do not want you to leave this serene city of Rome without greeting you with the devotion and affection that we always nourish in our hearts for our most worthy brothers in the episcopal office, nor without thanking you for coming here to give your counsel concerning the practice and ordered implementation of the restoration of the order of deacon in our Latin Church as a permanent degree of the sacred hierarchy.

Since it is a question of something new and, in no small part, entails canonical discipline, and wishing both to keep in mind the wishes made known to us as well as the difficulties that the situation itself can present, we have desired, before proceeding to legislative action, to bring you all up to date on the conclusions of the studies carried out on the subject by our command, and to examine the matter with you in its full context, and thus to bring it to a happy completion. Each one of you, in fact, has come to us to acquire the appropriate instruction and the necessary faculties that the conciliar Constitution *Lumen Gentium*, no. 29, reserves to this Apostolic See; and to each one of you, we have wished to give directly the pledge of our particular interest, discussing with all of you this not slight matter.

We now wait to find out what the success of these meetings is in order to give the matter its appropriate set of canonical norms.

In the meanwhile, we wish to say to you that from the time of the greatly awaited restoration of the diaconate in its own permanent state, we have had a great concept of this degree of Holy Orders. Its apostolic origin, its specific definition as service, its first member and representative the heroic protomartyr Stephen, "a man filled with faith and the holy Spirit" (Acts 6:5), the honor in which the permanent diaconate has been held for so much time in the Latin Church and still is in the Eastern Churches, the varied and extremely useful work that the deacons have offered the Church in so many periods and in so many events of its history, and finally the functions that the cited Conciliar Constitutions reserve to them—these are the many reasons for our esteem for the diaconal order. We would be very happy, therefore, to implement and support, as best as seems possible, the wishes that your pastoral charity has manifested to us.

Only one thing needs to be insisted upon: "Your every act should be done with love" (1 Cor 16:14), as the Apostle Paul says, here meaning not only the theological virtue that comes from God and unites us to him, but, more so, that harmony of mind and deeds that should mark mutual relations in the Church community and that involves a confluence of sentiments, of virtues, and of norms that make the very community's fullness of order and holiness become more enriched. We like to ponder the union, the docility, the affection that should unite the deacon to the bishop. We like to think of the spirit of service that should characterize the deacon who is defined precisely by service and, in service, becomes like Christ, who "did not come to be served but to serve" (Mt 20:28). We like to think also that the holy Church, in the permanent deacons, will have a new, pure example of that splendor of the chaste lifestyle that is duly demanded of the sacred ministry, whether they remain celibate or have the diaconal order bestowed on them when already married and of mature age.

May the Lord make this new reality a source of spiritual joy. May our veneration for those who are called in the Church to give service and witness in the sacred diaconate grow. May the efficiency of pastoral care and Christian apostolate, which we hope for from permanent deacons, grow. May the "sense of the Church," on which the Lord has desired to bestow sacred ministers whom he has deigned to mark with distinction and to bring together into the hierarchical and community ranks, grow. May his grace, wherever it is most needed and wherever he plans to provide for that need with new ministers, grow. And may our apostolic blessing fulfill these prayers.[3]

Apostolic Letter *Motu Proprio Sacrum Diaconatus Ordinem* (*General Norms for Restoring the Permanent Diaconate in the Latin Church*)

June 18, 1967

Sacrum Diaconatus Ordinem *is the pontifical document with which the decisions of the Council were put into motion.*

3 [Ibid.]

Listed among the diaconal functions are leadership of "scattered Christian communities" and "promoting and sustaining the apostolic activities of the laity."

General directives are laid out for the formation of candidates to the priesthood, formulating a distinction between "young deacons" and "deacons of mature age." In practice, this will have no follow-up: in fact, all of the episcopates, with the Holy See's permission, would apply the directives provided for deacons of mature age to all candidates.

It is also affirmed that it is up to the episcopal conferences to decide on the restoration of the diaconate among their various countries and to seek approval from the Holy See.

Beginning already in the early days of the Apostles, the Catholic Church has held in great veneration the sacred order of the diaconate, as the Apostle of the Gentiles himself bears witness. He expressly sends his greeting to the deacons, together with the bishops, and instructs Timothy[4] which virtues and qualities are to be sought in them in order that they may be regarded as worthy of their ministry.[5]

Furthermore, the Second Ecumenical Vatican Council, following this very ancient tradition, made honorable mention of the diaconate in the Constitution which begins with the words "*Lumen gentium*," where, after concerning itself with the bishops and the priests, it praised also the third rank of sacred orders, explaining its dignity and enumerating its functions.

Indeed while clearly recognizing on the one hand that "these functions very necessary to the life of the Church could in the present discipline of the Latin Church be carried out in many regions with difficulty," and while on the other hand wishing to make more suitable provision in a matter of such importance wisely decreed that the "diaconate in the future could be restored as a particular and permanent rank of the hierarchy."[6]

Although some functions of the deacons, especially in missionary countries, are in fact accustomed to be entrusted to lay men it is nevertheless "beneficial that those who perform a truly diaconal ministry be strengthened by the imposition of hands, a tradition going back to the Apostles, and be more closely joined to the altar so that they may more effectively carry out their ministry

4 Cf. Phil 1:1.

5 Cf. 1 Tm 3:8-13.

6 Cf. LG, no. 29; MS, no. 57 (1965), 36; EV I, 360.

through the sacramental grace of the diaconate."[7] Certainly in this way the special nature of this order will be shown most clearly. It is not to be considered as a mere step towards the priesthood, but it is so adorned with its own indelible character and its own special grace so that those who are called to it "can permanently serve the mysteries of Christ and the Church."[8]

Although the restoration of the permanent diaconate is not necessarily to be effected in the whole Latin Church since "it pertains to the competent territorial episcopal conferences, with the approval of the Supreme Pontiff, to decide whether and where it is timely that deacons of this kind be ordained for the care of souls,"[9] we therefore consider it not only proper but also necessary that specific and precise norms be given to adapt present discipline to the new precepts of the Ecumenical Council and to determine the proper conditions under which not only the ministry of the diaconate will be more advantageously regulated, but the training also of the candidates will be better suited to their different kinds of life, their common obligations and their sacred dignity.

Therefore, in the first place, all that is decreed in the *Code of Canon Law* about the rights and obligations of deacons, whether these rights and obligations be common to all clerics, or proper to deacons—all these, unless some other disposition has been made—we confirm and declare to be in force also for those who will remain permanently in the diaconate. In regard to these we moreover decree the following.

I

1. It is the task of the legitimate assemblies of bishops of episcopal conferences to discuss, with the consent of the Supreme Pontiff, whether and where—in view of the good of the faithful—the diaconate is to be instituted as a proper and permanent rank of the hierarchy.

2. When asking the Apostolic See for approval, the reasons must be explained which favor the introduction of this new practice in a region as well as the circumstances which give well-founded hope of success. Likewise, the manner will have to be indicated in which the new discipline will be implemented, that is to

---

7 AG, no. 16;/1/15'58 (1966), 967; EV I, 1140.

8 Cf. LG, no. 41: AAS 57 (1965), 46; EV I, 393.

9 LG, no. 29: AAS 57 (1965), 36; EV I, 360.

say, whether it is a matter of conferring the diaconate on "suitable young men for whom the law of celibacy must remain intact, or on men of more mature age, even upon those living in the married state," or on both kinds of candidates.

3. Once the approval of the Holy See has been obtained, it is within the powers of each Ordinary, within the sphere of his own jurisdiction, to approve and ordain the candidates, unless special cases are concerned which exceed his faculties.

Let the Ordinaries, in drawing up the report on the state of their diocese, also mention this restored discipline.

II

4. By the law of the Church, confirmed by the Ecumenical Council itself, young men called to the diaconate are obliged to observe the law of celibacy.

5. The permanent diaconate may not be conferred before the completion of the twenty-fifth year. Nevertheless, an older age can be required by the episcopal conferences.

6. Let young men to be trained for the diaconal office be received in a special institute where they will be put to the test and will be educated to live a truly evangelical life and prepared to fulfill usefully their own specific functions.

7. For the foundation of this institute, let the bishops of the same country, or, if advantageous, of several countries according to the diversity of circumstances, join their efforts. Let them choose, for its guidance, particularly suitable superiors and let them establish most accurate norms regarding discipline and the ordering of studies, observing the following prescriptions.

8. Let only those young men be admitted to training for the diaconate who have shown a natural inclination of the spirit to service of the sacred hierarchy and of the Christian community and who have acquired a sufficiently good store of knowledge in keeping the custom of their people and country.

9. Specific training for the diaconate should be spread over a period of at least three years. The series of subjects, however, should be arranged in such a way that the candidates are orderly and gradually led to carrying out the various

functions of the diaconate skillfully and beneficially. Moreover, the whole plan of studies can be so arranged that in the last year special training be given for the various functions which deacons especially will carry out.

10. To this moreover should be added practice and training in teaching the elements of the Christian religion to children and other faithful, in familiarizing the people with sacred chant and in directing it, in reading the sacred books of Scripture at gatherings of the faithful, in addressing and exhorting the people, in administering the sacraments which pertain to them, in visiting the sick, and in general in fulfilling the ministries which can be entrusted to them.

III

11. Older men, whether single or married, can be called to the diaconate. The latter, however, are not to be admitted unless there is certainty not only about the wife's consent, but also about her blameless Christian life and those qualities which will neither impede nor bring dishonor on the husband's ministry.

12. The older age in this case is reached at the completion of the thirty-fifth year. Nevertheless, the age requirement is to be understood in this sense, namely, that no one can be called to the diaconate unless he has gained the high regard of the clergy and the faithful by a long example of truly Christian life, by his unexceptionable conduct, and by his ready disposition to be of service.

13. In the case of married men care must be taken that only those are promoted to the diaconate who while living many years in matrimony have shown that they are ruling well their own household and who have a wife and children leading a truly Christian life and noted for their good reputation.[10]

14. It is to be desired that such deacons be possessed of no small learning about which we have spoken in numbers 8, 9, 10 above, or that they at least be endowed with that knowledge which in the judgment of the episcopal conference is necessary for them to carry out their specific functions. Consequently they are to be admitted for a time in a special school where they are to learn all that is necessary for worthily fulfilling the diaconal ministry.

10 Cf. 1 Tm 3:10-12.

15. Should this be impossible, let the candidate be entrusted for his education to an outstanding priest who will direct him, and instruct him and be able to testify to his prudence and maturity. Care must always and emphatically be taken that only suitable and skilled men may be admitted to the sacred order.

16. Once they have received the order of deacon, even those who have been promoted at a more mature age, can not contract marriage by virtue of the traditional discipline of the Church.

17. Let care be taken that the deacons do not exercise an art or a profession which in the judgment of the local Ordinary is unfitting or impedes the fruitful exercise of the sacred office.

IV

18. Any deacon who is not a professed member of a religious family must be duly enrolled in a diocese.

19. The norms in force with regard to caring for the fitting sustenance of priests and guaranteeing their social security are to be observed also in favor of the permanent deacons, taking into consideration also the family of married deacons and keeping article 21 of this letter in mind.

20. It is the function of the episcopal conference to issue definite norms on the proper sustenance of the deacon and his family if he is married in keeping with the various circumstances of place and time.

V

21. According to the above-mentioned *Constitution* of the Second Vatican Council it pertains to the deacon,[11*] to the extent that he has been authorized by the local Ordinary, to attend such functions:

1. To assist the bishop and the priest during liturgical actions in all things which the rituals of the different orders assign to him;
2. To administer baptism solemnly and to supply the ceremonies which may have been omitted when conferring it on children or adults;
3. To reserve the Eucharist and to distribute it to himself and to others, to bring it as a Viaticum to the dying and to impart to the people benediction with the Blessed Sacrament with the sacred ciborium;
4. In the absence of a priest, to assist at and to bless marriages in the name of the Church by delegation from the bishop or pastor,[12**] observing the rest of the requirements which are in the *Code of Canon Law*,[13] with Canon 1098 remaining firm and where what is said in regard to the priest is also to be understood in regard to the deacon;
5. To administer sacramentals and to officiate at funeral and burial services;
6. To read the sacred books of Scripture to the faithful and to instruct and exhort the people;
7. To preside at the worship and prayers of the people when a priest is not present;
8. To direct the liturgy of the word, particularly in the absence of a priest;
9. To carry out, in the name of the hierarchy, the duties of charity and of administration as well as works of social assistance;

---

11 * The same duties outlined here are valid for the deacon who does not stay in this degree but wants to ascend to priesthood (cf. *Responsum* to the Pontifical Commission for the Interpretation of the Decrees of the Second Vatican Council, March 26, 1968: AAS 60, 1968, 363).

It should be held in account that the deacon can impart only those blessings and can administer only those sacramentals that are granted to him expressly by the law (cf. *Responsum ad propositum dubium de Diaconi facultatibus quoad sacramentalia et benedictiones* of the Pontifical Commission for the Interpretation of the Decrees of the Second Vatican Council, November 13, 1974: AAS 66, 1974, 667).

12 ** The phrase *in the absence of a priest* is not required "for the validity of a delegation given to the deacon to preside at a wedding" (cf. *Responsum ad propositum dubium de Diaconi facultatibus quoad sacramentalia et benedictiones* of the Pontifical Commission for the Interpretation of the Decrees of the Second Vatican Council, April 4, 1969, 348).

13 Cf. CIC cc. 1095 §2, and 1096.

10. To guide legitimately, in the name of the parish priest and of the bishop, remote Christian communities;
11. To promote and sustain the apostolic activities of laymen.

23. All these functions must be carried out in perfect communion with the bishop and with his presbytery, that is to say, under the authority of the bishop and of the priest who are in charge of the care of souls in that place.

24. Deacons, as much as possible, should have their part in pastoral councils.

VI

25. Let the deacons, as those who serve the mysteries of Christ and of the Church, abstain from all vice and endeavor to be always pleasing to God, "ready for every good work"[14] for the salvation of men. By reason, therefore, of the order received they must surpass by far all the others in the practice of liturgical life, in the love for prayer, in the divine service, in obedience, in charity, in chastity.

26. It will be the task of the episcopal conference to establish more efficacious norms to nourish the spiritual life of the deacons, both celibate and married. Let the local Ordinaries, however, see to it that all the deacons:

1. Devote themselves assiduously to reading and meditating on the word of God;
2. Frequently, and if possible every day, participate actively in the sacrifice of the Mass, receive the sacrament of the Most Holy Eucharist and devoutly visit the Sacrament;
3. Purify their souls frequently with the sacrament of Penance and, for the purpose of receiving it worthily, examine their conscience each day;
4. Venerate and love the Virgin Mary, the Mother of God with fervent devotion.

14 Cf. 2 Tm 2:21.

27. It is a supremely fitting thing that permanent deacons recite every day at least part of the Divine Office, to be determined by the episcopal conference.

28. Diocesan deacons must, at least every third year, attend spiritual exercises in a religious house or pious institution designated by the Ordinary.

29. Deacons are not to neglect studies, particularly the sacred ones; let them read assiduously the sacred books of the Scripture; let them devote themselves to ecclesiastical studies in such a way that they can correctly explain Catholic teaching to the rest and become daily more capable of instructing and strengthening the minds of the faithful.

For this purpose, let the deacons be called to meetings to be held at specified times at which problems regarding their life and the sacred ministry are treated.

30. Because of the special character of the ministry entrusted to them they are bound to show reverence and obedience to the bishop; the bishops, however, should in the Lord highly esteem these ministers of the people of God and love them with the love of a father. If for a just cause a deacon lives for a time outside his own diocese he should willingly submit to the supervision and authority of the local Ordinary in those matters which pertain to the duties and functions of the diaconal state.[15]

31. In the matter of wearing apparel the local custom will have to be observed according to the norms set down by the episcopal conference.

VII

32. The institution of the permanent diaconate among the Religious is a right reserved to the Holy See, which is exclusively competent to examine and approve the recommendations of the general chapters in the matter.

33. Let the Religious deacons exercise the diaconal ministry under the authority of the bishop and of their own superiors, according to the norms in force for Religious priests; they are also bound by the laws to which the members of the same Religious family are obliged.

---

15 Pius XII, *Motu proprio Cleri Sanctitati*, c. 87: MS 49 (1957), 462.

34. A Religious deacon who lives either permanently or for a specified time in a region which lacks a permanent diaconate may not exercise diaconal functions except with the consent of the local Ordinary.

35. The provisions in numbers 32-34 regarding the Religious must be regarded as applying likewise to members of other institutes who profess the evangelical counsels.

VIII

36. Finally as regards the rite to be followed in conferring the sacred order of the diaconate and those orders which precede the diaconate, let the present discipline be observed until it is revised by the Holy See.

Finally, after issuing these norms the desire springs spontaneously from our heart that deacons in performing their arduous functions in the modern world follow the examples which we propose for their imitation; the example of St. Stephen the protomartyr, who as St. Irenaeus says "was the first chosen for diaconal service by the Apostles,"[16] and of St. Lawrence of Rome "who was illustrious not only in the administration of the sacraments but also in the stewardship of the possessions of the Church."[17]

We order, then, that what has been established by us in this letter, given "*motu proprio*," be firm and valid, all things to the contrary notwithstanding.

Given at Rome, at St. Peter's on the feast of St. Ephrem the Syrian, June 18, 1967, in the fourth year of our pontificate.

Ad Pascendum (*Apostolic Letter Establishing Some Norms Concerning the Sacred Order of Deacons*)

August 15, 1972

The profile of the diaconal ministry is even better outlined in the document Ad Pascendum, *in which Paul VI reemphasizes that the deacon is "encourager of*

16 *Adv. Haereses IV*, 15, 1: *Patrologia Graeco-Latina* (PG) 7, 1013.
17 St. Leo Magnus, *Serm. 85:* PL 54, 436.

service—or rather of the Church's diakonia*—in local communities, sign and instrument of Christ the Lord himself.*"

To look after the People of God and work for its growth, Christ the Lord instituted various ministries in the Church directed toward the good of his whole Body. In the context of such ministries, since the first apostolic age, the diaconate has been of particular visibility and has been held in great honor by the Church. This is attested to explicitly by the apostle Paul in his letter to the Philippians, where he addresses his greeting not only to the bishops but also to the deacons; this is also seen in a letter to Timothy, where he reveals the qualities and virtues indispensable for deacons so that they can live up to the level of the ministry entrusted to them.

Later, while extolling the dignity of deacons, ancient Church writers do not neglect to exalt the spiritual gifts and virtues needed to accomplish this ministry, namely fidelity to Christ, moral integrity, and submission to the bishop. St. Ignatius of Antioch clearly affirms that the office of deacon is none other than "the ministry of Jesus Christ, who before all ages was with the Father and has appeared at the end times" and observes: "It is necessary that even deacons, who are ministers of Jesus Christ's mysteries, in every way succeed at satisfying everyone. They are not, in fact, deacons distributing food and drink, but ministers of God's Church." St. Polycarp of Smyrna exhorts deacons to be "in everything temperate, merciful, zealous, inspired by the Lord's truth in their conduct." The author of the work titled *Didascalia Apostolorum*, remembering Christ's words: "Anyone who wishes to be the greatest among you, let him be your servant," addresses deacons with this fraternal exhortation: "It is then necessary that you deacons do the same, meaning that, should you find yourself needing to give your very life for your brother while exercising your ministry, you have to give it. . . . So if the Lord of heaven and earth has made himself our servant and has patiently suffered every sort of pain for us, how much more should we do this for our brothers, since we are imitators of him and have received Christ's same mission?"

And again, the authors of the first centuries of the Church, while they emphasize the importance of the ministry of the diaconate, often explain the multiple, serious functions entrusted to them and openly declare the great prestige they have gained in the Christian communities as well as the great contribution they have made to the apostolate. The deacon is defined as "the eye, the mouth, the heart, and the soul of the bishop." The deacon is at the bishop's disposal to serve the whole People of God and take care of the sick and the poor; therefore, he is precisely and rightly called "the friend of orphans, of devout persons, and of widows, fervent in spirit and lover of good." Furthermore, to him has been entrusted the duty of carrying the Holy Eucharist to the homebound sick, of administering Baptism, and of seeing to the preaching of God's Word according to the bishop's bidding.

For these reasons, the diaconate in the Church experienced a marvelous flourishing and offered a magnificent testimony of love for Christ and for the brethren in carrying out works of charity, in celebrating the sacred rites, and in fulfilling pastoral duties. Those who would become priests would prove themselves precisely by the exercise of their diaconal duty, demonstrating the merit of their work, and, moreover, acquiring the preparation necessary for attaining priestly dignity and the pastoral office.

Still, with the passing of time, the discipline concerning this sacred order underwent changes. Certainly, the prohibition against conferring ordination by skipping over intermediate degrees became more rigid, but the number of those who preferred to remain deacons for life rather than ascend to a higher degree lessened little by little. It was thus that the permanent diaconate almost disappeared completely in the Latin Church. It is worthwhile to remember what was established by the Council of Trent, proposing to restore the sacred orders to their proper nature as the primal functions of the Church; much later, the intention of restoring this important sacred order as a truly permanent degree did in fact mature. Even our predecessor of venerable memory, Pius XII, had the occasion to make brief mention of the matter. Finally, the Second Vatican Council met the wishes and prayers to see the permanent diaconate restored—on the condition that it be for the good of souls—as an intermediate degree between the higher degrees of the Church hierarchy and the rest of God's people, so that it would be, in a certain way, the interpreter of the Christian community's needs and desires, an encourager of service, or rather of the *diakonia* of the Church in local Christian communities, a sign or sacrament of Christ the Lord himself, "who came not to be served, but to serve."

Therefore, during the Council's third session, in October 1964, the Fathers confirmed the principle of renewing the diaconate and, in the following month of November, the *Dogmatic Constitution on the Church* (*Lumen Gentium*) was promulgated; in number 29, it presents the main features proper to this state:

"At a lower level of the hierarchy are deacons, upon whom hands are imposed 'not unto the priesthood, but unto a ministry of service.' For strengthened by sacramental grace, in communion with the bishop and his group of priests, they serve the People of God in the ministry of the liturgy, of the word, and of charity." By way of stability in the diaconal degree, the same constitution declares the following: "These duties, so very necessary for the life of the Church, can in many areas be fulfilled only with difficulty according to the prevailing discipline of the Latin Church. For this reason, the diaconate can in the future be restored as a proper and permanent rank of the hierarchy."

Now, on one hand, this restoration of the permanent diaconate demanded a detailed elaboration of the Council's directives, and, on the other, a mature examination of the deacon's juridical condition, whether celibate or married. At the same time, it was necessary that the elements concerning the diaconate of those who are becoming priests be adapted to present conditions so that the exercise of their diaconate would truly provide that life experience and test of maturity and aptitude for priestly ministry, just as ancient discipline has demanded of candidates to the priesthood.

This is why on June 18, 1967, with our *motu proprio*, we published the Apostolic Letter *Sacrum Diaconatus Ordinem*, that determined appropriate canonical norms for the permanent diaconate. On June 17 of the following year, with the Apostolic Constitution *Pontificalis Romani Recognitio*, we established the new rite for conferring the sacred orders of diaconate, presbyterate, and episcopate, defining the matter and form of ordination itself.

And while now in our present day, in order to further develop this matter, we are promulgating the Apostolic Letter *Ministeria Quaedam*, we deem it appropriate to enact precise norms concerning the diaconate; we equally want candidates to the diaconate to know what ministries they should exercise before sacred ordination, and in what time and way they should assume the obligations of celibacy and liturgical prayers.

It is particularly appropriate that the ministries of lector and acolyte be conferred on those who desire to consecrate themselves in a special way to God and the Church as candidates to the order of diaconate or presbyterate. The Church, in fact, precisely because it "never ceases to be nourished by the bread of life from the table, whether of the Word of God or of the Body of Christ, and to offer it to the faithful," highly recommends that candidates to sacred orders, both with study and with the gradual exercise of the ministry of the Word and altar, should, through intimate contact, come to know and meditate on this double aspect of priestly duty. This is how the authenticity of their ministry will shine forth with the greatest efficacy. The candidates will then approach sacred orders, fully aware of their vocation, "fervent in spirit, ready to serve the Lord, persevering in prayer, concerned with the needs of the saints."

Therefore, having pondered every aspect of the issue and having asked for the opinion of experts, after having consulted the episcopal conferences and taken into account the judgments they have expressed, having listened to the opinion of our venerated brethren that are members of authorized, sacred congregations, by the power of our apostolic authority, we establish the following norms, repealing—if and insofar as it is necessary—the prescriptions of the *Codex Iuris Canonici* (*Code of Canon Law* [CIC]) in force until now, and we promulgate them with this letter:

I. a. A rite of admission of candidates for the diaconate and priesthood shall be introduced. In order for such admission to be valid, the aspirant's free request must be made, written, and signed, as well as written acceptance by the competent ecclesiastical superior, by virtue of which the Church's choice is made. This is not required of the professed members of clerical religious communities who prepare themselves for the priesthood.

b. The competent superior for this acceptance is the ordinary (the bishop and, in fully approved clerical institutes, the major superior). Capable of being accepted are those who show the signs of a true vocation and, being of sound behavior and immune from psychological and physical defects, intend to dedicate their own life to the service of the Church for the glory of God and for the good of souls. It is necessary that those who aspire to the transitional diaconate be at least twenty years of age and have begun their theological studies.

c. By force of his acceptance, the candidate is expected to take special care of his vocation and develop it, and [he] gains the right to have the necessary spiritual supports in order to be able to cultivate his vocation and align himself with God's will without letting any conditions interfere.

II. The candidate to the diaconate, whether permanent or transitional, and candidates to the priesthood should receive, if they have not already done so, the ministries of lector and acolyte, and have exercised them for a convenient period of time in order to better prepare themselves for the future services of the Word and altar. For the candidates themselves, dispensation from receiving the ministries is reserved to the Holy See.

III. The liturgical rites through which admission of the candidates to the diaconate or priesthood takes place, and that confer the aforementioned ministries, should be completed by the aspirant's ordinary (the bishop or, in fully approved clerical institutes, the major superior).

IV. As they are established by the Holy See or by the episcopal conferences, the intervals between conferral of the ministries of lector and acolyte, as well as acolyte and deacon, should be respected.

V. Before ordination, candidates to the diaconate must hand their ordinary (the bishop or, in fully approved clerical institutes, the major superior) a handwritten, signed declaration in which they attest to their free and spontaneous desire to receive Holy Orders.

VI. Consecration to celibacy, to be observed for the Kingdom of Heaven, and the obligation to it for candidates to the priesthood and for unmarried candidates to the diaconate, are really connected with the diaconate. Public commitment to sacred celibacy before God and the Church should be celebrated with a special rite that should precede diaconal ordination, even by religious. Celibacy, when committed to in this way, constitutes a diriment impediment against marriage. Even married deacons, if they lose their wives, according to the Church's traditional discipline, are unable to contract a new marriage.

VII. a. Deacons called to priesthood should not be ordained unless they have first completed the course of studies as it is defined by the prescriptions of the Holy See.

b. Regarding the course of theological studies that should precede the ordination of permanent deacons, it is the competency of the episcopal conferences to issue, based on local circumstances, the proper norms and to submit them for approval to the sacred congregation for Catholic education.

VIII. In keeping with numbers 29-30 of "Principles and Norms for the Liturgy of the Hours":

a. Deacons called to priesthood, by virtue of their very ordination, are obliged to celebrate the Liturgy of the Hours.
b. It is highly appropriate that permanent deacons every day recite at least part of the Liturgy of the Hours, as is defined by the episcopal conference.

IX. Entrance into the clerical state and incardination into a diocese occur with the diaconal ordination itself.

X. The admission rite of candidates to the diaconate or the presbyterate, as well as that of consecration to sacred celibacy, will be published shortly thereafter by the competent dicastery of the Roman curia.

Transitional norm.—Candidates to the Sacrament of Holy Orders who have already received first tonsure before the promulgation of this letter, conserve all duties, rights, and privileges proper to clerics; those who have been promoted to the subdiaconate are obligated to celibacy and to the Liturgy of the Hours; they must, however, again celebrate their public commitment to celibacy before God and the Church according to the new, special rite that precedes diaconal ordination. We hereby command that all that has been decreed by us with this letter in the form of *motu proprio* be upheld, any disposition to the contrary notwithstanding. We also decree that these norms come into effect on January 1, 1973.[1]

Rome, St. Peter's, August 15, 1972, Solemnity of the Assumption of the Blessed Virgin Mary, in the tenth year of our pontificate.

Post-Synodal Apostolic Exhortation *Evangelii Nuntiandi* (*On Evangelization in the Modern World*)

December 8, 1975

To the Episcopate, to the Clergy, and to all the Faithful of the entire world.

68. In union with the Successor of Peter, the bishops, who are successors of the apostles, receive through the power of their episcopal ordination the authority to teach the revealed truth in the Church. They are teachers of the faith.

Associated with the bishops in the ministry of evangelization and responsible by a special title are those who through priestly ordination "act in the

1 [*Ad Pascendum* is a translation of the Italian text.]

person of Christ." They are educators of the People of God in the faith and preachers, while at the same time being ministers of the Eucharist and of the other sacraments.

We pastors are therefore invited to take note of this duty, more than any other members of the Church. What identifies our priestly service, gives a profound unity to the thousand and one tasks which claim our attention day by day and throughout our lives, and confers a distinct character on our activities, is this aim, ever present in all our action: to proclaim the Gospel of God.

A mark of our identity which no doubts ought to encroach upon and no objection eclipse is this: as pastors, we have been chosen by the mercy of the Supreme Pastor, in spite of our inadequacy, to proclaim with authority the Word of God, to assemble the scattered People of God, to feed this People with the signs of the action of Christ which are the sacraments, to set this People on the road to salvation, to maintain it in that unity of which we are, at different levels, active and living instruments, and unceasingly to keep this community gathered around Christ faithful to its deepest vocation. And when we do all these things, within our human limits and by the grace of God, it is a work of evangelization that we are carrying out. This includes ourself as Pastor of the universal Church, our brother bishops at the head of the individual Churches, priests and deacons united with their bishops and whose assistants they are, by a communion which has its source in the sacrament of Orders and in the charity of the Church.

The Breath of the Holy Spirit

75. Evangelization will never be possible without the action of the Holy Spirit. The Spirit descends on Jesus of Nazareth at the moment of His baptism when the voice of the Father—"This is my beloved Son with whom I am well pleased"—manifests in an external way the election of Jesus and His mission. Jesus is "led by the Spirit" to experience in the desert the decisive combat and the supreme test before beginning this mission. It is "in the power of the Spirit" that He returns to Galilee and begins His preaching at Nazareth, applying to Himself the passage of Isaiah: "The Spirit of the Lord is upon me." And He proclaims: "Today this Scripture has been fulfilled." To the disciples whom He was about to send forth He says, breathing on them, "Receive the Holy Spirit."

In fact, it is only after the coming of the Holy Spirit on the day of Pentecost that the apostles depart to all the ends of the earth in order to begin the great work of the Church's evangelization. Peter explains this event as the fulfillment of the prophecy of Joel: "I will pour out my spirit." Peter is filled with the Holy Spirit so that he can speak to the people about Jesus, the Son of God. Paul too is filled with the Holy Spirit before dedicating himself to his apostolic ministry, as is Stephen when he is chosen for the ministry of service and later on for the witness of blood. The Spirit, who causes Peter, Paul and the Twelve to speak, and who inspires the words that they are to utter, also comes down "on those who heard the word."

Authentic Witnesses

76. Let us now consider the very persons of the evangelizers.

It is often said nowadays that the present century thirsts for authenticity. Especially in regard to young people, it is said that they have a horror of the artificial or false and that they are searching above all for truth and honesty.

These "signs of the times" should find us vigilant. Either tacitly or aloud—but always forcefully—we are being asked: *Do you really believe what you are proclaiming? Do you live what you believe? Do you really preach what you live?* The witness of life has become more than ever an essential condition for real effectiveness in preaching. Precisely because of this, we are, to a certain extent, responsible for the progress of the Gospel that we proclaim.

"What is the state of the Church ten years after the Council?" we asked at the beginning of this meditation. Is she firmly established in the midst of the world and yet free and independent enough to call for the world's attention? Does she testify to solidarity with people and at the same time to the divine Absolute? Is she more ardent in contemplation and adoration and more zealous in missionary, charitable and liberating action? Is she ever more committed to the effort to search for the restoration of the complete unity of Christians, a unity that makes more effective the common witness "so that the world may believe?" We are all responsible for the answers that could be given to these questions.

We therefore address our exhortation to our brethren in the Episcopate, placed by the Holy Spirit to govern the Church. We exhort the priests and deacons, the bishops' collaborators in assembling the People of God and in animating spiritually the local communities.

John Paul II

Even though John Paul II never left an explicit document on the diaconate, we can certainly refer widely to some of the pope's speeches given during encounters with deacons. Of particular significance are those addressed to deacons of Italy and of the United States.[2]

Among the many aspects highlighted by the pope, of particular importance is the affirmation that the deacon's service is the sacramentalized *service of the Church. The pope also speaks of a "special witness" that deacons are called to give in society precisely for the fact that their* secular occupation *grants them access to the temporal sphere in a special way that is normally not granted to other members of the clergy. In the same way, the contribution that the married deacon offers for the transformation of family life by the double sacramentality that marks his ministry is also remarkable. Of particular significance is the fact that he emphasizes how the involvement of the deacon's wife in her husband's public ministry in the Church is brought about through* the enrichment and deepening of the sacrificial love between husband and wife.

The pope dealt with the theme of the diaconate in a systematic way during some Wednesday catecheses.[3] *On the occasion of the Plenary Assembly of the Congregation for the Clergy, which examined an* Instrumentum laboris *with the intention of preparing a document concerning the life and ministry of permanent deacons similar to that for priests, John Paul II*[4] *gave a speech that constitutes an important contribution in the configuration of diaconal ministry.*

---

2 Speech given by John Paul II to the bishop delegates for the permanent diaconate and to deacons for the meeting promoted by the Episcopal Commission for the Clergy of the CEI, Rome, March 3, 1995; Speech given to deacons of the United States on September 19, 1987.

3 The pope gave these catecheses on October 6, 13, and 20 of 1993 (*L'Osservatore Romano*, October 7, 14, and 21, 1993, 4.)

4 Cf. John Paul II, speech given November 30, 1995, for the occasion of the Plenary Assembly for the Clergy, in *L'Osservatore Romano*, CXXXV (1995) 277, 5.

Homily at the Eucharistic Celebration with a Group of New Deacons

April 21, 1979

Dearly beloved Deacons,

In the long history of the Church in Rome, it is not uncommon to see deacons associated with the Pope in his ministry, to see deacons at his side. And this morning it is a special joy for me to be surrounded by deacons, as our relationship—our ecclesial communion—reaches its highest expression in the holy Sacrifice of the Mass.

Our joy is enhanced—yours and mine—to have some of your parents and loved ones here. All of us have come to celebrate the Paschal Mystery and to experience the love of Jesus. His is a sacrificial love—a love that moved him to lay down his life for his people and to take it up again. And his sacrificial love has been manifested with great generosity in your parents' lives, and today it is very fitting that they should have an exceptional moment of serenity, satisfaction and wholesome pride.

As we commemorate the Resurrection of the Lord Jesus, we reflect on his various appearances, as recorded in the reading from the Acts of the Apostles: his appearance to Mary Magdalen, to the two disciples, to the Eleven Apostles. We renew our faith—our holy Catholic faith—and we rejoice and exult because the Lord is truly risen, alleluia! Today more than ever before we are conscious of what it means to be an Easter people and to have the alleluia as our song.

The Easter event—the bodily Resurrection of Christ—pervades the life of the whole Church. It gives to Christians everywhere strength at every turn in life. It makes us sensitive to humanity with all its limitations, sufferings and needs. The Resurrection has immense power to liberate, to uplift, to bring about justice, to effect holiness, to cause joy.

But for you, Deacons, there is a particular message this morning. By your sacred ordination you have been associated in a special way with the Gospel of the Risen Christ. You have been commissioned to render a special type of service, *diaconia*, in the name of the Risen Lord. During the ordination ceremony the Bishop told each of you: "Receive the Gospel of Christ, whose herald you now are. Believe what you read, teach what you believe, and practice what you teach." And so you are called to take the words of the Acts of the Apostles to heart. In the rank of deacons you have come to be associated with Peter and John and all the apostles. You support the apostolic ministry and share in its proclamation. Like the Apostles you too must feel impelled to proclaim by word and deed the Resurrection of the Lord Jesus. You too must experience the need to do good, to render service in the name of the crucified and Risen Jesus—to bring God's word into the lives of his holy people.

In today's first reading we hear the Apostles saying: "We cannot but speak of what we have seen and heard." And you are called, in the obedience of faith, to proclaim on the basis of their testimony—on the basis of what has been handed down in the Church under the guidance of the Holy Spirit—the great mystery of the Risen Lord, who in his very act of Resurrection communicates eternal life to all his brethren because he communicates his victory over sin and death. Remember that the Apostles by their proclamation of the Resurrection were a challenge and reproof to many. And they were warned never to speak again in the name of the Risen Jesus. But their response was immediate and clear: "You must judge whether in God's eyes it is right to listen to you and not to God."

And in this obedience to God they found the supreme measure of paschal joy.

It is the same for you, the new deacons of this Easter season. As the associates of the Bishops and priests of the Church, your discipleship will be marked by these two characteristics: obedience and joy. Each, in his own way, will show the authenticity of your lives. Your ability to communicate the Gospel will depend on your adherence to the faith of the Apostles. The effectiveness of your *diaconia* will be measured by fidelity of your obedience to the mandate of the Church. It is the Risen Christ who has called you, and it is his Church that sends you forth to proclaim the message transmitted by the Apostles. And it is the Church that authenticates your ministry. Be confident that the very power of the Gospel you proclaim will fill you with the most sublime joy: sacrificial joy, yes, but the transforming joy of being intimately associated with the Risen Jesus in his triumphant mission of salvation. All the disciples of Jesus and you Deacons by a special title, are called to share the immense Easter joy experienced by Blessed Mother. At the Resurrection of her Son, we see Mary as *Mater plena sanctae laetitiae,* becoming for all of us *Causa nostrae laetitiae.*

Obedience and joy are then true expressions of your discipleship. But they are also conditions for your effective ministry, and at the same time gifts of God's grace—effects of the very mystery of the Resurrection that you proclaim.

Dear Deacons, I speak to you as sons and brothers and friends. This is a day of special joy. But let it also be a day of special resolve. In the presence of the Pope, under the gaze of the Apostles Peter and Paul, in the company of Stephen, before the witness of your parents, and in the communion of the universal Church, renew again your ecclesial consecration to Jesus Christ, whom you serve and whose life-giving message you are called to transmit in all its purity and integrity, with all its exigencies and in all its power. And know that it is with immense love that I repeat to you and to your brother deacons throughout the Church the words of this morning's Gospel, the words of our Lord Jesus Christ: "Go out to the whole world, proclaim the Good News to all creation."

This is the meaning of your ministry. This will be your greatest service to humanity. This is your response to God's love. Amen.

Apostolic Exhortation *Catechesi Tradendae* (*On Catechesis in Our Time*)

October 16, 1979

Catechesis in the Apostolic Age

11. The apostles were not slow to share with others the ministry of apostleship. They transmitted to their successors the task of teaching. They entrusted it also to the deacons from the moment of their institution: Stephen, "full of grace and power," taught unceasingly, moved by the wisdom of the Spirit. The apostles associated "many others" with themselves in the task of teaching, and even simple Christians scattered by persecution "went about preaching the word." St. Paul was in a pre-eminent way the herald of this preaching, from Antioch to Rome, where the last picture of him that we have in Acts is that of a person "teaching about the Lord Jesus Christ quite openly." His numerous letters continue and give greater depth to his teaching. The letters of Peter, John, James and Jude are also, in every case, evidence of catechesis in the apostolic age.

The Priests

64. For your part, priests, here you have a field in which you are the immediate assistants of your Bishops. The Council has called you "instructors in the

faith"; there is no better way for you to be such instructors than by devoting your best efforts to the growth of your communities in the faith. Whether you are in charge of a parish, or are chaplains to primary or secondary schools or universities, or have responsibility for pastoral activity at any level, or are leaders of large or small communities, especially youth groups, the Church expects you to neglect nothing with a view to a well-organized and well-oriented catechetical effort. The deacons and other ministers that you may have the good fortune to have with you are your natural assistants in this. All believers have a right to catechesis; all pastors have the duty to provide it. I shall always ask civil leaders to respect the freedom of catechetical teaching; but with all my strength I beg you, ministers of Jesus Christ: Do not, for lack of zeal or because of some unfortunate preconceived idea, leave the faithful without catechesis. Let it not be said that "the children beg for food, but no one gives to them."

Apostolic Exhortation *Familiaris Consortio* (*On the Role of the Christian Family in the Modern World*)

November 22, 1981

Agents in the Pastoral Care of the Family

Bishops and Priests

73. The Bishops avail themselves especially of the priests, whose task—as the Synod expressly emphasized—constitutes an essential part of the Church's ministry regarding marriage and the family. The same is true of deacons to whose care this sector of pastoral work may be entrusted.

Priests and deacons, when they have received timely and serious preparation for this apostolate, must unceasingly act toward families as fathers, brothers, pastors and teachers, assisting them with the means of grace and enlightening them with the light of truth. Their teaching and advice must therefore always be in full harmony with the authentic Magisterium of the Church, in such a way as to help the People of God to gain a correct sense of the faith, to be subsequently applied to practical life. Such fidelity to the Magisterium will also enable priests to make every effort to be united in their judgments, in order to avoid troubling the consciences of the faithful.

Speech to Italian Deacons

March 16, 1985

Dear brothers!

1. I am sincerely happy to be able to meet with you today while you have been gathered these seven days for the National Convention of Episcopal Delegates for the Permanent Diaconate and of Permanent Deacons, promoted by the Episcopal Commission for the Clergy of the Italian Episcopal Conference. These are days of study that have as their purpose reflection on the two documents, published by the same Episcopal Conference in 1972, on the very matter of "The Restoration of the Permanent Diaconate in Italy" and "The Diaconal Ministry."

One of the fruits of the Second Ecumenical Vatican Council was that of wishing to restore the diaconate as its own, permanent degree within the hierarchy (cf. LG, no. 29; AG, no. 16). The *Dogmatic Constitution on the Church* clearly and profoundly synthesized the theological aspects of the order of diaconate and the specific functions of candidates. Deacons, sustained by sacramental grace, serve the People of God—in communion with the bishop and his presbyterate—in the *ministry* of the *liturgy*, of *preaching*, and of *charity*. Regarding the ministry of the liturgy, several duties can be entrusted to the deacon by the competent authority: solemnly administering Baptism; keeping and distributing the Eucharist; bringing Viaticum to the dying; presiding over Matrimony and blessing it in the name of the Church; presiding at the worship and prayer of the faithful; administering sacramentals; directing funeral rites and burial. For the ministry of *preaching*, the deacon can read the Sacred Scriptures to the faithful, instruct, and exhort the people (cf. LG, no. 29).

The ministry of *charity*, in particular, has reference in the pages of the *Acts of the Apostles*, which describes the choice of the "seven"—among whom were Stephen and Phillip—to offer service (*diakonia*) to the tables (cf. Acts 6:1-6). Of special note are the recommendations given to deacons in the *Didascalia of the Apostles*: "As our Lord and Savior said in the Gospel: *Whoso among you desireth to be chief, let him be your servant: even as the Son of Man came not to be ministered unto, but to minister, and to give his life* [*as*] *a ransom for many* (Mt 20:26-28). So ought you the deacons also to do [sic], if it fall to you to lay down your life for your brethren in the ministry which is due to them" (*Didascalia Apostolorum*, XVI, 13).

2. In his degree, the deacon personifies Christ, servant of the Father, participating in the triple function of the Sacrament of Holy Orders: he is a teacher insofar as he proclaims and expounds on the Word of God; he is a sanctifier insofar as he administers the Sacrament of Baptism, the Eucharist, and sacramentals; he is a *guide* insofar as he is a promoter in communities or sectors of Church life.

In this sense, the deacon contributes to making the Church a reality of communion, of service, and of mission.

Often in the liturgy we hear the words with which St. Paul presented the ideal image of the deacon to the first generation of Christians (cf. 1 Tm 3:8-13); and I like to remember also those of the great Apostolic Fathers, St. Ignatius, Bishop of Antiochia and martyr: "All of you, follow the bishop, just as Jesus Christ follows the Father, and the presbyterate as the Apostles; as regards the deacons, venerate them as the Law of God" (*Ad Smyrnenses*, VIII, I); "listen to the bishop and God will listen to you; I am ready to give my life for those who are in submission to the bishop, to the presbyters, and to the deacons; with them, may I have a part of the possession of God!" (*Ad Polycarpum*, VI, 1).

3. Participation in Holy Orders, with the duties cited, demands that candidates to the permanent diaconate have a *serious preparation* in the field of the sacred sciences and a *profound commitment* to the interior life, nourished by consistent contact with Christ, especially through the Sacraments of the Eucharist and Reconciliation (cf. Paul VI, *Motu Proprio Sacrum Diaconatus Ordinem*: AAS 59 [1967], 697-704; Sacred Congregation for Catholic Education, *Circular Letter on the Ordination of Candidates to the Permanent Diaconate*, July 16, 1969).

In a special way, a continuous, lengthy study of the Word of God, of theology, of the Magisterium's teaching, and of Christian spirituality will be necessary according to the directives, indications, and programs of the competent Church authority.

I hope with all my heart that the National Convention will represent an important step for the further promotion of the permanent diaconate in Italy. To you here present, to all the episcopal delegates, and to the permanent deacons that already minister in the dioceses and to those who are preparing to receive the order of diaconate, I will remember you affectionately in prayer, and impart to you my apostolic blessing.[5]

Speech to the Deacons of the United States

September 19, 1987

Dear Brothers in the service of our Lord,

Dear Wives and Collaborators of these men ordained to the Permanent Diaconate,

1. I greet you in the love of our Lord Jesus Christ, in whom, as St. Paul tells us, God has chosen us, redeemed us and adopted us as his children (cf. Eph 1:3ff.). Together with St. Paul, and together with you today, *I praise our heavenly Father* for these wonderful gifts of grace.

It is a special joy for me to meet you because you represent *a great and visible sign of the working of the Holy Spirit* in the wake of the Second Vatican Council, which provided for the restoration of the permanent diaconate in the Church. The wisdom of that provision is evident in your presence in such numbers today and in the fruitfulness of your ministries. With the whole Church, *I give thanks to God for the call you have received and for your generous response*. For the majority of you who are married, this response has been made possible by the love and support and collaboration of your wives. It is a great encouragement to know that in the United States over the past two decades almost eight thousand permanent deacons have been ordained for the service of the Gospel.

It is above all *the call to service* that I wish to celebrate with you today. In speaking of deacons, the *Vatican Council* said that "strengthened by sacramental grace, in communion with the bishop and his presbyterate, they serve the People of God in the service of the liturgy, the word, and charity" (*Lumen Gentium*, no. 29). Reflecting further on this description, my predecessor Paul VI was in agreement with the Council that "the permanent diaconate should be restored . . . as a driving force for the Church's service (*diakonia*) toward the local Christian communities, and as a sign or sacrament of the Lord Christ himself, who 'came not to be served but to serve'" (Paul VI, *Ad Pascendum*, Intro.). These words recall *the ancient tradition of the Church* as expressed by the early Fathers such

5 [Translation of the Italian text.]

as Ignatius of Antioch, who says that deacons are "ministers of the mysteries of Jesus Christ . . . ministers of the Church of God" (St. Ignatius of Antioch, *Ad Trallianos*, II, 3). You, dear brothers, belong to the life of the Church that goes back to saintly deacons, like Lawrence, and before him to Stephen and his companions, whom the Acts of the Apostles consider "deeply spiritual and prudent" (Act 6:3).

This is at the very heart of the diaconate to which you have been called: *to be a servant of the mysteries of Christ and, at one and the same time, to be a servant of your brothers and sisters.* That these two dimensions are inseparably joined together in one reality shows the important nature of the ministry which is yours by ordination.

2. How are we to understand the mysteries of Christ of which you are ministers? A profound description is given to us by St. Paul in the reading we heard a few moments ago. *The central mystery* is this: God the Father's plan of glory to bring *all things in the heavens and on earth into one under the headship of Christ*, his beloved Son. It is for this that all the baptized are predestined, chosen, redeemed and sealed with the Holy Spirit. This plan of God is at the center of our lives and the life of the world.

At the same time, if service to this redemptive plan is the mission of all the baptized, what is the specific dimension of your service as deacons? The Second Vatican Council explains that *a sacramental grace conferred through the imposition of hands* enables you to carry out your service of the Word, the altar and charity with a special effectiveness (cf. *Ad Gentes*, no. 16). *The service of the deacon is the Church's service sacramentalized.* Yours is not just one ministry among others, but it is truly meant to be, as Paul VI described it, a "driving force" for the Church's *diakonia.* By your ordination you are configured to Christ in his servant role. You are also meant to be *living signs of the servanthood of his Church.*

3. If we keep in mind the deep spiritual nature of this *diakonia*, then we can better appreciate *the interrelation of the three areas of ministry* traditionally associated with the diaconate, that is, the ministry of the word, the ministry of the altar, and the ministry of charity. Depending on the circumstances, one or another of these may receive particular emphasis in an individual deacon's work, but these three ministries are *inseparably joined together as one in the service of God's redemptive plan*. This is so because the word of God inevitably leads us to

the Eucharistic worship of God at the altar; in turn, this worship leads us to a new way of living which expresses itself in acts of charity.

This charity is both *love of God and love of neighbor*. As the First Letter of John teaches us, "one who has no love for the brother whom he can see cannot love the God whom he has not seen . . . whoever loves God must also love his brother" (1 Jn 4:20-21). By the same token, acts of charity which are not rooted in the word of God and in worship cannot bear lasting fruit. "*Apart from me*," Jesus says, "*you can do nothing*" (Jn 15:5). The ministry of charity is confirmed on every page of the Gospel; it demands a constant and radical conversion of heart. We have a forceful example of this in the Gospel of Matthew proclaimed earlier. We are told: "offer no resistance to injury." We are commanded: "Love your enemies and pray for your persecutors." All of this is an essential part of the ministry of charity.

4. Certainly *today's world* is not lacking in opportunities for such a ministry, whether in the form of the simplest acts of charity or the most heroic witness to the radical demands of the Gospel. All around us many of our brothers and sisters live in either *spiritual or material poverty* or both. So many of the world's people are *oppressed by injustice* and the denial of their fundamental human rights. Still others are troubled or suffer from a loss of faith in God, or are tempted to give up hope.

In the midst of the human condition it is a great source of satisfaction to learn that so many permanent deacons in the United States are involved in *direct service to the needy*: to the ill, the abused and battered, the young and old, the dying and bereaved, the deaf, blind and disabled, those who have known suffering in their marriages, the homeless, victims of substance abuse, prisoners, refugees, street people, the rural poor, the victims of racial and ethnic discrimination, and many others. As Christ tells us, "as often as you did it for one of my least brothers, you did it for me" (Mt 25:40).

At the same time, the Second Vatican Council reminds us that the ministry of charity at the service of God's redemptive plan also obliges us to be *a positive influence for change* in the world in which we live, that is, to be a leaven—to be the soul of human society—so that society may be renewed by Christ and transformed into the family of God (cf. *Gaudium et Spes*, no. 40ff.). The "*temporal order*" includes marriage and the family, the world of culture, economic and social life, the trades and professions, political institutions, the solidarity of peoples, and issues of justice and peace (cf. *Apostolicam Actuositatem*, no. 7; *Gaudium et Spes*, no. 46ff.). The task is seldom an easy one. The truth about ourselves and the world, revealed in the Gospel, is not always what the world wants to hear. *Gospel truth often contradicts commonly accepted thinking*, as we see so clearly today with regard to evils such as racism, contraception, abortion, and euthanasia—to name just a few.

5. Taking an active part in society belongs to the baptismal mission of every Christian in accordance with his or her state in life, but the permanent deacon has *a special witness to give*. The sacramental grace of his ordination is meant to strengthen him and to make his efforts fruitful, even as his *secular occupation* gives him entry into the temporal sphere in a way that is normally not appropriate for other members of the clergy. At the same time, the fact that he is an ordained minister of the Church brings a special dimension to his efforts in the eyes of those with whom he lives and works.

Equally important is the contribution that a married deacon makes to *the transformation of family life*. He and his wife, having entered into a communion of life, are called to help and serve each other (cf. *Gaudium et Spes*, no. 48). So intimate is their partnership and unity in the sacrament of marriage, that the Church fittingly requires the wife's consent before her husband can be ordained a permanent deacon (*Codex Iuris Canonici*, c. 1031 §2). As the current guidelines for the permanent diaconate in the United States point out, the *nurturing and deepening of mutual, sacrificial love between husband and wife* constitute perhaps the most significant involvement of a deacon's wife in her husband's public ministry in the Church (*Guidelines*, NCCB, 110). Today especially, this is no small service.

In particular, the deacon and his wife must be a living example of *fidelity and indissolubility in Christian marriage* before a world which is in dire need of such signs. By facing *in a spirit of faith* the challenges of married life and the demands of daily living, they strengthen the family life not only of the Church community but of the whole of society. They also show how the obligations of family, work and ministry can be harmonized in the *service of the Church's mission*. Deacons and their wives and children can be a great encouragement to all others who are working to promote family life.

Mention must also be made of another kind of family, namely, the *parish*, which is the usual setting in which the vast majority of deacons fulfill the mandate of their ordination "to help the bishop and his presbyterate." The parish provides *an ecclesial context* for your ministry and serves as a reminder that your labors are not carried out in isolation, but in communion with the bishop, his priests and all those who in varying degrees share in the public ministry of the Church. Permanent deacons have an obligation to respect the office of the priest and to cooperate conscientiously and generously with him and with the parish staff. The deacon also has a right to be accepted and fully recognized by them and by all for what he is: an ordained minister of the word, the altar and charity.

6. Given the dignity and importance of the permanent diaconate, what is expected of you? As Christians we must not be ashamed to speak of *the qualities of a servant* to which all believers must aspire, and especially deacons, whose ordination rite describes them as "servants of all." A deacon must be known for *fidelity, integrity and obedience*, and so it is that fidelity to Christ, moral integrity and obedience to the bishop must mark your lives, as the ordination rite makes clear (cf. also Paul VI, *Ad Pascendum*, Intro.). In that rite *the Church* also *expresses her hopes and expectations* for you when she prays:

> "Lord, may they excel in every virtue: in love . . . concern . . . unassuming authority . . . self-discipline and in holiness of life. May their conduct exemplify your commandments and lead your people to imitate their purity of life. May they remain strong and steadfast in Christ, giving to the world the witness of a pure conscience. May they . . . imitate your Son, who came, not to be served but to serve."

Dear brothers: this prayer commits you to *lifelong spiritual formation* so that you may grow and persevere in rendering a service that is truly edifying to the People of God. You who are wives of permanent deacons, being close collaborators in their ministry, are likewise challenged with them *to grow in the knowledge and love of Jesus Christ*. And this of course means growth in prayer—personal prayer, family prayer, liturgical prayer.

Since deacons are ministers of the word, the Second Vatican Council invites you to *constant reading and diligent study of the Sacred Scriptures*, lest—if you are a preacher—you become an empty one for failing to hear the word in your own heart (cf. *Dei Verbum*, no. 25). In your lives as deacons you are called to *hear* and *guard* and *do* the word of God, in order to be able to proclaim it worthily. To preach to God's people is an honor that entails a serious preparation and a real commitment to holiness of life.

As ministers of the altar you must be *steeped in the spirit of the liturgy*, and be convinced above all that it is "the summit toward which the activity of the Church is directed and at the same time the source from which all her power flows" (cf. *Sacrosanctum Concilium*, no. 10). You are called to discharge your office with the dignity and reverence befitting the liturgy, which the Council powerfully describes as being "above all, the worship of the divine majesty" (ibid., no. 33). I join you in thanking *all those who devote themselves to your training*, both before and after your ordination, through programs of spiritual, theological, and liturgical formation.

7. "Sing a new song unto the Lord! Let your song be sung from mountains high!" *Sing to him as servants*, but also sing *as friends* of Christ, who has made known to you all that he has heard from the Father. It was not you who chose him, but he who *chose you, to go forth and bear fruit*—fruit that will last. This you do by loving one another (cf. Jn 15:15ff.). By the standards of this world, servanthood is despised, but in the wisdom and providence of God it is *the mystery through which Christ redeems the world. And you are ministers of that mystery*, heralds of that Gospel. You can be sure that one day you will hear the Lord saying to each of you: "Well done, good and faithful servant, enter into the joy of your Lord" (cf. Mt 25:21).

Dear brothers and sisters: as one who strives to be "the servant of the servants of God," I cannot take leave of you until, together, we turn to Mary, as she continues to proclaim: "I am the servant of the Lord" (Lk 1:38). And in *the example of her servanthood*, we see the perfect model of our own call to the discipleship of our Lord Jesus Christ and to the service of his Church.

Apostolic Letter *Vicesimus Quintus Annus* (*On the 25th Anniversary of the Promulgation of the Conciliar Constitution "Sacrosanctum Concilium" On the Sacred Liturgy*)

December 4, 1988

Attention to New Problems

17. The effort toward liturgical renewal must furthermore respond to the needs of our time. The Liturgy is not disincarnate. In these twenty-five years new problems have arisen or have assumed new importance, for example: the exercise of a diaconate open to married men; liturgical tasks in celebrations which can be entrusted to laypeople; liturgical celebrations for children, for young people, and the disabled; the procedures for the composition of liturgical texts appropriate to a particular country.

In the Constitution *Sacrosanctum Concilium* there is no reference to these problems, but the general principles are given which serve to coordinate and promote liturgical life.

Post-Synodal Apostolic Exhortation *Christifideles Laici* (*On the Vocation and the Mission of the Lay Faithful in the Church and in the World*)

December 30, 1988

States of Life and Vocations

55. Simply in *being* Christians, even before actually *doing* the works of a Christian, all are branches of the one fruitful vine which is Christ.

All are living members of the one Body of the Lord built up through the power of the Spirit. The significance of "being" a Christian does not come about simply from the life of grace and holiness which is the primary and more productive source of the apostolic and missionary fruitfulness of Holy Mother Church. Its meaning also arises from the state of life that characterizes the clergy, men and women religious, members of secular institutes and the lay faithful.

Post-Synodal Apostolic Exhortation *Pastores Dabo Vobis* (*On the Formation of Priests in the Circumstances of the Present Day*)

March 25, 1992

The Fundamental Relationship with Christ the Head and Shepherd

15. In their turn, the apostles, appointed by the Lord, progressively carried out their mission by calling—in various but complementary ways—other men as bishops, as priests and as deacons in order to fulfill the command of the risen Jesus who sent them forth to all people in every age.

47. A loving knowledge of the word of God and a prayerful familiarity with it are specifically important for the prophetic ministry of the priest. They are a fundamental condition for such a ministry to be carried out suitably, especially if we bear in mind the "new evangelization" which the Church today is called to undertake. The Council tells us: "All clerics, particularly priests of Christ and others who, as deacons or catechists, are officially engaged in the ministry of the word, should immerse themselves in the Scriptures by constant sacred reading and diligent study. For it must not happen that anyone becomes 'an empty preacher of the word of God to others, not being a hearer of the word of God in his own heart'" (St. Augustine, Sermon 179, 1: PL 8:966) (cf. *Dogm. Const. on Divine Revelation Dei Verbum*, no. 25).

58. If the training is to be suitable, the different experiences which candidates for the priesthood have should assume a clear "ministerial" character and should be intimately linked with all the demands that befit preparation to the priesthood and (certainly not neglecting their studies) in relation to the services of the proclamation of the word, of worship, and of leadership. These services can become a specific way of experiencing the ministries of lector, acolyte, and deacon.

The Diaconate in the Ministerial Communion and Hierarchy of the Church

General Audience, *October 6, 1993*

1. In addition to presbyters, in the Church there is another category of ministers with specific tasks and charisms as the Council of Trent recalls when it discusses the Sacrament of Orders: "In the Catholic Church, there is a hierarchy established by divine ordinance that includes bishops, presbyters, and ministers."[1] The New Testament books already attest to the presence of ministers, "deacons," who gradually formed a distinct category from the presbyterate and episcopate. One need only recall that Paul addressed his greeting to the bishops and ministers of Philippi (cf. Phil 1:1). The First Letter to Timothy lists the qualities that deacons should have, with the recommendation that they be tested before they are entrusted with their functions. They must be dignified and honest, faithful in marriage, and must manage their children and households well, having "much confidence in their faith in Christ Jesus" (cf. 1 Tm 3:8-13).

The Acts of the Apostles (6:1-6) speaks of seven "ministers" for service at table. Although the question of a sacramental ordination of deacons is not clear from the text, a long tradition has interpreted the episode as the first evidence of the institution of deacons. By the end of the first century or the beginning of the second, the deacon's place, at least in some Churches, was already well established as a rank in the ministerial hierarchy.

2. An important witness is given especially by St. Ignatius of Antioch, according to whom the Christian community lives under the authority of a bishop, surrounded by presbyters and deacons. "There is only one Eucharist, one Body of the Lord, one chalice, one altar, just as there is only one bishop with the college of presbyters and deacons, fellow servants."[2] In Ignatius' letters, deacons are always mentioned as a lower rank in the ministerial hierarchy. A deacon is praised for "being subject to the bishop as to the grace of God, and to the presbyter as to the law of Jesus Christ."[3] Nevertheless, Ignatius highlights the

---

1 Denzinger-Schönmetzer, *Enchiridion Symbolorum, definitionum et declarationum de rebus fidei et morum* (1965) (DS), no. 1776.

2 St. Ignatius of Antioch, To the Philadelphians (*Ad Philad.*) 4:1.

3 St. Ignatius of Antioch, To the Magnesians (*Ad Magnes.*) 2.

magnitude of the ministry of the deacon, because it is "the ministry of Jesus Christ, who was with the Father before the beginning of time, and in the end was revealed."[4] As "ministers of the mysteries of Jesus Christ," deacons must "in every way be pleasing to all."[5] When Ignatius urges Christians to obey the bishop and the priests, he adds: "Respect the deacons as God's commandment."[6]

We find other witnesses in St. Polycarp of Smyrna,[7] St. Justin,[8] Tertullian,[9] St. Cyprian,[10] and later in St. Augustine.[11]

3. In the early centuries, the deacon carried out liturgical functions. In the Eucharistic celebration, he read or chanted the Epistle and the Gospel; he brought the offerings of the faithful to the celebrant; he distributed Communion and brought it to those absent; he was responsible for the orderliness of the ceremonies and, at the end, dismissed the assembly. In addition, he prepared catechumens for Baptism, instructed them, and assisted the priest in administering this sacrament. In certain circumstances, he himself baptized and preached. He also shared in the administration of ecclesiastical property and cared for the poor, widows, orphans, and prisoners.

In Tradition, there are witnesses to the distinction between the deacon's functions and those of the priest. For example, St. Hippolytus states (second to third century) that the deacon is ordained "not to the priesthood, but for service to the bishop, to do what he commands."[12] Actually, according to the Church's mind and practice, the diaconate belongs to the Sacrament of Holy Orders, but is not part of the priesthood and does not entail functions proper to priests.

4. With the passage of time, the presbyterate in the West assumed almost exclusive importance in relation to the diaconate, which was reduced to being merely a step on the way to the priesthood. This is not the place to retrace the historical process and explain the reasons for these changes. It is rather a question of pointing out that, on the basis of ancient teaching, the awareness of the diaconate's importance for the Church became greater and greater in theological and

---

4 St. Ignatius of Antioch, To the Magnesians (*Ad Magnes.*) 6:1. [This sentence and footnote were missing from the English translation used, but appear in the Italian compendium, and so are included here.]

5 St. Ignatius of Antioch, To the Trallians (*Ad Trall.*) 2:3.

6 St. Ignatius of Antioch, To the Smyrnaeans (*Ad Smyrn.*) 8:1.

7 St. Polycarp of Smyrna, To the Philippians (*Ad Phil.,*) 5,2.

8 St. Justin, *Apologia,* I, 65, 5; 67, 5

9 Tertullian, *De Baptismo,* 17, 1

10 St. Cyprian, *Epistolae,* 15 and 16.

11 St. Augustine, *De catechizandis rudibus,* 1, c. 1, 1

12 St. Hippolytus, *Sources Chrétiennes,* 11, 39; cf. *Constitutiones Aegypt.,* 3, 2: ed. Funk, *Didascalia,* 103; *Statuta Ecclesiae Ant.,* 37-41: Mansi 3, 954.

pastoral circles, as did the appropriateness of reestablishing it as an order and permanent state of life. Pope Pius XII also referred to this in his address to the Second World Congress of the Lay Apostolate (October 5, 1957). He stated that although the idea of reintroducing the diaconate as a function distinct from the priesthood was not yet ripe, it could become such. In any case, the diaconate was to be put in the context of the hierarchical ministry determined by the most ancient tradition.[1]

The time was ripe at the Second Vatican Council. It considered the proposals of the preceding years and decided on its [the diaconate's] reestablishment.[2] Pope Paul VI later implemented the decision, determining the complete canonical and liturgical discipline for this order.[3]

5. There were two main reasons for the theologians' proposals and the conciliar and papal decisions. First of all, it was considered fitting that certain charitable services, guaranteed in a stable way by laymen conscious of being called to the Church's Gospel mission, should be concretely expressed in a form recognized by virtue of an official consecration. It was also necessary to provide for the scarcity of priests, as well as to assist them in many responsibilities not directly connected to their pastoral ministry. Some saw the permanent diaconate as a bridge between pastors and the faithful.

Clearly, the Holy Spirit, who has the leading role in the Church's life, was mysteriously working through these reasons connected with historical circumstances and pastoral perspectives. He was bringing about a new realization of the complete picture of the hierarchy, traditionally composed of bishops, priests, and deacons. Thus a revitalization of Christian communities was fostered, making them more like those founded by the Apostles that flourished in the early centuries, always under the impulse of the Paraclete, as the Acts of the Apostles attest.

6. A deeply felt need in the decision to reestablish the permanent diaconate was and is that of a greater and more direct presence of Church ministers in the various spheres of the family, work, school, etc., in addition to existing pastoral structures. Among other things, this fact explains why the Council, while not totally rejecting the idea of celibacy for deacons, permitted this order to be

1 Cf. Pius XII, *Speeches and Radio Messages of His Holiness Pius XII*, vol. 9, 458.

2 Cf. LG, no. 29.

3 Paul VI, *Sacrum Diaconatus Ordinem* (SDO): June 18, 1967; cf. *Pontificalis Romani Recognitio*: June 17, 1968; cf. *Ad Pascendum*: August 15, 1972.

conferred on "mature married men." It was a prudent, realistic approach, chosen for reasons that can be easily understood by anyone familiar with different people's ages and concrete situations according to the level of maturity reached. For the same reason, it was then decided, in applying the Council's provisions, that the diaconate would be conferred on married men under certain conditions: they would be at least thirty-five years of age and have their wife's consent, be of good character and reputation, and receive an adequate doctrinal and pastoral preparation given either by institutes or priests specially chosen for this purpose.[4]

7. However, it should be noted that the Council maintained the ideal of a diaconate open to younger men who would devote themselves totally to the Lord with the commitment to celibacy as well. It is a life of "evangelical perfection" that can be understood, chosen, and loved by generous men who want to serve the Kingdom of God in the world without entering the priesthood to which they do not feel called. Nevertheless, they receive a consecration that guarantees and institutionalizes their special service to the Church through the conferral of sacramental grace. These men are not lacking today. Certain provisions were given for them: for ordination to the diaconate they must be at least twenty-five years of age and receive formation for at least three years in a special institute,[5] "where they are tested, trained to live a truly evangelical life, and prepared to carry out effectively their own specific functions." These provisions show the importance the Church puts on the diaconate and her desire that this ordination occur after due consideration and on a sound basis. But they are also a sign of the ancient yet ever new ideal of dedicating oneself to the Kingdom of God that the Church takes from the Gospel and raises as a banner especially before young people in our time too.

Functions of the Deacon in Pastoral Ministry

General Audience, *October 13, 1993*

1. The Second Vatican Council determined the place deacons have in the Church's ministerial hierarchy in accordance with the most ancient tradition:

4 Cf. SDO, nos. 11-15: *Ench. Vaticanum,* 2, 1381-1385.

5 Cf. SDO, nos. 5-9: *Ench. Vaticanum,* 2, 1375-1379.

"At a lower level of the hierarchy are deacons, upon whom hands are imposed 'not unto the priesthood, but unto a ministry of service.' For strengthened by sacramental grace, in communion with the bishop and his group of priests, they serve the people of God in the ministry of the liturgy, of the word, and of charity" (LG, no. 29). The formula "not unto the priesthood, but unto a ministry" is taken from a text of Hippolytus' Apostolic Tradition, and the Council sets it against a broader horizon. In this ancient text, the "ministry" is specified as a "service to the bishop"; the Council stresses the service to the People of God. Actually, this basic meaning of the deacon's service was asserted at the beginning by St. Ignatius of Antioch, who called deacons the "ministers of God's Church," recommending that for this reason they should be pleasing to everyone.[6] Down through the centuries, in addition to being the bishop's helper, the deacon was also considered to be at the service of the Christian community.

2. In order to be allowed to carry out their functions, deacons receive, before ordination, the ministries of lector and acolyte. The conferral of these two ministries shows the essential twofold orientation of the deacon's functions as Paul VI explains in his Apostolic Letter (*Ad Pascendum*) (1972):

"It is especially fitting that the ministries of lector and acolyte should be entrusted to those who, as candidates for the order of diaconate or priesthood, desire to devote themselves to God and to the Church in a special way. For the Church, which 'does not cease to take the Bread of Life from the table of the Word of God and the Body of Christ and offer it to the faithful,' considers it to be very opportune that both by study and by gradual exercise of the ministry of the Word and of the altar, candidates for Holy Orders should, through intimate contact, understand and reflect upon the double aspect of the priestly office."[7]

This orientation is valid not only for the role of priests but also for that of deacons.

3. It should be kept in mind that before Vatican II, the lectorate and acolytate were considered minor orders. In a letter to a bishop in 252, Pope Cornelius listed the seven ranks in the Church of Rome:[8] priests, deacons, subdeacons, acolytes, exorcists, lectors, and porters. In the tradition of the Latin Church, three were considered major orders: those of the priest, deacon, and subdeacon;

6 Cf. St. Ignatius of Antioch, To the Trallians (Ad Trall.), 2:3.

7 Pope Paul VI, Apostolic Letter *Ad Pascendum* (1972); AAS 64 (1972); *Ench. Vat.*, IV, 1781.

8 Cf. Eusebius, *Church History*, VI, 43: PG 20, 622.

four were minor orders: those of the acolyte, exorcist, lector, and porter. This arrangement of the ecclesiastical structure was due to the needs of Christian communities over the centuries and was determined by the Church's authority.

When the permanent diaconate was reestablished, this structure was changed. As to the sacramental framework, it was restored to the three orders of divine institution: the diaconate, presbyterate, and episcopate. In fact, in his Apostolic Letter on ministries in the Latin Church (*Ministeria Quaedam*, 1972), Pope Paul VI suppressed tonsure, which marked the entrance into the clerical state, and the subdiaconate, whose functions were given to lectors and acolytes. He kept the lectorate and the acolytate; however, they were no longer considered orders, but ministries conferred by installation rather than by ordination. These ministries must be received by candidates to the diaconate and presbyterate and are also open to laymen in the Church who want to assume only the responsibilities corresponding to them: the lectorate, as the office of reading the Word of God in the liturgical assembly, except for the Gospel, carrying out certain roles (such as leading the singing and instructing the faithful); and the acolytate, instituted to help the deacon and to minister to the priest.[9]

4. The Second Vatican Council lists the deacon's liturgical and pastoral functions: "to administer baptism solemnly, to be custodian and dispenser of the Eucharist, to assist at and bless marriages in the name of the Church, to bring Viaticum to the dying, to read the sacred Scripture to the faithful, to instruct and exhort the people, to preside at the worship and prayer of the faithful, to administer sacramentals, to officiate at funeral and burial services" (LG, no. 29).

Pope Paul VI laid down in addition that the deacon, "in the name of the parish priest or bishop, could legitimately lead dispersed Christian communities."[10] This is a missionary function to be carried out in territories, surroundings, social contexts, and groups where a priest is lacking or not easily available. Especially in those places where no priest is available to celebrate the Eucharist, the deacon gathers and leads the community in a celebration of the Word with the distribution of the sacred species duly reserved. This is a supply function that the deacon fulfills by ecclesial mandate when it is a case of providing for the shortage of priests. This substitution, which can never be complete, reminds

9 *Ench. Vaticanum*, 4, 1762-1763; cf. Paul VI, *Ministeria Quaedam*, August 15, 1972: AAS 64 (1972), 529-534.

10 SDO, no. 22, 10: *Ench. Vat.*, II, 1392.

communities lacking priests of the urgent need to pray for priestly vocations and to do their utmost to encourage them as something good both for the Church and for themselves. The deacon too should foster this prayer.

5. Again, according to the Council, the functions assigned to the deacon can in no way diminish the role of laypeople called and willing to cooperate in the apostolate with the hierarchy. On the contrary, the deacon's tasks include that of "promoting and sustaining the apostolic activities of the laity." To the extent that he is present and more involved than the priest in secular environments and structures, he should feel encouraged to foster closeness between the ordained ministry and lay activities, in common service to the Kingdom of God.

The deacon has a charitable function as well that also entails an appropriate service in the administration of property and in the Church's charitable works. In this area, the function of deacons is: "on behalf of the hierarchy, to exercise the duties of charity and administration in addition to social work."[1]

In this regard, the Council recommends to deacons what stems from the oldest tradition of Christian communities: "Dedicated to duties of charity and of administration, let deacons be mindful of the admonition of Blessed Polycarp: 'Be merciful, diligent, walking according to the truth of the Lord, who became the servant of all.'"[2]

6. According to the Council, the diaconate seems of particular value in the young Churches. This is why *Ad Gentes* (*Decree on the Church's Missionary Activity*) establishes: "Where Episcopal Conferences deem it opportune, the order of the diaconate should be restored as a permanent state of life, according to the norms of the *Constitution on the Church*. For there are men who are actually carrying out the functions of the deacon's office, either preaching the word of God as catechists, or by presiding over scattered Christian communities in the name of the pastor and the bishop, or by practicing charity in social or relief work. It will be helpful to strengthen them by that imposition of hands which has come down from the apostles, and to bind them more closely to the altar. Thus they can carry out their ministry more effectively because of the sacramental grace of the diaconate."[3]

1 Pope Paul VI, SDO, no. 22, 9; *Ench. Vaticanum*, 2, 1392.

2 LG, no. 29; cf. Polycarp, *Ad Philippenses*, 5:2.

3 AG, no. 16.

It is known that wherever missionary activity has led to the formation of new Christian communities, catechists often play an essential role. In many places, they lead the community, instruct it, and encourage it to pray. The order of the diaconate can confirm them in the mission they are exercising through a more official consecration and a mandate that is more expressly granted by the authority of the Church through the conferral of a sacrament. In this sacrament, in addition to a sharing in the grace of Christ the Redeemer poured out in the Church through the Holy Spirit, the source of every apostolate, an indelible character is received that in a special way configures the Christian to Christ, "who made himself the 'deacon' or servant of all."[4]

4 *Catechism of the Catholic Church* (CCC), no. 1570.

Features of Diaconal Spirituality

General Audience, *October 20, 1993*

1. Among the catechetical topics on the diaconate, the one about the spirit of the diaconate is especially important and attractive for it concerns and involves all who receive this sacrament in order to carry out its functions in a Gospel perspective. This is the way that leads its ministers to Christian perfection and allows them to give truly effective service (*diakonia*) in the Church, "for building up the body of Christ" (Eph 4:12).

Here is the source of diaconal spirituality, which is rooted in what the Second Vatican Council calls the "sacramental grace of the diaconate."[5] In addition to being a valuable help in carrying out various tasks, it deeply affects the deacon's heart, spurring him to offer his whole self to serving the Kingdom of God in the Church. As the very word "diaconate" indicates, the spirit of service characterizes the interior mind and will of the one who receives the sacrament. In the diaconate, an effort is made to carry out what Jesus stated about his mission: "The Son of Man did not come to be served but to serve and to give his life as a ransom for many" (Mk 10:45; Mt 20:28).

Doubtless Jesus addressed these words to the Twelve, whom he chose for the priesthood, to make them understand that, although endowed with authority conferred by him, they should act as he did, as servants. The advice applies to all ministers of Christ; however, it has particular meaning for deacons. For them, the aspect of service is stressed by virtue of their ordination. Although they do not exercise the pastoral authority of priests, in carrying out all their functions, their particular aim is to show an intention to serve. If their ministry is consistent with this spirit, they shed greater light on that identifying feature of Christ's face—service. They are not only "servants of God" but also of their brothers and sisters.

2. This teaching of the spiritual life is of Gospel origin and entered the earliest Christian Tradition as that ancient third-century text called the *Didascalia Apostolorum* (*Didascalia of the Apostles*) confirms. It encourages deacons to take their inspiration from the Gospel incident of the washing of feet. "If the Lord did this," it says, "then you deacons should not hesitate to do it for the sick and

5 AG, no. 16.

infirm since you are workers of the truth, who have put on Christ."[6] The diaconate commits one to following Jesus with this attitude of humble service, which is expressed not only in works of charity but shapes and embraces one's whole way of thinking and acting.

This perspective explains the condition set by the document *Sacrum Diaconatus Ordinem* (*General Norms for Restoring the Permanent Diaconate in the Latin Church*) for admitting young men to formation as deacons: "Only those young men should be enrolled to train for the diaconate who have shown a natural inclination for service to the hierarchy and the Christian community."[7] The "natural inclination" should not be understood in the sense of a simple spontaneity of natural dispositions although this too is a presupposition to be considered. It is rather an inclination of nature inspired by grace with a spirit of service that conforms human behavior to Christ's. The sacrament of the diaconate develops this inclination. It makes the subject share more closely in Christ's spirit of service and imbues the will with a special grace so that in all his actions, he will be motivated by a new inclination to serve his brothers and sisters.

This service should first of all take the form of helping the bishop and the priest both in liturgical worship and the apostolate. It scarcely needs remarking here that anyone whose dominant attitude was one of challenging or opposing authority could not properly carry out the functions of a deacon. The diaconate can only be conferred on those who believe in the value of the bishop's and priest's pastoral mission and in the Holy Spirit's assistance guiding them in their actions and their decisions. In particular, it must again be said that the deacon should "profess reverence and obedience to the bishop."

However, the deacon's service is also directed to his own Christian community and to the whole Church, to which he must foster a deep attachment because of her mission and divine institution.

3. The Second Vatican Council also speaks of the duties and the obligations that deacons assume by virtue of their own sharing in the mission and grace of the high priesthood: "Since they are servants of the mysteries of Christ and the Church, [deacons] should keep themselves free from every fault, be pleasing to God, and be a source of all goodness in the sight of men (cf. 1 Tm 3:8-10,

6 *Didascalia of the Apostles*, XVI, 36: ed. Connolly, 1904, 151.

7 SDO, no. 8: *Ench. Vaticanum*, 2, 1378.

12-13)."[8] Theirs, then, is a duty of witness that embraces not only their service and apostolate but also their whole life.

In the document cited above, *Sacrum Diaconatus Ordinem*, Paul VI called attention to this responsibility and the obligations it entails: "Deacons serve the mysteries of Christ and the Church, and must abstain from any vice, strive to please God, and be 'ready for any good work' for the salvation of men. Therefore, because of their reception of this order, they should far excel others in their liturgical lives, in devotion to prayer, in the divine ministry, in obedience, charity, and chastity."[9]

With particular regard to chastity, young men who are ordained deacons commit themselves to observing celibacy and to leading a life of more intense union with Christ. Here too, even those who are older and "have received ordination . . . may not, in accordance with traditional Church discipline, enter into marriage."[10]

4. In order to fulfill these obligations and, even more deeply, to respond to the spiritual demands of the diaconate with the help of sacramental grace, the exercises of the spiritual life must be practiced as described in Paul VI's Apostolic Letter. Deacons should (1) apply themselves to reading carefully and to meditating attentively on the Word of God, (2) attend Mass frequently, even daily if possible, receive the Blessed Sacrament of the Eucharist and visit it out of devotion, (3) purify their souls frequently through the Sacrament of Penance having prepared for it worthily through a daily examination of conscience, and (4) show a deep, filial love and veneration for the Virgin Mary, the Mother of God.[11]

Moreover, Pope Paul VI adds: "It is very fitting for permanent deacons to recite daily at least some part of the Divine Office—to be specified by the episcopal conference."[12] The episcopal conferences are also responsible for establishing more detailed norms for the lives of deacons in accordance with the circumstances of time and place.

Lastly, whoever receives the diaconate is obliged to ongoing doctrinal formation that continually improves and updates the formation required before

8 LG, no. 41.
9 SDO, no. 25: *Ench. Vat.*, 2, 1395.
10 SDO, no. 16: *Ench. Vat.*, 2, 1386.
11 Cf. SDO, no. 26; *Ench. Vaticanum*, 2, 1397.
12 SDO, no. 27; *Ench. Vaticanum*, 2, 1397.

ordination: "Deacons should not slacken in their studies especially of sacred doctrine; they should carefully read the Scriptures; they should devote themselves to ecclesiastical studies in such a way that they can correctly explain Catholic doctrine to others and day by day become better fitted to train and strengthen the souls of the faithful. With this in mind, deacons should be called to regular meetings at which matters concerning their life and sacred ministry will be treated."[13]

5. The catechesis I have given on the diaconate, to complete the picture of the ecclesiastical hierarchy, highlights what is most important in this order as in those of the presbyterate and the episcopate: a specific spiritual participation in the priesthood of Christ and the commitment to a life in conformity to him by the action of the Holy Spirit. I cannot conclude without recalling that deacons, like priests and bishops, who are committed to following Christ in the way of service, share most especially in his redeeming sacrifice. This is according to the principle Jesus formulated when speaking to the Twelve about the Son of Man, who came "to serve and to give his life as a ransom for many" (Mk 10:45). Therefore, deacons are called to participate in the mystery of the cross, to share in the Church's sufferings, and to endure the hostility she encounters in union with Christ the Redeemer. This painful aspect of the deacon's service makes it most fruitful.

Post-Synodal Apostolic Exhortation *Ecclesia in Africa* (*On the Church in Africa and Its Evangelizing Mission Toward the Year 2000*)

September 14, 1995

Deacons

96. Where pastoral conditions lend themselves to respect and understanding of this ancient ministry in the Church, Episcopal Conferences and Assemblies are to study the most suitable ways of promoting and encouraging the permanent diaconate "as an ordained ministry and also as an instrument of evangelization."

13 SDO, no. 29; *Ench. Vaticanum*, 2, 1397.

Where deacons already exist they should be provided with an integrated and thorough program of permanent formation.

Speech to the Plenary Assembly of the Congregation for the Clergy

November 30, 1995

Fidelity to Catholic Tradition, to the Magisterium, to the Responsibility of Re-Evangelization that the Holy Spirit has Inspired in the Church

1. I am pleased to meet you on the occasion of the plenary assembly of the Congregation for the Clergy, which is examining a question of particular importance for the Church: "The Ministry and Life of Permanent Deacons." I affectionately greet Cardinal José Sánchez, the prefect, whom I thank for his words. I also greet Archbishop Crescenzio Sepe, the secretary, and the members of the congregation, together with the officials and experts who give you their valuable service.

You have organized these intense days of reflection and dialogue on the basis of a working paper, which has taken into account the suggestions and contributions of every episcopal conference. In addition to your satisfaction at the work achieved and the results so far reached, you intend to prepare a document concerning the life and ministry of the permanent deacon similar to that for priests, which you saw to at your last plenary session. Thus it will be possible to offer *providential practical guidance* following Vatican Council II's decisions. I encourage and bless your efforts, motivated as they are by a deep love for the Church and for our brother deacons.

Fidelity to Catholic Tradition Should Mark a Deacon's Ministry

2. Since the diaconate has been restored to the Latin Church "as a proper and permanent rank of the hierarchy,"[14] the directives and guidance of the magisterium in its regard have increased. One need only recall Pope Paul VI's teachings and, in particular, those contained in the *motu proprio Sacrum Diaconatus Ordinem*[15]

14 LG, no. 29.

15 June 18, 1967, AAS 59 (1967), 697-704.

and *Ad Pascendum*,[16] which remain a basic reference point. The doctrine and discipline explained in these documents have found their juridical expression in the new *Code of Canon Law*, which must inspire the development of this sacred ministry. Several catecheses which I addressed to the faithful during the month of October 1993 were also devoted to the permanent diaconate.

Reflecting on the ministry and life of permanent deacons, and in the light of the experience acquired so far, it is necessary to proceed with careful theological research and prudent pastoral sense, in view of the new evangelization on the threshold of the third millennium. The vocation of the permanent deacon is a great gift of God to the Church and for this reason is "an important enrichment for the Church's mission."[17]

What is specific to the life and ministry of deacons could be summarized in a single word: "fidelity"—fidelity to the Catholic tradition, especially as witnessed to by the *lex orandi*, fidelity to the magisterium, fidelity to the task of re-evangelization which the Holy Spirit has brought about in the Church. This commitment to fidelity is, first of all, an invitation carefully to promote throughout the Church *a sincere respect for the theological, liturgical and canonical identity* proper to the sacrament conferred on deacons, as well as for the demands required by the ministerial functions which, in virtue of receiving holy orders, are assigned to them in the particular churches.

3. In fact, the sacrament of orders has its own nature and effects, whatever the degree in which it is received (episcopate, presbyterate or diaconate). "Catholic doctrine, expressed in the liturgy, the magisterium and the constant practice of the Church, recognizes that there are two degrees of ministerial participation in the priesthood of Christ: the episcopacy and the presbyterate. The diaconate is intended to help and serve them. . . . Yet Catholic doctrine teaches that the degrees of priestly participation (episcopate and presbyterate) and the degree of service (diaconate) are all three conferred by a sacramental act called 'ordination,' that is, by the sacrament of holy orders."[18]

By the imposition of the bishop's hands and the specific prayer of consecration, the deacon receives *a particular configuration to Christ*, the Head and

16 August 15, 1972, AAS 64 (1972), 534-540.

17 CCC, no. 1571.

18 CCC, no. 1554.

Shepherd of the Church, who for love of the Father made himself the least and the servant of all (cf. Mk 10:43-45; Mt 20:28; 1 Pt 5:3).

Sacramental grace gives deacons the necessary strength to serve the people of God in the *diakonia* of the liturgy, of the word and of charity, in communion with the bishop and his presbyterate.[19] By virtue of the sacrament received, *an indelible spiritual character* is impressed upon him, which marks the deacon permanently and precisely as a minister of Christ. Consequently he is no longer a layman nor can he return to the lay state in the strict sense.[20] These essential characteristics of his ecclesial vocation must pervade his readiness to give himself to the Church and must be reflected in his outward behavior. The Church expects of the permanent deacon a faithful witness to his ministerial state.

Magisterium Has Clearly Described Deacon's Tasks

In particular he must *show a strong sense of unity* with the successor of Peter, with the bishop and with the presbyterate of the Church for whose service he was ordained and incardinated. It is of great importance for the formation of the faithful that the deacon, in exercising the duties assigned to him, should promote an authentic and effective ecclesial communion. His relations with his own bishop, with the priests, with other deacons and with all the faithful should be marked by a *diligent respect for the various charisms and duties*. Only when one keeps to one's own tasks does communion become effective, and each can fulfill his own mission.

4. Deacons are ordained *to exercise a ministry of their own*, which is not that of a priest, because they "receive the imposition of hands 'not unto the priesthood but unto the ministry.'"[21] Therefore they have specific tasks whose content has been clearly described by the magisterium: "To assist the bishop and priests in the celebration of the divine mysteries, above all the Eucharist, in the distribution of Holy Communion, in assisting at and blessing marriages—if they are delegated by the ordinary or the parish priest[22]—in the proclamation of the

19 Cf. CCC, no. 1588.
20 Cf. CCC, no. 1583.
21 LG, no. 29.
22 Cf. CIC, c. 1108 §1.

Gospel and preaching, in presiding over funerals and in dedicating themselves to the various ministries of charity."[23]

The exercise of the diaconal ministry—like that of other ministries in the Church—requires *per se* of all deacons, celibate or married, *a spiritual attitude of total dedication*. Although in certain cases it is necessary to make the ministry of the diaconate compatible with other obligations, to think of oneself and to act in practice as a "part-time deacon" would make no sense.[24] The deacon is not a part-time employee or ecclesiastical official, but a minister of the Church. His is not a profession, but a mission! It is the circumstances of his life—prudently evaluated by the candidate himself and by the bishop before ordination—which should, if necessary, be adapted to the exercise of his ministry by facilitating it in every way.

The many problems which are still to be resolved and are of concern to pastors should be examined in this light. The deacon is called to be a person open to all, ready to serve people, generous in promoting just social causes, avoiding attitudes or positions which could make him appear to show favoritism. In fact, a minister of Jesus Christ, even as a citizen, must always promote unity and avoid, as far as possible, being a source of disunity or conflict. May the attentive study which you have undertaken in these days provide useful guidelines in this area.

5. With the restoration of the permanent diaconate, the possibility was recognized of conferring this order on men of a mature age who are already married, but once ordained they cannot remarry should they be widowed.[25]

It should be noted, however, that the council maintained the ideal of a diaconate open to younger men who would devote themselves totally to the Lord, with the commitment of celibacy as well. It is a life of "evangelical perfection" which can be understood, chosen and loved by generous men who want to serve the kingdom of God in the world, without entering the priesthood to which they do not feel called, but nevertheless receiving a consecration that guarantees and institutionalizes their special service to the Church through the conferral of sacramental grace. These men are not lacking today.[26]

23 Cf. CCC, no. 1570; cf. LG, no. 29; SC, no. 35; AG, no. 16.

24 Cf. *Directory for the Ministry and Life of Priests*, no. 44.

25 SDO, no. 16, AAS, no. 59 (1967), 701.

26 *Catechesis* at the General Audience, October 6, 1993, 7; *L'Osservatore Romano*, English edition, October 13, 1993, 11.

Spiritual Life Must Be Sustained by Personal Prayer

6. The spirituality of the diaconate "has its source in what Vatican Council II calls 'the sacramental grace of the diaconate' (*Ad Gentes*, no. 16)."[27] By virtue of ordination this is defined by *the spirit of service*. "This service should first of all take the form of helping the bishop and the priest, both in liturgical worship and the apostolate. . . . However, the deacon's service is also directed to his own Christian community and to the whole Church, to which he must foster a deep attachment because of her mission and divine institution."[28]

To fulfill his mission, the deacon therefore needs a *deep interior life* sustained by the exercises of piety recommended by the Church.[29] Carrying out ministerial and apostolic activities, fulfilling possible family and social responsibilities and, lastly, practicing an intense personal life of prayer require of the deacon, whether celibate or married, that *unity of life* which can only be attained, as Vatican Council II taught, through deep union with Christ.[30]

Dear brothers and sisters, as I thank you for your active involvement in this plenary assembly, I would also like to put into the hands of her who is the *ancilla Domini*, the fruit of the work to which you have applied yourselves. I ask the immaculate Virgin to accompany the Church's effort in this important field of pastoral activity in view of the new evangelization.

With these sentiments, I willingly impart my blessing to all.

---

27 *Catechesis* at the General Audience, October 20, 1993, 1; *L'Osservatore Romano*, English edition, October 27, 1993, 11.

28 *Catechesis* at the General Audience, October 20, 1993, 2; *L'Osservatore Romano*, English edition, October 27, 1993, 11.

29 Cf. SDO, nos. 26-27; AAS, no. 59 (1967) 702-703.

30 Cf. Second Vatican Ecumenical Council, Decree on the Ministry and Life of Priests, (*Presbyterorum Ordinis* [PO]), no. 14.

Apostolic Letter *Dies Domini* (*On Keeping the Lord's Day Holy*)

May 31, 1998

The Eucharistic Assembly: Heart of Sunday

A Celebration Involving All

51. There is a need too to ensure that all those present, children and adults, take an active interest, by encouraging their involvement at those points where the liturgy suggests and recommends it. Of course, it falls only to those who exercise the priestly ministry to effect the Eucharistic Sacrifice and to offer it to God in the name of the whole people. This is the basis of the distinction, which is much more than a matter of discipline, between the task proper to the celebrant and that which belongs to deacons and the non-ordained faithful. Yet the faithful must realize that, because of the common priesthood received in Baptism, "they participate in the offering of the Eucharist." Although there is a distinction of roles, they still "offer to God the divine victim and themselves with him. Offering the sacrifice and receiving holy communion, they take part actively in the liturgy," finding in it light and strength to live their baptismal priesthood and the witness of a holy life.

Post-Synodal Exhortation *Ecclesia in America* (*On Encountering the Living Jesus Christ Through Conversion, Communion, and Solidarity in the Americas*)

January 22, 1999

The Bishops as Builders of Communion

36. Precisely because it signifies life, communion in the Church must constantly increase. Therefore, the Bishops, remembering that "each of them is the visible principle and foundation of the unity of his particular Church," cannot but feel duty-bound to promote communion in their dioceses, so that the drive for a new evangelization in America may be more effective. Working in favor of this communion are the structures which the Second Vatican Council called for as

a means of supporting the diocesan Bishop's work, and which post-conciliar legislation has spelled out in greater detail. "It is up to the Bishop, with the help of the priests, deacons, religious and lay people to implement a coordinated pastoral plan, which is systematic and participatory, involving all the members of the Church and awakening in them a missionary consciousness" (Chap. IV, 36).

The Permanent Diaconate

42. For serious pastoral and theological reasons, the Second Vatican Council decided to restore the diaconate as a permanent element of the hierarchy of the Latin Church, leaving to the Episcopal Conferences, with the approval of the Supreme Pontiff, the task of assessing whether and where to establish permanent deacons. The experience has varied significantly, not only in the different parts of America but even between dioceses of the same area. "Some dioceses have trained and ordained a good number of deacons, and they are fully satisfied with their integration and their ministry." Here we see with joy how deacons "sustained by the grace of the Sacrament, in the ministry (*diakonia*) of the Liturgy, of the word and of charity are at the service of the People of God, in communion with the Bishop and his priests." Other dioceses have not followed this path, while elsewhere there have been difficulties in integrating permanent deacons into the hierarchical structure.

With due respect for the freedom of the particular Churches to restore the permanent diaconate, with the approval of the Supreme Pontiff, it is clear that for such a move to be successful there has to be a careful selection process, solid formation and continuous attention to the suitability of the candidates, as well as constant concern for them once they are ordained, and—in the case of married deacons—concern as well for their families, wives and children (Chap. IV, 42).

Angelus for the Jubilee of Permanent Deacons

February 20, 2000

Dear Brothers and Sisters,

1. The celebrations for the Jubilee of Permanent Deacons, organized by the Congregation for the Clergy, are closing today. I would first like to extend a

warm greeting to the many deacons who have come to Rome from all over the world, together with their families, for this special occasion. In particular, I greet you, dear brothers, who were ordained to the diaconate this morning in the Vatican Basilica.

I am very pleased that all of you are here because you give me the opportunity to stress the importance of your role: by sacramental ordination, the deacon takes on a special "*diakonia*," which is expressed particularly in service to the Gospel. During the rite, the ordaining Bishop says these words: "Receive the Gospel of Christ, whose herald you now are. Believe what you read, teach what you believe and practice what you teach." This is your mission, dear brothers: embrace the Gospel, reflect on its message in faith, love it and bear witness to it in word and deed. The work of the new evangelization needs your contribution, marked by consistency and dedication, by courage and generosity, in the daily service of the liturgy, of the word and of charity. Live your mission joyously and faithfully, you deacons who are called by celibacy to a life that is totally dedicated to God and his kingdom. Live it, you married deacons, whom Christ asks to be models of true love in family life. The Lord has chosen all of you to cooperate with him in the work of salvation.

2. Next Tuesday I will have the joy of celebrating the Jubilee of the Roman Curia together with my collaborators. This has been preceded by several meetings of reflection and prayer in which the members of the Curia have prepared intensely to live this moment of grace, which invites us to conversion of heart. Everyone who works in the service of the Holy See—Cardinals, Archbishops, Bishops, priests, religious and laity—will enter together through the Holy Door, a symbol of mercy and a call to the renewal of life.

A very close bond joins the Curia family to the Successor of Peter, who avails himself of its service in exercising the ministry entrusted to him by Christ for the benefit of the entire Ecclesial Community. It is therefore important that he be able to count not only on the ability and efficiency of his collaborators, but also on their communion in a love so profound as to make the Curia, as Pope Paul VI liked to say, a "permanent Upper Room," totally dedicated to the good of the Church. The purification which is a goal of the Jubilee experience will certainly make a positive contribution in this regard.

3. To the Virgin Mary I entrust all my collaborators in the Curia, as well as the permanent deacons and other members of the Ecclesial Community: through

the intercession of Mary most holy may the harmonious fusion of all the energies of God's People make the Church's work in the world for humanity's salvation ever more effective.

Apostolic Letter *Novo Millennio Ineunte* (*At the Close of the Great Jubilee of the Year 2000*)

January 6, 2001

45. Communion must be cultivated and extended day by day and at every level in the structures of each Church's life. There, relations between Bishops, priests and deacons, between Pastors and the entire People of God, between clergy and Religious, between associations and ecclesial movements must all be clearly characterized by communion. To this end, the structures of participation envisaged by Canon Law, such as the *Council of Priests* and the *Pastoral Council*, must be ever more highly valued. These of course are not governed by the rules of parliamentary democracy, because they are consultative rather than deliberative; yet this does not mean that they are less meaningful and relevant. The theology and spirituality of communion encourage a fruitful dialogue between Pastors and faithful: on the one hand uniting them *a priori* in all that is essential, and on the other leading them to pondered agreement in matters open to discussion.

Post-Synodal Apostolic Exhortation *Ecclesia in Oceania* (*On Jesus Christ and the Peoples of Oceania: Walking His Way, Telling His Truth, Living His Life*)

November 22, 2001

The Permanent Diaconate

50. The Second Vatican Council decided to restore the permanent diaconate as part of the ordained ministry of the Latin Church. It has been introduced into some Dioceses of Oceania, where it has been well received. A particular advantage of the permanent diaconate is its adaptability to a great variety of local pastoral needs. The Bishops in Synod gave thanks for the untiring work

and dedication of the permanent deacons in Oceania, and were conscious of the generosity of the families of married deacons. The proper formation of the deacons is vital, as is a thorough catechesis and preparation throughout the Diocese, especially in the communities where they will serve. It is also important that they receive continuing formation. It is good for priests and deacons, each responding to his particular vocation, to work together closely in preaching the Gospel and administering the Sacraments.

Post-Synodal Apostolic Exhortation *Ecclesia in Europa* (*On Jesus Christ Alive in His Church: The Source of Hope for Europe*)

June 28, 2003

36. Together with priests, I also wish to mention *deacons*, who share, albeit to a different degree, in the one Sacrament of Holy Orders. Sent forth in service to ecclesial communion, they exercise, under the leadership of the Bishop and his presbyterate, the "*diakonia*" of liturgy, word and charity. In their own way, *they are at the service of the Gospel of hope.*

By the Witness of Life

49. Europe calls out for *credible evangelizers, whose lives*, in communion with the Cross and Resurrection of Christ, *radiate the beauty of the Gospel.* Such evangelizers must be *properly trained.* Now more than ever a *missionary consciousness* is needed in all Christians, beginning with Bishops, priests, deacons, consecrated persons, catechists and teachers of religion: "All the baptized, since they are witnesses of Christ, should receive a training appropriate to their circumstances, not only so that their faith does not wither for lack of care in a hostile environment such as the secularist world, but also so that their witness to the Gospel will receive strength and inspiration."

Post-Synodal Exhortation *Pastores Gregis* (*On the Bishop, Servant of the Gospel of Jesus Christ for the Hope of the World*)

October 16, 2003

Servants of the Gospel for the Hope of the World

5. As we gaze upon the face of our Master and Lord at that hour when he "loved his own to the end," all of us, like the Apostle Peter, allow our feet to be washed so that we might have a part in him (cf. Jn 13:1-9). And with the strength that comes to us from him in the Church, in the presence of our priests and deacons, before all men and women of the consecrated life, and all our beloved laypeople, we repeat aloud: "Whatever we may be, let not your hope be placed in us: if we are good, we are your servants; if we are bad, we are still your servants. But if we are good and faithful servants, it is then that we are truly your servants."

The Trinitarian Foundation of the Episcopal Ministry

7. The tradition which sees the Bishop as an image of God the Father is quite ancient. As St. Ignatius of Antioch wrote, the Father is like an invisible Bishop, the Bishop of all. Every Bishop, therefore, stands in the place of the Father of Jesus Christ in such a way that, precisely because of this representation, he is to be revered by all. Consonant with this symbolism, the Bishop's chair, which especially in the tradition of the Eastern Churches evokes God's paternal authority, can only be occupied by the Bishop. This same symbolism is the source of every Bishop's duty to lead the holy people of God as a devoted father and to guide them—together with his priests, his co-workers in the episcopal ministry, and with his deacons—in the way of salvation. Conversely, as an ancient text exhorts, the faithful are to love their Bishops who are, after God, their fathers and mothers. For this reason, in accordance with a custom widespread in certain cultures, one kisses the Bishop's hand as one would kiss the hand of the loving Father, the giver of life.

The Bishop's Spiritual Path

13. The spiritual journey of the Bishop coincides, from this perspective, with that pastoral charity which must rightly be considered the soul of his apostolate,

as it is of the apostolate of priests and deacons. Here it is not only a matter of an *existentia* but indeed of a *pro-existentia*, that is to say, of a way of living inspired by the supreme model of Christ the Lord and which is spent totally in worship of the Father and in service of neighbor. The Second Vatican Council rightly states that pastors, in the image of Christ, must carry out their ministry with holiness and zeal, with humility and fortitude, "which, fulfilled in this way, will be for them an excellent means of sanctification" (*Lumen Gentium*, no. 41). No Bishop can fail to realize that the summit of Christian holiness is the crucified Christ in his supreme self-oblation to the Father and to his brothers and sisters in the Holy Spirit. For this reason configuration to Christ and a share in his sufferings (cf. 1 Pt 4:15) becomes the royal road of the Bishop's holiness in the midst of his people.

Prayer and the Liturgy of the Hours

17. Every Bishop therefore prays with his people and for his people. He himself is supported and assisted by the prayer of his faithful: priests, deacons, consecrated persons and the lay people of all ages. In their midst the Bishop is a teacher and a promoter of prayer. He not only hands down what he himself has contemplated, but he opens to Christians the way of contemplation itself. The well-known motto *contemplata aliis tradere* thus becomes *contemplationem aliis tradere.*

The Proponent of a Spirituality of Communion and Mission

22. In that same Apostolic Letter I indicated the broad outlines of this promotion of a spirituality of communion. Here it will suffice to add that a Bishop must encourage this spirituality especially among his presbyterate, as well as among deacons and men and women religious. He will do so in personal dialogue and encounters, but also in community meetings. To this end he will make an effort to provide in his own particular Church special occasions which facilitate listening, especially to the Spirit "who speaks to the Churches" (Acts 2:7, 11 et al.). Examples of the latter would be retreats, spiritual exercises and days of spirituality, and also a prudent use of new communications media, should this prove useful and effective.

The Bishop, Hearer and Keeper of the Word

28. The Spirit also makes himself heard as he awakens in the Church different forms of charisms and services. For this reason too, there were frequent calls during the Synod for Bishops to have direct and personal contact with the faithful living in the communities entrusted to their pastoral care, following the example of the Good Shepherd who knows his sheep and calls each by name. Indeed, frequent meetings of the Bishop with his priests, in the first place, and then with the deacons, consecrated persons and their communities, and with the laity, individually and in their various forms of association, are of great importance for the exercise of effective ministry among the People of God.

Authentic and Authoritative Service of the Word

29. Conscious, then, of his responsibility in the area of transmitting and teaching the faith, every Bishop must ensure that a corresponding concern is shown by all those who by their vocation and mission are called to hand down the faith. This means priests and deacons, the faithful who have embraced the consecrated life, fathers and mothers of families, pastoral workers and in a special way catechists, as well as teachers of theology and teachers of the ecclesiastical sciences and religious education. The Bishop will thus take care to provide them with both initial and ongoing training.

The Bishop and Permanent Deacons

49. As ministers of Holy Orders, Bishops also have direct responsibility for permanent deacons, in whom the Synodal Assembly saw authentic gifts of God for proclaiming the Gospel, instructing Christian communities and promoting the service of charity within God's family.

Each Bishop will therefore show great care for these vocations, for the discernment and formation of which he is ultimately responsible. Although he must normally exercise this responsibility through trusted collaborators committed to acting in conformity with the prescriptions of the Holy See, the Bishop will seek in every way possible to know personally all the candidates for the diaconate. After their ordination he will continue to be a true father for them, encouraging them to love the Body and Blood of Christ whose ministers they are, and Holy Church which they have committed themselves to serve; he will also exhort married deacons to lead an exemplary family life.

74. The duty of Bishops at the beginning of a new millennium is thus clearly marked out. It is the same duty as ever: to proclaim the Gospel of Christ, the salvation of the world. But it is a duty which has a new urgency and which calls for cooperation and commitment on the part of the whole People of God. The Bishop needs to be able to count on the members of his diocesan presbyterate and on his deacons, the ministers of the Blood of Christ and of charity; he needs to be able to count on his consecrated sisters and brothers, called to be for the Church and the world eloquent witnesses of the primacy of God in the Christian life and the power of his love amid the frailty of the human condition; and he needs to be able to count on the lay faithful, whose greater scope for the apostolate represents for their pastors a source of particular support and a reason for special comfort.

Benedict XVI

Deus Caritas Est (*God Is Love*)

December 25, 2005

Charity as a Duty of the Church

21. A decisive step in the difficult search for ways of putting this fundamental ecclesial principle into practice is illustrated in the choice of the "seven," which marked the origin of the diaconal office (cf. Acts 6:5-6). In the early Church, in fact, with regard to the daily distribution to widows, a disparity had arisen between Hebrew speakers and Greek speakers. The Apostles, who had been entrusted primarily with "prayer" (the Eucharist and the liturgy) and the "ministry of the word," felt overburdened by "serving tables," so they decided to reserve to themselves the principal duty and to designate for the other task, also necessary in the Church, a group of seven persons. Nor was this group to carry out a purely mechanical work of distribution: they were to be men "full of the Spirit and of wisdom" (cf. Acts 6:1-6). In other words, the social service which

they were meant to provide was absolutely concrete, yet at the same time it was also a spiritual service; theirs was a truly spiritual office which carried out an essential responsibility of the Church, namely a well-ordered love of neighbor. With the formation of this group of seven, "*diaconia*"—the ministry of charity exercised in a communitarian, orderly way—became part of the fundamental structure of the Church.

23. Here it might be helpful to allude to the earliest legal structures associated with the service of charity in the Church. Toward the middle of the fourth century we see the development in Egypt of the "*diaconia*": the institution within each monastery responsible for all works of relief, that is to say, for the service of charity. By the sixth century this institution had evolved into a corporation with full juridical standing, which the civil authorities themselves entrusted with part of the grain for public distribution. In Egypt not only each monastery, but each individual Diocese eventually had its own *diaconia*; this institution then developed in both East and West. Pope Gregory the Great († 604) mentions the *diaconia* of Naples, while in Rome the *diaconiae* are documented from the seventh and eighth centuries. But charitable activity on behalf of the poor and suffering was naturally an essential part of the Church of Rome from the very beginning, based on the principles of Christian life given in the Acts of the Apostles. It found a vivid expression in the case of the deacon Lawrence († 258). The dramatic description of Lawrence's martyrdom was known to St. Ambrose († 397) and it provides a fundamentally authentic picture of the saint. As the one responsible for the care of the poor in Rome, Lawrence had been given a period of time, after the capture of the Pope and of Lawrence's fellow deacons, to collect the treasures of the Church and hand them over to the civil authorities. He distributed to the poor whatever funds were available and then presented to the authorities the poor themselves as the real treasure of the Church. Whatever historical reliability one attributes to these details, Lawrence has always remained present in the Church's memory as a great exponent of ecclesial charity.

Audience for the Permanent Deacons of the Diocese of Rome

February 18, 2006

Dear Roman Deacons,

I am particularly glad to meet you today on the twenty-fifth anniversary of the reestablishment of the permanent diaconate in the Diocese of Rome. I greet with affection the Cardinal Vicar, whom I thank for his words on behalf of you all. I also greet Bishop Vincenzo Apicella, until now in charge of the Diocesan Center for the Permanent Diaconate, and Msgr. Francesco Peracchi, Delegate of the Cardinal Vicar, who has supervised your formation for years. I offer my most cordial welcome to each one of you and to your families.

In a famous passage from his Letter to the Philippians, the Apostle Paul says that Christ "emptied himself, taking the form of a servant" (2:7). He, Christ, is the example at which to look. In the Gospel, he told his disciples he had come "not to be served but to serve" (cf. Mt 20:28). In particular, during the Last Supper, after having once again explained to the Apostles that he was among them "as one who serves" (Lk 22:27), he made the humble gesture of washing the feet of the Twelve, a duty of slaves, setting an example so that his disciples might imitate him in service and in mutual love.

Union with Christ, to be cultivated through prayer, sacramental life and in particular, Eucharistic adoration, is of the greatest importance to your ministry, if it is truly to testify to God's love. Indeed, as I wrote in my Encyclical *Deus Caritas Est*, "Love can be 'commanded' because it has first been given" (no. 14).

Dear deacons, accept with joy and gratitude the love the Lord feels for you and pours out in your lives, and generously give to people what you have received as a free gift. The Church of Rome has a long tradition of service to the city's poor. In these years new forms of poverty have emerged.

Indeed, many people have lost the meaning of life and do not possess a truth upon which to build their existence; a great many young people ask to meet men and women who can listen to and advise them in life's difficulties. Beside material poverty, we also find spiritual and cultural poverty.

Our Diocese, aware that the encounter with Christ, "gives life a new horizon and a decisive direction" (*Deus Caritas Est*, no. 1) is devoting special attention to the topic of the transmission of the faith.

Dear deacons, I am grateful to you for the services you carry out with great generosity in many parish communities of Rome, dedicating yourselves in particular to the ministries of Baptism and the family. By teaching Christ's Gospel, a faculty conferred upon you by the Bishop on the day of your ordination, you help parents who ask for Baptism for their children to reflect more deeply on the mystery of the divine life that has been given to us, and that of the Church, the great family of God.

Meanwhile, you also proclaim the truth about human love to engaged couples who desire to celebrate the sacrament of marriage, explaining that "marriage based on exclusive and definitive love becomes the icon of the relationship between God and his people and vice versa" (*Deus Caritas Est*, no. 11).

Many of you work in offices, hospitals and schools: in these contexts you are called to be servants of the Truth. By proclaiming the Gospel, you will be able to convey the Word that can illumine and give meaning to human work, to the suffering of the sick, and you will help the new generations to discover the beauty of the Christian faith.

Thus you will be deacons of the liberating Truth, and you will lead the inhabitants of this city to encounter Jesus Christ.

Welcoming the Redeemer into their lives is a source of deep joy for human beings, a joy that can bring peace even in moments of trial. Therefore, be servants of the Truth in order to be messengers of the joy that God desires to give to every human being.

However, it is not enough to proclaim the faith with words alone for, as the Apostle James recalls, "faith by itself, if it has no works, is dead" (Jas 2: 17). Thus, it is necessary to back up the proclamation of the Gospel with a practical witness of charity, so that "for the Church, charity is not a kind of welfare activity . . . but is a part of her nature, an indispensable expression of her very being" (*Deus Caritas Est*, no. 25).

The practice of charity has been part of the diaconal ministry from the outset: the "seven" of which the Acts of the Apostles speak were chosen "to serve at tables."

You, who belong to the Church of Rome, are the heirs of a long tradition, of which the Deacon Lawrence is a singularly fine and luminous example. Many of the poor who come knocking at the doors of parish communities to ask for the help they need to get through moments of serious difficulty often come from countries very far from Italy.

Welcome these brothers and sisters with great warmth and willingness, and do all you can to help them in their need, always remembering the Lord's words: "As you did it to one of the least of these my brethren, you did it to me" (Mt 25:40).

I express my gratitude to those of you who are employed in this silent and daily witness of charity. Indeed, through your service, the poor realize that they too belong to that great family of God's children: the Church.

Dear Roman deacons, by living and witnessing to God's infinite love, may you always be, in your ministry, at the service of building the Church as communion. In your work you are sustained by the affection and prayer of your families. Your vocation is a special grace for your family life, which in this way is called to be ever more open to the will of the Lord and to the needs of the Church. May the Lord reward the availability with which your wives and children accompany you in your service to the entire ecclesial community.

May Mary, the humble handmaid of the Lord who gave the Savior to the world, and the Deacon Lawrence who loved the Lord to the point of giving up his life for him, always accompany you with their intercession. With these sentiments, I wholeheartedly impart to each one of you the Apostolic Blessing, which I gladly extend to all your loved ones and to everyone you meet in your ministry.

Post-Synodal Apostolic Exhortation *Sacramentum Caritatis* (*On the Eucharist as the Source and Summit of the Church's Life and Mission*)

February 22, 2007

Gratitude and Hope

26. Finally, we need to have ever greater faith and hope in God's providence. Even if there is a shortage of priests in some areas, we must never lose confidence that Christ continues to inspire men to leave everything behind and to dedicate themselves totally to celebrating the sacred mysteries, preaching the Gospel and ministering to the flock. In this regard, I wish to express the gratitude of the whole Church for all those Bishops and priests who carry out their respective missions with fidelity, devotion and zeal. Naturally, the Church's gratitude also goes to

deacons, who receive the laying on of hands "not for priesthood but for service." As the Synod Assembly recommended, I offer a special word of thanks to those *Fidei Donum* priests who work faithfully and generously at building up the community by proclaiming the word of God and breaking the Bread of Life, devoting all their energy to serving the mission of the Church. Let us thank God for all those priests who have suffered even to the sacrifice of their lives in order to serve Christ. The eloquence of their example shows what it means to be a priest to the end. Theirs is a moving witness that can inspire many young people to follow Christ and to expend their lives for others, and thus to discover true life.

The Bishop, Celebrant Par Excellence

39. While it is true that the whole People of God participates in the eucharistic liturgy, a correct *ars celebrandi* necessarily entails a specific responsibility on the part of those who have received the sacrament of Holy Orders. Bishops, priests, and deacons, each according to his proper rank, must consider the celebration of the liturgy as their principal duty. Above all, this is true of the Diocesan Bishop: as "the chief steward of the mysteries of God in the particular Church entrusted to his care, he is the moderator, promoter, and guardian of the whole of its liturgical life." This is essential for the life of the particular Church, not only because communion with the Bishop is required for the lawfulness of every celebration within his territory, but also because he himself is the celebrant par excellence within his Diocese. It is his responsibility to ensure unity and harmony in the celebrations taking place in his territory. Consequently the Bishop must be "determined that the priests, the deacons, and the lay Christian faithful grasp ever more deeply the genuine meaning of the rites and liturgical texts, and thereby be led to an active and fruitful celebration of the Eucharist." I would ask that every effort be made to ensure that the liturgies which the Bishop celebrates in his Cathedral are carried out with complete respect for the *ars celebrandi*, so that they can be considered an example for the entire Diocese.

The Dismissal: "Ite, missa est"

51. Finally, I would like to comment briefly on the observations of the Synod Fathers regarding the dismissal at the end of the eucharistic celebration. After the blessing, the deacon or the priest dismisses the people with the words: *Ite, missa est.* These words help us to grasp the relationship between the Mass

just celebrated and the mission of Christians in the world. In antiquity, *missa* simply meant "dismissal." However in Christian usage it gradually took on a deeper meaning. The word "dismissal" has come to imply a "mission." These few words succinctly express the missionary nature of the Church. The People of God might be helped to understand more clearly this essential dimension of the Church's life, taking the dismissal as a starting point. In this context, it might also be helpful to provide new texts, duly approved, for the prayer over the people and the final blessing, in order to make this connection clear.

Participation and the Priestly Ministry

53. The beauty and the harmony of the liturgy find eloquent expression in the order by which everyone is called to participate actively. This entails an acknowledgment of the distinct hierarchical roles involved in the celebration. It is helpful to recall that active participation is not per se equivalent to the exercise of a specific ministry. The active participation of the laity does not benefit from the confusion arising from an inability to distinguish, within the Church's communion, the different functions proper to each one. There is a particular need for clarity with regard to the specific functions of the priest. He alone, and no other, as the tradition of the Church attests, presides over the entire eucharistic celebration, from the initial greeting to the final blessing. In virtue of his reception of Holy Orders, he represents Jesus Christ, the head of the Church, and, in a specific way, also the Church herself. Every celebration of the Eucharist, in fact, is led by the Bishop, "either in person or through priests who are his helpers." He is helped by a deacon, who has specific duties during the celebration: he prepares the altar, assists the priest, proclaims the Gospel, preaches the homily from time to time, reads the intentions of the Prayer of the Faithful, and distributes the Eucharist to the faithful. Associated with these ministries linked to the sacrament of Holy Orders, there are also other ministries of liturgical service which can be carried out in a praiseworthy manner by religious and properly trained laity.

Large-Scale Concelebrations

61. The Synod considered the quality of participation in the case of large-scale celebrations held on special occasions and involving not only a great number of the lay faithful, but also many concelebrating priests. On the one hand, it is easy to appreciate the importance of these moments, especially when the Bishop

himself celebrates, surrounded by his presbyterate and by the deacons. On the other hand, it is not always easy in such cases to give clear expression to the unity of the presbyterate, especially during the Eucharistic Prayer and the distribution of Holy Communion. Efforts need to be made lest these large-scale concelebrations lose their proper focus. This can be done by proper coordination and by arranging the place of worship so that priests and lay faithful are truly able to participate fully. It should be kept in mind, however, that here we are speaking of exceptional concelebrations, limited to extraordinary situations.

Sunday Assemblies in the Absence of a Priest

75. Rediscovering the significance of the Sunday celebration for the life of Christians naturally leads to a consideration of the problem of those Christian communities which lack priests and where, consequently, it is not possible to celebrate Mass on the Lord's Day. Here it should be stated that a wide variety of situations exists. The Synod recommended first that the faithful should go to one of the churches in their Diocese where the presence of a priest is assured, even when this demands a certain sacrifice. Wherever great distances make it practically impossible to take part in the Sunday Eucharist, it is still important for Christian communities to gather together to praise the Lord and to commemorate the Day set apart for him. This needs, however, to be accompanied by an adequate instruction about the difference between Mass and Sunday assemblies in the absence of a priest. The Church's pastoral care must be expressed in the latter case by ensuring that the liturgy of the word—led by a deacon or a community leader to whom this ministry has been duly entrusted by competent authority—is carried out according to a specific ritual prepared and approved for this purpose by the Bishops' Conferences. I reiterate that only Ordinaries may grant the faculty of distributing holy communion in such liturgies, taking account of the need for a certain selectiveness. Furthermore, care should be taken that these assemblies do not create confusion about the central role of the priest and the sacraments in the life of the Church. The importance of the role given to the laity, who should rightly be thanked for their generosity in the service of their communities, must never obscure the indispensable ministry of priests for the life of the Church. Hence care must be taken to ensure that such assemblies in the absence of a priest do not encourage ecclesiological visions incompatible with the truth of the Gospel and the Church's tradition. Rather,

they should be privileged moments of prayer for God to send holy priests after his own heart. It is touching, in this regard, to read the words of Pope John Paul II in his *Letter to Priests* for Holy Thursday 1979 about those places where the faithful, deprived of a priest by a dictatorial regime, would meet in a church or shrine, place on the altar a stole which they still kept and recite the prayers of the eucharistic liturgy, halting in silence "at the moment that corresponds to the transubstantiation," as a sign of how "ardently they desire to hear the words that only the lips of a priest can efficaciously utter." With this in mind, and considering the incomparable good which comes from the celebration of the Eucharist, I ask all priests to visit willingly and as often as possible the communities entrusted to their pastoral care, lest they remain too long without the sacrament of love.

Conclusions

94. Dear brothers and sisters, the Eucharist is at the root of every form of holiness, and each of us is called to the fullness of life in the Holy Spirit. How many saints have advanced along the way of perfection thanks to their eucharistic devotion! From St. Ignatius of Antioch to St. Augustine, from St. Anthony Abbot to St. Benedict, from St. Francis of Assisi to St. Thomas Aquinas, from St. Clare of Assisi to St. Catherine of Siena, from St. Paschal Baylon to St. Peter Julian Eymard, from St. Alphonsus Liguori to Blessed Charles de Foucauld, from St. John Mary Vianney to St. Thérèse of Lisieux, from St. Pius of Pietrelcina to Blessed Teresa of Calcutta, from Blessed Piergiorgio Frassati to Blessed Ivan Merz, to name only a few, holiness has always found its center in the sacrament of the Eucharist.

This most holy mystery thus needs to be firmly believed, devoutly celebrated and intensely lived in the Church. Jesus' gift of himself in the sacrament which is the memorial of his passion tells us that the success of our lives is found in our participation in the trinitarian life offered to us truly and definitively in him. The celebration and worship of the Eucharist enable us to draw near to God's love and to persevere in that love until we are united with the Lord whom we love. The offering of our lives, our fellowship with the whole community of believers and our solidarity with all men and women are essential aspects of that *logiké latreía*, spiritual worship, holy and pleasing to God (cf. Rom 12:1), which transforms every aspect of our human existence, to the glory of God. I therefore ask all pastors to spare no effort in promoting an authentically eucharistic

Christian spirituality. Priests, deacons and all those who carry out a eucharistic ministry should always be able to find in this service, exercised with care and constant preparation, the strength and inspiration needed for their personal and communal path of sanctification. I exhort the lay faithful, and families in particular, to find ever anew in the sacrament of Christ's love the energy needed to make their lives an authentic sign of the presence of the risen Lord. I ask all consecrated men and women to show by their eucharistic lives the splendor and the beauty of belonging totally to the Lord.

Recitation of the Holy Rosary and Meeting with Priests, Men Religious, Women Religious, Seminarians, and Deacons

To the Deacons of Brazil

May 12, 2007

Dear Deacons and Seminarians, you have a special place in the Pope's heart, and so I extend to you too my most fraternal and heartfelt greetings. Your exuberance, enthusiasm, idealism, and encouragement to face new challenges boldly serve to give the People of God a renewed openness, make the faithful more dynamic and help the community to grow, to progress, and to become more trusting, joyful, and optimistic. I thank you for the witness that you bear, working together with your Bishops in the pastoral activities of your dioceses. Always keep before your eyes the figure of Jesus, the Good Shepherd, who "came not to be served but to serve, and to give his life as a ransom for many" (Mt 20:28). Be like the first deacons of the Church: men of good reputation, filled with the Holy Spirit, with wisdom and with faith (cf. Acts 6:3-5).

Meeting with the Parish Priests and the Clergy of the Diocese of Rome

February 7, 2008

I am grateful for this testimony from one of Rome's more than one hundred deacons. I would also like to express my joy and gratitude to the Council for restoring this important ministry in the universal Church. I must say that when I became Archbishop of Munich I did not find more than perhaps three or four deacons. I have strongly encouraged this ministry because it seems to me that it enhances the riches of the Church's sacramental ministry. At the same time, it can also serve as a link between the secular world, the professional world and the world of the priestly ministry, since many deacons continue to carry out their professions and keep their posts—both important and also simple positions—while on Saturdays and Sundays they work in church. Thus, they witness in the contemporary world as well as in the world of work to the presence of the faith, the sacramental ministry and the diaconal dimension of the Sacrament of Orders. I consider this very important: the visibility of the diaconal dimension.

Every priest, of course, also continues to be a deacon and must always be aware of this dimension, for the Lord himself became our minister, our deacon. Recall the act of the washing of the feet, where it is explicitly shown that the Teacher, the Lord, acts as a deacon and wants those who follow him to be deacons and carry out this ministry for humanity, to the point that they even help us to wash the dirty feet of the people entrusted to our care. This dimension seems to me to be of paramount importance.

On this occasion, a small experience noted by Paul VI springs to mind—although it may not be quite relevant to our subject. Every day of the Council, the Gospel was enthroned. The Pontiff once told the masters of ceremonies that he himself would like to be the one who enthroned the Gospel. They said: No, this is a task for deacons and not for the Pope, the Supreme Pontiff, or the Bishops. He noted in his diary: But I am also a deacon, I am still a deacon, and I too would like to exercise my diaconal ministry by enthroning the Word of God. Thus, this concerns us all. Priests remain deacons and deacons clarify this diaconal dimension of our ministry in the Church and in the world. The liturgical enthronement of the Word of God every day during the Council was always an act of great importance: it told us who was the true Lord of that Assembly, it told us that the Word of God is on the throne and that we exercise the ministry to listen to and interpret this Word in order to offer it to others. To enthrone the Word of God, the living Word or Christ, in the world underlies the meaning of all we do. May it truly be he who governs our personal life and our life in the parishes.

You then asked me a question which, I have to say, somewhat exceeds my capacity: What should be the proper tasks of deacons in Rome? I am aware that the Cardinal Vicar is far better acquainted than I am with the real situation of the city and of the diocesan community of Rome. I think that one characteristic of the diaconal ministry is precisely the multiplicity of its applications.

A few years ago, in the International Theological Commission, we studied the diaconate at length in the Church's history and present. We discovered precisely this: there is no single profile. What must be done varies according to a person's formation and situation. Applications and implementation can vary widely but are naturally always in communion with the Bishop and parish. In these different situations, different possibilities are revealed which depend on the professional training these deacons may have possibly received: they may be employed in the cultural sector, so important in our day, or they may have a voice and important place in the educational sector. This year we are thinking precisely of the problem of education as central to our future, to the future of all humanity.

There is no doubt that in Rome the sector of charity was the original sector, because presbyteral titles and deaconries were centers of Christian charity. This context was fundamental in the city of Rome from the outset. In my Encyclical *Deus Caritas Est* I showed that not only are preaching and the liturgy essential to the Church and the Church's ministry, but that they also exist for the poor, for the needy, for the service of *caritas* in its multiple dimensions. I therefore hope that despite the differing situations, charity will continue in every age and every diocese to be a fundamental as well as a key dimension for the commitment of deacons, although not the only one. We see this in the primitive Church where the seven deacons were elected precisely to enable the Apostles to devote themselves to prayer, the liturgy and preaching. Even if Stephen later found he was required to preach to Hellenists and to Greek-speaking Jews, the field of preaching was in this way extended. He was conditioned, we can say, by the cultural situations in which he had a voice in order to make the Word of God present in this field in such a way as also to extend as far as possible the universality of Christian witness. Thus, he opened the door to St. Paul, who was a witness to his stoning and subsequently, in a certain sense, his successor in the universalization of the Word of God.

CHAPTER VI

The Diaconate in the Documents of the Holy See

CONGREGATION FOR CATHOLIC EDUCATION (FOR SEMINARIES AND EDUCATIONAL INSTITUTIONS)

Circular Letter on the Diaconate

July 16, 1969

The Circular Letter of the Congregation for Catholic Education is the first of the preliminary documents for the formation of permanent deacons. In it, the indispensible elements of the deacon's formation are indicated in brief. Contextually, it underlines that the proposed action should be adjusted to the varying situations, the level of the candidates' culture, and the ministry that they will likely be called to undertake, all according to the judgment of the various episcopal conferences.

To the Most Reverend Pontifical Representatives

Most Reverend Monsignor,

As is already known to Your Most Reverend Lordship, with his *Motu Proprio, Sacrum Diaconatus Ordinem* (*General Norms for Restoring the Permanent Diaconate in the Latin Church*), and according to the wishes expressed in the Second Vatican Council, the Holy Father granted permission for the Latin Church to restore the permanent diaconate.

Since some episcopal conferences have asked the Holy See for such a permission for their own nations, it is urgent and necessary to define some norms for preparing candidates for the permanent diaconate.

The first step to carry out on the part of each episcopal conference should consist—in cases where this is not already done—in naming a commission of experts. This commission shall study the problem in depth according to the needs of that nation, in order to examine if there are valid reasons for introducing the new institution and in what way it may be most effectively implemented.

It would be best in such a study to keep some basic principles in mind, already indicated in the aforementioned *Motu Proprio*. Finding ourselves before a new problem for our times, establishing *a priori* a *ratio studiorum* and formation program for candidates to the permanent diaconate is not without its difficulties.

First and foremost, it is necessary to determine the functions proper to the deacon, intermediary between the priest and the faithful, functions that are outlined differently by the various episcopal conferences as already took place during the discussion in the Council Hall.

Furthermore, it must be remembered that candidates to the diaconate can be of two types, as is provided by the Council and by the *Motu Proprio*: young men vowing celibacy and older men already married and having a profession or other form of employment. Another difference is the destination of deacons: the same formation cannot be required of deacons destined for mission territory or for developing countries as is of those exercising their functions in more civilized nations with a rather high culture.

It is left to each episcopal conference, therefore, to determine the type—or the types—of diaconate that most fit the needs of the country and, consequently, the preparation that should be given to them.

Having considered the various sorts of formation, it follows that the study programs should also differ.

For the young men vowing celibacy, thought should be given to creating special institutes with well-organized curricula and spiritual formation that prepares the candidates for the future diaconal ministry. On the other hand, for men who are already married, courses should be compatible with their work duties, and it may thus be convenient to organize more or less prolonged nightly or weekly courses. For this second category of candidates, one must take into account the level of learning already acquired, and, in this case, the courses can be more accelerated. For others who have barely undertaken basic courses, preparation will certainly require more time. In any case, a hurried or superficial preparation must be absolutely avoided since the duties of deacons, according to what is established in the *Lumen Gentium* (*Dogmatic Constitution on the Church*) (no. 29) and in the *Motu Proprio* (no. 22), are of such importance as to demand a solid, efficient formation. Deacons, in fact, should prepare catechumens for Baptism; explain and comment on the Word of God with preaching; prepare the faithful for Matrimony and observe all that regulates the celebration of that sacrament; and fill in for the priest, when he is missing, in preparing the faithful for death and administering Viaticum to them.

All of this entails a doctrinal formation that is above that of a simple catechist and, in some way, analogous to that of the priest.

The courses should then include the study of:

a. Sacred Scripture, with all of the background that makes the deacons able to comprehend and explain the Word of God to the faithful in a way that leads to the development of their spiritual life. Therefore, the deacon should be capable, in the absence of the priest, of giving the homily and presiding over the Liturgy of the Word;
b. Dogma. Such study can be similar to that provided for in the Institute of Catechesis, destined for non-priestly religious. We can give as an example that undertaken by the Brothers of the Christian Schools or by the graduate courses in religion taken by educated laity. The structure should also be largely biblical and kerygmatic. It is certainly possible to avoid the largely controversial aspects, making mention of these problems, however, by reading passages chosen from the Fathers of the Church, from theologians, and from ascetical authors.
c. Moral theology, concerning the deepening of individual, social, and political morality, at least at the level of catechists or of courses that deal with the writings of Catholic Action;
d. Canon law, especially regarding Matrimony, and understanding the pastoral care to give for preparing the faithful for such a sacrament;
e. Liturgy, possibly within the framework of the dogmatic courses. It should also include concepts surrounding the development of sacred ceremonies;
f. Specialized fields that will prepare the candidate for certain ministerial activities, such fields as psychology, catechetical training, public speaking, sacred chant, setting up Catholic organizations, church administration, updating of sacramental records for Baptism, Confirmation, Matrimony, funerals, etc.

Although future deacons should not be required to take everything demanded of aspirants to the priesthood (such as Church history, a complete course in canon law, philosophy), in certain regions—and especially those destined for urban settings—it would still be best for them to complete their cultural formation with those disciplines that their specific, local situation requires, for example: the study of pagan religions; ecumenism; a full survey of philosophical matters, especially those in vogue; the study of certain economic problems, politics, etc.

It is up to the bishops of every nation to decide on the fields of study for diaconal ministry in their own territory.

Moreover, it should be kept in mind that cultural formation does not end with diaconal ordination, but that a "permanent" or ongoing formation should be provided, one with courses to keep them up to date and participating in the study weeks set aside for priests.

May Your Most Reverend Lordship have the kindness to present these indications of ours to the president of the episcopal conference of this nation so that we may arrive—should the bishops deem it fit—at the creation of the aforementioned commission of experts, which will be of service to the same conference in studying this important matter. Furthermore, Your Lordship, when you make known to said president all that was stated above, kindly ask him to share with us what has currently been established in this country concerning the permanent diaconate, and, above all, concerning the initiatives that may be taken for preparing future deacons.

We also venture to cordially invite you, Most Reverend Monsignor, to keep us constantly informed of the question, because this sacred dicastery wishes to be kept abreast of all that happens in this nation with regard to this new sector that is opening up in the organization of the Church.

Thanking you from this time forward for the inconvenience we bring you, with heartfelt esteem and respect, we remain your most devoted in the Lord.[1]

1 [The 1969 Circular Letter is a translation of the Italian text.]

CODEX IURIS CANONICI (*CODE OF CANON LAW*)

February 22, 1983

With the Apostolic Constitution Sacrae Disciplinae Leges (For the Promulgation of the New Code of Canon Law), *Pope John Paul II, on January 25, 1983, promulgated the new Code of Canon Law. In regard to the permanent diaconate, the new code largely drew on the norms of the previous documents: the Motu Proprio* Sacrum Diaconatus Ordinem (General Norms for Restoring the Permanent Diaconate in the Latin Church) *and the Motu Proprio* Ad Pascendum (Apostolic Letter Establishing Some Norms Concerning the Sacred Order of Deacons).

Everything that is stated about the Sacrament of Holy Orders in general applies to the diaconate while some canons deal in particular with the permanent diaconate.

Quoted below are two introductory canons on the Sacrament of Holy Orders: the canon that pertains to the spiritual life of clerics, i.e., of ordained ministers, insofar as it is applicable to deacons, with some references to them; and then canons that expressly pertain to the permanent diaconate.

Can. 1008. By divine institution, the sacrament of orders establishes some among the Christian faithful as sacred ministers through an indelible character which marks them. They are consecrated and designated, each according to his grade, to nourish the people of God, fulfilling in the person of Christ the Head the functions of teaching, sanctifying, and governing.

Can. 1009 §1. The orders are the episcopate, the presbyterate, and the diaconate.

§2. They are conferred by the imposition of hands and the consecratory prayer which the liturgical books prescribe for the individual grades.

Can. 276 §1. In leading their lives, clerics are bound in a special way to pursue holiness since, having been consecrated to God by a new title in the reception of orders, they are dispensers of the mysteries of God in the service of His people.

§2. In order to be able to pursue this perfection:

1° they are first of all to fulfill faithfully and tirelessly the duties of the pastoral ministry;
2° they are to nourish their spiritual life from the two-fold table of sacred scripture and the Eucharist; therefore, priests are earnestly invited to offer the eucharistic sacrifice daily and deacons to participate in its offering daily;
3° priests and deacons aspiring to the presbyterate are obliged to carry out the liturgy of the hours daily according to the proper and approved liturgical books; permanent deacons, however, are to carry out the same to the extent defined by the conference of bishops;
4° they are equally bound to make time for spiritual retreats according to the prescripts of particular law;
5° they are urged to engage in mental prayer regularly, to approach the sacrament of penance frequently, to honor the Virgin Mother of God with particular veneration, and to use other common and particular means of sanctification.

Can. 236. According to the prescripts of the conference of bishops, those aspiring to the permanent diaconate are to be formed to nourish a spiritual life and instructed to fulfill correctly the duties proper to that order:

1° young men are to live at least three years in some special house unless the diocesan bishop has established otherwise for grave reasons;
2° men of a more mature age, whether celibate or married, are to spend three years in a program defined by the conference of bishops.

Can. 287 §1. Most especially, clerics are always to foster the peace and harmony based on justice which are to be observed among people.

§2. They are not to have an active part in political parties and in governing labor unions unless, in the judgment of competent ecclesiastical authority, the protection of the rights of the Church or the promotion of the common good requires it.

Can. 288. The prescripts of cc. 284, 285, §§3 and 4, 286, and 287, §2 do not bind permanent deacons unless particular law establishes otherwise.

Can. 1035 §1. Before anyone is promoted to the permanent or transitional diaconate, he is required to have received the ministries of lector and acolyte and to have exercised them for a suitable period of time.

Can. 1031 §2. A candidate for the permanent diaconate who is not married is not to be admitted to the diaconate until after completing at least the twenty-fifth year of age; one who is married, not until after completing at least the thirty-fifth year of age and with the consent of his wife.

§3. The conference of bishops is free to establish norms which require an older age for the presbyterate and the permanent diaconate.

§4. A dispensation of more than a year from the age required according to the norm of §§1 and 2 is reserved to the Apostolic See.

CATECHISM OF THE CATHOLIC CHURCH (2ND EDITION)

September 8, 1997

I. The Hierarchical Constitution of the Church

Why the Ecclesial Ministry?

875. "How are they to believe in him of whom they have never heard? And how are they to hear without a preacher? And how can men preach unless they are sent?" (Rom 10:14-15). No one—no individual and no community—can proclaim the Gospel to himself: "Faith comes from what is heard" (Rom 10:17). No one can give himself the mandate and the mission to proclaim the Gospel. The one sent by the Lord does not speak and act on his own authority, but by virtue of Christ's authority; not as a member of the community, but speaking to it in the name of Christ. No one can bestow grace on himself; it must be given and offered. This fact presupposes ministers of grace, authorized and empowered by Christ. From him, bishops and priests receive the mission and faculty ("the sacred power") to act *in persona Christi Capitis*; deacons receive the strength to serve the people of God in the *diaconia* of liturgy, word and charity, in communion with the bishop and his presbyterate. The ministry in which Christ's

emissaries do and give by God's grace what they cannot do and give by their own powers, is called a "sacrament" by the Church's tradition. Indeed, the ministry of the Church is conferred by a special sacrament.

The Episcopal College and Its Head, the Pope

886. "The individual *bishops* are the visible source and foundation of unity in their own particular Churches" (LG, no. 23). As such, they "exercise their pastoral office over the portion of the People of God assigned to them" (LG, no. 23), assisted by priests and deacons. But, as a member of the episcopal college, each bishop shares in the concern for all the Churches (cf. CD, no. 3). The bishops exercise this care first "by ruling well their own Churches as portions of the universal Church," and so contributing "to the welfare of the whole Mystical Body, which, from another point of view, is a corporate body of Churches" (LG, no. 23). They extend it especially to the poor (cf. Gal 2:10), to those persecuted for the faith, as well as to missionaries who are working throughout the world.

The Governing Office

896. The Good Shepherd ought to be the model and "form" of the bishop's pastoral office. Conscious of his own weaknesses, "the bishop . . . can have compassion for those who are ignorant and erring. He should not refuse to listen to his subjects whose welfare he promotes as of his very own children. . . . The faithful . . . should be closely attached to the bishop as the Church is to Jesus Christ, and as Jesus Christ is to the Father" (LG, no. 27 §2).

"Let all follow the bishop, as Jesus Christ follows his Father, and the college of presbyters as the apostles; respect the deacons as you do God's law. Let no one do anything concerning the Church in separation from the bishop" (St. Ignatius of Antioch, *Ad Smyrnaeos*, 8,1; *Apostolic Fathers*, II/2, 309).

939. Helped by the priests, their co-workers, and by the deacons, the bishops have the duty of authentically teaching the faith, celebrating divine worship, above all the Eucharist, and guiding their Churches as true pastors. Their responsibility also includes concern for all the Churches, with and under the Pope.

V. Who Can Baptize?

1256. The ordinary ministers of Baptism are the bishop and priest and, in the Latin Church, also the deacon (cf. CIC, c. 861 §1; CCEO, c. 677 §1). In case of necessity, anyone, even a non-baptized person, with the required intention, can baptize (CIC, c. 861 §2), by using the Trinitarian baptismal formula. The intention required is to will to do what the Church does when she baptizes. The Church finds the reason for this possibility in the universal saving will of God and the necessity of Baptism for salvation (cf. 1 Tm 2:4).

PONTIFICAL COUNCIL FOR THE PROMOTION OF CHRISTIAN UNITY

Directory for the Application of Principles and Norms on Ecumenism

March 25, 1993

I. The Search for Christian Unity

The Church and Its Unity in the Plan of God

12. The People of God in its common life of faith and sacraments is served by ordained ministers: bishops, priests and deacons. Thus united in the three-fold bond of faith, sacramental life and hierarchical ministry, the whole People of God comes to be what the tradition of faith from the New Testament onward has always called *koinonia*/communion. This is a key concept which inspired the ecclesiology of the Second Vatican Council and to which recent teaching of the magisterium has given great importance.

III. Ecumenical Formation in the Catholic Church

B. Formation of Those Engaged in Pastoral Work

1. Ordained Ministers

70. Among the principal duties of every future ordained minister is to shape his own personality, to the extent possible, in such a way as will serve his mission of helping others to meet Christ. In this perspective, the candidate for the ministry needs to develop fully those human qualities which make a person acceptable and credible among people, checking regularly his own language and capacity for dialogue so as to acquire an authentically ecumenical disposition. If this is essential for one who has the office of teacher and shepherd in a particular Church, like the Bishop, or one who as a priest takes care of souls, it is no less important for the deacon, and in a particular way for the permanent deacon, who is called to serve the community of the faithful.

a-2) The Ecumenical Dimension of Theological Disciplines in General

76. Ecumenical openness is a constitutive dimension of the formation of future priests and deacons: "Sacred theology and other branches of knowledge, especially those of a historical nature, must be taught with due regard for the ecumenical point of view so that they may correspond as exactly as possible with the facts." The ecumenical dimension in theological formation should not be limited to different categories of teaching. Because we are talking about interdisciplinary teaching—and not only "pluridisciplinary"—this will involve cooperation between the professors concerned and reciprocal coordination. In each subject, even in those which are fundamental, the following aspects may be suitably emphasized:

a. The elements of the Christian patrimony of truth and holiness which are common to all Churches and ecclesial Communities, even though these are sometimes presented according to varying theological expressions

b. The riches of liturgy, spirituality and doctrine proper to each communion, but which can help Christians toward a deeper knowledge of the nature of the Church

c. Points of disagreement on matters of faith and morals which can nonetheless encourage deeper exploration of the Word of God and lead to distinguishing real from apparent contradictions.

D. Permanent Formation

91. Doctrinal formation and learning experience are not limited to the period of formation, but ask for a continuous "*aggiornamento*" of the ordained ministers and pastoral workers, in view of the continual evolution within the ecumenical movement.

Bishops and religious superiors, when organizing pastoral renewal programs for clergy—through meetings, conferences, retreats, days of recollection or study of pastoral problems—should give careful attention to ecumenism along the following lines:

a. Systematic instruction of priests, religious, deacons and laity on the present state of the ecumenical movement, so that they may be able to introduce the ecumenical viewpoint into preaching, catechesis, prayer and Christian life in general. If it seems suitable and possible, it would be good to invite a minister of another Church to expound its tradition or speak on pastoral problems which are often common to all.

IV. Communion in Life and Spiritual Activity Among the Baptized

B. Sharing Spiritual Activities and Resources

b) Sharing Sacramental Life with Christians of Other Churches and Ecclesial Communities

134. In the Catholic Eucharistic Liturgy, the homily which forms part of the liturgy itself is reserved to the priest or deacon, since it is the presentation of the mysteries of faith and the norms of Christian living in accordance with Catholic teaching and tradition.

C. Mixed Marriages

146. It is the abiding responsibility of all, especially priests and deacons and those who assist them in pastoral ministry, to provide special instruction and support for the Catholic party in living his or her faith as well as for the couples in mixed marriages both in the preparation for the marriage, in its sacramental celebration and for the life together that follows the marriage ceremony. This pastoral care should take into account the concrete spiritual condition of each partner, their formation in their faith and their practice of it. At the same time, respect should be shown for the particular circumstances of each couple's situation, the conscience of each partner and the holiness of the state of sacramental marriage itself. Where judged useful, diocesan Bishops, Synods of Eastern Catholic Churches or Episcopal Conferences could draw up more specific guidelines for this pastoral care.

148. In preparing the necessary marriage preparation programs, the priest or deacon, and those who assist him, should stress the positive aspects of what the couple share together as Christians in the life of grace, in faith, hope and love, along with the other interior gifts of the Holy Spirit. Each party, while continuing to be faithful to his or her Christian commitment and to the practice of it, should seek to foster all that can lead to unity and harmony, without minimizing real differences and while avoiding an attitude of religious indifference.

157. With the previous authorization of the local Ordinary, and if invited to do so, a Catholic priest or deacon may attend or participate in some way in the celebration of mixed marriages, in situations where the dispensation from canonical form has been granted. In these cases, there may be only one ceremony in which the presiding person receives the marriage vows. At the invitation of this celebrant, the Catholic priest or deacon may offer other appropriate prayers, read from the Scriptures, give a brief exhortation and bless the couple.

CONGREGATION FOR DIVINE WORSHIP AND THE DISCIPLINE OF THE SACRAMENTS

Circular Letter *(June 6, 1997)*

To the Diocesan Ordinaries and General Superiors of the Institutes of Consecrated Life and the Societies of Apostolic Life

On the dispensation from *diriment impediment* for contracting a new marriage and remaining in ministry on the part of widowed permanent deacons (CIC, cc. 1087-1088).

6. Following both the new discipline surrounding the permanent diaconate and the norms put forth by the Holy See and by numerous episcopates relative to the formation, lifestyle, and ministerial duties of deacons, there is as of yet a difficulty posed by the impediment for "married permanent deacons who become widowed after ordination" to contract another marriage, the result being the canonical nullity of a possible second marriage contracted after ordination.[1]

7. For some time now, we have had to take note that, on the basis of such a prohibition, grave difficulties arise for those who, having become widowers after ordination, are available to remain in ministry.

8. This dicastery, in order to implement a new practice allowing for dispensation from the preclusion of canon 1087, which previously required three cumulative, simultaneous conditions as valid exceptions, has petitioned and obtained from the Holy Father that only one of the following conditions may be sufficient for obtaining said dispensation:

- The great and proven usefulness of the deacon's ministry for the pertinent diocese
- The presence of very young children in need of motherly care

1 Cf. Paul VI, Apostolic Letter *Ad Pascendum* (August 15, 1972), no. VI: *l.c.* 539; CIC, c. 1087 compared with c. 1078 §2, 1.

- The presence of aging parents or in-laws in need of assistance

9. The Cardinal Secretary of State, in letter no. 402.629 from February 27, 1997, communicated that the Holy Father, on February 10, 1997, had approved of the new criteria cited above concerning dispensation from celibacy for priests younger than forty years of age; and with the letter of March 22, 1997, of like number, consent was given for the new conditions providing for dispensation in favor of deacons who became widowers, providing that this Circular Letter, with the new dispensations to be brought to their attention, should be sent to diocesan and religious ordinaries.

10. Diocesan and religious ordinaries are therefore asked to duly consider the aforementioned guidelines when forwarding requests for dispensation to this dicastery.[2]

Jorge Medina Estevez
Pro-prefect Archbishop

Gerardo Majella
Agnelo Secretary Archbishop

2 [The 1997 Circular Letter is a translation of the Italian text.]

CONGREGATION FOR CATHOLIC EDUCATION

Pontifical Work for Ecclesiastical Vocations

New Vocations for a New Europe: Final Document of the Congress on Vocations to the Priesthood and to Consecrated Life in Europe

January 6, 1998

New Evangelization

12. All of this opens up new directions and requires that a new impulse be given to the very process of evangelization of the old and the new Europe. For some time now the Church and the present Pope have been asking for a profound renewal of the contents and method of proclaiming the Gospel, "in order to make the Church of the twentieth century ever more able to proclaim the Gospel to the people of the twentieth century." And, as we have been reminded by the Congress, "there is no need to be afraid of being in a period of passing from one shore to the other."

The Icon of the Early Church

24. Historical situations change, but the point of reference in the life of the believer and the believing community remains the same, that point of reference that is represented by the Word of God, especially where it recounts the events of the early Church. These events of the early Church and their way of living them constitute for us the *exemplum*, the model for being Church. This is true also in regard to the pastoral care of vocations. We shall examine only some essential and particularly exemplary elements as they are proposed to us in the Acts of the Apostles, at the time when the early Church was numerically very poor and weak. The pastoral care of vocations is the same age as the Church; it arose at the same time as the Church, in that poverty unexpectedly inhabited by the Spirit.

At the dawn of this singular history, that is the history of all of us, *there is the promise of the Holy Spirit*, made by Jesus before He ascended to the Father.

"It is not for you to know times or seasons which the Father has fixed by his own authority. But you shall receive power when the Holy Spirit has come upon you; and you shall be my witnesses in Jerusalem and Samaria and to the end of the earth" (Acts 1:7-8). The Apostles gather together in the cenacle "and *with one accord devoted themselves to prayer* . . . with Mary, the mother of Jesus" (1:14), and immediately they act to fill the post left vacant by Judas with another chosen from among those who had been with Jesus from the beginning: so that "he might become with us a *witness to His resurrection*" (1:22). And the promise is fulfilled: the Holy Spirit descends with riotous effect and fills the house and the lives of those who before had been timid and fearful, with a rumble, a wind, a fire . . . "And they began to speak in other tongues . . . *and each one heard them speaking in his own language*" (2:4, 6). And "Peter stood up . . . raised his voice, and proclaimed to them" about the history of salvation (2:14), an address that cuts those that hear it "to the heart" and provokes the decisive question about life: "What shall we do?" (2:37).

At this point the Book of the Acts [of the Apostles] describes the life of the early community, which was marked by some essential elements, such as their diligence in listening to the teachings of the Apostles, brotherly union, the breaking of bread, prayer, sharing of material goods; but at the same time the feelings and goods of the Spirit (cf. 2:42-48).

In the meantime, Peter and the Apostles continue to work wonders in the name of Jesus and to proclaim the *kerygma* of salvation, regularly risking their lives but always supported by the community, within which the believers form "one heart and soul" (4:32). In it, as well, needs begin to grow and diversify, and so deacons are instituted to meet these needs of the community, even the material needs, especially of the weakest (cf. 6:1-7).

Vocational Pastoral Itineraries

27. The biblical icon around which we have articulated our reflection allows us to make a further advance, moving from theoretical principles to the identification of some vocational pastoral programs.

Service of Charity

This is one of the most typical functions of the ecclesial community. It consists in living the experience of freedom in Christ, at that supreme point which is constituted by service. "Whoever would be great among you must be your servant" (Mt 20:26), and "if anyone would be first, he must be last of all and servant of all" (Mk 9:35). In the early Church it seems that this lesson was very quickly learned, given that service appears as one of the structural components of it, to the point that deacons are instituted precisely for "service at table."

Rome, January 6, 1998, the Epiphany of the Lord.

Pio Card. Laghi
President

José Saraiva Martins
Titular Archbishop of Tuburnica,
Vice-President

CONGREGATION FOR CATHOLIC EDUCATION, CONGREGATION FOR THE CLERGY

The two documents Ratio Fundamentalis Institutionalis Diaconorum Permanentium (Basic Norms for the Formation of Permanent Deacons) *and the* Directory for the Ministry and Life of Permanent Deacons *were promulgated by the Congregation for the Clergy and by the Congregation for Catholic Education, respectively. While each conserved its own identity and specific juridical value, they were published together, drawing on one another and mutually integrating with each other by reason of their logical continuity. For this very reason, they were preceded by a joint declaration and introduction.*

The documents respond to the urgency felt in many places to clarify and regulate a wide range of experiences, whether on the level of discernment and preparation or that of implementation in ministry and permanent formation.

The need was also motivated by the fact that, after the restoration of the diaconate called for by Vatican II, many ecclesiastical regions saw a veritable explosion *of diaconal vocations, a sign of the enthusiasm and hopes it had awakened.*

Basic Norms for the Formation of Permanent Deacons

Directory for the Ministry and Life of Permanent Deacons

Joint Declaration and Introduction

Joint Declaration

The permanent Diaconate, restored by the Second Vatican Council, in complete continuity with ancient Tradition and the specific decision of the Council of Trent, has flourished in these last decades in many parts of the Church—with promising results, especially for the urgent missionary work of new evangelization. The Holy See and many Episcopates, in promoting this ecclesial experience, have continually afforded norms and guidelines for the life and formation of deacons. The growth of the permanent Diaconate, however, now gives rise to a need for a certain unity of direction and clarification of concepts, as well as for practical encouragement and more clearly defined pastoral objectives. The total reality of the Diaconate—embracing its fundamental doctrinal vision, discernment of vocation, as well as the life, ministry, spirituality and formation of deacons—calls for a review of the journey thus far made, so as to arrive at a global vision of this grade of Sacred Orders corresponding to the desire and intention of the Second Vatican Council.

Following the publication of the *Ratio Fundamentalis Institutionis Sacerdotalis* on priestly formation and the *Directory on the Ministry and Life of Priests*, the Congregation for Catholic Education and the Congregation for the Clergy, completing the treatment of what pertains to the Diaconate and the Priesthood, the objects of their competence, now wish to devote particular consideration to the subject of the permanent Diaconate. Both Congregations, having consulted the Episcopate throughout the world and numerous experts, discussed the permanent Diaconate at their Plenary Assemblies in November 1995. The Cardinal Members together with the Archbishop and Bishop Members carefully considered the various consultations and numerous submissions made in the matter. As a result, the final texts of the *Ratio Fundamentalis Institutionis Diaconorum*

Permanentium and the *Directory for the Ministry and Life of Permanent Deacons* were drafted by the two Congregations and faithfully reflect points and proposals from every geographical area represented at the Plenary Assemblies. The work of both Plenaries illustrated convergence on many points and agreement concerning the clear need for greater uniformity in training so as to ensure the pastoral effectiveness of the Sacred Ministry in confronting the challenges which face it on the eve of the Third Millenium. Therefore, both Dicasteries were requested to undertake the drafting of these documents which are published simultaneously and prefaced by a single, comprehensive introduction. The *Ratio Fundamentalis Institutionis Diaconorum Permanentium*, prepared by the Congregation for Catholic Education, is intended not only as a guideline for the formation of permanent Deacons but also as a directive of which due account is to be taken by the Episcopal Conferences when preparing their respective "Rationes." As with the *Ratio Fundamentalis Institutionis Sacerdotalis*, the Congregation offers this aid to the various Episcopates to facilitate them in discharging adequately the prescriptions of canon 236 of the *Code of Canon Law* and to ensure for the Church, unity, earnestness and completeness in the formation of permanent Deacons.

The *Directory for the Ministry and Life of Permanent Deacons*, as in the case of the *Directory on the Ministry and Life of Priests*, has, together with its hortative character, juridically binding force where its norms "recall disciplinary norms of the *Code of Canon Law*" or "determine with regard to the manner of applying universal laws of the Church, explicitate their doctrinal basis and inculcate or solicit their faithful observance."[1] In these specific cases, it is to be regarded as a formal, general, executory Decree (cf. c. 32).

While retaining their proper identity and their own specific juridical quality, both of these documents, published with the authority of the respective Dicasteries, mutually reflect and complete each other by virtue of their logical continuity. It is to be hoped that they will be presented, received and applied everywhere in their entirety. The introduction, here conjointly published with these documents, is intended as a reference point and a normative source for both, while remaining an inextricable part of each document.

The introduction restricts itself to the historical and pastoral aspects of the permanent Diaconate, with specific reference to the practical dimension of

1 Cf. Pontifical Council for the Interpretation of Legislative Texts, *Chiarimenti circa il valore vincolante dell'art. 66 del Direttorio per il Ministero e la Vita dei Presbiteri* (October 22, 1994), in "*Sacrum Ministerium*" 2 (1995), 263.

formation and ministry. The doctrinal reasons for the arguments advanced are drawn from those expressed in the documents of the Second Vatican Council and subsequent Magisterium.

The documents produced here are intended as a response to a widely felt need to clarify and regulate the diversity of approaches adopted in experiments conducted up to now, whether at the level of discernment and training or at that of active ministry and ongoing formation. In this way it will be possible to ensure a certain stability of approach which takes account of legitimate plurality and in turn guarantees that indispensable unity, necessary for the success of the ministry of the permanent Diaconate which has been fruitful and which, at the threshold of the Third Millenium, promises to make an important contribution to New Evangelization.

The directives contained in the following documents pertain to permanent deacons of the secular clergy, although many, with due adaptation, may also be applied to permanent deacons who are members of institutes of consecrated life or societies of apostolic life.

Introduction[2]

I. The Ordained Ministry

1. "In order to shepherd the People of God and to increase its numbers without cease, Christ the Lord set up in the Church a variety of offices which aim at the good of the whole body. The holders of office, who are invested with a sacred power, are, in fact, dedicated to promoting the interests of their brethren, so that all who belong to the People of God, and are consequently endowed with true Christian dignity, may, through their free and well-ordered efforts towards a common goal, attain to salvation."[3]

The Sacrament of Orders "configures the recipient to Christ by a special grace of the Holy Spirit, so that he may serve as Christ's instrument for his Church. By ordination he is enabled to act as a representative of Christ, Head of the Church, in his triple office of priest, prophet and king."[4]

---

2 This introduction is common both to the "Ratio" and to the "Directory." It should always be included in both documents in the event of their being printed separately.

3 LG, no. 18.

4 CCC, no. 1581.

Through the Sacrament of Orders, the mission entrusted by Christ to his Apostles continues to be exercised in the Church until the end of time. It is thus the sacrament of apostolic ministry.[5] The sacramental act of ordination surpasses mere election, designation or delegation by the community, because it confers a gift of the Holy Spirit enabling the exercise of sacred power which can only come from Christ himself through his Church.[6] "The one sent by the Lord does not speak and act of his own authority, but by virtue of Christ's authority; not as a member of the community but speaking to it in the name of Christ. No one can bestow grace on himself; it must be given and offered. This fact presupposes ministers of grace, authorized and empowered by Christ."[7]

The sacrament of apostolic ministry comprises three degrees. Indeed "the divinely instituted ecclesiastical ministry is exercised in different degrees by those who even from ancient times have been called bishops, priests and deacons."[8]

Together with priests and deacons as their helpers, the bishops have received pastoral charge of the community, and preside in God's stead over the flock of which they are shepherds inasmuch as they are teachers of doctrine, priests of sacred worship and ministers of pastoral government.[9]

The sacramental nature of ecclesial ministry is such that it has "intrinsically linked . . . *its character of service*. Entirely dependent on Christ who gives mission and authority, ministers are truly 'slaves of Christ' (cf. Rom 1:11), in the image of him who freely took 'the form of a slave'" for us (cf. Phil 2:7).[10]

The sacred ministry also has a *collegial form*[11] and a *personal character*[12] by which "sacramental ministry in the Church . . . is at once a collegial and a personal service, exercised in the name of Christ."[13]

II. The Diaconate

2. The service of deacons in the Church is documented from apostolic times. A strong tradition, attested already by St. Ireneus and influencing the liturgy

---

5 CCC, no. 1536.
6 CCC, no. 1538.
7 CCC, no. 875.
8 LG, no. 28.
9 Cf. LG, no. 20; CIC, c. 375 §1.
10 CCC, no. 876.
11 Cf. CCC, no. 877.
12 Cf. CCC, no. 878.
13 CCC, no. 879.

of ordination, sees the origin of the diaconate in the institution of the "seven" mentioned in the Acts of the Apostles (6:1-6). Thus, at the initial grade of sacred hierarchy are deacons, whose ministry has always been greatly esteemed in the Church.[14] St. Paul refers to them and to the bishops in the exordium of his *Epistle to the Philippians* (cf. Phil 1:1), while in his first *Epistle to Timothy* he lists the qualities and virtues which they should possess so as to exercise their ministry worthily (cf. 1 Tm 3:8-13).[15]

From its outset, patristic literature witnesses to this hierarchical and ministerial structure in the Church, which includes the diaconate. St. Ignatius of Antioch[16] considers a Church without bishop, priest or deacon, unthinkable. He underlines that the ministry of deacons is nothing other than "the ministry of Jesus Christ, who was with the Father before time began and who appeared at the end of time." They are not deacons of food and drink but ministers of the Church of God. The *Didascalia Apostolorum*,[17] the Fathers of subsequent centuries, the various Councils[18] as well as ecclesiastical praxis[19] all confirm the continuity and development of this revealed datum.

Up to the fifth century the Diaconate flourished in the western Church, but after this period, it experienced, for various reasons, a slow decline which ended in its surviving only as an intermediate stage for candidates preparing for priestly ordination.

14 Cf. LG, no. 29; Paul VI, Apostolic Letter *Ad Pascendum* (August 15, 1972), *AAS* 64 (1972), 534.

15 Moreover, he also describes several of the sixty who collaborated with him as deacons: Timothy (1 Thes 3:2), Epophros (Col 1:7), Tychicus (Col 3:7; Eph 6:2).

16 Cf. *Epistula ad Philadelphenses*, 4; *Epistula ad Smyrnaeos*, 12, 2: *Epistula ad Magnesios*, 6, 1; F. X. Funk (ed.) *Patres Apostolici*, Tubingae 1901; 266-267; 286-287; 234-235; 244-245.

17 Cf. *Didascalia Apostolorum* (Syriac), capp. III, XI: A. Vööbus (ed.) *The Didascalia Apostolorum* (Syriac with English translation), *Corpus Scriptorum Christianorum Orientalium* (CSCO), vol. I, no. 402 (t. 176), 29-30; vol. II, no. 408 (t. 180), 120-129; *Didascalia Apostolorum*, III, 13 (19), 1-7: F. X. Funk (ed.), *Didascalia et Constitutiones Apostolorum*, Paderborn 1906, I, 212-216.

18 Cf. cc. 32 and 33 of the Council of Elvira (300-303): PL 84, 305; cc. 16 (15), 18, 21 of the first Council of Arles. CCL, 148, 12-13; cc. 15, 16, and 18 of the Council of Nicea: *Conciliorum Oecumenicorum Decreta*, bilingual edition of G. Alberigo, G. L. Dossetti, Cl. Leonardi, P. Prodi, cons. of H. Jedin, ed. Dehoniane, Bologna 1991, 13-15.

19 In the first period of Christianity, every local Church needed a number of deacons proportionate to her numbers so that they might be known and helped (cf. *Didascalia Apostolorum*, III, 12 (16): F. X. Funk, ed. cit., I, 208). In Rome, Pope St. Fabian (236-250) divided the city into seven zones (or "regiones," later called "diaconiae") in charge of each of which was placed a deacon ("regionarius") for the promotion of charity and assistance to the poor. Analogous diaconal structures were to be found in many cities of the east and west during the third and fourth centuries.

The Council of Trent disposed that the permanent Diaconate, as it existed in ancient times, should be restored, in accord with its proper nature, to its original function in the Church.[20] This prescription, however, was not carried into effect.

The second Vatican Council established that "it will be possible for the future to restore the diaconate as a proper and permanent rank of the hierarchy. . . . (and confer it) even upon married men, provided they be of more mature age, and also on suitable young men for whom, however, the law of celibacy must remain in force,"[21] in accordance with constant tradition. Three reasons lay behind this choice: (1) a desire to enrich the Church with the functions of the diaconate, which otherwise, in many regions, could only be exercised with great difficulty; (2) the intention of strengthening with the grace of diaconal ordination those who already exercised many of the functions of the Diaconate; (3) a concern to provide regions, where there was a shortage of clergy, with sacred ministers. Such reasons make clear that the restoration of the permanent Diaconate was in no manner intended to prejudice the meaning, role or flourishing of the ministerial priesthood, which must always be fostered because of its indispensability.

With the Apostolic Letter *Sacrum Diaconatus Ordinem*[22] of June 18, 1967, Pope Paul VI implemented the recommendations of the Second Vatican Council by determining general norms governing the restoration of the permanent Diaconate in the Latin Church. The Apostolic Constitution *Pontificalis Romani Recognitio*[23] of June 18, 1968, approved the new rite of conferring the Sacred Orders of the Episcopate, the Presbyterate and the Diaconate and determined the matter and form of these sacramental ordinations. Finally, the Apostolic Letter *Ad Pascendum*[24] of August 15, 1972, clarified the conditions for the admission and ordination of candidates to the diaconate. The essential elements of these norms subsequently passed into the *Code of Canon Law* promulgated by Pope John Paul II on January 25, 1983.[25]

20 Cf. Council of Trent, Session XXIII, *Decreta de Reformatione*, c. 17: *Conciliorum Oecumenicorum Decreta*, ed. cit., 750.

21 LG, no. 29.

22 *AAS* 59 (1967), 697-704.

23 *AAS* 60 (1968), 369-373.

24 *AAS* 64 (1972), 534-540.

25 Ten canons speak explicitly of permanent deacons: 236; 276 §2, 3°; 288; 1031 §§2-3; 1032 §3; 1035 §1; 1037; 1042, 1°; 1050, 3°.

In the wake of this universal legislation, several Episcopal Conferences, with the prior approbation of the Holy See, have restored the permanent Diaconate in their territories and have drawn up complementary norms for its regulation.

III. The Permanent Diaconate

3. The experience of the Church over several centuries has generated the norm of conferring the priesthood only on those who have already received the Diaconate and exercised it appropriately.[26] The Order of deacons, however, "should not be considered merely a step toward the Priesthood."[27]

"One of the fruits of the Second Vatican Council was the desire to restore the diaconate as a proper and stable rank of the hierarchy."[28] On the basis of the "historical circumstances and pastoral purposes noted by the Council Fathers, the Holy Spirit, protagonist of the Church's life, worked mysteriously to bring about a new and more complete actualization of the hierarchy which traditionally consists of bishops, priests and deacons. In this manner the Christian community was revitalized, configured more closely to that of the Apostles which, under the influence of the Paraclete, flourished as the Acts of the Apostles[29] testifies.

The permanent Diaconate is an important enrichment for the mission of the Church.[30] Since the *munera* proper to deacons are necessary to the Church's life,[31] it is both convenient and useful, especially in mission territories,[32] that men who are called to a truly diaconal ministry in the Church, whether liturgical or pastoral, charitable or social, "be strengthened by the imposition of hands, which has come down from the Apostles, and more closely united to

---

26 Cf. CIC, c. 1031 §1.

27 SDO: *AAS* 59 (1967), 698.

28 Cf. LG, no. 29; AG, no. 16; Second Vatican Ecumenical Council, Decree on Eastern Catholic Churches, *Orientalium Ecclesiarum* (OE), no. 17; Allocution of John Paul II of March 16, 1985, no. 1: *Insegnamenti*, VIII, 2 (1985), 648.

29 Catechesis of John Paul II at the General Audience of October 6, 1993, no. 5, *Insegnamenti*, XVI, 2 (1993), 954.

30 "A particularly felt need behind the decision to restore the permanent diaconate was that of a greater and more direct presence of sacred ministers in areas such as the family, work, schools, etc., as well as in the various ecclesial structures." Catechesis of John Paul II at the General Audience of October 6, 1993, no. 6, *Insegnamenti*, XVI, 2 (1993), 954.

31 Cf. LG, no. 29b.

32 Cf. AG, no. 16.

the altar so as to exercise their ministry more fruitfully through the sacramental grace of the diaconate."[33]

Vatican City, February 22, 1998, Feast of the Chair of Peter.

CONGREGATION FOR CATHOLIC EDUCATION

Pio Card. Laghi
Prefect

✠ José Saraiva Martins
Titular Archbishop of Tuburnica
Secretary

CONGREGATION FOR THE CLERGY

Darío Card. Castrillón Hoyos
Prefect

✠ Csaba Ternyák
Titular Archbishop of Eminenziana
Secretary

33 AG, no. 16; cf. CCC, 1571.

CONGREGATION FOR CATHOLIC EDUCATION

Ratio Fundamentalis Institutionis Diaconorum Permanentium (Basic Norms for the Formation of Permanent Deacons)

Introduction

1. The Paths of Formation

1. The first indications about the formation of permanent deacons were given by the Apostolic Letter Sacrum Diaconatus Ordinem.[34]

These indications were then taken up and further refined in the Circular Letter of the Sacred Congregation for Catholic Education of July 16, 1969, *Come è a conoscenza*, in which were foreseen "different types of formation" according to the "different types of diaconate" (for celibates, married people, "those destined

34 Cf. Paul VI, Apostolic Letter *Sacrum Diaconatus Ordinem* (SDO): *AAS* 59 (1967), 697-704. The Apostolic Letter, at Chapter II, which is dedicated to younger candidates, prescribes: "6. Young men who are to be trained for the office of deacon should go to a special institution where they can be tested, trained to live a truly evangelical life, and instructed on how to perform usefully the duties of their future state. 9. The period of preparation for the diaconate as such should run for a period of at least three years. The course of studies should be arranged in such a way that the candidates make orderly and gradual progress toward gaining an understanding of the various duties of the diaconate and toward being able to carry them out effectively. The whole course of studies might well be so planned that in the last year special training will be given in the principal functions to be carried out by the deacon. 10. In addition, there should be practice in teaching the fundamentals of the Christian religion to children and others of the faithful, in teaching people to sing sacred music and lead them in it, in reading the books of Scripture at gatherings of the faithful, in giving talks to the people, in administering those sacraments which deacons may administer, in visiting the sick, and, in general, in carrying out the ministries which may be required of them." The same Apostolic Letter, at Chapter III, which is dedicated to older candidates, prescribes: "14. It is desirable for these deacons, too, to acquire a good deal of doctrine, as was said in nos. 8, 9, and 10 above, or at least for them to have the knowledge which the episcopal conference may judge they will need to fulfill their functions properly. They should therefore be admitted to a special institution for a certain length of time in order to learn all they will have to know to carry out worthily the office of deacon. 15. But if for some reason this cannot be done, then the candidate should be entrusted to some priest of outstanding virtue who will take a special interest in him and teach him, and who will be able to testify to his maturity and prudence."

for mission territories or for countries which were still developing," those called "to carry out their function in countries with a certain level of civilization and a fairly developed culture"). Regarding doctrinal formation, it was specified that it must be above that required for a simple catechist and, in some way, analogous to that of the priest. The material which had to be taken into consideration when drawing up the program of studies was then listed.[35]

The subsequent Apostolic Letter *Ad Pascendum* specified that "in regard to the course of theological studies that are to precede the ordination of permanent deacons, the Episcopal Conferences, according to the local situation, are competent to issue the appropriate norms and submit them to the Sacred Congregation for Catholic Education for approval."[36]

The new *Code of Canon Law* brought together the essential elements of this norm into canon 236.

2. After about thirty years from the first directives, and with the contribution of subsequent experiences, it has been thought opportune now to draw up the present *Ratio Fundamentalis Institutionis Diaconorum Permanentium*. Its purpose is that of providing an instrument for guiding and harmonizing, while respecting legitimate diversity, the educational projects drawn up by the Episcopal Conferences and dioceses, which at times vary greatly from one to another.

2. Reference to a Sure Theology of the Diaconate

3. The effectiveness of the formation of permanent deacons depends to a great extent on the theological understanding of the diaconate that underlies it. In fact it offers the coordinates for establishing and guiding the formation process and, at the same time, lays down the end to be attained.

The almost total disappearance of the permanent diaconate from the Church of the West for more than a millennium has certainly made it more difficult to understand the profound reality of this ministry. However, it cannot be said for that reason that the theology of the diaconate has no authoritative points of reference, completely at the mercy of different theological opinions.

35 The Circular Letter of the Congregation indicated that courses must take into consideration the study of Sacred Scripture, dogma, moral, canon law, liturgy, "technical training, in order to prepare the candidates for certain activities of the ministry, such as psychology, catechetical pedagogy, public speaking, sacred song, organization of Catholic groups, ecclesiastical administration, keeping up to date the registers of Baptism, Confirmation, marriage, deaths, etc."

36 Paul VI, Apostolic Letter, *Ad Pascendum* (August 15, 1972), VII b): *AAS* 64 (1972), 540.

There are points of reference, and they are very clear, even if they need to be developed and deepened. Some of the most important of these will now follow, without, however, any claim to completeness.

4. First of all we must consider the diaconate, like every other Christian identity, from within the Church which is understood as a mystery of Trinitarian communion in missionary tension. This is a necessary, even if not the first, reference in the definition of the identity of every ordained minister insofar as its full truth consists in being a specific participation in and representation of the ministry of Christ.[37] This is why the deacon receives the laying on of hands and is sustained by a specific sacramental grace which inserts him into the sacrament of Orders.[38]

5. The diaconate is conferred through a special outpouring of the Spirit (*ordination*), which brings about in the one who receives it a specific conformation to Christ, Lord and servant of all. Quoting a text of the *Constitutiones Ecclesiae Aegypticae*, *Lumen Gentium* (no. 29) defines the laying on of hands on the deacon as being not "*ad sacerdotium sed ad ministerium*,"[39] that is, not for the celebration of the Eucharist, but for service. This indication, together with the admonition of St. Polycarp, also taken up again by *Lumen Gentium*, no. 29,[40] outlines the specific theological identity of the deacon: as a participation in the one ecclesiastical ministry, he is a specific sacramental sign, in the Church, of Christ the servant. His role is to "express the needs and desires of the Christian communities" and to be "a driving force for service, or *diakonia*,"[41] which is an essential part of the mission of the Church.

6. The *matter* of diaconal ordination is the laying on of the hands of the Bishop; the *form* is constituted by the words of the prayer of ordination, which is

37 Cf. John Paul II, Post-synodal Apostolic Exhortation, *Pastores Dabo Vobis* (PDV) (March 25, 1992), 12: *AAS* 84 (1992), 675-676.

38 Cf. LG, nos. 28 and 29.

39 The *Pontificale Romanum—De Ordinatione Episcopi, Presbyterorum et Diaconorum*, Editio typica altera, Typis Polyglottis Vaticanis 1990, 101, cites at no. 179 of the "*Praenotanda*," relative to the ordination of deacons, the expression "*in ministerio Episcopi ordinantur*" taken from the *Traditio Apostolica*, 8 (*SCh*, 11bis, 58-59), as taken from the *Constitutiones Ecclesiae Aegypticae* III, 2: F. X. Funk (ed.), *Didascalia et Constitutiones Apostolorum*, II, Paderbornae 1905, 103.

40 "(They should be) compassionate, industrious, walking according to the truth of the Lord, who was the servant of all" (St. Polycarp, *Epist. Ad Philippenses*, 5, 2: F. X. Funk [ed.], *Patres Apostolici*, I, Tubingae 1901, 300-302.

41 Paul VI, Apostolic Letter *Ad Pascendum*, Introduction: *l.c.*, 534-538.

expressed in the three moments of anamnesis, epiclesis and intercession.[42] The anamnesis (which recounts the history of salvation centered in Christ) goes back to the "levites," recalling worship, and to the "seven" of the Acts of the Apostles, recalling charity. The epiclesis invokes the power of the seven gifts of the Spirit so that the ordinand may imitate Christ as "deacon." The intercession is an exhortation to a generous and chaste life.

The *essential form* of the sacrament is the epiclesis, which consists of the words: "Lord, send forth upon them the Holy Spirit, that they may be strengthened by the gift of your sevenfold grace to carry out faithfully the work of the ministry." The seven gifts originate in a passage of Isaiah 11:2, from the fuller version given by the Septuagint. These are the gifts of the Spirit given to the Messiah, which are granted to the newly ordained.

7. Insofar as it is a grade of holy orders, the diaconate imprints a character and communicates a specific sacramental grace. The diaconal character is the configurative and distinguishing sign indelibly impressed in the soul, which configures the one ordained to Christ, who made himself the deacon or servant of all.[43] It brings with it a specific sacramental grace, which is strength, *vigor specialis*, a gift for living the new reality wrought by the sacrament. "With regard to deacons, 'strengthened by sacramental grace they are dedicated to the People of God, in conjunction with the bishop and his body of priests, in the service (*diakonia*) of the liturgy, of the Gospel and of works of charity.'"[44] Just as in all sacraments which imprint character, grace has a permanent virtuality. It flowers again and again in the same measure in which it is received and accepted again and again in faith.

8. In the exercise of their power, deacons, since they share in a lower grade of ecclesiastical ministry, necessarily depend on the Bishops, who have the fullness of the sacrament of orders. In addition, they are placed in a special relationship with the priests, in communion with whom they are called to serve the People of God.[45]

---

42 Cf. *Pontificale Romanum—De Ordinatione Episcopi, Presbyterorum et Diaconorum*, no. 207: *ed. cit.*, 115-122.

43 Cf. CCC, no. 1570.

44 CCC, no. 1588.

45 Cf. CD, no. 15.

From the point of view of discipline, with diaconal ordination, the deacon is incardinated into a particular Church or personal prelature to whose service he has been admitted, or else, as a cleric, into a religious institute of consecrated life or a clerical society of apostolic life.[46] Incardination does not represent something which is more or less accidental, but is characteristically a constant bond of service to a concrete portion of the People of God. This entails ecclesial membership at the juridical, affective and spiritual level and the obligation of ministerial service.

3. The Ministry of the Deacon in Different Pastoral Contexts

9. The ministry of the deacon is characterized by the exercise of the three *munera* proper to the ordained ministry, according to the specific perspective of *diakonia.*

In reference to the *munus docendi* the deacon is called to proclaim the Scriptures and instruct and exhort the people.[47] This finds expression in the presentation of the Book of the Gospels, foreseen in the rite of ordination itself.[48]

The munus sanctificandi of the deacon is expressed in prayer, in the solemn administration of baptism, in the custody and distribution of the Eucharist, in assisting at and blessing marriages, in presiding at the rites of funeral and burial and in the administration of sacramentals.[49] This brings out how the diaconal ministry has its point of departure and arrival in the Eucharist, and cannot be reduced to simple social service.

Finally, the *munus regendi* is exercised in dedication to works of charity and assistance[50] and in the direction of communities or sectors of church life, especially as regards charitable activities. This is the ministry most characteristic of the deacon.

10. As can be seen from original diaconal practice and from conciliar indications, the outlines of the ministerial service inherent in the diaconate are very well defined. However, even if this inherent ministerial service is one and the same in every case, nevertheless the concrete ways of carrying it out are diverse;

---

46 Cf. CIC, c. 266.
47 Cf. LG, no. 29.
48 Cf. *Pontificale Romanum–De Ordinatione Episcopi, Presbyterorum et Diaconorum*, no. 210: *ed. cit.*, 125.
49 Cf. LG, no. 29.
50 Cf. LG, no. 29.

these must be suggested, in each case, by the different pastoral situations of the single Churches. In preparing the formation to be imparted, these should obviously be taken into account.

4. Diaconal Spirituality

11. The outlines of the specific spirituality of the deacon flow clearly from his theological identity; this spirituality is one of service.

The model "par excellence" is Christ the servant, who lived totally at the service of God, for the good of men. He recognized himself as the one announced in the servant of the first song of the Book of Isaiah (cf. Lk 4:18-19), he explicitly qualified his action as *diakonia* (cf. Mt 20:28; Lk 22:27; Jn 13:1-17; Phil 2:7-8; 1 Pt 2:21-25), and he entrusted his disciples to do the same (cf. Jn 13:34-35; Lk 12:37).

The spirituality of service is a spirituality of the whole Church, insofar as the whole Church, in the same way as Mary, is the "handmaid of the Lord" (Lk 1:28), at the service of the salvation of the world. And so that the whole Church may better live out this spirituality of service, the Lord gives her a living and personal sign of his very being as servant. In a specific way, this is the spirituality of the deacon. In fact, with sacred ordination, he is constituted a living icon of Christ the servant within the Church. The *Leitmotiv* of his spiritual life will therefore be service; his sanctification will consist in making himself a generous and faithful servant of God and men, especially the poorest and most suffering; his ascetic commitment will be directed toward acquiring those virtues necessary for the exercise of his ministry.

12. Obviously such a spirituality must integrate itself harmoniously, in each case, with the spirituality related to the state of life. Accordingly, the same diaconal spirituality acquires diverse connotations according to whether it be lived by a married man, a widower, a single man, a religious, a consecrated person in the world. Formation must take account of these variations and offer differentiated spiritual paths according to the types of candidates.

5. The Role of Episcopal Conferences

13. "It is the competence of legitimate assemblies of Bishops or Episcopal Conferences to decide, with the consent of the Supreme Pontiff, whether and

where the diaconate is to be established as a permanent rank in the hierarchy for the good of souls."[51]

The *Code of Canon Law* likewise attributes to the Episcopal Conferences the competence to specify, by means of complementary dispositions, the discipline regarding the recitation of the liturgy of the hours,[52] the required age for admission,[53] and the formation given; canon 236 is dedicated to this. The canon lays down that it is the Episcopal Conferences, on the basis of local circumstances, which issue the appropriate norms to ensure that candidates for the permanent diaconate, whether young or of a more mature age, whether single or married are "formed in the spiritual life and appropriately instructed in the fulfillment of the duties proper to that order."

14. To assist the Episcopal Conferences in preparing a formation which, as well as being attentive to diverse particular situations, will still be in harmony with the universal direction of the Church, the Congregation for Catholic Education has prepared the present (*Ratio Fundamentalis Institutionis Diaconorum Permanentium*) which is intended as a point of reference for defining the criteria of vocational discernment and the various aspects of formation. This document—by its very nature—establishes only some basic guidelines of a general character, which constitute the norm to which the Episcopal Conferences must make reference for the preparation or eventual perfecting of their respective national *rationes*. In this way the principles and criteria on the basis of which the formation of permanent deacons can be programmed with surety and in harmony with the other Churches shall be illustrated, without stifling the creativity or originality of the particular Churches.

15. In the same way that the Second Vatican Council established for the *Rationes Institutionis Sacerdotalis*,[54] with this document, the Episcopal Conferences which have restored the permanent diaconate are requested to submit their respective *Rationes Institutionis Diaconorum Permanentium* for examination and approval by the Holy See. The same will approve them, firstly, *ad experimentum*, and, then for a specified number of years, so as to guarantee periodic revisions.

51 SDO, I, 1: *l.c.*, 699.
52 Cf. CIC, c. 276 §2, 3°.
53 Cf. CIC, c. 1031 §3.
54 Second Vatican Ecumenical Council, Decree on Priestly Formation, *Optatam Totius* (OT), no. 1.

6. Responsibility of Bishops

16. The restoration of the permanent diaconate in a nation does not imply the obligation of restoring it in all its dioceses. The diocesan Bishop will proceed or not in this regard, after having prudently heard the recommendation of the Council of Priests and, if it exists, the Pastoral Council, and taking account of concrete needs and the specific situation of his particular Church.

If he opts for the restoration of the permanent diaconate, he will take care to promote a suitable catechesis on the subject, both among laity and priests and religious, in such a way that the diaconal ministry may be fully understood. In addition, he will provide for the setting up of the structures necessary for the work of formation and for nominating suitable associates to assist him by being directly responsible for formation, or, according to circumstances, he will commit himself to employing the formation structures of other dioceses, or those of the region or nation.

The Bishop will then take care that, on the basis of the national *ratio* and actual experience, an appropriate rule be drafted and periodically revised.

7. The Permanent Diaconate in Institutes of Consecrated Life and in Societies of Apostolic Life

17. The institution of the permanent diaconate among the members of institutes of consecrated life and societies of apostolic life is regulated by the norms of the Apostolic Letter *Sacrum Diaconatus Ordinem*. It establishes that "Institution of the permanent diaconate among religious is a right reserved to the Holy See, which alone is competent to examine and approve the votes of general chapters in the matter."[55] The document continues: "Whatever is said . . . is to be understood as applying to the members of other institutes professing the evangelical counsels."[56]

Each institute or society which has obtained the right to reestablish the permanent diaconate assumes the responsibility of guaranteeing the human, spiritual, intellectual and pastoral formation of its candidates. Such an institute or society must commit itself therefore to preparing its own formation program which incorporates the specific charism and spirituality of the

55 SDO, VII, 32: *l.c.*, 703.
56 SDO, VII, 35: *l.c.*, 704.

institute or society and, at the same time, is in harmony with the present *Ratio Fundamentalis*, especially as regards intellectual and pastoral formation.

The program of each institute or society should be submitted for examination and approval to the Congregation for Institutes of Consecrated Life and Societies of Apostolic Life or the Congregation for the Evangelization of Peoples and the Congregation for the Oriental Churches for territories where they are competent. The competent Congregation, having obtained the opinion of the Congregation for Catholic Education as regards intellectual formation, will approve it, firstly *ad experimentum*, and then for a specific number of years, so as to guarantee periodic revisions.

I. Those Involved in the Formation of Permanent Deacons

1. The Church and the Bishop

18. The formation of deacons, like that of other ministers and all the baptized, is a duty which involves the whole Church. Hailed by the Apostle Paul as "the heavenly Jerusalem" and like Mary "our mother" (Gal 4:26), "by preaching and baptism she brings forth sons, who are conceived of the Holy Spirit and born of God, to a new and immortal life."[57] And not only this: imitating the motherhood of Mary, she accompanies her children with maternal love and cares for them so that they all may come to the fullness of their vocation.

The Church's care for her children is expressed in the offering of the Word and sacraments, in love and solidarity, in prayer and in the solicitude of the various ministries. However, in this care, which is, so to speak, visible, the care of the Holy Spirit is made present. In fact "the social structure of the Church serves the Spirit of Christ who vivifies it, in the building up of the body,"[58] both in its universality and in the singularity of its members.

In the Church's care for her children, the first figure, therefore, is the Spirit of Christ. It is He who calls them, accompanies them and molds their hearts so that they can recognize his grace and respond generously to it. The Church must be well aware of this *sacramental* relevance of its educational work.

57 LG, no. 64.
58 LG, no. 8.

19. In the formation of permanent deacons, the first *sign and instrument* of the Spirit of Christ is the proper Bishop (or the competent Major Superior).[59] He is the one ultimately responsible for their discernment and formation.[60] While ordinarily exercising this duty through the assistants who have been chosen, nevertheless he will he commit himself, as far as is possible, to knowing personally those who are preparing for diaconate.

2. Those Responsible for Formation

20. Those persons who, in dependence upon the Bishop (or competent Major Superior) and in strict collaboration with the diaconal community, have a special responsibility in the formation of candidates for the permanent diaconate are: the director of formation, the tutor (where the number requires it), the spiritual director and the pastor (or the minister to whom the candidate is entrusted for the diaconal placement).

21. The director of formation, nominated by the Bishop (or the competent Major Superior) has the task of coordinating the different people involved in the formation, of supervising and inspiring the whole work of education in its various dimensions, and of maintaining contacts with the families of married aspirants and candidates and with their communities of origin. In addition, he has the responsibility of presenting to the Bishop (or to the competent Major Superior) the judgment of suitability on aspirants for their admission among the candidates, and on candidates for their promotion to the order of diaconate after having heard the opinion of the other formators,[61] excepting the spiritual director.

Because of his decisive and delicate duties, the director of formation must be chosen with great care. He must be a man of lively faith and a strong ecclesial sense, have had a wide pastoral experience and have given proof of wisdom, balance and capacity for communion; in addition he must have acquired a solid theological and pedagogical competence.

59 Equivalent to the diocesan bishop in this regard are those to whom the following have been entrusted: territorial prelature, territorial abbey, apostolic vicariate, apostolic prefecture, and a stably erected apostolic administration (cf. CIC, cc. 368; 381 §2) as well as the personal prelature (cf. CIC, cc. 266 §1; 295) and the military ordinariate (cf. John Paul II, Apostolic Constitution *Spirituali Militum Curae* [April 21, 1986], art. I, § 1; art. II, § 1: *AAS* 78 [1986], 482; 483).

60 Cf. CIC, cc. 1025; 1029.

61 This also includes the director of the specific house of formation, wherever it exists (cf. CIC, c. 236, 1°).

He could be a priest or a deacon and, preferably, not be at the same time also responsible for ordained deacons. In fact, it would be better for this responsibility to remain distinct from that of forming aspirants and candidates.

22. The tutor, designated by the director of formation from among the deacons or priests of proven experience and nominated by the Bishop (or the competent Major Superior), is the direct companion of each aspirant and of each candidate. He is charged with closely following the formation of each one, offering his support and advice for the resolution of any problems which may arise and for helping to make personal the various moments of formation. He is also called to collaborate with the director of formation in the programming of the different formational activities and in the preparation of the judgment of suitability to be presented to the Bishop (or the competent Major Superior). According to circumstances, the tutor will be responsible for only one person or for a small group.

23. The spiritual director is chosen by each aspirant or candidate and must be approved by the Bishop or Major Superior. His task is that of discerning the workings of the Spirit in the soul of those called and, at the same time, of accompanying and supporting their ongoing conversion; he must also give concrete suggestions to help bring about an authentic diaconal spirituality and offer effective incentives for acquiring the associated virtues. Because of all this, aspirants and candidates are invited to entrust themselves for spiritual direction only to priests of proven virtue, equipped with a good theological culture, of profound spiritual experience, of marked pedagogical sense, of strong and refined ministerial sensibility.

24. The pastor (or other minister) is chosen by the director of formation in agreement with the other members of the formation team and taking account of the different situations of the candidates. He is called to offer to the one who has been entrusted to him a lively ministerial communion and to introduce him to and accompany him in those pastoral activities which he considers most suitable; he will also be careful to make a periodic check on the work done with the candidate himself and to communicate the progress of the placement to the director of formation.

3. Professors

25. The professors contribute in a relevant way to the formation of the future deacons. In fact, by teaching the *sacrum depositum* held by the Church, they nourish the faith of the candidates and qualify them to be teachers of the People of God. For that reason they must occupy themselves not only with acquiring the necessary scientific competence and an adequate pedagogical ability, but also with witnessing with their lives to the Truth which they teach.

In order to harmonize their specific contribution with the other dimensions of formation, it is important that they be willing, depending on circumstances, to collaborate and be open to discussion with the others involved in formation. In this way they will contribute to providing the candidates with a unified formation and help them in the necessary work of synthesis.

4. The Formation Community of Permanent Deacons

26. Aspirants and candidates for the permanent diaconate, naturally constitute a unique context, a distinct ecclesial community which strongly influences the formation process.

Those entrusted with the formation must take care that this community be characterized by a profound spirituality, a sense of belonging, a spirit of service and missionary thrust, and have a definite rhythm of meetings and prayer.

The formation community of permanent deacons can thus be for aspirants and candidates for the diaconate a precious support in the discernment of their vocation, in human growth, in the initiation to the spiritual life, in theological study and pastoral experience.

5. Communities of Origin

27. The communities of origin of aspirants and candidates for the diaconate can exercise some influence on their formation.

For younger aspirants and candidates, the family can be an extraordinary help. It must be invited to "accompany the formative journey with prayer, respect, the good example of the domestic virtues and spiritual and material help, especially in difficult moments . . . Even in the case of parents or relatives who are indifferent or opposed to the choice of a vocation, a clear and calm facing of the situation and the encouragement which derives from it can be a great help to the deeper and more determined maturing of a . . . vocation."[62] As far as married aspirants and candidates are concerned, their commitment must be such that their married communion might contribute in a real way to inspiring their formation journey toward the goal of the diaconate.

The parish community is called to accompany the path of its member toward the diaconate with the support of prayer and an appropriate catechesis which, while it makes the faithful aware of this ministry, gives to the candidate a strong aid to his vocational discernment.

Those other ecclesial groupings from which aspirants and candidates for the diaconate come can also continue to be for them a source of help and support, of light and warmth. However, they must show, at the same time, respect for the ministerial call of their members, not obstructing them, but rather promoting in them the maturing of an authentic diaconal spirituality and readiness.

6. Aspirant and Candidate

28. Finally, the man preparing for diaconate "is a necessary and irreplaceable agent in his own formation: all formation . . . is ultimately a self-formation."[63]

Self-formation does not imply isolation, closure to or independence from formators, but responsibility and dynamism in responding with generosity to God's call, valuing to the highest the people and tools which Providence puts at one's disposition.

Self-formation has its root in a firm determination to grow in life according to the Spirit and in conformity with the vocation received, and it is nourished in being humbly open to recognizing one's own limitations and one's own gifts.

II. Characteristics of Candidates for the Permanent Diaconate

29. "The history of every priestly vocation, as indeed of every Christian vocation, is the history of an *inexpressible dialogue between God and human beings*, between the love of God who calls and the freedom of individuals who respond lovingly to him."[64] However, alongside God's call and the response of individuals, there is another element constitutive to a vocation, particularly a ministerial

62 PDV, no. 68: *l.c.*, 775-776.
63 PDV, no. 69: *l.c.*, 778.
64 PDV, no. 36: *l.c.*, 715-716.

vocation: the public call of the Church. "*Vocari a Deo dicuntur qui a legitimis Ecclesiae ministris vocantur.*"[65] The expression should not be understood in a predominantly juridical sense, as if it were the authority that calls which determines the vocation, but in a *sacramental* sense, that considers the authority that calls as the sign and instrument for the personal intervention of God, which is realized with the laying on of hands. In this perspective, every proper *election* expresses an *inspiration* and represents a choice of God. The Church's discernment is therefore decisive for the choice of a vocation; how much more so, due to its ecclesial significance, is this true for the choice of a vocation to the ordained ministry.

This discernment must be conducted on the basis of objective criteria, which treasure the ancient tradition of the Church and take account of present day pastoral needs. For the discernment of vocations to the permanent diaconate, some requirements of a general nature and others responding to the particular state of life of those called should be taken into account.

1. General Requirements

30. The first diaconal profile was outlined in the First Letter of St. Paul to Timothy: "Deacons likewise must be serious, not double-tongued, not addicted to much wine, not greedy for gain; they must hold the mystery of the faith with a clear conscience. And let them also be tested first; then if they prove themselves blameless let them serve as deacons . . . Let deacons be the husband of one wife, and let them manage their children and their households well; for those who serve well as deacons gain a good standing for themselves and also great confidence in the faith which is in Jesus Christ" (1 Tm 3:8-10,12-13).

The qualities listed by Paul are prevalently human, almost as if to say that deacons could carry out their ministry only if they were acceptable models of humanity. We find echoes of Paul's exhortation in texts of the Apostolic Fathers, especially in the *Didachè* and St. Polycarp. The *Didachè* urges: "Elect for yourselves, therefore, bishops and deacons worthy of the Lord, meek men, not lovers of money, honest and proven,"[66] and St. Polycarp counsels: "In like manner should the deacons be blameless before the face of his righteousness, as being

65 *Catechismus ex decreto Concilii Tridentini ad Parochos*, pars II, c. 7, no. 3, Turin 1914, 288.
66 *Didachè*, 15, 1: F. X. Funk (ed.), *Patres Apostolici*, I, *o.c.*, 32-35

the servants of God and Christ, and not of men. They must not be slanderers, double-tongued, or lovers of money, but temperate in all things, compassionate, industrious, walking according to the truth of the Lord, who was the servant of all."[67]

31. The Church's tradition subsequently finalized and refined the requirements which support the authenticity of a call to the diaconate. These are firstly those which are valid for orders in general: "Only those are to be promoted to orders who . . . have sound faith, are motivated by the right intention, are endowed with the requisite knowledge, enjoy a good reputation, and have moral probity, proven virtue and the other physical and psychological qualities appropriate to the order to be received."[68]

32. The profile of candidates is then completed with certain specific human qualities and evangelical virtues necessary for *diakonia*. Among the human qualities which should be highlighted are: psychological maturity, capacity for dialogue and communication, sense of responsibility, industriousness, equilibrium and prudence. Particularly important among the evangelical virtues: prayer, Eucharistic and Marian devotion, a humble and strong *sense of the Church*, love for the Church and her mission, spirit of poverty, capacity for obedience and fraternal communion, apostolic zeal, openness to service,[69] charity toward the brothers and sisters.

33. In addition, candidates for the diaconate must be active members of a Christian community and already have exercised praiseworthy commitment to the apostolate.

34. They may come from every social grouping and carry out any work or professional activity, providing that it is not, according to the norms of the Church and the prudent judgment of the Bishop, inconsistent with the diaconal state.[70] Furthermore, such activity must be compatible in practice with commitments of formation and the effective exercise of the ministry.

---

67 St. Polycarp, *Epist. ad Philippenses*, 5, 1-2: F. X. Funk (ed.), *Patres Apostolici*, I, *o.c.*, 300-302.
68 CIC, c. 1029. Cf. c. 1051, 1°.
69 Cf. SDO, II, 8: *l.c.*, 700.
70 Cf. CIC, cc. 285 §§1-2; 289; SDO, III, 17: *l.c.*, 701.

35. Regarding the minimum age, the *Code of Canon Law* prescribes that: "the candidate for the permanent diaconate who is not married may be admitted to the diaconate only when he has completed at least his twenty-fifth year; if he is married, not until he has completed at least his thirty-fifth year."[71]

Lastly, candidates must be free of irregularities and impediments.[72]

2. Requirements Related to the Candidate's State of Life

a) Unmarried

36. "On the basis of Church law, confirmed by the same Ecumenical Council, young men called to the diaconate are obliged to observe the law of celibacy."[73] This is a particularly appropriate law for the sacred ministry, to which those who have received the charism freely submit.

The permanent diaconate, lived in celibacy, gives to the ministry a certain unique emphasis. In fact, the sacramental identification with Christ is placed in the context of the *undivided heart*, that is within the context of a nuptial, exclusive, permanent and total choice of the unique and greatest Love; service of the Church can count on a total availability; the proclamation of the Kingdom is supported by the courageous witness of those who have left even those things most dear to them for the sake of the Kingdom.

b) Married

37. "In the case of married men, care should be taken that only those are promoted to the diaconate who have lived as married men for a number of years and

---

71 CIC, c. 1031 §2. Cf. SDO, II, 5; III, 12: *l.c.*, 699; 700. Canon 1031 §3 prescribes that " the conference of bishops is free to establish norms which require an older age for the presbyterate and the permanent diaconate."

72 Cf. CIC, cc. 1040-1042. The irregularities (perpetual impediments) listed by canon 1041 are (1) any form of *insanity* or other *psychological infirmity*, because of which he is, after experts have been consulted, judged incapable of properly fulfilling the ministry; (2) the offenses of *apostasy*, *heresy* or *schism*; (3) *attempted marriage*, even a civil marriage; (4) *willful homicide* or actually *procured abortion*; (5) *grave mutilation* of self or others, and *attempted suicide*; (6) *illicit completion of acts of order*. The simple impediments, listed by canon 1042, are (1) the *exercise of an office or administration forbidden to, or inappropriate to, the clerical state*; (2) the *state of being a neophyte* (except when the ordinary decides otherwise).

73 SDO, II, 4: *l.c.*, 699. Cf. LG, no. 29.

have shown themselves to be capable of running their own homes, and whose wives and children lead a truly Christian life and have good reputations."[74]

Moreover, in addition to stability of family life, married candidates cannot be admitted unless "their wives not only consent, but also have the Christian moral character and attributes which will neither hinder their husbands' ministry nor be out of keeping with it."[75]

c) Widowers

38. "Those who have received the order of deacon, even those who are older, may not, in accordance with traditional Church discipline, enter into marriage."[76] The same principle applies to deacons who have been widowed.[77] They are called to give proof of human and spiritual soundness in their state of life.

Moreover, a precondition for accepting widowed candidates is that they have already provided, or have shown that they are capable of providing adequately for, the human and Christian upbringing of their children.

d) Members of Institutes of Consecrated Life and of Societies of Apostolic Life

39. Permanent deacons belonging to institutes of consecrated life or to societies of apostolic life[78] are called to enrich their ministry with the particular charism which they have received. In fact, their pastoral activity, while being under the jurisdiction of the local Ordinary,[79] is nevertheless characterized by particular traits of their religious or consecrated state of life. They will therefore commit themselves to integrating their religious or consecrated vocation with the ministerial vocation and to offering their special contribution to the mission of the Church.

---

74 SDO, III, 13: *l.c.*, 700.

75 SDO, III, 11: *l.c.*, 700. Cf. CIC, cc. 1031 §2; 1050, 3°.

76 SDO, III, 16: *l.c.*, 701; Ap. Lett. *Ad Pascendum*, VI: *l.c.*, 539; CIC, c. 1087.

77 The Circular Letter, Prot. n. 26397 of June 6, 1997, of the Congregation for Divine Worship and the Discipline of the Sacraments envisages that one only of the following conditions be sufficient for obtaining dispensation from the impediment found in canon 1087: the great and proven usefulness of the ministry of the deacon to the diocese to which he belongs; that he has children of such a tender age as to be in need of motherly care; that he has parents or parents in law who are elderly and in need of care.

78 Cf. SDO, VII, 32-35: *l.c.*, 703-704.

79 Cf. Paul VI, Apostolic Letter *Ecclesiae Sanctae* (August 6, 1966), I, 25 §1: *AAS* 58 (1966), 770.

III. The Path of Formation Toward the Permanent Diaconate

1. The Presentation of Aspirants

40. The decision to undertake the path of diaconal formation can come about either upon the initiative of the aspirant himself or by means of an explicit proposal of the community to which the aspirant belongs. In each case, the decision must be accepted and shared by the community.

On behalf of the community, it is the pastor (or the superior in religious houses) who must present to the Bishop (or competent Major Superior) the aspirant to the diaconate. He will do so accompanying the candidacy with an illustration of the motivations which support it and with a *curriculum vitae* and pastoral history of the aspirant.

The Bishop (or competent Major Superior), after having consulted the director of formation and the formation team, will decide whether or not to admit the aspirant to the propaedeutic period.

2. The Propaedeutic Period

41. With admission among the aspirants to diaconate there begins a propaedeutic period, which must be of an appropriate length. During this period, the aspirants will be introduced to a deeper knowledge of theology, of spirituality, and of the ministry of deacon, and they will be led to a more attentive discernment of their call.

42. The director of formation is responsible for the propaedeutic period; depending on the cases, he may entrust the aspirants to one or more tutors. It is to be hoped that, where circumstances permit, the aspirants may form their own community with its own cycle of meetings and prayer which also foresees times in common with the community of candidates.

The director of formation will ensure that each aspirant is accompanied by an approved spiritual director and will make contact with the pastor of each one (or another priest) in order to program the pastoral placement. In addition, he will make contact with the families of married aspirants to make sure of their openness to accepting, sharing and accompanying the vocation of their relative.

43. The program of the propaedeutic period, usually, should not provide school lessons, but rather meetings for prayer, instructions, moments of reflection and comparison directed toward ensuring the objective nature of the vocational discernment, according to a well-structured plan.

Even during this period, care should be taken, wherever possible, to involve the wives of the aspirants.

44. The aspirants are invited to carry out a free and self-conscious discernment, basing it on the requirements necessary for the diaconal ministry, without allowing themselves to be conditioned by personal interests or external pressures of any sort.[80]

At the end of the propaedeutic period, the director of formation, after having consulted the formation team and taking account of all the elements in his possession, will present to the proper Bishop (or competent Major Superior) a declaration which outlines the profile of the aspirants' personalities and also, on request, a judgment of suitability.

For his part, the Bishop (or the competent Major Superior) will enlist among the candidates for the diaconate only those about whom he will have reached a moral certainty of suitability, whether because of personal knowledge or because of information received from the formators.

3. The Liturgical Rite of Admission to Candidacy for Ordination as Deacon

45. Admission to candidacy for ordination as deacon comes about by means of a special liturgical rite "by which one who aspires to the diaconate or priesthood publicly manifests his will to offer himself to God and the Church so that he may exercise sacred orders. The Church, accepting this offering, chooses and calls him to prepare himself to receive a sacred order, and in this way, he is rightly numbered among candidates for the diaconate."[81]

46. The competent superior for this acceptance is the Bishop himself or, for members of a clerical religious institute of pontifical rite or of a clerical society of apostolic life of pontifical right, the Major Superior.[82]

---

80 Cf. CIC, c. 1026.

81 Paul VI, Apostolic Letter *Ad Pascendum*, Introduction; cf. I a): *l.c.*, 537-538. Cf. CIC, c. 1034 §1. The rite for admission among the candidates for Holy Orders is found in the *Pontificale Romanum—De Ordinatione Episcopi, Presbyterorum et Diaconorum*, Appendix, II: *ed. cit.*, 232ff.

82 Cf. CIC, cc. 1016, 1019.

47. By reason of its public character and its ecclesial significance, the rite is to be held in proper esteem and celebrated preferably on a feast day. The aspirant is to prepare himself for it by a spiritual retreat.

48. The liturgical rite of admission must be preceded by a request for enrollment among the candidates, which must be prepared and personally signed by the aspirant himself and accepted in writing by the proper Bishop or Major Superior to whom it is addressed.[83]

Enrollment among the candidates for the diaconate does not constitute any right necessarily to receive diaconal ordination. It is a first official recognition of the positive signs of the vocation to the diaconate, which must be confirmed in the subsequent years of formation.

4. Time of Formation

49. The formation program must last at least three years, in addition to the propaedeutic period, for all candidates.[84]

50. The *Code of Canon Law* prescribes that young candidates receive their formation residing "for at least three years in a special house, unless the diocesan Bishop for grave reasons decides otherwise."[85] "The Bishops of a region—or, where it would be useful, those of several regions in the same country—should join in establishing a college of this kind, depending on local circumstances. They should choose particularly well-fitted men to be in charge of it and should make clear rules regarding discipline and studies."[86] Care should be taken that these candidates have good relationships with the deacons of the diocese to which they belong.

51. For those more mature candidates, whether single or married, the *Code of Canon Law* prescribes that they "prepare for three years in a manner determined by the Episcopal Conference."[87] Where circumstances permit, this preparation must be undertaken in the context of a full participation in the community of candidates, which will have its own calendar of meetings for prayer and

---

83 Cf. CIC, c. 1034 §1; Paul VI, Apostolic Letter *Ad Pascendum*, I a): *l.c.*, 538.

84 Cf. CIC, c. 236 and numbers 41-44 of the present *Ratio.*

85 CIC, c. 236, 1°. Cf. SDO, II, 6: *l.c.*, 699.

86 Cf. SDO, II, 7: *l.c.*, 699.

87 CIC, c. 236, 2°.

formation and will also foresee meetings in common with the community of aspirants.

Different ways of organizing the formation are possible for these candidates. Due to work and family commitments, the most common models foresee formational and scholastic meetings in the evenings, during weekends, at holiday time, or with a combination of the various possibilities. Where geographical factors might present particular difficulties it will be necessary to consider other models, extending over a longer time period or making use of modern means of communication.

52. For candidates belonging to institutes of consecrated life or societies of apostolic life, formation will be carried out according to the directives of the eventual *ratio* of the person's institute or society, or by using the structures of the diocese in which the candidates are to be found.

53. In the cases in which the above-mentioned ways of formation might not be set up or be impracticable, "then the candidate should be entrusted to some priest of outstanding judgment who will take a special interest in him and teach him, and who will be able to testify to his maturity and prudence. Great care must always be taken that only those who have enough learning and are suitable are enrolled in the sacred order."[88]

54. In all cases the director of formation (or the priest responsible) will check that during the whole time of formation every candidate will maintain his commitment to spiritual direction with his own approved spiritual director. In addition, he will ensure the accompaniment, evaluation and eventual modification of each one's pastoral internship.

55. The formation program, which will be outlined in general in the next chapter, must integrate in a harmonious manner the different areas of formation (human, spiritual, theological and pastoral), it must be theologically well founded, have a specific pastoral finality and be adapted to local needs and pastoral programs.

56. The wives and children of married candidates and the communities to which they belong should also be involved in appropriate ways. In particular,

88 SDO, III, 15: *l.c.*, 701.

there should be also a specific program of formation for the wives of candidates, to prepare them for their future mission of accompanying and supporting their husband's ministry.

5. *Conferral of the Ministries of Lectorate and Acolytate*

57. "Before anyone may be promoted to the diaconate, whether permanent or transitory, he must have received the ministries of lector and acolyte, and have exercised them for an appropriate time,"[89] so that he may "be better disposed for the future service of the word and the altar."[90] In fact the Church "considers it to be very opportune that both by study and by gradual exercise of the ministry of the word and of the altar, candidates for sacred orders should through intimate contact understand and reflect upon the double aspect of the priestly office. Thus it comes about that the authenticity of the ministry shines out with the greatest effectiveness. In this way the candidates come to sacred orders fully aware of their vocation, 'fervent in spirit, serving the Lord, constant in prayer and aware of the needs of the faithful' (Rom 12:11-13)."[91]

The identity of these ministries and their pastoral relevance are illustrated in the Apostolic Letter *Ministeria Quaedam*, to which reference should be made.

58. Aspirants to lectorate and acolytate, on the invitation of the director of formation, will make a request for admission, which has been compiled and signed freely, and present it to the Ordinary (the Bishop or Major Superior) who has the authority to accept it.[92] Having accepted the request, the Bishop or Major Superior will proceed to the conferral of the ministries, according to the rite of the *Roman Pontifical.*[93]

59. It is appropriate that a certain period of time elapse between the conferring of lectorate and acolytate in such a way that the candidate may exercise the

89 CIC, c. 1035 §1.

90 Paul VI, Apostolic Letter *Ad Pascendum*, II: *l.c.*, 539; Apostolic Letter *Ministeria Quaedam* (August 15, 1972), XI: *AAS* 64 (1972), 533.

91 Paul VI, Apostolic Letter *Ad Pascendum*, Introduction: *l.c.*, 538.

92 Cf. Idem, Apostolic Letter *Ministeria Quaedam*, VIII a): *l.c.*, 533.

93 Cf. *Pontificale Romanum–De Institutione Lectorum et Acolythorum*, Editio typica, Typis Polyglottis Vaticanis 1972.

ministry he has received.[94] "Between the conferring of the ministry of acolyte and the diaconate there is to be an interval of at least six months."[95]

6. Diaconate Ordination

60. At the conclusion of the formation journey, the candidate who, in agreement with the director of formation, considers himself to have the necessary prerequisites for ordination, may address to the proper Bishop or competent Major Superior "a declaration written in his own hand and signed by him, in which he attests that he is about to receive the sacred order freely and of his own accord and will devote himself permanently to the ecclesiastical ministry, asking at the same time that he be admitted to receive the order."[96]

61. With this request the candidate must enclose the certificate of baptism, of confirmation and of the ministries mentioned in canon 1035, and the certificate of studies duly completed in accordance with canon 1032.[97] If the ordinand to be promoted is married, he must present his marriage certificate and the written consent of his wife.[98]

62. Having received the request of the ordinand, the Bishop (or competent Major Superior) will evaluate his suitability by means of a diligent scrutiny. First of all he will examine the certificate which the director of formation is obliged to present to him "concerning the qualities required in the candidate for the reception of the order, namely sound doctrine, genuine piety, good moral behavior, fitness for the exercise of the ministry; likewise, after proper investigation, a certificate of the candidate's state of physical and psychological health."[99] "The diocesan Bishop or Major Superior may, in order properly to complete the investigation, use other means which, taking into account the circumstances of time and place, may seem useful, such as testimonial letters, public notices or other sources of information."[100]

---

94 Cf. Paul VI, Apostolic Letter *Ministeria Quaedam*, X: *l.c.*, 533; Apostolic Letter *Ad Pascendum*, IV: *l.c.*, 539.

95 CIC, c. 1035 §2.

96 CIC, c. 1036. Cf. Paul VI, Apostolic Letter *Ad Pascendum*, V: *l.c.*, 539.

97 Cf. CIC, c. 1050.

98 Cf. CIC, cc. 1050, 3°; 1031 §2.

99 Cf. CIC, c. 1051, 1°.

100 Cf. CIC, c. 1051, 2°.

After having verified the suitability of a candidate and having been assured that he is aware of the new obligations which he is assuming,[101] the Bishop or competent Major Superior will promote him to the order of the diaconate.

63. Before ordination, unmarried candidates must assume publicly, in the prescribed rite, the obligation of celibacy;[102] candidates belonging to an institute of consecrated life or a society of apostolic life who have taken perpetual vows or other form of definitive commitment in the institute or society are also obliged to this.[103] All candidates are bound personally, before ordination, to make a profession of faith and an oath of fidelity, according to the formulae approved by the Apostolic See, in the presence of the Ordinary of the place or his delegate.[104]

64. "Each candidate is to be ordained . . . to the diaconate by his proper Bishop, or with lawful dimissorial letters granted by that Bishop."[105] If the candidate belongs to a clerical religious institute of pontifical right or to a clerical society of apostolic life of pontifical right it belongs to the Major Superior to grant him dimissorial letters.[106]

65. The ordination, carried out according to the rite of the *Roman Pontifical*,[107] is to be celebrated during solemn Mass, preferably on a Sunday or holy day of obligation, and generally in the Cathedral Church.[108] The ordinands prepare themselves for it by making "a retreat for at least five days, in a place and in the manner prescribed by the Ordinary."[109] During the rite special attention should be given to the participation of the wives and children of the married ordinands.

---

101 Cf. CIC, c. 1028. For the obligations that ordinands assume with the diaconate, see canons 273-289. In addition, for married deacons, there is the impediment to contracting new marriages (cf. c. 1087).

102 Cf. CIC, c. 1037; Paul VI, Apostolic Letter *Ad Pascendum*, VI: *l.c.*, 539.

103 Cf. *Pontificale Romanum—De Ordinatione Episcopi, Presbyterorum et Diaconorum*, no. 177: *ed. cit.*, 101.

104 Cf. CIC, c. 833, 6°; Congregation for the Doctrine of the Faith, *Professio Fidei et Iusiurandum Fidelitatis in Suscipiendo Officio Nomine Ecclesiae Exercendo*: *AAS* 81 (1989), 104-106; 1169.

105 CIC, c. 1015 §1.

106 Cf. CIC, c. 1019.

107 *Pontificale Romanum–De Ordinatione Episcopi, Presbyterorum et Diaconorum*, cap. III, *De Ordinatione diaconorum*: *ed. cit.*, 100-142.

108 Cf. CIC, cc. 1010-1011.

109 CIC, c. 1039.

IV. The Dimensions of the Formation of Permanent Deacons

1. Human Formation

66. The scope of human formation is that of molding the personality of the sacred ministers in such a way that they become "a bridge and not an obstacle for others in their meeting with Jesus Christ the Redeemer of man."[1] Accordingly they must be educated to acquire and perfect a series of human qualities which will permit them to enjoy the trust of the community, to commit themselves with serenity to the pastoral ministry, to facilitate encounter and dialogue.

Similar to the indications of *Pastores Dabo Vobis* for the formation of priests, candidates for the diaconate, too, must be educated "to love the truth, to be loyal, to respect every person, to have a sense of justice, to be true to their word, to be genuinely compassionate, to be men of integrity and, especially, to be balanced in judgment and behavior."[2]

67. Of particular importance for deacons, called to be men of communion and service, is the capacity to relate to others. This requires that they be affable, hospitable, sincere in their words and heart, prudent and discreet, generous and ready to serve, capable of opening themselves to clear and brotherly relationships, and quick to understand, forgive and console.[3] A candidate who was excessively closed in on himself, cantankerous and incapable of establishing meaningful and serene relationships with others must undergo a profound conversion before setting off with conviction on the path of ministerial service.

68. At the root of the capacity to relate to others is affective maturity, which must be attained with a wide margin of certainty in both celibate and married candidates. Such a maturity presupposes in both types of candidate the discovery of the centrality of love in their own lives and the victorious struggle against their own selfishness. In reality, as Pope John Paul II wrote in the Encyclical *Redemptor Hominis*, "man cannot live without love. He remains a being that is incomprehensible for himself, his life is senseless, if love is not revealed to him, if he does not encounter love, if he does not experience it and make it his own, if

1 PDV, no. 43: *l.c.*, 732.
2 PDV, no. 43: *l.c.*, 732-733.
3 Cf. PDV, no. 43: *l.c.*, 733.

he does not participate intimately in it."[4] As the Pope explains in *Pastores Dabo Vobis*, this is a love which involves all the aspects of the person, physical, psychological and spiritual and which therefore demands full dominion over his sexuality, which must become truly and fully personal.[5]

For celibate candidates, to live love means offering the totality of one's being, of one's energies and readiness, to Christ and the Church. It is a demanding vocation, which must take into account the inclinations of affectivity and the pressures of instinct and which therefore requires renunciation, vigilance, prayer and fidelity to a precise rule of life. A decisive assistance can come from the presence of true friends, who represent a precious help and a providential support in living out one's own vocation.[6]

For married candidates, to live love means offering themselves to their spouses in a reciprocal belonging, in a total, faithful and indissoluble union, in the likeness of Christ's love for his Church; at the same time it means welcoming children, loving them, educating them and showing forth to the whole Church and society the communion of the family. Today, this vocation is being hard tested by the worrying degradation of certain fundamental values and the exaltation of hedonism and a false conception of liberty. To be lived out in all its fullness, the vocation to family must be nourished by prayer, the liturgy and a daily offering of self.[7]

69. A precondition for an authentic human maturity is training in freedom, which is expressed in obedience to the truth of one's own being. "Thus understood, freedom requires the person to be truly master of himself, determined to fight and overcome the different forms of selfishness and individualism which threaten the life of each one, ready to open out to others, generous in dedication and service to one's neighbor."[8] Training in freedom also includes the education of the moral conscience, which prepares one to listen to the voice of God in the depths of one's heart and to adhere closely to it.

70. These many aspects of human maturity—human qualities, ability to relate, affective maturity, training in freedom and education of the moral

4 John Paul II, Encyclical Letter *Redemptor Hominis* (March 4, 1979), no. 10: *AAS* 71 (1979), 274.

5 Cf. PDV, no. 44: *l.c.*, 734.

6 Cf. PDV, no. 44: *l.c.*, 734-735.

7 Cf. John Paul II, Apostolic Exhortation *Familiaris Consortio* (November 22,1981): *AAS* 74 (1982), 81-191.

8 PDV, no. 44: *l.c.*, 735.

conscience—must be considered, taking into account the age and previous formation of the candidates, when planning programs tailored to the individual. The director of formation and the tutor will contribute in the area of their competence; the spiritual director will take these aspects into consideration and check them during spiritual direction. Encounters and conferences which encourage development and give some incentive to maturity are also of use. Community life—in the various forms in which it can be programmed—will constitute a privileged forum for fraternal checks and correction. In those cases where it may be necessary, in the judgment of the formators, and with the consent of the individual concerned, recourse may be made to a psychological consultation.

2. Spiritual Formation

71. Human formation leads to and finds its completion in spiritual formation, which constitutes the heart and unifying center of every Christian formation. Its aim is to tend to the development of the new life received in Baptism.

When a candidate begins the path of formation for the diaconate, generally he has already had a certain experience of the spiritual life, such as, recognition of the action of the Spirit, listening to and meditating upon the Word of God, the thirst for prayer, commitment to service of the brothers and sisters, willingness to make sacrifices, the sense of the Church, apostolic zeal. Also, according to his state of life, he will already have matured a certain defined spirituality: of the family, of consecration in the world or of consecration in the religious life. The spiritual formation of the future deacon, therefore, cannot ignore this experience which he has already had, but must seek to affirm and strengthen it, so as to impress upon it the specific traits of diaconal spirituality.

72. The element which most characterizes diaconal spirituality is the discovery of and sharing in the love of Christ the servant, who came not to be served but to serve. The candidate must therefore be helped progressively to acquire those attitudes which are specifically diaconal, though not exclusively so, such as simplicity of heart, total giving of self and disinterest for self, humble and helpful love for the brothers and sisters, especially the poorest, the suffering and the most needy, the choice of a lifestyle of sharing and poverty. Let Mary, the handmaid of the Lord, be present on this journey and be invoked as mother and auxiliatrix in the daily recitation of the Rosary.

73. The source of this new capacity to love is the Eucharist, which, not by chance, characterizes the ministry of the deacon. In fact, service of the poor is the logical consequence of service of the altar. Therefore the candidate will be invited to participate every day, or at least frequently, within the limits of his family and professional commitments, in the celebration of the Eucharist and will be helped to penetrate ever deeper into its mystery. Within the context of this Eucharistic spirituality, care will be taken to give adequate appreciation to the sacrament of Penance.

74. Another characteristic element of diaconal spirituality is the Word of God, of which the deacon is called to be an authoritative preacher, believing what he proclaims, teaching what he believes, living what he teaches.[9] The candidate must therefore learn to know the Word of God ever more deeply and to seek in it constant nourishment for his spiritual life by means of its loving and thorough study and the daily exercise of *lectio divina.*

75. There should also be an introduction to the meaning of the Prayer of the Church. Indeed praying in the name of the Church and for the Church is part of the ministry of the deacon. This requires a reflection on the uniqueness of Christian prayer and the meaning of the Liturgy of the Hours, but especially a practical initiation into it. To this end, it is important that time be dedicated to this prayer during all meetings of the future deacons.

76. Finally, the deacon incarnates the charism of service as a participation in the ministry of the Church. This has important repercussions on his spiritual life, which must be characterized by obedience and fraternal communion. A genuine education in obedience, instead of stifling the gifts received with the grace of ordination, will ensure ecclesial authenticity in the apostolate. Communion with his ordained confreres is also a balm for supporting and encouraging generosity in the ministry. The candidate must therefore be educated to a sense of belonging to the body of ordained ministers, to fraternal collaboration with them and to spiritual sharing.

77. The means for this formation are monthly retreats and annual spiritual exercises; instructions, to be programmed according to an organic and progressive

9 Cf. the presentation of the Book of the Gospels, in *Pontificale Romanum—De Ordinatione Episcopi, Presbyterorum et Diaconorum*, no. 210: *ed. cit.*, 125.

plan, which takes account of the various stages of the formation; and spiritual accompaniment, which must be constant. It is a particular task of the spiritual director to assist the candidate to discern the signs of his vocation, to place himself in an attitude of ongoing conversion, to bring to maturity the traits proper to the spirituality of the deacon, drawing on the writings of classical spirituality and the example of the saints, and to bring about a balanced synthesis of his state of life, his profession and the ministry.

78. Moreover, provision should be made that wives of married candidates may grow in awareness of their husbands' vocation and their own mission at his side. They are to be invited, therefore, to participate regularly in the spiritual formation meetings.

Appropriate efforts should also be directed toward educating children about the ministry of the deacon.

3. Doctrinal Formation

79. Intellectual formation is a necessary dimension of diaconal formation insofar as it offers the deacon a substantial nourishment for his spiritual life and a precious instrument for his ministry. It is particularly urgent today, in the face of the challenge of the new evangelization to which the Church is called at this difficult juncture of the millennium. Religious indifference, obscuring of values, loss of ethical convergence, and cultural pluralism demand that those involved in the ordained ministry have an intellectual formation which is complete and serious.

In the Circular Letter of 1969, *Come è a conoscenza*, the Congregation for Catholic Education invited Episcopal Conferences to prepare a doctrinal formation for candidates to the diaconate which would take account of the different situations, personal and ecclesial, yet at the same time would absolutely exclude "a hurried or superficial preparation, because the duties of the Deacon, as laid down in the Constitution *Lumen Gentium* (no. 29) and in the *Motu Proprio* (no. 22),[10] are of such importance as to demand a formation which is solid and effective."

80. The criteria which must be followed in preparing this formation are:

10 This refers to the Apostolic Letter of Paul VI, *Sacrum Diaconatus Ordinem* (SDO), no. 22: *l.c.*, 701-702.

a. Necessity for the deacon to be able to explain his faith and bring to maturity a lively ecclesial conscience
b. Attention to his formation for the specific duties of his ministry
c. Importance of acquiring the capacity to read a situation and an adequate inculturation of the Gospel
d. Usefulness of knowing communication techniques and group dynamics, the ability to speak in public, and to be able to give guidance and counsel

81. Taking account of these criteria, the following contents must be taken into consideration:[11]

a. Introduction to Sacred Scripture and its right interpretation; the theology of the Old and New Testament; the interrelation between Scripture and Tradition; the use of Scripture in preaching, catechesis and pastoral activity in general
b. Introduction to the study of the Fathers of the Church and an elementary knowledge of the history of the Church
c. Fundamental theology, with illustration of the sources, topics and methods of theology, presentation of the questions relating to Revelation and the formulation of the relationship between faith and reason, which will enable the future deacons to explain the reasonableness of the faith
d. Dogmatic theology, with its various treatises: Trinity, creation, Christology, ecclesiology and ecumenism, mariology, Christian anthropology, sacraments (especially theology of the ordained ministry), eschatology
e. Christian morality, in its personal and social dimensions and, in particular, the social doctrine of the Church
f. Spiritual theology
g. Liturgy
h. Canon law

11 Cf. Congregation for Catholic Education, Circular Letter *Come è a Conoscenza* (July 16, 1969), 2.

According to particular situations and needs, the program of studies will be integrated with other disciplines such as the study of other religions, philosophical questions, a deepening of certain economic and political problems.[12]

82. For theological formation, use may be made, where possible, of institutes of religious sciences which already exist or of other institutes of theological formation. Where special schools for the theological formation of deacons must be instituted, this should be done in such a way that the number of hours of lectures and seminars be not less than a thousand in the space of the three years. The fundamental courses at least are to conclude with an examination and, at the end of the three years there is to be a final comprehensive examination.

83. For admission to this program of formation, a previous basic formation is required; this is to be determined according to the cultural situation of the country.

84. Candidates should be predisposed to continuing their formation after ordination. To this end, they are encouraged to establish a small personal library with a theological-pastoral emphasis and to be open to programs of ongoing formation.

4. Pastoral Formation

85. In the wide sense, pastoral formation coincides with spiritual formation: it is formation for an ever greater identification with the *diakonia* of Christ. This attitude must guide the articulation of the various aspects of formation, integrating them within the unitary perspective of the diaconal vocation, which consists in being a sacrament of Christ, servant of the Father.

In the strict sense, pastoral formation develops by means of a specific theological discipline and a practical internship.

86. This theological discipline is called *pastoral theology*. It is "a scientific reflection on the Church as she is built up daily, by the power of the Spirit, in history; on the Church as the 'universal sacrament of salvation,' as a living sign and instrument of the salvation wrought by Christ through the word, the

12 Cf. Congregation for Catholic Education, Circular Letter *Come è a Conoscenza* (July 16, 1969), 3.

sacraments and the service of charity."[13] The scope of this discipline, therefore, is the presentation of the principles, the criteria and the methods which guide the apostolic-missionary work of the Church in history.

The *pastoral theology* programmed for the deacons will pay particular attention to those *fields* which are eminently diaconal, such as

a. Liturgical praxis: administration of the sacraments and sacramentals, service at the altar
b. Proclamation of the Word in the varied contexts of ministerial service: kerygma, catechesis, preparation for the sacraments, homily
c. The Church's commitment to social justice and charity
d. The life of the community, in particular the guidance of family teams, small communities, groups and movements, etc.

Certain technical subjects, which prepare the candidates for specific ministerial activities, can also be useful, such as psychology, catechetical pedagogy, homiletics, sacred music, ecclesiastical administration, information technology, etc.[14]

87. At the same time as (and possibly in relationship with) the teaching of pastoral theology a practical internship should be provided for each candidate, to permit him to meet in the field what he has learned in his study. It must be gradual, tailored to the individual and under continual supervision. For the choice of activities, account should be taken of the instituted ministries received, and their exercise should be evaluated.

Care is to be taken that the candidates be actively introduced into the pastoral activity of the diocese and that they have periodic sharing of experiences with deacons already involved in the ministry.

88. In addition, care should be taken that the future deacons develop a strong missionary sensitivity. In fact, they too, in an analogous way to priests, receive with sacred ordination a spiritual gift which prepares them for a universal mission, to the ends of the earth (cf. Acts 1:8).[15] They are to be helped, therefore, to be strongly aware of their missionary identity and prepared to undertake the

---

13 PDV, 57: *l.c.*, 758.

14 Cf. Congregation for Catholic Education, Circular Letter *Come è a Conoscenza*, 3.

15 Cf. PO, no. 10; AG, no. 20.

proclamation of the truth also to non-Christians, particularly those belonging to their own people. However, neither should the prospect of the mission *ad gentes* be lacking, wherever circumstances require and permit it.

Conclusion

89. The *Didascalia Apostolorum* recommends to the deacons of the first century: "As our Savior and Master said in the Gospel: *let he who wishes to be great among you, make himself your servant, in the same way as the Son of Man came not to be served but to serve and give his life as a ransom for many,* you deacons must do the same, even if that means giving your life for your brothers and sisters, because of the service which you are bound to fulfill."[16] This invitation is most appropriate also for those who are called today to the diaconate, and urges them to prepare themselves with great dedication for their future ministry.

90. May the Episcopal Conferences and Ordinaries of the whole world, to whom the present document is given, ensure that it becomes an object of attentive reflection in communion with their priests and communities. It will be an important point of reference for those Churches in which the permanent diaconate is a living and active reality; for the others, it will be an effective invitation to appreciate the value of that precious gift of the Spirit which is diaconal service.

The Supreme Pontiff John Paul II has approved this "Ratio Fundamentalis Institutionis Diaconorum Permanentium" and ordered it to be published.

Rome, given at the Offices of the Congregations, February 22, 1998, Feast of the Chair of Peter.

Pio Card. Laghi
Prefect

✠ José Saraiva Martins
Titular Archbishop of Tuburnica
Secretary

16 *Didascalia Apostolorum*, III, 13 (19), 3: F. X. Funk (ed.), *Didascalia et Constitutiones Apostolorum*, I, *o.c.*, 214-215.

CONGREGATION FOR THE CLERGY

Directorium pro Ministerio et Vita Diaconorum Permanentium (*Directory for the Ministry and Life of Permanent Deacons*)

1. The Juridical Status of the Deacon

Sacred Minister

1. The origin of the diaconate is the consecration and mission of Christ, in which the deacon is called to share.[17] Through the imposition of hands and the prayer of consecration, he is constituted a sacred minister and a member of the hierarchy. This condition determines his theological and juridical status in the Church.

Incardination

2. At the time of admission to the diaconate, all candidates shall be required to express clearly in writing their intention to serve the Church[18] for the rest of their lives in a specific territorial or personal circumscription, in an institute of consecrated life, or in a society of apostolic life which has the faculty to incardinate.[19] Written acceptance of a request for incardination is reserved to him who has authority to incardinate and determines the candidate's Ordinary.[20]

Incardination is a juridical bond. It has ecclesiological and spiritual significance inasmuch as it expresses the ministerial dedication of the deacon to the Church.

3. A deacon already incardinated into one ecclesiastical circumscription may be incardinated into another in accordance with the norm of law.[21] Written

17 Cf. LG, no. 28a.

18 Cf. CIC, c. 1034 §1; Paul VI, *Ad Pascendum*, I, a: *l.c.*, 538.

19 Cf. CIC, cc. 265-266.

20 Cf. CIC, cc. 1034 §1, 1016, 1019; Apostolic Constitution *Spirituali Militum Curae*, VI, §§3-4; CIC, c. 295 §1.

21 Cf. CIC, cc. 267-268 §1.

authorization must be obtained from both the bishop *a quo* and the bishop *ad quem* in the case of deacons who, for just reasons, wish to exercise their ministry in a diocese other than that into which they were incardinated. Bishops should encourage deacons of their own dioceses who wish to place themselves either permanently or for a specified time period at the service of other particular Churches with a shortage of clergy. They should also support in a particular way those who, after specific and careful preparation, seek to dedicate themselves to the *missio ad gentes.* The terms on which deacons afford such service should be duly regulated by contract and agreed upon by the bishops concerned.[22]

It is a duty incumbent on the bishop to care for the deacons of his diocese with particular solicitude.[23] This is to be discharged either personally or through a priest acting as his delegate. Special pastoral care should always be shown to those in particular difficulties because of personal circumstances.

4. The deacon incardinated into an institute of consecrated life or society of apostolic life shall exercise ministry under the jurisdiction of the bishop in all that pertains to the pastoral ministry, acts of public worship, and the apostolate. He is, however, also subject to his own superiors' competence and to the discipline of his community.[24] When a deacon is transferred to a community in another diocese, the superior shall be obliged to present him to the local Ordinary and obtain permission for him to exercise his ministry in accordance with the procedures agreed upon, between the bishop and the superior.

5. The specific vocation to the permanent Diaconate presupposes the stability of this Order. Hence ordination to the Priesthood of non-married or widowed deacons must always be a very rare exception, and only for special and grave reasons. The decision of admission to the Order of Presbyters rests with the diocesan bishop, unless impediments exist which are reserved to the Holy See.[25] Given the exceptional nature of such cases, the diocesan bishop should consult the Congregation for Catholic Education with regard to the intellectual and theological preparation of the candidate, and also the Congregation for the

22 Cf. CIC, c. 271.

23 Cf. SDO, VI, 30: *l.c.*, 703.

24 Cf. CIC, c. 678 §§1-3; 715; 738; cf. also SDO, VII, 33-35: *l.c.*, 704.

25 Letter of the Secretariat of State to the Cardinal Prefect of the Congregation for Divine Worship and the Discipline of the Sacraments, Prot. N. 122.735, of January 3, 1984.

Clergy concerning the program of priestly formation and the aptitude of the candidate to the priestly ministry.

6. By virtue of their ordination, deacons are united to each other by a sacramental fraternity. They are all dedicated to the same purpose—building up the Body of Christ—in union with the Supreme Pontiff[26] and subject to the authority of the bishop. Each deacon should have a sense of being joined with his fellow deacons in a bond of charity, prayer, obedience to their bishops, ministerial zeal and collaboration.

With the permission of the bishop and in his presence or that of his delegate, it would be opportune for deacons periodically to meet to discuss their ministry, exchange experiences, advance formation and encourage each other in fidelity. Such encounters might also be of interest to candidates to the permanent Diaconate. The local Ordinary should foster a "spirit of communion" among deacons ministering in his diocese and avoid any form of "corporatism" which was a factor in the decline and eventual extinction of the permanent Diaconate in earlier centuries.

7. The Diaconate brings with it a series of rights and duties as foreseen by canons 273-283 of the *Code of Canon Law* with regard to clerics in general and deacons in particular.

8. The rite of ordination includes a promise of obedience to the bishops: "Do you promise respect and obedience to me and to my successors?"[27] In making this promise to his bishop the deacon takes Christ, obedient par excellence (cf. Phil 2:5-11), as his model. He shall conform his own obedience in listening (Heb 10:5ff; Jn 4:34) and in radical availability (cf. Lk 9:54ff, 10:1ff) to the obedience of Christ. He shall therefore dedicate himself to working in complete conformity with the will of the Father and devote himself to the Church

26 Cf. CD, no. 15; SDO, 23; *l.c.*, 702.

27 *Pontificale Romanum, De Ordinatione Episcopi, Presbyterorum et Diaconorum,* no. 201 (*editio typica altera*), *Typis Polyglottis Vaticanis*, 1990, 110; cf. CIC, c. 273.

by means of complete availability.[28] In a spirit of prayer, with which he should be permeated, the deacon, following the example of the Lord who gave himself "unto death, death on a cross" (Phil 2:8), should deepen every day his total gift of self. This vision of obedience also predisposes acceptance of a more concrete detailing of the obligation assumed by the deacon at ordination, in accordance with the provisions of law: "Unless excused by a lawful impediment, clerics are obliged to accept and faithfully fulfill the office committed to them by their Ordinary."[29] This obligation is based on participation in the bishop's ministry conferred by the Sacrament of Holy Orders and by canonical mission. The extent of obedience and availability is determined by the diaconal ministry itself and by all that is objectively, immediately and directly in relation to it.

The Deacon receives office by a decree of the bishop. In his decree of appointment, the bishop shall ascribe duties to the deacon which are congruent with his personal abilities, his celibate or married state, his formation, age, and with his spiritually valid aspirations. The territory in which his ministry is to be exercised or those to whom he is to minister should be clearly specified. The decree must also indicate whether the office conferred is to be discharged on a partial or full-time basis and the priest who has the "*cura animarum*" where the deacon's ministry is exercised, must be named.

9. Clerics are obliged to live in the bond of fraternity and of prayer, collaborate with each other and with the bishop to recognize and foster the mission of the faithful in the Church and in the world[30] and live in a simple, sober manner which is open to fraternal giving and sharing.[31]

---

28 "Those dominated by an outlook of contestation or of opposition to authority cannot adequately fulfill the functions of the diaconate. The diaconate can only be conferred on those who believe in the value of the pastoral mission of bishops and priests and in the assistance of the Holy Spirit who helps them in their activities and in the decisions they take. It should be recalled that the deacon must 'profess respect and obedience to the bishop.' The service of the deacon is directed to a particular Christian community for which he should develop a profound attachment both to its mission and divine institution" (Catechesis of John Paul II at the General Audience of October 20, 1993, no. 2, *Insegnamenti*, XVI, 2, [1993], 1055).

29 CIC, c. 274 §2.

30 "Among the duties of the deacon there is that of 'promoting and sustaining the apostolic activities of the laity.' Being more present and active in the secular world than priests, deacons should strive to promote greater closeness between ordained ministers and activities of the laity for the common service of the Kingdom of God" (Catechesis of John Paul II at the General Audience of October 13, 1993, no. 5, *Insegnamenti*, XVI, 2 [1993], 1002-1003); cf. CIC, c. 275.

31 Cf. CIC, c. 282.

10. Unlike deacons to be ordained to the priesthood,[32] who are bound by the same norms as priests in the matter,[33] permanent deacons are not obliged to wear clerical garb. Deacons who are members of institutes of consecrated life or societies of apostolic life shall adhere to the norms prescribed for them by the *Code of Canon Law*.[34]

11. In its canonical discipline, the Church recognizes the right of deacons to form associations among themselves to promote their spiritual life, to carry out charitable and pious works and pursue other objectives which are consonant with their sacramental consecration and mission.[35] As with other clerics, deacons are not permitted to found, participate in, or be members of any association or group, even of a civil nature, which is incompatible with the clerical state or which impedes the diligent execution of their ministerial duties. They shall also avoid all associations whose nature, objectives and methods are insidious to the full hierarchical communion of the Church. Likewise, associations which are injurious to the identity of the diaconate and to the discharge of its duties for the Church's service, as well as those groups or associations which plot against the Church, are to be avoided.[36]

Associations too which, under the guise of representation, organize deacons into a form of *trade(s) unions* or *pressure groups*, thus reducing the sacred ministry to a secular profession or trade, are completely irreconcilable with the clerical state. The same is true of any form of association which would prejudice the direct and immediate relationship between every deacon and his bishop.

All such associations are forbidden because they are injurious to the exercise of the sacred ministry, which, in this context, is considered as no more than a subordinate activity, and because they promote conflict with the bishops who are similarly regarded purely as employers.[37]

It should be recalled that no private association may be considered an ecclesial association unless it shall have obtained prior *recognitio* of its statutes by the

32 Cf. CIC, c. 288 referring to c. 284.

33 Cf. CIC, c. 284; *Directory for the Ministry and Life of Priests* of the Congregation for the Clergy (January 31, 1994), 66-67. Clarification of the Pontifical Council for the Interpretation of Legislative Texts on the binding character of article 66 (October 22, 1994) in *Sacrum Ministerium*, 2 (1995), 263.

34 Cf. CIC, c. 669.

35 Cf. CIC, c. 278 §§1-2, explicating c. 215.

36 Cf. CIC, c. 278 §3 and c. 1374; also the declaration of the German Bishops' Conference "The Church and Freemasonry" (February 28, 1980).

37 Congregation for the Clergy, *Quidam Episcopi* (March 8, 1982), IV: AAS 74 (1982), 642-645.

competent ecclesiastical authority.[38] Such authority has the right and duty to be vigilant concerning associations and the fulfillment of their statutory ends.[39]

Deacons who come from ecclesial associations or movements may continue to enjoy the spiritual benefits of such communities and may continue to draw help and support from them in their service of a particular Church.

12. The professional activity of deacons assumes a significance which distinguishes it from that of the lay faithful.[40] Thus the secular work of permanent deacons is in some sense linked with their ministry. They should be mindful that the lay members of the faithful, in virtue of their own specific mission, are "particularly called to make the Church present and fruitful in those places and circumstances where it is only through them that she can become the salt of the earth."[41]

Derogating from what is prescribed for other clerics,[42] the present discipline of the Church does not prohibit to permanent deacons professions which involve the exercise of civil authority or the administration of temporal goods or accountable secular offices. Particular law, however, may determine otherwise, should such derogation prove inopportune.

In those commercial and business activities[43] permitted under particular law, deacons should exhibit honesty and ethical rectitude. They should be careful to fulfill their obligations to civil law where it is not contrary to the natural law, to the Magisterium or to the canons of the Church and to her freedom.[44]

The aforementioned derogation is not applicable to permanent deacons who are incardinated into institutes of consecrated life or societies of apostolic life.[45]

Permanent deacons must make prudent judgments and they should seek the advice of their bishops in more complex instances. Some professions, while

38 Cf. CIC, c. 299 §3, and c. 304.

39 Cf. CIC, c. 305.

40 Cf. Allocution of John Paul II to the Bishops of Zaire on "*Ad Limina*" visit, April 30, 1983, *Insegnamenti*, VI, 1 (1983), 112-113. Allocution to Permanent Deacons (March 16, 1985), *Insegnamenti*, VIII, 1 (1985), 648-650. Cf. also John Paul II, Allocution at the Ordination of Eight New Bishops in Kinshasa (May 4, 1980), 3-5 *Insegnamenti*, 1 (1980), 1111-1114; Catechesis at the General Audience of October 6, 1983 *Insegnamenti*, XVI, 2 (1983), 951-955.

41 LG, no. 33; cf. CIC, c. 225.

42 Cf. CIC, c. 288, referring to c. 285 §§3-4.

43 Cf. CIC, c. 288, referring to c. 286.

44 Cf. CIC, c. 222 §2, and also c. 225 §2.

45 Cf. CIC, c. 672.

of undoubted benefit to the community, can, when exercised by a permanent deacon, in certain circumstances, become incompatible with the pastoral responsibilities of his ministry. The competent authority, bearing in mind the requirements of ecclesial communion and of the fruitfulness of pastoral ministry, shall evaluate individual cases as they arise, including a change of profession after ordination to the permanent Diaconate.

Where there is conflict of conscience, deacons must act in conformity with the doctrine and discipline of the Church, even if this should require of them great sacrifices.

13. As sacred ministers, deacons are required to give complete priority to their ministry and to pastoral charity and "do their utmost to foster among people peace and harmony based on justice."[46] Active involvement in political parties or trades unions, in accordance with the dispositions of the Episcopal Conference,[47] may be permitted in particular circumstances "for the defense of the rights of the Church or to promote the common good."[48] Deacons are strictly prohibited from all involvement with political parties or trade(s) union movements which are founded on ideologies, policies or associations incompatible with Church doctrine.

14. Should a deacon wish to absent himself from his diocese for "a considerable period of time," he should normally obtain the permission of his Ordinary or Major Superior in accordance with the provisions of particular law.[49]

15. Deacons who are professionally employed are required to provide for their own upkeep from the ensuing emoluments.[50]

It is entirely legitimate that those who devote themselves fully to the service of God in the discharge of ecclesiastical office,[51] be equitably remunerated, since "the laborer is deserving of his wage" (Lk 10:7) and the Lord has disposed that those who proclaim the Gospel should live by the Gospel (cf. 1 Cor 9:14). This does not however exclude the possibility that a cleric might wish to renounce

46 Cf. CIC, c. 287 §1.
47 Cf. CIC, c. 288.
48 Cf. CIC, c. 287 §2.
49 Cf. CIC, c. 283.
50 Cf. SDO, 21: *l.c.*, 701.
51 Cf. CIC, c. 281.

this right, as the Apostle himself did (1 Cor 9:12), and otherwise make provision for himself.

It is not easy to draw up general norms concerning the upkeep of deacons which are binding in all circumstances, given the great diversity of situations in which deacons work, in various particular Churches and countries. In this matter, due attention must also be given to possible stipulations made in agreements between the Holy See or Episcopal Conferences and governments. In such circumstances, particular law should determine appropriately in the matter.

16. Since clerics dedicate themselves in an active and concrete way to the ecclesiastical ministry, they have a right to sustenance which includes "a remuneration that befits their condition"[52] and to social security.[53]

With regard to married deacons the *Code of Canon Law* provides that: "married deacons who dedicate themselves full-time to the ecclesiastical ministry deserve remuneration sufficient to provide for themselves and their families. Those, however, who receive remuneration by reason of a secular profession which they exercise or have exercised are to see to their own and to their families' needs from that income."[54] In prescribing "adequate" remuneration, parameters of evaluation are also: personal condition, the nature of the office exercised, circumstances of time and place, material needs of the minister (including those of the families of married deacons), just recompense of those in his service—the same general criteria, in fact, which apply to all clerics.

In order to provide for the sustenance of clerics ministering in dioceses, every particular Church is obliged to constitute a special fund which "collects offerings and temporal goods for the support of the clergy."[55]

Social security for clerics is to be provided by another fund, unless other provision has been made.[56]

---

52 "Since clerics dedicate themselves to the ecclesiastical ministry, they deserve the remuneration which is consistent with their condition, taking into account the nature of their function and the condition of places and times, and by which they can provide for the necessities of their life as well as for the equitable payment of those whose services they need" (CIC, c. 281 §1).

53 "Provision must also be made so that they possess that social assistance which provides for their needs suitably if they suffer from illness, incapacity, or old age" (CIC, c. 281 §2).

54 CIC, c. 281 §3. The canonical term "remuneration" as distinct from civil law usage, denotes more than a stipend in the technical sense of this term. It connotes that income, due in justice, that permits a decent upkeep, congruent with the ministry.

55 CIC, c. 1274 §1.

56 CIC, c. 1274 §2.

17. Celibate deacons who minister full-time in a diocese, have a right to be remunerated according to the general principle of law[57] should they have no other source of income.

18. Married deacons who minister full-time and who do not receive income from any other source are to be remunerated, in accordance with the aforementioned general principle, so that they may be able to provide for themselves and for their families.[58]

19. Married deacons who minister full-time or part-time and who receive income from a secular profession which they exercise or have exercised are obliged to provide for themselves and for their families from such income.[59]

20. It is for particular law to provide opportune norms in the complex matter of reimbursing expenses, including, for example, that those entities and parishes which benefit from the ministry of a deacon have an obligation to reimburse him those expenses incurred in the exercise of his ministry.

Particular law may also determine the obligations devolving on the diocese when a deacon, through no fault of his own, becomes unemployed. Likewise, it will be opportune to define the extent of diocesan liability with regard to the widows and orphans of deceased deacons. Where possible, deacons, before ordination, should subscribe to a mutual assurance (insurance) policy which affords cover for these eventualities.

21. Trusting to the perennial fidelity of God, the deacon is called to live his Order with generous dedication and ever renewed perseverance. Sacred ordination, once validly received, can never be rendered null. Nevertheless, loss of the clerical state may occur in conformity with the canonical norms.[60]

57 CIC, c. 281 §1.
58 Cf. CIC, c. 281 §3.
59 Cf. CIC, c. 281 §3.
60 Cf. CIC, cc. 290-293.

2. The Diaconal Ministry

Diaconal Functions

22. The Second Vatican Council synthesized the ministry of deacons in the threefold "diaconia of the liturgy, the word and of charity."[61] In this way diaconal participation through the ordained ministry in the one and triple *munus* of Christ is expressed. The deacon "is *teacher* insofar as he preaches and bears witness to the word of God; he *sanctifies* when he administers the Sacrament of Baptism, the Holy Eucharist and the sacramentals, he participates at the celebration of Holy Mass as a 'minister of the Blood,' and conserves and distributes the Blessed Eucharist; he is a *guide* inasmuch as he animates the community or a section of ecclesial life."[62] Thus deacons assist and serve the bishops and priests who preside at every liturgy, are watchful of doctrine and guide the people of God.

The ministry of deacons, in the service of the community of the faithful, should "collaborate in building up the unity of Christians without prejudice and without inopportune initiatives."[63] It should cultivate those "human qualities which make a person acceptable to others, credible, vigilant about his language and his capacity to dialogue, so as to acquire a truly ecumenical attitude."[64]

Diaconia of the Word

23. The bishop, during the rite of ordination, gives the book of the Gospels to the deacon saying: "Receive the Gospel of Christ whose herald you have become."[65] Like priests, deacons are commended to all by their conduct, their preaching of the mystery of Christ, by transmitting Christian doctrine and by devoting attention to the problems of our time. The principal function of the deacon, therefore, is to collaborate with the bishop and the priests in the exercise of a

61 LG, no. 29.

62 John Paul II, Allocution to Permanent Deacons (March 16, 1985), no. 2: *Insegnamenti*, VIII, 1 (1985), 649; cf. LG, no. 29; CIC, c. 1008.

63 Pontifical Council for the Promotion of Christian Unity *Directory on the Applications of the Principles and Norms on Ecumenism*, (March 25, 1993), 71: *AAS* 85 (1993), 1069; cf. Congregation for the Doctrine of the Faith, *Communionis Notio* (May 28, 1992), *AAS* 85 [1993], 838f.

64 Pontifical Council for the Promotion of Christian Unity *Directory on the Applications of the Principles and Norms on Ecumenism*, (March 25, 1993), 70: *l.c.*, 1068.

65 *Pontificale Romanum*, no. 210: ed. cit., 125: "*Accipe Evangelium Christi, cuius praeco effectus es; et vide, ut quod legeris credas, quod credideris doceas, quod docueris imiteris.*"

ministry[66] which is not of their own wisdom but of the word of God, calling all to conversion and holiness.[67] He prepares for such a ministry by careful study of Sacred Scripture, of Tradition, of the liturgy and of the life of the Church.[68] Moreover, in interpreting and applying the sacred deposit, the deacon is obliged to be directed by the Magisterium of those who are "witnesses of divine and Catholic truth,"[69] the Roman Pontiff and the bishops in communion with him,[70] so as to teach and propose the mystery of Christ fully and faithfully.[71]

It is also necessary that he learn the art of communicating the faith effectively and integrally to contemporary man, in diverse cultural circumstances and stages of life.[72]

24. It is for the deacon to proclaim the Gospel and preach the word of God.[73] Deacons have the faculty to preach everywhere, in accordance with the conditions established by law.[74] This faculty is founded on the Sacrament of Ordination and should be exercised with at least the tacit consent of the rector of the churches concerned and with that humility proper to one who is servant and not master of the word of God. In this respect the warning of the Apostle is always relevant: "Since we have this ministry through the mercy shown to us, we are not discouraged. Rather we have renounced shameful, hidden things; not acting deceitfully or falsifying the word of God, but by the open declaration of the truth we commend ourselves to everybody's conscience in the sight of God" (2 Cor 4:1-2).[75]

---

66 Cf. LG, no. 29. "It is also for deacons to serve the people of God in the ministry of the word in communion with the bishop and his presbyterate" (CIC, c. 757); "By their preaching, deacons participate in the priestly ministry" (John Paul II, Allocution to Priests, Deacons, Religious, and Seminarians in the Basilica of the Oratory of St. Joseph, Montreal, Canada (September 11, 1984), no. 9: *Insegnamenti*, VII, 2 (1984), 436.

67 Cf. PO, no. 4.

68 Cf. DV, no. 25; Congregation for Catholic Education, Circular Letter *Come è a Conoscenza*; CIC, c. 760.

69 LG, no. 25a; DV, no. 10a.

70 Cf. CIC, c. 753.

71 Cf. CIC, c. 760.

72 Cf. CIC, c. 769.

73 Cf. *Institutio Generalis Missalis Romani* (IGMR), no. 61: *Missale Romanum, Ordo lectionis Missae, Praenotanda*, nos. 8, 24, and 50: ed. typica altera, 1981.

74 Cf. CIC, c. 764.

75 Congregation for the Clergy, Directory on the Ministry and Life of Priests, *Tota Ecclesia* (January 31, 1994), nos. 45-47: *l.c.*, 43-48.

25. When the deacon presides at a liturgical celebration, in accordance with the relevant norms,[76] he shall give due importance to the homily, since it "proclaims the marvels worked by God in the mystery of Christ, present and effective in the liturgical celebrations."[77] Deacons should be trained carefully to prepare their homilies in prayer, in study of the sacred texts, in perfect harmony with the Magisterium and in keeping with the situation of those to whom they preach.

In order to assist the Christian faithful to grow in knowledge of their faith in Christ, to strengthen it by reception of the sacraments and to express it in their family, professional and social lives,[78] much attention must be given to catechesis of the faithful of all stages of Christian living. With growing secularization and the ever greater challenges posed for man and for the Gospel by contemporary society, the need for complete, faithful and lucid catechesis becomes all the more pressing.

26. Contemporary society requires a new evangelization which demands a greater and more generous effort on the part of ordained ministers. Deacons, "nourished by prayer and above all by love of the Eucharist,"[79] in addition to their involvement in diocesan and parochial programs of catechesis, of evangelization and of preparation for the reception of the Sacraments, should strive to transmit the word in their professional lives, either explicitly or merely by their active presence in places where public opinion is formed and ethical norms are applied—such as the social services or organizations promoting the rights of the family or life. They should also be aware of the great possibilities for the ministry of the word in the area of religious and moral instruction in schools,[80] in Catholic and civil universities[81] and by adequate use of modern means of social communication.[82]

---

76 Cf. *Institutio Generalis Missalis Romani*, nos. 42, 61; Congregation for the Clergy, Pontifical Council for the Laity, Congregation for the Doctrine of the Faith, Congregation for Divine Worship and the Discipline of the Sacraments, Congregation for Bishops, Congregation for the Evangelization of Peoples, Congregation for the Institutes of Consecrated Life and the Societies of Apostolic Life, Pontifical Council for the Interpretation of Legislative Texts, Instruction concerning some questions on the collaboration of the lay faithful in the ministry of priests, *Ecclesiae de Mysterio* (August 15, 1997), art. 3.

77 SC, no. 35; cf. 52; CIC, c. 767 §1.

78 Cf. CIC, c. 779; cf. Congregation for the Clergy, *General Directory for Catechesis* (GDC), (August 15, 1997) no. 216.

79 Paul VI, Apostolic Exhortation, *Evangelii Nuntiandi* (EN), December 8, 1975: *AAS* 68 (1976), 576.

80 Cf. CIC, cc. 804-805.

81 Cf. CIC, c. 810.

82 Cf. CIC, c. 761.

In addition to indispensable orthodoxy of doctrine, these *new fields demand* specialized training, but they are very effective means of bringing the Gospel to contemporary man and society.[83]

Finally, deacons are reminded that they are obliged to submit, before its publication, written material concerning faith or morals,[84] to the judgment of their Ordinaries. It is also necessary to obtain the permission of the Ordinary before writing in publications which habitually attack the Catholic religion or good morals. They are also bound to adhere to the norms established by the Episcopal Conference[85] when involved in radio or television broadcasts.

In every case, the deacon should hold before him the primary and indefeasible necessity of always presenting the truth without compromise.

27. The deacon will be aware that the Church is missionary[86] by her very nature, both because her origin is in the missions of the Son and the Holy Spirit, according to the eternal plan of the Father and because she has received an explicit mandate from the risen Lord to preach the Gospel to all creation and to baptize those who believe (cf. Mk 16:15-16; Mt 28:19). Deacons are ministers of the Church and thus, although incardinated into a particular Church, they are not exempt from the missionary obligation of the universal Church. Hence they should always remain open to the *missio ad gentes* to the extent that their professional or—if married—family obligations permit.[87]

The deacon's ministry of service is linked with the missionary dimension of the Church: the missionary efforts of the deacon will embrace the ministry of the word, the liturgy, and works of charity which, in their turn, are carried into daily life. Mission includes witness to Christ in a secular profession or occupation.

Diaconia of the Liturgy

28. The rite of ordination emphasizes another aspect of the diaconal ministry—ministry at the altar.[88]

---

83 Cf. CIC, c. 822.
84 Cf. CIC, c. 823 §1.
85 CIC, c. 831 §§1-2.
86 AG, no. 2a.
87 Cf. CIC, cc. 784, 786.
88 AG, no. 16; *Pontificale Romanum*, no. 207: ed. cit., 122 (*Prex Ordinationis*).

Deacons receive the Sacrament of Orders, so as to serve as a vested minister in the sanctification of the Christian community, in hierarchical communion with the bishop and priests. They provide a sacramental assistance to the ministry of the bishop and, subordinately, to that of the priests which is intrinsic, fundamental and distinct.

Clearly, this *diaconia* at the altar, since founded on the Sacrament of Orders, differs in essence from any liturgical ministry entrusted to the lay faithful. The liturgical ministry of the deacon is also distinct from that of the ordained priestly ministry.[89]

Thus, in the Eucharistic Sacrifice, the deacon does not celebrate the mystery: rather, he effectively represents on the one hand, the people of God and, specifically, helps them to unite their lives to the offering of Christ; while on the other, in the name of Christ himself, he helps the Church to participate in the fruits of that sacrifice.

Since "the liturgy is the summit toward which the activity of the Church is directed and the font from which all her power flows,"[90] this prerogative of diaconal ordination is also the font of sacramental grace which nourishes the entire ministry. Careful and profound theological and liturgical preparation must precede reception of that grace to enable the deacon to participate worthily in the celebration of the sacraments and sacramentals.

29. While exercising his ministry, the deacon should maintain a lively awareness that "every liturgical celebration, because it is an action of Christ the Priest and of his Body which is the Church, is a sacred action surpassing all others. No other action of the Church can equal its efficacy by the same title and to the same degree."[91] The liturgy is the source of grace and sanctification. Its efficacy derives from Christ the Redeemer and does not depend on the holiness of the minister. This certainty should cause the deacon to grow in humility since he can never compromise the salvific work of Christ. At the same time it should inspire him to holiness of life so that he may be a worthy minister of the liturgy. Liturgical actions cannot be reduced to mere private or social actions which can be celebrated by anybody since they belong to the Body of the universal Church.[92] Deacons shall observe devoutly the liturgical norms proper to the

89 Cf. LG, no. 29.
90 SC, no. 10.
91 SC, no. 7d.
92 Cf. SC, no. 22 §3; CIC, cc. 841, 846.

sacred mysteries so as to bring the faithful to a conscious participation in the liturgy, to fortify their faith, give worship to God and sanctify the Church.[93]

30. According to the tradition of the Church and the provisions of law,[94] deacons "assist the bishop and priests in the celebration of the divine mysteries."[95] They should therefore work to promote liturgical celebrations which involve the whole assembly, fostering the interior participation of the faithful in the liturgy and the exercise of the various ministries.[96]

They should be mindful of the importance of the aesthetical dimension which conveys to the whole person the beauty of what is being celebrated. Music and song, even in its simplest form, the preached word and the communion of the faithful who live the peace and forgiveness of Christ, form a precious heritage which the deacon should foster.

The deacon is to observe faithfully the rubrics of the liturgical books without adding, omitting or changing of his own volition[97] what they require. Manipulation of the liturgy is tantamount to depriving it of the riches of the mystery of Christ, whom it contains, and may well signify presumption toward what has been established by the Church's wisdom. Deacons, therefore, should confine themselves to those things, and only to those things, in which they are properly competent.[98] For the Sacred Liturgy they should vest worthily and with dignity, in accordance with the prescribed liturgical norms.[99] The dalmatic, in its appropriate liturgical colors, together with the alb, cincture and stole, "constitutes the liturgical dress proper to deacons."[100]

---

93 Cf. CIC, c. 840.

94 CCC, no. 1570; cf. *Caeremoniale Episcoporum*, nos. 23-26.

95 "Deacons have a part in the celebration of divine worship according to the norm of the prescripts of the law" (CIC, c. 835 §3).

96 Cf. SC, nos. 26-27.

97 Cf. CIC, c. 846 §1.

98 Cf. SC, no. 28.

99 Cf. CIC, c. 929.

100 Cf. *Institutio generalis Missalis Romani*, nos, 81b, 300, 302; *Institutio generalis Liturgiae Horarum*, no. 255; *Pontificale Romanum*, nos. 23, 24, 28, 29, editio typica, Typis Polyglottis Vaticanis 1977, 29 and 90; *Rituale Romanum*, no. 36, editio typica, Typis Polyglottis Vaticanis 1985, 18; *Ordo Coronandi Imaginem Beatae Mariae Virginis*, no. 12, editio typica, Typis Polyglottis Vaticanis 1981, 10; Congregation for Divine Worship, Directory for celebrations in the absence of a priest, *Christi Ecclesia*, no. 38, in "Notitiae" 24 (1988), 388-389; *Pontificale Romanum*, nos. 188: ("Immediate post Precem Ordinationis, Ordinati stola diaconali et dalmatica induuntur quo eorum ministerium abhinc in liturgia peragendum manifestatur") and 190; ed. cit., 102, 103; *Caeremoniale Episcoporum*, no. 67, editio typica, Libreria Editrice Vaticana 1995, 28-29.

The ministry of deacons also includes preparation of the faithful for reception of the sacraments and their pastoral care after having received them.

31. The deacon, together with the bishop and priest, is the ordinary minister of Baptism.[101] The exercise of this power requires either the permission of the parish priest, since he enjoys the particular right of baptizing those entrusted to his pastoral care,[102] or the presence of necessity.[103] In preparing for the reception of this sacrament, the ministry of the deacon is especially important.

Holy Eucharist

32. At the celebration of the Holy Eucharist, the deacon assists those who preside at the assembly and consecrate the Body and Blood of the Lord—that is the bishop and his priests[104]—according to the norms established by the *Institutio Generalis* of the Roman Missal,[105] and thus manifests Christ, the Servant. He is close to the priest during the celebration of the Mass[106] and helps him, especially if the priest is blind, infirm or feeble. At the altar he serves the chalice and the book. He proposes the intentions of the bidding prayers to the faithful and invites them to exchange the sign of peace. In the absence of other ministers, he discharges, when necessary, their office too.

The deacon may not pronounce the words of the eucharistic prayer, nor those of the collects nor may he use the gestures which are proper to those who consecrate the Body and Blood of the Lord.[107]

The Deacon Properly Proclaims from the Books of Sacred Scripture108

As an ordinary minister of Holy Communion,[109] the deacon distributes the Body of Christ to the faithful during the celebration of the Mass and, outside

101 CIC, c. 861 §1.
102 Cf. CIC, c. 530, 1°.
103 Cf. CIC, c. 862.
104 Cf. SDO, V, 22, 1: *l.c.*, 701.
105 Cf. *Institutio Generalis Missalis Romani*, nos. 61, 127-141.
106 Cf. CIC, c.930 §2.
107 Cf. CIC, c. 907; Congregation for the Clergy, etc., Instruction *Ecclesiae de Mysterio* (August 15, 1997), art. 6.
108 Cf. SDO, V, 22, 6: *l.c.*, 702.
109 Cf. CIC, c. 910 §1.

of it, administers Viaticum[110] to the sick. He is equally an ordinary minister of exposition of the Most Blessed Sacrament and of eucharistic benediction.[111] It falls to the deacon to preside at Sunday celebrations in the absence of a priest.[112]

33. The pastoral care of families, for which the bishop is primarily responsible, may be entrusted to deacons. In supporting families in their difficulties and sufferings,[113] this responsibility will extend from moral and liturgical questions to difficulties of a social and personal nature, and can be exercised at diocesan or, subject to the authority of the parish priest, local level in promoting the catechesis of Christian marriage, the personal preparation of future spouses, the fruitful celebration of marriage and help offered to couples after marriage.[114]

Married deacons can be of much assistance in promoting the Gospel value of conjugal love, the virtues which protect it and the practice of parenthood which can truly be regarded as responsible, from a human and Christian point of view.

Where deacons have been duly delegated by the parish priest or the local Ordinary, they may assist at the celebration of marriages *extra Missam* and pronounce the nuptial blessing in the name of the Church.[115] They may also be given general delegation, in accordance with the prescribed conditions,[116] which may only be subdelegated, however, in the manner specified by the *Code of Canon Law.*[117]

34. It is defined doctrine,[118] that the administration of the Sacrament of the Anointing of the Sick is reserved to bishops and priests since this sacrament involves the forgiveness of sins and the worthy reception of the Holy Eucharist, but, the pastoral care of the sick may be entrusted to deacons. Active service to alleviate the suffering of the sick, catechesis in preparation for the reception of

110 Cf. CIC, c. 911 §2.

111 Cf. CIC, c. 943 and also SDO, V, 22, 3: *l.c.*, 702.

112 Cf. Congregation for Divine Worship, Directory for Celebrations in the Absence of a Priest, *Christi Ecclesia*, no. 38: *l.c.*, 388-389; Congregation for the Clergy, etc., Instruction *Ecclesiae de Mysterio* (August 15, 1997), art. 7.

113 Cf. John Paul II, Post-Synodal Apostolic Exhortation *Familiaris Consortio* (FC), 73: *AAS* 74 (November 22, 1982), 107-171.

114 Cf. CIC, c. 1063.

115 Cf. LG, no. 29; CIC, c. 1108 §§1-2; *Ordo Celebrandi Matrimonii*, ed. typica altera 1991, 24.

116 Cf. CIC, c. 1111 §§1-2.

117 Cf. CIC, c. 137 §§3-4.

118 *Exultate Deo* of the Council of Florence (DS 1325); *Doctrina de sacramento extremae unctionis* of the Council of Trent, cap. 3 (DS 1697) and cap. 4 *de extrema unctione* (DS 1719).

the Sacrament of Anointing of the Sick, preparing the faithful for death in the absence of a priest, and the administration of Viaticum according to the prescribed rites, are means by which deacons may bring the love of the Church to the suffering faithful.[119]

35. Deacons have an obligation, established by the Church, to celebrate the Liturgy of the Hours with which the entire Mystical Body is united to the prayer Christ the Head offers to the Father. Mindful of this obligation, they shall celebrate the Liturgy of the Hours every day according to the approved liturgical books and in the manner determined by the respective Episcopal Conference.[120] Furthermore, they should strive to promote participation by the greater Christian community in this Liturgy, which is never private, but an action proper to the entire Church,[121] even when celebrated individually.

36. The deacon is the minister of sacramentals, that is of "sacred signs which bear a resemblance to the sacraments (and) signify effects, particularly of a spiritual nature, which are obtained through the Church's intercession."[122]

The deacon may therefore impart those blessings most closely linked to ecclesial and sacramental life that are expressly permitted to him by law.[123] It is for the deacon to conduct *exequies* celebrated outside of Holy Mass, as well as the rite of Christian burial.[124]

When a priest is present or available, however, such tasks must be given to him.[125]

The Diaconia of Charity

37. In virtue of the Sacrament of Orders, deacons, in communion with the bishop and the diocesan presbyterate, participate in the same pastoral functions,[126] but exercise them differently in serving and assisting the bishop and his

119 Cf. SDO, II, 10: *l.c.*, 699; Congregation for the Clergy, etc., Instruction, *Ecclesiae de Mysterio* (August 15, 1997), art. 9.

120 Cf. CIC, c. 276 §2, 3°.

121 Cf. *Institutio Generalis Liturgiae Horarum*, nos. 20, 255-256.

122 Cf. SC, no. 60; CIC, cc. 1166 and 1168; CCC, 1667.

123 Cf. CIC, c.1169 §3.

124 Cf. SDO, V, 22, 5: *l.c.*, 702; also *Ordo Exsequiarum*, 19; Congregation for the Clergy, etc., Instruction *Ecclesiae de Mysterio* (August 15, 1997), art. 12.

125 Cf. *Rituale Romanum—De Benedictionibus*, no. 18 c.: ed. cit, 14.

126 Cf. CIC, c.129 §1.

priests. Since this participation is brought about by the sacrament, they serve God's people in the name of Christ. For this reason, they exercise it in humility and charity, and, according to the words of St. Polycarp, they must always be "merciful, zealous and let them walk according to the truth of the Lord who became servant of all."[127] Their authority, therefore, exercised in hierarchical communion with the bishop and his priests, and required by the same unity of consecration and mission,[128] is a service of charity which seeks to help and foster all members of a particular Church, so that they may participate, in a spirit of communion and according to their proper charisms, in the life and mission of the Church.

38. In the ministry of charity, deacons should conform themselves in the likeness of Christ the Servant, whom they represent and, above all, they should be "dedicated to works of charity and to administration."[129] Thus, in the prayer of ordination, the bishop implores God the Father that they may be "full of all the virtues, sincere in charity, solicitous toward the weak and the poor, humble in their service . . . may they be the image of your Son who did not come to be served but to serve."[130] By word and example they should work so that all the faithful, in imitation of Christ, may place themselves at the constant service of their brothers and sisters.

Diocesan and parochial works of charity, which are among the primary duties of bishops and priests are entrusted by them, as attested by Tradition, to servants in the ecclesiastical ministry, that is, to deacons.[131] So too is the service of charity in Christian education; in training preachers, youth groups, and lay groups; in promoting life in all its phases and transforming the world according to the Christian order.[132] In all of these areas the ministry of deacons is particularly valuable, since today the spiritual and material needs of man, to which

127 St. Polycarp, *Epist. Ad Philippenses,* 5, 2; F. X. Funk (ed.), I, 300; cited in LG, no. 29.

128 Cf. SDO *l.c.,* 698.

129 LG, no. 29.

130 *Pontificale Romanum—De Ordinatione Episcopi, Presbyterorum et Diaconorum,* no. 207, 122 (Prex Ordinationis).

131 Hippolytus, *Traditio Apostolica,* 8, 24; *S. Ch.* 11 bis 58-63, 98-99; *Didascalia Apostolorum* (Syriac), chapters III and IX; A. Vööbus (ed) *The "Didascalia Apostolorum" in Syriac* (original text in Syriac with an English translation), *Corpus Scriptorum Christianorum Orientalium* (CSCO) vol. I, no. 402 (tome 176), 29-30; vol. II, no. 408 (tome 180), 120-129; *Didascalia Apostolorum,* III (19), 1-7: F. X. Funk (ed.), *Didascalia et Constitutiones Apostolorum,* Paderbornae 1906, I, 212-216; CD, no. 13.

132 GS, nos. 40-45.

the Church is called to respond, are greatly diversified. They should, therefore, strive to serve all the faithful without discrimination, while devoting particular care to the suffering and the sinful. As ministers of Christ and of his Church, they must be able to transcend all ideologies and narrow party interests, lest they deprive the Church's mission of its strength which is the love of Christ. *Diaconia* should bring man to an experience of God's love and move him to conversion by opening his heart to the work of grace.

The charitable function of deacons "also involves appropriate service in the administration of goods and in the Church's charitable activities."[133] In this regard, deacons "discharge the duties of charity and administration in the name of the hierarchy and also provide social services."[134] Hence, deacons may be appointed to the office of diocesan *oeconomus*[135] and likewise nominated to the diocesan finance council.[136]

The Canonical Mission of Permanent Deacons

39. The three contexts of the diaconal ministry, depending on circumstances, may absorb, to varying degrees, a large proportion of every deacon's activity. Together, however, they represent a unity in service at the level of divine Revelation: the ministry of the word leads to ministry at the altar, which in turn prompts the transformation of life by the liturgy, resulting in charity. "If we consider the deep spiritual nature of this *diaconia*, then we shall better appreciate the interrelationship between the three areas of ministry traditionally associated with the diaconate, that is, the ministry of the word, the ministry of the altar and the ministry of charity. Depending on the circumstances, one or other of these may take on special importance in the individual work of a deacon, but these three ministries are inseparably joined in God's plan for redemption."[137]

40. Throughout history the service of deacons has taken on various forms so as to satisfy the diverse needs of the Christian community and to enable that

133 John Paul II, Functions of the Deacon in Pastoral Ministry at the General Audience of October 13, 1993, no. 5.

134 SDO, V, 22, 9; *l.c.*, 702. Cf. John Paul II, Catechesis at the General Audience of October 13, 1993, no. 5: *Insegnamenti* XVI, 2 (1993), 1000-1004.

135 Cf. CIC, c. 494.

136 Cf. CIC, c. 493.

137 Cf. John Paul II, Address to the Permanent Deacons of the USA, Detroit (September 19, 1987), no. 3, *Insegnamenti*, X, 3 (1987), 656.

community to exercise its mission of charity. It is for the bishops alone,[138] since they rule and have charge of the particular Churches "as Vicars and legates of Christ,"[139] to confer ecclesiastical office on each deacon according to the norm of law. In conferring such office, careful attention should be given to both the pastoral needs and the personal, family (in the case of married deacons), and professional situation of permanent deacons. In every case it is important, however, that deacons fully exercise their ministry, in preaching, in the liturgy and in charity to the extent that circumstances permit. They should not be relegated to marginal duties, be made merely to act as substitutes, nor discharge duties normally entrusted to non-ordained members of the faithful. Only in this way will the true identity of permanent deacons as ministers of Christ become apparent and the impression avoided that deacons are simply laypeople particularly involved in the life of the Church.

For the good of the deacon and to prevent improvisation, ordination should be accompanied by a clear investiture of pastoral responsibility.

Parish

41. While assuming different forms, the diaconal ministry ordinarily finds proper scope for its exercise in the various sectors of diocesan and parochial pastoral action.

The bishop may give deacons the task of cooperating with a parish priest in the parish[140] entrusted to him or in the pastoral care of several parishes entrusted *in solidum* to one or more priests.[141]

Where permanent deacons participate in the pastoral care of parishes which do not, because of a shortage, have the immediate benefit of a parish priest,[142] they always have precedence over the non-ordained faithful. In such cases, it is necessary to specify that the moderator of the parish is a priest and that he is its proper pastor. To him alone has been entrusted the *cura animarum*, in which he is assisted by the deacon.

138 Cf. CIC, c. 157.
139 LG, no. 27a.
140 Cf. CIC, c. 519.
141 Cf. CIC, c. 517 §1.
142 Cf. CIC, c. 517 §2.

Deacons may also be called to guide dispersed Christian communities in the name of the bishop or the parish priest.[143] "This is a missionary function to be carried out in those territories, environments, social strata and groups where priests are lacking or cannot be easily found. In particular, in those areas where no priest is available to celebrate the Eucharist, the deacon brings together and guides the community in a celebration of the word with the distribution of Holy Communion which has been duly reserved.[144] When deacons supply in places where there is a shortage of priests, they do so by ecclesial mandate."[145] At such celebrations, prayers will always be offered for an increase of vocations to the priesthood whose indispensable nature shall be clearly emphasized. Where deacons are available, participation in the pastoral care of the faithful may not be entrusted to a layperson or to a community of laypersons. Similarly where deacons are available, it is they who preside at such Sunday celebrations.

The competence of deacons should always be clearly specified in writing when they are assigned office.

Those means which encourage constructive and patient collaboration between deacons and others involved in the pastoral ministry should be promoted with generosity and conviction. While it is a duty of deacons to respect the office of parish priest and to work in communion with all who share in his pastoral care, they also have the right to be accepted and fully recognized by all. Where the bishop has deemed it opportune to institute parish pastoral councils, deacons appointed to participate in the pastoral care of such parishes are members of these councils by right.[146] Above all else, a true charity should prevail which recognizes in every ministry a gift of the Spirit destined to build up the Body of Christ.

42. Numerous opportunities for the fruitful exercise of the ministry of deacons arise at the diocesan level. Indeed, when they possess the necessary requirements, deacons may act as members of diocesan bodies, in particular diocesan pastoral councils[147] and diocesan finance councils, and take part in diocesan synods.[148]

---

143 Cf. SDO, V, 22, 10; *l.c.*, 702.

144 Cf. CIC, c. 1248 §2; Congregation for Divine Worship, Directory for Celebrations in the Absence of a Priest, *Christi Ecclesia*, 29, *l.c.*, 386.

145 John Paul II, Catechesis at the General Audience of October 13, 1993, no. 4: *Insegnamenti* XVI, 2 (1993), 1002.

146 Cf. SDO, V, 24; *l.c.*, 702; CIC, c. 536.

147 Cf. SDO, V, 24; *l.c.*, 702; CIC, c. 512 §1.

148 Cf. CIC, c. 463 §2.

They may not, however, act as members of the council of priests, since this body exclusively represents the presbyterate.[149]

In the diocesan curia, deacons in possession of the necessary requirements may exercise the office of chancellor,[150] judge,[151] assessor,[152] auditor,[153] *promotor iustitiae, defensor vinculi,*[154] and notary.[155]

Deacons may not, however, be constituted judicial vicars, adjunct judicial vicars or vicars forane, since these offices are reserved for priests.[156]

Other areas in which deacons may exercise their ministry include diocesan commissions, pastoral work in specific social contexts—especially the pastoral care of the family—or among particular groups with special pastoral needs, such as ethnic minorities.

In the exercise of the above offices, the deacon should recall that every action in the Church should be informed by charity and service to all. In judicial, administrative and organizational matters, deacons should always strive to avoid unnecessary forms of bureaucracy, lest they deprive their ministry of pastoral meaning and value. Those deacons who are called to exercise such offices should be placed so as to discharge duties which are proper to the diaconate, in order to preserve the integrity of the diaconal ministry.

3. The Spirituality of the Deacon

Contemporary Context

43. The Church, gathered together by Christ and guided by the Holy Spirit according to the providence of God the Father, lives and proclaims the Gospel in concrete historical circumstances. While present in the world, she is nonetheless a pilgrim[157] on the way to the fullness of the Kingdom.[158] "The world which she has in mind is the whole human family seen in the context of everything which envelops it: it is the world as the theatre of human history, bearing the

149 Cf. LG, no. 28; CD, no. 27; PO, no. 7; CIC, c. 495 §1.
150 CIC, c. 482.
151 CIC, c. 1421 §1.
152 CIC, c. 1424.
153 CIC, c. 1428 §2.
154 CIC, c. 1435.
155 CIC, c. 483 §1.
156 CIC, c. 1420 §4, c. 553 §1.
157 SC, no. 2.
158 LG, no. 5.

marks of its travail, its triumphs and failures, the world, which in the Christian vision has been created and is sustained by its Maker, which has been freed from the slavery of sin by Christ, who was crucified and rose again in order to break the stranglehold of the evil one, so that it might be fashioned anew according to God's design and brought to its fulfillment."[159]

The deacon, as a member and minister of the Church, should be mindful of this reality in his life and ministry. He should be conversant with contemporary cultures and with the aspirations and problems of his times. In this context, indeed, he is called to be a living sign of Christ the Servant and to assume the Church's responsibility of "reading the signs of the time and of interpreting them in the light of the Gospel, so that, in language intelligible to every generation, she may be able to answer the ever-recurring questions which men ask about this present life and of the life to come and how one is related to the other."[160]

Vocation to Holiness

44. The universal call to holiness has its origin in the "baptism of faith" by which all are "truly made sons of God and sharers in the divine nature and thus are made holy."[161]

By the Sacrament of Holy Orders, deacons receive "a new consecration to God" through which they are "anointed by the Holy Spirit and sent by Christ" [162] to serve God's people and "build up the Body of Christ" (Eph 4:12).

From this stems the *diaconal spirituality* with its source in what the Second Vatican Council calls "the sacramental grace of the diaconate."[163] In addition to helping the deacon to fulfill his functions this also affects his deepest being, imbuing it with a willingness to give his entire self over to the service of the Kingdom of God in the Church. As is indicated by the term "diaconate" itself, what characterizes the inner feelings and desire of those who receive the sacrament, is the *spirit of service.* Through the diaconate, what Jesus said of his mission is continually realized: "The Son of Man did not come to be served but to serve and to give his life as a ransom for many" (Mt 20:28).[164] Thus, through

159 GS, no. 2b.
160 GS, no. 4a.
161 LG, no. 40.
162 PO, no. 12a.
163 AG, no. 16.
164 John Paul II, Catechesis at the General Audience of October 20, 1993, no. 1: *Insegnamenti*, XVI, 2 (1993), 1053.

his ministry, the deacon lives the virtue of obedience: in faithfully carrying out those duties assigned to him, the deacon serves the episcopate and the presbyterate in the *munera* of Christ's mission and what he does is truly pastoral ministry, for the good of the faithful.

45. Hence, the deacon should accept with gratitude the invitation to follow Christ the Servant and devote himself to it throughout the diverse circumstances of life. The character received in ordination conforms to Christ to whom the deacon should adhere ever more closely.

Sanctification is a duty binding all the faithful.[165] For the deacon it has a further basis in the special consecration received.[166] It includes the practice of the Christian virtues and the various evangelical precepts and counsels according to one's own state of life. The deacon is called to live a holy life because he has been sanctified by the Holy Spirit in the sacraments of Baptism and Holy Orders and has been constituted by the same Spirit a minister of Christ's Church to serve and sanctify mankind.[167]

For deacons the call to holiness means "following Jesus by an attitude of humble service which finds expression not only in works of charity but also in imbuing and forming thoughts and actions."[168] When "their ministry is consistent with this spirit [deacons] clearly highlight that quality which best shows the face of Christ: service[169] which makes one not only 'servants of God' but also servants of God in our own brethren."[170]

---

165 "All the Christian faithful must direct their efforts to lead a holy life and to promote the growth of the Church and its continual sanctification, according to their own condition" (CIC, c. 210).

166 As "servants of the mysteries of Christ and the Church, they should keep themselves free from every fault, be pleasing to God, and be a source of all goodness in the sight of men" (cf. 1 Tm 3:8-10, 12-13): LG, no. 41; Cf. also SDO, VI, 25: *l.c.*, 702.

167 "Clerics are bound in a special way to pursue holiness since, having been consecrated to God by a new title in the reception of orders, they are dispensers of the mysteries of God in the service of His people" (CIC, c. 276 §1).

168 John Paul II, Catechesis at the General Audience of October 20, 1993, no. 2: *Insegnamenti*, XVI, 2 (1993), 1054.

169 John Paul II, Catechesis at the General Audience of October 20, 1993, no. 1. *Insegnamenti*, XVI, 2 (1993), 1054.

170 John Paul II, Catechesis at the General Audience of October 20, 1993, no. 1: *Insegnamenti*, XVI, 2 (1993), 1054.

The Relations of Holy Orders

46. By a special sacramental gift, Holy Orders confers on the deacon a particular participation in the consecration and mission of Him who became servant of the Father for the redemption of mankind, and inserts him in a new and specific way in the mystery of Christ, of his Church and the salvation of all mankind. Hence the spiritual life of the deacon should deepen this threefold relationship by developing a community spirituality which bears witness to that communion essential to the nature of the Church.

47. The primary and most fundamental relationship must be with Christ, who assumed the condition of a slave for love of the Father and mankind.[171] In virtue of ordination, the deacon is truly called to act in conformity with Christ the Servant.

The eternal Son of the Father "emptied himself assuming the form of a slave" (Phil 2:7) and lived this condition in obedience to the Father (Jn 4:34) and in humble service to the brethren (Jn 13:4-15). As servant of the Father in the work of salvation Christ constitutes the way, the truth and the life for every deacon in the Church.

All ministerial activity is meaningful when it leads to knowing, loving and following Christ in his *diaconia.* Thus deacons should strive to model their lives on Christ, who redeemed mankind by his obedience to the Father, an obedience "unto death, death on a cross" (Phil 2:8).

48. Indissolubly associated with this fundamental relationship with Christ is the Church[172] which Christ loves, purifies, nourishes and cares for (cf. Eph 5:25-29). The deacon cannot live his configuration to Christ faithfully without sharing His love for the Church "for which he cannot but have a deep attachment because of her mission and her divine institution."[173]

The Rite of Ordination illustrates the connection which comes about between the bishop and the deacon: the bishop alone imposes hands on the candidate and invokes the outpouring of the Holy Spirit on him. Every deacon,

171 John Paul II allocution of March 6, 1985, no. 2: *Insegnamenti*, VIII, 1 (1985), 649. *Pastores Dabo Vobis* (PDV), 3, 21: *l.c.*, 661, 688.

172 Cf. PDV, 16: *l.c.*, 681.

173 John Paul II, Catechesis at the General Audience of October 20, 1993, no. 2: *Insegnamenti*, XVI, 2 (1993), 1055.

therefore, finds the point of reference for his own ministry in hierarchical communion with the bishop.[174]

Diaconal ordination also underlines another ecclesial aspect: it communicates a ministerial sharing in Christ's *diaconia* with which God's people, governed by the Successor of Peter and those Bishops in communion with him, and in cooperation with the presbyterate, continues to serve the work of redemption. Deacons, therefore, are called to nourish themselves and their ministry with an ardent love for the Church, and a sincere desire for communion with the Holy Father, their own bishops and the priests of their dioceses.

49. It must not be forgotten that the object of Christ's *diaconia* is mankind.[175] Every human being carries the traces of sin but is called to communion with God. "God so loved the world that He gave His only Son, so that all who believe in Him might not die but have eternal life" (Jn 3:16). It was for this plan of love, that Christ became a slave and took human flesh. The Church continues to be the sign and instrument of that *diaconia* in history.

In virtue of the Sacrament of Orders deacons are at the service of their brothers and sisters needing of salvation. As mankind can see the fullness of the Father's love by which they are saved in the words and deeds of Christ the Servant, so too this same charity must be apparent in the life of the deacon. Growth in imitation of Christ's love for mankind—which surpasses all ideologies—is thus an essential component of the spiritual life of every deacon.

A "natural inclination of service to the sacred hierarchy and to the Christian community"[176] is required of those who seek admission to the diaconate. This should not be understood "in the sense of a simple spontaneity of natural disposition . . . it is rather an inclination of nature inspired by grace, with a spirit of service that conforms human behavior to Christ's. The sacrament of the diaconate develops this inclination: it makes the subject to share more closely in Christ's spirit of service and imbues the will with a special grace so that in all his actions he will be motivated by a *new inclination* to serve his brothers and sisters."[177]

174 Cf. SDO, V, 23: *l.c.*, 702.

175 Cf. John Paul II, Encyclical Letter *Redemptor Hominis* (March 4, 1979), nos. 13-17: *AAS* 71 (1979), 282-300.

176 SDO, II, 8: *l.c.*, 700.

177 John Paul II, Catechesis at the General Audience of October 20, 1993, no. 2: *Insegnamenti*, XVI, 2 (1993), 1054.

Aids to the Spiritual Life

50. The aforementioned points of reference emphasize the primacy of the spiritual life. The deacon, mindful that the *diaconia* of Christ surpasses all natural capacities, should continually commit himself in conscience and in freedom to His invitation: "Remain in me and I in you. As the branch cannot bear fruit unless it remain in the vine, so also with you unless you remain in me" (Jn 15:4).

Following Christ in the diaconate is an attractive but difficult undertaking. While it brings satisfaction and rewards, it can also be open to the difficulties and trials experienced by the followers of the Lord Jesus Christ. In order to live this ministry to the full, deacons must know Christ intimately so that He may shoulder the burdens of their ministry. They must give priority to the spiritual life and live their *diaconia* with generosity. They should organize their ministry and their professional and, when married, family obligations, so as to grow in their commitment to the person and mission of Christ the Servant.

51. Progress in the spiritual life is achieved primarily by faithful and tireless exercise of the ministry in integrity of life.[178] Such ministry not only develops the spiritual life but promotes the theological virtues, a disposition to selflessness, service to the brethren and hierarchical communion. What has been said of priests, *mutatis mutandis*, also applies to deacons: "Through the sacred actions they perform every day . . . they are set on the right course to perfection of life. The very holiness of priests is of the greatest benefit for the fruitful fulfillment of their ministry."[179]

52. The deacon should always be mindful of the exhortation made to him in the Rite of Ordination: "Receive the Gospel of Christ of which you are the herald; believe what you preach, teach what you believe and put into practice what you teach."[180] For a worthy and fruitful proclamation of the word of God, deacons should "immerse themselves in the Scriptures by constant sacred reading and diligent study. For it must not happen that anybody becomes 'an empty preacher of the word of God to others, not being a hearer of the word in his own

178 Cf. PO, nos. 14, 15: CIC, c. 276 §2, 1°.

179 PO, no. 12.

180 *Pontificale Romanum—De Ordinatione Episcopi, Presbyterorum et Diaconorum*, no. 210; ed. cit., 125.

heart' when he should be sharing the boundless riches of the divine word with the faithful committed to his care, especially in the sacred Liturgy."[181]

Moreover, deacons, under the guidance of those in the Church who are true teachers of divine and Catholic truth,[182] should strive to deepen their knowledge of the word, so as to hear its call and experience its saving power (cf. Rom 1:16). Their sanctification is based on their consecration and on their mission. This is true also with regard to the word and they should be conscious that they are its ministers. As members of the hierarchy, the actions and public pronouncements of deacons involve the Church. Consequently, it is essential for pastoral charity that deacons should ensure the authenticity of their own teaching. Likewise, in the spirit of the profession of faith and the oath of fidelity,[183] taken prior to ordination, they should preserve their own clear and effective communion with the Holy Father, the episcopal order and with their own bishops, not only with regard to the articles of the Creed, but also with regard to the teaching of ordinary Magisterium and the Church's discipline. Indeed, "such is the force and power of the word of God that it can serve the Church as her support and vigor, and the children of God for their strength, food for the soul, and for a pure and lasting fount of spiritual life."[184] The closer deacons come to the word of God, therefore, the greater will be their desire to communicate it to their brothers and sisters. God speaks to man in Sacred Scripture[185]: by his preaching, the sacred minister fosters this salvific encounter. Then, lest the faithful be deprived of the word of God through the ignorance or indolence of its ministers, deacons should devote themselves to preach the word tirelessly and yet be mindful that the exercise of the ministry of the word is not confined to preaching alone.

53. Likewise, when the deacon baptizes or distributes the Body and Blood of Christ or serves at the celebration of the other sacraments and sacramentals, he confirms his identity in the Church: he is a minister of the Body of Christ, both mystical and ecclesial. Let him remember that, when lived with faith and

181 DV, no. 25; cf. SDO, VI, 26, 1; *l.c.*, 703; CIC, c. 276 §2, 2°.

182 Cf. LG, no. 25a.

183 Cf. CIC, c. 833; Congregation for the Doctrine of the Faith, *Professio fidei et iusiurandum fidelitatis in suscipiendo officio nomine Ecclesiae exercendo*: *AAS* 81 (1989), 104-106 and 1169.

184 DV, no. 21.

185 Cf. SC, no. 7.

reverence, these actions of the Church contribute much to growth in the spiritual life and to the increase of the Christian community.[186]

54. With regard to the spiritual life, deacons should devote particular importance to the sacraments of grace whose purpose "is to sanctify men, to build up the Body of Christ, and finally to give worship to God."[187]

Above all, they should participate with particular faith at the daily celebration of the eucharistic sacrifice,[188] possibly exercising their own proper liturgical *munus*, and adore the Lord, present in the Sacrament,[189] because in the Blessed Eucharist, source and summit of all evangelization, "the whole spiritual good of the Church is contained."[190] In the Blessed Eucharist they truly encounter Christ who, for love of man, became an expiatory victim, the food of life eternal and friend of all who suffer.

Conscious of his own weakness and trusting the mercy of God the deacon should regularly approach the Sacrament of Penance,[191] in which sinful man encounters Christ the Redeemer, receives forgiveness of sin and is impelled toward the fullness of charity.

55. In performing the works of charity entrusted to them by their bishops, deacons should always be guided by the love of Christ for all men instead of personal interests and ideologies which are injurious to the universality of salvation or deny the transcendent vocation of man. They should be ever conscious that the *diaconia* of charity necessarily leads to a growth of communion within the particular Churches since charity is the very soul of ecclesial communion. Deacons are thus obliged to foster fraternity and cooperation with the priests of their dioceses and sincere communion with their bishops.

Prayer Life

56. The deacon shall always remain faithful to the Lord's command: "But watch at all times, praying that you may have strength to escape all these things that will take place, and to stand before the Son of man" (Lk 21:36; cf. Phil 4:6-7).

186 Cf. SC, no. 7.
187 SC, no. 59a.
188 Cf. CIC, c. 276 §2, 2°; SDO, VI, 26, 2: *l.c.*, 703.
189 Cf. SDO, VI, 26, 2: *l.c.*, 703.
190 PO, no. 5b.
191 Cf. CIC, c. 276 §2, 5°; SDO, VI, 26, 3: *l.c.*, 703.

Prayer, which is a personal dialogue with God, confers the strength needed to follow Christ and serve the brethren. In the light of this certainty, deacons should form themselves according to the various types of prayer: the celebration of the Liturgy of the Hours, as prescribed by the various Episcopal Conferences,[192] should inform their whole prayer life since deacons, as ministers, intercede for the entire Church. Such prayer is carried over into the *lectio divina*, arduous mental prayer and the spiritual retreat prescribed by particular law.[193]

The habit of penance should also be taken to heart together with other means of sanctification which foster personal encounter with God.[194]

57. Participation in the mystery of Christ the Servant necessarily directs the deacon's heart to the Church and her most holy Mother. Christ indeed cannot be separated from the Church which is his Body. True union with Christ the Head cannot but foster true love for His body which is the Church. This love will commit the deacon to work diligently to build up the Church by faithful discharge of his ministerial duties, through fraternity and hierarchical communion with his own bishop and with the presbyterate. The deacon should be concerned for the entire Church: the universal Church, the principle and perpetually visible foundation of whose unity is the Roman Pontiff, the Successor of St. Peter,[195] as well as the particular Church which "adhering to its pastor and united by him in the Holy Spirit through the Gospel and the Eucharist . . . in which the one, holy, Catholic and apostolic Church of Christ is present."[196]

Love for Christ and for His Church is profoundly linked to love of the Blessed Virgin Mary, handmaid of the Lord. With her unique title of Mother, she was the selfless helper of her divine Son's *diaconia* (cf. Jn 19:25-27). Love of the Mother of God, based on faith and expressed in daily recitation of the Rosary, imitation of her virtues and trust in her, are indeed signs of authentic filial devotion.[197]

With deep veneration and affection Mary looks on every deacon. Indeed, "the creature who more than any other who has lived the full truth of vocation

192 Cf. CIC, c. 276 §2, 3°.
193 Cf. CIC, c. 276 §2, 4°.
194 Cf. CIC, c. 276 §2, 5°.
195 LG, no. 23a.
196 CD, no. 11; CIC, c. 369.
197 Cf. CIC, c. 276 §2, 5°; SDO, VI, 26, 4: *l.c.*, 703.

is Mary the Virgin Mother, and she did so in intimate communion with Christ: no one has responded with a love greater than hers to the immense love of God."[198] This love of the Virgin Mary, handmaid of the Lord, which is born and rooted in the word, will cause deacons to imitate her life. In this way a Marian dimension is introduced into the Church which is very close to the vocation of the deacon.[199]

58. Regular spiritual direction is truly of the greatest assistance to deacons. Experience clearly shows how much can be gained in sincere and humble dialogue with a wise spiritual director, not only in the resolution of doubts and problems which inevitably arise throughout life, but also in employing the necessary discernment to arrive at better self-knowledge and to grow in faithful fellowship of Christ.

Spirituality of Deacons and States of Life

59. In contrast with the requirement for the priesthood, not only celibate men, in the first place and widowers, may be admitted to the permanent Diaconate but also men who live in the Sacrament of Matrimony.[200]

60. With gratitude, the Church recognizes the gift of celibacy which God gives to some of her members and, in different ways, both in the East and West, she has linked it to the ordained ministry with which it is always particularly consonant.[201] The Church is conscious that this gift, accepted and lived for the sake of the Kingdom of God (cf. Mt 19:12), directs the whole person of the deacon toward Christ who devoted Himself in chastity to the service of the Father so as to bring man to the fullness of the Kingdom. Loving God and serving the brethren by this complete choice, so far from impeding the personal development of deacons, fosters man's true perfection which is found in charity. In celibate life, indeed, love becomes a sign of total and undivided consecration to Christ and

---

198 PDV, 36, quoting *Propositio* 5 of the Synodal fathers: *l.c.*, 718.

199 Cf. John Paul II, Allocution to the Roman Curia, December 22, 1987: *AAS* 80 (1988), 1025-1034; Apostolic Letter *Mulieris Dignitatem*, 27: *AAS* 80 (1988), 1718.

200 Cf. LG, no. 29b.

201 "His rationibus in mysteriis Christi Eiusque missione fundatis, coelibatus . . . omnibus ad Ordinem sacrum promovendis lege impositum est" "For these reasons, which are based on the mystery of the Church and her mission, celibacy was at first recommended to priests. Then, in the Latin Church, it was imposed by law on all who were to be promoted to sacred orders": PO, no. 16; cf. CIC, c. 247 §1; c. 277 §1, c. 1037.

of greater freedom to serve God and man.[202] The choice of celibacy is not an expression of contempt for marriage nor of flight from reality but a special way of serving man and the world.

Contemporary man, very often submerged in the ephemeral, is particularly sensitive to those who are a living witness of the eternal. Hence, deacons should be especially careful to give witness to their brothers and sisters by their fidelity to the celibate life the better to move them to seek those values consonant with man's transcendent vocation. "Celibacy 'for the sake of the Kingdom' is not only an eschatological sign. It also has a great social significance in contemporary life for service to the People of God."[203]

In order to conserve this special gift of God throughout life for the benefit of the entire Church, deacons should not depend excessively on their own resources, but should be faithful to the spiritual life and the duties of their ministry in a spirit of prudence and vigilance, remembering that "the spirit is willing but the flesh is weak" (Mt 26:41).

They should be particularly careful in their relationships with others lest familiarity create difficulties for continence or give rise to scandal.[204]

They must finally be aware that in contemporary society, it is necessary to exercise careful discernment when using the means of social communications.

61. The Sacrament of Matrimony sanctifies conjugal love and constitutes it a sign of the love with which Christ gives himself to the Church (cf. Eph 5:25). It is a gift from God and should be a source of nourishment for the spiritual life of those deacons who are married. Since family life and professional responsibilities must necessarily reduce the amount of time which married deacons can dedicate to the ministry, it will be necessary to integrate these various elements in a unitary fashion, especially by means of shared prayer. In marriage, love becomes an interpersonal giving of self, a mutual fidelity, a source of new life, a support in times of joy and sorrow: in short, love becomes service. When lived in faith, this *family service* is for the rest of the faithful an example of the love of Christ. The married deacon must use it as a stimulus of his *diaconia* in the Church.

202 Cf. CIC, c. 277 §1; OT, no. 10.
203 John Paul II, Letter to Priests on Holy Thursday, April 8, 1979, 8: *AAS* 71 (1979), 408.
204 Cf. CIC, c. 277 §2.

Married deacons should feel especially obliged to give clear witness to the sanctity of marriage and the family. The more they grow in mutual love, the greater their dedication to their children and the more significant their example for the Christian community. "The nurturing and deepening of mutual, sacrificial love between husband and wife constitutes perhaps the most significant involvement of a deacon's wife in her husband's public ministry in the Church."[205] This love grows thanks to chastity which flourishes, even in the exercise of paternal responsibilities, by respect for spouses and the practice of a certain continence. This virtue fosters a mutual self-giving which soon becomes evident in ministry. It eschews possessive behavior, undue pursuit of professional success and the incapacity to program time. Instead, it promotes authentic interpersonal relationships, OIC, and the capacity to see everything in its proper perspective.

Special care should be taken to ensure that the families of deacons be made aware of the demands of the diaconal ministry. The spouses of married deacons, who must give their consent to their husbands' decision to seek ordination to the diaconate,[206] should be assisted to play their role with joy and discretion. They should esteem all that concerns the Church, especially the duties assigned to their husbands. For this reason it is opportune that they should be kept duly informed of their husbands' activities in order to arrive at a harmonious balance between family, professional and ecclesial responsibilities. In the children of married deacons, where such is possible, an appreciation of their father's ministry can also be fostered. They in turn should be involved in the apostolate and give coherent witness in their lives.

In conclusion, the families of married deacons, as with all Christian families, are called to participate actively and responsibly in the Church's mission in the contemporary world. "In particular, the deacon and his wife must be a living example of *fidelity and indissolubility in Christian marriage* before a world which is in dire need of such signs. By facing in a *spirit of faith* the challenges of married life and the demands of daily living, they strengthen the family life not only of the Church community but of the whole of society. They also show how the obligations of family life, work and ministry can be harmonized *in the*

205 John Paul II, Allocution to the Permanent Deacons of the USA in Detroit (September 19, 1987), no. 5: *Insegnamenti*, X, 3 (1987), 658.

206 Cf. CIC, c. 1031 §2.

service of the Church's mission. Deacons and their wives and children can be a great encouragement to others who are working to promote family life."[207]

62. It is necessary to reflect on the situation of the deacon following the death of his wife. This is a particular moment in life which calls for faith and Christian hope. The loss of a spouse should not destroy dedication to the rearing of children nor lead to hopelessness. While this period of life is difficult, it is also an opportunity for interior purification and an impetus for growth in charity and service to one's children and to all the members of the Church. It is a call to grow in hope since faithful discharge of the ministry is a way of reaching Christ and those in the Father's glory who are dear to us.

It must be recognized, however, that the loss of a spouse gives rise to a new situation in a family which profoundly influences personal relationships and in many instances can give rise to economic difficulties. With great charity, therefore, widowed deacons should be helped to discern and accept their new personal circumstances and to persevere in providing for their children and the new needs of their families.

In particular, the widowed deacon should be supported in living perfect and perpetual continence.[208] He should be helped to understand the profound ecclesial reasons which preclude his remarriage (cf. 1 Tm 3:12), in accordance with the constant discipline of the Church in the East and West.[209] This can be achieved through an intensification of one's dedication to others for the love of God in the ministry. In such cases the fraternal assistance of other ministers, of the faithful and of the bishop can be most comforting to widowed deacons.

With regard to the widows of deacons, care should be taken, where possible, by the clergy and the faithful to ensure that they are never neglected and that their needs are provided for.

207 John Paul II, Allocution to the Permanent Deacons of the USA in Detroit, September 19, 1987, no. 5; *Insegnamenti,* X, 3 (1987), 658-659.

208 Cf. CIC, c. 277 §1.

209 SDO, III, 16: *l.c.*, 701; Apostolic Letter *Ad Pascendum*, VI: *l.c.*, 539; CIC, c. 1087. Provision is made for possible exceptions to this discipline in the circular letter of the Congregation for Divine Worship and the Discipline of the Sacraments, N. 26397, of June 6, 1997, no. 8.

4. Continuing Formation of Deacons

Characteristics

63. The continuing formation of deacons is a human necessity which must be seen in continuity with the divine call to serve the Church in the ministry and with the initial formation given to deacons, to the extent that these are considered two initial moments in a single, living, process of Christian and diaconal life.[210] Indeed, "those who are ordained to the diaconate are obliged to ongoing doctrinal formation which perfects and completes what they received prior to ordination,"[211] so that, by a periodic renewal of the "I am" pronounced by deacons at their ordination, the vocation *to* the diaconate continues and finds expression as vocation *in* the diaconate. On the part of both the Church which provides ongoing formation and of deacons who are its recipients, such formation should be regarded as a mutual obligation and duty arising from the nature of the vocational commitment which has been assumed.

The continuing need to provide and receive adequate, integral formation is an indispensable obligation for both bishops and deacons.

Ecclesiastical norms regarding ongoing formation[212] have constantly emphasized the obligatory nature of such formation for the apostolic life and stressed the need for it to be global, interdisciplinary, profound, scientific and propedeutic. Application of these norms is all the more necessary in those instances where initial formation did not adhere to the ordinary model.

Continuing formation should be informed with the characteristics of fidelity to Christ, to the Church and to "continuing conversion" which is a fruit of sacramental grace articulated in the pastoral charity proper to every moment of ordained ministry. This formation is similar to the fundamental choice, which must be reaffirmed and renewed throughout the permanent diaconate by a long series of coherent responses which are based on and animated by the initial acceptance of the ministry.[213]

---

210 PDV, no. 42.

211 John Paul II, Catechesis at the General Audience of October 20, 1993, no. 4: *Insegnamenti*, XVI, 2 (1993), 1056.

212 SDO, II, 8-10; III, 14-15: *l.c.*, 699-701; Apostolic Letter *Ad Pascendum*, VII: *l.c.*, 540; CIC, cc. 236, 1027, 1032 §3.

213 Cf. PDV, no. 70: *l.c.*, 780.

Motivation

64. Inspired by the prayer of ordination, ongoing formation is based on the need of every deacon to love Christ in such manner as to imitate him ("may they be images of your Son"). It seeks to confirm him in uncompromising fidelity to a personal vocation to ministry ("may they fulfill faithfully the works of the ministry") and proposes a radical, sincere following of Christ the Servant ("may the example of their lives be a constant reminder of the Gospel . . . may they be sincere . . . solicitous . . . and vigilant").

The basis and motivation of this formation, therefore, "is the dynamism of the order itself,"[214] while its nourishment is the Holy Eucharist, compendium of the entire Christian ministry and endless source of every spiritual energy. St. Paul's exhortation to Timothy can also be applied, in a certain sense, to deacons: "I remind you to fan into a flame the gift of God that you have" (2 Tm 1:6; cf. 1 Tm 4:14-16). The theological demands of their call to a singular ministry of ecclesial service requires of them a growing love for the Church, shown forth by their faithful carrying out of their proper functions and responsibilities. Chosen by God to be holy, serving the Church and all mankind, the deacon should continually grow in awareness of his own ministerial character in a manner that is balanced, responsible, solicitous and always joyful.

Subjects

65. From the perspective of the deacon, primary protagonist and primary subject of the obligation, ongoing formation is first and foremost a process of continual conversion. It embraces every aspect of his person as deacon, that is to say, consecrated by the Sacrament of Orders and placed at the service of the Church, and seeks to develop all of his potential. This enables him to live to the full the ministerial gifts that he has received in diverse circumstances of time and place and in the tasks assigned to him by the bishop.[215] The solicitude of the Church for the permanent formation of deacons would, however, be ineffective without their cooperation and commitment. Thus formation cannot be reduced merely to participating at courses or study days or other such activities: it calls for every deacon to be aware of the need for ongoing formation and to cultivate it with

214 PDV, no. 70: *l.c.*, 779.
215 PDV, no. 76; 79: *l.c.*, 793; 796.

interest and in a spirit of healthy initiative. Books approved by ecclesiastical authority should be chosen as material for reading; periodicals known for their fidelity to the Magisterium should be followed; time should be set aside for daily meditation. Constant self-formation which helps him to serve the Church ever better is an important part of the service asked of every deacon.

Formators

66. From the perspective of the bishops[216] (and their fellow workers in the presbyterate), who bear responsibility for formation, ongoing formation consists in helping the deacon to overcome any dualism that might exist between spirituality and ministry and, more fundamentally, any dichotomy between their civil profession and diaconal spirituality and "respond generously to the commitment demanded by the dignity and the responsibility which God conferred upon them through the sacrament of Orders; in guarding, defending, and developing their specific identity and vocation; and in sanctifying themselves and others through the exercise of their ministry."[217]

Both dimensions are complementary and reciprocal since they are founded, with the help of supernatural gifts, in the interior unity of the person.

The assistance which formators are called to offer deacons will be successful inasmuch as it responds to the personal needs of each deacon, since every deacon lives his ministry in the Church as a unique person placed in particular circumstances.

Personalized assistance to deacons also assures them of that love with which mother Church is close to them as they strive to live faithfully the sacramental grace of their calling. It is thus of supreme importance that each deacon be able to choose a spiritual director, approved by the bishop, with whom he can have regular and frequent contact.

The entire diocesan community is also, in some sense, involved in the formation of deacons.[218] This is particularly true of the parish priest or other priests charged with formation who should personally support them with fraternal solicitude.

---

216 Cf. CD, no. 15; PDV, no. 79: *l.c.*, 797.

217 Congregation for the Clergy, *Tota Ecclesia*, Directory for the Ministry and Life of Priests (January 31, 1994), no. 71: 76.

218 Cf. PDV, no. 78: *l.c.*, 795.

Specificity

67. Personal concern and commitment in ongoing formation are unequivocal signs of a coherent response to divine vocation, of sincere love for the Church and of authentic pastoral zeal for the Christian faithful and all men. What has been said of priests can also be applied to deacons: "ongoing formation is a necessary means of reaching the object of one's vocation which is service of God and one's people."[219]

It must be seen in continuity with initial formation since it pursues the same ends as initial formation and seeks to integrate, conserve and deepen what was begun in initial formation.

The essential availability of the deacon to others is a practical expression of sacramental configuration to Christ the Servant, received through ordination and indelibly impressed upon the soul. It is a permanent reminder to the deacon in his life and ministry. Hence permanent formation cannot be reduced merely to complementary education or to a form of training in better *techniques*. Ongoing formation cannot be confined simply to updating, but should seek to facilitate a practical configuration of the deacon's entire life to Christ who loves all and serves all.

Dimensions

68. Ongoing formation must include and harmonize all dimensions of the life and ministry of the deacon. Thus, as with the permanent formation of priests, it should be complete, systematic and personalized in its diverse aspects whether human, spiritual, intellectual or pastoral.[220]

69. As in the past, attention to the various aspects of the human formation of deacons is an important task for Pastors. The deacon, aware that he is chosen as a man among men to be at the service of the salvation of all, should be open to being helped in developing his human qualities as valuable instruments for ministry. He should strive to perfect all those aspects of his personality which might render his ministry more effective.

219 Congregation for the Clergy, Directory for the Ministry and Life of Priests, *Tota Ecclesia*, 71: 76.

220 Cf. PDV, no. 71: *l.c.*, 783; Congregation for the Clergy, Directory for the Ministry and Life of Priests, *Tota Ecclesia*, no. 74; 78.

To fulfill successfully his vocation to holiness and his particular ecclesial mission, he should, above all, fix his gaze on Him who is true God and true man and practice the natural and supernatural virtues which conform him more closely to the image of Christ and make him worthy of the respect of the faithful.[221] In their ministry and daily life particularly, deacons should foster in themselves kindheartedness, patience, affability, strength of character, zeal for justice, fidelity to promises given, a spirit of sacrifice and consistency with tasks freely undertaken. The practice of these virtues will assist in arriving at a balanced personality, maturity and discernment.

Conscious of the example of integrity in his social activity, the deacon should reflect on his ability to dialogue, on correctness in human relationships and on cultural discernment. He should also give careful consideration to the value of friendship and to his treatment of others.[222]

70. Ongoing spiritual formation is closely connected with diaconal spirituality, which it must nourish and develop, and with the ministry, which is sustained by "a truly personal encounter with Jesus, a relationship with the Father and a profound experience of the Spirit."[223] Hence, deacons should be encouraged by the Pastors of the Church to cultivate their spiritual lives in a responsible manner, for it is from this life that springs up that love which sustains their ministry and makes it fruitful, and prevents its reduction to mere "functionalism" or bureaucracy.

In particular, the spiritual formation of deacons should inculcate those attitudes related to the triple *diaconia* of word, liturgy and charity.

Assiduous meditation on Sacred Scripture will achieve familiarity and worshipful dialogue with the living God and thus an assimilation of the revealed word.

A profound knowledge of Tradition and of the liturgical books will help the deacon to discover continually the riches of the divine mysteries and thus become their worthy minister. A solicitude for fraternal charity will impel him

---

221 Cf. St. Ignatius of Antioch: "Deacons, who are ministers of Christ Jesus, must be acceptable to all in every respect. They are not servants of food and drink. They are ministers of the Church of God" (*Epist. ad Trallianos*, 2, 3: F. X. Funk, *o.c.*, I, 244-245).

222 Cf. PDV, no. 72: *l.c.*, 783; Congregation for the Clergy, Directory for the Ministry and Life of Priests, *Tota Ecclesia*, 75, ed. cit., 75-76.

223 PDV, no. 72: *l.c.*, 785.

to practice the spiritual and corporal works of mercy, and provide living signs of the Church's love.

All of this requires careful planning and organization of time and resources. Improvisation should be avoided. In addition to spiritual direction, deacons should try to pursue study courses on the great themes of the theological tradition of Christian spirituality, intensive sessions in spirituality and pilgrimages to places of spiritual interest.

While on retreat, which should be at least every other year,[224] deacons should work out a spiritual program which they should periodically share with their spiritual directors. This program should include a period of daily eucharistic adoration and provide for exercises of Marian devotion, liturgical prayer, personal meditation and the habitual ascetical practices.

The center of this spiritual itinerary must be the Holy Eucharist since it is the touchstone of the deacon's life and activity, the indispensable means of perseverance, the criterion of authentic renewal and of a balanced synthesis of life. In this way, the spiritual formation of the deacon will reveal the Holy Eucharist as Passover, in its annual articulation in Holy Week, in its weekly articulation on Sunday and in its constant articulation at daily Mass.

71. The insertion of deacons into the mystery of the Church, in virtue of Baptism and their reception of the first grade of the Sacrament of Orders, requires that ongoing formation strengthen in them the consciousness and willingness to live in intelligent, active and mature communion with their bishops and the priests of their dioceses, and with the Supreme Pontiff who is the visible foundation of the entire Church's unity.

When formed in this way, they can become in their ministry effective promoters of communion. In situations of conflict they, in particular, should make every effort to restore peace for the good of the Church.

72. The doctrine of the faith should be deepened by suitable initiatives such as study days, renewal courses and the frequentation of academic institutions. For the same reason, it would be particularly useful to promote careful, in-depth and systematic study of the *Catechism of the Catholic Church*.

It is necessary that deacons have an accurate knowledge of the Sacraments of Holy Orders, the Holy Eucharist, Baptism and Matrimony. They must develop

224 Cf. SDO, VI, 28: *l.c.*, 703; CIC, c. 276 §4.

a knowledge of those aspects of philosophy, ecclesiology, dogmatic Theology, Sacred Scripture, and Canon Law which most assist them in their ministry.

Such courses, while aimed at theological renewal, should also lead to prayer, ecclesial communion and greater pastoral efforts in response to the urgent need for new evangelization.

Under sure guidance, the documents of the Magisterium should be studied in common, and in relation to the needs of the pastoral ministry, especially those documents in which the Church responds to the more pressing moral and doctrinal questions. Thus, with a sense of communion, deacons will be enabled to achieve and express due obedience to the Pastor of the universal Church and to diocesan bishops, as well as to promote fidelity to the doctrine and discipline of the Church.

In addition, it is of the greatest use and relevance to study, appropriate and diffuse the social doctrine of the Church. A good knowledge of that teaching will permit many deacons to mediate it in their different professions, at work and in their families. The diocesan bishop may also invite those who are capable to specialize in a theological discipline and obtain the necessary academic qualifications at those pontifical academies or institutes recognized by the Apostolic See which guarantee doctrinally correct formation.

Deacons should pursue systematic study not only to perfect their theological knowledge but also to revitalize constantly their ministry in view of the changing needs of the ecclesial community.

73. Together with study of the sacred sciences, appropriate measures should be taken to ensure that deacons acquire a pastoral methodology[225] for an effective ministry. Permanent pastoral formation consists, in the first place, in constantly encouraging the deacon to perfect the effectiveness of his ministry of making the love and service of Christ present in the Church and in society without distinction, especially to the poor and to those most in need. Indeed it is from the pastoral love of Christ that the ministry of deacons draws its model and inspiration. This same love urges the deacon, in collaboration with his bishop and the priests of his diocese, to promote the mission of the laity in the world. He will thus be a stimulus "to become ever better acquainted with the real situation of the men and women to whom he is sent, to discern the call of the Spirit in the historical circumstances in which he finds himself, and to seek the most suitable

225 Cf. CIC, c. 279.

methods and the most useful forms for carrying out his ministry today,"[226] in loyal and convinced communion with the Supreme Pontiff and with his own bishop.

The effectiveness of the apostolate sometimes calls also for group work requiring a knowledge and respect of the diversity and complementarity of the gifts and respective functions of priests, deacons and the lay faithful, within the organic nature of ecclesial communion.

Organization and Means

74. The diversity of circumstances in the particular Churches makes it difficult to give an exhaustive account of how best to organize the suitable ongoing formation of permanent deacons. Yet it is necessary that all such formation be accomplished by means which accord with theological and pastoral clarity.

A few general criteria, easily applicable to diverse concrete circumstances, may be mentioned in this respect.

75. The primary locus of ongoing formation for deacons is the ministry itself. The deacon matures in its exercise and by focusing his own call to holiness on the fulfillment of his social and ecclesial duties, in particular, of his ministerial functions and responsibilities. The formation of deacons should, therefore, concentrate in a special way on awareness of their ministerial character.

76. Permanent formation must follow a well-planned program drawn up and approved by competent authority. It must be unitary, divided into progressive stages, and at the same time, in perfect harmony with the Magisterium of the Church. It is better that the program should insist on a basic minimum to be followed by all deacons and which should be distinct from later specialization courses.

Programs such as this should take into consideration two distinct but closely related levels of formation: the diocesan level, in reference to the bishop or his delegate, and the community level in which the deacon exercises his own ministry, in reference to the parish priest or some other priest.

77. The first appointment of a deacon to a parish or a pastoral area is a very sensitive moment. Introducing the deacon to those in charge of the community (the parish priest, priests), and the community to the deacon, helps them not only

226 PDV, no. 72: *l.c.*, 783.

to come to know each other but contributes to a collaboration based on mutual respect and dialogue, in a spirit of faith and fraternal charity. The community into which a deacon comes can have a highly important formative effect, especially when he realizes the importance of respect for well-proven traditions and knows how to listen, discern, serve and love as Jesus Christ did.

Deacons in their initial pastoral assignments should be carefully supervised by an exemplary priest especially appointed to this task by the bishop.

78. Periodic meetings should be arranged for deacons which treat of liturgical and spiritual matters, of continuous theological renewal and study, either at the diocesan or supra-diocesan level.

Under the bishop's authority and without multiplying existent structures, periodic meetings should be arranged between priests, deacons, religious and laity involved in pastoral work both to avoid compartmentalization or the development of isolated groups and to guarantee coordinated unity for different pastoral activities.

The bishop should show particular solicitude for deacons since they are his collaborators. When possible he should attend their meetings and always ensure the presence of his representative.

79. With the approval of the diocesan bishop, a realistic program of ongoing formation should be drawn up in accordance with the present dispositions, taking due account of factors such as the age and circumstances of deacons, together with the demands made on them by their pastoral ministry.

To accomplish this task, the bishop might constitute a group of suitable formators or seek the assistance of neighboring dioceses.

80. It is desirable that the bishop set up a diocesan *organization for the coordination of deacons* to plan, coordinate, and supervise the diaconal ministry from the discernment of vocation,[227] to the exercise of ministry and formation—including ongoing formation. This organization should be composed of the Bishop as its president, or a priest delegated by him for this task, and a proportionate number of deacons. This organization should not be remiss in maintaining the necessary links with the other diocesan organizations.

227 Cf. CIC, c. 1029.

The Bishops should regulate the life and activity of this organization by the issuance of appropriate norms.

81. In addition to the usual permanent formation offered to deacons, special courses and initiatives should be arranged for those deacons who are married. These courses should involve, where opportune, their wives and families. However, they must always be careful to maintain the essential distinction of roles and the clear independence of the ministry.

82. Deacons should always be appreciative of all those initiatives for the ongoing formation of the clergy promoted by Conferences of bishops or various dioceses—spiritual retreats, conferences, study days, conventions, theological and pastoral courses. They should avail themselves of such initiatives especially when they concern their own ministry of evangelization, worship and loving service.

The Sovereign Pontiff, Pope John Paul II, has approved this present Directory and ordered its publication.

Rome, at the Office of the Congregations, February 22, 1998, Feast of the Chair of Peter.

Darío Card. Castrillón Hoyos
Prefect

✠ Csaba Ternyák
Titular Archbishop of Eminenziana
Secretary

Prayer to the Blessed Virgin Mary

MARY,

Who as teacher of faith, by your obedience to the Word of God, has co-operated in a remarkable way with the work of redemption, make the ministry of deacons effective by teaching them to hear the Word and to proclaim it faithfully.

MARY,

Teacher of charity, who by your total openness to God's call, has co-operated in bringing to birth all the Church's faithful, make the ministry and the life of deacons fruitful by teaching them to give themselves totally to the service of the People of God.

MARY,

Teacher of prayer, who through your maternal intercession has supported and helped the Church from her beginnings, make deacons always attentive to the needs of the faithful by teaching them to come to know the value of prayer.

MARY,

Teacher of humility, by constantly knowing yourself to be the servant of the Lord you were filled with the Holy Spirit, make deacons docile instruments in Christ's work of redemption by teaching them the greatness of being the least of all.

MARY,

Teacher of that service which is hidden, who by your everyday and ordinary life filled with love, knew how to co-operate with the salvific plan of God in an exemplary fashion, make deacons good and faithful servants, by teaching them the joy of serving the Church with an ardent love.

Amen.

CONGREGATION FOR THE CLERGY

Instruction *The Priest, Pastor, and Leader of the Parish Community*

19. Another basic element for the idea of parish is that of the *cura pastoralis* or *cura animarum* which is proper to the office of parish priest and principally expressed by preaching the Word of God, administering the sacraments, and in the pastoral government of the community. In the parish, which is the normal context for pastoral care, "the parish priest is the proper shepherd of the parish entrusted to him. He exercises the pastoral care of that community under the authority of the diocesan bishop with whom he has been called to share in the ministry of Christ so that, in the service of that community, he may discharge the duties of teaching, sanctifying and governing, with the cooperation of other priests or deacons and the assistance of the lay members of the faithful and in accordance with the norms of law." The concept of parish priest is redolent of great theological significance while permitting a Bishop to establish other forms of the *cura animarum* in accordance with the norms of law.

24. The foregoing has already been clarified by John Paul II in the Post-Synodal Apostolic Exhortation *Christifideles Laici*: "The Church's mission of salvation in the world is realized not only by the ministers in virtue of the Sacrament of Orders but also by all the lay faithful; indeed, because of their Baptismal state and their specific vocation, in the measure proper to each person, the lay faithful participate in the priestly, prophetic and kingly mission of Christ.

"The Pastors, therefore, ought to acknowledge and foster the ministries, offices and roles of the lay faithful that find their *foundation in the Sacraments of Baptism and Confirmation*, and indeed, for a good many of them, *in the Sacrament of Matrimony*. When necessity in the Church requires it, the Pastors, according to the established norms of universal law, can entrust to the lay faithful, *ad tempus*, certain offices and roles, connected with their pastoral ministry which do not require the character of Orders." This same document recalls the basic principles underlying this collaboration and sets the limits for it: the exercise of such tasks does not make Pastors of the lay faithful: in fact, a person is not a minister simply in performing a task, but through sacramental ordination.

Only the Sacrament of Orders gives the ordained minister a particular participation in the office of Christ, the Shepherd and Head, and in his Eternal Priesthood. Supplying certain tasks by the laity takes its legitimacy, formally and immediately, from the official deputation given by the Pastors to the laity, as well as from its concrete exercise under the guidance of ecclesiastical authority.

In those cases where a collaboration with the ordained ministry has been entrusted to the non-ordained faithful, a priest must necessarily be appointed as moderator and vested with the power and duties of a parish priest, personally to direct pastoral care.

Clearly, the office of parish priest exercised by a priest who has been designated to direct pastoral activity—i.e., one invested with the faculties of a parish priest—and exercise those functions which are exclusively priestly differs completely from the subsidiary collaboration of the non-ordained faithful in the other functions of the office. A non-ordained male religious, a female religious, a layperson may exercise administrative functions, as well as that of promoting spiritual formation. They may not, however, exercise functions which belong fully to the care of souls since such requires priestly character. They may, nevertheless, *supply for the ordained minister in those liturgical functions which are consonant with their canonical condition* and enumerated in canon 230 §3: "exercise the ministry of the word, preside over liturgical prayers, confer Baptism, and distribute Holy Communion in accordance with the prescriptions of law." Even Deacons, who cannot be equated with other members of the faithful, cannot exercise the full *cura animarum.*

25. "Where permanent deacons participate in the pastoral care of parishes which, because of a shortage of priests, do not have the immediate benefit of a parish priest, they should have precedence over the non-ordained faithful." In virtue of Sacred Orders, "the deacon is teacher insofar as he preaches and bears witness to the word of God; he sanctifies when he administers the Sacrament of Baptism, the Holy Eucharist and the sacramentals, he participates at the Holy Eucharist as 'a minister of the Blood,' and conserves and distributes the Blessed Eucharist; he is a guide inasmuch as he animates the community or a section of ecclesial life."

Deacons who are candidates for ordination to the priesthood should be especially welcome when they offer their pastoral services in a parish. In agreement with the seminary authorities, the parish priest should be a guide and a teacher, conscious that a sincere and total self-offering to Christ on the part of a candidate for the priesthood can depend on his own coherent witness to priestly identity and to the missionary generosity of his service and love for the parish.

The Supreme Pontiff John Paul II approved this present Instruction and ordered its publication.

Rome, at the offices of the Congregation for the Clergy, August 4, 2002, liturgical memorial of St. John Mary Vianney, Curé d'Ars, patron of parish priests.

Dario Card. Castrillon Hoyos
Prefect

Csaba Ternyak
Titular Archbishop of Eminenziana
Secretary

INTERNATIONAL THEOLOGICAL COMMISSION

From the *Diakonia* of Christ to the *Diakonia* of the Apostles*

(2002)

The document of the International Theological Commission (ITC) "From the Diakonia *of Christ to the* Diakonia *of the Apostles" is identified in the "preliminary note" as the fruit of ten years of work by two Subcommissions and a review of the entire draft by the Commission in a plenary session. It represents a significant expression of theological reflection on the diaconate and contributes in no small way toward achieving a more mature awareness of the diaconal ministry in the post-conciliar Church. In continuity with Tradition and the fruits that have matured from Vatican II until today, the document engages in dialogue with the today of our history and opens the way for further study and research.*

Introduction

The Second Vatican Council, with the aim of the *aggiornamento* of the Church, sought inspiration and resources in its origins and history in order to announce, and more effectively make present, the mystery of Jesus Christ. Among these

* **Preliminary Note:** *The International Theological Commission had already addressed the theme of the diaconate in the quinquennium 1992-1997. The work was carried out by a Subcommission charged with studying a number of ecclesiological problems, headed by Bishop Max Thurian and comprising the following members: Bishop Christian Schönborn, OP, Bishop Joseph Osei-Bobsu, Rev. Charles Acton, Msgr. Giuseppe Colombo, Msgr. Joseph Doré, PSS, Prof. Gösta Hallonstein, Rev. Stanislaw Nagy, SCI, Rev. Henrique de Noronha Galvão. Since this Subcommission was unable to conclude its work with the publication of a document, the study was taken up again in the following quinquennium on the basis of the work already done. To this end a new Subcommission was formed, headed by the Rev. Henrique de Noronha Galvão and comprising the Rev. Santiago Del Cura Elena, Rev. Pierre Gaudette, Msgr. Richard Minnerath, Msgr. Gerhard Ludwig Müller, Msgr. Luis Tagle and Rev. Ladislaus Nagy. General discussions on this theme took place during numerous meetings of the Subcommission and during the plenary sessions of the International Theological Commission held in Rome from 1998 to 2002. The present text was approved in* forma specifica *by unanimous vote of the Commission on September 30, 2002, and was then submitted to its president, Cardinal Joseph Ratzinger, Prefect of the Congregation for the Doctrine of the Faith, who approved its publication.* [Preliminary note is a translation of the Italian text.]

riches of the Church are found the diaconate ministry, to which the texts of the New Testament bear witness, and which has rendered important services in the life of Christian communities, above all in the time of the ancient Church. Having fallen into decline during the Middle Ages, it eventually disappeared as a permanent ministry and only endured as a time of transition towards the presbyterate and episcopate. This has not altered the fact that, from Scholastic times to the present day, there has been interest in its theological meaning, especially with regards to the question of its sacramental value as a grade of Holy Orders.

Following its restoration as an effective ministry, placed by the Vatican II at the disposal of the particular Churches, different receptive processes have been witnessed. Each Church has tried to become aware of the true reach of the Conciliar initiative. Taking into account the particular circumstances of ecclesial life in each context, variation according to country and continent, the ecclesial authorities continue to evaluate the opportunity or inopportunity of including the permanent diaconate in the reality of their communities.

In this receptive process, some questions have arisen regarding the interpretation of both New Testament and historical data, the theological implications of the Conciliar decision and of the extensions which have been conferred on the ecclesial Magisterium. Furthermore, although the Council did not make a pronouncement on the feminine diaconal ministry, of which mention is found in the past, this must be studied in order to establish its ecclesial status and the current reality in which it could be accommodated and examined.

The International Theological Commission has examined these questions with the aim of clarifying them, through a greater knowledge of both historical and theological sources, as well as of the current life of the Church.

While it is true that facts must be rigorously established by the historical method, their consideration does not become *locus theologicus* except in so far that this is carried out in the light of the *sensus fidei*. It is necessary to distinguish between that which can be identified as the essence of Tradition itself, from its origins, and regional variations or links to a particular era of this same

Tradition.[2] From this perspective, it is essential to highlight the function of the interventions in the Church which pertain to the competence of the hierarchy, namely the decisions of Ecumenical Councils and the declarations of the Magisterium. Briefly, in order to arrive at properly theological conclusions efforts of discernment have to be made in the light of these interventions, allowing for the fact that knowledge of history and its generality have the inestimable advantage of making known the life of the Church, in a specific time and place, within whom there is always a truly human element and a truly divine element (*Lumen Gentium*, no. 8). Only faith is capable of distinguishing the action of the Spirit of God therein. Man, a material and spiritual being, both historical and transcendent, becomes the providential recipient of an opening of God in his Word made flesh and his Spirit who, being *pneuma* and *dynamis*, grants men the capacity to identify God, who communicates by words and signs, in historical phenomena. Precisely because He opens his mystery to the community of faith by his Word and his Spirit, God erects the Church as a community of witnesses, whose testimony emanates from Revelation and represents it. Dogma is the verbalization of the Word who is God and was made flesh, according to the expression of the Church's profession of faith, the response to divine Revelation.

Scripture, which with Tradition is the supreme rule of faith (*Dei Verbum*, no. 21), presents us in living, frequently symbolic language, the mystery and mission of Christ; language which speculative theology especially tries to rigorously interpret. However, it cannot be forgotten that in all its forms, theological language always remains somewhat analogical, its ultimate criterion really residing in its capacity to tell of Revelation. The *regula fidei* is the *regula veritatis*.

The present investigation has remained attentive to the divergence which characterizes the diaconate ministry and the course of the different historical periods and which even today animate the debate which it stirs. The reflection presented herein is founded on the living awareness of the gift made by Jesus Christ to his Church when he communicated to the Twelve a particular

2 Cf. W. Kasper, *Theologie und Kirche*, Mainz, 1987, 99: "Einzelne Zeugnisse haben theologisch normative Bedeutung nur, insofern sie massgebliche Repräsentanten des gemeinsamen Glaubens der Kirche sind. Es gilt also in der Vielfalt und Fülle der Traditionszeugnisse den 'roten Faden' herauszufinden. Dafür genügt historische Erudition, so unverzichtbar sie ist, nicht. Es bedarf vielmehr eines geistlichen Gespürs und Feinsinns, um die eine und gemeinsame Tradition in den vielen Traditionen erkennen zu können. Allein der *sensus fidei* vermag festzustellen, wo wirklicher *consensus fidei* und nicht verbreitete, aber zeitbedingte Meinung vorliegt." The classic work on this subject remains Y. Congar, *La Tradition et les traditions*, 2 vols., Paris, 1960-63.

responsibility in fulfilling the mission which he himself had received from the Father. The Church has never been without the Spirit, who both enables the discovery of the riches which God has made available to her and continues to bear fresh witness of her faithfulness to the salvific project which He offers us in his Son. It is because of his condition as a servant, by his diaconate assumed in obedience to the Father and for the benefit of man as, according to Scripture and Tradition, Jesus Christ carried out the divine design of salvation. Only by starting from this primordial Christological fact can the vocation and mission of the diaconate in the Church, manifested in her ministries, be understood. In this light we initially ask about the historical and theological significance of the ministry of deacons in the course of the Church's history and what the reasons for its disappearance were in order to finally ask about the extent of introducing an effective diaconal ministry at the service of the Christian community in the present day.

Chapter I

From the Diakonia of Christ to the Diakonia of the Apostles

I. Diakonia of Christ and Christian Existence

Through the incarnation of the Word who is God and by whom all was made (cf. Jn 1:1-18) the strangest revolution imaginable has come about. The *Kyrios*, Lord, becomes the *diakonos*, servant, of all. The Lord God comes out to meet us in his Servant Jesus Christ, the only Son of God (Rom 1:3), who, being in the "form of God," "did not see in the form of God a prize to be coveted, but emptied himself, taking the form of a slave. Having become like men . . . he abased himself and became obedient to death, even death on a cross" (Phil 2:6-8).

The essence of being a Christian can thus be grasped in a Christological perspective. Christian existence is a sharing in the *diakonia* or service which God himself fulfilled in favor of mankind; it likewise leads to an understanding of the fulfillment of mankind. Being a Christian means following Christ's example in putting oneself at the service of others to the point of self-renunciation and self-giving, for love.

Baptism confers this *diakonein*, power of service, on every Christian. Through it, by virtue of their participation in the *diakonia*, *leiturgia* and *martyria*, the service, worship and witness of the Church, Christians cooperate in Christ's own *diakonia* for the salvation of mankind. As members of the Body of Christ, all should become servants of one another, using the charisms which they have received for the building up of the Church and their brethren in faith and love: "If anyone claims to serve, let it be as by a command received from God" (1 Pt 4:11-12; cf. Rom 12:8; 1 Cor 12:5).

This *diakonia* done to others by Christians can take the form of different expressions of fraternal charity, service to the physically or spiritually sick, to the needy, to prisoners (Mt 25); the help given to the Churches (Rom 15:25; 1 Tm 5:3-16); or different kinds of assistance given to Apostles, as can be seen in the case of the men and women collaborators of St. Paul, who sends them his greetings (Rom 16:3-5; Phil 4:3).

II. Diakonia of the Apostles

Because he was the *doulos*, or slave, carrying out the Father's saving will in total obedience, Jesus Christ was made Lord of all creation. He made himself the instrument through which God's sovereignty was achieved, by giving his life: "The Son of Man has not come to be served but to serve, and to give his life as a ransom for many" (Mk 10:45). In the same way, Jesus instituted the Twelve "to be his companions, and sent them out to preach, giving them the power to cast out demons" (Mk 3:14-15). In a way that was radically opposed to the lords and rulers of this world who abuse their power to oppress and exploit others, the disciple must be ready to become *diakonos* and *doulos* of all (Mk 10:42-43).

Diakonein, to serve, is the essential characteristic of the Apostle's ministry. Apostles are collaborators and servants of God (cf. 1 Thes 3:2; 1 Cor 3:9; 2 Cor 6:1), "servants of Christ and witnesses of God's mysteries" (1 Cor 4:1). They are "ministers of a new covenant" (2 Cor 3:6) and ministers of the Gospel (cf. Col 1:23; Eph 3:6ff.), "servants of the word" (Acts 6:4). They are, in their function as Apostles, "ministers of the Church" in order to bring about the coming of the word of Christ in its fullness to believers (cf. Col 1:25), and to organize the building up of the Church, the Body of Christ, in love (cf. Eph 4:12). The Apostles become the servants of believers because of Christ, since it is not themselves whom they are proclaiming, but Christ Jesus the Lord (2 Cor 4:5).

They are sent in the name of Christ, the word having been passed on to them so that they may proclaim it in the service of reconciliation. Through them, God himself *exhorts* and *acts* in the Holy Spirit and in Christ Jesus, who has reconciled the world with him (cf. 2 Cor 5:20).

III. Diakonia of the Apostles' Collaborators

Within the Pauline communities, with, as well as, or after St. Paul, St. Peter and the other eleven Apostles (cf. 1 Cor 15:3-5; Gal 2), are to be found direct collaborators with St. Paul in the apostolic ministry (for example, Sylvanus, Timothy, Titus, Apollos) as well as many others allied to him in apostolic activities and service to local Churches (2 Cor 8:23). These include Epaphroditus (Phil 2:25), Epaphras (Col 4:12) and Archippus (Col 4:17), who are named as servants of Christ. In the opening words of the Epistle to the Philippians (around AD 50) St. Paul sends a special greeting to "their bishops and their deacons" (Phil 1:1). This necessarily calls to mind the ministries that were then taking shape in the Church.

It is of course recognized that the terminology of these ministries was not yet fixed. Reference is made to the *proistamenoi* (Rom 12:8) "who are at your head in the Lord and who reprimand you," and whom the Thessalonians are to hold "in extreme charity, by reason of their work" (1 Thes 5:12); reference is also made to leaders (*hegoumenoi*), "who have made you hear the word of God"; the Epistle to the Hebrews adds, "Obey your leaders and be docile to them" (13:7, 17; cf. 13:24; cf. 1 Clem 1:3; 21:6); and reference is made to the "men who were sent" who guide the communities (cf. Acts 15:22), to apostles, prophets, and teachers (cf. 1 Cor 12:28; Gal 6:6; Acts 13:1; 4:14), and to "evangelists, or rather shepherds and teachers" (Eph 4:11). St. Paul says of Stephanas, Fortunatus and Achaicus, "the first-fruits of Achaia," "that they spontaneously put themselves at the service of the saints" (1 Cor 16:15); and he exhorts the Corinthians: "Place yourselves under such men, and under whoever works arid labors with them" (1 Cor 16:16).

The activity expressed in these terms points to the official titles which were to take shape soon afterwards. It is clear from these documents that the early Church attributed the formation of the various ministries to the action of the Holy Spirit (1 Cor 12:28; Eph 4:11; Acts 20:28) and to the personal initiative of the Apostles, who owed their sending forth on their mission to the Most High and Lord of this world, and who anchored their role of upholding the Church in the power they had received from him (Mk 3:13-19; 6:6-13; Mt 28:16-20; Acts 1:15-26; Gal 1:10-24).

Diakonein is shown to be a radical determination of *Christian life*, expressing itself in the sacramental basis of Christian existence, of the charismatic building up of the Church, and also of the sending out of the Apostles on their mission and of the *ministry* which flows from the apostolate, of the proclamation of the Gospel, and of the sanctification and governance of Churches.

Chapter II

The Diaconate in the New Testament and in the Writings of the Fathers

I. The Diaconate in the New Testament

1. Difficulties in Terminology

The word *diakonos* is almost absent from the Old Testament, by contrast with *presbyteros* which is abundantly used. In the Septuagint, in the rare places where the word *diakonos* is attested, it means messenger or servant.[3] The Latin Bible (Vulgate) renders it in a general sense by *minister* or, in a specific sense, by transliterating the Greek word to give *diaconus*. But the terms *minister*, *ministerium*, and *ministrare* are also used to render other Greek terms, such as *hyperetes* and *leitourgos*. In the Vulgate the use of *diaconus* is found three times,[4] and in the remaining cases the word is translated by *minister*.[5]

Apart from the words *diakoneo*, *diakonia*, and *diakonos*, Greek could choose between the following words: *douleuo* (to serve as a servant), *therapeuo* (someone who volunteers to serve), *latreuo* (to serve for wages), *leitourgeo* (someone

3 Neh 1:10: "They are your servants and your people, whom you redeemed by your great power and your strong hand"; 6:3: "I sent messengers to them, saying"; 6:5: "Sanballat sent his servant to me"; Prov 10:4a (Septuagint); 1 Mac 11:58; 4 Mac 9:17; Esther (Greek) 6:13.

4 Phil 1:1; 1 Tm 3:8, 12.

5 Cf. E. Cattaneo, *I ministeri nella chiesa antica, testi patristici dei primi tre secoli* (Milan, 1997), 33ff.; J. Lecuyer, *Le sacrement de l'ordination*, ThH 65 (Paris, 1983), 131.

who holds public office), and *hypereteo* (governor).[6] In any case, it is characteristic that the verbal form *diakonein* is unknown in the Septuagint, the functions of service being translated by the verbs *leitourgein* or *latreuein*. Philo only used it in the sense of "to serve."[7] Josephus knew it in the sense of "to serve," "to obey" and "priestly service."[8] In the New Testament, the word *douleuo* meant service of a very personal kind: the service of charity. In the language of the Gospels[9] and at Acts 6:2, *diakoneo* means "ministering at table." Making a collection whose proceeds Paul would take to Jerusalem was a service of this kind.[10] The Apostle goes to Jerusalem for "a ministry to the saints."[11] As for the use of the words *cheirotonia, cheirotesia, ordinatio*, there is a degree of uncertainty with regard to these terms.[12]

2. *Data from the New Testament*

The first fundamental fact of relevance from the New Testament is that the verb *diakonein* designates Christ's actual mission as servant (Mk 10:45 and parallels; cf. Mt 12:18; Acts 4:30; Phil 2:6-11). This word or its derivatives also designate the exercise of service or ministry by his disciples (Mk 10:43ff.; Mt 20:26ff.; 23:11; Lk 8:3; Rom 15:25), the ministries of different kinds in the Church,

---

6 H. W. Beyer, *diakoneo, diakonia, diakonos*, in *Theölogisches Wörterbuch zum Neuen Testament* [ThWNT] 2:81-93.

7 *De vita contemplativa* 70 and 75.

8 *Antiquitates* 7, 365; 10, 72.

9 Lk 17:8; 12:37; 22:26; Jn 12:2.

10 2 Cor 8:19.

11 Rom 15:25.

12 "The meaning of the laying on of the hands in Acts 6:6 and 13:3 has been much disputed, but the stress laid on this gesture in both texts makes it difficult to see it as a mere act of blessing and not as an ordination rite. . . . The usual verb to denote the election of a minister by the community is *eklegein*, Latin *eligere*. The verb *cheirotonein* may have the same meaning, 'to choose by stretching out the hand' (Did. 15, 1), but it becomes a technical term for the appointment, i.e., the ordination of a minister, in Latin *ordinate*. In this meaning it is synonymous with *kathistanai*, Latin *instituere*. Another synonym is *procheirizein*. It is less usual and sometimes denotes the aspect of election and appointment by God. All these verbs are synonymous with *cheira(s) epitheinai*, but whereas the former group denotes the juridical aspect, the latter lays emphasis on the liturgical act. Moreover all the terms of the former group can be used for an appointment/ordination which does not include an imposition of hands, but there is apparently a preference for *cheirotonein/cheirotonia*, as they are composed with *cheir-*, when the imposition of the hand (or of both hands) is included. A first attempt for such a distinction is made by Hippolytus, *Trad. A* 10." J. Ysebaert, "The Deaconesses in the Western Church of Late Antiquity and Their Origin," in *Eulogia: Mélanges offerres à Antoon A. R. Bastiaensen*, IP 24 (Steenbrugis, 1991), 423.

especially the apostolic ministry of preaching the Gospel, and other charismatic gifts.[13]

The words *diakonein* and *diakonos* are widely used, with a wide range of meanings, in the language of the New Testament.[14]

The *diakonos* may mean the servant who waits at table (e.g., Jn 2:5 and 9), the servant of the Lord (Mt 22:13; Jn 12:26; Mk 9:35; 10:43; Mt 20:26; 23:11), the servant of a spiritual power (2 Cor 11:14; Eph 3:6; Col 1:23; Gal 2:17; Rom 15:8; 2 Cor 3:6), the servant of the Gospel, of Christ or of God (2 Cor 11:23). Pagan authorities are also in the service of God (Rom 13:4); the deacons are the servants of the Church (Col 1:25; 1 Cor 3:5). In the case where the deacon belongs to one of the Churches, the Vulgate does not use the word *minister*, but retains the Greek word *diaconus*.[15] This fact shows clearly that in Acts 6:1-6 it is not the institution of the diaconate which is being referred to.[16]

"Diaconate" and "apostolate" are sometimes synonymous, as in Acts 1:17-25, where, on the occasion of the addition of Matthias to the eleven Apostles, Peter calls the apostolate "a share in our service" (v. 17: *ton kleron tes diakonias tautes*)

---

13 Rom 11:13; 12:6ff.; 1 Cor 12:5; 2 Cor 4:1; Eph 4:llff.; Heb 1:14: "*leitourgika pneumata*"; Acts 21:19; Col 4:17.

14 "Amt im Sinne Jesu muss immer 'diakonia' sein; nicht zufällig, nicht nebenbei, sondern sehr bewusst und ausdrücklich wählt die Heilige Schrift dieses Wort zu seiner Wesensbestimmung. Die griechische Sprache bot eine ganze Reihe von Möglichkeiten, das Amt in einer menschlichen Gemeinschaft—auch im religiös-kultischen Bereich—zu charakterisieren (archai, exousiai, archontes). Das Neue Testament wählte keine davon, sondern entschied sich für eine Bezeichnung, die weder in der jüdischen, noch in der hellenistischen Umwelt üblich war." E. Dassmann, *Ämter und Dienste in der frühchristlichen Gemeinden*, Hereditas 8 (Bonn, 1994), 37.

15 Phil 1:1: "*cum episcopis et diaconis*"; 1 Tm 3:8, 12: "*diaconos similiter . . . [sicut episcopi] diaconi sint.*"

16 "Dieser Tatbestand zeigt, dass der Ursprung des Diakonenamtes nicht in Ag 6 zu finden ist. . . . Der Diakonos ist nicht nur Diener seiner Gemeinde, sondern auch seines Bischofes." Beyer, *diakoneo, diakonia, diakonos*, 90. Cf. M. Dibelius, "Bischöfe und Diakonen in Philippi" (1937), in *Das kirchliche Amt im Neuen Testament*, WdF 439 (Darmstadt, 1977), 413ff.; E. Schweizer, "Das Amt: Zum Amtsbegriff im Neuen Testament", in *Gemeinde und Gemeindeordnung im Neuen Testament*, AThANT 35 (Zürich, 1955), 154-64: "Als allgemeine Bezeichnung dessen, was wir 'Amt' nennen, also des Dienstes Einzelner innerhalb der Gemeinde, gibt es mit wenigen Ausnahmen nur ein einziges Wort: 'diakonia,' Diakonie. Das NT wählt also durchwegs und einheitlich ein Wort, das völlig unbiblisch und unreligiös ist und nirgends eine Assoziation mit einer besonderen Würde oder Stellung einschliesst. Im griechischen AT kommt das Wort nur einmal rein profan vor. . . . In der griechischen Sprachentwicklung ist die Grundbedeutung 'zu Tischen dienen' auch zum umfassenden Begriff 'dienen' ausgeweitet worden. Es bezeichnet fast durchwegs etwas Minderwertiges, kann aber im Hellenismus auch die Haltung des Weisen gegen Gott (nicht gegen den Mitmenschen) umschreiben"; K. H. Schelke, "Dienste und Diener in den Kirchen der Neutestamentlichen Zeit," *Concilium* 5 (1969): 158-64; J. Brosch, *Charismen und Ämter in der Urkirche* (Bonn, 1951). Cf. B. Kötting, "Amt und Verfassung in der Alten Kirche," in *Ecclesia peregrinans: Das Gottesvolk unterwegs*, METh 54, 1 (Münster, 1988), 429; G. Schöllgen, *Die Anfänge der Professionalisierung des Klerus und das kirchliche Amt in der Syrischen Didaskalie*, JAC, Ergbd 26 (Münster, 1998), 93.

and speaks of service and apostolate (v. 25: *ton topon tes diakonias kai apostoles*, which is sometimes translated as "the service of the apostolate." This text from Acts also quotes Psalm 109:8: "Let another take over his position [*ten episkopen*]." The question therefore arises as to whether *diakonia*, *apostole*, and *episkope* are equivalent to each other or not. In the opinion of M.J. Schmitt and J. Colson, "apostolate" is "an editorial term correcting 'diakonias.'"[17]

Acts 6:1-6 describes the institution of the "Seven"[18] "to serve at tables." The reason for this is given by Luke as stemming from internal tensions within the community: "The Hellenists complained [*egeneto goggysmos*] against the Hebrews because their widows were being neglected in the daily distribution of food" (Acts 6:1). It has not yet been ascertained whether the widows of the "Hellenists" belonged to the community or not, according to strict respect for ritual purity. Were the Apostles hoping to send to the provinces the rebellious "Hellenists" of Jerusalem who, in their preaching in the synagogue, were responsible for much provocation? Is this why the Apostles chose "Seven," which was the number of provincial community magistrates attached to a synagogue? But at the same time, through the imposition of hands, they wished to preserve the unity of the Spirit and avoid a schism.[19] Commentators on Acts do not explain the significance of this laying on of the Apostles' hands.

It is possible that the Apostles appointed the Seven to be at the head of the "Hellenists" (baptized Greek-speaking Jews) to fulfill the same task as the presbyters among the "Hebrew" Christians.[20]

The reason given for the designation of the chosen Seven (complaints by the Hellenists) is in contradiction with their actual activity as later described by Luke. We hear nothing about serving at tables. Out of the Seven, Luke only speaks of the activities of Stephen and Philip; or more precisely, Stephen's discourse in the

---

17 Cf. J. Colson, *Ministre de Jésus-Christ ou le Sacerdoce de l'Évangile*, ThH 4 (Paris, 1966), 191.

18 It was lrenaeus of Lyons (*Adv. haer.* 3, 12, 10) who first referred to the "Seven" as "deacons."

19 "Die Siebenzahl wohl nach Analogie der sieben Mitglieder, aus denen in den jüdischen Gemeinden meist der Ortsvorstand sich zusammensetzte. Dieser hiess deshalb geradezu 'die Sieben einer Stadt' oder 'die Sieben Besten einer Stadt,' während seine einzelnen Mitglieder . . . 'Hirten' oder 'Vorsteher' genannt wurden." H. L. Strack and P. Billerbeck, *Kommentar zum Neuen Testament aus Talmud und Midrasch*, vol. 2 (Munich, 1969), 641.

20 E. Haenchen, *Die Apostelgeschichte*, Neu übersetzt und erklärt, 12. neubearb. Auflage, Kritisch--exegetischer Kommentar (Göttingen, 1959), 228-22; Dassmann, *Ämter und Dienste*, 232: "Über die Entstehung des Diakonenamtes sind keine genauere Angaben bekannt, seitdem feststeht, dass Apg 6 nicht die Bestellung von Diakonen, sondern von Beauftragten für die griechisch sprechende Gruppe der Urgemeinde beschreibt."

synagogue at Jerusalem, and his martyrdom, and the apostolate carried out in Samaria by Philip, who also baptized people.[21] There is no word of the others.[22]

In the Churches entrusted to St. Paul's apostolic care, deacons appear beside the *episkopoi* as exercising a ministry subordinate to or coordinated with theirs (Phil 1:1; 1 Tm 3:1-13). In the apostolic writings mention is often made of deacons with the bishop, or else of the bishop with priests. However, historical sources which cite all three together, bishop, priest and deacon, are very rare.

II. The Apostolic Fathers

The first epistle of St. Clement of Rome to the Corinthians (first century) mentions that the bishops and deacons have a spiritual function in the community: "The Apostles received for us the good news through the Lord Jesus Christ; Jesus, the Christ, was sent by God. Therefore the Christ comes from God, the Apostles come from Christ; both proceeded in due order from the will of God [*egenonto oun amphotera eutaktos ek thelematos Theou*]. They therefore received instructions and, filled with conviction by the resurrection of our Lord Jesus Christ, strengthened by the word of God, with the full conviction of the Holy Spirit, they set out to announce the good news of the coming of God's kingdom. They preached in the countryside and in the towns and they established [*kathistanon*] its first-fruits, they tested them by the Spirit, so as to make them bishops and deacons [*eis episkopous kai diakonous*] of those who were to believe. And there was nothing new [*ou kainos*] in this; for long ago Scripture spoke of bishops and deacons [*egegrapto peri episkopon kai diakonon*]; for it is written somewhere, 'I shall establish their bishops in justice and their deacons in faith.'"[23]

When the author of the Epistle of Clement speaks of liturgical functions he refers to the Old Testament;[24] when he explains the institution of the *episkopoi kai diakonoi*, he refers to the will of God, and to the Apostles.[25] The order of bishops

21 Cf. Acts 8:12, 26-40 and 21:8, where Philip is called "the evangelist." "The next day we left and came to Caesarea; and went into the house of Philip the evangelist, one of the seven [*Philippou tou euaggelistou, ontos ek ton epta*], and stayed with him."

22 "Nicolaitae autem magistrum quidem habent Nicolaum, unum ex VII qui primi ad diaconium ab apostolis ordinati sunt: qui indiscrete vivunt." *Adv. haer.* 1, 26, 3; Harvey, 1:214. Hippolytus, *Philosophomena* 7, 36; Tertullian, *De praescriptione* 33. For the opposing view, Clement of Alexandria, *Strom.* 2, 118, 3 and 3, 25, 5-26, 2.

23 Cf. Is 60:17, where the Septuagint does not mention "deacons," which must be an addition by St. Clement; cf. 1 Clem 42:1-5; Sources Chrétiennes (SCh) 167, 173, 168-71.

24 Cf. 40:1 and 41:2-4.

25 Colson, *Ministre de Jésus-Christ*, 228ff.

and deacons was not an innovation, but was founded on the will of God, and therefore was a "due order"; their sending originated in God himself. The successors chosen by the Apostles were the first-fruits offered to God. The Apostles had tested the chosen ones by the Spirit; those who succeeded them would be established by the choice of the whole assembly.[26] Here we find the tradition of the pastoral letters in reverse order: (1) the testing in the Spirit (cf. 1 Tm 3:1-7 and 8:10ff.); (2) the use side by side of the terms *episkopos kai diakonos* (cf. Phil 1:1), where *episkopos* does not yet correspond to the present definition of bishop.[27] It is worth noting the way St. Polycarp linked the ministry of deacons with the service of Christ the Savior: "Let them walk in the truth of the Lord who became the servant [*diakonos*] of all" (Letter of St. Polycarp to the Philippians 5:2).

The text of the *Didache* (written before AD 130) at 15, 1 only mentions bishops and deacons as the successors of the prophets and the *didaskaloi*, and says nothing of priests: "Choose yourselves therefore bishops and deacons worthy of the Lord, mild men, fair-minded, truthful and reliable, for they too fulfill toward you the offices of prophets and teachers."[28] J.-P. Audet comments, "The two words admittedly sound different to us. But in Greek, at the time of the Didache, an *episkopos* was a supervisor, foreman, guardian, moderator, warden or steward . . . whereas a *diakonos* was simply a servant able to fulfill different functions according to the particular conditions of his service. The two terms are widely used with a variety of meanings. . . . The specific way they were appointed (*cheirotonesate*) remains unclear. They were chosen and appointed, perhaps by election; that is all that can be said."[29] The *Didache* does not say anything about ordination. According to K. Niederwimmer, the term *cheirotonein* means election.[30]

It is certain that at that period the deacons were responsible for the life of the Church with regard to works of charity towards widows and orphans, as was the case in the first community at Jerusalem. Their activities were doubtless linked to catechesis and also probably to the liturgy. However information on

26 1 Clem 44:3; SCh 167, 172-73.

27 "Von den zwei erwähnten Ämtern, *episkopoi* und *diakonoi*, wurde das erste mit 'Episkopen' wiedergegeben, um das sehr missverständliche 'Bischöfe' zu vermeiden. Denn auf keinen Fall handelt es sich dabei um die Institution des Monepiskopats." H. E. Lona, *Der erste Clemensbrief*, Kommentar zu den Apostolischen Vätern 2 (Göttingen, 1998), 446. Cf. Dassmann, *Ämter und Dienste*, 40.

28 J.-P. Audet, *La Didachè: Instructions des Apôtres* (Paris, 1958), 241.

29 Ibid., 465.

30 "'*Cheirotonein*' heisst hier (natürlich) 'wählen' und nicht 'ernennen.'" *Die Didache*, Kommentar zu den Apostolischen Vätern 1 (Göttingen, 1989), 241.

this subject is so brief[31] that it is difficult to learn from it the precise range of their functions.

The letters of St. Ignatius of Antioch point to a new stage. His statements about the ecclesiastical hierarchy with its three grades are similar to those of Clement of Rome: "Let everyone revere the deacons as Jesus Christ, the bishop as the image of the Father, and the presbyters as the senate of God and the assembly of the Apostles. For without them one cannot speak of the Church."[32] And again, "All of you, follow the bishop, as Jesus Christ [follows] his Father, and the presbyterium as the Apostles; as for the deacons, respect them as the law of God."[33] St. Ignatius speaks of the bishop in the singular and of priests and deacons in the plural, but says nothing on the character of the diaconate, simply exhorting the faithful to venerate the deacons as appointed by God.

St. Justin (fl65) gives information especially about the liturgical activity of deacons. He describes the role of deacons in the Eucharist during the *oblatio* and the *communio*: "Then there is brought to him who presides over the assembly of the brethren, some bread and a cup of water and wine mixed. . . . Once the prayers and giving of thanks are over, all the people present express their assent by replying Amen. When the president of the assembly has finished the prayer of thanksgiving [eucharist] and all the people have made their response, those who among us are called deacons [*oi kaloumenoi par 'emin diakonoi'*] give to each of those present to share in the bread and in the wine mixed with water over which has been said the prayer of thanksgiving [eucharist], and they carry it to those who are absent."[34]

III. Consolidation and Development of the Diaconate in the Third and Fourth Centuries

According to Clement of Alexandria there are in the Church, as in the life of civil society, positions which are intended to benefit either the body or the soul (*therapeia beltiotike, hyperetike*). There are also people who in themselves are ordered to the service of people of a higher grade. Priests are of the first kind,

31 *Did.* 14, 1-3; 15, 1.

32 *Letter to the Trallians* 3, 1; SCh 10, 113.

33 *Letter to the Smyrnaeans* 8, 1; SCh 10, 163.

34 *Apol.* 1, 65, 3-5. St. Justin, *Apologies*, introduction, texte critique, traduction, commentaire et index par A. Wartelle (Paris, 1987), 188-91.

and deacons of the second.[35] In Origen, the *diakonia* of the bishop is always the service of the whole Church (*ekklesiastike diakonia*). The bishop is called "prince" and, at the same time, also called "servant of all."[36] Deacons are often criticized by Origen because they are particularly infected by the spirit of covetousness. Because of their responsibility for charitable works, they were more in contact with money. In a passage on the expulsion of the traders from the Temple, Origen speaks of those "deacons who do not administer rightly the tables of the money of the Church [*sc.* of the poor], but always act fraudulently towards them."[37] "They amass riches for themselves, misappropriating money meant for the poor."[38]

The *Didascalia* (third century) evidences a degree of supremacy of deacons over priests, since deacons are compared to Christ, while priests are only compared to the Apostles.[39] But in the first place, priests are presented as the senate of the Church and the bishop's assessors; they are placed around the altar and the episcopal throne. The deacons are called the "third ones," which probably suggests that they come after the bishop and the priests. However, the status and activity of deacons undoubtedly seem to have surpassed those of priests. The laity ought to have great confidence in the deacons and not importune the head, but make their wishes known to him through the *hyperetai*, that is through the deacons, for no one can approach the almighty Lord and God either except through Christ.[40] In the *Didascalia* the increase in the status of the diaconate in the Church is remarkable, resulting in a growing crisis in the reciprocal relations of priests and deacons. To the deacons' social and charitable responsibilities was added that of providing various services during liturgical assemblies: ushering in newcomers and pilgrims; taking care of the offerings; supervising orderliness and silence; and ensuring that people were suitably dressed.

The *Traditio Apostolica* of Hippolytus of Rome (f235) presents the theological and juridical status of the deacon in the Church for the first time. It includes them among the group of the *ordinati* by the imposition of hands (*cheirotonein*), contrasting them with those in the hierarchy who are called *instituti*. The "ordination" of deacons is done only by the bishop (Chapter 8). This

35 *Strom.* 7, 1, 3; GCS 17, 6.

36 *Comm. in Mat.* 16:8; GCS 40, 496.

37 Ibid., 16:22; GCS 40, 552.

38 Ibid., 16:22; GCS 40, 553.

39 *Didascalia apostolorum*, ed. R.H. Connolly (Oxford, 1969), 89.

40 Cf. A. Vilela, *La condition collégiale des prêtres au Me siècle*, ThH 14 (Paris, 1971).

connection defines the scope of the tasks of the deacon, who is at the disposition of the bishop, to fulfill his orders, but is excluded from taking part in the council of priests.

A comparison should be made between the two texts for the ordination of deacons, that of the *Veronense* (L, Latin version) and that of the Sahidic Ethiopian (S[AE]), because there are some differences between them. L says: "*Diaconus vero cum ordinatur, eligatur secundum ea, quae praedicta sunt, similiter imponens manus episcopus solus sicuti praecipimus.*" S[AE] is clearer: "*Episcopus autem instituet [kathistasthat] diaconum qui electus est, secundum quod praedictum est.*" There is still, however, a difference between *ordinatio* and *institutio*. The tenth chapter, speaking of the widows of the *Traditio Apostolica* contributes some significant elements. "*Non autem imponetur manus super eam, quia non offert oblationem neque habet liturgiam. Ordinatio [cheirotonia] autem fit cum clero [kleros] propter liturgiam. Vidua [xera] autem instituitur [kathistasthai] propter orationem: haec autem est omnium.*"[41] According to this text, if the imposition of hands is absent from the rite, then it is only an institution (*katastasis, institutio*) and not an *ordinatio*. Thus, in the course of the third century, the imposition of hands already constituted the distinctive sign of the rite of ordination to major orders. In the fourth century it was extended to minor orders as well.

In what concerns the liturgy, the task of the deacon was to bring the offerings and distribute them. In the administration of baptism, his role was to accompany the priest and serve him "the oil of the catechumens and the chrism and also to go down into the water with the person who was to receive baptism" (Chapter 21). Another field of work for the deacons was teaching: "Let them come together and instruct those with whom they are in the Church" (Chapter 39). Their social activity is emphasized, specifically in close union with the bishop.

According to St. Cyprian, "The deacons should not forget that the Lord himself chose the Apostles, that is, the bishops and the heads of the Church, while in the case of deacons, it was the Apostles who instituted them after the Lord's Ascension, to be ministers of their episcopate and of the Church. Hence, just as we cannot undertake anything in defiance of God who makes us bishops, neither can they too undertake anything in defiance of us, who make

41 SCh 11(2), 66.

them deacons."[42] It seems that, from time to time, even at Carthage, the deacons wished to take the place of the priests. They had to be warned that deacons came in third place in the order of the hierarchy. While the see was vacant they also had an important role in the governance of the Church. In exile, Cyprian normally addressed his letters "to the priests and deacons" to discuss disciplinary problems. In Cyprian's writings priests and deacons were sometimes designated by the word *clerus*, and less frequently were called *praepositi*.[43] The priest Gains Didensis and his deacons were both charged to offer the Eucharist, but the fifth letter indicates that in reality it was the priests who offered it, attended by the deacons.[44] To deacons, on the other hand, falls the practice of charity by prison-visiting. They are described as "*boni viri et ecclesiasticae administrationis per omnia devoti*."[45] The word *administratio* is found in the expression *sancta administratio* applied to the deacon Nicostratus in regard to the Church money that he looked after. Thus deacons would be charged not only with the practice of charity toward the poor, but also with the administration of the finances belonging to the community.[46]

To sum up, as well as the fact of the existence of the diaconate in all the Churches from the beginning of the second century, and the fact of the ecclesiastical nature of the diaconate as such, it can be said that the role fulfilled by deacons was basically the same everywhere, although the emphasis placed on the various elements of their commitment may have differed in different regions. The diaconate was stabilized in the course of the fourth century. In the synodal and conciliar directives of this period the diaconate was regarded as an essential element of the hierarchy of the local Church. At the synod of Elvira (c. 306-309) the diaconate's preeminent role in the administrative sector of the Church was primarily underlined. Paradoxically, at the same time as it imposed a certain limitation on the involvement of deacons in the liturgical sector, this synod attributed to them the possibility of giving absolution of sins in urgent cases. This tendency to invade the field of competences of priests, which was

42 *Ep.* 3, 3: "Meminisse autem diaconi debent quoniam apostolos id est episcopos et praepositos Dominus elegit, diaconos autem post ascensum Domini in caelos apostoli sibi constituerunt episcopatus sui et ecclesiae ministros. Quod si nos aliquid audere contra Deum possumus qui episcopos facit, possunt et contra nos audere diaconi a quibus fiunt."

43 *Ep.* 15, 2; 16, 3.

44 *Ep.* 34, 1; *Ep.* 5, 2.

45 *Ep.* 15, 1; 43, 1.

46 *Ep.* 52, 1.

also manifested in the claim to preside at the Eucharist (albeit as an exception) was put a stop to by the synod of Aries (314) and particularly by the Council of Nicaea (325, c. 18).

The *Constitutiones Apostolorum* (CA), which forms the most impressive of the juridical collections drawn up in the fourth century, cites the different parts of the *Didache* and the *Didascalia* which refer to deacons, and comments on them in ways which reflect the point of view of the period. Also included are the statements of St. Ignatius in his letters, thus providing a considerable amount of information. The text is characterized by a tendency to historicism, the more so since the author-editor looks for prefigurations in parallel passages of the Old Testament. He introduces his discourse with a solemn formula (cf. Dt 5:31 and 27:9): "Hear, O sacred and catholic Church.... For these are your pontiffs; your priests are the presbyters, and your Levites are now the deacons, these are your lectors, cantors and door-keepers, these are your deaconesses, your widows, your virgins and your orphans.... The deacon will attend him as Christ attends the Father."[47] He describes the relation of the bishop with the deacon through the prefigurations of the Old Covenant and the heavenly models: "For you now, Aaron is the deacon and Moses the bishop; if therefore Moses was called a god by the Lord, among you the bishop shall be likewise honored as a god and the deacon as his prophet... and as the Son is the angel and prophet of the Father, in the same way the deacon is the angel and prophet of the bishop."[48] The deacon represents the eye, the ear, and the mouth of the bishop "so that the bishop does not have to concern himself with a multitude of matters, but only with the most important ones, as Jethro established for Moses, and his counsel was well received."[49] The prayer of ordination of a deacon by the bishop attests that the diaconate was envisaged as a transitory grade towards the presbyterate: "Grant that he may satisfactorily accomplish the service which has been entrusted to him, in a seemly manner, without deviation or blame or reproach, to be judged worthy of a higher rank [*meizonos axiothenai bathmou*], through the mediation of your Christ, your onlybegotten Son."[50]

In the *Euchologion* of Serapion (toward the end of the fourth century) there appears a prayer of ordination of a deacon whose terminology is similar to that

47 *Constitutiones Apostolorum* (CA) 2, 26, 4.5.6; SCh 320, 239-41.
48 Ibid., 30, 1-2; SCh 320, 249-51.
49 Ibid., 44, 4; SCh 285.
50 CA 8, 18, 3; SCh 336, 221.

of the Sahidic version of the *Traditio Apostolica*. The text of the prayer alludes to the canons of the Church, to the three hierarchical grades, and refers to the Seven in Acts chapter 6; to designate the ordination of the deacon it employs the verb *katisthanai*: "*Pater unigeniti, qui* jilium misisti *tuum et ordinasti res super terra atque ecclesiae canones et ordines dedisti in utilitatem et salutem gregum, qui elegisti episcopos et presbyteros et diaconos in ministerium catholicae tuae ecclesiae, qui elegisti per unigenitum tuum septem diaconos eisque largitus es spiritum sanctum: constitue* [*katasteson*] *et hunc diaconum ecclesiae tuae catholicae et da in eo* spiritum cognitionis ac discretionis, *ut possit inter populum sanctum pure et immaculate ministrare in hoc ministerio per unigenitum tuum Iesum Christum, per quern tibi gloriam et imperium in sancto spiritu et nunc et in omnia saecula saeculorum, amen*."[51]

The prayer of consecration of a deacon in the *Sacramentarium Veronense* speaks of the service of the holy altar, and, like the text in the *Constitutiones Apostolorum,* considers the diaconate to be a transitory grade. "*Oremus . . . quos consecrationis indultae propitius dona conservet . . . quos ad officium levitarum vocare dignaris, altaris sancti ministerium tribuas sufficienter implere . . . trinis gradibus ministrorum nomini tuo militare constituehs . . . dignisque successibus de inferiori gradu per gratiam tuam capere potiora mereantur*."[52] The *Sacramentarium Gregorianum* is similar at every point to the texts already cited. It also recalls the three grades, and uses the word *constituere* to designate the ordination of the deacon.[53]

Behind their apparent unanimity, the declarations of the Fathers of the Church in the fourth century give a glimpse of certain dissensions which had

51 *Sacramentarium Serapionis*, in *Didascalia et Constitutiones Apostolorum*, ed. F. X. Funk, vol. 2, *Testimonia et Scripturae propinquae* (Paderbornae, 1905), 188. The quotation is given here in the Latin translation of the editor. The same use of the word (*constituat*) is found in c. 3 (33) of *Constitutiones Ecclesiae Aegyptiacae*, De diaconis, ibid., 103-4.

52 *Sacramentarium Veronense*, ed. L. C. Mohlberg (Rome, 1966), 120-21.

53 *Le Sacramentaire Grégorien,* ed. J. Deshusses, vol. 1 (Fribourg [Switzerland], 1992), 96-97.

been well known since the third century, as for example the deacons' claim to appropriate the places, rank and tasks of the priests.[54]

There is also evidence of the idea that the three grades (bishop, priest and deacon) were like elements of one and the same order. Pseudo-Athanasios speaks of this in his work *De Trinitate* as a "consubstantiality."[55] In addition, Christianity was beginning to spread in provincial areas, with bishops or priests leaving the town against their will, and deacons doing so very willingly, but abusing the situation in that they used to appropriate certain of priests' rights. The historical context also contributed to this development. What had happened was that the Arians had compromised the standing of the episcopate. Contrasting with bishops and priests avid for power and money, the popularity of deacons grew strongly because of their close links with monks and laypeople. The widespread opinion in the fourth century was that deacons had been instituted by the Apostles and the bishop ordained them in the same way as priests. Deacons belonged to the clergy, but only assisted at the liturgy.[56]

The sources show us that even Chrysostom did not manage to place the three grades of the ecclesial order in a clear historical continuity. There were Jewish models for the priesthood, but the episcopate and diaconate were instituted by the Apostles. It is not clear what should be understood by these notions.[57] Chrysostom stated that the diaconate had been instituted by the

54 Jerome, *Ep.* 146, 1; PL 22, 1192-95: "Audio quemdam in tantam erupisse vecordiam, ut diaconos, presbyteris, id est episcopis anteferret. Nam cum Apostolus perspicue doceat eosdem esse presbyteros, quos episcopos, quid patitur mensarum et viduarum minister, ut super eos se tumidus efferat, ad quorum preces Christi corpus sanguinisque conficitur?" Jerome, *Comm. in Ez.* 6, 17, 5-6; PL 25, 183B: "Quod multos facere conspicimus, clientes et pauperes, et agricolas, ut taceam de militantium et iudicum violentia, qui opprimunt per potentiam, vel furta committunt, ut de multis parva pauperibus tribuant, et in suis sceleribus glorientur, publiceque diaconus, in Ecclesiis recitet offerentium nomina. Tantum offert ilia, tantum ille pollicitus est, placentque sibi ad plausum populi, torquente eis conscientia."

55 *De Trinitate* 1, 27; *Patrologia Graeco-Latina* (PG) 28, 1157B: "episkopos, presbyteros, diakonoi homoousioi eisin."

56 Origen, *Horn, in Jer.* 11, 3; *Concilium Ancyranum*, c. 14.

57 *Horn. 14, 3 in Act.;* PG 60:116: "Quam ergo dignitatem habuerunt illi [*sc.* the deacons and the bishops]. . . . Atqui haec in Ecclesiis non erat; sed presbyterorum erat oeconomia. Atqui nullus adhuc episcopus erat, praeterquam apostoli tantum. Unde puto nec diaconorum nec presbyterorum tunc fuisse nomen admissum nec manifestum."

Holy Spirit.[58] In the course of this century the Latins also took up the use of the Greek word *diaconus*, as St. Augustine attests.[59]

The fourth century marked the end of the process which led to the recognition of the diaconate as a grade or degree in the ecclesial hierarchy, placed after the bishop and the priests, with a well-defined role. Linked to the bishop himself and his mission, this role encompassed three tasks: the service of the liturgy, the service of preaching the Gospel and teaching catechesis, and a vast social activity concerning the works of charity and administrative action in accordance with the bishop's directives.

IV. The Ministry of Deaconesses

In the apostolic era different forms of diaconal assistance offered to the Apostles and communities by women seem to have been institutional. Thus Paul recommends to the community at Rome "our sister Phoebe, servant [*he diakonos*] of the Church at Cenchreae" (cf. Rom 16:1-4). Although the masculine form of *diakonos* is used here, it cannot therefore be concluded that the word is being used to designate the specific function of a "deacon"; firstly because in this context *diakonos* still signifies servant in a very general sense, and secondly because the word "servant" is not given a feminine suffix but preceded by a feminine article. What seems clear is that Phoebe exercised a recognized service in the community of Cenchreae, subordinate to the ministry of the Apostle. Elsewhere in Paul's writings the authorities of the world are themselves called *diakonos* (Rom 13:4), and in Second Corinthians 11:14-15 he refers to *diakonoi* of the devil.

Exegetes are divided on the subject of 1 Timothy 3:11. The mention of "women" following the reference to deacons may suggest women deacons (by parallel reference), or the deacons' wives who had been mentioned earlier. In this epistle, the functions of the deacon are not described, but only the conditions for admitting them. It is said that women must not teach or rule over men

58 "And rightly so; for it is not a man, nor an angel, nor an archangel, nor any other created power, but the Paraclete himself who instituted this order, persuading men who are still in the flesh to imitate the service of the angels," *De sacerdotio* 3, 4, 1-8; SCh 272, 142.

59 "Graecum codicem legite, et diaconum invenietis. Quod enim interpretatus est latinus, Minister; graecus habet, Diaconus; quia vere diaconus graece, minister latine; quomodo martyr graece, testis latine; apostolus graece, missus latine. Sed iam consuevimus nominibus graecis uti pro latinis. Nam multi codices Evangeliorum sic habent: 'Ubi sum ego, illic et diaconus meus,'" V *Sermo* 329, *De Stephano martyre* 6, 3, PL 38, 1441.

(1 Tm 2:8-15). But the functions of governance and teaching were in any case reserved to the bishop (1 Tm 3:5) and to priests (1 Tm 5:17), and not to deacons. Widows constituted a recognized group in the community, from whom they received assistance in exchange for their commitment to continence and prayer. First Timothy 5:3-16 stresses the conditions under which they may be inscribed on the list of widows receiving relief from the community, and says nothing more about any functions they might have. Later on they were officially "instituted" but "not ordained";[60] they constituted an "order" in the Church,[61] and would never have any other mission apart from good example and prayer.

At the beginning of the second century a letter from Pliny the Younger, governor of Bithynia, mentioned two women who were described by the Christians as *ministrae*, the probable equivalent of the Greek *diakonoi* (10, 96-97). It was not until the third century that the specific Christian terms *diaconissa* or *diacona* appeared.

From the end of the third century onwards, in certain regions of the Church[62] (and not all of them), a specific ecclesial ministry is attested to on the part of women called deaconesses.[63] This was in Eastern Syria and Constantinople. Toward 240 there appeared a singular canonico-liturgical compilation, the *Didascalia Apostolorum* (DA), which was not official in character. It attributed to the bishop the features of an omnipotent biblical patriarch (cf. DA 2, 33-35, 3). He was at the head of a little community which he governed mainly with the help of deacons and deaconesses. This was the first time that deaconesses appeared in an ecclesiastical document. In a typology borrowed from Ignatius of Antioch, the bishop held the place of God the Father, the deacon the place of Christ, and the deaconess that of the Holy Spirit (the word for "Spirit" is feminine in Semitic languages), while the priests (who are seldom mentioned)

60 *Traditio Apostolica* 10; SCh 11(2), 67.

61 Cf. Tertullian, *To His Wife* 1, 7, 4; SCh 273; *Exhortation to Chastity* 13, 4; SCh 319.

62 "It is at the Eastern limits of the Roman Empire that deaconesses finally make their appearance. The first document to refer to them, which is in some sort their birth certificate, is the *Didascalia Apostolorum* . . . known since the publication in 1854 . . . of its Syriac text." A. G. Martimort, *Les diaconesses: Essai historique* (Rome, 1982), 31.

63 The most ample collection of all the testimony about this ecclesiastical ministry, accompanied by a theological interpretation, is that of John Pinius, *De diaconissamm ordinatione*, in *Acta Sanctorum*, September 1 (Antwerp, 1746), 1-27. Most of the Greek and Latin documents referred to by Pinius are reproduced by J. Mayer, *Monumenta de viduis diaconissis virginibusque tractantia* (Bonn, 1938). Cf. R. Gryson, *Le ministère des femmes dans l'Église ancienne*, Recherches et synthèses: Section d'histoire 4 (Gembloux, 1972).

represented the Apostles, and the widows, the altar (DA 2, 26, 4-7). There is no reference to the ordination of these ministers.

The *Didascalia* laid stress on the charitable role of the deacon and the deaconess. The ministry of the diaconate should appear as "one single soul in two bodies." Its model is the *diakonia* of Christ, who washed the feet of his disciples (DA 3, 13, 1-7). However, there was no strict parallelism between the two branches of the diaconate with regard to the functions they exercised. The deacons were chosen by the bishop to "concern themselves about many necessary things," and the deaconesses only "for the service of women" (DA 3, 12, 1). The hope was expressed that "the number of deacons may be proportionate to that of the assembly of the people of the Church" (DA 3, 13, l).[64] The deacons administered the property of the community in the bishop's name. Like the bishop, they were maintained at its expense. Deacons are called the ear and mouth of the bishop (DA 2, 44, 3-4). Men from among the faithful should go through the deacons to have access to the bishop, as women should go through the deaconesses (DA 3, 12, 1-4). One deacon supervised the entries into the meeting place, while another attended the bishop for the Eucharistic offering (DA 2, 57, 6).

Deaconesses should carry out the anointing of women in the rite of baptism, instruct women neophytes, and visit the women faithful, especially the sick, in their homes. They were forbidden to confer baptism themselves, or to play a part in the Eucharistic offering (DA 3, 12, 1-4). The deaconesses had supplanted the widows. The bishop may still institute widows, but they should not either teach or administer baptism (to women), but only pray (DA 3, 5, 1-3, 6, 2).

The *Constitutiones Apostolorum*, which appeared in Syria towards 380, used and interpolated the *Didascalia*, the *Didache* and the *Traditio Apostolica*. The *Constitutiones* were to have a lasting influence on the discipline governing ordinations in the East, even though they were never considered to be an official canonical collection. The compiler envisaged the imposition of hands with the epiklesis of the Holy Spirit not only for bishops, priests and deacons, but also

64 This norm is repeated in the *Constitutiones Apostolorum* 3, 19, 1. On the origins of the professionalization of the clergy, cf. Schöllgen, *Die Anfänge der Professionalisierung.*

for the deaconesses, sub-deacons and lectors (cf. CA 8, 16-23).[65] The concept of *kleros* was broadened to all those who exercised a liturgical ministry, who were maintained by the Church, and who benefited from the privileges in civil law allowed by the Empire to clerics, so that the deaconesses were counted as belonging to the clergy while the widows were excluded. Bishop and priests were paralleled with the high priest and the priests respectively of the Old Covenant, while to the Levites corresponded all the other ministries and states of life: "deacons, lectors, cantors, door-keepers, deaconesses, widows, virgins and orphans" (CA 2, 26, 3; CA 8, 1, 21). The deacon was placed "at the service of the bishop and the priests" and should not impinge on the functions of the latter.[66] The deacon could proclaim the Gospel and conduct the prayer of the assembly (CA 2, 57, 18), but only the bishop and the priests exhorted (CA 2, 57, 7). Deaconesses took up their functions through an *epithesis cheirôn* or imposition of hands that conferred the Holy Spirit,[67] as did the lectors (CA 8, 20, 22). The bishop pronounced the following prayer: "Eternal God, Father of our Lord Jesus Christ, creator of man and woman, who filled Myriam, Deborah, Anne and Hulda with your spirit; who did not deem it unworthy for your Son, the Only-Begotten, to be born of a woman; who in the tent of witness and in the temple did institute women as guardians of your sacred doors, look now upon your servant before you, proposed for the diaconate: grant her the Holy Spirit and purify her of all defilement of flesh and spirit so that she may acquit herself worthily of the office which has been entrusted to her, for your glory and

65 The compiler was attentive to the nuances of vocabulary. At CA 2, 11, 3 he says, "We do not allow the priests to ordain [*cheirotonein*] deacons, deaconesses, lectors, servants, cantors or door-keepers: that belongs to the bishops alone." However, he reserves the term *cheirotonia* to the ordination of bishops, priests, deacons and sub-deacons (8, 4-5; 8, 16-17; 8, 21). He employs the expression *epitithenai tēn (tas) cheira(s)* for deaconesses and lectors (8, 16, 2; 8, 17, 2). He does not seem to wish to give these expressions a different meaning, since all these impositions of hands are accompanied by an epiklesis of the Holy Spirit. For confessors, virgins, widows, and exorcists, he specifies that there is no *cheirotonia* (8, 23-26). The compiler additionally distinguishes between *cheirotonia* and *cheirothesia*, which is simply a gesture of blessing (cf. 8, 16, 3 and 8, 28, 2-3). *Cheirothesia* may be practiced by priests in the baptismal rite, the re-integration of penitents, or the blessing of catechumens (cf. 2, 32, 3; 2, 18, 7; 7, 39, 4).

66 Cf. CA 3, 20, 2; 8, 16, 5; 8, 28, 4; 8, 46, 10-11.

67 Canon 19 of the Council of Nicaea (325) could be interpreted not as refusing the imposition of hands to all deaconesses in general, but as the simple statement that the deaconesses from the party of Paul of Samosata did not receive the imposition of hands, and "were anyway counted among the laity," and that it was also necessary to re-ordain them, after having re-baptized them, like the other ministers of this dissident group who returned to the Catholic Church. Cf. G. Alberigo, *Les conciles oecuméniques*, vol. 2 *Les décrets*, bk. 1 (Paris, 1994), 54.

to the praise of your Christ, through whom be glory and adoration to you, in the Holy Spirit, world without end. Amen."[68]

The deaconesses were named before the sub-deacon who, in his turn, received a *cheirotonia* like the deacon (CA 8, 21), while the virgins and widows could not be "ordained" (8, 24-25). The *Constitutiones* insist that the deaconesses should have no liturgical function (3, 9, 1-2), but should devote themselves to their function in the community which was "service to the women" (CA 3, 16, 1) and as intermediaries between women and the bishop. It is still stated that they represent the Holy Spirit, but they "do nothing without the deacon" (CA 2, 26, 6). They should stand at the women's entrances in the assemblies (2, 57, 10). Their functions are summed up as follows: "The deaconess does not bless, and she does not fulfill any of the things that priests and deacons do, but she looks after the doors and attends the priests during the baptism of women, for the sake of decency" (CA 8, 28, 6).

This is echoed by the almost contemporary observation of Epiphanius of Salamis in his *Panarion,* in around 375: "There is certainly in the Church the order of deaconesses, but this does not exist to exercise the functions of a priest, nor are they to have any undertaking committed to them, but for the decency of the feminine sex at the time of baptism."[69] A law of Theodosius of June 21, 390, revoked on August 23 of the same year, fixed the age for admission to the ministry of deaconesses at sixty. The Council of Chalcedon (c. 15) reduced the age to 40, forbidding them subsequent marriage.[70]

Even in the fourth century the way of life of deaconesses was very similar to that of nuns. At that time the woman in charge of a monastic community of women was called a deaconess, as is testified by Gregory of Nyssa among others.[71] Ordained abbesses of the monasteries of women, the deaconesses wore the *maforion*, or veil of perfection. Until the sixth century they still attended women in the baptismal pool and for the anointing. Although they did not serve at the altar, they could distribute communion to sick women. When the practice of anointing the whole body at baptism was abandoned, deaconesses were simply consecrated virgins who had taken the vow of chastity. They lived either in monasteries or at home. The condition for admission was virginity

68 CA, 8, 20, 1-2; SCh 336; Metzger, 221-23.

69 Epiphanius of Salamis, *Panarion haer.* 79, 3, 6, ed. K. Holl, GCS 37 (1933), p. 478.

70 Cf. Alberigo, *Décrets*, bk. 1, 214.

71 Gregory of Nyssa, *Life of St. Macrina* 29, 1; SCh 178; Maraval, 236-37.

or widowhood and their activity consisted of charitable and health-related assistance to women.

At Constantinople the best-known of the fourth-century deaconesses was Olympias, the superior of a monastery of women, who was a protegee of St. John Chrysostom and had put her property at the service of the Church. She was "ordained" (*cheirotonein*) deaconess with three of her companions by the patriarch. Canon 15 of the Council of Chalcedon (451) seems to confirm the fact that deaconesses really were "ordained" by the imposition of hands (*cheirotonia*). Their ministry was called *leitourgia* and after ordination they were not allowed to marry.

In eighth-century Byzantium, the bishop still imposed his hands on a deaconess, and conferred on her the orarion or stole (both ends of which were worn at the front, one over the other); he gave her the chalice, which she placed on the altar without giving communion to anyone. Deaconesses were ordained in the course of the Eucharistic liturgy, in the sanctuary, like deacons.[72] Despite the similarities between the rites of ordination, deaconesses did not have access to the altar or to any liturgical ministry. These ordinations were intended mainly for the superiors of monasteries of women.

It should be pointed out that in the West there is no trace of any deaconesses for the first five centuries. The *Statuta Ecclesiae Antiqua* laid down that the instruction of women catechumens and their preparation for baptism was to be entrusted to the widows and women religious "chosen *ad ministerium baptizandarum mulierum*."[73] Certain councils of the fourth and fifth centuries reject every *ministerium feminae*[74] and forbid any ordination of deaconesses.[75] According to the *Ambrosiaster* (composed at Rome at the end of the fourth century), the female diaconate was an adjunct of Montanist ("Cataphrygian") heretics.[76] In the sixth century women admitted into the group of widows were sometimes referred to as deaconesses. To prevent any confusion the Council of

72 Byzantine Ritual of ordination of deaconesses: *Euchologe du manuscrit grec Barberini* 336, in Vatican Library, ff. 169R-17/v. Quoted by J.-M. Aubert, *Des femmes diacres*, Le Point Théologique 47 (Paris, 1987), 118-19.

73 Cf. c. 100 (Munier, 99). In addition, it is expressly forbidden to women, "even well-instructed and holy" ones, to teach men and to baptize (cf. c. 37, 41; Munier, 86).

74 Council of Nimes (394-396), c. 2. Cf. J. Gaudemet, *Conciles gaulois du IVe siècle*, SCh 241 (Paris, 1977), 127-29.

75 First Council of Orange (441), c. 26.

76 Cf. ed. H. I. Vogels, *Corpus Scriptorum Ecclesiasticorum Latinorum* (CSEL) 81/3 (Vienna, 1969), 268.

Epaone forbade "the consecrations of widows who call themselves deaconesses."[77] The Second Council of Orleans (533) decided to exclude from communion women who had "received the blessing for the diaconate despite the canons forbidding this and who had remarried."[78] Abbesses, or the wives of deacons, were also called *diaconissae*, by analogy with *presbyterissae* or even *episcopissae*.[79]

The present historical overview shows that a ministry of deaconesses did indeed exist, and that this developed unevenly in the different parts of the Church. It seems clear that this ministry was not perceived as simply the feminine equivalent of the masculine diaconate. At the very least it was an ecclesial function, exercised by women, sometimes mentioned together with that of sub--deacon in the lists of Church ministries.[80] Was this ministry conferred by an imposition of hands comparable to that by which the episcopate, the priesthood and the masculine diaconate were conferred? The text of the *Constitutiones Apostolorum* would seem to suggest this, but it is practically the only witness to this, and its proper interpretation is the subject of much debate.[81] Should the imposition of hands on deaconesses be considered the same as that on deacons, or is it rather on the same level as the imposition of hands on sub-deacons and lectors? It is difficult to tackle the question on the basis of historical data alone. In the following chapters some elements will be clarified, and some questions

77 Council of Epaone (517), c. 21 (C. de Clercq, *Concilia Galliae 511-695*, 250: 148A [1963], 29). Blessings of women as deaconesses had become widespread because the ritual did not provide a blessing for widows, as was noted in the Second Council of Tours (567), c. 21 (ibid., 187).

78 Ibid., 101.

79 Cf. Second Council of Tours, c. 20 (ibid., 184).

80 Many commentators have followed the model of *Ambrosiaster* in his Commentary on 1 Tm 3:11 (CSEL 81, 3; G. L. Muller, ed., *Der Empfänger des Weihesakraments: Quellen zur Lehre und Praxis der Kirche, nur Männern das Weihesakrament zu spenden* [Würzburg, 1999], 89): "But the Cataphrygians, seizing this opportunity of falling into error, uphold in their foolish rashness, under the pretext that Paul addressed women after deacons, that it is also necessary to ordain deaconesses. They know however that the Apostles chose seven deacons (cf. Acts 6:1-6); is it to be supposed that no woman was found suitable at that point, when we read that there were holy women grouped around the eleven Apostles (cf. Acts 1:14)? . . . And Paul orders women to keep silence in church (cf. 1 Cor 14:34-35)." See also John Chrysostom, *In 1 Tm horn.* 11; PG 62, 555; Epiphanius, *Haer.* 79, 3 (Müller, *Quellen*, 88); Council of Orange (Müller, *Quellen*, 98); Council of Dovin (Armenia, 527): "*Feminis non licet ministeria diaconissae praestare nisi ministerium baptismi*" (Müller, *Quellen*, 105); Isidore of Seville, *De Eccl. Off* 2, 18, 11 (Müller, *Quellen*, 109); *Decretum Gratiani*, c. 15 (Müller, *Quellen*, 115); Magister Ruftnus, *Summa Decretorum*, c. 27, q. 1 (Müller, *Quellen*, 320); Robert of Yorkshire, *Liber poenitentialis*, q. 6, 42 (Müller, *Quellen*, 322); Thomas Aquinas, *In 1 Tm* 3, 11 (Müller, *Quellen*, 333); etc.

81 Cf. Vanzan, "*Le diaconat permanent feminin: Ombres et lumieres*", in *Documentation Catholique* 2203 (1999): 440-46. The author refers to the discussions which have taken place between R. Gryson, A. G. Martimort, C. Vagaggini and C. Marucci. Cf. L. Scheffczyk, ed., *Diakonat und Diakonissen* (St. Ottilien, 2002), especially M. Hauke, "Die Geschichte der Diakonissen: Nachwort und Literaturnachtrag zur Neuauflage des Standardwerkes von Martimort über die Diakonissen," 321-76.

will remain open. In particular, one chapter will be devoted to examining more closely how the Church through her theology and Magisterium has become more conscious of the sacramental reality of Holy Orders and its three grades. But first it is appropriate to examine the causes which led to the disappearance of the permanent diaconate in the life of the Church.

Chapter III

The Disappearance of the Permanent Diaconate

I. The Changes in the Diaconal Ministry

At Rome, from the third century onward, each deacon was at the head of one of the seven pastoral regions, while the priests had a smaller *titulus* (the future parish). Deacons were charged with administering funds and organizing charitable works. The Council of Neo-Caesarea, at the beginning of the fourth century, had asked that each Church, however big it was, should have no more than seven deacons, in memory of Acts 6:1-6.[82] This provision, still remembered by Isidore of Seville[83] but infrequently observed, particularly in the East,[84] heightened the prestige of the diaconal order and encouraged deacons still more to leave their original functions to other members of the clergy. They were to define themselves more and more explicitly by reference to their liturgical attributes, and come into conflict with the priests.

The functions of deacons were progressively being taken over by other ministers. As early as the *Traditio Apostolica* (13), "sub-deacons" were appointed "to follow the deacon." Those who "followed the deacon" soon became his "acolytes."[85] The acolytes had the job of taking the *fermentum*, the portion of the bishop's Eucharist, to the priests of the *tituli* in the town. It was also the acolytes who took it to those who were absent. The "door-keepers" also fulfilled a

82 Council of Neo-Caesarea (314 or 319), c. 15, in Mansi, *Sacrorum conciliomm nova et amplissima collectio*, vol. 2, new ed. (Paris-Leipzig, 1901), 539.

83 Isidore of Seville, *De Eccl. Off.* 2, 8.

84 There were one hundred deacons at Constantinople in the time of Justinian. Cf. Justinian, *Novellae* 3, 1 (*Corpus juris civilis*, ed. Kriegel, vol. 3 [Leipzig, 1887], 20).

85 Cf. CA 2, 28, 6.

function which had originally been the task of the deacons. It may be considered that the minor ministries resulted from a sharing-out of diaconal functions.

The state of sub-deacon approached that of deacon more closely. Toward 400, in the East, the Council of Laodicea tried to prevent sub-deacons from encroaching on the liturgical functions of deacons, stating that they should content themselves with looking after the doors.[86] Sub-deacons adopted the rule of life of deacons. The African councils of the last part of the fourth century demanded continence on the part of clergy "who serve at the altar."[87] The *Canones in causa Apiarii* (419-425) extended this requirement to sub-deacons, "who touch the sacred mysteries."[88] Leo the Great (440-461) confirmed this requirement for sub-deacons.[89] Leo made a ready distinction between *sacerdotes* (the bishop and priests), *levitae* (the deacons and sub-deacons), and *clerici* (the other ministers).[90]

Cyprian had already found it necessary to remind people that deacons had been instituted by the Apostles and not by the Lord himself.[91] In certain places deacons must have been tempted to take the place of priests. The Council of Aries (314) reminded them that they could not offer the Eucharist (c. 15) and that they should show due honor to priests (c. 18). Nicaea forbade them to give communion to priests, or to receive it before the bishops: they were to receive communion from the bishop or from a priest, and after them. They were not to sit among the priests. "Let the deacons remain within the limits of their competence, knowing that they are the servants of the bishop and are inferior to priests in rank" (c. 19).[92]

Toward 378 the anonymous *Ambrosiaster*, composed at Rome, witnessed to the persistent tension between the presbyterate and the diaconate.[93] Jerome went further, exclaiming that deacons were not superior to priests![94] Priests came to exercise more and more of the functions reserved to deacons, at the

86 Cf. cc. 21, 22, 43, in P.-P. Joannou, *Discipline generate antique IIe—IXe siecle*, 1/2 (Rome, 1962), 139-48.

87 Council of Carthage sub Genethlio (390), c. 2, in C. Munier, *Concilia Africae*, CCSL 259 (Turnhout, 1974), 13.

88 Cf. c. 25 (ibid., 108-9).

89 Leo the Great, *Ep.* 14, 4 to Anastasius of Thessalonica; PL 54, 672-73.

90 Ibid.

91 Cf. chapter II supra, note 40.

92 Cf. Alberigo, *Décrets*, 54.

93 The short treatise *De jactantia Romanorum diaconum* (CSEL 50, 193-98) reproves deacons for wanting to work their way up into the ranks of the priests, for refusing tasks of service, and for concerning themselves with liturgical singing alone.

94 Jerome, *Letter 146 to Evangelus*; PL 22, 1192-95.

same time as they received progressively more autonomy in their responsibilities within the urban *tituli* and the rural parishes. Deacons, who had wanted to exercise the liturgical and teaching functions reserved to priests, now suffered from a backlash against such an attitude: they became subordinate to the priests, their direct link with the bishop faded away, and they ended up having no specific function. The clergy of the Church in the Empire progressively forgot about their function of service and maintained the concept of the sacredness of the priesthood, toward which all the other degrees of the clerical career tended. The deacons were the first to suffer the consequences of this.

Toward the end of the fifth century the thinking of Pseudo-Dionysius began to have a lasting influence both in the East and in the West. In Dionysius' hierarchically structured view of heaven and the Church, every being received its specific determination and function from the order to which it belonged. The ecclesiastical hierarchy was composed of two groups of three. The first group contained the order of the hierarchs or bishops, the order of priests, and the order of "liturges" or ministers. This latter order included the ecclesiastical orders from deacon to door-keeper. The diaconate no longer had any specific mark to distinguish it from the other orders beneath the priests.[95]

Still toward the end of the fifth century, the career path of the clergy was defined in function of their liturgical attributes as well as the demand of continence for those who served in the sanctuary, or related positions. Leo the Great considered that the ideal path, before proceeding to the priesthood and the episcopate, was to go through all the degrees of the clergy with an appropriate interval between each.[96] The number and names of the different degrees (*gradus*) of the clergy fluctuated. There were eight at Rome in the time of Pope Cornelius.[97] In the fifth century, the door-keeper and the exorcist were no longer included among them.[98] The author of *De Septem Ordinibus* at the beginning of the fifth century speaks of grave-diggers, door-keepers, lectors, sub-deacons, deacons, priests and bishops.[99] The *Statuta Ecclesiae Antiqua*, also composed in the south of Gaul toward 480, re-proposed a list of eight *officiates*

95 Pseudo-Dionysius, *Ecclesiastical Hierarchy* 5, 7; 5, 6; PG 3, 506-8.

96 Leo the Great, *Ep.* 6, 6 to Anastasius of Thessalonica; PL 54, 620. Leo himself was a deacon when he was elected to the episcopate. See also L. Duchesne, *Liber Pontijicalis*, vol. 1 (Paris: de Boccard, 1981), 238-39.

97 Cf. Eusebius of Caesarea, *Hist. Eccl.* 6, 43.

98 Cf. *The Decretals of Siricius*, PL 13, 1142-43; *The Decretals of Innocent I*, PL 20, 604-5.

99 Pseudo-Jerome, *Ep. XII de septem ordinibus ecclesiae*, PL 30, 150-62.

ecclesiae who received an *ordinatio*: bishop, priest and deacon received an imposition of hands, [while] the candidates for orders inferior to these (sub-deacon, acolyte, exorcist, lector and doorkeeper) were installed by a rite of handing over of the instruments of their office.[100] Thus the functions which had in the past been autonomous and practical, became stages in the career path toward the priesthood. The sacramentary of Verona (around 560-580) contained a prayer of "consecration" for the bishop and the priest, and a prayer of "blessing" for the deacon. It said that the deacon was essentially ordained in view of liturgical ministry; he should be an example of chastity.[101]

Progress through the clerical career path was still often made *per saltum*. At Rome in the ninth century the sub-diaconate was the only obligatory degree before major orders. All the popes between 687 and 891 had been sub-deacons. Five had then become deacons before being raised to the episcopate, and nine passed directly from the sub-diaconate to the priesthood and then to the episcopate.

One of the former competencies of deacons, the management of the funds of the community, was also lost to them. The Council of Chalcedon (451) sanctioned this development, laying down that each bishop should entrust this responsibility to an officer chosen from "among his own clergy" (c. 26), not necessarily from among the deacons. Aid to the poor was often looked after by monasteries. Under Gregory the Great, the huge "Patrimony of St. Peter" was managed by *defensores* or *notarii*, who were added to the clergy, in other words at least given the tonsure.

In the East, the Byzantine Council in Trullo in 692 analyzed the contents of Acts 6:1-6. The Seven, it observed, were neither deacons nor priests nor bishops. They were people who were "charged with administering the common property of the community of that time. . . . They are an example of charity" (c. 7).[102] At the end of the ninth century in the East, the deacons still formed a permanent order of clergy, but for liturgical needs alone. The Byzantine rite had two preparatory stages for the sacred ministry: those of lector (or cantor) and sub-deacon,

100 Cf. C. Munier, *Les Statuta Ecclesiae antiqua*, editions-études critiques (Paris, 1960), 95-99. The author adds the psalmist to this list. Isidore of Seville, *Etymologies* 7, 12 (PL 82, 290) spoke of nine degrees, including the psalmist. In his terminology, all nine *ordines* were also called *sacramenta*; cf. *De Eccl. Off.* 2, 21.

101 Cf. L. C. Mohlberg, *Sacramentarium Veronense*, RED.F 1 (Rome, 1956), 120-21.

102 P.-Joannou, *Discipline générale antique IIe-IXe siècle*, vol. 1, pt. 1, *Les canons des conciles oecuméniques* (Rome, 1962), 132-34.

conferred by *cheirothesia*, and obligatory before the diaconate.[103] But the sub-diaconate was often conferred at the same time as the lectorate, or just before the diaconate. According to the ritual of the *Constitutiones Apostolorum*, which was still applied in the East, admission to the minor orders of sub-diaconate and lectorate was accomplished by the imposition of hands and the handing over of the instruments of office. In the West too, the activity of deacons was reduced, in practice, to their liturgical functions.[104] When rural parishes were created the Councils insisted that they should be endowed with a priest. It did not occur to them to call for deacons.[105]

From the tenth century onward, at least in the Holy Roman Empire, the rule was ordination *per gradum*. The reference document was the *Pontifical Romano-Germanique*,[106] composed at Mainz in around 950. It was in direct continuity with the tradition of the *Ordines Romani* of the preceding centuries,[107] to which it added plentiful elements from the Germanic ritual. The ordination of deacons included the handing over of the book of the Gospels, signifying their function of proclaiming the Gospel in the liturgy. The deacon here appears closer to the sub-deacon than to the priest. The priest was the man of the Eucharist; the deacon attended him at the altar. This ritual was introduced at Rome through the Germanic emperors' zeal for reform at the end of the tenth century. Rome fell into line with the *per gradum* career path for clergy which was the rule in the Empire. From that time on the history of the ordination rites

103 Cf. F. Mercenier and F. Paris, *La prière des Églises de rite byzantin*, 2 vols. (Prieuré d'Ainay sur Meuse, 1937). From the eighth century onward, usage became fixed. The term *cheirotonia* was now reserved to the ordinations of bishops, priests and deacons, while *cheirothesia* was the term used for orders below those. Thus canon 15 of the Second Council of Nicaea (ed. G. Alberigo, vol. 2/1, 149). Cf. C. Vogel, "Chirotonie et chirothésie," in *Irénikon* 37 (1972): 7-21; 207-38.

104 Pseudo-Jerome, *De septem ordinibus*, says that deacons "do not leave the temple of the Lord. . . . They are the altar of Christ. . . . Without the deacon, the priest has no name nor origin nor function" (PL 30, 153).

105 Cf. Council of Aix-la-Chapelle (817), c. 11 (C. J. Hefele and H. Leclercq, *Histoire des conciles*, vol. 4 [Paris, 1910], 27).

106 C. Vogel, *Le Pontifical romano-germanique du dixième siècle*, 3 vols., Studi e testi 226, 227, 269 (Vatican, 1963-1972).

107 See M. Andrieu, *Les Ordines Romani du haut moyen âge*, SSL 24 (Louvain, 1951).

attests perfect continuity.[108] The First Lateran Council (1123) canon 7, and the Second Lateran Council (1139) canon 6, deprived of their office any clergy who contracted marriage, from the sub-diaconate inclusive. Canon 7 of the Second Lateran Council declared that such a marriage would be null and void.[109] From that time on the Latin Church normally ordained only celibate men.

The patristic and liturgical texts of the first millennium all mentioned the ordination of bishops, priests and deacons, but they did not yet explicitly raise the question of the sacramentality of each of these ordinations.

The history of the ministries shows that the priesthood has had a tendency to take over the functions of the lesser orders. When the progression through the various orders became stabilized, each grade possessed the competencies of the previous grade, plus some additional ones—what a deacon can do, a priest can also do. The bishop, being at the summit of the hierarchy, can exercise all the ecclesiastical functions. The fact that the different competencies fitted together in this way and that lesser functions were taken over by higher ones; the fragmentation of the original role of deacons into many different functions to be performed by subordinate clergy; and the progression to the higher functions *per gradum*, all go to explain how the diaconate as a permanent ministry lost its reason for existing. All that was left were liturgical tasks exercised for a given time by candidates for the priesthood.

II. Toward the Disappearance of Deaconesses

After the tenth century deaconesses were only named in connection with charitable institutions. A Jacobite author of that time notes: "In ancient times, deaconesses were ordained. Their function was to look after women so that they should not have to uncover themselves before the bishop. But when religion spread more widely and it was decided to administer baptism to infants, this

108 The various Roman Pontificals of the twelfth century had as their common foundation the tenth-century *Pontifical Romano-Germanique*. Cf. M. Andrieu, *Le Pontifical romain au moyen âge*, vol. 1 *Le Pontifical du XIIe siècle*, Studi e testi 86 (Vatican, 1938). This was widely used in the Latin Church and was brought up to date by Innocent III. See M. Andrieu, ibid., vol. 2, *Le Pontifical de la Curie romaine du XIIe siècle*, Studi e testi 87 (Vatican, 1940). This in its turn was included in the Pontifical composed by Guillaume Durand, bishop of Mende at the end of the thirteenth century. Cf. M. Andrieu, ibid., vol. 3, *Le Pontifical de Guillaume Durand*, Studi e testi 88 (Vatican, 1940). It was to serve as a model for the edition printed by Burchard of Strasbourg in 1485.

109 Cf. Alberigo, *Les Conciles oecumeniques*, bk. 1, 419 and 435.

function was abolished."[110] We find the same statement in the Pontifical of Patriarch Michael of Antioch (1166-1199).[111] When commenting on canon 15 of the Council of Chalcedon, Theodore Balsamon, at the end of the twelfth century, observed that "the topic of this canon has altogether fallen into disuse. For today deaconesses are no longer ordained, although the name of deaconesses is wrongly given to those who belong to communities of ascetics."[112] Deaconesses had become nuns. They lived in monasteries which no longer practiced works of *diakonia* except in the field of education, medical care, or parish service.

The presence of deaconesses is still attested in Rome at the end of the eighth century. While the Roman rituals had previously not mentioned deaconesses, the sacramentary *Hadrianum*, sent by the pope to Charlemagne and spread by him throughout the Frankish world, includes an *Oratio ad Diaconam Faciendum*. It was in fact a blessing, placed as an appendix among other rites of first institution. The Carolingian texts often combined deaconesses and abbesses. The Council of Paris of 829 contained a general prohibition on women performing any liturgical function.[113] The Decretals of Pseudo-Isidore contain no mention of deaconesses; and neither does a Bavarian Pontifical from the first half of the ninth century.[114] A century later, in the Pontifical Romano-Germanique of Mainz, the prayer *Ad Diaconam Faciendum* is to be found after the *ordinatio abbatissae*, between the *consecratio virginum* and the *consecratio viduarum*. Once again, this was merely a blessing accompanied by the handing over of the stole and veil by the bishop, as well as the nuptial ring and the crown. Like widows, the deaconess promised continence. This is the last mention of "deaconesses" found in the Latin rituals. In fact the Pontifical of Guillaume Durand at the end of the thirteenth century speaks of deaconesses only with reference to the past.[115]

110 Cf. G. Khouri-Sarkis, "Le livre du guide de Yahya ibn Jarîr," *Orient syrien* 12 (1967): 303-18.

111 "Long ago the *cheirotonia* or ordination was also done for deaconesses: and for that reason the rite concerning them was given in ancient manuscripts. In those times deaconesses were needed mainly for the baptism of women" (quoted by Martimort, *Les diaconesses*, 167).

112 *Scholia in concilium Chalcedonense*; PG 137, 441 (quoted by Martimort, *Les diaconesses*, 171).

113 Cap. 45 (ed. A. Werminghoff, *Concilia aevi Karolini*, 1:639).

114 Cf. F. Unterkircher, *Das Kollectar-Pontifikale des Bischofs Baturich von Regensburg (817-848)*, Spicilegium Friburgense 8 (Freiburg, 1962).

115 Between *De ordinatione abbatissae* and *De benedictione et consecratione virginum*, the passage *De ordinatione diaconissae* occupies a few lines phrased as follows: "*Diaconissa olim, non tamen ante annum quadragesimum, ordinabatur hoc modo.*" See Andrieu, *Pontifical de Guillaume Durand*, vol. 3 (1, 21-23), 411.

In the Middle Ages, the nursing and teaching religious orders of nuns fulfilled in practice the functions of *diakonia* without, however, being ordained for this ministry. The title, with no corresponding ministry, was given to women who were instituted as widows or abbesses. Right up until the thirteenth century, abbesses were sometimes called deaconesses.

Chapter IV

The Sacramentality of the Diaconate from the Twelfth to the Twentieth Centuries

The sacramentality of the diaconate is a question which remains *implicit* in biblical, patristic and liturgical texts which have just been discussed. We now need to see how the Church first became *explicitly* conscious of it in a period in which, apart from certain rare exceptions, the diaconate was simply a stage on the way to the priesthood.

I. In the First Scholastic Teaching

Although "sacramentality" can have a broad, generic meaning, in the strict sense it refers to the seven sacraments (outward and effective signs of grace), among which is the sacrament of "Holy Orders." Within this sacrament were different "orders" or "grades," between seven and nine in number. The diaconate and the priesthood were always listed among the *ordines sacri* of the sacrament, and the sub-diaconate began to be included among them because of its requirement of celibacy; the episcopate was excluded from them in most cases.[116]

According to Peter Lombard († 1160),[117] the diaconate was an *ordo* or *gradus officiorum* (the sixth). Although he held that all the *ordines* were *spirituales et sacri*, he underlined the excellence of the diaconate and the priesthood, the only ones which existed in the primitive Church by the will of the Apostles, while

116 For these variations, see L. Ott, *Das Weihesakrament*, HbDG 4/5 (Freiburg am Breisgau, 1964).

117 Peter Lombard introduced in *IV Sent.*, d. 24 the treatise *De ordinibus ecclesiasticis* which, with the exception of certain lines, was copied from Hugh of St. Victor († 1141), Yves of Chartres († 1040-1115) and the *Decretum Gratiani;* all these authors depend in their turn on *De septem ordinibus ecclesiae* (fifth to seventh centuries), one of the first treatises of the Western Church (cf. St. Isidore of Seville) devoted to an exposition of the competencies of the different grades of the hierarchy.

the others had been instituted by the Church in the course of time. He did not consider the episcopate to share in this excellence, saying that it did not belong to the sacramental *ordines* but rather to the domain of dignities and offices.[118]

II. From St. Thomas Aquinas († 1273) to Trent (1563)

1. Affirmation of Sacramentality

St. Thomas' teaching on the diaconate[119] included the fact that it was a sacrament insofar as it belonged to Holy Orders, one of the seven sacraments of the new law. He considered that each of the different orders constituted in some way a sacramental reality; however, only three (priest, deacon and sub-deacon) could strictly be said to be *ordines sacri* by reason of their special relation to the Eucharist.[120] But it should not be concluded that their sacramentality meant that the priesthood and the diaconate were different sacraments; the distinction between the orders did not indicate that each was a universal or integral whole, but indicated a potestative wholeness.[121]

The way that the unity and oneness of the sacrament of Holy Orders was bound together in its different grades had to do with their reference to the Eucharist, *Sacramentum Sacramentorum.*[122] Because of that, the different orders needed a sacramental consecration depending on their type of power with respect to the Eucharist. Through ordination priests received the power to consecrate, while deacons received the power to serve the priests in the administration of the sacraments.[123]

The relationship of each order to the Eucharist became the deciding factor in avoiding the idea that each order gave the power to administer a specific sacrament. The same criterion also served to exclude the orders of psalmist and cantor from the sacramental orders. But this criterion was also used to exclude the episcopate from sacramentality.[124] In spite of everything, although St. Thomas refuses to recognize in the episcopate any sort of power superior to that of the priest in relation to the *verum corpus Christi*, he considers the episcopate to be

118 IV *Sent*, d. 24, c. 14.

119 Cf. *In IV Sent*, d. 24-25; *Suppl*, qq. 34-40; SCG 4, 74-77, *De art. fidei et Eccl sacramentis.*

120 *In IV Sent.*, d. 24, q. 2, a. 1 ad 3.

121 Ibid., d. 24, q. 2, a. 1, sol. 1.

122 Ibid., d. 24, q. 2, a. 1, sol. 2.

123 Ibid.

124 Ibid., d. 24, q. 3, a. 2, sol. 2.

also an *ordo* in a certain way, by reason of the powers which the bishop holds over the *corpus mysticum*.[125]

Because the diaconate is a sacrament, it is an *ordo* which imprints a character on the soul. St. Thomas applies this doctrine to baptism, confirmation and Holy Orders. His thinking on this developed with time. Starting from the priesthood of Christ he defined Holy Orders alone as imprinting a character (*In IV Sent*), but finally defined the complete doctrine of character (*STh*).[126]

On the subject of the diaconate, he explained all its *potestates*, in relation to the *dispensatio* of the sacraments, as something that seemed to belong rather within the domain of what was "licit" and not within the domain of a new radical enablement with regard to the "validity" of the functions in question.[127] In his turn, in *Summa Theologiae*, III, q. 67, a. 1, he asks whether evangelizing and baptizing are part of the deacon's office, and he answers that no direct administration of the sacraments belongs to the diaconate *quasi ex proprio officio*, any more than any task in relation with *docere*, but only with *cathechizare*.[128]

2. Sacramentality Called into Question

Durandus of Saint-Pourfain († 1334) represented a doctrinal line which was to reappear intermittently up until the present day. According to this line, only ordination to the priesthood is a "sacrament"; the other orders, including the diaconate, were only "sacramentals."[129] The reasons for his position were as follows:

a. With regard to the Eucharist, the distinction between the power of consecrating, which belonged exclusively to the order of the priesthood (which should be considered a sacrament) and the preparatory actions, which belonged to the other orders (merely considered as sacramentals).
b. In the same way as with baptism, there was a *potestas ad suscipiendum sacramenta*; but it was only the priesthood that was granted a *postestas*

125 Ibid., d. 24, q. 3, a. 2, sol. 2.

126 Cf. *In IV Sent*, d. 7, q. 2 ad 1; STh III, q. 63, a. 3.

127 *In IV Sent*, d. 24, q. 1, a. 2, sol. 2.

128 STh III, q. 67, a. 1.

129 As for the episcopate, he tended to state that it was "*ordo et sacramentum, non quidem praecise distinctum a sacerdotio simplici, sed est unum sacramentum cum ipso, sicut perfectum et imperfectum*." Durandus of Saint-Pourcain, *Super Sententias Comm. Libri quatuor* (Parisii, 1550), 4, d. 24, q. 6.

ordinis ad conficiendum vel conferendum ea, which was not granted to any of the orders inferior to the priesthood, not even to the diaconate.

c. Ordination to the priesthood grants a power *ad posse* and not *ad licere*, so that the ordained priest can really do something which he could not do before his ordination. The diaconate, on the other hand, grants the capacity to do *licite* something that he could in fact do before, although illicitly, and this is why the diaconate can be considered as an institution or ecclesial deputation to exercise certain functions.

d. It is also demanded by the unity of the sacrament of Orders and the evaluation of the priesthood as the fullness of this sacrament, since otherwise it would be hard to preserve the meaning of what St. Thomas said on the unity and oneness of the sacrament of Holy Orders.[130]

e. The distinction between *sacramentum* and *sacramentalia* did not, however, prevent Durandus from saying that each of the orders imprints a "character." He distinguished in his turn between a *deputatio* which had its origin in God himself, and made the order in question a *sacramentum*, and an ecclesiastical *deputatio* instituted by the Church, which only made the orders in question (all the other orders) *sacramentalia*. In this sense it could be said that the diaconate imprints a character; the doubt or debate concerned exactly when the character was imprinted, since some maintained that it would come *in traditione libri evangeliorum* (an opinion which Durandus rejected) while others held that it came *in impositione manuum* (an opinion which he appeared to adopt).[131]

3. The Teaching of Trent (1563)

The Council of Trent chose to make a dogmatic definition of Holy Orders as a sacrament; the direction of its doctrinal statements leaves no doubt on the subject. However, it is not clear to what extent the sacramentality of the diaconate should be considered as being included in this definition. The question has remained a controversial one to the present day, although very few people

130 Ibid., q. 2 for what is said under a, b, c and d.

131 Ibid., q. 3.

indeed now debate the subject. This makes it necessary to interpret the statements of the Council of Trent.

As against the denials of the Reformers, Trent declared the existence of a *hierarchia in Ecclesia ordinatione divina* (which led to a rejection of the statement "*omnes christianos promiscue Novi Testamenti sacerdotes esse*") and also a *hierarchia ecclesiastica* (which led to the distinction between the different grades within the sacrament of Holy Orders).[132]

The references by Trent to the diaconate (which it also refers to explicitly) need to be set within the general theology of the sacrament of Holy Orders. However, it is not entirely certain that the dogmatic declarations of Trent on the sacramentality and the sacramental character of the priesthood, to which Trent refers explicitly, include an intention on the part of the Council to define the sacramentality of the diaconate as well.

According to Trent deacons are mentioned directly in the New Testament, although it is not stated that they were instituted directly by Christ the Savior. In accordance with the way the other orders are envisaged, the diaconate is also conceived of as a help to exercising *dignius et maiore cum veneratione ministerium tarn Sancti sacerdotii* and to serve the priesthood *ex officio* (it is not said to be *ad ministerium episcopi*). Furthermore, the diaconate appears to be a stage on the way to the priesthood—there is no explicit mention of a permanent diaconate.[133]

When Trent defined dogmatically that *ordo* or *sacra ordinatio* was "*vere sacramentum*,"[134] there was no explicit mention of the diaconate, which was included among the *ordines ministrorum*.[135] Thus, if the dogmatic statement of sacramentality is to be applied to the diaconate, it should perhaps be applied equally to the other *ordines ministrorum*, which seems excessive and unjustified.

Something similar can be said on the subject of the doctrine of "sacramental character."[136] In view of the expressions used by the Council, there can be no doubt that Trent referred explicitly and directly to the "priests of the New Testament," to distinguish them clearly from the "laypeople." There is no mention made of "deacons," either direct or indirect; therefore it would be difficult

132 Cf. Denzinger-Schönmetzer (DS), *Enchiridion Symbolorum, Definitionum et Declarationum de Rebus Fidei et Morum* 1767, 1776.
133 Cf. DS 1765, 1772.
134 Cf. DS 1766, 1773.
135 Cf. DS 1765.
136 Cf. DS 1767, 1774.

to see in the text of Trent any intention to establish the dogma of character for the diaconate.

Canon 6 merits particular attention ("*si quis dixerit in Ecclesia catholica non esse hierarchiam, divina ordinatione institutam, quae constat ex episcopis, presbyteris et ministris, a.s.*"[137]) because of different interpretations of the word *ministris*: deacons, or deacons and other ministers, or all the other orders? Right up until the day before its approval (July 14, 1563), the text of canon 6 said "*et aliis ministris*." That day, in view of petitions made by a Spanish group, the expression *aliis ministris* was altered to exclude the word *aliis*. But the reasons and scope of this change are not very clear.[138]

How should the term *ministris*, and their inclusion in the *hierarchia*, be interpreted? The exclusion of the word *aliis* means, according to some, that the dividing line within the ecclesiastical hierarchy should be drawn between *sacerdotes* (bishops and priests) on the one hand, and *ministri* on the other; the suppression of the word *aliis* was intended to stress once again that the bishops and priests are not *nudi ministri* but *sacerdotes Novi Testamenti*. The history of the text in question, in the light of its previous formulations, would seem to suggest a broad understanding of *ministri*, to include *diaconos caeterosque ministros*, corresponding to a triple division of the hierarchy (*praecipue episcopi, deinde praesbyteri, diaconi et alii ministri*). But it must not be forgotten that according to other authors the suppression of the term *aliis* meant that the subdiaconate and other minor orders were excluded from the hierarchy "*divina ordinatione instituta*"—an expression whose interpretation is in its turn polemical.[139]

To sum up, whether one interprets it exclusively or inclusively, it cannot be doubted that deacons are included in the term *ministri*. But the dogmatic consequences concerning their sacramentality and their inclusion in the hierarchy will differ, depending on whether the word *ministri* refers to deacons alone, or includes the other orders too.

137 Cf. DS 1776.

138 Cf. Council of Trent, 3, 682f., 686, 690; 7/2, 603, 643.

139 Cf. K. J. Becker, *Wesen und Vollmachten des Priestertums nach dem Lehramt*, QD 47 (Freiburg, 1970), 19-156; J. Freitag, *Sacramentum ordinis aus dem Konzil von Trient: Ausgeblendeter Disserts und erreichter Konsens* (Innsbruck, 1991), 218ff.

III. Theological Nuances after Trent

After the Council of Trent, in the theology of the sixteenth and seventeenth centuries, a majority of opinions maintained the sacramentality of the diaconate, with only a minority questioning or denying it. However, the form in which this sacramentality was defended had many differing nuances, and it was generally considered to be a point which had not been dogmatically defined by Trent, and which was reasserted doctrinally in the *Roman Catechism* where it describes the functions of deacons.[140]

Thus for example, F. de Vitoria († 1546) considers as *probabilissima* the opinion that "*solum sacramentum est sacerdotium*" and that all the other orders are sacramentals. D. de Soto († 1560), for his part, although in favor of the sacramentality of both the diaconate and the sub-diaconate, considered that anyone who followed Durandus was not to be reprehended.[141]

Robert Bellarmine († 1621) well described the *status quaestionis* at that point. He established the sacramentality of Holy Orders ("*vere ac proprie sacramentum novae legis*") as a fundamental principle admitted by all Catholic theologians and denied by (Protestant) heretics. But as regarded the sacramentality of the individual orders he felt it necessary to make a distinction, because although there was unanimous agreement on the sacramentality of the priesthood, this was not the case for the other orders.[142]

Bellarmine declared himself clearly in favor of the sacramentality of the episcopate ("*ordinatio episcopalis sacramentum est vere ac proprie dictum*"), as against the scholastics of old who denied it; and he considered this an *assertio certissima*, based on Scripture and Tradition. Moreover, he spoke of an episcopal character which was distinct from and superior to the character of the presbyterate.

As regards the doctrine of the sacramentality of the diaconate, Bellarmine adopted it, considering it very probable; however, he did not take it as a certainty *ex fide*, since it could not be deduced from the evidence of Scripture nor Tradition nor any explicit pronouncement on the part of the Church.[143]

140 Cf. *Catechismus Romanus*, p. 2, c. 7, q. 20.

141 Cf. F. de Vitoria, *Summa sacramentorum*, no. 226 (Venice, 1579), f. 136v; D. de Soto, *In Sent.* 4, d. 24, q. 1, a. 4, concl. 5 (633ab).

142 Cf. R. Bellarminus, *Controversiarum de sacramento ordinis liber unicus*, in *Opera omnia*, vol. 5 (Paris, 1873), 26.

143 Ibid., 27-28.

Bellarmine was also in favor of the sacramentality of the sub-diaconate, basing his opinion on the doctrine of character, on celibacy, and on the common opinion of theologians, although he recognized that this doctrine was not as certain as that of the diaconate.[144] Still less certain, in his view, was the sacramentality of the other minor orders.

IV. The Sacramentality of the Diaconate in Vatican II

Concerning deacons or the diaconate in the texts of Vatican II (SC, no 86; LG, nos. 20, 28, 29, 41; OE, no. 17; CD, no. 15; DV, no. 25; AG, nos. 15, 16) the sacramentality of both modes (permanent and transitory) was taken for granted. Sometimes it was stated simply in passing, or indirectly, or faintly. Taken all together, the texts of Vatican II repeated what had been the majority opinion in theology up to that time, but went no further. Neither did the Council clarify a number of uncertainties which were expressed in the course of the debates.

1. In the Conciliar Debates

The sacramentality of the diaconate was a theme tackled in several interventions in the second period of the Council (1963). The result was a majority in favor, particularly among those who upheld the institution of the permanent diaconate; among who opposed such an institution, there was no majority in favor of the sacramentality of the diaconate.[145]

In the *relatio* of the doctrinal Commission, some explanatory notes on the text are presented which are of interest in interpreting it. The notes give the exegetical reason for not directly mentioning Acts 6:1-6,[146] and also explain the moderate way in which the sacramentality of the diaconate is mentioned, as caused by unwillingness to give the impression of condemning those who

144 Ibid., 30.

145 Cf., in favor: *Acta Synodalia Sacrosancti Concilii Oecumenici Vaticani II (AS)* 2/2, 227f., 314f., 317f., 359, 431, 580; raising doubts about or calling into question the sacramentality of the diaconate: AS 2/2, 378, 406, 447f.

146 "Quod attinet ad Act. 6, 1-6, inter exegetas non absolute constat viros de quibus ibi agitur diaconis nostris corresponded" (AS 3/1, 260).

questioned it.[147] The conciliar debate did not in fact reach unanimity on the sacramental nature of the diaconate.

Also of interest for interpretation of the texts are the nuances introduced into the summary of the discussion. Among the arguments in favor of restoration, mention was first made of the sacramental nature of the diaconate, of which the Church ought not to be deprived. Among the arguments against restoration the main one was undoubtedly that of celibacy. But others were added, such as whether or not the diaconate was needed for tasks which could be carried out by laypeople. The following questions were asked under this heading: whether all tasks were to be considered, or only some of them; whether those tasks were of a regular nature or were exceptional; whether or not there was a privation of the special graces linked to the sacramentality of the diaconate; whether negative or positive influences on the apostolate of the laity could be considered; whether it was appropriate to recognize ecclesially, by ordination, the diaconal tasks which were in fact already being carried out; and whether deacons' (and especially married deacons') possible situation as a "bridge" between the higher clergy and the laity could be considered.[148]

2. *In the Texts of Vatican II*

In *Lumen Gentium* (no. 29), the proposition according to which there was an imposition of hands on deacons "*non ad sacerdotium, sed ad ministerium*" was to become a key reference for the theological understanding of the diaconate. However, many questions have been left open up until the present day for the following reasons: the suppression of the reference to the bishop in the formula which was settled upon;[149] the dissatisfaction felt by certain people about the

---

147 "De indole sacramentali diaconatus, statutum est, postulantibus pluribus . . . eam in schemate caute indicare, quia in Traditione et Magisterio fundatur. Cf. praeter canonem citatum Tridentini: Pius XII, Apost. Const. *Sacramentum Ordinis*, DS 3858f. . . . Ex altera tamen parte cavetur ne Concilium paucos illos recentes auctores, qui de hac re dubia moverunt, condemnare videatur," ibid.

148 Cf. AS 3/1, 260-64; AS 3/2, 214-18.

149 The original text said: "in ministerio episcopi." On the origin of and variations on this formula, cf. A. Kerkvoorde, "Esquisse d'une theologie du diaconat," in P. Winninger and Y. Congar, eds., *Le Diacre dans l'Église et le monde d'aujour'hui*, UnSa 59 (Paris, 1966), 163-71, which, for its part, includes the warning that "it would be a mistake . . . to make it [*sc.* this formula] the basis for a future theology of the diaconate."

ambiguity in that formula;[150] the interpretation given by the Commission;[151] and the scope of the actual distinction between *sacerdotium* and *ministerium*.

In *Lumen Gentium* (no. 28a), the term *ministerium* is used in a double sense in turn: (a) to refer to the ministry of the bishops, who as successors of the Apostles partake of the "consecration" and "mission" received by Christ from his Father, which they hand on in various degrees to different individuals, without explicit mention being made of deacons;[152] [and] (b) to refer to the "ecclesiastical ministry" as a whole, divinely established on different levels, embracing those who from antiquity have been called bishops, priests and deacons.[153] In the relevant note, Vatican II gives a reference to Trent, session 23, cap. 2 and canon 6.[154] The same sort of caution can be observed in both sources in the expressions which relate to the diversity of grades: "*ordinatione divina*" (Trent), "*divinitus institutum*" (Vatican II); "*ab ipso Ecclesiae initio*" (Trent), "*ab antiquo*" or else "*inde ab Apostolis*" according to *Ad Gentes* (no. 16) (Vatican II).[155]

The statement which relates most directly to the sacramentality of the diaconate is found in *Lumen Gentium* (no. 29a): "*gratia enim sacramentali roborati, in diaconia liturgiae, verbi et caritatis populo Dei, in communione cum Episcopo eiusque presbyterio, inserviunt*"; and also in *Ad Gentes* (no. 16): "*lit ministerium suum per gratiam sacramentalem diaconatus efficacius expleant*." The expression *gratia sacramentalis* is prudent, appropriate for an interjection, and much more nuanced than the formula "sacramental ordination" employed in the previous project of *Lumen Gentium* in 1963. Why was this caution apparent in the expressions finally used? The doctrinal Commission referred to the basis in tradition of what is affirmed, and to the concern to avoid giving the impression that those who had doubts on the subject were being condemned.[156]

150 The expression is ambiguous: "nam sacerdotium est ministerium" (AS 3/8, 101).

151 The words of the *Statuta* are interpreted as follows: "significant diaconos non ad corpus et sanguinem Domini offerendum sed ad *servitium caritatis* in Ecclesia," ibid.

152 "Christus . . . consecrationis missionisque suae per Apostolos suos, eorum successores, videlicet Episcopos participes effecit, qui *munus ministerii sui*, vario gradu, variis subiectis in Ecclesia legitime tradiderunt," LG, no. 28a.

153 "Sic *ministerium ecclesiasticum* divinitus instituturn diversis ordinibus exercetur ab illis qui iam ab antiquo Episcopi, Presbyteri, Diaconi vocantur," ibid.

154 DS 1765, 1776.

155 Cf. the different references to Trent in the conciliar debates. Some identified *ministry* with *diaconi*, although their semantic equivalence does not justify making an instant theological identification between the two; others considered it to have been *dogmatically* defined at Trent that the diaconate constitutes the third grade of the hierarchy, but this evaluation seems to go beyond what was intended at Trent. Cf. notes 136 and 143 supra.

156 Cf. AS 3/1, 260.

3. *The Sacramentality of the Diaconate in Post-Conciliar Developments*

1. Mention must first be made of the document which puts the Council's decisions into effect, i.e., the *Motu Proprio* of Pope Paul VI, *Sacrum Diaconatus Ordinem* (1967). In what concerns the theological nature of the diaconate, it takes up what Vatican II said about the *gratia* of the diaconate, while adding a reference to the indelible "character" (absent from the Council texts), and it is understood as a "stable" service.[157]

As a grade of the sacrament of Holy Orders, it bestows the capacity to exercise tasks which mostly belong to the domain of the liturgy (eight out of the eleven mentioned). In some expressions these appear as tasks which are deputized or delegated.[158] Thus it is not clear up to what point the diaconal "character" confers the capacity for some competencies or powers which could only be exercised by reason of previous sacramental ordination; since there is another way of accessing them (by delegation or deputizing, and not by reason of the sacrament of Holy Orders).

2. The most recent step taken in the *Motu Proprio* of Pope Paul VI, *Ad Pascendum* (1972) refers to the instituting of the permanent diaconate (not excluding it as a transitory stage) as a "middle order" between the upper hierarchy and the rest of the People of God. In what concerns sacramentality, as well as considering this *medius ordo* as "*signum vel sacramentum ipsius Christi Domini, qui non venit ministrari, sed ministrare*," the document presupposes the sacramentality of the diaconate and limits itself to repeating the aforementioned expressions such as *sacra ordinatio* or *sacrum ordinem*.[159]

3. Following some positions which had already been taken up before Vatican II, certain authors expressed their doubts with regard to the sacramentality of the diaconate more explicitly and with detailed arguments, after the Council too. Their motives were varied. J. Beyer (1980) primarily presented his analysis of the conciliar texts, whose silence on the distinction between the power of "order" and of "jurisdiction" seemed to him to avoid rather than provide a solution to the questions which were still unresolved.[160] The same would apply

157 Cf. AAS 59 (1967): 698.

158 Cf. ibid., 702.

159 Cf. AAS 64 (1972): 536, 534, 537.

160 Cf. J. Beyer, "Nature et position du sacerdoce," *NRTh* 76 (1954): 356-73, 469-80; J. Beyer, "De diaconatu animadversiones," *Periodica* 69 (1980): 441-60.

to the fluctuation in meaning which could be accorded to the term *ministerium*, and the contrast between it and *sacerdotium*. He further evaluated the caution shown in the Council texts not only as the result of concern to avoid condemning anyone, but also as a result of doctrinal hesitations.[161] This was why further clarification was needed of the question: "*Estne diaconatus pars sacerdotii sicut et episcopatus atque presbyteratus unum sacerdotium efficiunt?*" This need was not satisfied by referring to the "common priesthood" of the faithful and excluding deacons from the "sacrificing" priesthood (cf. Philips). According to Tradition, the ministerial priesthood was *unum* and *unum sacramentum*. If it was this sacramental priesthood alone which rendered someone capable of acting *in persona Christi* with effect *ex opere operato*, then it would be hard to call the diaconate a "sacrament" because it was not instituted to accomplish any act *in persona Christi* with effect *ex opere operato*.

Additionally, further careful investigation was needed into the statements of Trent and also into the normative value of its references to the diaconate.[162] The acts of Vatican II, the development of the schemas, the various interventions and the *relatio* of the relevant Commission, also needed a careful re-reading. It could be concluded from this *relatio* that a solution had not altogether been found of the difficulties with regard to the following points: (a) the exegetical foundation of the institution of the diaconate (Acts 6:1-6 was excluded because it was open to debate, and consideration was limited to the simple mentions of deacons in Philippians 1:1 and 1 Timothy 3:8-12); and (b) the theological justification of the sacramental nature of the diaconate, in connection with the intention of re-establishing its permanent mode.

In conclusion: if Vatican II spoke cautiously and *ex obliquo* of the sacramental nature of the diaconate, it was not only from a concern not to condemn anyone, but rather because of the *incertitudo doctrinae*.[163] Therefore, to confirm

161 Beyer especially disagreed with G. Philips' evaluation of this caution. Given that the Council wished to act *non dogmatice, sed pastorale*, even a much more explicit statement would not *ipso facto* imply condemnation of the contrary opinion. Hence in Beyer's view the reason for this caution was due to the fact that in what concerned the sacramentality of the diaconate the *haesitatio* was indeed "manifesta et doctrinalis quidem."

162 According to Beyer, the term *ministri* had a generic sense; it had not been intended to give a dogmatic statement only of what the Protestant reform refused. The sense in which Trent was now invoked often went "ultra eius in Concilio Tridentino pondus et sensum."

163 The biggest reason for this uncertainty lay in the fact of affirming "diaconum non ad sacerdotium sed ad ministerium ordinari, atque nihil in hoc ministerio agere diaconum quin et laicus idem facere non possit."

its sacramental nature, neither the majority opinion of theologians (which had also existed concerning the sub-diaconate), nor the mere description of the rite of ordination (which needed to be clarified from other sources) nor the mere imposition of hands (which could be non-sacramental in character) was sufficient.

4. In the new *Codex Iuris Canonici* (CIC) of 1983, the diaconate is spoken of from the standpoint of its sacramentality, introducing certain developments which deserve comment.

This is true of canons 1008-1009. The diaconate is one of the three orders, and the CIC seems to apply to it the general theology of the sacrament of Holy Orders in its integrity.[164] If this application is valid, then it follows from it that the diaconate is a sacramental reality, of divine institution, which makes deacons *sacri ministri* (in the CIC, those who are baptized and ordained), imprints on them an "indelible character" (taking for granted what was said by Paul VI) and by reason of their consecration and deputation (*consecrantur et deputantur*) renders them capable of exercising *in persona Christi Capitis* and in the grade which corresponds to them (*pro suo quisque gradu*) the tasks of teaching, sanctifying and ruling, in other words the functions proper to those who are called to guide the People of God.

Integrating the diaconate within the general theology of the sacrament of Holy Orders in this way raises certain questions. Can it be theologically maintained that deacons, *even pro suo gradu*, really exercise the "*munera docendi, sanctificandi et regendi*" *in persona Christi Capitis* as do bishops and priests? Is that not something particular and exclusive to those who have received sacramental ordination and the consequent power to *conficere corpus et sanguinem Christi*, i.e., to consecrate the Eucharist, which does not belong to deacons in any way? Should the CIC's expression *in persona Christi Capitis* be understood in a broader sense so that it can also be applied to the functions of deacons? How, then, should the Council's statement be interpreted, which says that deacons are "*non ad sacerdotium, sed ad ministerium*"? Can the task of *pascere populum Dei* be considered an effect of the sacramentality of the diaconate? Would not arguing over its "powers" lead to an impasse?

164 "Sacramento ordinis ex divina institutione inter christifideles quidam, charactere indelebili suo signantur, constituuntur sacri ministri, qui nempe consecrantur et deputantur ut, pro suo quisque gradu, in persona Christi Capitis munera docendi, sanctificandi et regendi adimplentes, Dei populum pascant," CIC, c. 1008.

It is very natural that the CIC should concern itself specially and at length with the faculties proper to deacons, and it does so in several canons.[165] In canons 517, 2 and 519 deacons are mentioned with reference to cooperation with the parish priest as *pastor proprius*, and to the possibility of granting them a share in the exercise of the *cura pastoralis* (c. 517, 2). This possibility of sharing in the exercise of the *cura pastoralis paroeciae* (which refers in the first place to deacons, although it can also be granted to laypeople) raises the question of the capacity of the deacon to assume the pastoral guidance of the community, and takes up again, with different nuances, what had already been established by *Ad Gentes* (no. 16), and *Sacrum Diaconatus* (no. 22). Although these points referred directly to *regere*, canon 517, 2 speaks in a more nuanced way of *participatio in exercitio curae pastoralis*. In any case, with reference to the possibility opened by canon 517, which is presented as a last solution, more precise thought needs to be given to the real participation of deacons, by reason of their diaconal ordination, in the *cura animarum* and the task of *pascere populum Dei*.[166]

5. The recent *Catechismus Catholicae Ecclesiae* (CCE), in its definitive 1997 edition, seems to speak more decidedly in favor of the sacramentality of the diaconate.

It states that the *potestas sacra* to act *in persona Christi* only corresponds to the bishops and priests, whereas deacons hold *vim populo Dei serviendi* in their various diaconal functions (no. 875). It also mentions deacons when, concerning the sacrament of Holy Orders, it considers "ordination" as a "sacramental act" enabling recipients to exercise a "sacred power" which proceeds ultimately from Jesus Christ alone (no. 1538).

On the one hand it seems that according to the CCE deacons could also be included in a certain way in a general understanding of the sacrament of Holy

165 In cc. 757, 764, 766, 767 (the homily is reserved "sacerdoti aut diacono," while laypeople may also be admitted "ad praedicandum"), 835, 861, 910, 911, 1003 (deacons are not ministers of the anointing of the sick, for "unctionem infirmorum valide administrat omnis et solus sacerdos": is this an application of the principle which speaks of deacons as "non ad sacerdotium, sed ad ministerium"?), 1079, 1081, 1108, 1168, 1421, 1425, 1428, 1435 (they can be "judges," something which forms part of the power of governance or jurisdiction).

166 Such reflection is necessary, because the principle is maintained that the *pastor proprius* and the final moderator of the *plena cura animarum* can only be one who has received ordination to the priesthood (the *sacerdos*). This raises the possibility of an extreme case of a *sacerdos* (who is not in fact a *parochus*, although he has all the attributes of one) and a *diaconus* (who is a *quasi-parochus*, since he has in fact the responsibility for the *cura pastoralis*, though not in its totality because he lacks the sacramental powers relating to the Eucharist and Reconciliation).

Orders under some categories of the priesthood, since it mentions them from this point of view at the same time as bishops and priests in numbers 1539-43. On the other hand, in the definitive version of number 1554, it justifies the restriction of the term *sacerdos* to bishops and priests, excluding deacons, while maintaining that deacons also belong to the sacrament of Holy Orders (no. 1554).

Finally, the idea of sacramentality is strengthened by the explicit attribution of the doctrine of "character" to deacons as a special configuration with Christ, deacon and servant of all (no. 1570).

6. The recent *Ratio Fundamentalis* (1998), which recognizes the difficulties that exist in reaching an understanding of the *germana natura* of the diaconate, nevertheless firmly upholds the clarity of the doctrinal elements ("*clarissime definita*," nos. 3 and 10) on the basis of original diaconal practice and conciliar indications.

There is no doubt that we have here a way of speaking of the specific identity of the deacon which offers certain novelties in comparison with what has usually been the case up till now. The deacon has a specific configuration with Christ, Lord and Servant.[167] To this configuration there corresponds a spirituality whose distinguishing mark is "serviceability," which by ordination makes the deacon into a living "icon" of Christ the Servant in the Church (no. 11). This is offered in justification of restricting the configuration with Christ the Head and Shepherd to priests. But configuration with Christ the "Servant," and "service" as a characteristic of the ordained minister, are also valid for priests; so that it is not very clear what is "specifically diaconal" in this service, what it is that might express itself in functions or "*munera*" (cf. no. 9) which were the exclusive competence of deacons by reason of their sacramental capacity.

All in all, the *Ratio* clearly affirms the sacramentality of the diaconate as well as its sacramental character, in the perspective of a common theology of the sacrament of Holy Orders and the respective character which it confers.[168] Here the language is decisive and explicit, although it is not altogether clear to

167 "Specificam configurationem cum Christo, Domino et Servo omnium . . . specificam diaconi identitatem . . . is enim, prout unici ministerii ecclesiastici particeps, est in Ecclesia specificum signum sacramentale Christi Servi," *Ratio*, 5.

168 "Prout gradus ordinis sacri, diaconatus characterem imprimit et specificam gratiam sacramentalem communicat . . . signum configurativum-distinctivum animae modo indelebili impressum, quod . . . configurat Christo, qui diaconus, ideoque servus omnium, factus est," *Ratio*, 7.

what extent it is the expression of more consistent theological developments or a new or better-justified base.

Conclusion

The doctrinal position in favor of the sacramentality of the diaconate is broadly speaking the majority opinion of theologians from the twelfth century to the present day and it is taken for granted in the practice of the Church and in most documents of the Magisterium; it is upheld by those who defend the permanent diaconate (for celibate or married people) and constitutes an element which includes a large number of the propositions in favor of the diaconate for women.

Despite everything, this doctrinal position faces questions which need to be clarified more fully, either through the development of a more convincing theology of the sacramentality of the diaconate, or through a more direct and explicit intervention by the Magisterium, or by a more successful attempt to connect and harmonize the various elements. The path which was followed concerning the sacramentality of the episcopate could be taken as a decisive and instructive reference point. Among the questions requiring deeper or more fully developed theology are the following: (a) the normative status of the sacramentality of the diaconate as it was fixed by the doctrinal interventions of the Magisterium, especially in Trent and in Vatican II; (b) the "unity" and "oneness" of the sacrament of Holy Orders in its diverse grades; (c) the exact scope of the distinction *non ad sacerdotium, sed ad ministerium* (*episcopi*); (d) the doctrine of the character of the diaconate and its specificity as a configuration with Christ; [and] (e) the "powers" conferred by the diaconate as a sacrament.

To reduce sacramentality to the question of *potestates* would undoubtedly be an overly narrow approach; ecclesiology offers broader and richer perspectives. But in the case of the sacrament of Holy Orders, this question cannot be passed over with the excuse that it is too narrow. The other two grades of Holy Orders, the episcopate and the priesthood, give a capacity, by reason of sacramental ordination, for tasks which an unordained person cannot perform validly. Why should it be otherwise for the diaconate? Does the difference lie in the *way* in which the *munera* are exercised or in the personal quality of the person performing them? But how could this be rendered theologically credible? If in fact these functions can be exercised by a layperson, what justification is there for the argument that they have their source in a new and distinct sacramental ordination?

The discussion of diaconal powers gives rise once again to general questions on: the nature or condition of the *potestas sacra* in the Church, the connection of the sacrament of Holy Orders with the *potestas conficiendi eucharistiam*, and the need to widen ecclesiological perspectives beyond a narrow view of this connection.

Chapter V

The Restoration of the Permanent Diaconate at Vatican II

In three places, Vatican II uses different terms to describe what it intends to do when it speaks of the diaconate as a stable rank of the hierarchy of the Church. *Lumen Gentium* (no. 29b) uses the notion of *restitutio*,[169] *Ad Gentes* (no. 16f.) uses that of *restauratio*,[170] while *Orientalium Ecclesiarum* (no. 17) employs the word *instauratio*.[171] All three connote the idea of restoring, renewing, re-establishing, and re-activating. In the present chapter two points will be dealt with. First, it is important to know the reasons why the Council restored the permanent diaconate, and secondly, to examine the figure it wished to bestow upon it.

I. The Intentions of the Council

The idea of re-establishing the diaconate as a permanent grade of the hierarchy did not originate with Vatican II. It was already current before the Second World War, but was developed as a definite possibility after 1945, especially in German-speaking countries.[172] The challenge of responding to the pastoral needs of communities at a time when priests were facing imprisonment, deportation

169 "Diaconatus in futurum tamquam proprius ac permanens gradus hierarchiae restitui poterit," LG, no. 29b.

170 "Ordo diaconatus ut status vitae permanens restauretur ad normam constitutions de ecclesia," AG, no. 16f.

171 "Exoptat haec sancta synodus, ut institutum diaconatus permanentis, ubi in desuetudinem venerit, instauretur," OE, no. 17.

172 Cf. J. Hornef and P. Winninger, "Chronique de la restauration du diaconat (1945-1965)," in Winninger and Congar, *Le Diacre dans l'Église*, 205-22.

or death led to serious consideration being given to this idea. Various specialists soon produced studies on the theological and historical aspects of the diaconate.[173] Some men who were thinking about a vocation to the diaconate even established a group called the "Community of the Diaconate."[174] A renewed theology of the Church issuing from biblical, liturgical and ecumenical movements opened up the way to the possibility of restoring the diaconate as a stable order of the hierarchy.[175]

Thus on the eve of the Council the idea of a permanent diaconate was very much alive in certain significant sectors of the Church, and influenced a certain number of bishops and experts during the Council.

The motivations which led Vatican II to open the possibility of restoring the permanent diaconate are mainly given in the Dogmatic Constitution on the Church *Lumen Gentium* and the Decree on the missionary activity of the Church *Ad Gentes*. Because of the doctrinal nature of *Lumen Gentium*, the origin of its formulations concerning the permanent diaconate will be considered first.

During the first stage of the Council (1962)[176] the question of the diaconate did not attract much attention as a particular topic: this led certain Council Fathers to point to the absence of all mention of the diaconate in the chapter dealing with the episcopate and the priesthood.[177] But during the first intersession (1962-1963), a certain number of Council Fathers began to evoke the possibility of a restoration of the permanent diaconate, some pointing out its advantages in the missionary or ecumenical field, others recommending caution. However, most of them addressed practical questions rather than theoretical

173 A huge dossier of theological and historical studies, edited by K. Rahner and H. Vorgrimler, was published in Germany, entitled *Diaconia in Christo: Über die Erneuerung des Diakonates*, QD 15/16 (Freiburg am Breisgau, 1962).

174 Cf. Hornef and Winninger, "Chronique," 207-8.

175 For example, Yves Congar explored the impact of the theology of the People of God and the ontology of grace on a renewed understanding of the ministries which could open the possibility of restoring the diaconate. Cf. "Le diaconat dans la théologie des ministères," in Winninger and Congar, *Le Diacre dans l'Église*, especially 126f.

176 The Council discussed the first draft of *De Ecclesia* from the 31st General Congregation, December 1, 1962, to the 36th General Congregation, December 7, 1962.

177 Joseph Cardinal Bueno y Monreal (31 GC, December 1, 1962), AS 1/4, 131. Msgr. Raphael Rabban, for his part, asked why the schema made mention "de duobus gradibus ordinis, de episcopatu scilicet et de sacerdotio" and not of the diaconate "qui ad ordinem pertinet," ibid., 236.

matters: they discussed in particular the question of the admission of married men and its consequences for the celibacy of the clergy.[178]

In comparison with the level of discussion of the first period, that of the second period (1963) covered more ground and proved essential for an understanding of the Council's intentions.[179] Three interventions on the permanent diaconate could be considered "foundational" in the sense that they established in some measure the directions and the parameters, both doctrinal and practical, which were taken in the course of the debate. These interventions were those of Julius Cardinals Dopfher,[180] Joannes Landazuri Ricketts[181] and Leo Joseph Suenens.[182] The other interventions took up themes which had been raised by these three.

Beginning with the Council Fathers who favored the re-establishment of a permanent diaconate, it should be said that they stressed the fact that the Council was only examining the *possibility* of re-establishing the permanent diaconate at the time and in the places that the competent ecclesiastical authority should judge opportune. There was no indication to the effect that the establishment of a permanent diaconate might be something *obligatory* on all local Churches. The same contributors considered how the Church would benefit from such a decision from a practical and pastoral viewpoint. The presence of permanent deacons could help to resolve some of the pastoral problems caused by the shortage of priests in mission countries and in areas subject to persecution.[183] The encouragement of vocations to the diaconate could thus give greater prominence to the priesthood.[184] It could also help to improve the ecumenical relations of the Latin Church with the other Churches which have preserved the permanent diaconate.[185] Additionally, men who wanted to commit themselves more deeply to the apostolate, or those who were already engaged in a

178 Cf. G. Caprile, 17 *Concilio Vaticano II: Il primo periodo 1962-1963* (Rome, 1968), 337, 410, 413, 494, 498, 501, 536.

179 The Council discussed the chapter on the hierarchical structure of the Church from October 4 to 30, 1963.

180 Julius Cardinal Döpfner (43 GC, October 7, 1963), AS 2/2, 227-30.

181 Joannes Cardinal Landazuri Ricketts (43 GC, October 8, 1963), ibid., 314-17.

182 Leo Joseph Cardinal Suenens (43 GC, October 8, 1963), ibid., 317-20.

183 Cf. Msgr. Franciscus Seper (44 GC, October 9, 1963), ibid., 359; Msgr. Bernardus Yago (45 GC, October 10, 1963), ibid., 406; Msgr. Joseph Clemens Maurer (45 GC, written intervention), ibid., 412; and Msgr. Paul Yu Pin (45 GC), ibid., 431.

184 Cf. Paul Cardinal Richaud (44 GC, October 9, 1963), ibid., 346-47; Mgr. Bernardus Yago, ibid., 406.

185 Msgr. E. Seper, ibid., 359.

certain form of ministry could belong to the hierarchy.[186] Finally, the admission of married men to the diaconate could mean that the celibacy of priests shone out more clearly as a charism embraced in a spirit of freedom.[187]

The interventions also pointed to the theological basis for a re-establishing of the permanent diaconate. Some Council Fathers highlighted the fact that the question of the permanent diaconate was not merely a disciplinary matter, but was properly speaking a theological one.[188] As a rank within the sacred hierarchy of the Church, the diaconate had been part of the constitution of the Church from its beginnings.[189] Cardinal Dopfher stated vigorously: "*Schema nostrum, agens de hierarchica constitutione Ecclesiae, ordinem diaconatus nullo modo silere potest, quia tripartitio hierarchiae ratione ordinis habita in episcopatum, presbyteratum et diaconatum est juris divini et constitutioni Ecclesiae essentialiter propria.*"[190] If the Council revived the permanent diaconate, it would not be altering the constitutive elements of the Church, but would only be reintroducing something that had been left aside. The teaching of the Council of Trent (session 23, c. 17) was often invoked. Moreover, the Fathers maintained that the diaconate was a sacrament conferring grace and a character.[191] A deacon should not be considered as the same as a layman who was in the service of the Church, because the diaconate confers the grace to exercise a particular office.[192] Thus a deacon is not a layman who has been raised to a higher degree of the lay apostolate, but a member of the hierarchy by reason of sacramental grace and the character received at the moment of ordination. But as it was assumed that permanent deacons would live and work in the middle of the lay population and the secular world, they could exercise the role of "bridge or mediation between the hierarchy and the faithful."[193] Thus there was the intention on the part of the Fathers to restore the diaconate as a permanent rank of the hierarchy destined to penetrate secular society in the same way as laypeople. The permanent diaconate was not perceived as a call to the priesthood, but as a distinct ministry in the

186 Card. Landazuri Ricketts, ibid., 315; Card. J. Döpfner, ibid., 229.

187 Cf. Msgr. J. Maurer, ibid., 411; Msgr. Emmanuel Talamas Camandari (46 GC, October 11, 1963), ibid., 450; and Msgr. George Kemere (47 GC, October 14, 1963), ibid., 534.

188 Cf. Card. J. Döpfner, ibid., 227; Card. J. Landazuri Ricketts, ibid., 314.

189 Cf. Card. L. Suenens, ibid., 317; Msgr. Joseph Slipyj (46 GC, October 10, 1963), ibid., 445.

190 Card. J. Döpfner, ibid., 227.

191 Cf. Msgr. Armandus Fares (47 GC, October 14, 1963), ibid., 530-31; Msgr. Narcissus Jubany Arnau (48 GC, October 15, 1963), ibid., 580; Msgr. J. Maurer, ibid., 411.

192 Card. J. Landazuri Ricketts, ibid., 314-15; Card. L. Suenens, ibid., 318; Msgr. Seper, ibid., 319.

193 Msgr. Yü Pin, ibid., 431.

service of the Church.[194] It could thus be a sign of the Church's vocation to be the servant of Christ and of God.[195] The presence of the deacon, consequently, could renew the Church in the evangelical spirit of humility and service.

These opinions in favor of the restoration of the diaconate met with objections. Certain Fathers underlined the fact that the permanent diaconate would not be useful in resolving the shortage of priests because deacons cannot replace priests completely.[196] A number expressed the fear that the fact of accepting married men as deacons might endanger the celibacy of priests.[197] It would create a group of clergy inferior to the members of secular institutes, who took a vow of chastity.[198] The Fathers suggested solutions which seemed less prejudicial, such as giving a share of pastoral work to a larger number of men and women, committed lay-people and members of secular institutes.[199]

The definitive text of *Lumen Gentium*, promulgated on November 21, 1964, expresses some objectives which the Council set in re-establishing the diaconate as a proper and permanent rank of the hierarchy in the Latin Church.[200]

In the first place, according to number 28a of *Lumen Gentium*, Vatican II re-established the diaconate as a proper and permanent rank of the hierarchy in recognition of the divinely established ecclesiastical ministry, just as it had evolved in the course of history. Hence a motive of faith, namely the recognition of the gift of the Holy Spirit in the complex reality of Holy Orders, furnished the ultimate justification for the Council's decision to re-establish the diaconate.

---

194 Msgr. B. Yago, ibid., 407.

195 Msgr. J. Maurer, ibid., 410.

196 Anicetus Fernández, O.P. (45 GC, October 10, 1963), ibid., 424; Msgr. Joseph Drzazga (49 GC, October 16, 1963), ibid., 624.

197 Msgr. Franciscus Franic (44 GC, October 10, 1963), ibid., 378; Msgr. Dinus Romoli (48 GC, October 15, 1963), ibid., 598; Msgr. Petrus Cule (47 GC, October 14, 1963), ibid., 518.

198 Msgr. Joseph Carraro, ibid., 525-26.

199 Card. F. Spellman, ibid., 83; A. Fernández, ibid., 424; Msgr. Victorius Costantini, ibid., 447.

200 On September 15, 1964, Mgr. Aloysius Eduardo Henríquez Jiménez read the *relatio* explaining the text of the Doctrinal Commission on the priesthood and the diaconate, before the Fathers proceeded to vote on the chapter of *Lumen Gentium* dealing with the hierarchy. Explaining the position of the text, he stated that in the Church bishops, priests and deacons shared in power in different ways and to different degrees. As at Trent, the text taught that the diaconate belongs to the sacred hierarchy, of which it is the lowest degree. Ordained for ministry and not for the priesthood, deacons have received sacramental grace and have been charged with a triple service of the liturgy, of the word and of charity. The diaconate could be conferred on married men. Cf. AS 3/2, 211-18. Msgr. Franciscus Franic presented the opposing views, ibid., 193-201.

Lumen Gentium (no. 29), however, presented what might be termed the "circumstantial reason" for the restoration of the permanent diaconate.[201] Vatican II foresaw deacons as engaging in tasks (*munera*) which were very necessary to the life of the Church (*ad vitam ecclesiae summopere necessaria*), but which in many regions could be fulfilled only with difficulty because of the discipline of the Latin Church as it existed at the time. The present difficulties caused by the shortage of priests demanded some response. Care for the faithful (*pro cura animarum*) was the determining factor in re-establishing the permanent diaconate in a local Church. The re-establishment of the permanent diaconate was therefore intended to respond to pastoral needs which were grave, not merely peripheral ones. This explains in part why it was the responsibility of the territorial episcopal conferences, and not the pope, to determine whether it was opportune to ordain such deacons, because they would have a more immediate grasp of the needs of the local Churches.

Indirectly, Vatican II was also to initiate a clarification of the identity of the priest, who did not have to fulfill all the tasks necessary to the life of the Church. In consequence, the Church would be able to experience the riches of different degrees of Holy Orders. At the same time Vatican II enabled the Church to go beyond a narrowly sacerdotal understanding of the ordained minister.[202] Since deacons were ordained *non ad sacerdotium, sed ad ministerium*, it was possible to conceive of clerical life, the sacred hierarchy and ministry in the Church beyond the category of the priesthood.

It is also worth noting that the permanent diaconate could be conferred upon men of more mature age (*viris maturioris aetatis*), even upon those living in the married state, but that the law of celibacy remained intact for younger candidates. *Lumen Gentium* does not give the reasons for this decision. But the conciliar debates indicate that the Fathers wished to make of the permanent diaconate an order which would unite the sacred hierarchy and the secular life of laypeople more closely together.

Further motivations emerge from *Ad Gentes* (no. 16). Here it can be seen that the Council was not re-establishing the permanent diaconate merely because of a shortage of priests. There were already men who were in fact exercising the diaconal ministry. By the imposition of hands these were "to be

201 K. Rahner, "L'Enseignement de Vatican II sur le diaconat et sa restauration," in Winninger and Congar, *Le Diacre dans l'Église*, 221.

202 Cf. A. Borras and B. Pottier, *La grâce du diaconat* (Brussels, 1998), 22-40.

strengthened and more closely associated with the altar" (*corroborari et altari arctius conjungi*). The sacramental grace of the diaconate would render them capable of exercising their ministry more effectively. Here Vatican II was not motivated only by current pastoral difficulties, but by the need to recognize the existence of the diaconal ministry in certain communities. It desired to confirm by sacramental grace those who were already exercising the diaconal ministry, or showing forth its charism.

From *Lumen Gentium* to *Ad Gentes*, there was a shift in the Council's intentions. These intentions can be of great importance in understanding not only the diaconate but the true nature of the sacrament. Three main reasons can be discerned in favor of the restoration of the permanent diaconate. In the first place, the restoration of the diaconate as a proper degree of Holy Orders enabled the constitutive elements of the sacred hierarchy willed by God to be recognized. Secondly, it was a response to the need to guarantee indispensable pastoral care to communities which had been deprived of this because of a shortage of priests. Finally, it was a confirmation, a reinforcement and a more complete incorporation into the ministry of the Church of those who were already de facto exercising the ministry of deacons.

II. The Form of the Permanent Diaconate Restored by Vatican II

Six of the documents promulgated by Vatican II contain some teachings concerning the diaconate: *Lumen Gentium*, *Ad Gentes*, *Dei Verbum*, *Sacrosanctum Concilium*, *Orientalium Ecclesiarum* and *Christus Dominus*. The following paragraphs will cover the key elements of the teaching of Vatican II in order to identify more precisely the form or "figure" of the permanent diaconate which has been restored.

1. Vatican II recognized the diaconate as one of the sacred Orders. *Lumen Gentium* (no. 29a), established that deacons belong to the lowest degree of the hierarchy (*in gradu inferiori hierarchiae sistunt diaconi*). They are "sustained by sacramental grace" (*gratia sacramentali roborati*) and receive the imposition of hands *non ad sacerdotium, sed ad ministerium*. But this important expression, drawn from the *Statuta Ecclesiae Antiqua*, and a variation on a still more

ancient expression from the *Traditio Apostolica* of Hippolytus, is not explained anywhere in the conciliar documents.[203]

Vatican II taught that Christ instituted the sacred ministries for the nurturing and constant growth of the People of God. Those ministers are endowed with a sacred power to serve the Body of Christ, so that all may arrive at salvation (LG, no. 18a). Like the other sacred ministers, deacons should therefore consecrate themselves to the growth of the Church and the pursuit of its plan of salvation.

Within the body of ministers, bishops, who possess the fullness of the priesthood, have taken up the service of the community, presiding in place of God over the flock as teachers, priests and shepherds. Deacons, with the priests, help the bishops in their ministry (LG, no. 20c). Belonging to the lowest order of the ministry, deacons grow in holiness through the faithful fulfillment of their ministry as a share in the mission of Christ the Supreme Priest. "*Missionis autem et gratiae supremi Sacerdotis peculiari modo participes sunt inferioris quoque ordinis ministri, imprimis Diaconi, qui mysteriis Christi et ecclesiae servientes*" (LG, no. 41d). Although they occupy different ranks within the hierarchy, all three orders deserve to be called ministers of salvation (AG, no. 16a), exercising one single ecclesiastical ministry in the hierarchical communion. Strictly speaking deacons belong to the mission of Christ, but not to that of the bishop or to that of the priest. However, the specific ways of exercising this participation are determined by the demands of the communion within the hierarchy. Far from degrading the orders of priest and deacon within the hierarchy, hierarchical communion situates them within the single mission of Christ, shared in by the different orders in different degrees.

2. The functions assigned to deacons by the Council also provide indications concerning the way it envisaged the diaconal order. It is good to remember that the basic function of all the sacred ministers, according to Vatican II, is to nurture the People of God and lead them to salvation. Thus *Lumen Gentium* (no. 29b), declared that the permanent diaconate can be re-established if the competent authorities decide that it is opportune to choose deacons, even from among married men, *pro cura animarum*. All the tasks which deacons are authorized to

203 Cf. Kerkvoorde, "Esquisse d'une Théologie du diaconat," in Winninger and Congar, *Le Diacre dans l'Église*, 157-71.

fulfill are at the service of the basic duty of building up the Church and taking care of the faithful.

As for their specific tasks, *Lumen Gentium* (no. 29a), presented the service which the deacon renders to the People of God in terms of the triple ministry of the liturgy, the word and charity. The particular tasks of the deacon are seen as falling within the framework of one or other of these ministries. The ministry of the liturgy, or sanctification, is developed at length in *Lumen Gentium.* It includes the faculty of administering baptism solemnly (cf. SC, no. 68), of being custodian and dispenser of the Eucharist, assisting at and blessing weddings in the name of the Church, bringing Viaticum to the dying, presiding over the worship and prayer of the faithful, administering sacramentals, and finally officiating at funeral and burial services. The function of teaching includes reading the Sacred Scripture to the faithful, and instructing and exhorting the people. *Dei Verbum* (no. 25a) and *Sacrosanctum Concilium* (no. 35) include deacons among those who are officially engaged in the ministry of the word. The ministry of "government" is not mentioned as such, but rather termed the ministry of charity. Administration is at least mentioned.

It is clear that the function of the deacon as described by *Lumen Gentium* is above all liturgical and sacramental. Questions inevitably arise about the specific notion of diaconal ordination *non ad sacerdotium sed ad ministerium.* The form of the diaconal ministry based on *Lumen Gentium* invites a deeper exploration of the meaning of *sacerdotium* and *ministerium.*

Ad Gentes gave a different configuration to the permanent diaconate, as can be seen by looking at the functions it assigned to it, probably because it sprang from the experience of mission territories. In the first place, *Ad Gentes* contained little about the liturgical ministry of the deacon. Preaching the word of God was mentioned in connection with catechism teaching. What is called the ministry of "government" received broader treatment in *Ad Gentes* (no. 16f). Deacons preside over scattered Christian communities in the name of the parish priest and the bishop. They also practice charity in social or relief work.

Vatican II showed some hesitation in its description of the permanent diaconate which it was restoring. In the more doctrinal perspective of *Lumen Gentium,* it tended to place the emphasis on the liturgical image of the deacon and his ministry of sanctification. In the missionary perspective of *Ad Gentes,* the focus shifted towards the administrative, charitable aspect of the figure of the deacon, and his ministry of government. It is however interesting to note that nowhere did the Council claim that the form of the permanent diaconate which it was proposing was a restoration of a previous form. This explains why certain theologians avoid the term "restoration," because it might easily suggest something being brought back to its original state. But Vatican II never aimed to do that. What it re-established was *the principle of the permanent exercise of the diaconate*, and not one particular form which the diaconate had taken in the past."[204] Having established the possibility of re-establishing the permanent diaconate, the Council seemed open to the kind of form it might take in the future, in function of pastoral needs and ecclesial practice, but always in fidelity to Tradition. Vatican II could not be expected to provide a clearly defined picture of the permanent diaconate, because of the gap that existed in the pastoral life of those times, unlike the case of the episcopate or the priesthood. The most it could do was to open the possibility of reinstalling the diaconate as a proper, permanent degree in the hierarchy and as a stable way of life, give some general theological principles even though they might appear timid, and establish some general norms of practice. Beyond that it could do no more than wait for the contemporary form of the permanent diaconate to develop. Finally, the apparent indecision and hesitancy of the Council might serve as an invitation to the Church to continue working to discern the type of ministry appropriate to the diaconate through ecclesial practice, canonical legislation, and theological reflection.[205]

Chapter VI

The Reality of the Permanent Diaconate Today

More than thirty-five years after Vatican II, what is the reality of the permanent diaconate?

To examine the available statistics is to realize the huge disparity which exists in the distribution of deacons around the world. Out of a total of 25,122 deacons in 1998,[206] North America alone accounts for 12,801, i.e., just over

---

204 Borras and Pottier, *La grâce du diaconat*, 20.

205 Cf. Kerkvoorde, "*Esquisse d'une Théologie du diaconat*," 155-56.

206 These figures and the analysis of them were kindly supplied to us in the course of the fall 1999 session of the Commission, by Prof. Enrico Nenna, Ufficio centrale statistica della Chiesa, Segretaria di Stato.

half (50.9 percent), while Europe has 7,864 (31.3 percent): this means a total of 20,665 deacons (82.2 percent) in the industrialized countries of the northern hemisphere. The remaining 17.8 percent are distributed as follows: South America 2,370 (9.4 percent); Central America and the Caribbean 1,387 (5.5 percent); Africa 307 (1.22 percent); Asia 219 (0.87 percent). Finally comes Australasia and the Pacific, with 174 deacons, or 0.69 percent of the total.[207]

One very striking point is that it is in the advanced industrialized countries of the North[208] that the diaconate has developed particularly. Now that was not at all what the Council Fathers envisaged when they asked for a "reactivation" of the permanent diaconate. They expected, rather, that there would be a rapid increase among the young Churches of Africa and Asia, where pastoral work relied on a large number of lay catechists.[209] But they had laid down that it would pertain "to the competent territorial bodies of bishops, of one kind or another, with the approval of the Supreme Pontiff, to decide whether and where it [was] opportune for such deacons to be established for the care of souls" (LG, no. 29b). It is therefore unsurprising that the diaconate did not develop uniformly throughout the Church, since the evaluation of the needs of the People of God made by the different episcopates could vary according to the specific circumstances of the Churches and their modes of organization.

What these statistics enable us to see is that there were two very different situations to be dealt with. On the one hand, after the Council most of the Churches in Western Europe and North America were faced with a steep reduction in the numbers of priests, and had to undertake a major reorganization of ministries. On the other hand, the Churches which were mainly in former mission territories had long since adopted a structure which relied on the commitment of large numbers of laypeople, the catechists.

---

207 If a comparison is made between the numbers of priests and deacons in the different continents, the same differences are observable as before. While in America as a whole there are 7.4 priests per deacon (mainly because of the high number of deacons in North America), in Asia there are 336 priests to one deacon. In Africa there are 87 priests per permanent deacon, in Europe 27, and in Australasia and the Pacific, 31. The relative weight of the deacons within the ordained ministry therefore varies greatly from one place to another.

208 Another source of information gives a list of countries where there are the greatest numbers of permanent deacons: United States (11,589), Germany (1,918), Italy (1,845), France (1,222), Canada (824), Brazil (826).

209 Cf. H. Legrand, "Le diaconat dans sa relation à la théologie de l'Église et aux ministères: Réception et devenir du diaconate depuis Vatican II", in A. Haquin and P. Weber, eds., *Diaconate, 21e siècle* (Brussels, Paris, and Montreal, 1997), 13 and 14.

These two typical situations need to be studied separately, without losing sight of the fact that many variations exist; and also that in both cases, a certain number of bishops may have wanted to institute the permanent diaconate in their dioceses not so much for pastoral reasons as from a theological motive which had also been invoked by Vatican II: to enable the ordained ministry to be expressed better, through the three degrees traditionally recognized.

First Typical Situation: Churches with a Low Number of Deacons

Many Churches, then, did not feel the need to develop the permanent diaconate. These were mainly Churches which had long since been accustomed to function with a restricted number of priests, and to rely on the commitment of a very large number of laypeople, mainly as catechists. The case of Africa is an example in this regard.[210] It is undoubtedly matched by the experience of other young Churches.

It will be remembered that in the 1950s many missionaries and bishops in Africa had asked for the reactivation of the diaconate while thinking particularly of the catechists in mission countries. They saw it as a way of responding to the liturgical demands of the missions and the shortage of priests. These new deacons would thus be able to take care of the liturgy in the branch Churches, lead the Sunday gatherings in the absence of the missionary, officiate at funerals, assist at weddings, look after catechesis and the proclamation of the Word of God, take charge of *caritas* and the Church administration, confer certain sacraments, and so on.[211] This perspective was what many Council Fathers had in mind at Vatican II when, in *Ad Gentes*, the Council referred to "the ranks of men and women catechists, well deserving of missionary work to the nations."[212]

But in the years that followed the Council, the African bishops displayed considerable reservations and did not undertake the road to the reactivation of the diaconate. A participant at the eighth Kinshasa theological week held in 1973 noted that the proposal for a restoration of the permanent diaconate in Africa raised much more opposition than enthusiasm. The objections raised

210 For the following points, cf. J. Kabasu Bamba, "Diacres permanents ou catéchistes au Congo-Kinshasa?" (PhD thesis, University of Ottawa, 1999), 304 pages.

211 The author is here quoting Msgr. W. Van Bekkum, Mgr. Eugène D'Souza (India), Msgr. J. F. Cornelis (Élizabethville) and, at the time of the preparation of the Council, the (mostly European) Ordinaries of Congo and Rwanda, Bamba, *op. cit.*, 190.

212 Decree on the Missionary Activity of the Church, 17a. This calls to mind the interventions of Msgr. B. Yago and Mgr. Paul Yü Pin referred to in the previous chapter.

would be widely repeated elsewhere. They had to do with deacons' state in life, the financial situation of the young Churches, the consequences on vocations to the actual priesthood, confusion and uncertainty about the nature of the diaconal vocation, the clericization of laypeople who were committed to the apostolate, the conservatism and lack of critical spirit of certain candidates, the marriage of clergy and the depreciation of celibacy, and the reaction of faithful who would content themselves with the diaconate as a sort of half-measure.[213]

The Congolese bishops therefore adopted an attitude of caution. Why should catechists be ordained as deacons if no new power was being given to them? They decided that it would be preferable to embark on a revaluation of the lay state, and work to renew the role of catechists. Other countries would appeal for a greater participation of laypeople as "servants of the Word" or activity leaders of small communities. That could be done all the better now that the Council had so strongly highlighted the vocation of all the baptized to share in the Church's mission.

An often-heard objection, therefore, was "What can a deacon do that a layman can't?" It has to be recognized that the sacramental link which joins deacons to their bishop creates special, lifelong obligations for the bishop which can be difficult to manage, especially in the case of married deacons.[214] Furthermore, it is normally a question of Churches in which the place of the ordained ministry is well-defined and retains its full meaning, even though priests may be few in number.

That said, it is nevertheless worth mentioning initiatives such as that of the bishop of the Indian diocese of San Cristobal (Mexico), Msgr. Ruiz. Faced with the fact that his diocese had never succeeded in producing vocations to the priesthood among the indigenous Indians, he decided to undertake an intensive promotion of the permanent diaconate. Accordingly he put in place a long process of formation designed to lead married Amerindian men to the diaconate.

---

213 Cf. Bamba, *op. cit.*, 195, which has a reference to M. Singleton, "Les nouvelles formes de ministère en Afrique," *Pro Mundi Vita* 50 (1974): 33.

214 The archbishop of Santiago de Chile reported the objections of certain priests as follows: "They say for example that the diaconate is an unnecessary commitment, since its functions can be fulfilled by laymen and laywomen for given periods of time; if it works, their mandate is prolonged, and if not, it is not renewed." Msgr. C. Oviedo Cavada, "La promoción del diaconado permanente," *Iglesia de Santiago* (Chile), no. 24 (September 1992): 25.

These would thus be sacramentally associated to his episcopal ministry and form the beginnings of an indigenous Church.[215]

Second Typical Situation: Churches Where the Diaconate Is More Developed

The second typical situation is that of the Churches where the diaconate has undergone its greatest expansion. These are the Churches which have had to face a considerable drop in the number of priests: the United States, Canada, Germany, Italy, France, etc. The need to set about a reorganization of pastoral duties to respond to the needs of Christian communities which were accustomed to a wide range of services, and the obligation of finding new collaborators, all helped to stimulate the emergence of new ministries and an increase in the number of laypeople working full-time on parish or diocesan pastoral work.[216] This also favored the expansion of the diaconate. But at the same time it exercised a very strong pressure on the kind of tasks which were entrusted to deacons. Tasks which for a long time had been undertaken by priests without any problem because of their large numbers, now had to be given to other collaborators, some ordained (the deacons), others not ordained (lay pastoral officials). Because of this background the diaconate often came to be seen as a *supply ministry for the priesthood.*

This dynamic is reflected in the results of a broad study undertaken in the United States,[217] which is clearly representative of the situation existing in many countries. The study shows that deacons are mainly doing what priests used to do unaided before the restoration of the diaconate. They exercise their ministry in the parish where they live, and there they fulfill mainly liturgical and sacramental functions. Their parish priests find them particularly useful in sacramental activities such as baptisms, weddings and liturgical acts. The same applies to the care of the sick and homilies. The field in which they take least part is in the ministry to prisoners and the promotion of civil rights and human rights. Lay leaders, for their part, consider that deacons are most successful in more familiar and traditional roles such as the liturgy and the administration of the

215 See a long text published by the Diocese of San Cristobal de las Casas, *Directorio diocesano para el diaconado indigena permanente* (1999), 172 pages.

216 Depending on the country, these collaborators received different names: "pastoral officials," "pastoral workers or leaders," "pastoral auxiliaries," "pastoral lay agents," "parish auxiliaries," "parish assistants," "pastoral assistants" (*Pastoralassistenten und Pastoralassistentinnen*), etc. Cf. A. Borras, *Des laïcs en responsabilité pastorale?* (Paris, 1998).

217 NCCB, "National Study of the Diaconate, Summary Report," *Origins* 25, no. 30 (January 18, 1996).

sacraments. And it is predicted that their numbers will increase because of the reduction in the numbers of priests. Thus, as they accomplish tasks traditionally fulfilled by priests, there may be a danger of deacons being seen as "incomplete priests" or else as "more advanced laymen." The danger is the greater since the first generations of deacons have received much less detailed theological training than that of priests or that of pastoral officials.

A similar development is also to be found in other areas which likewise suffer from a marked reduction in the numbers of priests.[218] It is the result of an effort to respond to the real needs of the People of God. It enables these Churches to guarantee a wider presence of the ordained ministry within Christian communities which are in danger of losing sight of the real meaning of that ministry. Together with the bishop and the priest, the deacon will remind them that it is Christ who is the foundation of the Church in every place and that through the Spirit he is still acting in the Church today.

In this context, however, the identity of the deacon tends to take the figure of the priest as a reference point; the deacon is perceived as the person who helps or replaces the priest in activities which previously he carried out in person. Many consider this development to be problematical, because it makes it more difficult for the diaconal ministry to evolve an identity of its own.[219] For this reason, here and there efforts are made to modify this development by identifying charisms which might be those proper to the diaconate, and tasks which might suitably belong primarily to the diaconate.

Lines of Development

For their part, the most recent texts from the Roman Congregations list the tasks which can be entrusted to deacons, and group them under the three recognized diakonias, namely those of the liturgy, the word and charity.[220] Even when it is considered that one or other of these diakonias could take up the greater part of a deacon's activity, it is insisted on that the three diakonias taken together "represent a unity in the service of the divine plan of Redemption: the

---

218 See for example Maskens, "Un enquête sur les diacres francophones de Belgique," in Haquin and Weber, *Diaconat, 21e siècle*, 217-32.

219 Thus, B. Sesboüé, "Quelle est l'identité ministérielle du diacre?" in *L'Église à venir* (Paris, 1999), 255-57.

220 See for example the text of the Congregation for the Clergy, *Directorium pro ministerio et vita diaconarum permanentium*, February 22, 1998, published as *Directory for the Ministry and Life of Permanent Deacons*, in *The Permanent Diaconate* (London, 1998), 88.

ministry of the word leads to ministry at the altar, which in turn prompts the transformation of life by the liturgy, resulting in charity."[221] But it is recognized that in these tasks taken all together, "the service of charity"[222] is to be seen as particularly characteristic of the deacons' ministry.

In many regions, then, efforts have been made to identify a certain number of tasks for deacons which can be connected in one way or another to the "service of charity." Particular advantage may be taken of the fact that most of them are married men, earning their own living, immersed in the world of work, and, together with their wives, contributing their own life experience.[223]

For example, a text by the bishops of France published in 1970 expressed their preference "for deacons who, in daily contact with others through their family and work situation, can witness with their whole lives to the service that the People of God should render to men, following Christ's example. . . . Permanent deacons will thus share in their own special way in the efforts of the hierarchical Church to go out to meet unbelief and poverty, and to be more fully present in the world. They will keep all previous commitments which are compatible with the diaconal ministry."[224] The mission entrusted to them, therefore, may often be situated "in the sphere of work and association or trade-union life (or even political life, particularly at the level of local government). Their mission is directed toward the care of the poor and marginalized in such places, but also in their own district and their parish, starting with home and family life."[225]

---

221 Ibid., 39, 103. The text adds in the next paragraph: "It is important that deacons fully exercise their ministry, in preaching, in the liturgy and in charity, to the extent that circumstances permit. They should not be relegated to marginal duties, be made merely to act as substitutes, nor discharge duties normally entrusted to non-ordained members of the faithful."

222 See Congregation for Catholic Education, *Basic Norms for the Formation of Permanent Deacons*, 9: "Finally the *munus regendi* is exercised in devotion to works of charity and assistance and in motivating communities or sectors of the ecclesial life, especially in what has to do with charity. *This is the ministry which is most characteristic of the deacon*" (emphasis added). In *Permanent Diaconate*, 27.

223 "It is not the wife who is ordained and nevertheless the mission entrusted to the deacon obliges the couple to redefine themselves in some way, in function of this ministry," M. Cacouet and B. Viole, *Les diâcres*, quoted in a study document on the role of the deacon's wife (Quebec, 1993). For this reason, in many countries the wife joins her husband for the initial training period, and takes part in continued training activities with him.

224 Note of the Episcopal Commission for the Clergy, cited by F. Deniau, "Mille diâcres en France," *Études* 383, no. 5 (1995): 526.

225 Ibid., 527. This direction taken by the bishops was confirmed in 1996 during their gathering at Lourdes, where they expressed their desire that "the image given by deacons should not be that of supplying for priests, but of communion with them in the exercise of the sacrament of Holy Orders." "Points d'attention," *Documentation Catholique*, no. 2149 (1996): 1012-13.

Hence in various places particular efforts have been made to make the diaconate a "threshold ministry," which aims to look after "the frontier Church": work in surroundings where the priest is not present, and also with one-parent families, couples, prisoners, young people, drug addicts, AIDS victims, the elderly, disadvantaged groups, etc. The tasks of deacons may be oriented toward activities in the social, charitable or administrative spheres, without however neglecting the necessary link with liturgical and teaching duties. In Latin America, the focus is placed upon families who proclaim the Gospel in the midst of zones of conflict; a presence in extreme situations such as drugs, prostitution and urban violence; an active presence in the sector of education, the world of work and the professional sphere; a greater presence in densely populated zones and likewise in the countryside; and finally, leadership given in small communities.[226] Very often, efforts are directed toward ensuring that these deacons receive progressively more thorough theological and spiritual formation.

The outcome of all this very diverse experience makes it clear that it is not possible to characterize the totality of the diaconal ministry by delineating tasks which belong exclusively to deacons because of ecclesial tradition—which is far from clear—or through a rigid distribution of tasks among the different ministers.[227] A text of Vatican II seems to have intuited this, since one of the reasons it invoked for re-establishing the diaconate "as a permanent state of life" was to strengthen, "by the imposition of hands which has come down from the Apostles" and to unite more closely to the altar, "men who *accomplish a truly diaconal ministry*, either by preaching the word of God, or by governing far-off Christian communities in the name of the parish priest and bishop, or by exercising charity in social or charitable works" (AG, no. 16f.).[228] All of this leads certain people to propose that in order to define the character of the diaconate it is necessary to look rather at the *being* of the deacon. "It is in the aspect *of being* that the specificity of the permanent diaconate is to be sought, and not

226 J. G. Mesa Angulo, O.P., "Aportes para visualizar un horizonte pastoral para el diaconado permanente en América Latina, hacia el tercer milenio," in Consejo Episcopal Latinoamericano (CELAM), "I Congreso de diaconado permanente," Lima, August 1998, working document.

227 A certain number of tasks, of course, are reserved to deacons by canon law, but they do not account for the whole of the deacon's activity.

228 Emphasis added.

in the aspect of *doing*. It is what they *are* that gives its true meaning to what they do."[229]

It is in this perspective of configuration to Christ the Servant that theological and pastoral studies on the lines of development of the permanent diaconate are currently being made. This theological given is seen as providing the opportunity for an in-depth spiritual reflection which is particularly appropriate for the present era. It can also provide guidance to pastors in their choice of the tasks to entrust to deacons. In that case, the tasks selected for them will preferably be such as to highlight this particular characteristic of the diaconate. These will naturally include service to the poor and oppressed; a service which is not limited to mere assistance but which, following Christ's own example, will be a sharing of life with the poor in order to journey with them toward their total liberation.[230] Their tasks will include service to those who are on the threshold of the Church and who need to be led to the Eucharist. In many countries this perspective is prominent in the minds of those responsible for deacons' formation, and a spirituality and a pastoral practice of the "service of charity" can be seen to develop in the deacons themselves. The true figure of the deacon should thus emerge little by little in the performance of various ministries, and be manifest through a definite way of doing—in the spirit of service—what all are called to do, but also through a pronounced dedication to particular tasks or functions which make Christ the Servant ever more visible. However, it seems to be an established fact that the development of the diaconal ministry must always be thought of in relation to the real needs of the Christian community. Certain Churches will not feel the need to develop it very widely. Other Churches will, on occasions, require the deacons to perform tasks other than those listed above; here one could think of those tasks which contribute to pastoral leadership in parishes and small Christian communities. The essential objective for pastors, inspired by St. Paul, must always be that of seeing that the faithful are equipped "for the work of ministry, for building up the body of Christ, until all of us come to the unity of the faith and of the knowledge of the Son of God, to maturity, to the measure of the full stature of Christ" (Eph 4:12-13). At the service of the

229 R. Page, *Diaconat permanent et diversité des ministères: Perspectives du droit canonique* (Montreal, 1988), 61.

230 V. Gerardi, "El diaconado en la Iglesia," in CELAM, "I Congreso," p. 8, referring to the First International Congress held in Turin in 1977.

bishop and his presbyterium, the deacon should, in the way which is proper to him, go wherever pastoral care requires him to be.

Chapter VII

Theological Approach to the Diaconate in the Wake of Vatican II

A theological approach to the diaconate in the wake of Vatican II should start from the Council texts, examine how they were received and how they were later enlarged upon in the documents of the Magisterium, take account of the fact that the restoration of the diaconate was accomplished very unevenly in the post-Conciliar period, and above all pay special attention to the doctrinal fluctuations which have closely shadowed the various pastoral suggestions. Today there are numerous very different aspects which require an effort at doctrinal clarification. This chapter will attempt to contribute to these efforts at clarification as follows. First it will pinpoint the roots and reasons which make the theological and ecclesial identity of the diaconate (both permanent and transitory) into a real *quaestio disputata* in certain respects. Then it will outline a theology of the diaconal ministry which may serve as a firm common basis to inspire the fruitful re-creation of the diaconate in Christian communities.

I. The Texts of Vatican II and the Post-Conciliar Magisterium

In the Council texts which mention the diaconate specifically (cf. SC, no. 35; LG, nos. 20, 28, 29, 41; OE, no. 17; CD, no. 15; DV, no. 25; AG, nos. 15, 16), Vatican II did not aim to offer a dogmatic decision on any of the questions debated in the course of the Council, nor to lay down a strict doctrinal system. Its true interest was in opening a path to the restoration of the permanent diaconate which could be put into effect in a plurality of ways. This is perhaps why, in the texts taken as a whole, certain fluctuations can be seen in the theology, depending on the place or context in which the diaconate is mentioned. Both with reference to pastoral priorities and in what concerns objective doctrinal difficulties, the Council texts show a diversity of theological nuances which it is quite hard to harmonize.

After the Council the theme of the diaconate was developed or referred to in other documents of the post-Conciliar Magisterium: Paul VI's *Motu Proprio Sacrum diaconatus ordinem* (1967); the Apostolic Constitution *Pontificalis romani recognitio* (1968); Paul VI's *Motu Proprio Ad pascendum* (1972); the new *Codex luris Canonici* (1983); and the *Catechismus Catholicae Ecclesiae* (1992, 1997).[231] These new documents develop the basic elements of Vatican II and sometimes add important theological, ecclesial or pastoral clarifications; but they do not all speak from the same perspective, nor at the same doctrinal level.[232] For this reason, in order to attempt a theological approach in the wake of Vatican II, it is appropriate to bear in mind the possible relation between the doctrinal fluctuations (in Vatican II texts) and the diversity of theological approaches perceptible in post-Conciliar proposals about the diaconate.

II. Implications of the Sacramentality of the Diaconate

As stated above (cf. Chapter IV), the most reliable doctrine and that most in accord with ecclesial practice is that which holds that the diaconate is a sacrament. If its sacramentality were denied the diaconate would simply represent a form of ministry rooted in baptism; it would take on a purely functional character, and the Church would possess a wide faculty of decision-making with regard to restoring or suppressing it, and to its specific configuration. Whatever the context, the Church would have a much greater freedom of action than is granted to her over the sacraments instituted by Christ.[233] A denial of the sacramentality of the diaconate would dissipate the main reasons why the diaconate is a theologically disputed question. But to make such a denial would be to diverge from the path marked out by Vatican II. Hence it is with the sacramentality of

231 Cf. AAS 59 (1967): 697-704; AAS 60 (1968): 369-73; AAS 64 (1973): 534-40; *Codex Iuris Canonici* (Vatican City, 1983); *Catechismus Catholicae Ecclesiae* (CCE) (Vatican City, 1997). [English ed.: *Catechism of the Catholic Church*.]

232 This is the case of two recent guidance documents: Congregatio de Institutione Catholica/Congregatio pro Clericis, *Ratio fundamental institutionis diaconorum permanentium* and *Directorium pro ministerio et vita diaconorum permanentium* (Vatican City, 1998). According to Pio Cardinal Laghi, the *Ratio fundamentalis* is a document "di ordine eminentemente pedagogico e non dottrinale" and, according to Dario Cardinal Castrillon, the *Directorium* "intende presentare linee pratiche." *L'Osservatore Romano*, March 11, 1998, pp. 6-7.

233 "Christus, 'sedens ad dexteram Patris' et Spiritum Sanctum in Suum effundens corpus, quod est Ecclesia, iam operatur per sacramenta a Se instituta ad Suam gratiam communicandam. . . . Efficaciter gratiam efficiunt quam significant propter Christi actionem et per Spiritus Sancti virtutem," CCE 1084.

the diaconate as a starting point that the other questions concerning the theology of the diaconate should be dealt with.

1. The Diaconate as Rooted in Christ

As a sacrament, the diaconate must ultimately be rooted in Christ. The Church, herself rooted in the free gift of the Blessed Trinity, has no capacity to create sacraments or to confer on them their salvific effectiveness.[234] In order to affirm that the diaconate is a sacrament, it is theologically necessary to state that it is rooted in Christ. Moreover, this fact enables us to understand the various theological attempts to link the diaconate directly to Christ himself (whether in regard to the mission of the Apostles,[235] or to the washing of the feet at the Last Supper[236]). But that does not imply that it is necessary to maintain that Christ himself "instituted" the diaconate directly as a degree of the sacrament. The Church played a decisive role in its specific historical establishment. That fact was implicitly recognized in the opinion (a minority one today) which identified the institution of the Seven (cf. Acts 6:1-6) with the first deacons.[237] This has emerged clearly from the exegetical and theological studies on the complex of historical developments and the progressive differentiation of ministries

234 "Sunt efficacia quia in eis Ipse Christus operatur: Ipse est qui baptizat, Ipse est qui in Suis agit sacramentis ut gratiam communicet quam sacramentum significat. . . . Hic est sensus affirmationis Ecclesiae: sacramenta agunt ex opere operato . . . , i.e., virtute salvifici operis Christi, semel pro semper adimpleti," CCE 1127f.

235 Cf. CCJB 1536: "Ordo est sacramentum per quod missio a Christo Ipsius Apostolis concredita exerceri pergit in Ecclesia usque ad finem temporum: est igitur ministerii apostolici sacramentum. Tres implicat gradus: Episcopatum, presbyteratum et diaconatum."

236 For the application of the passage about the washing of the feet to deacons, cf. *Didascalia* 16, 13 (trans. E. Nau [Paris, 1912], 135f.) and H. Wasserschleben, *Die irische Canonensammlung* (Leipzig, 1885), 26: "Diaconus [fuit] Christus, quando lavit pedes discipulorum": cf. K. Rahner and H. Vorgrimmler, *Diaconia in Christo* (Freiburg, 1962), 104. Recently, W. Kasper proposed seeing in the washing of the feet and in the words of Jesus at John 13:15 "die Stiftung des Diakonats," "Der Diakon in ekklesiologischer Sicht angesichts der gegenwärtigen Herausforderungen in Kirche und Gesellschaft" in *Diakonia* 32/3-4 (1997): 22. In reality it is the whole of the passage at Mark 10:43-45 that *Didascalia* 3, 13 cites in relation to deacons. For his part, St. Ignatius of Antioch considers that deacons were entrusted with "the service of Jesus Christ" (*Magn.* 6, 1) and St. Polycarp exhorts them to walk in the truth of the Lord, who became the "diakonos" of all (*Phil.* 5, 2).

237 Current exegetical debate on the consideration of Acts 6:1-6 as the origin of the diaconate goes back to the patristic texts: St. Irenaeus (second century), *Adv. haer.* 1, 26, 3; 3, 12, 10 sees the ordination of the "Seven" as the beginning of the diaconate; St. John Chrysostom (circa 400), *In Acta Apost.* 14, 3 (PG 60, HSf.) does not consider the "Seven" to be deacons, although he does interpret their post as an ordination and a share in the apostolic mission. This second opinion was adopted by the synod in Trullo (692), a synod which has the status of an ecumenical council for the Orthodox Church; cf. Concilium Quinisextum, c. 16 (Mansi, 11:949; ed. Joannou, 1/1, 132-34).

and charisms, finally arriving at the tripartite structure of bishop, priest and deacon.[238] The cautious language used by Trent ("*divina ordinatione*") and Vatican II ("*divinitus institutum . . . iam ab antiquo*")[239] reflects the impossibility of totally identifying Christ's and the Church's activity with relation to the sacraments, and also reflects the complexity of the historical facts.

2. The Sacramental "Character" of the Diaconate and Its "Configuration" with Christ

Vatican II makes no explicit statement about the sacramental character of the diaconate; however, the post-Conciliar documents do. These speak of the "indelible character" linked to the stable condition of service (*Sacrum Diaconatus*, 1967) or of an imprint which cannot be removed and which configures the deacon to Christ, who made himself the "deacon" or servant of all (CCB, 1997).[240] The doctrine of the diaconal "character" is consistent with the sacramentality of the diaconate and is a specific application to it of what Trent (1563) said of the sacrament of Holy Orders as a whole.[241] It rests on the witness of theological tradition.[242] It corroborates God's fidelity to his gifts, and implies the unrepeatable nature of the sacrament and lasting stability in

---

238 The differentiation into three grades or degrees appears clearly in the post-Apostolic period, first perhaps with St. Ignatius of Antioch's *Ad Trail.* 3, 1. On this question, cf. E. Dassmann, *Ämter und Dienste in der frühchristlichen Gemeinden* (Bonn, 1994); E. Cattaneo, *I ministeri della Chiesa antica: Testi patristici dei primi tre secoli* (Milan, 1997).

239 "Sic ministerium ecclesiasticum divinitus institutum diversis ordinibus exercetur ab illis qui iam ab antiquo Episcopi, Presbyteri, Diaconi vocantur," LG, no. 28a, with references to Trent, DS 1765 ("in Ecclesiae ordinatissima dispositione plures et diversi essent ministrorum ordines . . . ab ipso Ecclesiae initio") and DS 1776 ("hierarchiam, divina ordinatione institutam, quae constat ex episcopis, presbyteris et ministris").

240 "Non tamquam merus ad sacerdotium gradus est existimandus, sed indelebile suo charactere ac praecipua sua gratia insignis ita locupletatur, ut qui ad ipsum vocentur, ii mysteriis Christi et Ecclesiae stabiliter inservire possint," Paul VI, *Sacrum diaconatus*, AAS 59 (1967): 698. "Diaconi missionem et gratiam Christi, modo speciali, participant. Ordinis sacramentum eos signat *sigillo* ('charactere') quod nemo delere potest et quod eos configurat Christo qui factus est 'diaconus,' id est, omnium minister," CCE 1570. "Prout gradus Ordinis sacri, diaconatus characterem imprimit et specificam gratiam sacramentalem communicat. Character diaconalis est signum configurativum-distinctivum animae modo indelebili impressum," *Ratio fundamentalis*, 7. In the measure in which c. 1008 of the CIC also refers to the diaconate, its indelible character may also be considered to be stated there.

241 "Quoniam vero in sacramento ordinis, sicut et in baptismo et confirmatione, character imprimitur, qui nec deleri nec auferri potest: merito sancta Synodus damnat eorum sententiam, qui asserunt, Novi Testamenti sacerdotes temporariam tantummodo potestatem habere, et semel rite ordinatos iterum laicos effici posse, si verbi Dei ministerium non exerceant." Council of Trent, DS 1767.

242 Cf. St. Thomas, *In IV Sent*, d. 7, q. 2 ad 1; *STh* HI, q. 63, a. 3.

ecclesial service.[243] Finally, it confers upon the diaconate a theological solidity which cannot be dissolved into something purely functional. However, this doctrine does raise certain questions which demand further theological clarifications. For instance, *Lumen Gentium* (no. 10) lays down that the distinction between the common priesthood of the faithful and the ministerial priesthood is "*essentia, non gradu tantum*": in what sense should this be applied to the diaconate?[244] While maintaining the unity of the sacrament of Holy Orders, how should the particularity of the diaconal character be further clarified in its distinctive relation to the priestly character and the episcopal character? What resources should be used to differentiate symbolically the specific configuration with Christ of each of the three grades?

Vatican II does not use the vocabulary of configuration but instead employs sober expressions which include sacramentality.[245] It also speaks of a special share in the mission and grace of the Supreme Priest.[246] In the *Motu Proprio Ad Pascendum* (1972) the permanent deacon is considered a sign or sacrament of Christ himself.[247] The *Catechismus Catholicae Ecclesiae* (1997) does make use of the vocabulary of configuration, and links it to the doctrine of character.[248] All these texts therefore give evidence of a further development of the Conciliar texts, starting from the deacon's immediate relation with Christ by virtue of the sacrament of Holy Orders. It only remains to describe its precise scope.

---

243 Although it does not specifically mention the doctrine of "character," as regards the diaconate the *Directorium* states (no. 21): "Sacra Ordinatio, semel valide recepta, numquam evanescit. Amissio tamen status clericalis fit iuxta normas iure canonico statutas."

244 The *Directorium* (no. 28) speaks of the "essential difference" which exists between the ministry of the deacon at the altar and that of every other liturgical minister; however, it gives a reference not to LG, no. 10, but to LG, no. 29: "Constat eius diaconiam apud altare, quatenus a sacramento Ordinis effectam, essentialiter differre a quolibet ministerio liturgico, quod pastores committere possint christifidelibus non ordinatis. Ministerium liturgicum diaconi pariter differt ab ipso ministerio sacerdotali."

245 "Gratia sacramentali roborati," LG, no. 29a; "gratiam sacramentalem diaconatus," AG, no. 16f.

246 "Missionis autem et gratiae supremi Sacerdotis peculiari modo participes sunt inferioris quoque ordinis ministri, imprimis Diaconi, qui mysteriis Christi et Ecclesiae servientes," LG, no. 41d.

247 "Diaconatus permanens . . . signum vel sacramentum ipsius Christi Domini, qui non venit ministrari, sed ministrare," Paul VI, *Ad Pascendum*, AAS 54 (1972): 536.

248 In reference to LG, no. 41, and AG, no. 16, the CCE says (no. 1570): "Diaconi missionem et gratiam Christi, modo speciali, participant. Ordinis sacramentum eos signat *sigillo* ('charactere') quod nemo delere potest et quod eos configurat Christo qui factus est 'diaconus,' id est, omnium minister." Meanwhile the *Ratio* (nos. 5, 7) links this configuration to the out pouring of the Spirit and identifies it specifically by its assimilation to Christ as Servant of all: "Diaconatus confertur per peculiarem effusionem Spiritus (*ordinatio*), quae in recipientis persona specificam efficit configurationem cum Christo, Domino et Servo omnium . . . is (diaconus) enim, prout unici ministerii ecclesiastici particeps, est in Ecclesia specificum signum sacramentale Christi servi. . . . Character diaconalis est signum configurativum-distinctivum animae modo indelebili impressum, quod sacro ordine auctos configurat Christo."

3. Diaconal Action, "in Persona Christi (Capitis)"?

The technical expression "*in persona Christi (Capitis)*" is used in different ways in the texts of Vatican II. It is employed in reference to the episcopal ministry, considered either as a whole or in one of the functions proper to it;[249] particularly noticeable is its application to the Eucharistic ministry of the ministerial priesthood (presbyterate) as the maximum expression of this ministry,[250] because to preside at and to consecrate the Eucharist belongs to its exclusive competence.[251] The perspective is much wider in other texts, where the expression may embrace the whole ministerial activity of the priest as a personification

249 The sacramentality of the episcopate implies that "Episcopi, eminenti ac adspectabili modo, ipsius Christi Magistri, Pastoris et Pontificis partes sustineant et in Eius persona agant," LG, no. 21b; at other points analogous formulas are used such as: "Episcopi sententiam de fide et moribus nomine Christi prolatam," LG, no. 25; "potestas qua, nomine Christi personaliter funguntur," LG, no. 27; "munus in ipsius nomine et potestate docendi, sanctificandi et regendi," AA 2b; "oves suas in nomine Domini pascunt," CD lib.

250 In LG, no. 10b, on the subject of the essential difference between the common priesthood of the faithful and the ministerial priesthood, it is said of the ministerial priesthood that "potestate sacra qua gaudet, populum sacerdotalem efformat ac regit, sacrificium eucharisticum in persona Christi conficit illudque nomine totius populi Deo offert"; in turn, LG, no. 28a states of priests that "suum vero munus sacrum maxime exercent in eucharistico cultu vel synaxi, qua in persona Christi agentes . . . unicum sacrificium . . . repraesentant"; likewise PO, no. 13b, states that "praesertim in Sacrificio Missae, Presbyteri personam specialiter gerunt Christi."

251 The connection of "in persona Christi" with the exclusive competence of the priest to consecrate the Eucharist was underlined in the post-Conciliar documents: the synod of 1971 stated that "solus sacerdos in persona Christi agere valet ad praesidendum et perficiendum sacrificale convivium," *Ench. Vat.* 4, 1166; the letter of the Congregation for the Doctrine of the Faith, *Sacerdotium ministeriale*, 1983, stresses that "munus tam grave conficiendi mysterium eucharisticum adimplere valeant [episcopi et presbyteri] . . . ut ipsi . . . non communitatis mandato, sed agant in persona Christi," AAS 75 (1983): 1006; this is recalled in the 1983 CIC: "Minister, qui in persona Christi sacramentum Eucharistiae conficere valet, est solus sacerdos valide ordinatus," c. 900, 1.

of Christ the Head, or allude to other distinct specific functions.[252] However, in the Conciliar texts there is no question of applying this expression explicitly to the functions of the diaconal ministry. Nevertheless, such a mode of expression does emerge in the post-Conciliar documents.[253] That is currently a source of differences of opinion on the part of theologians (especially in what concerns the representation of Christ the "Head"), because of the diverse meaning which the expression has in the documents of the Magisterium and in theological propositions.

If it is applied to the sacrament of Holy Orders as a whole, as being a specific participation in the threefold *munus* of Christ, then it can be said that the deacon also acts "*in persona Christi (Capitis)*" (or other equivalent expressions of a specific "representing" of Christ in the diaconal ministry), since the diaconate constitutes one of the grades of this sacrament. Today, many theologians follow this line, which is consistent with the sacramentality of the diaconate,

252 "Presbyteri, unctione Spiritus Sancti, speciali charactere signantur et sic Christo Sacerdoti configurantur, ita ut in persona Christi Capitis agere valeant," PO, no. 2c; the equivalent expression in PO, no. 12a goes in the same direction: "omnis sacerdos, suo modo, ipsius Christi personam great." The priestly ministry as a whole is included in the references of AG, no. 39a ("Presbyteri personam Christi gerunt . . . in triplici sacro munere"), and LG, no. 37a ("illos, qui ratione sacri sui muneris personam Christi gerunt"); in SC, no. 33a, it is made more specific as a presiding at the celebration of the Eucharist: "Immo, preces a sacerdote, qui coetui in persona Christi praeest, . . . dicuntur." Post-Conciliar documents: in *Evangelii Nuntiandi* (EN), Paul VI applies the formula to the ministry of evangelization: "Cum Episcopis in ministerium evangelizationis consociantur . . . ii qui per sacerdotalem ordinationem personam Christi gerunt," EN 68, *Ench. Vat.* 5, 1683; John Paul II employs it when referring to the specific ministry of reconciliation in the sacrament of penance: "Sacerdos, Paenitentiae minister . . . agit 'in persona Christi,'" *Reconciliatio et Paenitentia* (1984), 29; according to *Pastores Dabo Vobis* (1992), the priest represents Christ the Head, Shepherd and Spouse of the Church: "connectuntur cum 'consecratione,' quae eorum propria est eosque ad Christum, Ecclesiae Caput et Pastorem configurat; vel cum 'missione' vel ministerio presbyterorum proprio, quod eos habiles efficit et instruit ut fiant 'Christi Sacerdotis aeterni viva instrumenta' et ad agendum provehit 'Ipsius Christi nomine et persona,'" 20; "Presbyter, per sacramentalem hanc consecrationem, configuratur Christo Iesu quatenus Capiti et Pastori Ecclesiae," 21; "Sacerdos ergo advocatur ut sit imago vivens Iesu Christi, Ecclesiae sponsi: remanet ipse quidem semper communitatis pars . . . , sed vi eiusdem configurationis ad Christum Caput et Pastorem, ipse presbyter positus est in eiusmodi relatione sponsali erga propriam communitatem," 22.

253 The 1983 CIC applies the formula to the whole of the sacrament of Holy Orders, and consequently to the diaconate as well: "Sacramento ordinis . . . consecrantur et deputantur ut, pro suo quisque gradu, in persona Christi Capitis munera docendi, sanctificandi et regendi adimplendi, Dei populum pascant. Ordines sunt episcopatus, presbyteratus et diaconatus," cc. 1008/9. An intervention by John Paul II includes the idea of personification, but applied to Christ the servant, cf. note 255 infra. The 1998 *Directorium* prefers the formula "in the name of Christ" to refer to the Eucharistic ministry of the deacon ("nomine ipsius Christi, inservit ad Ecclesiam participem reddendam fructuum sacrificii sui," 28) and in relation with the diakonia of charity ("Vi sacramenti Ordinis diaconus . . . munera pastoralia participat . . . quae participatio, utpote per sacramentum peracta, efficit ut diaconi Populum Dei inserviant nomine Christi," 37).

and is supported by some documents of the Magisterium and certain theological trends. By contrast, those who reserve the expression to the functions of the priest alone, especially those of presiding at and consecrating the Eucharist, do not apply it to the diaconate and find corroboration of this opinion in the latest edition of the CCE (1997).

In the final edition of number 875 of the CCE the expression "*in persona Christi Capitis*" is not applied to the diaconal functions of service.[254] In this case the capacity to act "*in persona Christi Capitis*" seems to be reserved to bishops and priests. Theological opinions are not unanimous on the question of whether this signifies a definitive exclusion or not. In a way, number 875 of the CCE is a return to the language of *Lumen Gentium* (no. 28a), *Presbyterorum Ordinis* (no. 2c, priestly ministry) and *Lumen Gentium* (no. 29a, triple *diakonia*). Furthermore, other texts from the CCE itself do seem to apply the expression to the whole of the sacrament of Holy Orders,[255] while recognizing a primordial role on the part of bishops and priests.[256] Thus there is a diversity of tendencies which are difficult to bring into harmony, and which are clearly reflected in the various theological understandings of the diaconate. And even if it is considered theologically sound to understand the diaconal ministry as an action "*in persona Christi (Capitis)*," it still has to be clarified what characterizes the diaconate's specific way (the "*specificum*") of rendering Christ present as distinct from that of the episcopal ministry and the priestly ministry.

4. *"In Persona Christi Servi" as the Specificity of the Diaconate?*

One way of doing this is to underline the aspect of "service" and see the specific characteristic, or a particularly distinctive element, of the diaconate, in the representation of Christ the "Servant." This course appears in the most recent

254 "Ab Eo [Christo] Episcopi et presbyteri missionem et facultatem ('sacram potestatem') agendi *in persona Christi Capitis* accipiunt, diaconi vero vim populo Dei serviendi in 'diaconia' liturgiae, verbi et caritatis," CCE 875.

255 "Per ordinationem recipitur capacitas agendi tamquam Christi legatus, Capitis Ecclesiae," CCE 1581; "sacramento ordinis, cuius munus est, nomine et in persona Christi Capitis, in communitate servire," CCE 1591; "In ecclesiali ministri ordinati servitio, Ipse Christus, Ecclesiae suae est praesens, quatenus Caput Sui corporis," CCE 1548.

256 "Per ministerium ordinatum, prasertim Episcoporum et presbyterorum, praesentia Christi, tamquam Capitis Ecclesiae, in communitate credentium, visibilis fit," CCE 1549.

documents[257] and in some theological essays. However, difficulties arise, not because of the central importance of the notion of service for every ordained minister, but because this is made the specific criterion of the diaconal ministry. Could "headship" and "service" in the representation of Christ be separated so as to make each of the two a principle of specific differentiation? Christ the Lord is at the same time the supreme Servant and the servant of all.[258] The ministries of the bishop[259] and the priest, precisely in their function of presiding and of representing Christ the Head, Shepherd and Spouse of his Church, also render Christ the Servant visible,[260] and require to be exercised as services. This is why it would seem problematic to aim to distinguish the diaconate through its exclusive representation of Christ as Servant. Given that service should be considered a characteristic common to every ordained minister,[261] the point in any case would be to see how in the diaconate it takes on predominant importance and particular solidity. To avoid disproportionate theological exchanges on this matter, it is appropriate to bear in mind simultaneously the unity of the person of Christ, the unity of the sacrament of order, and the symbolic character of the terms used to represent Christ ("head," "servant," "shepherd," "spouse").

257 For example, the *Ratio Fundamentalis* stresses the simultaneous configuration of the deacon "cum Christo, Domino et Servo omnium" and considers it to be "specificum signum sacramentale Christi Servi," 5. John Paul II, for his part, stated (March 16, 1985): "II diacono nel suo grado personifica Cristo servo del Padre, partecipando alia triplice funzione del sacramento dell'Ordine," *Insegnamenti* VIII, 1, 649.

258 The same text of St. Polycarp, *Ad Phil* 5, 2 (ed. Funk, 1:300), which LG, no. 29a, and the *Ratio* no. 5 apply to deacons, considers Christ as Lord and Servant (minister): "Misericordes, seduli, incedentes iuxta veritatem Domini, qui omnium minister factus est."

259 On the subject of bishops, LG, no. 24a, declares: "Munus autem illud quod Dominus pastoribus populi sui commisit, verum est servitium quod in sacris Litteris 'diakonia' seu ministerium significanter nuncupatur (cf. Acts 1:17 and 25; 21:19; Rom 11:13; 1 Tm 1:12)."

260 Cf. *Pastores Dabo Vobis*, no. 21: "Christus est Ecclesiae Caput, sui scilicet Corporis. 'Caput' est eo quidem novo et sibi proprio modo, 'servum' scilicet significandi, prout ab Ipsius verbis evincitur (Mk 10:45).... Quod servitium seu 'ministerium' plenitudinem sui attigit per mortem in cruce acceptam, id est per totale sui donum, in humilitate at amore (Phil 2:7-8).... Auctoritas autem Christi Iesu Capitis eadem est ac Ipsius servitium, donum, totalis deditio, humilis atque dilectionis plena, erga Ecclesiam. Idque in perfecta erga Patrem oboedientia. Ille enim, unicus verusque est afflictus et dolens Domini Servus, idemque Sacerdos et Hostia seu Victima."

261 The CCE states (no. 876): "Intrinsece coniuncta naturae sacramentali ministerii eccle-sialis est *eius indoles servitii.* Ministri etenim, prorsus dependentes a Christo qui missionem praebet et auctoritatem, vere sunt 'servi Christi' ad imaginem Christi qui libere propter nos 'formam servi' (Phil 2:7) accepit. Quia verbum et gratia quorum sunt ministri, eorum non sunt, sed Christi qui ilia eis pro aliis concredidit, ipsi libere omnium fient servi."

5. Specific Diaconal "Functions"?

In Vatican II and the post-Conciliar documents, the functions attributed to deacons are many and diverse in varied fields, or, as *Lumen Gentium* (no. 29a) puts it, "*in diaconia liturgiae, verbi et caritatis.*" These documents do not discuss the fact that all those tasks and functions can be carried out (as happens today in many communities) by Christians who have not received diaconal ordination. Now, according to *Ad Gentes* (no. 16f) there do seem to exist "actual functions of the deacon's office" previous to ordination; and in this case ordination would merely strengthen, bind more closely to the altar, and make more effective because of the sacramental grace of the diaconate.[262] This statement confirms the doubts felt by some in regard to the sacramentality of the diaconate. How can this sacramentality be said to exist if it does not confer any specific *potestas* like that conferred by the priesthood and the episcopate? This same statement is taken by certain local Churches as justifying mistrust and a negative attitude toward the institution of the permanent diaconate: Why, they ask, proceed to this ordination if the same functions can be fulfilled by laypeople and lay ministers, who may be more effective and more adaptable? This theological matter thus has practical and pastoral repercussions which Vatican II did not deal with explicitly and which need to be tackled in the perspective of an ecclesiology of communion (cf. section IV infra). The desire of the Council was to make it clear how each *potestas sacra* in the Church was rooted in the sacraments, and that was why the Council did not consider it indispensable to have recourse to the traditional distinction between "power of order" and "power

262 "Iuvat enim viros, qui ministerio vere diaconali fungantur . . . per impositionem manuum inde ab Apostolis traditam corroborari et altari arctius coniungi, ut ministerium suum per gratiam sacramentalem diaconatus efficacius expleant," AG, no. 16f.

of jurisdiction."[263] In any case that did not prevent it from reappearing in the post-Conciliar documents.[264]

III. The Diaconate in the Perspective of the Episcopate as "Plenitudo Sacramenti Ordinis"

Vatican II gave a clear and authentic statement of the sacramentality of the episcopate, considering it as the "fullness of the sacrament of Orders" (*Lumen Gentium*, no. 21b).[265] The reversal of views implied in this statement does not make the episcopal "fullness" any reason for depriving the priesthood and the diaconate of their proper consistency, as though their only meaning lay in being preparatory stages for the episcopate. In their participation in the one priesthood of Christ and the mission of salvation, priests cooperate with bishops and depend on them in the pastoral exercise of the ministry.[266] It now remains to be seen how the diaconate should be understood theologically from the same point of view.

---

263 Vatican II does not use the expression "potestas iurisdictionis" and only in PO, no. 2b, does it speak of "sacra ordinis potestas." However, in the *Explanatory Note*, no. 2, of LG, it affirms with reference to episcopal consecration: "In consecratione datur ontologica participatio sacrorum munerum, ut indubie constat ex Traditione, etiam liturgica. Consulto adhibetur vocabulum munerum, non vero potestatum, quia haec ultima vox de potestate ad actum expedita intelligi posset. Ut vero talis expedita potestas habeatur, accedere debet canonica seu iuridica determinatio per auctoritatem hierarchicam. Quae determinatio potestatis consistere potest in concessione particularis officii vel in assignatione subditorum, et datur iuxta normas a suprema auctoritate adprobatas. Huiusmodi ulterior norma ex natura rei requiritur, quia agitur de muneribus quae a pluribus subiectis, hierarchice ex voluntate Christi cooperantibus, exerceri debent." On the different interpretations of the "potestas sacra," cf. Kramer, *Dienst und Vollmacht in der Kirche: Eine rechtstheologische Untersuchung zur Sacra Potestas-Lehre des II. Vatikanischen Konzils* (Trier, 1973), 38f.; A. Celeghin, *Origine e natura della potestà sacra: Posizioni postconciliari* (Brescia, 1987).

264 CIC, c. 966, distinguishes between "potestate ordinis" and "facultate eandem exercendi."

265 "Docet autem Sancta Synodus episcopali consecratione plenitudinem conferri sacramenti Ordinis, quae nimirum et liturgica Ecclesiae consuetudine et voce Sanctorum Patrum summum sacerdotium, sacri ministerii summa nuncupatur," LG, no. 21b. The doctrinal *relatio* understands the expression finally used (*plenitudo sacramenti*) as "totalitas omnis partes includens," AS 3/1, 238. LG, no. 41b, considers bishops to be "ad imaginem summi et aeterni Sacerdotis, Pastoris et Episcopi . . . ad plenitudinem sacerdotii electi."

266 "Presbyteri, quamvis pontificatus apicem non habeant et in exercenda sua potestate ab Episcopis pendeant, cum eis tamen sacerdotali honore coniuncti sunt et vi sacramenti Ordinis, ad imaginem Christi, summi atque aeterni Sacerdotis . . . consecrantur, ut veri sacerdotes Novi Testamenti. Muneris unici Mediatoris Christi (cf. 1 Tm 2:5) participes in suo gradu ministerii. . . . Presbyteri, ordinis Episcopalis providi cooperatores eiusque adiutorium," LG, no. 28.

1. The Unity of the Sacrament of Holy Orders

The statement of the unity of the sacrament of Holy Orders can be considered to form part of the common theological patrimony, and to have done so from the time (in the twelfth and following centuries) when the question was raised as to the sacramentality of the different degrees of Holy Orders.[267] This unity is maintained by Vatican II in speaking of the different orders, including the diaconate, in which the ecclesiastical ministry is exercised.[268] The post-Conciliar documents take the same line. The difficulties arise not from the assertion of this unity, but from the theological path taken in order to justify it. Traditionally, this unity was justified by the relation of this sacrament to the Eucharist, while respecting the different modalities proper to each degree.[269] Vatican II modified the viewpoints and the formulations. Hence the need to seek another path to justify it. Such a path might well take as its starting point some consideration of the episcopate as the "fullness" of the sacrament of Holy Orders and the foundation of its unity.

2. "Profile" and "Consistency" of the Diaconate

There is a theological understanding of the ordained ministry perceived as "hierarchy," which has been preserved by Vatican II and in subsequent documents. This understanding[270] leads to the doctrine of the different "degrees" of Holy Orders. Here deacons represent the "lowest" degree in the hierarchical scale, in relation to bishops and priests.[271] The internal unity of the sacrament of Holy Orders means that each degree participates *suo modo* in the triple ministerial *munus*, on a descending scale on which the higher degree includes and surpasses the whole reality and functions of the lower. This hierarchized and

267 Cf. several references in L. Ott, *Das Weihesakrament*, HbDG 4/5 (Freiburg, 1969). Trent, cf. DS 1763-78, takes its unity for granted as a starting point when speaking of the "sacrament of Order," as in the case of baptism and confirmation (cf. DS 1767).

268 "Sic ministerium ecclesiasticum divinitus institutum diversis ordinibus exercetur ab illis qui iam ab antiquo Episcopi, Presbyteri, Diaconi vocantur," LG, no. 28a.

269 Cf. St. Thomas, STh III, *Supply* q. 37, a. 2, resp.: "Distinctio ordinis est accipienda secundum relationem ad Eucharistiam. Quia potestas ordinis aut est ad consecrationem Eucharistiae ipsius, aut ad aliquod ministerium ordinandum ad hoc. Si primo modo, sic est ordo sacerdotum."

270 Cf. LG, no. 10b: "sacerdotium ministeriale seu hierarchicum"; the CCE gives the heading "Hierarchica Ecclesiae constitutio" to the doctrine on the ecclesial ministry which it sets out in nos. 874-96.

271 "In gradu inferiori hierarchiae sistunt Diaconi," LG, no. 29a. With the suppression of the other degrees in *Ministeria Quaedam* (1972), the diaconate became in fact the last degree.

graded "participation" in one and the same sacrament means that the deacon is a minister who depends on the bishop and the priest.

The difficulty in giving the (permanent) diaconate its own profile and consistency in this hierarchized scheme of things has led to the proposal of other models of interpretation. It is obviously not compatible with the Conciliar texts to consider the episcopate, the priesthood and the diaconate as three totally autonomous sacraments, juxtaposed and equal. The unity of the sacrament of Holy Orders would be seriously damaged, and such a view would prevent the episcopate from being seen as the "fullness" of the sacrament. For this reason certain contemporary theological approaches highlight the tradition of ancient sources and rites of ordination in which the diaconate appears "*ad ministerium* episcopi." The diaconate's direct and immediate relation to the episcopal ministry[272] would make deacons the natural collaborators of the bishop: that would imply for them the possibility of performing (preferentially) tasks in the super-parochial and diocesan field.

In that case what still remains to be explained more fully is the relation of the (permanent) diaconate with the priesthood. According to certain people, priests and deacons are on the same level with regard to the "fullness" of the sacrament represented by the episcopal ministry. Such people see this reflected in the ancient practice of ordinations (a deacon could be ordained bishop without necessarily passing through the priesthood, and a layman could be ordained a priest without passing through the diaconate[273]). These are historical facts which need to be borne in mind when delineating the ecclesiological profile of the diaconate today However, it does not seem theologically justifiable to exclude deacons from every form of help and cooperation with priests,[274] and

272 The *Directorium* (8) speaks explicitly of "participation" in the episcopal ministry: "Fundamentum obligationis consistit in ipsa participatione ministerii episcopalis, quae per sacramentum Ordinis et missionem canonicam confertur." Further on, no. 11 warns against what would prejudice the "relatio directa et inmediata, quam quilibet diaconus cum proprio episcopo habere debet."

273 Cf. M. Andrieu, "La carrière ecclésiastique des papes et les documents liturgiques du Moyen-Âge," *RevScRel* 21 (1947): 90-120.

274 In regard to their relation with bishops, the *Ratio Fundamentalis* (1998), no. 8, says that deacons "depend" on bishops in the exercise of their power; and speaks of a "special relationship" of deacons with priests: "Diaconi, cum ecclesiasticum ministerium in inferiore gradu participent, in sua potestate exercenda necessario ex Episcopis pendent prout plenitudinem sacramenti habentibus. Praeterea, necessitudinem peculiarem cum presbyteris ineunt, quippe in communione quorum ad populum Dei serviendum sunt vocati."

especially not with the *presbyterium* as a whole.[275] The hypothesis of a "diaconal college" around the bishop, as a manifestation of the *ordo diaconorum* similar to the *presbyterium*[276] and in communion with it, would require further theological study. The Conciliar and post-Conciliar texts say practically nothing about this possibility.[277] On the other hand, some contemporary theologico-pastoral essays maintain that the idea of a diaconal college would contribute solidity to the ecclesial profile required by a ministry which entails the demand of stability (the permanent diaconate).[278]

3. The Imposition of Hands "non ad sacerdotium . . ."

According to *Lumen Gentium* (no. 29a), deacons receive the imposition of hands "*non ad sacerdotium, sed ad ministerium.*" On this point Vatican II refers to text such as the *Statuta Ecclesiae Antiqua*[279] whose formula has remained the

275 "[Diaconi] Populo Dei, in communione cum Episcopo eiusque *presbyterio*, inserviunt," LG, no. 29a. The Motu Proprio *Sacrum Diaconatus*, no. 23, which applies the Conciliar decisions, underlines submission to the authority of the bishop and the priest: "Quae omnia munera in perfecta cum episcopo eiusque presbyterio communione exsequenda sunt, videlicet sub auctoritate episcopi et presbyteri, qui eo loci fidelium curae praesunt." The *Caeremoniale Episcoporum* . . . , Typ. Pol. Vat. 1985, no. 24, says with regard to deacons: "Spiritus Sancti dono roborati, Episcopo eiusque *presbyterio* adiumentum praestant in ministerio verbi, altar is et caritatis."

276 Deacons cannot be members of the council of priests; cf. LG, no. 28; CD, no. 27; PO, no. 7; and CIC, c. 495, 1, This is confirmed by the *Directorium*, 42: "Nequeunt tamen esse membra consilii presbyteralis, quia ipsum exclusive presbyterium repraesentat."

277 The 1998 *Directorium* (6) recalls the "sacramental fraternity" which unites deacons, the importance of the bonds of charity, prayer, unity and cooperation, and that it is opportune for them to meet together; but it says nothing about the possibility of a collegial "ordo diaconorum," and it warns against the risks of "corporatism" which was a factor in the disappearance of the permanent diaconate in earlier centuries: "Diaconi, vi ordinis accepti, fraternitate sacramentali inter se uniti sunt. . . . Praestat ut diaconi, consentiente Episcopo et ipso Episcopo praesente aut eius delegato, statutis temporibus congregentur. . . . Ad Episcopum loci spectat inter diaconos in dioecesi operantes spiritum communionis alere, evitando ne ille 'corporativismus' efformetur, qui praeteritis saeculis tantopere ad diaconatum permanentem evanescendum influxit."

278 "Specifica vocatio diaconi permanentis stabilitatem in hoc ordine supponit. Fortuitus igitur transitus ad presbyteratum diaconorum permanentium, non uxoratorum vel viduorum, rarissima exceptio semper erit, quae admitti non poterit, nisi graves et speciales rationes id suadeant," *Directorium*, no. 5.

279 LG, no. 29a, gives a reference to *Constitutiones Ecclesiae Aegypciacae* 3, 2 (ed. Funk, *Didascalia* 2, 103); *Statuta Eccl. ant* 37-41 (Mansi, 3:954) (but in fact it is taken from *Statuta Eccl ant.* 4 [Mansi, 3:951]). The text of the *Statuta* 92 (4), CChr SL 148, 181, says: "Diaconus cum ordinatur, solus episcopus, qui eum benedicit, manum super caput illius ponat, quia non ad sacerdotium sed ad ministerium consecratur."

same until our own times in the Roman Pontifical.[280] However, the formula goes back to the *Traditio Apostolica* (second and third centuries), which specifies something which is absent from the Council texts: "*in ministerio episcopi*."[281] Moreover, the interpretation of the precise meaning of this divergence is disputed in the current theology of the diaconate.[282] What seems excluded in this formulation (*sacerdotium*) will be looked at first; after that, what seems to be stated in it (the relationship to *ministerium*). The diaconate is not *ad sacerdotium*. How should this exclusion be interpreted? In a stricter sense the ministerial *sacerdotium* has been traditionally linked with the power *conficiendi eucharistiam*,[283] *offerendi sacrificium in Ecclesia*,[284] or *consecrandi verum corpus et sanguinem Domini*.[285] Down the centuries, the basis for the sacramental equality of bishops and priests as "priests," i.e., those who offer sacrifice,[286] and the attribution of a solely jurisdictional origin to the distinction between the two,[287] has been based on this close connection between priesthood and Eucharist.

280 Cf. *Pontifical Romano-Germanique* (950), vol. 1 (Citta del Vaticano, 1963), 24. In the present *Pontificale Romanum* (ed. typ. 1968, 1989), the following expressions are found: "The mission of the deacon is a help for the bishop and his priests [episcopo eiusque presbyterio adiumentum] in the service of the word, of the altar and of charity" (opening address by the bishop); the deacon is ordained "in the service of the Church [ad ministerium Ecclesiae]" and "to provide help to the order of priests [in adiutorium ordinis sacerdotalis]" (bishop's questions to the ordinands). In the consecratory prayer it is recalled that the Apostles "chose seven men to help them in daily service." It will be noted that in the case of a priest, the question asked is whether he "wishes to become a priest, collaborator with the bishops in the priesthood, to serve and guide the people of God under the guidance of the Holy Spirit."

281 The Latin version (L) says: "In diacono ordinando solus episcopus imponat manus, propterea quia non in sacerdotio ordinatur, sed in ministerio episcopi, ut faciat ea quae ab ipso iubentur." *Trad. Apost.* (ed. B. Botte), SCh 11(2) (Paris, 1968), 58.

282 The interpretation given by the Council Commission is also controversial: "Verba desumuntur ex Statutis Eccl. Ant. . . . et significant diaconos non ad corpus et sanguinem Domini offerendum, sed ad servitium caritatis in Ecclesia ordinari," AS 3/8, 101.

283 "Et utique sacramentum nemo potest conficere, nisi sacerdos, qui rite fuerit ordinatus," Fourth Lateran Council (1215), DS 802; cf. *Trad. Apost.* 4.

284 "Forma sacerdotii talis est: 'Accipe potestatem offerendi sacrificium in Ecclesia pro vivis et mortuis,'" Council of Florence (1439), DS 1326.

285 Council of Trent (1563), DS 1771; cf. likewise DS 1764: "Apostolis eorumque successoribus in sacerdotio potestatem traditam consecrandi, offerendi et ministrandi corpus et sanguinem eius, nec non et peccata dimittendi et retinendi."

286 "Distinctio ordinis est accipienda secundum relationem ad Eucharistiam. Quia potestas ordinis aut est ad consecrationem Eucharistiae ipsius, aut ad aliquod ministerium ordinandum ad hoc. Si primo modo, sic est ordo sacerdotum. Et ideo, cum ordinantur, accipiunt calicem cum vino et patenam cum pane, potestatem accipientes consecrandi corpus et sanguinem Christi." St. Thomas, STh HI, *Supply* q. 37, a. 2, resp.

287 "Episcopatus non est ordo, secundum quod ordo est quoddam sacramentum . . . ordinatur omnis ordo ad eucharistiae sacramentum; unde, cum Episcopus non habeat potestatem superiorem sacerdote quantum ad hoc, non erit episcopatus ordo." St. Thomas, *In IV Sent,* d. 24, q. 3, a. 2, sol. 2.

This same reason, then, is why deacons are not ordained *ad sacerdotium*, given the impossibility for them of presiding at and validly consecrating the Eucharist, which is a power reserved exclusively to "priests." Does this restriction also imply that the diaconate is excluded from *sacerdotium* understood in a less strict sense? Vatican II did indeed place the relationship between the ministerial priesthood and the Eucharist in a wider context: that of an ecclesiology centered on the Eucharist seen as *totius vitae christianaefons et oilmen*[1] and that of a ministerial priesthood whose constitutive relationship with the Eucharist is rooted in a broader *potestas sacra*, also relating to the other ministerial *munera*.[2] If the diaconate is totally excluded from the "priesthood" in all senses of the term, then it will be necessary to re-think the unity of the sacrament of Holy Orders as "ministerial or hierarchical priesthood" (cf. *Lumen Gentium*, no. 10b), as well as the use of "sacerdotal" categories to make a global definition or description of the sacrament. Different tendencies are to be observed on this point in the Conciliar texts, in later developments, and in theological studies of the diaconate.

On one hand the texts of Vatican II which explicitly mention the diaconate do not apply terms or categories of priesthood to it, but ministerial ones.[3] The same is true of the modifications introduced for the sake of greater precision into the latest edition of the CCE, which distinguishes clearly, within the single sacrament of Holy Orders, between a degree of sacerdotal participation (episcopate and priesthood) and a degree of service (deacons), and which excludes

1 LG, no. 11a. The statement of the central value of the Eucharist is repeated several times. Cf. PO, no. 5b ("in Sanctissima . . . Eucharistia totum bonum spirituale Ecclesiae continetur"), UR, no. 15a ("celebrationem eucharisticam, fontem vitae ecclesiae et pignus futurae gloriae"), CD, no. 30f. ("ut celebratio Eucharistici Sacrificii centrum sit et culmen totius vitae communitatis christianae").

2 "Sacerdos quidem minister ialis, potestate sacra qua gaudet, populum sacerdotalem efformat ac regit, sacrificium eucharisticum in persona Christi conficit illudque nomine totius populi Dei offert," LG, no. 10b.

3 Cf. SC, no. 35d ("authorized person," which also includes deacons), LG, no. 20c ("adiutoribus . . . diaconis"), LG, no. 28a ("ministerium ecclesiasticum . . . Diaconi"), LG, no. 29a ("ad ministerium"), LG, no. 41d ("ministri, imprimis Diaconi"), OE, no. 17 ("institutum diaconatus"), CD, no. 15a ("diaconi, qui ad ministerium ordinati"), DV, no. 25a ("clericos omnes . . . qui ut diaconi"), AG, no. 15i ("munera . . . diaconorum"), AG, no. 16a, f ("salutis ministros in ordine . . . Diaconorum . . . ordo diaconatus").

the application of the term *sacerdos* to deacons.[4] On the other hand, when Vatican II speaks from the perspective of the single sacrament of Holy Orders, it seems to consider the "priestly" categories as all-inclusive and extends them beyond the distinction between *sacerdotium* and *ministerium*. This is the case in *Lumen Gentium* (no. 10b), which states that there is a difference of essence and not merely of degree between the common priesthood of the faithful and the ministerial or hierarchical priesthood.[5] In the same way, when it speaks of the spirituality of different states of life in *Lumen Gentium* (no. 41d), the Council seems to attribute an intermediate role to deacons in the collection of different ministries (it should be noted that at that point the minor orders had not yet been suppressed), by attributing to deacons a special share in the mission and grace of the High Priest.[6] For its part, the 1983 CIC, in cc. 1008-9, includes deacons within the *sacri ministri*, who by their consecration are enabled to pasture the People of God and to execute *pro suo quisque gradu* the functions of teaching, sanctifying and ruling *in persona Christi Capitis*.[7]

Since this was the state of affairs it is not surprising to find that the post-Conciliar efforts to arrive at a theological understanding of the diaconate

---

4 "Doctrina catholica, in liturgia, Magisterio et constant! Ecclesiae explicita praxi, agnoscit duos gradus paiticipationis ministerialis exsistere sacerdotii Christi: Episcopatum et presbyteratum. Diaconatus ad illos adiuvandos atque ad illis serviendum destinatur. Propterea verbum *sacerdos* designat, in usu hodierno, Episcopos et presbyteros, sed non diaconos. Tamen doctrina catholica docet gradus paiticipationis sacerdotalis (Episcopatum et presbyteratum) et gradum servitii (diaconatum) conferri, hos omnes tres, actii sacramentali qui 'ordinatio' appellatur, id est, sacramento Ordinis," CCE, no. 1554. The *Ratio Fundamentalis*, nos. 4 and 5, also avoids applying terms of "priesthood" etc. to deacons: "Ad eius [cuiusque ministri ordinati] plenam veritatem pertinet esse participatio specifica et repraesentatio ministerii Christi ... manuum impositio diaconum non est 'ad sacerdotium sed ad ministerium,' id est non ad celebrationem eucharisticam sed ad servitium . . . is [diaconus] enim, prout unici ministerii ecclesiastici particeps, est in Ecclesia specificum signum sacramentale Christi servi."

5 "Sacerdotium autem commune fidelium et sacerdotium ministeriale seu hierarchicum, licet essentia et non gradu tantum differant, ad invicem tamen ordinantur; unum enim et alterum suo peculiari modo de uno Christi sacerdotio participant," LG, no. 10b.

6 "Missionis autem et gratiae supremi Sacerdotis peculiari modo participes sunt inferioris quoque ordinis ministri, imprimis Diaconi," LG, no. 41d. Referring to this text, CCE, no. 1570, replaces the expression "supremi Sacerdotis" by that of "Christi": "Diaconi missionem et gratiam Christi, modo speciali participant."

7 "Sacramento ordinis ex divina institutione inter christifideles quidam charactere indelebili quo signantur, constituuntur sacri ministri, qui nempe consecrantur et deputantur ut, pro suo quisque gradu, in persona Christi Capitis munera docendi, sanctificandi et regendi adimplentes, Dei populum pascant," c. 1008. "Ordines sunt episcopatus, presbyteratus et diaconatus," c. 1009. The 1983 CIC uses the expression "sacri ministri" to designate the baptized faithful who have received sacramental ordination. On one hand its expressions are briefer than those of Vatican II, and do not quote LG, no. 29; on the other, despite the qualification "pro suo gradu," it goes further than the explicit texts of Vatican II in applying the notion of "in persona Christi Capitis" to the diaconate.

were marked by tensions born of whether the diaconate was excluded from or included in the priestly categories. As long as the diaconate was merely a step on the way to the priesthood, these tensions were manageable. From the moment when the diaconate was instituted as a permanent state, and took shape and started to grow in many Churches,[8] the theological tensions became more pronounced and developed in two different directions.

On the basis of the unity of the sacrament of Holy Orders, and in the conviction that they were being faithful to the Conciliar and post-Conciliar texts, some people stressed the unity of the sacrament and applied to the diaconate theological principles which were valid in proportionate ways for the three degrees of the sacrament. They maintained, with some differences of emphasis, that it should be generally understood and described as "*sacerdotium ministeriale seu hierarchicum*" (cf. *Lumen Gentium*, no. 10b), which, they held, was borne out by the language used in the ancient tradition of the Church.[9] In this line of argument the diaconate is a sacramental reality which implies a difference "*essentia, non gradu tantum*" (cf. *Lumen Gentium*, no. 10b) in comparison with the common priesthood of the faithful. Hence the statement that the diaconate is "*non ad sacerdotium*" would then exclude only what related to the consecration of the Eucharist (and the sacrament of Reconciliation).[10] But both because of its integration within the single sacrament of Holy Orders, and because of its special relationship with the Eucharistic ministry, both by reason of the broadly "priestly" significance of the *munera* of teaching and government and by its specific participation in the mission and grace of the High Priest, the diaconate should still be included within the "ministerial or hierarchical priesthood," as distinct from the "common priesthood" of the faithful.

Other opposing tendencies insist strongly on the distinction expressed by the formula "*non ad sacerdotium, sed ad ministerium*." In a line of argument contrary to that just outlined, these writers tend to exclude all "priestly" conceptualization or terminology from the correct understanding of the diaconate. At

8 Cf. the data given in Chapter VI.

9 Cf., e.g., Tertullian, *De exh. cast.* 7, 5 (CCh SL 319, 94), in which bishops, priests and deacons constitute the "ordo sacerdotalis" or "sacerdotium"; Leo I, *Ep.* 12, 5; 14, 3f. (PL 54, 652, 672f.), who also adds sub-deacons as members of the "ordo sacerdotalis"; Optatus of Milevis, *Contra Parmen.* 1, 13 (SCh 412, 200), for whom deacons formed part of the "third priesthood" ("Quid diaconos in tertio, quid presbyteros in secundo sacerdo-tio constitutos?"); also St. Jerome, *Ep.* 48, 21 (CSEL 54, 387): "Episcopi, presbyteri, diaconi aut virgines eliguntur aut vidui aut certe post sacerdotium in aeternum pudici."

10 Cf. Council of Trent, DS 1764.

the same time they highlight this distinction as a decisive step towards overcoming the "sacerdotalization" of the sacrament of Holy Orders. They hold that this sacrament comprises three degrees, of which two (the episcopate and the priesthood) belong to the *sacerdotium* and one (the diaconate) is only *ad ministerium.* In this way they avoid a theological understanding of the deacon in the image of a priest whose competencies are (still) limited. It would likewise enable a greater consistency and identity to be recognized in the deacon as a minister of the Church. However, the identity of the deacon is still to be defined in the light of *Lumen Gentium* (no. 10b), because, as a sacramental reality, the diaconate is not to be identified with the functions, services and ministries rooted in baptism.

4. "... Sed ad Ministerium (Episcopi)"

Certain theologico-pastoral studies of the (permanent) diaconate see the specific mention "*in ministerio episcopi*"[11] as a basis for asserting that the diaconate has a direct link with the episcopal ministry.[12] While maintaining that this link does exist,[13] Vatican II softened the force it had in the *Traditio Apostolica* by stating that the diaconate was only *ad ministerium*, in other words a service for the people exercised in the domain of the liturgy, the word and charity, in communion with the bishop and his presbyterium.[14] John Paul II stressed this dimension of service to the People of God.[15] However, when it comes to specifying the theological scope of the expression "*ad ministerium* (*episcopi*)" and the possible integration of the diaconate into the ministry of apostolic succession, they return in a way to the divergences outlined above. Here too, the Conciliar and post-Conciliar texts are ambivalent.

---

11 Cf. note 279 supra.

12 CCE, no. 1569 itself, citing the formula of the *Traditio* and LG, no. 29, underlines the fact that the bishop alone imposes his hands on the deacon at ordination, as a sign of a special connection with him: "Pro diacono ordinando, solus Episcopus manus imponit, ita significans diaconum in muneribus suae 'diaconiae' Episcopo speciatim annecti."

13 "Episcopos . . . qui munus ministerii sui, vario gradu, variis subiectis in Ecclesia legitime tradiderunt," LG, no. 28.

14 "Gratia etenim sacramentali roborati, in diaconia liturgiae, verbi et caritatis Populo Dei, in communione cum Episcopo eiusque presbyterio, inserviunt," LG, no. 29. The *Directorium* (no. 22) speaks of assistance given to "bishops" and "priests": "Sic diaconus auxiliatur et inservit episcopis et presbyteris, qui semper praesunt liturgiae, praevigilant super doctrinam et moderantur Populum Dei."

15 "In this ancient text the 'ministry' is described as 'service of the bishop'; the Council lays the stress on service to the People of God," *Insegnamenti* XVI, 2, 1000.

In the light of *Lumen Gentium* (nos. 20 and 24a), it has been stated that the bishops are the successors of the Apostles so as to prolong the first apostolic mission until the end of time.[16] As for *Lumen Gentium* (no. 28a), it also seems to include deacons in the line of succession which prolongs the mission of Christ in that of the Apostles, that of the bishops and that of the ecclesiastical ministry.[17] The CCE defines the sacrament of Holy Orders in its three degrees as "the sacrament of apostolic ministry."[18] With these texts as a basis, despite the variations in their terminology ("ecclesiastical" and "apostolic" ministry),[19] the diaconate could be considered as an integral part of the ministry of apostolic succession. This would fit in with the unity of the sacrament of Holy Orders, as rooted ultimately in Christ and with the deacons participating in their own way in the mission which the Apostles and their successors received from Christ.[20]

However, this conclusion is not shared by those who retain the distinction between *sacerdotium* and *ministerium* as a difference of quality, and give decisive importance to the latest modifications to CCE (no. 1154, where the term *sacerdos* is reserved to bishops and priests). They see these modifications as going beyond what had been said up until that point, and as a key reference point for future developments. The apostolic ministry is understood as the continuation of the *diakonia* of Christ, which cannot be dissociated from his "priesthood": the priestly offering which he makes of his life actually constitutes his diaconal service for the salvation of the world. In this sense the *diakonia* or service characterizes the *munus* of the pastors (bishops) of the People of God,[21] and it would not be sufficient to represent deacons as the specific heirs of the diaconal

16 "Inter varia ilia ministeria quae inde a primis temporibus in Ecclesia exercentur, teste traditione, praecipuum locum tenet munus illorum qui, in episcopatum constituti, per successionem ab initio decurrentem, apostolici seminis traduces habent. . . . Proinde docet Sacra Synodus Episcopos ex divina institutione in locum Apostolorum successisse, tamquam Ecclesiae pastores," LG, no. 20; "Episcopi, utpote apostolorum successores, a Domino . . . missionem accipiunt," LG, no. 24a. In the same sense, cf. DS 1768, 3061, CCE, no. 1555.

17 "Christus, quem Pater sanctificavit et misit in mundum (Jn 10:36), consecrationis missionisque suae per Apostolos suos, eorum successores, videlicet Episcopos participes effecit, qui munus ministerii sui, vario gradu, variis subiectis in Ecclesia legitime tradiderunt. Sic ministerium ecclesiasticum divinitus institutum diversis ordinibus exercetur ab illis qui iam ab antiquo Episcopi, Presbyteri, Diaconi vocantur," LG, no. 28a.

18 "Ordo est sacramentum per quod missio a Christo Ipsius Apostolis concredita exerceri pergit in Ecclesia usque ad finem temporum: est igitur ministerii apostolici sacramentum. Tres implicat gradus: Episcopatum, presbyteratum et diaconatum," CCE, no. 1536.

19 See, even, the expression "ministerial or hierarchical priesthood" in LG, no. 10b.

20 "Apostolis eorumque successoribus a Christo collatum est munus in ipsius nomine et potestate docendi, sanctificandi et regendi," AA, no. 2b; cf. LG, no. 19a.

21 "Munus autem illud quod Dominus pastoribus populi sui commisit, verum est servitium quod in sacris Litteris 'diakonia' seu ministerium significanter nuncupatur," LG, no. 24a.

dimension of the ministry. The diaconate should be recognized as apostolic in its foundation, and not in its theological nature. That is to say, therefore, that the ministry of apostolic succession should be restricted to "priests"[22] (bishops and priests), while deacons would form part of the "ecclesiastical" ministry[23] and should be considered, consequently, as auxiliary collaborators towards the ministry of apostolic succession, and not, strictly speaking, an integral part of it.

5. *The Diaconate as Mediating Function or* Medius Ordo?

The interventions made at the Council, and the notes of the relevant Conciliar Commission, already attributed to the permanent diaconate a mediating or bridging function between the hierarchy and the people.[24] Although this idea was not retained in the definitive Council texts, it was in a way reflected in the order adopted in *Lumen Gentium* (no. 29): the text speaks of deacons at the end of Chapter III as the last degree of the hierarchy, just before dealing with the subject of laypeople in Chapter IV. The same order is found in *Ad Gentes* (no. 16). The actual expression "*medius ordo*" applied explicitly to the (permanent) diaconate is found only in the *Motu Proprio Ad Pascendum* (1972) and is presented as one way of putting into effect the hopes and intentions which had led Vatican II to restore it.[25] The idea spread widely in contemporary theology, and gave rise to different ways of conceiving this mediating function: between clergy and laity, between the Church and the world, between worship and ordinary life, between charity work and the Eucharist, between the center and the periphery of the Christian community. Whatever the context, the notion merits some theological clarifications.

---

22 Cf. Council of Trent, DS 1764 ("Apostolis eorumque successoribus in sacerdotio potestatem traditam consecrandi"), DS 1771 ("sacerdotium visibile et externum"), DS 1765 ("tam sancti sacerdotii ministerium . . . ministrorum ordines, qui sacerdotio ex officio deservirent"), DS 1772 ("alios ordines, et maiores et minores, per quos velut per gradus quosdam in sacerdotium tendatur").

23 Cf. LG, no. 29a.

24 E.g., Msgr. Yü Pin thought that permanent deacons could exercise a function "pontis seu mediationis inter hierarchiam et christifideles," AS 2/2, 431; likewise the Conciliar Commission retained the idea that married deacons could constitute "quasi pontem" between the clergy and the people, AS 3/1, 267.

25 "Concilium denique Vaticanum II optatis et precibus suffragatum est, ut Diaconatus permanens, ubi id animarum bono conduceret, instauretur veluti medius ordo inter superiores ecclesiasticae hierarchiae gradus et reliquum populum Dei, quasi interpres necessitatum ac votorum christianorum communitatum, instimulator famulatus seu *diaconiae* Ecclesiae apud locales Christianas communicates, signum vel sacramentum ipsius Christi Domini, qui non venit ministrari, sed ministrare." Paul VI, *Ad Pascendum*, 536.

It would be a theological error to identify the diaconate as *medius ordo* with a kind of intermediate (sacramental?) reality between the baptized and the ordained faithful. The fact that the diaconate belongs to the sacrament of Holy Orders is sure doctrine. Theologically the deacon is not a "layperson." Vatican II considers that the deacon is a member of the hierarchy and the CIC refers to him as *sacer minister* or *clericus*.[26] It is true that it belongs to the deacon to accomplish some sort of task of mediation, but it would not be theologically correct to make that task into the expression of the diaconate's theological nature or its specifying note. Additionally, there is a certain risk that the fixing of the diaconate in ecclesiological terms, and institutionalizing it in pastoral terms as *medius ordo* might end up by sanctioning and deepening, through that very function, the gap which it was supposed to fill.

These theological clarifications do not imply a total rejection of all mediating function on the part of the deacon. The notion is based on the witnesses of ecclesial tradition.[27] In a certain way it is reflected in the ecclesiological position which current canon law (CIC 1983) attributes to deacons between the mission of laypeople and that of priests. On the one hand, (permanent) deacons live in the middle of the world with a lay style of life (although there is the possibility of a religious permanent diaconate) and with certain "concessions" which are not (or not always) accorded to all clergy and priests.[28] On the other hand there are certain functions in which deacons and priests share alike, and in which both alike take precedence over the laity.[29] That does not mean that deacons

---

26 "Per receptum diaconatum aliquis fit clericus et incardinatur Ecclesiae particulari vel Praelaturae personali pro cuius servitio promotus est," CIC c. 266; cf. also cc. 1008-9, which are echoed in the 1998 *Directorium*, no. 1: "Per impositionem manuum et consecrationis precem ipse minister sacer et hierarchiae membrum constituitur. Haec condition ipsius statum theologicum et iuridicum in Ecclesia determinat."

27 Cf. *Trad. Apost.* 4, 8, 21, 24 (bridging function between the bishop and the Christian people); STh III, q. 82, a. 3 ad 1 ("diaconi sunt inter sacerdotes et populum").

28 Thus they can be married (c. 281 §3), they are not obliged to wear ecclesiastical dress (c. 284), or to abstain from holding public office in the civil sphere (c. 285 §3) or from administering property; they can devote themselves to business and commerce (c. 286) and take an active part in party politics and trades unions (c. 287 §2; cf. c. 288). In this regard, see the further clarifications made in the *Directorium*, nos. 7-14.

29 E.g.: the capacity to exercise power of government or jurisdiction by reason of one's order (c. 129); to obtain posts whose exercise requires the power of order or government (c. 274 §1) although they cannot be vicars-general or bishops (c. 475); deacons can be appointed diocesan judges (c. 1421 §l) and even the only judge (c. 1425 §4); they can also confer certain dispensations (c. 89; c. 1079 §2), or, as a general faculty, assist at weddings (c. llllf.); they are ordinary ministers of baptism (c. 861 §1), of communion (c. 910 §1) and of the exposition of the Eucharist (c. 943); they can preach everywhere (c. 764) and the homily is reserved to them as it is to the priests (c. 767 §1).

can exercise completely all the functions which belong to priests (Eucharist, Reconciliation, Anointing of the Sick). However, except in certain exceptional cases, what the CIC lays down for "clergy" in general is, in principle, applied to deacons (cf. cc. 273ff.).

IV. The Diaconate in an "Ecclesiology of Communion"

Although it is based on the texts of Vatican II, what can be called the "ecclesiology of communion" was developed in greater depth in and after the synod of 1985.[30] This ecclesiology grants a clearer understanding of the Church as a "universal sacrament of salvation" (cf. *Lumen Gentium*, nos. 1, 9) which finds in the communion of the Trinitarian God the source and ecclesial model for all the dynamism of salvation. *Diakonia* is the realization of this model in history. It now remains to be seen how the specific sacramental configuration of the diaconal ministry is integrated within this *diakonia* as a whole.

1. The Munera of the Diaconate: Plurality of Functions, and Varying Priorities

Lumen Gentium (no. 29a) lists and explains the diaconal functions in the field of the liturgy (which includes tasks where the deacon presides), of the word and of charity, to which administrative tasks are connected.[31] *Ad Gentes* (no. 16f.) follows another order: ministry of the word/of the government of communities, and of charity.[32] For its part, *Sacrum Diaconatus* singles out eleven tasks, eight of which belong to the liturgical sphere (which is given first rank in this way) although sometimes they have the character of "supply" tasks. The

30 Cf. *Zukunft aus der Kraft des Konzils: Die ausserordentliche Bischofssynode 1985; Die Dokumente mit einem Kommentar von W. Kasper* (Freiburg, 1986); W. Kasper, *Kirche als Communio*, in *Theologie und Kirche* (Mainz, 1987), 272-89.

31 "In diaconia liturgiae, verbi et caritatis Populo Dei... inserviunt... fidelium cultui et orationi praesidere ... caritatis et administrationis officiis dediti," LG, no. 29a. The Conciliar Commission clarified it in these terms: "Indicantur officia diaconorum in primis modo generali, brevi sed gravi sententia, in triplici campo, scilicet 'in diaconia liturgiae, verbi et caritatis': quod deinde magis specificatur per 'caritatis et administrationis officia,'" AS 3/1, 260. The stress laid on the charitable dimension is also evident in the explanation given by the same Commission with regard to the formula "non ad sacerdotium, sed ad ministerium": "significant diaconos non ad corpus et sanguinem Domini offerentes, sed ad servitium caritatis in Ecclesia ordinari," AS 3/8, 101.

32 "Iuvat enim viros, qui ministerio vere diaconali fungantur, vel verbum divinum tamquam catechistae praedicantes, vel nomine parochi et episcopi dissitas communitates Christianas moderantes, vel caritatem exercentes in operibus socialibus seu caritativis, per impositionem manuum inde ab Apostolis traditam corroborari et altari arctius coniungi, ut ministerium suum per gratiam sacramentalem diaconatus efficacius expleant," AG, no. 16f.

charitable and social work is done in the name of the hierarchy, and also includes the duty of stimulating the lay apostolate.[33] The CIC goes into details on the faculties and tasks which properly belong to deacons; the possibility is there mentioned of conferring on deacons a share in the exercise of the *cura pastoralis* of the parish.[34] With reference to the Conciliar texts of *Lumen Gentium* (no. 29), *Sacrosanctum Concilium* (no. 35) and *Ad Gentes* (no. 16), the CCE takes up the familiar list of relationships to liturgical life (with an explicit mention of assistance to bishops and priests), to pastoral life, and to charitable and social works.[35] The *Ratio Fundamental* presents the diaconal ministry as an exercise of the three *munera* in the specific light of *diakonia*, enumerated as the *munus docendi*, the *munus sanctificandi* (with the Eucharist as its point of departure and its destination) and the *munus regendi* (where charitable activities are given as the most characteristic ministry of the deacon).[36] And the *Directorium* takes up again the triple *diakonia* of *Lumen Gentium* (no. 29), though changing the order (word, liturgy, charity). In this way it retains the *diakonia* of the word as the main function of the deacon; it underlines the *diakonia* of the liturgy as an intrinsic and organic assistance to the priestly ministry, and it considers the *diakonia* of charity as a different way of participating in the pastoral tasks of the bishops and priests.[37]

---

33 "Ubi sacerdos deest, Ecclesiae nomine matrimoniis celebrandis assistere et benedicere ex delegatione episcopi vel parochi . . . funeris ac sepulturae ritibus praeesse . . . praesidere, ubi sacerdos non adest . . . caritatis et administrationis officiis atque socialis subsidii operibus, Hierarchiae nomine, perfungi . . . apostolica laicorum opera fovere et adiuvare," *Sacrum Diaconatus*, no. 22, pp. 701f.

34 On the tasks appointed to them and the questions raised by c. 517 §2, cf. supra Chapter IV, notes 162-63.

35 When it speaks of deacons, it says quite simply: "Ad diaconos pertinet, inter alia, Episcopo et presbyteris in mysteriorum divinorum celebratione assistere, maxime Eucharistiae, eamque distribuere, Matrimonio assistere idque benedicere, Evangelium proclamare et praedicare, exsequiis praesidere atque se diversis caritatis consecrare servitiis," CCE, no. 1570. When it makes an explicit reference to the permanent diaconate, citing AG, no. 16, it reaffirms that it is appropriate and useful to give sacramental ordination to "viros qui in Ecclesia ministerium vere diaconale explent sive in vita liturgica et pastorali sive in operibus socialibus et caritativis," CCE, no. 1571.

36 "Ad munus docendi . . . quidem elucet ex libri Evangelii traditione, in ipso ordinationis ritu praescripta. Diaconi munus sanctificandi impletur . . . quo pacto apparet quomodo ministerium diaconale ex Eucharistia procedat ad eandemque redeat, nec in mero servitio sociali exhauriri possit. Munus regendi denique exercetur per deditionem operibus caritatis . . . peculiari habito ad caritatem, quae praeeminentem diaconalis ministerii notam constituit," *Ratio*, no. 9.

37 "Diaconi proprium officium est Evangelium proclamare et Verbum Dei praedicare . . . quae facultas oritur e sacramento. . . . Ministerio Episcopi et, subordinate, ministerio presbyterorum, diaconus praestat auxilium sacramentale, ac proinde intrinsecum, organicum, a confusione alienum. . . . Opera caritatis, dioecesana vel paroecialia, quae sunt inter primaria officia Episcopi et presbyterorum, ab his transmittuntur, secundum testimonium Traditionis Ecclesiae, servis ministerii ecclesiastici, hoc est diaconis," *Directorium*, nos. 24, 28, 37.

The different functions attributed to the (permanent) diaconate in the Conciliar and post-Conciliar texts generally come down to us from ancient liturgical tradition, from the rites of ordination and theological studies of them. These functions are also open to contemporary pastoral situations and needs, although in that case a certain reserve is noticeable in the documents. In general a sort of triple *diakonia* or a sort of triple *munus* is recognized and serves as the basis for the diaconal functions taken together. In the documents and in numerous theological studies, charitable works are given a certain pre-eminence;[38] however, it would be problematic to consider these as being specific to the diaconate, because they are also properly the responsibility of the bishops and the priests, whose auxiliaries the deacons are. Moreover, the witness of ecclesial tradition suggests that the three functions ought to be integrated into a single whole. From that point of view it is possible to point out different characteristic features in the figure of the diaconal ministry. This ministry may be more strongly focused either on charity, or on the liturgy, or on evangelization; it may be exercised in a service directly linked to the bishop, or else in the sphere of the parish; and the permanent diaconate and the transitory diaconate may be preserved alike, or a clear option for one single figure may be determined. How plausible, and how viable, would such diversity prove to be in the long term? That would depend not only on the way the diaconate is understood theologically, but also on the real situation of different local Churches.

2. *Communion in a Plurality of Ministries*

The specific way the diaconate is exercised in different surroundings will also help to define its ministerial identity, modifying if necessary an ecclesial framework in which its proper connection with the ministry of the bishop hardly appears and in which the figure of the priest is identified with the totality of the ministerial functions. The living consciousness that the Church is "communion" will contribute to this development. However, it would be hard to arrive at a solution to the theological queries about the specific "powers" of the diaconate through practical experience alone. Not everyone considers this question to be an insoluble difficulty. Thus different propositions of contemporary theology

38 E.g.: "Itaque Diaconatus in Ecclesia mirabiliter effloruit simulque insigne praebuit testimonium amoris erga Christum ac fratres in caritatis operibus exsequendis, in ritibus sacris celebrandis atque in pastoralibus perfungendis muneribus," Paul VI, *Ad Pascendum*, p. 535.

may be observed which aim to give the diaconate theological substance, ecclesial acceptance and pastoral credibility.

There are some people who consider this question of the "powers" of the deacon to have only relative importance. For them, to make it into a central question would be a kind of reductionism, and would disfigure the true meaning of the ordained minister. Moreover, the observation, which was true in ancient times as well, that a layman can exercise the tasks of the deacon did not in practice prevent this ministry from being considered sacramental from every point of view. Additionally, neither would it be possible to reserve the exclusive exercise of certain functions to bishops and priests in great detail, save in the case of the *potestas conficiendi eucharistiam*,[39] of the sacrament of Reconciliation[40] and the ordination of bishops.[41] Other people distinguish between what is or should be the normal and ordinary exercise of the whole collection of functions attributed to deacons, and what could be considered as an extraordinary exercise of them on the part of Christians,[42] determined by pastoral needs or emergencies, even on a long-term basis. A certain analogy could be drawn between this and the normal or ordinary competencies of the bishop in regard to confirmation (which the priest can also administer)[43] and in regard to the ordination of priests (which according to certain papal bulls seems to have been performed by priests too in exceptional cases).[44]

Finally, there are some who also throw doubt on whether in fact a non-ordained member of the faithful does perform exactly the same *munera* in the same way and with the same salvific effect as an ordained deacon.[45] Even if they

39 Cf. notes 249, 281, 282 supra.

40 Cf. note 283 supra.

41 LG, no. 21b notes succinctly: "Episcoporum est per Sacramentum Ordinis novos electos in corpus episcopale assumere."

42 E.g.: "Minister ordinarius sacrae communionis est Episcopus, presbyter et diaconus. Extraordinarius sacrae communionis minister est acolythus necnon alius christifidelis ad normam c. 230 §3 deputatus." CIC, c. 910.

43 "Confirmationis minister ordinarius est Episcopus; valide hoc sacramentum confert presbyter quoque hac facultate vi iuris communis aut peculiaris concessionis competentis auctoritatis instructus." CIC, c. 882.

44 LG, no. 26c, considers bishops to be "dispensatores sacrorum ordinum," while CIC, c. 1012, states that "sacrae ordinationis minister est Episcopus consecratus"; cf. likewise DS 1326 and 1777. Nevertheless, the problem raised by some papal documents which seemed to grant a priest the faculty of conferring the diaconate (cf. DS 1435) and even the priesthood (cf. DS 1145, 1146, 1290) does not appear to have been settled doctrinally.

45 The *Ratio Fundamentalis* itself (no. 9) says this: "Ministerium diaconale distinctum est exercitio trium munerum, ministerio ordinato propriorum, in specifica luce diaconiae."

seem to be the same functions as are exercised by a non-ordained member of the faithful, the deciding factor would be what the deacon *was* rather than what he *did*: the action of the deacon would bring about a special presence of Christ the Head and Servant that was proper to sacramental grace, configuration with Him, and the community and public dimension of the tasks which are carried out in the name of the Church. The viewpoint of faith and the sacramental reality of the diaconate would enable its particular distinctiveness to be discovered and affirmed, not in relation to its functions but in relation to its theological nature and its representative symbolism.

V. Conclusion

From the point of view of its theological meaning and its ecclesial role the ministry of the diaconate presents a challenge to the Church's awareness and practice, particularly through the questions that it still raises today. With reference to deacons, plenty of witnesses from Tradition recall that the Lord chose acts of humble service to express and render present the reality of the *morphe doulou* (Phil 2:7) which he assumed for the sake of his saving mission. Specifically, the diaconate was born as a help to the Apostles and their successors, who were themselves perceived as servants of Christ. If the diaconate has been restored as a permanent ministry by Vatican II it is especially to respond to specific needs (cf. *Lumen Gentium*, no. 29b) or to grant sacramental grace to those who were already carrying out the functions of the deacon's office (*Ad Gentes*, no. 16f.). But the task of identifying these needs and these functions more clearly in Christian communities is still to be done, although the rich experience of the particular Churches which, after the Council, gave the permanent diaconate a place in their pastoral practice, is already available.

In the current consciousness of the Church there is only one single sacrament of Holy Orders. Vatican II, taking up the teaching of Pius XII,[46] affirmed this unity and saw the episcopate, the priesthood and the diaconate as included within it. According to the decision of Paul VI it is only these three ordained ministries which constitute the clerical state.[47] However, concerning the diaconate the Council cautiously speaks only of "sacramental grace." After Vatican II,

46 Constitutio apostolica *Sacramentum Ordinis*, art. 4-5 (DS 3857-3861). On the imposition of hands and the prayer of consecration, cf. also Gregory IX, *Ep. Presbyter et diaconus* ad episc. Olaf de Lund (DS 826; cf. 1326).

47 *Ministeria Quaedam*, AAS 64 (1972): 531.

Paul VI[48] and the CCE (no. 1570) teach that the deacon, through ordination, receives the character of the sacrament of Holy Orders. Canon 1008 of the CIC states that the three ordained ministries are exercised *in persona Christi Capitis.*[49] Following *Lumen Gentium* (no. 29), which attributed to the deacon the solemn administration of baptism (cf. *Sacrosanctum Concilium*, no. 68), canon 861 §1 spoke of each of the three ordained ministers as ordinary ministers of this sacrament; canon 129 recognized that the *potestas regiminis* belonged to all those who have received the sacrament of Holy Orders.[50]

On the other hand, the difference between the sacerdotal ministries and the diaconal ministry is also underlined. The Council statement that the deacon is not ordained for priesthood but for ministry was taken up by various documents of the post-Conciliar Magisterium. Most clearly of all, the CCE (no. 154) distinguishes within one and the same *ordinatio*, the *gradus participations sacerdotalis* of the episcopate and the priesthood, and the *gradus servitii* of the diaconate. The diaconate, by the very nature of its *way of participating* in the one mission of Christ, carries out this mission in the manner of an auxiliary service. It is "*icona vivens Christi servi in Ecclesia*" but, precisely as such, it maintains a constitutive link with the priestly ministry to which it lends its aid (cf. *Lumen Gentium*, no. 41). It is not just any service which is attributed to the deacon in the Church: his service belongs to the sacrament of Holy Orders, as a close collaboration with the bishop and the priests, in the unity of the same ministerial actualization of the mission of Christ. The CCE (no. 1554) quotes St. Ignatius of Antioch: "Let everyone revere the deacons as Jesus Christ, the bishop as the image of the Father, and the presbyters as the senate of God and the assembly of the Apostles. For without them one cannot speak of the Church."[51]

With regard to the ordination of women to the diaconate, it should be noted that two important indications emerge from what has been said up to this point:

48 *Sacrum Diaconatus*, p. 698.

49 The International Theological Commission has been notified that a revised version of this canon is in preparation, aiming to distinguish the priestly ("sacerdotal") ministries from the diaconal ministry.

50 Cf. Erdö, "Der ständige Diakon: Theologisch-systematische und rechtliche Erwägungen," *AKathKR* 166 (1997): 79-80.

51 *Ad Trail* 3, 1; SCh 10(2), 96.

1. The deaconesses mentioned in the tradition of the ancient Church—as evidenced by the rite of institution and the functions they exercised—were not purely and simply equivalent to the deacons;
2. The unity of the sacrament of Holy Orders, in the clear distinction between the ministries of the bishop and the priests on the one hand and the diaconal ministry on the other, is strongly underlined by ecclesial tradition, especially in the teaching of the Magisterium.

In the light of these elements which have been set out in the present historico-theological research document, it pertains to the ministry of discernment which the Lord established in his Church to pronounce authoritatively on this question.

Over and above all the questions raised by the diaconate, it is good to recall that ever since Vatican II the active presence of this ministry in the life of the Church has aroused, in memory of the example of Christ, a more vivid awareness of the value of service for Christian life.

CONGREGATION FOR BISHOPS

Apostolorum Successores (Directory for the Pastoral Ministry of Bishops)

(2004)

The present Directory, an updated and revised version of the one issued on February 22, 1973, has been prepared by the Congregation for Bishops in order to offer to the "Shepherds of Christ's flock" a useful guide that will help them to exercise more fruitfully every aspect of their complex and difficult pastoral ministry in the Church and in the modern world. It is intended to help the Bishops to address, with humble trust in God and with constant courage, the challenges and new problems of the present day, amid the great progress and the rapid changes that mark the beginning of this third millennium.

This Directory belongs to a rich tradition: from the sixteenth century onward, many ecclesiastical writers have produced documents with such titles as *Enchiridion*, *Praxis*, *Statutes*, *Ordo*, *Dialogues*, *Aphorisms*, *Munera*, *Instructions*, *Officium*, with a view to offering Bishops comprehensive pastoral manuals to assist them in the exercise of their ministry.

The principal sources of this Directory are the documents of the Second Vatican Council, as well as more recent pontifical teaching and the 1983 *Code of Canon Law*. Significantly, this Directory is being published shortly after the promulgation of the Post-Synodal Apostolic Exhortation *Pastores Gregis*, which brought together the ideas and proposals of the Tenth Ordinary General Assembly of the Synod of Bishops, held in 2001 and devoted to a study of the episcopal ministry under the heading: "The Bishop, minister of the Gospel of Jesus Christ for the hope of the world." This recent Apostolic Exhortation completed the series of Post-Synodal Magisterial reflections by the Holy Father on the different vocations of the People of God, in the context of the ecclesiology of communion set out by the Second Vatican Council, focusing on the diocesan Bishop as the visible sign and central principle. Hence, this Directory is closely linked to the Apostolic Exhortation *Pastores Gregis* with regard to its doctrinal and pastoral foundations. It was produced after wide consultation, taking note of suggestions and comments received from various diocesan Bishops and from some Bishops Emeritus.

The Directory is fundamentally pastoral and practical in nature, offering suggestions and concrete guidelines for the activity of Bishops, without prejudice to the prudent discretion of each individual Bishop in judging how best to apply them in the particular conditions of his diocese, taking into account the local mentality and social situation, and the growth of his people's faith. In this Directory, whatever is drawn from the discipline of the Church retains the same force that it has in its original source.

Chapter II

The Bishop's Solicitude for the Universal Church

17. Missionary Activity

Insofar as the situation of the diocese permits, and having secured the agreement of the Holy See and the Ordinary concerned, the Bishop is encouraged to establish a relationship with a *particular missionary Church*, sending missionaries and material resources in accordance with agreed commitments. Moreover, he is urged to promote and support in his particular Church the *Pontifical Missionary Societies*, securing the necessary spiritual and financial aid.[1] With this end in view, the Bishop should appoint a competent priest, deacon or layperson to organize the various diocesan initiatives, such as the annual World Mission Day and the annual collection for the missionary societies.[2]

In the same way, the Bishop should join his own efforts with those of the Holy See in order to assist Churches which suffer persecution or are afflicted with serious shortages of clergy or of resources.[3]

The bond of communion between the Churches is clearly manifested in the *fidei donum* priests, chosen from among those who are suitable and sufficiently trained. Through these priests, older dioceses contribute effectively to the evangelization of newer Churches, and receive, in their turn, freshness and vitality of faith from the younger Christian communities.[4]

---

1 Cf. CD, no. 6.

2 Cf. John Paul II, Encyclical Letter *Redemptoris Missio*, nos. 81, 84.

3 Cf. CD, nos. 6-7.

4 Cf. John Paul II, Encyclical Letter *Redemptoris Missio*, no. 68; PDV, no. 18.

When a *suitable cleric* (priest or deacon) expresses a desire to join the *fidei donum* priests, the Bishop should, as far as possible, accede to the request, even if this involves a short-term sacrifice for his diocese. He should ensure that the cleric's rights and duties are clearly established by means of a written agreement with the Bishop in the territory of destination. A temporary transfer need not involve excardination, thereby allowing the cleric on his return to retain all the rights he would have enjoyed had he remained in the diocese.[5]

The Bishops of younger Churches in mission countries should also be prepared to send their priests to other regions in the same country, the same Continent or other Continents which have greater need of evangelization or of clergy.

Chapter IV

VI. Permanent Deacons

92. The Diaconal Ministry

The Second Vatican Council, according to the venerable tradition of the Church, defined the diaconate as a ministry "of the liturgy, of the Gospel and of works of charity."[6] The deacon, therefore, participates in his own way in the three functions of *teaching, sanctifying and governing*, which belong properly to the members of the hierarchy.

He proclaims and expounds the Word of God, he administers baptism, Communion and the sacramentals, and he animates the Christian community mainly in those areas relating to the exercise of charity and the administration of goods.

The ministry of these clerics, in its different aspects, is pervaded by the *sense of service* which gives rise to the very name "deacon." As in the case of any other sacred ministry, diaconal service should be directed in the first place to God, and, in God's name, to the brethren. Yet the diaconate is also a service to the episcopate and to the presbyterate, to which the order of deacons is joined by bonds of obedience and communion, according to canonical discipline. In this way, the entire diaconal ministry constitutes a unity in the service of the divine

5 Cf. CIC, c. 271.
6 Cf. LG, no. 29.

plan of redemption, and its different elements are closely interconnected: the ministry of the Word leads to the ministry of the altar, which in turn implies the exercise of charity. Therefore, the Bishop should take steps to ensure that all the faithful, and priests in particular, appreciate and hold in esteem the ministry of deacons, which in all its aspects (e.g., liturgical, catechetical, charitable, pastoral, administrative) serves to build up the Church and may help to compensate for any shortage of priests.

93. Functions and Offices Entrusted to Permanent Deacons

It is very important to enable deacons, as far as possible, to exercise their ministry in its fullness: in preaching, in the liturgy, and in works of charity.[7] Deacons should understand that their various tasks are not a mere aggregate of different activities, but are *strictly linked* by virtue of the sacrament received. While some of these tasks may also be performed by the lay faithful, they are always diaconal when performed by a deacon in the name of the Church, and sustained by the grace of the sacrament.[8]

For this reason, it is preferable that any office which involves *supplying for the presence of a priest* be assigned to a deacon rather than to a layperson, especially when it is a question of providing some form of stable leadership for a Christian community without a priest, or assisting widely dispersed groups of Christians in the name of the Bishop or the pastor.[9] Yet at the same time, it is important to ensure that deacons exercise their *proper functions*, rather than simply supplying for a priest.

94. Relationships of Deacons with One Another

Like Bishops and priests, deacons constitute an order of the faithful united by bonds of solidarity in the exercise of a common activity. For this reason, the Bishop should encourage human and spiritual fellowship among deacons, so that they come to sense a special sacramental fraternity. This can be achieved through standard means of ongoing diaconal formation and also through

---

7 Cf. John Paul II, Post-Synodal Apostolic Exhortation *Pastores Gregis*, no. 49.

8 Cf. AG, no. 16.

9 Cf. CIC, cc. 517 §§1-2, 519; SDO, V, 22, 10; Congregation for the Clergy, *Directory for the Ministry and Life of Permanent Deacons*, 11.

regular meetings, called by the Bishop, to evaluate the exercise of the ministry, to share experiences and to receive support in order to persevere in their vocation.

Deacons, like other members of the faithful and other clerics, have the *right of association* with others, lay and clerical, for the purpose of deepening their spiritual life and performing works of charity or apostolate suited to their clerical state and compatible with the fulfillment of their proper duties.[10] Nevertheless, this right of association should not lead to an undue corporativism for the protection of their interests, which would be an inappropriate imitation of secular models, irreconcilable with the sacramental bonds that unite deacons with one another, with the Bishop and with other sacred ministers.[11]

95. Deacons Engaged in a Profession or a Secular Occupation

The diaconal ministry is compatible with the exercise of a profession or civil office. Depending on local circumstances and the particular ministry assigned to the individual deacon, it is desirable that he should have work and a profession of his own, so that he has sufficient means of support.[12] It goes without saying that his involvement in secular business does not transform the deacon into a layperson.

Those deacons who practice a profession should be able to offer an example of honesty and a true spirit of service, so that their professional and human relationships serve to bring people closer to God and to the Church. They should be zealous in conforming their work to individual and social moral norms. They should not fail to consult their pastor when the practice of their profession becomes more an obstacle than a means to sanctification.[13]

Deacons may exercise any honest profession or activity, provided that they are not prevented in principle from doing so by the prohibitions established by canonical discipline for clerics.[14] Nevertheless, it is preferable that deacons should perform those professional activities more closely linked to the *transmission of Gospel truth and the service of the brethren*: such as education—principally

10 Cf. CIC, c. 278.

11 Cf. Congregation for the Clergy, Decree *Quidam Episcopi* (1982), IV; *Directory for the Ministry and Life of Permanent Deacons*, 7, 11.

12 Regarding the remuneration due to a deacon, cf. CIC, c. 281, and Congregation for the Clergy, *Directory for the Ministry and Life of Permanent Deacons*, 15-20.

13 Cf. Congregation for the Clergy, *Directory for the Ministry and Life of Permanent Deacons*, 12.

14 Cf. CIC, cc. 288, 285 §§3-4.

religious education—various social services, communications media, and some areas of medical research and practice.

96. Married Deacons

The married deacon's witness of fidelity to the Church and to his vocation of service is also expressed through family life. It follows that the *consent of the wife* is necessary for her husband's ordination.[15] Particular pastoral attention should be given to the deacon's family, so that they can live with joy the commitment made by their husband or father and support him in his ministry. Nevertheless, functions and activities proper to the ministry should not be entrusted to the deacon's wife or children, because the diaconal state is properly and exclusively his. Naturally, this does not prevent family members from assisting the deacon as he fulfills his responsibilities. Moreover, the experience of family life makes married deacons especially well suited to the *pastoral care of families*, at diocesan or parochial levels, for which they should receive appropriate preparation.

97. The Formation of Permanent Deacons

The initial and ongoing formation of deacons has considerable importance for their life and ministry. In order to determine what is needed for the formation of candidates for the permanent diaconate, the norms issued by the Holy See and the Episcopal Conference should be observed. It is preferable that permanent deacons should not be too young, but should have arrived at human as well as spiritual maturity, and that they should be formed in a suitable community for three years, unless in a particular case serious reasons suggest otherwise.[16]

Their formation comprises similar elements to that of priests, but with some specific differences:

- The *spiritual formation* of the deacon[17] helps him on his path to Christian holiness with particular emphasis on the distinctive feature of his ministry, i.e., the spirit of service. Avoiding, therefore, every risk of merely maintaining a façade or of a dichotomy between his vocation

---

15 Cf. CIC, c. 1031 §2.

16 Cf. CIC, c. 236; Congregation for Catholic Education, *Basic Norms for the Formation of Permanent Deacons*.

17 Cf. Congregation for the Clergy, *Directory for the Ministry and Life of Permanent Deacons*, chapters 3-4.

and his manner of life, the deacon should wish to conform his entire existence to Christ, who loves and serves all people.

- The exercise of the deacon's ministry, especially preaching and teaching the Word of God, presupposes a continuous *doctrinal formation*, directed by suitably qualified professors.
- Every deacon should receive *personal support*, enabling him to address his particular life circumstances, in his relations with other members of the People of God, in his professional work, and in his family ties.

Chapter V

II. The Bishop, Moderator of the Ministry of the Word

124. The Bishop's Co-Workers in the Ministry of the Word

By virtue of the sacrament of orders, the ministry of preaching belongs properly to priests—predominantly parish priests and those entrusted with the care of souls—and also to deacons, in communion with the Bishop and his *presbyterium*.[18] The Bishop has a duty to monitor the *suitability of ministers* of the Word.

Chapter VI

III. Structures of Participation in the Pastoral Ministry of the Bishop

192. The Diocesan Finance Council and the Finance Officer

In every diocese a *finance council* is to be established over which the Bishop or his delegate presides.[19] Similar councils are to be established for each parish and for other juridical persons.[20] The members of these councils should be chosen from among those faithful who are knowledgeable in financial affairs and civil law, renowned for their honesty and their love for the Church and its apostolate. In those places where the permanent diaconate has been instituted, steps

18 Cf. CIC, c. 757.
19 Cf. CIC, c. 492.
20 Cf. CIC, cc. 537, 1280.

should be taken to arrange the participation of the deacons in finance councils, according to the charism of their order.

Together with the diocesan finance council, the Bishop examines work proposals, budgets, and plans for financing them, and he makes the necessary decisions in conformity with the law. Moreover, the diocesan finance council, jointly with the college of consultors, *must be consulted* for acts of administration which, given the economic situation of the diocese, are of *greater importance*; for the acts of *extraordinary administration* (established by the Episcopal Conference), the Bishop needs the *consent* of the college of consultors and the diocesan finance council. In placing various acts of administration, the Bishop, without prejudice to his own competence, will avail himself of the collaboration of the diocesan finance officer.[21]

In every diocese, after having heard the college of consultors and the finance council, the Bishop is to appoint a *finance officer* for a five-year renewable term.

The finance officer, who may be a permanent deacon or a layperson, must possess extensive experience in the administration of financial affairs. He must have a good knowledge of civil and canonical legislation concerning temporal goods and of any legal agreements with the civil authority concerning ecclesiastical goods.

Under the authority of the Bishop, the diocesan finance officer must administer the goods of the diocese according to the parameters approved by the finance council.

---

21 Cf. CIC, cc. 1277, 1292.

CONGREGATION FOR DIVINE WORSHIP AND THE DISCIPLINE OF THE SACRAMENTS

Instruction *Redemptionis Sacramentum (On Certain Matters to be Observed or to be Avoided Regarding the Most Holy Eucharist)*

The Diocesan Bishop, High Priest of his Flock

20. Indeed, the preeminent manifestation of the Church is found whenever the rites of Mass are celebrated, especially in the Cathedral Church, "with the full and active participation of the entire holy People of God, joined in one act of prayer, at one altar at which the Bishop presides," surrounded by his presbyterate with the Deacons and ministers. Furthermore, "every lawful celebration of the Eucharist is directed by the Bishop, to whom is entrusted the office of presenting the worship of the Christian religion to the Divine Majesty and ordering it according to the precepts of the Lord and the laws of the Church, further specified by his own particular judgment for the Diocese."

22. The Bishop governs the particular Church entrusted to him, and it is his task to regulate, to direct, to encourage, and sometimes also to reprove; this is a sacred task that he has received through episcopal Ordination, which he fulfills in order to build up his flock in truth and holiness. He should elucidate the inherent meaning of the rites and the liturgical texts, and nourish the spirit of the Liturgy in the Priests, Deacons and lay faithful so that they are all led to the active and fruitful celebration of the Eucharist, and in like manner he should take care to ensure that the whole body of the Church is able to grow in the same understanding, in the unity of charity, in the diocese, in the nation and in the world.

Deacons

34. Deacons "upon whom hands are imposed not for the Priesthood but for the ministry," as men of good repute, must act in such a way that with the help of God they may be recognized as the true disciples of him "who came not to be served but to serve," and who was among his disciples "as one who serves." Strengthened by the gift of the Holy Spirit through the laying on of hands, they are in service to the People of God, in communion with the Bishop and his presbyterate. They should therefore consider the Bishop as a father, and give assistance to him and to the Priests "in the ministry of the word, of the altar, and of charity."

35. Let them never fail, "as the Apostle says, to hold the mystery of faith with a clear conscience, and to proclaim this faith by word and deed according to the Gospel and the tradition of the Church," in wholehearted, faithful and humble service to the Sacred Liturgy as the source and summit of ecclesial life, "so that all, made children of God through faith and Baptism, may come together as one, praising God in the midst of the Church, to participate in the Sacrifice and to eat the Lord's Supper." Let all Deacons, then, do their part so that the Sacred Liturgy will be celebrated according to the norms of the duly approved liturgical books.

59. The reprobated practice by which Priests, Deacons or the faithful here and there alter or vary at will the texts of the Sacred Liturgy that they are charged to pronounce, must cease. For in doing thus, they render the celebration of the Sacred Liturgy unstable, and not infrequently distort the authentic meaning of the Liturgy.

The Distribution of Holy Communion

88. The faithful should normally receive sacramental Communion of the Eucharist during Mass itself, at the moment laid down by the rite of celebration, that is to say, just after the Priest celebrant's Communion. It is the Priest celebrant's responsibility to minister Communion, perhaps assisted by other Priests or Deacons; and he should not resume the Mass until after the Communion of the faithful is concluded. Only when there is a necessity may extraordinary ministers assist the Priest celebrant in accordance with the norm of law.

147. When the Church's needs require it, however, if sacred ministers are lacking, lay members of Christ's faithful may supply for certain liturgical offices according to the norm of law. Such faithful are called and appointed to carry out certain functions, whether of greater or lesser weight, sustained by the Lord's grace. Many of the lay Christian faithful have already contributed eagerly to this service and still do so, especially in missionary areas where the Church is still of small dimensions or is experiencing conditions of persecution, but also in areas affected by a shortage of Priests and Deacons.

149. More recently, in some dioceses long since evangelized, members of Christ's lay faithful have been appointed as "pastoral assistants," and among them many have undoubtedly served the good of the Church by providing assistance to the Bishop, Priests and Deacons in the carrying out of their pastoral activity. Let care be taken, however, lest the delineation of this function be assimilated too closely to the form of pastoral ministry that belongs to clerics. That is to say, attention should be paid to ensuring that "pastoral assistants" do not take upon themselves what is proper to the ministry of the sacred ministers.

150. The activity of a pastoral assistant should be directed to facilitating the ministry of Priests and Deacons, to ensuring that vocations to the Priesthood and Diaconate are awakened and that lay members of Christ's faithful in each community are carefully trained for the various liturgical functions, in keeping with the variety of charisms and in accordance with the norm of law.

152. These purely supplementary functions must not be an occasion for disfiguring the very ministry of Priests, in such a way that the latter neglect the celebration of Holy Mass for the people for whom they are responsible, or their personal care of the sick, or the baptism of children, or assistance at weddings or the celebration of Christian funerals—matters which pertain in the first place to Priests assisted by Deacons. It must therefore never be the case that in parishes Priests alternate indiscriminately in shifts of pastoral service with Deacons or laypersons, thus confusing what is specific to each.

The Extraordinary Minister of Holy Communion

154. As has already been recalled, "the only minister who can confect the Sacrament of the Eucharist *in persona Christi* is a validly ordained Priest."

Hence the name "minister of the Eucharist" belongs properly to the Priest alone. Moreover, also by reason of their sacred Ordination, the ordinary ministers of Holy Communion are the Bishop, the Priest and the Deacon, to whom it belongs therefore to administer Holy Communion to the lay members of Christ's faithful during the celebration of Mass. In this way their ministerial office in the Church is fully and accurately brought to light, and the sign value of the Sacrament is made complete.

Preaching

161. As was already noted above, the homily on account of its importance and its nature is reserved to the Priest or Deacon during Mass. As regards other forms of preaching, if necessity demands it in particular circumstances, or if usefulness suggests it in special cases, lay members of Christ's faithful may be allowed to preach in a church or in an oratory outside Mass in accordance with the norm of law. This may be done only on account of a scarcity of sacred ministers in certain places, in order to meet the need, and it may not be transformed from an exceptional measure into an ordinary practice, nor may it be understood as an authentic form of the advancement of the laity. All must remember besides that the faculty for giving such permission belongs to the local Ordinary, and this as regards individual instances; this permission is not the competence of anyone else, even if they are Priests or Deacons.

164. "If participation at the celebration of the Eucharist is impossible on account of the absence of a sacred minister or for some other grave cause," then it is the Christian people's right that the diocesan Bishop should provide as far as he is able for some celebration to be held on Sundays for that community under his authority and according to the Church's norms. Sunday celebrations of this specific kind, however, are to be considered altogether extraordinary. All Deacons or lay members of Christ's faithful who are assigned a part in such celebrations by the diocesan Bishop should strive "to keep alive in the community a genuine 'hunger' for the Eucharist, so that no opportunity for the celebration of Mass will ever be missed, also taking advantage of the occasional presence of a Priest who is not impeded by Church law from celebrating Mass."

186. Let all Christ's faithful participate in the Most Holy Eucharist as fully, consciously and actively as they can, honoring it lovingly by their devotion and

the manner of their life. Let Bishops, Priests and Deacons, in the exercise of the sacred ministry, examine their consciences as regards the authenticity and fidelity of the actions they have performed in the name of Christ and the Church in the celebration of the Sacred Liturgy. Let each one of the sacred ministers ask himself, even with severity, whether he has respected the rights of the lay members of Christ's faithful, who confidently entrust themselves and their children to him, relying on him to fulfill for the faithful those sacred functions that the Church intends to carry out in celebrating the sacred Liturgy at Christ's command. For each one should always remember that he is a servant of the Sacred Liturgy.

All things to the contrary notwithstanding.

This Instruction, prepared by the Congregation for Divine Worship and the Discipline of the Sacraments by mandate of the Supreme Pontiff John Paul II in collaboration with the Congregation for the Doctrine of the Faith, was approved by the same Pontiff on the Solemnity of St. Joseph, March 19, 2004, and he ordered it to be published and to be observed immediately by all concerned.

From the offices of the Congregation for Divine Worship and the Discipline of the Sacraments, Rome, on the Solemnity of the Annunciation of the Lord, March 25, 2004.

Francis Card. Arinze
Prefect

Domenico Sorrentino
Archbishop Secretary

VII INTERNATIONAL CONGRESS FOR THE PASTORAL CARE OF CIRCUS AND TRAVELING SHOW PEOPLE

Final Document

III. Pastoral Proposals

1. During the Congress it was pointed out that circus and carnival families live and work in the same place and that it would be a good thing to bolster this up from a pastoral point of view in order to:

> think out and put into practice suitable training for pastoral workers (priests, deacons, religious, laity), involving also seminarians and religious in formation.[22]

IV. Recommendations

1. Particular Churches, parishes, must become "homes open to all," "missionary parishes" at the service of the faith of men and women, including persons who are transient, which also means circus, carnival and traveling show people.

2. These people in fact, though living the inconvenience always of leaving for somewhere else, are nevertheless members of the Christian community for the short time of their stay. The community must therefore adopt the attitude and relationship toward them that our Lord asks of his Church, resisting temptations and subterfuge incompatible with the gospel.

3. It would also be desirable for the local Church to take on the task of promotion and correct discernment of this particular sector of pastoral care of human mobility, preparing a culture of welcome in its own territory. Furthermore a specific ministry should also be envisaged, keeping in mind the diaconate and "lay ministries" in the service of mission.

Rome, Italy, December 12-16, 2004

22 This phrase is a translation of the Italian.

SYNOD OF BISHOPS, XII ORDINARY GENERAL ASSEMBLY

Instrumentum Laboris The Word of God in the Life and Mission of the Church

The Task of Priests and Deacons

49. Knowledge of and familiarity with the Word of God is also of prime importance for priests and deacons in their calling to the ministry of evangelization. The Second Vatican Council states that, by necessity, all the clergy, primarily priests and deacons, ought to have continual contact with the Scriptures, through assiduous reading and attentive study of the sacred texts, so as not to become idle preachers of the Word of God, hearing the Word only with their ears while not hearing it with their hearts (cf. DV, no. 25; PO, no. 4). In keeping with this conciliar teaching, canon law speaks of the ministry of the Word of God entrusted to priests and deacons as collaborators of the Bishop.[23]

By being in daily contact with the Word, priests and deacons draw the life necessary to resist being conformed to the mentality of the world and receive the ability wisely to discern personal matters and those of the community so that, in their apostolic activity, they can zealously guide the People of God in the ways of the Lord. Consequently, instruction and pastoral formation inspired by the Word of God are a necessity. Developments in biblical learning, various needs and the ever-changing pastoral situation demand an ongoing formation.

The task of proclamation calls for recourse to specific initiatives, for example, a full appreciation of the Bible in all pastoral projects. In every diocese a biblical pastoral program, under the guidance of the bishop, can insert the Bible into the Church's great initiatives in evangelization and catechesis. If this is done, the Word of God can be seen as the basis for and manifestation of communion among the clergy and laity, and, consequently, among parishes, communities of the consecrated life and ecclesial movements.

From the vantage point of priestly service, seminary formation increasingly calls for a greater, up-to-date knowledge of exegesis and theology, a solid

23 Cf. CIC c. 757; CCEO, cc. 608; 614.

formation in the pastoral use of the Bible and a true and proper initiation into biblical spirituality, without neglecting an instruction in a passionate love for the Word expressed in service to the People of God. Members of the clergy, then, are asked to dedicate themselves to being students of Sacred Scripture, even through higher studies.

APPENDIX

National Directory for the Formation, Ministry, and Life of Permanent Deacons in the United States

NATIONAL DIRECTORY FOR THE FORMATION, MINISTRY, AND LIFE OF PERMANENT DEACONS IN THE UNITED STATES

Including the Secondary Documents
BASIC STANDARDS FOR READINESS
and
VISIT OF CONSULTATION TEAMS TO DIOCESAN PERMANENT DIACONATE FORMATION PROGRAMS

This *National Directory for the Formation, Ministry, and Life of Permanent Deacons in the United States* is intended to serve the entire Catholic Church in the United States. Its principles, norms, and pastoral applications are directed specifically to the Latin Rite. Nonetheless, it may be of assistance as a consistent reference for all Churches *sui iuris* in the United States in the preparation of the adaptations necessary to address the particular traditions, pastoral life, and requirements of the *Code of Canons of the Eastern Churches*.

UNITED STATES CONFERENCE OF CATHOLIC BISHOPS

The document *National Directory for the Formation, Ministry, and Life of Permanent Deacons in the United States* was developed by the Bishops' Committee on the Diaconate of the United States Conference of Catholic Bishops (USCCB). It was approved by the full body of the United States Conference of Catholic Bishops at its June 2003 General Meeting, received the subsequent *recognitio* of the Holy See, and has been authorized for publication by the undersigned.

Msgr. William P. Fay
General Secretary, USCCB

Office of the President

3211 FOURTH STREET NE · WASHINGTON DC 20017-1194 · 202-541-3100 · FAX 202-541-3166

Cardinal Francis George, OMI
Archbishop of Chicago

United States Conference of Catholic Bishops

DECREE OF PROMULGATION

In June 2003, the members of the United States Conference of Catholic Bishops approved the *National Directory for the Formation, Life and Ministry of Permanent Deacons in the United States.*

This action, made in accord with canon 236 of the *Code of Canon Law* and with n. 15 of the *Ratio fundamentalis institutionis diaconorum permanentium*, was confirmed *ad quinquennium experimenti gratia* by the Congregation for Catholic Education and the Congregation for Clergy (Prot. N. 78/2000), signed by Zenon Cardinal Grocholewski, Prefect of the Congregation for Catholic Education and Darío Cardinal Castrillón-Hoyos, Prefect of the Congregation for Clergy, and dated October 30, 2004.

By a subsequent decree of the same aforementioned Congregations dated October 12, 2009 (Prot. N. 78/2000), and signed by Zenon Cardinal Grocholewski, Prefect of the Congregation for Catholic Education, and Cláudio Cardinal Hummes, Prefect of the Congregation for Clergy, approval was granted *ad alterum quinquennium* for the text of the *National Directory for the Formation, Life and Ministry of Permanent Deacons in the United States* as originally approved by the United States Conference of Catholic Bishops in June 2003.

As President of the United States Conference of Catholic Bishops I hereby decree that the effective date of this Decree of Promulgation will be December 26, 2009, the Feast of St. Stephen, Deacon and Martyr.

Given at the offices of the United States Conference of Catholic Bishops in the city of Washington, the District of Columbia, on the 4th day of November, in the year of our Lord 2009, the Feast of St. Charles Borromeo.

Francis Cardinal George, O.M.I.
Archbishop of Chicago
President

Monsignor David J. Malloy
General Secretary, USCCB

TABLE OF CONTENTS

National Directory for the Formation, Ministry, and Life of Permanent Deacons in the United States

INTRODUCTION
I. Foreword 434
II. Abbreviations 436
III. Prayer to the Blessed Virgin Mary 438

PREFACE
I. The Diaconate in the Second Vatican Council and the Post-Conciliar Period: A Historical Overview . . . 441
II. The Diaconate in the United States 442
III. Recent Developments 444
IV. The Development of This *National Directory* 446
V. The Objective and Interpretation of This *National Directory* 446
VI. Acknowledgments 447

CHAPTER ONE

DOCTRINAL UNDERSTANDING OF THE DIACONATE
I. Introduction 453
II. The Sacramental Nature of the Church 453
III. Ecclesial Communion and Mission 454
IV. The Reestablished Order of Deacons 456
V. The Church's Ministry of the Word: The Deacon as Evangelizer and Teacher. 458
VI. The Church's Ministry of Liturgy: The Deacon as Sanctifier
VII. The Church's Ministry of Charity and Justice: The Deacon as Witness and Guide 460
VIII. An Intrinsic Unity 461
IX. Concluding Reflection 462

CHAPTER TWO

THE MINISTRY AND LIFE OF DEACONS

I. The Relationships of the Deacon 465
II. Diaconal Spirituality 472
III. The Deacon in His State of Life 473
IV. The Permanency of the Order of Deacons 477
V. The Obligations and Rights of Deacons 477
VI. United States Conference of Catholic Bishops; Particular Law Governing Deacons in the United States 480
Norms 483

CHAPTER THREE

DIMENSIONS IN THE FORMATION OF DEACONS

I. Introduction 491
II. Dimensions in Formation 491
III. Additional Considerations 502
IV. Assessment: Integrating the Four Dimensions in Formation Programming 507
Norms 509

CHAPTER FOUR

VOCATION, DISCERNMENT, AND SELECTION

I. Promotion and Recruitment 515
II. The Mystery of Vocation 517
III. The Discernment of the Call 518
IV. Admission and Selection Procedures 519
V. Admission into the Aspirant Path in Formation 521
Norms 522

CHAPTER FIVE

ASPIRANT PATH IN DIACONAL FORMATION

I. Introduction 525
II. The Dimensions of Formation in the Aspirant Path . . . 526
III. Assessment for Nomination into the Candidate Path in Formation 529

IV. The Rite of Admission to Candidacy 530
Norms 531

CHAPTER SIX

CANDIDATE PATH IN DIACONAL FORMATION

I. Introduction 535
II. The Length of the Candidate Path in Formation. 535
III. Formation Environments 536
IV. The Dimensions of Formation in the Candidate Path . . . 538
V. The Assessment of Candidates 540
VI. Scrutinies for Installation into the Ministries of Lector and Acolyte and Ordination to the Diaconate 544
Norms 546

CHAPTER SEVEN

POST-ORDINATION PATH IN DIACONAL FORMATION

I. Introduction 553
II. The Dimensions of Formation in the Post-Ordination Path 554
III. Additional Considerations 558
IV. Diocesan Organization for Post-Ordination Path Formation 559
Norms 560

CHAPTER EIGHT

ORGANIZATION, STRUCTURE, AND PERSONNEL FOR DIACONAL FORMATION

I. Organization 563
II. Structures 564
III. The Role of the Diocesan Bishop in Diaconate Formation . 566
IV. Recruitment and Preparation of Formation Personnel . . . 566
V. Aspirant/Candidate Formation Personnel 567
VI. Advisory Structures for Aspirant and Candidate Paths of Formation 571
VII. Post-Ordination Formation Personnel. 572
VIII. Post-Ordination Advisory Structures 574
Norms 575

CONCLUSION 581

FOREWORD

Throughout the last decade of the twentieth century, the Congregation for Catholic Education and the Congregation for the Clergy devoted considerable attention to the ordained ministries of priest and deacon. After the publication of the *Basic Norms for the Formation of Priests* and the *Directory on the Ministry and Life of Priests* in 1994, these two Congregations took up the same issues related to the ordained ministry of permanent deacons. In February 1998, they promulgated the *Basic Norms for the Formation of Permanent Deacons* and the *Directory on the Life and Ministry of Permanent Deacons*. In a Joint Declaration and Introduction, the prefects of these two Congregations offered these documents as directives "of which due account is to be taken by the Episcopal Conferences when preparing their respective 'Rationes.' As with the *Ratio fundamentalis institutionis sacerdotalis*, the Congregation offers this aid to the various Episcopates to facilitate them in discharging adequately the prescriptions of canon 236 of the Code of Canon Law and to ensure for the Church, unity, earnestness and completeness in the formation of permanent Deacons."[1]

After years of extensive consultation and preparation, the *National Directory for the Formation, Ministry, and Life of Permanent Deacons in the United States* received the *recognitio* from the Holy See on October 30, 2004. The *National Directory* was then officially promulgated by the president of the United States Conference of Catholic Bishops, on December 26, 2004, the Feast of St. Stephen, Deacon and Martyr.

On behalf of my predecessors who served as chairmen of the Bishops' Committee on the Diaconate in directing the preparation of this *National Directory*—Bishop Edward U. Kmiec, Bishop Gerald F. Kicanas, and Bishop Robert C. Morlino—and all the bishops who served on the committee during this period, I wish to acknowledge the extraordinary contribution made by the Rev. Msgr. Theodore W. Krauss of the Diocese of Oakland, California, who served as the project coordinator of the *National Directory* project. His most generous and skillful service in guiding the efforts of the many consultants, researchers, and other experts who contributed to the work of the committee is most gratefully appreciated.

Through much of the process, the work of the committee was greatly aided by two expert consultants: Rev. Kevin Irwin who served as theological consultant, and the Rev. Msgr. William A. Varvaro who served as canonical consultant. Providing overall wisdom and guidance were Cardinal Adam Maida and Bishop Donald W. Wuerl of Pittsburgh, who served as episcopal consultants to the committee.

I would like to offer a word about the organization of the documents presented in this volume. There are two major sections to this book. The first section contains the official *National Directory for the Formation, Ministry, and Life of Permanent Deacons in the United States*. This is the primary text, the text for which the *recognitio* has been received.

The second section consists of two secondary documents prepared as resources for the implementation of the *National Directory*. The first of these resource documents contains the *Basic Standards* for the formation of permanent deacons in the United States. Prepared by the Bishops' Committee on the Diaconate following considerable consultation in tandem with the *National Directory*, these *Standards* were approved by a vote of the full body of bishops in June 2000.

The second of these resource documents is the sixth revision of the committee document *Visit of Consultation Teams to Diocesan Permanent Diaconate Formation Programs*. This document is designed as an aid to the diocesan bishop and his staff in providing a mechanism for both program self-evaluation and for a formal visit and consultation by the Bishops' Committee on the Diaconate as outlined in the *National Directory*. This continues a resource offered by the Bishops' Committee on the Diaconate since the earliest days of the implementation of the permanent diaconate in the United States.

In the name of the Bishops' Committee on the Diaconate and the United States Conference of Catholic Bishops, I express our gratitude for the participation of all who assisted in the preparation of the *National Directory* and its related resources. Our heartfelt thanks to all those who serve so generously as deacons, as well as their families, pastors, and co-workers in ministry.

Bishop Frederick F. Campbell
Diocese of Columbus, Ohio
Chair, Bishops' Committee on the Diaconate

1 Congregation for Catholic Education and Congregation for the Clergy, "Joint Declaration and Introduction," *Basic Norms for the Formation of Permanent Deacons/Directory for the Ministry and Life of Permanent Deacons* (Vatican City: Libreria Editrice Vaticana, 1998), p. 8.

ABBREVIATIONS

ADUS Pope John Paul II, *The Heart of the Diaconate: Servants of the Mysteries of Christ and Servants of Your Brothers and Sisters*, Address to Deacons of the United States, Detroit, Michigan (September 19, 1987)

BNFPD Congregation for Catholic Education, *Basic Norms for the Formation of Permanent Deacons (Ratio Fundamentalis Institutionis Diaconorum Permanentium)* (Washington, DC: United States Catholic Conference, 1998)

CCC *Catechism of the Catholic Church*, 2nd ed. (Washington, DC: United States Conference of Catholic Bishops-Libreria Editrice Vaticana, 2000)

CIC Canon Law Society of America, trans., *Code of Canon Law Latin-English Edition (Codex Iuris Canonici)* (Washington, DC: Canon Law Society of America, 1983)

CL Congregation for Divine Worship and Discipline of the Sacraments, Circular Letter, *Scrutinies Regarding Suitability of Candidates for Orders*, Prot. No. 589/97 (November 28, 1997)

DMLPD Congregation for the Clergy, *Directory for the Ministry and Life of Permanent Deacons (Directorium Pro Ministerio et Vita Diaconorum Permanentium)* (Washington, DC: United States Catholic Conference, 1998)

FP Bishops' Committee on Marriage and Family, National Conference of Catholic Bishops, A *Family Perspective in Church and Society, Tenth Anniversary Edition* (Washington, DC: United States Catholic Conference, 1998)

GS Second Vatican Council, *Pastoral Constitution on the Church in the Modern World (Gaudium et Spes)* (Washington, DC: United States Catholic Conference, 1965)

LG Second Vatican Council, *Dogmatic Constitution on the Church*

(Lumen Gentium) (Washington, DC: United States Catholic Conference, 1964)

NSD (1996) Bishops' Committee on the Permanent Diaconate, National Conference of Catholic Bishops, *A National Study on the Permanent Diaconate of the Catholic Church in the United States, 1994-1995* (Washington, DC: United States Catholic Conference, 1996)

OE Second Vatican Council, *Decree on the Catholic Eastern Churches (Orientalium Ecclesiarum)*. In *Vatican Council II: Vol. 1: The Conciliar and Post Conciliar Documents*, Austin Flannery, ed. (Northport, NY: Costello, 1996).

PDG (1984) Bishops' Committee on the Permanent Diaconate, National Conference of Catholic Bishops, *Permanent Deacons in the United States: Guidelines on Their Formation and Ministry, 1984 Revision* (Washington, D.C.: United States Catholic Conference, 1985)

PDO Pope John Paul II, *The Permanent Deacon's Ordination*, Address to the Plenary Assembly of the Congregation for the Clergy (November 30, 1995)

PDV Pope John Paul II, Post-Synodal Apostolic Exhortation, *I Will Give You Shepherds (Pastores Dabo Vobis)* (Washington, DC: United States Catholic Conference, 1992)

SC Second Vatican Council, *Constitution on the Sacred Liturgy (Sacrosanctum Concilium)*. In *Vatican Council II: Vol. 1: The Conciliar and Post Conciliar Documents*, Austin Flannery, ed. (Northport, NY: Costello, 1996).

STVI Bishops' Committee on the Liturgy and Bishops' Committee on the Permanent Diaconate, National Conference of Catholic Bishops, *The Deacon: Minister of Word and Sacrament, Study Text VI* (Washington, DC: United States Catholic Conference, 1979)

PRAYER TO THE BLESSED VIRGIN MARY

MARY
Teacher of faith, who by your obedience to the Word of God have cooperated in a remarkable way with the work of redemption, make the ministry of deacons effective by teaching them to hear the Word and to proclaim it faithfully.

MARY
Teacher of charity, who by your total openness to God's call have cooperated in bringing to birth all the Church's faithful, make the ministry and the life of deacons fruitful by teaching them to give themselves totally to the service of the People of God.

MARY
Teacher of prayer, who through your maternal intercession have supported and helped the Church from her beginnings, make deacons always attentive to the needs of the faithful by teaching them to come to know the value of prayer.

MARY
Teacher of humility, who by constantly knowing yourself to be the servant of the Lord were filled with the Holy Spirit, make deacons docile instruments in Christ's work of redemption by teaching them the greatness of being the least of all.

MARY
Teacher of that service which is hidden, who by your everyday and ordinary life filled with love knew how to cooperate with the salvific plan of God in an exemplary fashion, make deacons good and faithful servants by teaching them the joy of serving the Church with an ardent love.[1]

NOTE

1 Adapted from DMLPD, p. 141.

NATIONAL DIRECTORY FOR THE FORMATION, MINISTRY, AND LIFE OF PERMANENT DEACONS IN THE UNITED STATES

PREFACE

I. The Diaconate in the Second Vatican Council and the Post-Conciliar Period: A Historical Overview[1]

1. One of the great legacies of the Second Vatican Council was its renewal and encouragement of the order of deacons throughout the entire Catholic Church. The Council's decisions on the diaconate flowed out of the bishops' discussions on the sacramental nature of the Church. The Fathers of the Council present in concise, descriptive, and complementary images a comprehensive magisterial teaching: The Church is "mystery," "sacrament," "communion," and "mission."[2] The Church is "like a sacrament or as a sign and instrument both of a very closely knit union with God and of the unity of the whole human race. . . ."[3] "In her whole being and in all her members, the Church is sent to announce, bear witness, make present, and spread the mystery of the communion of the Holy Trinity."[4] This "missionary mandate"[5] is the Church's sacred right and obligation.[6] Through the proclamation of God's word, in sacramental celebrations, and in response to the needs of others, especially in her ministry of charity and justice, "the Church is Christ's instrument . . . 'the universal sacrament of salvation,' by which Christ is 'at once manifesting and actualizing the mystery of God's love for men.'"[7]

The diaconate: legacy of the Second Vatican Council

2. Central to the Second Vatican Council's teaching on the Church is the service or ministry bestowed by Christ upon the apostles and their successors. The office of bishop "is a true service, which in sacred literature is significantly called a 'diakonia' or ministry."[8] The Council Fathers teach that the bishops, with priests and deacons as helpers, have by divine institution taken the place of the apostles as pastors of the Church.[9] Priests and deacons are seen as complementary but subordinate participants in the one apostolic ministry bestowed by Christ upon the apostles, with Peter as their head, and continued through their successors, the bishops, in union with the Roman Pontiff.[10] When discussing Holy Orders as one of the sacraments "at the service of communion" (along with Matrimony), the *Catechism of the Catholic Church* teaches that these two sacraments "are directed towards the salvation of others; if they

An apostolic ministry

contribute as well to personal salvation, it is through service to others that they do so. They confer a particular mission in the Church and serve to build up the People of God."[11]

The deacon's ministry of service is linked with the missionary dimensions of the Church

3. In the Dogmatic Constitution on the Church, the Decree on the Missionary Activity of the Church, and the Decree on the Catholic Eastern Churches, the Second Vatican Council reestablished the diaconate "as a proper and permanent rank of the hierarchy."[12] The Sacred Order of Deacons is to be "a driving force for the Church's service or diakonia toward the local Christian communities, and as a sign or sacrament of the Lord Christ himself, who 'came not to be served but to serve.'"[13] "The deacon's ministry of service is linked with the missionary dimension of the Church: the missionary efforts of the deacon will embrace the ministry of the word, the liturgy, and works of charity which, in their turn, are carried into daily life. Mission includes witness to Christ in a secular profession or occupation."[14] Further, "neither should the prospect of the mission ad gentes be lacking, wherever circumstances require and permit it."[15] In its renewal the Order of Deacons is permanently restored as "a living icon of Christ the Servant within the Church."[16]

The restoration of the diaconate in the Church

4. Following the closing of the Second Vatican Council, Pope Paul VI formally implemented the renewal of the diaconate. In his apostolic letter *Sacrum Diaconatus Ordinem*, he reestablished the Order of Deacons as a permanent ministry in the Catholic Church.[17] The apostolic constitution *Pontificalis Romani Recognito* promulgated new liturgical rites for the conferral of the Sacrament of Holy Orders upon bishops, priests, and deacons in the Latin Rite.[18] The apostolic letter *Ad Pascendum* established norms concerning the Order of Deacons.[19] The apostolic letter *Ministeria Quaedam* addressed the suppression in the Latin Rite of first tonsure, the minor orders, and the subdiaconate; established norms for entrance into the clerical state; and instituted the ministries of reader and acolyte.[20]

II. The Diaconate in the United States

The vision for the diaconate in the United States

5. Since the Second Vatican Council consigned the decision of the restoration of the diaconate to individual episcopal conferences, the bishops of the United States voted in the spring of 1968

to petition the Holy See for authorization. In their letter of May 2, 1968, the bishops presented the following reasons for the request:

1. To complete the hierarchy of sacred orders and to enrich and strengthen the many and various diaconal ministries at work in the United States with the sacramental grace of the diaconate
2. To enlist a new group of devout and competent men in the active ministry of the Church
3. To aid in extending needed liturgical and charitable services to the faithful in both large urban and small rural communities
4. To provide an official and sacramental presence of the Church in areas of secular life, as well as in communities within large cities and sparsely settled regions where few or no priests are available
5. To provide an impetus and source for creative adaptations of diaconal ministries to the rapidly changing needs of our society

USCCB Committee on the Diaconate

6. On August 30, 1968, the Apostolic Delegate informed the United States bishops that Pope Paul VI had agreed to their request. In November of that year, a standing committee on the diaconate was created by the National Conference of Catholic Bishops (NCCB).21 In 1971, the conference approved and authorized the publication of the committee's document, *Permanent Deacons in the United States: Guidelines on Their Formation and Ministry.*[22] These *Guidelines* served the Church in the United States well as it began to assimilate the new ministry of deacons.[23] In February 1977, the committee organized a comprehensive study "to assess the extent to which the vision" for the diaconate had been realized.[24] The results of that appraisal were published in 1981 under the title *A National Study of the Permanent Diaconate in the United States.*[25] The report acknowledged that the purpose of the diaconate and its integration into the life of the Church in the United States had not yet been fully realized. Building on this *Study*, the NCCB commissioned the revision of the 1971 *Guidelines*. In November 1984, new guidelines were published with the release of *Permanent Deacons in the United States: Guidelines on Their Formation and Ministry, 1984 Revision.*[26]

A national catechesis

7. The committee approved and authorized the publication of a series of monographs as part of a structured national catechesis on the diaconate. In collaboration with the committee, the Bishops' Committee on the Liturgy issued the document *The Deacon: Minister of Word and Sacrament, Study Text VI* (1979), which was devoted to the liturgical ministries of the deacon.[27] A second monograph addressed *The Service Ministry of the Deacon* (1988),[28] and a third monograph, *Foundations for the Renewal of the Diaconate* (1993), offered an international and historical perspective on the theology of the diaconate.[29] In 1998, the committee sponsored the production of a videotape, *Deacons: Ministers of Justice and Charity*, that highlighted some of the diverse service ministries of deacons in the United States.[30]

III. Recent Developments

8. The documents of the Second Vatican Council convey "a great deal about bishops and laity and very little about priests and deacons."[31] In 1990, Pope John Paul II convened an Extraordinary Synod of Bishops to consider the life and ministry of priests within the Church in order "to close this gap on behalf of priests with the completion of some important initiatives . . . for example . . . the publication of the post-synodal Apostolic Exhortation *Pastores Dabo Vobis*[32] and, as an implementation of this document, the *Directory on the Ministry and Life of Priests*.[33]"[34]

Vatican Congregations' plenary assembly

9. Seeking further to promote "a certain unity of direction and clarification of concepts, as well as . . . practical encouragement and more clearly defined pastoral objectives,"[35] the Congregation for the Clergy and the Congregation for Catholic Education organized a plenary assembly to study the diaconate. This gathering responded to concerns that had surfaced through the *ad limina* visits and reports of the bishops since the restoration of the diaconate was begun.[36] The members of the congregations and their consultants convened in November 1995. Pope John Paul II met with the participants and focused his comments on the identity, mission, and ministry of the deacon in the Church.[37]

10. Following this plenary assembly, the Congregation for the Clergy published a *Directory for the Ministry and Life of Permanent Deacons* and concurrently, the Congregation for Catholic Education issued *Basic Norms for the Formation of Permanent Deacons*. Both documents provide episcopal conferences with directives and norms on the selection, formation, and pastoral care of aspirants, candidates, and deacons in accord with the intent of the Second Vatican Council and the subsequent teachings of Pope Paul VI and Pope John Paul II.[38] These documents were promulgated as a joint text by Pope John Paul II on February 22, 1998, the Feast of the Chair of Peter.[39]

Directory for the Ministry and Life of Permanent Deacons

Basic Norms for the Formation of Permanent Deacons

11. In 1995-1996, the Bishops' Committee on the Diaconate, under the chairmanship of Most Rev. Dale J. Melczek, issued three documents: (1) *Protocol for the Incardination/Excardination of Deacons*, (2) *Policy Statement: Self-Study Instrument and Consultation Team Procedures*,[40] and (3) A *National Study on the Permanent Diaconate in the Catholic Church in the United States, 1994-1995*.[41] This *Study* focused on concerns that had surfaced at a special assembly of the Conference that was convened to address vocations and future church leadership. Those concerns included the identity of the deacon, his effective incorporation into the pastoral ministries of dioceses and parishes, and the need for better screening and training.[42] The *Study* confirmed the success of the restoration of the diaconate in the United States in terms of the number of vocations and in its significant, almost indispensable service to parochial communities. However, the *Study* also substantiates the concerns raised by the bishops and provides guidance in addressing them.[43]

Development of the diaconate in the United States

12. In 1994, the committee organized a national conference for deacons. Its purpose was to celebrate the twenty-fifth anniversary of their restoration in the Church in the United States. The first National Catholic Diaconate Conference was convened in the Archdiocese of New Orleans. The theme of this conference was *Diaconate: A Great and Visible Sign of the Work of the Holy Spirit*. In June 1997, the participants gathered in the Archdiocese of Milwaukee and there explored the theme *The Deacon in a Diaconal Church: Minister of Justice and Charity*. A third conference was convened in June 2000 in the Diocese of Oakland; the theme of this Jubilee Year 2000 conference was *The Deacon in the Third Millennium—New Evangelization*.[44]

National Catholic Diaconate Conference

IV. The Development of This *National Directory*

13. In March 1997, Most Rev. Edward U. Kmiec, chairman of the Bishops' Committee on the Diaconate,[45] convened two subcommittees to oversee the revision of the 1984 *Guidelines*. He named Most Rev. Howard J. Hubbard, D.D., and Most Rev. William E. Lori, S.T.D., members of the committee, as co-chairmen for the revision. He appointed Rev. Msgr. Theodore W. Kraus, Ph.D., past president of the National Association of Diaconate Directors, to serve as the project director. The members of both subcommittees brought varied professional and personal experience to the work and were representative of the geographic, cultural, and social profile of the Church in the United States.[46] Their work was assisted by Rev. Kevin Irwin, S.T.D., theological consultant to the committee; Rev. Msgr. William A. Varvaro, S.T.L., J.C.D., canonical consultant; and Deacon John Pistone, then-Executive Director of the Secretariat for the Diaconate, National Conference of Catholic Bishops. In November 1998, Most Rev. Gerald F. Kicanas., S.T.L., Ph.D., was elected by the conference as chairman of the committee. He invited Adam Cardinal Maida, J.C.L., J.D., S.T.L., and Most Rev. Donald W. Wuerl, S.T.D., to assist the committee as episcopal consultants in furthering the development of the document. Extensive consultation with the bishops and the major superiors of men religious, as well as diocesan directors of the diaconate and the executives of national diaconate organizations, preceded the approval of the document by the National Conference of Catholic Bishops at its general meeting in June 2000. In November 2001, Most Rev. Robert C. Morlino, S.T.D., was elected by the conference as chairman of the committee. Under his chairmanship, the committee revised the document in response to the observations received in March, 2002, from the Congregation for Catholic Education and the Congregation for the Clergy. The document was then approved by the United States Conference of Catholic Bishops at its general meeting in June 2003.

V. The Objective and Interpretation of This *National Directory*

National directives

14. This *Directory* is prescribed for the use of the diocesan bishop, as well as those responsible for its implementation. The specifica-

tions published in this *Directory* are to be incorporated by each diocese of the conference when preparing or updating its respective diaconal formation program and in formulating policies for the ministry and life of their deacons.[47]

This *Directory* is normative

15. This *Directory* is normative throughout the United States Conference of Catholic Bishops and its territorial sees. Reflecting more than thirty-five years of experience with the reestablished diaconate in the United States, this *Directory* will guide and harmonize the formation programs drawn up by each diocese of the conference that "at times vary greatly from one to another."[48]

16. When a diaconal formation program is introduced or substantially modified, or a program previously "on hold" is reactivated, the diocesan bishop is encouraged to submit a proposal to the Bishops' Committee on the Diaconate for its evaluation. The specific elements to be included in the proposal and applied by the committee in its review are listed in Appendix I of this *Directory*.

This is "an important point of reference"

17. Finally, this document adopts as its own the concluding directive of the Congregation for Catholic Education: May the ordinaries, "to whom the present document is given, ensure that it becomes an object of attentive reflection in communion with their priests and communities. It will be an important point of reference for those Churches in which the permanent diaconate is a living and active reality; for the others, it will be an effective invitation to appreciate the value of that precious gift of the Spirit which is diaconal service."[49]

VI. Acknowledgments

18. Gratefully conscious of those who have served on the Bishops' Committee on the Diaconate, as well as its subcommittees, the United States Conference of Catholic Bishops acknowledges the direction of Most Rev. Edward U. Kmiec, under whose chairmanship the present effort was begun, and Most Rev. Gerald F. Kicanas, under whose chairmanship the *National Directory* was formulated, as well as Most Rev. Robert C. Morlino, under whose chairmanship it has been brought to conclusion.

NOTES

1 There is one Sacred Order of Deacons. Some deacons, who are in transition to ordination to the priesthood, usually exercise the Order of Deacons for a brief period of time. The vast majority of deacons live and exercise it, however, as a permanent rank of the hierarchy in both the Latin and Eastern Catholic Churches. This *Directory* addresses only the formation, ministry, and life of permanent deacons.

In 1995, as authorized by the General Secretary of the National Conference of Catholic Bishops, the word "permanent" was discontinued in the title of the bishops' committee, in the National Conference of Catholic Bishops' Secretariat for the Diaconate, and in its communiqués. In this text, therefore, the word "permanent" is not used unless it is contained in a specific quotation or in the title or committee of a publication. When the word "diaconate" is mentioned in this text, it refers to those who seek to be or are ordained permanent deacons.

In 2001, the National Conference of Catholic Bishops, the "canonical entity," and the United States Catholic Conference, the "the civil entity," were canonically and civilly reconstituted as the United States Conference of Catholic Bishops. This reconstituted entity is implied in this document except in those circumstances where the text requires reference to the previous nomenclatures.

2 Extraordinary Synod of Bishops, Final Report, *Ecclesia Sub Verbo Dei Mysteria Christi Celebrans Pro Salute Mundi* (December 7, 1995).

3 LG, no. 1.

4 CCC, no. 738.

5 Ibid., no. 849.

6 Second Vatican Council, *Decree on the Missionary Activity of the Church* (*Ad Gentes Divinitus*) (AGD) (December 7, 1965) (Washington, D.C.: United States Catholic Conference, 1965), nos. 15-16.

7 CCC, no. 776. Cf. LG, nos. 9-17, 48; GS, nos. 1-3, 26-30, 32, 45.

8 LG, no. 24. Cf. Acts 1:17, 25; 21:19; Rom 11:13; 1 Tm 1:12; Pope John Paul II, Post-Synodal Apostolic Exhortation, *The Vocation and the Mission of the Lay Faithful in the Church and in the World* (*Christifideles Laici*) (December 30, 1988) (Washington, D.C.: United States Catholic Conference, 1988), no. 22.

9 Ibid., nos. 18, 20.

10 Ibid., nos. 20; cf. nos. 22-23.

11 CCC, no. 1534.

12 LG, no. 29. Cf. AGD, op. cit., nos. 15-16; OE, no. 17.

13 Pope Paul VI, Apostolic Letter, *Ad Pascendum* (AP) (August 15, 1972), citing Mt 20:28.

14 DMLPD, no. 27.

15 BNFPD, no. 88.

16 Ibid., no. 11.

17 Pope Paul VI, Apostolic Letter, *Sacrum Diaconatus Ordinem* (June 18, 1967).

18 Pope Paul VI, Apostolic Constitution, *Pontificalis Romani Recognito* (June 18, 1968).

19 AP, op. cit.

20 Pope Paul VI, Apostolic Letter, *Ministeria Quaedem* (August 15, 1972).

21 The committee's responsibilities, as authorized by the United States Conference of Catholic Bishops, are specified in Appendix II of this *Directory*.

22 Bishops' Committee on the Permanent Diaconate, National Conference of Catholic Bishops, *Permanent Deacons in the United States: Guidelines on Their Formation and Ministry* (Washington, D.C.: United States Catholic Conference, 1971). The committee, under its first chairman, Most Rev. Ernest L. Unterkoefler, prepared these *Guidelines*.

23 The diaconate has grown remarkably in the United States. According to statistics of the USCCB Secretariat for the Diaconate, there were, in 1971, 58 deacons and 529 candidates, and in 1975, 1,074 deacons and 2,243 candidates. By 1980, the number of deacons had quadrupled to 4,656, with 2,514 candidates. As of December 31, 2001, more than 14,000 deacons were serving in the dioceses of the United States and territorial sees. Only six dioceses had no incardinated deacons.

24 Bishops' Committee on the Permanent Diaconate, National Conference of Catholic Bishops, *A National Study of the Permanent Diaconate in the United States* (Washington, D.C.: United States Catholic Conference, 1981), p. 1.

25 Ibid.

26 PDG (1984). The committee under the chairmanship of Most Rev. John J. Snyder began the revision. It was completed under the chairmanship of Most Rev. John F. Kinney.

27 STVI.

28 Bishops' Committee on the Permanent Diaconate, National Conference of Catholic Bishops, *Service Ministry of the Deacon*, Rev. Timothy J. Shugrue, author, (Washington, D.C.: United States Catholic Conference, 1988).

28 Bishops' Committee on the Permanent Diaconate, National Conference of Catholic Bishops, *Foundations for the Renewal of the Diaconate* (Washington, D.C.: United States Catholic Conference, 1993).

30 Bishops' Committee on the Diaconate, National Conference of Catholic Bishops, *Deacons: Ministers of Justice and Charity* [video], Deacon Richard Folger, editor, (1998).

31 Most Rev. Crescenzio Sepe, Secretary of the Congregation for the Clergy, Address to the National Catholic Diaconate Conference, New Orleans, La. (July 21, 1994).

32 PDV.

33 Congregation for the Clergy, *Directory on the Ministry and Life of Priests* (Washington, D.C.: Libreria Editrice Vaticana-United States Catholic Conference, 1994).

34 Most Rev. Crescenzio Sepe, op. cit.

35 BNFPD and DMLPD, Joint Declaration.

36 These concerns centered upon an incorrect understanding of the role of the deacon in the

hierarchical structure of the Church, of the doctrine on ministries, on the role of the laity and the role of women, as well as concerns regarding selection, adequate intellectual formation, and proper pastoral ministries for deacons. Cf. Most Rev. Crescenzio Sepe, op. cit.

37 PDO.

38 BNFPD and DMLPD, Introduction, no. 2; cf. BNFPD, no. 14.

39 BNFPD, no. 90; DMLPD, no. 82. Additional Vatican documents relevant to the formation and ministry of deacons include the following: (1) *Guide for Catechists* (1993), promulgated by the Congregation for Evangelization of Peoples, which proposes educational and formational models. As required by the Congregation for Catholic Education in BNFPD, diaconal formation is to encompass more than catechist formation and is to be more analogous to the formation of priests. *Guide for Catechists* provides universal norms for catechist formation. (2) The *General Directory for Catechesis* (1997), from the Congregation for the Clergy, provides insightful criteria in proposing appropriate adult education methodologies and for establishing perimeters for an authentic and complete theological study. The *Instruction on Certain Questions Regarding the Collaboration of the Non-Ordained Faithful in the Sacred Ministry of Priests* (1997), signed by the heads of eight dicasteries of the Holy See, establishes norms for appropriate collaboration between the ordained ministers of the Church and the non-ordained faithful. (3) In 1997, the Congregation for Divine Worship and the Discipline of the Sacraments issued a Circular Letter to diocesan bishops and religious ordinaries establishing criteria on the suitability of candidates to be admitted to sacred orders and further directing the establishment of a diocesan board to oversee the scrutinies of candidates before the reception of the rite of candidacy, the ministry of lector, the ministry of acolyte, and ordination to the diaconate and priesthood. [The text abbreviation in this document is CL.] This document is essential in the formulation of admission and selection policies for diaconal candidates. (4) The Pontifical Council for Promoting Christian Unity issued a supplementary document to its *Directory for the Application of Principles and Norms on Ecumenism* (1993), namely, *The Ecumenical Dimension in the Formation of Those Engaged in Pastoral Work* (1997). This document specifies that an ecumenical dimension is to be included in diaconal formation and ministry. (5) The encyclical letter *On the Relationship Between Faith and Reason* (1998), promulgated by Pope John Paul II, establishes academic parameters to be included in the intellectual and human dimensions of diaconal formation. (6) The post-synodal apostolic exhortation *The Church in America* (1999), promulgated by Pope John Paul II, addresses the new evangelization in the Church in America and makes reference to the role of the deacon in that ministry.

40 Bishops' Committee on the Diaconate, National Conference of Catholic Bishops, Protocol for the Incardination/Excardination of Deacons (1995) and Policy Statement: Self-Study Instrument and Consultation Team Procedures (1995).

41 NSD (1996).

42 Joseph Cardinal Bernardin, "Summary Comments on the Permanent Diaconate," Special Assembly of the National Conference of Catholic Bishops, St. John's Abbey, Collegeville,

Minn. (June 9-16, 1986), in *Vocations and Future Church Leadership* (Washington, D.C.: United States Catholic Conference, 1986).

43 NSD (1996), pp. 13-16.

44 In 1994, Most Rev. Crescenzio Sepe, D.D., Secretary of the Congregation for the Clergy, addressed the National Catholic Diaconate Conference on the background and preparations being made for the plenary assembly scheduled for November 1995. In 1997, Cardinal Darío Castrillón Hoyos, Pro-Prefect of the Congregation for the Clergy, spoke on "The Deacon in the Life and Mission of the Church," providing insight on the *Directory* being prepared by the Congregation. In 2000, Most Rev. Gabriel Montalvo, Apostolic Nuncio to the United States, addressed the role of the deacon in the Church's mission of new evangelization.

45 See Note 1 above regarding the removal of the word "permanent" from title of the Bishops' Committee on the Diaconate.

46 The members of the Subcommittee on Formation and Curriculum included the following: Most Rev. Howard Hubbard, Bishop of Albany, N.Y. (chairman); [Deacon Ministry and Life] Deacon James Swiler, Director of Diaconate Formation, Archdiocese of New Orleans, La. (facilitator); Mrs. Bonnie Swiler, Archdiocese of New Orleans, La.; Sr. Yvonne Lerner, OSB, Director of Diaconate Formation, Diocese of Little Rock, Ark.; [Formation] Dr. Ann Healey, Director of Deacon Formation, Fort Worth, Texas (facilitator); Rev. Michael Galvan, Pastor, St. Joseph Church, Pinole, Calif.; Deacon James Keeley, Director of Diaconate Formation, Diocese of San Diego, Calif.; Mrs. Jeanne Schrempf, Director of Religious Education, Diocese of Albany, N.Y.; Deacon Enrique Alonso, President, National Association of Hispanic Deacons; [Diocesan Structures and Selection] Mr. Timothy C. Charek, Director, Deacon Formation Program, Archdiocese of Milwaukee, Wis. (facilitator); Most Rev. Dominic Carmon, SVD, Auxiliary Bishop of the Archdiocese of New Orleans, La., member of the Bishops' Committee on the Diaconate; Rev. Richard W. Woy, Vicar for Clergy, Archdiocese of Baltimore, Md.; [Curriculum] Deacon Stephen Graff, Dean of Students, St. Bernard's Institute, Rochester, N.Y. (facilitator); Rev. Msgr. Ernest J. Fiedler, Rector, Cathedral of the Immaculate Conception, Diocese of Kansas City, Mo., and former Executive Director, NCCB Secretariat for the Diaconate; Rev. Bryan Massingale, Vice Rector, St. Francis Seminary, Milwaukee, Wis.; Rev. Alejandro Castillo, SVD, Director of the Office for Hispanic Affairs, California Catholic Conference, Sacramento, Calif.; Rev. Robert Egan, SJ, St. Michael's Institute, Spokane, Wash.; Mr. Neal Parent, Executive Director, National Conference of Catechetical Leadership, Washington, D.C.; Dr. Seung Ai Yang, Professor of Scripture, The Jesuit School of Theology, Berkeley, Calif. The members of the Subcommittee for Theological and Canonical Revision included Most Rev. William Lori, Auxiliary Bishop of Washington, D.C. (chairman); [Theology] Rev. Msgr. Paul Langsfeld, Vice Rector, St. Mary's Seminary, Emmitsburg, Md. (facilitator); Deacon Samuel M. Taub, Diocese of Arlington, Va., former Executive Director, NCCB Secretariat for the Diaconate; Sr. Patricia Simpson, OP, Prioress, Dominican Sisters of San Rafael, Calif., and former Director of Diaconate Formation, Diocese of Sacramento, Calif.; Rev. Frank Silva, Pastor, Immaculate

Conception Church, Malden, Mass., and former Director of Diaconate, Archdiocese of Boston, Mass.; [Spirituality] Deacon William T. Ditewig, Director of Pastoral Services and Ministry Formation, Diocese of Davenport, Iowa (facilitator); Mrs. Diann Ditewig, Davenport, Iowa; Most Rev. Allen H. Vigneron, Auxiliary Bishop of the Archdiocese of Detroit, Mich., and Rector, Sacred Heart Major Seminary, Detroit, Mich.; Deacon James Condill, President, National Association of Deacon Organizations; [Ministry] Rev. Msgr. Timothy Shugrue, Pastor, Immaculate Conception Church, Montclair, N.J., and former Director of Diaconate, Archdiocese of Newark, N.J. (facilitator); Rev. Edward Salmon, Vicar, Diaconate Community, Archdiocese of Chicago, Ill.; Rev. Msgr. Joseph Roth, President, National Association of Diaconate Directors; Deacon John Stewart, President, National Association of African-American Catholic Deacons. Rev. Msgr. Theodore W. Kraus, Director of Diaconate, Diocese of Oakland, the *Directory*'s project director, served *ex officio* on each subcommittee and working unit.

47 BNFPD and DMLPD, Joint Declaration; cf. BNFPD, nos. 14, 17.

48 BNFPD, nos. 2, 14.

49 BNFPD, no. 90.

CHAPTER ONE

DOCTRINAL UNDERSTANDING OF THE DIACONATE

I. Introduction

Theological points of reference

19. This *Directory* offers some theological points of reference based upon relevant magisterial teaching. As the Congregation for Catholic Education explains, "The almost total disappearance of the permanent diaconate from the Church of the West for more than a millennium has certainly made it more difficult to understand the profound reality of this ministry. However, it cannot be said for that reason that the theology of the diaconate has no authoritative points of reference. . . [T]hey are very clear, even if they need to be developed and deepened."[1]

II. The Sacramental Nature of the Church

Church: One complex reality

20. The Second Vatican Council spoke of the Church as "mystery," "sacrament," "communion," and "mission":[2] "The Church is in Christ like a sacrament or as a sign and instrument both of a very closely knit union with God and of the unity of the whole human race."[3] The Church is the People of God, the Body of Christ, and the Temple of the Holy Spirit.[4] It is "the community of faith, hope and charity" as well as "an entity with visible delineation."[5] "But, the society [formed] with hierarchical [structures] and the Mystical Body of Christ . . .[is] not to be considered as two realities, nor are the visible assembly and the spiritual community, nor the earthly Church and the Church enriched with heavenly things; rather they form one complex reality, which coalesces from a divine and a human element."[6]

Church as communion and mission

21. Jesus Christ, through his ministry, life, death, and resurrection, established in human society and history a new and distinct reality, a community of men and women, through whom "He communicated truth and grace to all."[7] Through the Church, the Good News of Jesus Christ continues to be told and applied to the changing circumstances and challenges of human life. As Christians

live their lives in the power of the Holy Spirit and in the assurance of Christ's return in glory, they offer to others a hope to live by, encouraging them also to embrace Christ and overcome the forces of evil. In the sacraments, which symbolize and make real again the gifts of God that are the origin, center, and goal of the Church's life, the power of Jesus Christ's redemption is again and again at work in the world. In her ministry of charity and justice, the Church "encompasses with love all who are afflicted with human suffering and in the poor and afflicted sees the image of her poor and suffering founder. She does all in her power to relieve their need and in them she strives to serve Christ "[8] Thus, in the communion of life, love, and service realized under the leadership of the successors of the apostles, a vision of reconciled humanity is offered to the world.

III. Ecclesial Communion and Mission

The Sacraments of Christian Initiation: Baptism, Confirmation, and Eucharist

Initiation into the Church's communion and mission

22. Initiation into the Church, the Body of Christ, comes about first through the Sacrament of Baptism—the outpouring of the Holy Spirit. In Baptism, every member of the Church receives new life in the Spirit and becomes a member of Christ's Body—a participant in the new creation. This new life is strengthened in the Sacrament of Confirmation, through which the baptized receives the Spirit and is more perfectly bound to the Church and obliged to bear witness to Christ, to spread and defend the faith by word and deed. In the Sacrament of the Eucharist, the child of God receives the food of new life, the body and blood of Christ. In this Holy Communion, Christ unites each of the baptized to all the faithful in one body—the Church:

> Baptism, Confirmation, and Eucharist are sacraments of Christian initiation. They ground the common vocation of all Christ's disciples, a vocation to holiness and to the mission of evangelizing the world. They confer the graces needed for the life according to the Spirit during this life as pilgrims on the march towards the homeland.[9]
>
> Communion and mission are profoundly connected with each other, they interpenetrate and mutually imply each other, to

> the point that communion represents both the source and the fruit of mission: communion gives rise to mission and mission is accomplished in communion. It is always the one and the same Spirit who calls together and unifies the Church and sends her to preach the Gospel "to the ends of the earth."[10]

The Sacrament of Holy Orders

23. The Church, itself the great sacrament of Christ's presence, rejoices in another "outpouring of the Spirit"[11]—the Sacrament of Holy Orders. Out of the body of initiated believers—anointed in the Holy Spirit through the Sacrament of Baptism, strengthened in the Sacrament of Confirmation, and nurtured with the Bread of Life—Christ calls some to ordained service. The Church, discerning their vocational charism, asks the bishop to ordain them to *diakonia*.

Some are called to ordained service

24. "Holy Orders is the sacrament through which the mission entrusted by Christ to his apostles [and their successors] continues to be exercised in the Church until the end of time."[12] Thus, it is the sacrament of apostolic ministry: "The mission of the Apostles, which the Lord Jesus continues to entrust to the Pastors of his people, is a true service, significantly referred to in Sacred Scripture as '*diakonia*,' namely, service or ministry."[13] This *diakonia* "is exercised on different levels by those who from antiquity have been called bishops, priests and deacons."[14] "The ordained ministries, apart from the persons who receive them, are a grace for the entire Church."[15]

Holy Orders: The sacrament of apostolic ministry

25. The *Catechism of the Catholic Church* speaks of the Sacrament of Holy Orders in this way:

Catechism of the Catholic Church: Sacrament of Holy Orders

> Catholic doctrine, expressed in the liturgy, the Magisterium, and the constant practice of the Church, recognizes that there are two degrees of ministerial participation in the priesthood of Christ: the episcopacy and the presbyterate. The diaconate is intended to help and serve them. For this reason the term *sacerdos* in current usage denotes bishops and priests but not deacons. Yet Catholic doctrine teaches that the degrees of priestly participation (episcopate and presbyterate) and the degree of service (diaconate) are all three conferred by a sacramental act called "ordination," that is, by the Sacrament of Holy Orders.[16]

The primacy of apostolic ministry

26. St. Paul points out that the Holy Spirit is the source of all ministries in the Church and that these services are quite distinct.[17] The distribution of ministerial gifts follows a design set by Christ:

> In the building up of Christ's Body various members and functions have their part to play. There is only one Spirit who, according to His own richness and the needs of the ministries, gives His different gifts for the welfare of the Church. What has a special place among these gifts is the grace of the apostles to whose authority the Spirit Himself subjected even those who are endowed with charisms.[18]

IV. The Reestablished Order of Deacons

Diaconate: A permanent rank in the hierarchy

27. The Fathers of the Second Vatican Council, taking seriously the role of the deacon to which St. Paul refers in his first letter to Timothy, remind us that "those who serve well as deacons gain good standing and much confidence in their faith in Christ Jesus."[19] It was for serious pastoral and theological reasons that the Council decided to reestablish the Order of Deacons as a permanent rank in the hierarchy of the Church.

The deacon: Configured to Christ the deacon

28. The Sacrament of Holy Orders marks deacons "with an *imprint* ('character') which cannot be removed and which configures them to Christ, who made himself the 'deacon' or servant of all."[20] For this level of Holy Orders, Christ calls and the Church asks the bishop to ordain deacons to be consecrated witnesses to service. In his post-synodal exhortation *The Church in America,* Pope John Paul II makes his own the words of the bishops of that gathering: "We see with joy how deacons 'sustained by the grace of the Sacrament, in the ministry (*diakonia*) of the liturgy, of the word and of charity are at the service of the People of God, in communion with the Bishop and his priests.'"[21]

Deacon: Neither a lay person nor a priest, but a cleric

29. Ordination confers an outpouring of the Holy Spirit. It configures the deacon to Christ's consecration and mission. It constitutes the deacon as "a sacred minister and a member of the hierarchy,"[22] with a distinct identity and integrity in the Church that marks him as neither a lay person nor a priest; rather, the deacon is a cleric who is ordained to *diakonia*, namely, a service to God's

People in communion with the bishop and his body of priests. "The principal function of the deacon, therefore, is to collaborate with the bishop and the priests in the exercise of a ministry which is not of their own wisdom but of the Word of God, calling all to conversion and holiness."[23]

Service to the People of God

30. Referring to the traditional description of the deacon's *diakonia* to the Church and the bishop, Pope John Paul II observes that in an ancient text, the deacon's ministry is defined as a "service to the bishop."[24] This observation highlights the constant understanding of the Church that the deacon enjoys a unique relationship with his bishop. The Pope clearly has in view, therefore, the reason for not only the diaconate but the whole apostolic ministry: serving the discipleship of God's people. Pope John Paul II notes that

> the deacon's tasks include that of "promoting and sustaining the apostolic activities of the laity." To the extent he is more present and more involved than the priest in secular environments and structures, he should feel encouraged to foster closeness between the ordained ministry and lay activities, in common service to the kingdom of God.[25]

In particular, "a deeply felt need in the decision to reestablish the permanent diaconate," the Pope recalls, "was and is that of a greater and more direct presence of Church ministers in the various spheres of the family, work, school, etc., in addition to existing pastoral structures."[26] Deacons, both married and celibate, serve God's People by their witness to the gospel value of sacrificial love, a quality of life too easily dismissed in today's society. In their secular employment, deacons also make evident the dignity of human work. Contemporary society is in need of a "new evangelization which demands a greater and more generous effort on the part of [all] ordained ministers."[27] This is especially an opportunity and obligation for deacons in their secular professions to boldly proclaim and witness to the Gospel of life.

V. The Church's Ministry of the Word: The Deacon as Evangelizer and Teacher

Herald of the Gospel

31. The deacon participates as an evangelizer and teacher in the Church's mission of heralding the word. In the liturgy of the word, especially in the Eucharist or in those liturgies where he is the presiding minister, the deacon proclaims the Gospel. He may preach by virtue of ordination and in accord with the requirements of Canon Law.[28] Other forms of the deacon's participation in the Church's ministry of the word include catechetical instruction; religious formation of candidates and families preparing for the reception of the sacraments; leadership roles in retreats, evangelization, and renewal programs; outreach to alienated Catholics; and counseling and spiritual direction, to the extent that he is properly trained.[29] The deacon also strives to "transmit the word in [his] professional [life] either explicitly or merely by [his] active presence in places where public opinion is formed and ethical norms are applied."[30]

Witnessing the Word in his own life, the deacon leads people to their practice of charity and justice

32. In these and many other formal and informal ways, the deacon leads the community to reflect on their communion and mission in Jesus Christ, especially impelling the community of believers to live lives of service. Because the deacon sacramentalizes service, he should proclaim the word in such a way that he first witnesses its empowerment in his own life. Then he can effectively challenge others to practice the Church's ministry of charity and justice in the social environments in which people live their baptismal vocation. By his own faithful practice of the spiritual and corporal works of mercy, the deacon "by word and example . . . should work so that all the faithful, in imitation of Christ, may place themselves at the constant service of their brothers and sisters."[31]

VI. The Church's Ministry of Liturgy: The Deacon as Sanctifier

Liturgical ministry

33. For the deacon, as for all members of the Church, the liturgy is "the summit toward which the activity of the Church is directed; at the same time it is the fount from which all the Church's power flows."[32] For the Church gathered at worship, moreover, the ministry of the deacon is a visible, grace-filled sign of the integral connection between sharing at the Lord's Eucharistic table and serving the

many hungers felt so keenly by all God's children. In the deacon's liturgical ministry, as in a mirror, the Church sees a reflection of her own diaconal character and is reminded of her mission to serve as Jesus did.

An integral *diakonia*

34. In the context of the Church's public worship, because of its centrality in the life of the believing community, the ministry of the deacon in the threefold diakonia of the word, of the liturgy, and of charity is uniquely concentrated and integrated. "The diaconate is conferred through a special outpouring of the Spirit (*ordination*), which brings about in the one who receives it a specific conformation to Christ, Lord and servant of all."[33] "Strengthened by sacramental grace, they are dedicated to the people of God, in conjunction with the bishop and his body of priests, in a service of the liturgy of the word and of charity."[34]

Liturgical functions

35. During the celebration of the Eucharistic liturgy, the deacon participates in specific penitential rites as designated in the *Roman Missal*. He properly proclaims the Gospel. He may preach the homily in accord with the provisions of Canon Law. He voices the needs of the people in the General Intercessions, needs with which he should have a particular and personal familiarity from the circumstances of his ministry of charity. The deacon assists the presider and other ministers in accepting the offerings of the people—symbolic of his traditional role in receiving and distributing the resources of the community among those in need—and he helps to prepare the gifts for sacrifice. During the celebration he helps the faithful participate more fully, consciously, and actively in the Eucharistic sacrifice,[35] may extend the invitation of peace, and serves as an ordinary minister of Communion. Deacons have a special responsibility for the distribution of the cup. Finally, he dismisses the community at the end of the eucharistic liturgy. Other liturgical roles for which the deacon is authorized include those of solemnly baptizing, witnessing marriages, bringing *viaticum* to the dying, and presiding over funerals and burials. The deacon can preside at the liturgies of the word and communion services in the absence of a priest. He may officiate at celebrations of the Liturgy of the Hours and at exposition and benediction of the Blessed Sacrament. He can conduct public rites of blessing, offer prayer services for the sick and dying, and administer the Church's sacramentals, as designated in the *Book of*

Blessings.[36] In the Eastern Catholic Churches, the liturgical ministries of deacons are prescribed by the legislative authority of each particular Church.

VII. The Church's Ministry of Charity and Justice: The Deacon as Witness and Guide

Service: The hallmark of faithfulness

36. The deacon's ministry, as Pope John Paul II has said, "is the Church's service sacramentalized."[37] Therefore, the deacon's service in the Church's ministry of word and liturgy would be severely deficient if his exemplary witness and assistance in the Church's ministry of charity and justice did not accompany it. Thus, Pope John Paul II affirms both: "This is at the very heart of the diaconate to which you have been called: to be a servant of the mysteries of Christ and, at one and the same time, to be a servant of your brothers and sisters. That these two dimensions are inseparably joined together in one reality shows the important nature of the ministry which is yours by ordination."[38]

Service: The hallmark of faithfulness

37. The deacon's service in the Church's ministry of charity and justice is integral to his service in the Church's ministry of word and liturgy. "The three contexts of the diaconal ministry . . . represent a unity in service at the level of divine Revelation: the ministry of the word leads to ministry at the altar, which in turn prompts the transformation of life by the liturgy, resulting in charity."[39] "As a [participant] in the one ecclesiastical ministry, [the deacon] is a specific sacramental sign, in the Church, of Christ the Servant. His role is to 'express the needs and desires of the Christian communities' and to be 'a driving force for service, or *diakonia*,' which is an essential part of the mission of the Church."[40] The ancient tradition appears to indicate that because the deacon was the servant at the table of the poor, he had his distinctive liturgical roles at the Table of the Lord. Similarly, there is a reciprocal correspondence between his role as a herald of the Gospel and his role as an articulator of the needs of the Church in the General Intercessions. In his formal liturgical roles, the deacon brings the poor to the Church and the Church to the poor. Likewise, he articulates the Church's concern for justice by being a driving force in addressing the injustices among God's people. He thus symbolizes in his roles the grounding of the Church's life in the Eucharist and the mission of the Church in

her loving service of the needy. In the deacon, in a unique way, is represented the integral relationship between the worship of God in the liturgy that recalls Jesus Christ's redemptive sacrifice sacramentally and the worship of God in everyday life where Jesus Christ is encountered in the needy. The deacon's service begins at the altar and returns there. The sacrificial love of Christ celebrated in the Eucharist nourishes him and motivates him to lay down his life on behalf of God's People.

The washing of feet: The foundational model of diaconal service

38. The apostles' decision to appoint ministers to attend to the needs of the Greek-speaking widows of the early Church at Jerusalem[41] has long been interpreted as a normative step in the evolution of ministry. It is seen as a practical response to Jesus' command during the Last Supper of mutual service among his followers. In washing his disciples' feet, Jesus as head and shepherd of the community modeled the service that he desired to be the hallmark of their faithfulness. This gave the disciples a powerful sign of the love of God that was, in Jesus himself, incarnate and intended to be forever enfleshed in the attitudes and behaviors of his followers.[42] The deacon, consecrated and conformed to the mission of Christ, Lord and Servant, has a particular concern for the vitality and genuineness of the exercise of *diakonia* in the life of the believing community. In a world hungry and thirsty for convincing signs of the compassion and liberating love of God, the deacon sacramentalizes the mission of the Church in his words and deeds, responding to the master's command of service and providing real-life examples of how to carry it out.

VIII. An Intrinsic Unity

An intrinsic unity among the deacon's service ministries

39. By ordination, the deacon, who sacramentalizes the Church's service, is to exercise the Church's *diakonia.* Therefore, "the diaconal ministries, distinguished above, are not to be separated; the deacon is ordained for them all, and no one should be ordained who is not prepared to undertake each in some way."[43] "However, even if this inherent ministerial service is one and the same in every case, nevertheless, the concrete ways of carrying it out are diverse; these must be suggested, in each case, by the different pastoral situations of the single churches."[44] A deacon may also have greater abilities in one aspect of ministry; and, therefore, his service may be marked by one of them more than by the others. Fundamentally, however,

there is an intrinsic unity in a deacon's ministry. In preaching the word, he is involved in every kind of missionary outreach. In sanctifying God's People through the liturgy, he infuses and elevates people with new meaning and with a Christian worldview. In bringing Christ's reign into every stratum of society, the deacon develops a Christian conscience among all people of good will, motivating their service and commitment to the sanctity of human life.

IX. Concluding Reflection

40. When one reflects upon the Order of Deacons, it is worthwhile to recall the words from the ordination ritual of deacons:

> Like those once chosen by the Apostles for the ministry of charity, you should be men of good reputation, filled with wisdom and the Holy Spirit. Firmly rooted and grounded in faith, you are to show yourselves chaste and beyond reproach before God and man, as is proper for the ministers of Christ and the stewards of God's mysteries. Never allow yourselves to be turned away from the hope offered by the Gospel. Now you are not only hearers of this Gospel but also its ministers. Holding the mystery of faith with a clear conscience, express by your actions the Word of God which your lips proclaim, so that the Christian people, brought to life by the Spirit, may be a pure offering accepted by God. Then on the last day, when you go out to meet the Lord you will be able to hear him say, "Well done, good and faithful servant, enter into the joy of your Lord."[45]

NOTES

1 BNFPD, no. 3.

2 Extraordinary Synod of Bishops, Final Report, *Ecclesia Sub Verbo Dei Mysteria Christi Celebrans Pro Salute Mundi* (December 7, 1995).

3 LG, no. 1.

4 Ibid., no. 17.

5 Ibid., no. 8.

6 Ibid.

7 Ibid.

8 Ibid.

9 CCC, no. 1533.

10 Pope John Paul II, post-synodal Apostolic Exhortation, *The Vocation and the Mission of the Lay Faithful in the Church and in the World* (*Christifideles Laici*) (December 30, 1988) (Washington, D.C.: United States Catholic Conference, 1988), no. 32, citing Acts 1:8.

11 BNFPD, no. 5.

12 CCC, no. 1536.

13 Ibid., no. 22; cf. LG, no. 24.

14 LG, no. 28.

15 Pope John Paul II, *Christifideles Laici*, op. cit., no. 22.

16 CCC, no. 1554.

17 Cf. 1 Cor 12:4-11; Rom 12:4-8.

18 LG, no. 7.

19 1 Tm 3:13.

20 CCC, no. 1570.

21 Pope John Paul II, post-synodal Apostolic Exhortation, *The Church in America* (*Ecclesia in America*) (January 22, 1999) (Washington, D.C.: United States Catholic Conference, 1999), no. 42, citing LG, no. 29.

22 DMLPD, no. 1.

23 DMLPD, no. 23.

24 Pope John Paul II, General Audience, *Deacons Have Many Pastoral Functions* (October 13, 1993), no. 1, citing Hippolytus, *Apostolic Tradition*.

25 Ibid., no. 5, citing Pope Paul VI, Apostolic Letter, *Sacrum Diaconatus Ordinem*, (June 18, 1967), no. 22.

26 Pope John Paul II, General Audience, *Deacons Serve the Kingdom of God* (October 5, 1993), no. 6.

27 DMLPD, no. 26.

28 CIC, c. 764: "With due regard for the prescription of can. 765, presbyters and deacons possess the faculty to preach everywhere, to be exercised with at least the presumed consent of the rector of the church, unless the faculty has been restricted or taken away by the competent ordinary or unless express permission is required by particular law."

29 Cf. BNFPD, no. 86.

30 DMLPD, no. 26.

31 Ibid., no. 38.

32 Second Vatican Council, *Constitution on the Sacred Liturgy* (*Sacrosanctum Concilium*) (December 4, 1963) (Washington, D.C.: United States Catholic Conference, 1963), no. 10.

33 BNFPD, no. 5.

34 LG, no. 29, cited in PDO.

35 SC, no. 14.

36 STVI, pp. 51-57.

37 ADUS.

38 Ibid.

39 DMLPD, no. 39.

40 BNFPD, no. 5.

41 Acts 6:1-7.

42 Cf. Jn 13:1-15.

43 PDG (1984), no. 43.

44 BNFPD, no. 10.

45 Roman Pontifical, Ordination of Deacons, no. 199, in *Rites of Ordination of a Bishop, of Priests, and of Deacons* (Washington, D.C.: USCCB, 2003); cf. Mt 25:21.

CHAPTER TWO
THE MINISTRY AND LIFE OF DEACONS

I. The Relationships of the Deacon

Relationship with the Diocesan Bishop

41. The deacon exercises his ministry within a specific pastoral context—the communion and mission of a diocesan Church.[1] He is in direct relationship with the diocesan bishop with whom he is in communion and under whose authority he exercises his ministry. In making his promise of respect and obedience to his bishop, the deacon takes as his model Christ, who became the servant of his Father. The diocesan bishop also enters into a relationship with the deacon since the deacon is his collaborator in the service of God's People. It is, therefore, a particular responsibility of the bishop to provide for the pastoral care of the deacons of his diocese. The bishop discharges this responsibility both personally and through the director of deacon personnel.[2]

Respect and obedience

42. The bishop appoints the deacon to a specific assignment normally by means of an official letter of appointment.[3] The principal criteria for the assignment are the pastoral needs of the diocesan Church and the personal qualifications of the deacon, as these have been discerned in his previous experience and the course of his formation. The assignment also acknowledges the deacon's family and occupational responsibilities.

The bishop appoints the deacon to a specific ministry

43. The bishop promotes "a suitable catechesis" throughout the diocesan Church to assist the lay faithful, religious, and clergy to have a richer and firmer sense about the deacon's identity, function, and role within the Church's ministry.[4] In fact, such a catechesis is also "an opportunity for the bishop, priests, religious, and laity to discern the needs and challenges of the local Church, to consider the types of services needed in order to meet them, to tailor a diaconal program to address them, and to begin the process of considering which men in the church might be called upon to undertake diaconal ministry."[5]

Suitable catechesis: An opportunity to discern needs, suitable nominees, and placement on the diocesan level

Letter of appointment

44. The assignment of a deacon to a specific ministry, the delineation of his duties and responsibilities, and the designation of his immediate pastor or pastoral supervisor, who must be a priest, should always be clearly stated in the letter of appointment signed by the diocesan bishop. This document should make as explicit as possible the implicit expectations of the participants, thereby establishing a clear line of mutual responsibility and accountability among them. The director of deacon personnel, together with the deacon's designated pastor or priest supervisor (if the deacon is assigned to an office or agency not directed by a priest), a representative of that office or agency, and the deacon are to be involved in the preparation of the letter of appointment. "For the good of the deacon and to prevent improvisation, ordination should be accompanied by clear investiture of pastoral responsibility."[6] Although the wife of a married deacon has already given her permission before her husband's ordination to the demands of the diaconal ministry, nevertheless she should be "kept duly informed of [her husband's] activities in order to arrive at an harmonious balance between family, professional and ecclesial responsibilities."[7] Until the letter of appointment is signed by the bishop and publicly announced by the bishop's office, all parties are bound to confidentiality.

Rights and duties

45. The diocesan bishop also ensures that the "rights and duties as foreseen by canons 273-283 of the *Code of Canon Law* with regard to clerics in general and deacons in particular"[8] are promoted.

Concerns for the newly ordained deacons

46. The transition from candidate formation into an active diaconal ministry requires sensitivity. "Introducing the deacon to those in charge of the community (the parish priest, priests), and the community to the deacon, helps them not only to come to know each other but contributes to a collaboration based on mutual respect and dialogue, in a spirit of faith and fraternal charity."[9] Newly ordained deacons, therefore, are to be appointed to and supervised by a priest. This pastoral care of a newly ordained deacon, coordinated by the director of deacon personnel, extends for the first three years after ordination. This time would include opportunities for ongoing formation, with an initial emphasis upon the issues and concerns voiced by the newly ordained as he gains ministerial experience. It is likewise a unique opportunity to assist the deacon's family as it begins to adjust to its new situation within the community.

47. With the approval of the diocesan bishop, a realistic program for the continuing education and formation of each deacon and the entire diaconal community should be designed "taking due account of factors such as age and circumstances of deacons, together with the demands made on them by their pastoral ministry."[10] The preparation, implementation, and evaluation of this program are to be coordinated by the director of deacon personnel. "In addition to the [continuing] formation offered to [all] deacons, special courses and initiatives should be arranged for those deacons who are married," including the participation of their wives and families, "where opportune. . . . However, [care must be given] to maintain the essential distinction of roles and the clear independence of the ministry."[11] Similarly, special initiatives in continuing formation should be arranged for deacons who are not married.

Continuing formation and education

Relationship with the Diocese

48. While assuming different forms of diaconal ministry, a deacon exercises his service in both a diocesan setting and in an individual assignment. Therefore, he may be given specific responsibility, if he meets the necessary requirements, in an administrative position at a diocesan or parochial level.[12] However, in discharging these administrative responsibilities, "the deacon should recall that every action in the Church should be informed by charity and service to all. . . . Those deacons who are called to exercise such offices should be placed so as to discharge duties which are proper to the diaconate, in order to preserve the integrity of the diaconal ministry."[13]

Every diaconal service is informed by charity and service

49. Deacons who possess the necessary requirements, experience, and talent may be appointed members of the diocesan pastoral council, finance council, or commissions. They may be assigned to diocesan pastoral work in specific social contexts: e.g., the pastoral care of the family or the pastoral needs of ethnic minorities.[14] They may also participate in a diocesan synod.[15] They may exercise the offices of chancellor, judge, assessor, auditor, promoter of justice, defender of the bond, and notary or may serve as the diocesan finance officer.[16] However, deacons do not "act as members of the council of priests, since this body exclusively represents the presbyterate."[17] Deacons may not "be constituted judicial vicars, adjunct judicial vicars, or vicars forane, since these offices are reserved for

Diocesan appointments

priests."[18] To strengthen the diaconal character of the diocesan Church, care is to be taken, therefore, to include, as much as possible, a diaconal presence within diocesan structures, as well as within parish communities.[19] Deacons who have parochial administrative training and experience may be entrusted, under a canonically appointed pastor or priest supervisor, to assist in the pastoral care of a parish or to temporarily guide a parish that lacks, because of a shortage, the immediate benefit of a resident pastor.[20] In these extraordinary situations, deacons "always have precedence over the non-ordained faithful," and their authority and responsibility "should always be clearly specified in writing when they are assigned office."[21]

Relationship with the Priesthood

Complementary ministries

50. Deacons exercise their ministry in communion not only with their bishop but also with the priests who serve the diocesan Church. As collaborators in ministry, priests and deacons are two complementary but subordinate participants in the one apostolic ministry bestowed by Christ upon the apostles and their successors. The diaconate is not an abridged or substitute form of the priesthood, but is a full order in its own right.[22] Permanent deacons ought to foster fraternal bonds with transitional deacons. Through formal contacts arranged by the diocesan diaconate and vocation offices with the seminary program, in collaborative diocesan and parochial ministries, and in opportunities for shared study and prayer, the Order of Deacons can more clearly be understood and appreciated among those to be ordained to the Order of Priests.

Pastoral care of a parish

51. The diocesan bishop may assign a deacon to assist a priest entrusted with the pastoral care of one or several parishes.[23] Deacons who possess administrative experience and have received pastoral theological training also may be called to guide Christian communities that do not have the immediate benefit of a resident priest.[24] "While it is a duty of deacons to respect the office of parish priest and to work in communion with all who share in his pastoral care, they also have the right to be accepted and fully recognized by all."[25] When a deacon is entrusted to guide a parish community, "it is necessary to specify that the moderator of the parish is a priest and that he is its proper pastor. To him alone has been entrusted the *cura animarum*, in which he is assisted by the deacon."[26] "When deacons supply in places where there is a shortage of priests, they do

so by ecclesial mandate. . . . It is they who preside at [such] Sunday celebrations"[27] in the absence of the priest. In dioceses where parish pastoral councils are constituted, these deacons are members of such councils by law.[28]

Witnesses to communion and mission

52. Deacons and priests, as ordained ministers, should develop a genuine respect for each other, witnessing to the communion and mission they share with one another and with the diocesan bishop in mutual service to the People of God.[29] To foster this communion, it is important for the diocese to offer opportunities annually for shared retreats, days of recollection, deanery meetings, continuing education study days, and mutual work on diocesan councils and commissions, as well as regularly scheduled occasions for socialization. Further, the Church's communion and mission "is realized not only by the ministers in virtue of the Sacrament of Orders but also by all the lay faithful."[30] Therefore, the bishop, priests, and deacons need to welcome, inspire, and form the lay faithful to participate in the communion and mission of the Church "because of their Baptismal state and their specific vocation."[31]

Theological formation and collaboration of priests

53. Priests should be informed about the sacramental identity of the deacon. They also are to be aware of the nature of diaconal spirituality and the specific functions the deacons will perform within the diocesan Church.[32] Priests need to collaborate with the diocesan bishop in planning for the inclusion of deacons into the life and ministry of the diocesan Church. Pastors especially are involved in the presentation, selection, and assessment processes of aspirants and candidates. Priests must serve as spiritual directors and pastoral supervisors and may serve as members of the faculty. They are expected to catechize the people on the ordained vocation of the deacon and to actively seek out, with the assistance of the parish community, competent nominees for this ministry.[33]

Relationship Among Deacons and Those in Formation

Sacramental fraternity

54. By virtue of their ordination, a sacramental fraternity unites deacons. They form a community that witnesses to Christ, the Deacon-Servant. "Each deacon should have a sense of being joined with his fellow deacons in a bond of charity, prayer, obedience to their bishops, ministerial zeal and collaboration."[34] Therefore, "with the permission of the bishop . . . it would be opportune for deacons

periodically to meet to discuss their ministry, exchange experiences, advance formation and encourage each other in fidelity."[35] Canonically, deacons may "form associations among themselves to promote their spiritual life, to carry out charitable and pious works and pursue other objectives which are consonant with their sacramental consecration and mission."[36] However, it must be noted that associations that form as pressure groups that could promote conflict with the bishop are completely irreconcilable with the clerical state.[37] It may be desirable, therefore, for the diocesan bishop to form a diocesan structure composed of a proportionate number of deacons to coordinate diaconal ministry and life within the diocese.[38] The diocesan bishop would serve as its president and approve its statutes.[39] Finally, the diaconal community should be, for those in the aspirant and candidate paths in formation, "a precious support in the discernment of their vocation, in human growth, in the initiation to the spiritual life, in theological study and pastoral experience."[40]

Deacons and religious: Collaborators in ministry

Relationship with Women and Men Religious

55. Deacons ought to promote collaboration between themselves and women and men religious who also have dedicated their lives to the service of the Church. Pastoral sensitivity between deacons and religious should be carefully nurtured. Opportunities for dialogue among deacons and religious could serve the Church well in developing and maintaining mutual understanding and support of each other's unique vocation, each of which accomplishes in its own way the common mission of service to the Church.

Foster the mission of the faithful

Relationship with the Laity

56. By ordination, deacons are members of the clergy.[41] The vast majority of deacons in the United States, married or celibate, have secular employment and do not engage exclusively in specific church-related ministries. This combination of an ordained minister with a secular occupation and personal and family obligations can be a great strength, opportunity, and witness to the laity on how they too might integrate their baptismal call and state in life in living their Christian faith in society.[42]

The Church: A communion of service

57. The laity, as members of the Church, have an obligation and right to share in the communion and mission of the Church. Through his ordination to service, the deacon promotes, in an

active fashion, the various lay apostolates and guides these in communion with the bishop and local priests.[43] In collaboration with his bishop and the priests of his diocese, the deacon has a special role to promote communion and to counter the strong emphasis on individualism prevalent in the United States. Set aside for service, the deacon links together the individual and diverse segments of the community of believers. In his works of charity, the deacon guides and witnesses to the Church "the love of Christ for all men instead of personal interests and ideologies which are injurious to the universality of salvation . . . the *diakonia* of charity necessarily leads to a growth of communion within the particular Churches since charity is the very soul of ecclesial communion."[44]

Relationship with Society

58. The diaconate is lived in a particularly powerful way in the manner in which a deacon fulfills his obligations to his secular occupation, to his civic and public responsibilities, and among his family and neighbors. This, in turn, enables the deacon to bring back to the Church an appreciation of the meaning and value of the Gospel as he discerns it in the lives and questions of the people he has encountered. In his preaching and teaching, the deacon articulates the needs and hopes of the people he has experienced, thereby animating, motivating, and facilitating a commitment among the lay faithful to an evangelical service in the world.[45]

Deacons must be involved in the world

59. Specifically, in the third Christian millennium, "the whole Church is called to greater apostolic commitment which is both personal and communitarian, renewed and generous."[46] At the heart of this call is an awareness of a new evangelization: i.e., "to rekindle the faith in the Christian conscience of many and cause the joyful proclamation of salvation to resound in society."[47] The deacon, as herald of the Gospel, has an important pastoral responsibility in new evangelization.[48] Pope John Paul II reminds the Church that "what moves me even more strongly to proclaim the urgency of missionary evangelization is the fact that it is the primary service which the Church can render to every individual . . . in the modern world."[49] The deacon is ordained precisely for service in both the sanctuary and the marketplace.

The deacon and the new evangelization

Ministry-employment compatibility

60. The secular employment of a deacon is also linked with his ministry.[50] Although his secular work may benefit the community, some professions can become incompatible with the pastoral responsibilities of his ministry. The bishop, "bearing in mind the requirements of ecclesial communion and of the fruitfulness of pastoral ministry, shall evaluate individual cases as they arise, [and may require] a change of profession after ordination."[51]

Diocese-coordinated services

Unity in Pastoral Activity

61. Under the diocesan bishop's authority, joint meetings and cooperative action "arranged between priests, deacons, religious, and laity involved in pastoral work [can] avoid compartmentalization or the development of isolated groups and . . . guarantee coordinated unity for different pastoral activities."[52]

II. Diaconal Spirituality

Jesus, the Servant

Introduction

62. The primary sources of a deacon's spirituality are his participation in the sacraments of Christian initiation, as well as his sacramental identity and participation in ordained ministry. For a deacon who is married, his spirituality is nurtured further in the Sacrament of Matrimony, which sanctifies conjugal love and constitutes it as a sign of the love with which Christ gives himself to the Church. For the celibate deacon, loving God and serving his neighbor roots his whole person in a total and undivided consecration to Christ. For each deacon, his model *par excellence* is Jesus Christ, the Servant, who lived totally at the service of his Father, for the good of every person.[53] To live their ministry to the fullest, "deacons must know Christ intimately so that He may shoulder the burdens of their ministry."[54]

The priority of the spiritual life

Spiritual Life

63. Deacons are obligated to give priority to the spiritual life and to live their *diakonia* with generosity. They should integrate their family obligations, professional life, and ministerial responsibilities so as to grow in their commitment to the person and mission of Christ, the Servant. Clerics have a special obligation to seek holiness in their lives "because they are consecrated to God by a new title in the reception of orders as dispensers of God's mysteries in the service of His people."[55]

Simplicity of Life

64. Deacons are charged at ordination to shape a way of life always according to the example of Christ and to imitate Christ who came not to be served but to serve. Therefore, deacons are called to a simple lifestyle. Simplicity of life enables a cleric "to stand beside the underprivileged, to practice solidarity with their efforts to create a more just society, to be more sensitive and capable of understanding and discerning realities involving the economic and social aspects of life, and to promote a preferential option for the poor."[56] The prophetic significance of this lifestyle, "so urgently needed in affluent and consumeristic societies,"[57] is its important witness in animating the *diakonia* of every Christian to serve "especially those who are poor or in any way afflicted."[58]

Simple lifestyle

Pastoral Service

65. As Pope John Paul II observed, "a deeply felt need in the decision to reestablish the diaconate was and is that of a greater and more direct presence of Church ministers in the various spheres such as family, work, school, etc., in addition to existing pastoral structures."[59] While transforming the world is the proper role of the laity, the deacon—in communion with his bishop and the diocesan presbyterate—exhorts, consecrates, and guides the People of God in living faithfully the communion and mission they share in Christ, especially in making the Gospel visible in their daily lives through their concern for justice, peace, and respect for life.[60]

Engaged in the world

III. The Deacon in His State of Life

The Married Deacon

66. The majority of deacons in the United States are married.[61] These men bring to the Sacrament of Holy Orders the gifts already received and still being nurtured through their participation in the Sacrament of Matrimony. This sacrament sanctifies the love of husbands and wives, making that love an efficacious sign of the love of Christ for his Church. Marriage requires an "interpersonal giving of self, a mutual fidelity, a source of [and openness to] new life, [and] a support in times of joy and sorrow."[62] Lived in faith, this ministry within the domestic Church is a sign to the entire Church of the love of Christ. It forms the basis of the married deacon's unique gift within the Church.[63]

Married love is a sign of the love of Christ for the Church

Family life, work, and ministry

67. "In particular the deacon and his wife must be a living example of fidelity and indissolubility in Christian marriage before a world which is in dire need of such signs. By facing in a spirit of faith the challenges of married life and the demands of daily living, they strengthen the family life not only of the Church community but of the whole of society. They also show how the obligations of family life, work and ministry can be harmonized in the service of the Church's mission. Deacons and their wives and children can be a great encouragement to others who are working to promote family life."[64]

Witness to the sanctity of marriage

68. A married deacon, with his wife and family, gives witness to the sanctity of marriage. The more they grow in mutual love, conforming their lives to the Church's teaching on marriage and sexuality, the more they give to the Christian community a model of Christ-like love, compassion, and self-sacrifice. The married deacon must always remember that through his sacramental participation in both vocational sacraments, first in Matrimony and again in Holy Orders, he is challenged to be faithful to both. With integrity he must live out both sacraments in harmony and balance. The wife of a deacon should be included with her husband, when appropriate, in diocesan clergy and parochial staff gatherings. A deacon and his wife, both as a spiritual man and woman and as a couple, have much to share with the bishop and his priests about the Sacrament of Matrimony. A diaconal family also brings a unique presence and understanding of the domestic family. "By facing in a spirit of faith the challenges of married life and the demands of daily living, [the married deacon and his family] strengthen the family life not only of the Church community but of the whole of society."[65]

Celibacy: Consecration to Christ with an undivided heart

The Celibate Deacon

69. The Church acknowledges the gift of celibacy that God grants to certain of its members who wholeheartedly live it "*according to its true nature* and according to its real purposes, that is for evangelical, spiritual and pastoral motives."[66] The essential meaning of celibacy is grounded in Jesus' preaching of the kingdom of God. Its deepest source is love of Christ and dedication to his mission. "In celibate life, indeed, love becomes a sign of total and undivided consecration to Christ and of greater freedom to serve God and man. The choice of celibacy is not an expression of contempt for marriage nor of flight from reality but a special way of serving man and the world."[67]

70. The celibate commitment remains one of the most fundamental expressions of Jesus' call to radical discipleship for the sake of the kingdom on earth and as an eschatological sign of the kingdom of heaven.[68] "This perfect continency, out of desire for the kingdom of heaven, has always been held in particular honor in the Church. The reason for this was and is that perfect continency for the love of God is an incentive to charity, and is certainly a particular source of spiritual fecundity in the world."[69]

Celibacy: Radical discipleship

71. If the celibate deacon gives up one kind of family, he gains another. In Christ, the people he serves become mother, brother, and sister. In this way, celibacy as a sign and motive of pastoral charity takes flesh. Reciprocity, mutuality, and affection shared with many become channels that mold and shape the celibate deacon's pastoral love and his sexuality. "Celibacy should not be considered just as a legal norm . . . but rather as a value . . . whereby [the celibate deacon] takes on the likeness of Jesus Christ . . . as a full and joyful availability in his heart for the pastoral ministry."[70]

Celibacy Affects Every Deacon

72. In one way or another, celibacy affects every deacon, married or unmarried. Understanding the nature of celibacy—its value and its practice—are essential to the married deacon. Not only does this understanding strengthen and nurture his own commitment to marital chastity, but it also helps to prepare him for the possibility of living celibate chastity should his wife predecease him. This concern is particularly unique within the diaconate. Tragically, some deacons who were married at the time of ordination only begin to face the issues involved with celibacy upon the death of their wives. As difficult as this process is, all deacons need to appreciate the impact celibacy can have on their lives and ministry.

Celibacy affects every deacon

The Widowed Deacon

73. The death of a married deacon's wife is a "particular moment in life which calls for faith and Christian hope."[71] The death of the wife of a married deacon introduces a new reality into the daily routine of his family and ministry. Charity should be extended to the widowed deacon as he assesses and accepts his new personal circumstances, so he will not neglect his primary duty as father to his children or any new needs his family might have.[72] As required, a widowed deacon should

Ministry to a widowed deacon

be assisted to seek professional counsel and spiritual direction as he encounters and integrates the bereavement process. Further, the fraternal closeness of his bishop, the priests with whom he ministers, and the diaconal community should offer comfort and reassurance in this special moment in his life.[73] This adjustment to a new state of life can be achieved only in time through prayer, counsel, and an "intensification of one's dedication to others for the love of God in the ministry."[74]

Ministry to a deacon's widow

74. A similar sensitivity also should be given to the widow of a deacon since she shared so intimately in her husband's life and ministerial witness. The bishop and her pastor, as well as the diaconal and parish communities, should extend appropriate and adequate support in her bereavement. Widows of deacons ought to remain connected with the diaconal community, not only because of support and encouragement, but because of the unique bonds that had been forged by virtue of her husband's ordination.

Dispensations for remarriage or from the obligations of the clerical state

75. In exceptional cases, the Holy See may grant a dispensation for a new marriage[75] or for a release from the obligations of the clerical state. However, to ensure a mature decision in discerning God's will, effective pastoral care should be provided to maintain that a proper and sufficient period of time has elapsed before either of these dispensations is sought. If a dispensation for a new marriage is petitioned and granted, additional time will be required for the formation of a stable relationship in the new marriage, as well as the enabling of his new wife to obtain sufficient understanding and experience about the diaconate in order to give her written, informed consent and support.

Pastoral care of a divorced deacon and his family

A Deacon and Family Confronting Divorce

76. Divorce between a deacon and his wife can happen. In this situation, suitable pastoral care should be offered to the deacon, his wife, and their children. This pastoral care, which may be facilitated by the director of deacon personnel or any other qualified person on behalf of the bishop, should include ample time to work through the various stages of grieving and adjustment caused by divorce. The determination of the divorced deacon's ministerial status will require sensitivity and prudence on the part of the bishop, the pastor or pastoral supervisor, the ministerial community, and other

institutions in which the deacon serves. Members of the diaconal community are also in a unique position to reach out, as appropriate, in order to help the divorced couple and family deal with the challenges the divorce may entail.

IV. The Permanency of the Order of Deacons

Order of Deacons: Permanent and stable

77. Underlying the restoration and renewal of the diaconate at the Second Vatican Council was the principle that the diaconate is a stable and permanent rank of ordained ministry. Since the history of the order over the last millennium, however, has been centered on the diaconate as a transitory stage leading to the priesthood, actions that may obfuscate the stability and permanence of the order should be minimized. This would include the ordination of celibate or widowed deacons to the priesthood. "Hence ordination [of a permanent deacon] to the Priesthood . . . must always be a very rare exception, and only for special and grave reasons . . . Given the exceptional nature of such cases, the diocesan bishop should consult the Congregation for Catholic Education with regard to the intellectual and theological preparation of the candidate, and also the Congregation for the Clergy concerning the program of priestly formation and the aptitude of the candidate to the priestly ministry."[76]

V. The Obligations and Rights of Deacons

Incardination

Incardination: A juridical bond

78. "Through the imposition of hands and the prayer of consecration, [the deacon] is constituted a sacred minister and a member of the hierarchy."[77] Having already clearly expressed in writing his intention to serve the diocesan Church for life, upon his ordination the deacon is incardinated into the diocesan Church. "Incardination is a juridical bond. It has ecclesiastical and spiritual significance in as much as it expresses the ministerial dedication of the deacon to a specific diocesan Church."[78]

The Church's Ministry of the Word

"Receive the Gospel of Christ, whose herald you now are."

79. As a participant in the Church's ministry of the word, the deacon heeds the charge given him at ordination: "Receive the Gospel of Christ, whose herald you now are. Believe what you read, teach what you believe, and practice what you teach."[79] The

deacon must always remain a student of God's word, for only when the word is deeply rooted in his own life can he bring that word to others.[80] The deacon ought to remember that since he is a member of the hierarchy, his actions and public pronouncements involve the Church and its Magisterium. Therefore, he is obligated to cherish the communion and mission that bind him to the Holy Father and his own bishop, especially in his preaching of the Scriptures, the Creed, Catholic teachings, and the disciplines of the Church.[81]

The *diakonia* of the Word

80. Deacons are ordained "to proclaim the Gospel and preach the Word of God."[82] They "have the faculty to preach everywhere, in accordance with the conditions established by [Canon Law]."[83] "Deacons should be trained carefully to prepare their homilies in prayer, in study of the sacred texts, in perfect harmony with the Magisterium and in keeping with the [age, culture, and abilities] of those to whom they preach."[84] Further, "by their conduct . . . by transmitting Christian doctrine and by devoting attention to the problems of our time . . . [deacons] collaborate with the bishop and the priests in the exercise of a ministry which is not of their wisdom but of the Word of God, calling all to conversion and holiness."[85]

Publication, use of public media, and the Internet

81. Deacons are obliged to obtain the permission of their bishop before submitting for publication written material concerning faith and morals. Deacons are required to adhere to the norms established by the United States Conference of Catholic Bishops or diocesan policies when participating in radio or television broadcasts, public media, and the Internet.[86]

The *diakonia* of the liturgy

The Church's Ministry of Liturgy

82. As an ordained participant in the Church's ministry of liturgy, the deacon confirms his identity as servant of the Body of Christ. In the celebration of the sacraments, whether he serves as a presider or assists the presider, "let him remember that, when lived with faith and reverence, these actions of the Church contribute much to growth in the spiritual life and to the increase of the Christian community."[87]

83. Deacons, in hierarchical communion with the bishop and priests, serve in the sanctification of the Christian community. "In the Eucharistic Sacrifice, the deacon does not celebrate the mystery: rather, he effectively represents on the one hand, the people of God

and, specifically, helps them to unite their lives to the offering of Christ; while on the other, in the name of Christ himself, he helps the Church to participate in the fruits of that sacrifice."[88] While exercising his liturgical ministries, "the deacon is to observe faithfully the rubrics of the liturgical books without adding, omitting or changing of his own volition what they require. . . . For the Sacred Liturgy they should vest worthily and with dignity, in accordance with the prescribed liturgical norms. The dalmatic, in its appropriate liturgical colors, together with the alb, cincture and stole, 'constitutes the liturgical dress proper to deacons.'"[89] Specific liturgical functions of the deacon in the Latin rite of the Catholic Church are contained in Chapter One of this *Directory*.

The Church's Ministry of Charity and Justice

84. As an ordained participant in the Church's ministry of charity and justice, the deacon assumes the duties entrusted to him by his bishop with humility and enthusiasm. At the core of his spirituality, a deacon puts on Christ and is guided by the love of Christ in caring for all in his charge: "Charity is the very soul of ecclesial communion."[90]

The *diakonia* of charity

85. In the prayer of diaconal ordination, the bishop implores God that the deacon may be "full of all the virtues, sincere in charity, solicitous towards the weak and the poor, humble in their service . . . [and] may . . . be the image of your Son who did not come to be served but to serve."[91] Therefore, "by word and example," the deacon places himself "at the constant service of [his] brothers and sisters."[92] This service will include diocesan and parochial works of charity, including the Church's concern for social justice. It will also extend into Christian formation—working with youth and adults in promoting justice and life in all its phases—transforming the world through personal witness in conformity with the Gospel of life and justice. The deacon must strive, therefore, to serve all of humanity "without discrimination, while devoting particular care to the suffering and the sinful."[93] Ultimately, the deacon's principal *diakonia*—a sign of the Church's mission—"should bring [all whom he serves] to an experience of God's love and move [them] to conversion by opening [their] heart[s] to the work of grace."[94]

VI. United States Conference of Catholic Bishops: Particular Law Governing Deacons in the United States

Particular law

86. A number of practical concerns have emerged regarding diaconal ministry. Because of the diverse responses that exist throughout the United States, the United States Conference of Catholic Bishops has published the following *particular law* to provide a more harmonious approach.

Age for Ordination

87. In accord with Canon Law, the United States Conference of Catholic Bishops establishes the minimum age for ordination to the permanent diaconate at thirty-five for all candidates, married or celibate. The establishment of a maximum age for ordination is at the discretion of the diocesan bishop, keeping in mind the particular needs and expectations of the diocese regarding diaconal ministry and life.

Clerical Title

88. While various forms of address have emerged with regard to deacons, the Congregation for the Clergy has determined that in all forms of address for permanent deacons, the appropriate title is "Deacon."[95]

Clerical Attire

89. The Code of Canon Law does not oblige permanent deacons to wear an ecclesiastical garb.[96] Further, because they are prominent and active in secular professions and society, the United States Conference of Catholic Bishops specifies that permanent deacons should resemble the lay faithful in dress and matters of lifestyle. Each diocesan bishop should, however, determine and promulgate any exceptions to this law, as well as specify the appropriate clerical attire if it is to be worn.[97]

Liturgy of the Hours

90. Permanent deacons are required to include as part of their daily prayer those parts of the Liturgy of the Hours known as Morning and Evening Prayer. Permanent deacons are obliged to pray for the universal Church. Whenever possible, they should lead these prayers with the community to whom they have been assigned to minister.

Participation in Political Office

91. A permanent deacon may not present his name for election to any public office or in any other general election, or accept a nomination or an appointment to public office, without the prior written permission of the diocesan bishop.[98] A permanent deacon may not actively and publicly participate in another's political campaign without the prior written permission of the diocesan bishop.

Temporary Absence from an Assignment

92. Permanent deacons may temporarily absent themselves from their place of assignment with the permission of their proper pastor or priest supervisor.

Decree of Appointment

93. A deacon shall receive a decree of appointment from his bishop,which should delineate his specific duties and responsibilities and the designation of his proper pastor or priest supervisor.[99]

Support of the Clergy

94. Permanent deacons are to take care of their own and their family's needs using income derived from their full-time employment by the diocese, parish, or secular profession. In an individual situation of need, the diocesan Church ought to assist the deacon and his family in charity.

Social Security Insurance

95. To provide for their own upkeep, every permanent deacon is obliged to satisfy the legal requirements for Social Security benefits or a comparable program.[100]

Remuneration

96. (1) Permanent deacons in full-time employment by the diocese, parish, or agency are to receive remuneration commensurate with the salaries and benefits provided to the lay men and women on staff for that particular occupation.[101]

(2) Permanent deacons in full-time secular employment, as well as those in part-time ministries, are to be reimbursed for legitimate expenses incurred in their ministry.[102]

Continuing Formation and Spiritual Retreat

97. Deacons are entitled to a period of time each year for continuing education and spiritual retreat. Norms should be established in each diocese regarding suitable length of time for these activities and the manner in which the deacon shall receive financial assistance for his expenses either from the diocese, from the current place of ministerial service, or from a combination of sources.

Financial Assistance to Those in Formation

98. The diocesan bishop is to determine the financial assistance, if any, that is to be provided to inquirers, as well as those enrolled in the aspirant path in diaconal formation. For those admitted into the candidate path in formation for the diaconate, some provision for financial assistance, at least partial, should be provided for educational needs (e.g., tuition, books, tapes) and for mandatory aspects of formation (e.g., required retreats, workshops).

Loss of Diaconal Status

99. A deacon can be returned to the lay state by canonical dismissal or because of a dispensation granted by the Holy See. Once dismissed or dispensed, he no longer enjoys any rights or privileges accorded clerics by the law of the Church.[103] Any responsibility, financial or liability, ceases on the part of the diocese.

Withdrawal of Diaconal Faculties

100. Bishops are reminded that if the ministry of a permanent deacon becomes ineffective or even harmful due to some personal difficulties or irresponsible behavior, his ministerial assignment and faculties are to be withdrawn by the diocesan bishop in accord with Canon Law.

Diocesan Liability

101. The diocesan bishop should provide for insurance regarding the liability of the diocese for actions taken by a permanent deacon in the course of his public official ministry. The same policies that govern liability for priests in the diocese should be applicable to permanent deacons.

Service of a Deacon from Another Diocesan Church

102. A diocesan bishop is under no obligation to accept a permanent deacon—ordained or incardinated elsewhere—for assignment

to a diocesan or parochial ministry. Nevertheless, since a permanent deacon is an ordained cleric, the bishop may not ordinarily forbid a visiting permanent deacon the exercise of his order provided that the deacon is not under censure.

Bi-Ritual Permanent Deacons

When a permanent deacon of the Eastern Catholic Churches is granted bi-ritual faculties to assist in the Roman Church, the theological understanding of the sacraments and the order of the diaconate in the Eastern Catholic Churches is to be respected. Practically, a deacon of the Eastern Catholic Churches is not to be allowed to solemnize marriages in the Roman Church.

Resignation and Retirement

103. Norms should be established in each diocese regarding the age, health, and other matters that need to be considered regarding a deacon's resignation from a ministerial office or his retirement from ministerial duties.

NORMS

(The number[s] found in parentheses after each norm refer[s] to the appropriate paragraph[s] in this *Directory*.)

1. It is incumbent on the bishop to provide for the pastoral care of deacons of the diocese. This is discharged personally and through the director of deacon personnel, who must always be a cleric. (41)
2. The principal criteria for the assignment of a deacon are the pastoral needs of the diocesan Church and the personal qualifications of the deacon, as these have been discerned in his previous experience and the course of his formation. (42)
3. A catechetical introduction for priests, religious, and laity to the diaconate at the time of its restoration and throughout its development in the diocese should be planned and well implemented. (43, 53)
4. Deacon assignments ought to provide ample opportunities for an integrated exercise of the threefold diaconal ministry: word, liturgy, and charity. (44)
5. A program for newly ordained deacons during the first three years of their ministry is to be coordinated and supervised by

the director of deacon personnel. (46) Under the bishop's authority, periodic meetings should be arranged between priests, deacons, religious, and laity involved in pastoral work "to avoid compartmentalization or the development of isolated groups and to guarantee coordinated unity for different pastoral activities in the diocese."[104] (61)

6. The deacon must give priority to the spiritual life. As minister of liturgy, the deacon confirms his identity as servant of the Body of Christ. (63, 82)
7. The vocation to the permanent diaconate presupposes the stability and permanency of the order. Hence, the ordination of a permanent deacon to the priesthood is always a rare exception, and must be done in consultation with the Congregation for Catholic Education and the Congregation for the Clergy. (77)
8. Deacons have the faculty to preach everywhere, in accordance with the conditions established by law. (80)
9. Deacons are obliged to obtain the permission of their bishop before submitting for publication written materials concerning faith and morals. They are to adhere to the norms established by the United States Conference of Catholic Bishops, or diocesan policies, in publicly representing the Church. (81)
10. The minimum age for ordination to the permanent diaconate is thirty-five. The establishment of a maximum age of ordination is at the discretion of the diocesan bishop, keeping in mind both diocesan needs and expectations of diaconal life and ministry. (87)
11. In all forms of address for permanent deacons, "Deacon" is preferred. (88)
12. The *Code of Canon Law* does not oblige permanent deacons to wear an ecclesiastical garb. Further, because they are more prominent and active in secular professions and society, the United States Conference of Catholic Bishops specifies that permanent deacons should resemble the lay faithful in dress and matters of lifestyle. Each ordinary should, however, determine and promulgate any exceptions to this law, as well as specify the appropriate clerical attire. (89)
13. Permanent deacons are required to include as part of their daily prayer those parts of the Liturgy of the Hours known as Morning and Evening Prayer. (90)
14. A permanent deacon may not present his name for election to any public office or in any other general election, or accept

a nomination or an appointment to public office, without the prior written permission of the diocesan bishop. A permanent deacon may not actively and publicly participate in another's political campaign without the prior written permission of the diocesan bishop. (91)

15. The deacon shall receive an official letter of appointment from his bishop. (44, 45, 93)
16. Until the decree of appointment is publicly announced by the bishop's office, all parties are bound to confidentiality. (44)
17. Every permanent deacon is obliged to satisfy the legal requirements of Social Security benefits or a comparable program. (95)
18. Deacons in full-time employment by the diocese or parish are to receive remuneration commensurate with the salaries and benefits provided to the lay men or women on staff for that particular occupation. (96)
19. Deacons in full-time secular employment, as well as those in part-time ministries, are to be reimbursed for legitimate expenses incurred in their ministry. (96)
20. For those admitted into the candidate path in formation, some provision for financial assistance should be provided for educational needs and mandatory aspects of formation. (98)
21. The diocesan bishop should provide for insurance regarding the liability of the diocese for actions taken by a permanent deacon in the course of his public official ministry. The same policies that govern liability for priests in the diocese should be applicable to permanent deacons. (101)
22. Norms should be established in each diocese regarding the age, health, and other matters that need to be considered regarding a deacon's resignation from a ministerial office or his retirement from ministerial duties. (103)

NOTES

1 DMLPD, nos. 1-2.

2 Ibid., nos. 8, 78, 80; cf. no. 3.

3 Cf. CIC, cc. 156, 157. DMLPD, no. 8, refers to this written conferral of office as a "decree of appointment." Cf. also "Appendix: Sample Documents," in *Clergy Procedural Handbook*, Randolph R. Calvo and Nevin J. Klinger, eds. (Washington, D.C.: Canon Law Society of America, 1992), 128ff, for examples of possible formulations of the letter of appointment.

4 BNFPD, no. 16.

5 PDG (1984), no. 51.

6 DMLPD, no. 40; cf., also, Ibid., no. 41. "The decree of appointment should specify the ministry of the deacon. A subsequent 'ministerial agreement' should not be necessary, nor should it be signed by the deacon's wife: this is [a] blurring of the lines of ministry and authority." Congregation for Catholic Education and the Congregation for the Clergy, *Joint Study of the US Draft Document—National Directory for the Formation, Ministry and Life of Permanent Deacons in the United States*, Prot. No. 78/2000 (March 4, 2002). Given the comprehensive nature of the information to be provided in the bishops' letter of appointment, the information that was formerly developed as a separate "ministerial agreement" may now be done as an integral part of the preparation of the bishop's letter of appointment.

7 DMLPD, no. 61.

8 Ibid., no. 7.

9 Ibid., no. 77.

10 Ibid., nos. 78-79.

11 Ibid., no. 81. Cf., also, no. 60, regarding the needs of celibate deacons.

12 Ibid., no. 41.

13 Ibid., no. 42.

14 Ibid.

15 Ibid.

16 Ibid., nos. 42, 38.

17 Ibid., no. 42.

18 Ibid.

19 Ibid., nos. 41-42.

20 Ibid., nos. 40-42.

21 Ibid., no. 41.

22 Ibid., no. 1, 41.

23 CIC, cc. 519, 517:1.

24 Ibid., no. 517:2; DMLPD, no. 41.

25 DMLPD, no. 41.

26 Ibid.

27 Ibid.

28 Ibid., no. 41; cf. CIC, c. 536.

29 Ibid.; cf. no. 37.

30 Pope John Paul II, *On the Vocation and the Mission of the Lay Faithful in the Church and in the World* (*Christifideles Laici*) (December 30, 1988) (Washington, D.C.: United States Catholic Conference, 1988), no. 23.

31 Ibid.

32 BNFPD, no. 90: "Ordinaries . . . to whom the present document is given, [should] ensure that it becomes an object of attentive reflection in communion with their priests and communities."

33 Ibid., no. 16.

34 DMLPD, no. 6.

35 Ibid., no. 6.

36 Ibid., no. 11.

37 Ibid.

38 Ibid., no. 80.

39 Ibid.

40 BNFPD, no. 26.

41 DMLPD, nos. 1, 7.

42 Ibid., no. 73.

43 Cf. Pope John Paul II, General Audience, *Deacons Have Many Pastoral Functions* (October 13, 1993), no. 5.

44 DMLPD, no. 55.

45 Ibid., no. 43; cf. nos. 25-27.

46 Congregation for the Clergy, *The Priest and the Third Christian Millennium* (March 19, 1999), (Washington, D.C.: United States Catholic Conference, 1999) Introduction.

47 Ibid.

48 DMLPD, no. 26.

49 Pope John Paul II, Encyclical Letter, *On the Permanent Validity of the Church's Missionary Mandate* (*Redemptoris Missio*) (December 7, 1990) (Washington, D.C.: United States Catholic Conference, 1990), no. 2.

50 DMLPD, no. 12.

51 Ibid.

52 Ibid., no. 78.

53 BNFPD, no. 11.

54 DMLPD, no. 50.

55 CIC, c. 276:1.

56 PDV, no. 30.

57 Ibid.

58 GS, no. 1.

59 Pope John Paul II, General Audience, *Deacons Serve the Kingdom of God* (October 5, 1993), no. 6.

60 ADUS.

61 NSD (1996) reports that 97 percent of all deacons in the United States are married (p. 2).

62 DMLPD, no. 61.

63 Ibid.

64 ADUS.

65 Ibid.

66 PDV, no. 50.

67 DMLPD, no. 60.

68 LG, no. 42.

69 Ibid.; cf. *The Roman Pontifical* (Washington, D.C.: International Commission on English in the Liturgy, 1978).

70 PDV, no. 50.

71 DMLPD, no. 62.

72 Ibid.

73 Ibid.

74 Ibid.

75 DMLPD, Note 193, citing Congregation for Divine Worship and the Discipline of the Sacraments, Circular Letter, Prot. No. 263/97 (June 6, 1997), no. 8.

76 Ibid., no. 5.

77 Ibid., no. 1.

78 Ibid., no. 2; cf. Bishops'Committee on the Diaconate, National Conference of Catholic Bishops, *Protocol for the Incardination/Excardination of Permanent Deacons* (1995, revised 1999).

79 The Roman Pontifical, op. cit., Ordination of Deacons, p. 171.

80 St. Augustine, *Serm.* 179, no. 1.

81 DMLPD, no. 23.

82 Ibid., no. 24.

83 Ibid.; cf. CIC, c. 764.

84 Ibid., no. 25.

85 Ibid., no. 23.

86 Ibid., no. 26.

87 Ibid., no. 53.

88 Ibid., no. 28.

89 Ibid., no. 30.

90 Ibid., no. 55.

91 Ibid., no. 38, citing *Pontificale Romanum-De Ordinatione Episcopi, Presbyterorum et Diaconorum*, no. 207, p. 122.

92 Ibid, no. 38.

93 Ibid.

94 Ibid.

95 "The introduction of the title 'Reverend Mr.' for permanent deacons could further complicate the issue of identity for deacons. The term 'Reverend' has traditionally been

associated with priests and used only for transitional deacons on their way to priesthood. As there is great sensitivity surrounding the issue of a deacon being seen as a 'mini-priest,' it would seem that the title 'Reverend Mr.' would lead to continued identification of the diaconate with the priesthood, rather than contributing to the independence and integrity of the Order of Deacon in itself. The title 'Deacon' would, of course, be appropriate." Congregation for Catholic Education and the Congregation for the Clergy, *Joint Study of the US Draft Document—National Directory for the Formation, Ministry and Life of Permanent Deacons in the United States*, Prot. No. 78/2000 (March 4, 2002).

96 CIC, c. 288.

97 Liturgical books clearly specify the liturgical garb of a deacon for various rites and liturgical celebrations. Here, the intent is to bring about harmony between dioceses, especially on a provincial level, as to the appropriate clerical attire, if any, for other formal clerical ministries of deacons. In some places, deacons wear a clerical shirt and Roman collar; others wear pectoral crosses or deacon lapel pins, while still others wear a modified dress shirt. There is confusion about what is appropriate clerical attire among deacons themselves and among the lay faithful. Recognizing the geographical and social diversity that exists in our country, the Bishops' Committee on the Diaconate offers this particular law as a practical response to a national concern.

98 DMLPD, no. 13. The rationale is that the identity of a political candidate becomes well known and any investigation regarding background or reputation of the permanent deacon should be the responsibility of ecclesial authorities so as to avoid any undue or unwarranted publicity in the public media. In making his determination to grant written permission, the bishop should investigate the background of the permanent deacon, including his many social relationships (e.g., memberships in clubs, organizations) so that nothing would become an embarrassment to the Church. The bishop should investigate the credit rating of the deacon so that there is no question of unreasonable indebtedness. He also should be concerned about fundraising that the permanent deacon, as a political candidate, will have to initiate, as well as improper reflections that might occur by associating the deacon, as a political candidate, with a particular party and its platform.

99 Ibid., no. 41; cf. no. 40.

100 Ibid., no. 15; cf. CIC, cc. 281, 1274.

101 Ibid., no. 16.

102 Ibid, no. 20. Examples include videos for baptismal preparation programs, handouts, refreshments for required gatherings, and distinctive clerical garb. It also could include reimbursement for the personal use of and gas for his car in ministry, using IRS mileage standards and records.

103 Ibid., no. 21; cf. CIC, cc. 290-293.

104 DMLPD, no. 78.

CHAPTER THREE

DIMENSIONS IN THE FORMATION OF DEACONS

I. Introduction

104. There are three separate but integral paths that constitute a unified diocesan formation program for deacons: aspirant, candidate, and post-ordination. Although this *Directory* addresses each path separately, they nevertheless become "one sole organic journey" in diaconal formation.[1] In each path, the four dimensions or specific areas in formation—human, spiritual, intellectual, and pastoral—are always essential.[2]

Separate paths: A unified formation program

II. Dimensions in Formation

105. One who will serve as a deacon requires a formation that promotes the development of the whole person. Therefore, the four dimensions in formation should be so interrelated as to achieve a continual integration of their objectives in the life of each participant and in his exercise of ministry.

Four dimensions in ministerial formation

Human Dimension

106. A participant comes to formation with a history of interrelationships with other people. Formation for ministry begins with human formation and development. Participants "should therefore cultivate a series of human qualities, not only out of proper and due growth and realization of self, but also with a view to the ministry."[3]

Growth in self-formation

OBJECTIVES

107. Deacons have an important role in the field of human development and the promotion of justice. Because of their close living and working situations in society, they can well understand, interpret, and try to bring solutions to personal and social problems in the light of the Gospel. Therefore, deacons need to be close to the people, helping them to understand the realities of social life so they can try to improve it. Deacons should have the courage to speak out for the weak and defend their rights. As a prophetic voice

Cultivate qualities with a view to diaconal ministry

for the needs of others, the deacon proclaims God's word in the contemporary world. In this evangelizing role, the deacon collaborates with the diocesan bishop in the latter's responsibility for catechesis in the local Church.[4] The Congregation for the Evangelization of Peoples, in its *Guide for Catechists*, offers the following attributes for catechists that apply equally to deacons:

a. on the purely human sphere: psychophysical equilibrium—good health, sense of responsibility, honesty, and dynamism; good professional and family conduct, spirit of sacrifice, strength, perseverance . . .;
b. with a view to the functions of a [deacon]: good human relations, a good ability to dialogue with those of other religions, grasp of one's culture, ability to communicate, willingness to work with others, leadership qualities, balance judgment, openness of mind, a sense of realism, a capacity to transmit consolation and hope . . .;
c. with a view to particular situations or roles: aptitudes for working in the fields of peacemaking, development, socio-cultural promotion, justice, health care. . . .[5]

To this list may be added other important qualities, such as the ability to manage conflict, collaborate, and organize.

Four aspects of human maturity

108. The Congregation for Catholic Education's *Basic Norms for the Formation of Permanent Deacons* highlights four aspects of human maturity that must be considered when developing formation programs for deacons. These include: (1) formation in the human virtues, (2) the capacity to relate to others, (3) affective maturity (including psychosexual maturity and health), and (4) training in freedom, which "includes the education of the moral conscience."[6] Deacons, above all, must be persons who can relate well to others.[7] This ability flows from an affective maturity that "presupposes . . . the victorious struggle against their own selfishness."[8] Mature ways of relating to others are important servant-leadership qualities. Those who aspire to this ministry need to collaborate well with others and to confront challenges in a constructive way. "A pre-condition for an authentic human maturity is training in freedom, which is expressed in obedience to the truth of one's own being."[9]

109. Human formation aims to enhance the personality of the minister in such a way that he becomes "a bridge and not an obstacle for others in their meeting with Jesus Christ."[10] Accordingly, formation processes need to be structured so as to nurture and encourage the participants "to acquire and perfect a series of human qualities which will permit them to enjoy the trust of the community, to commit themselves with serenity to the pastoral ministry, to facilitate encounter and dialogue."[11] Therefore, all of these various aspects of human maturity must be carefully considered when planning the formation program and when assessing a participant's effective integration of them. If warranted, a participant may also consult (or be asked to do so) with a qualified professional, approved by the director of formation, to assist in this assessment.

Human formation aims to enhance the personality of the minister

Spiritual Dimension

110. "Human formation leads to and finds its completion in the spiritual dimension of formation, which constitutes the heart and unifying center of every Christian formation. Its aim is to tend to the development of the new life received in Baptism."[12] Many directions lead to this goal, all of them fundamentally the work of the Holy Spirit. The spiritual life is, therefore, dynamic and never static. The first goal of spiritual formation is the establishment and nourishment of attitudes, habits, and practices that will set the foundation for a lifetime of ongoing spiritual discipline.

Spiritual foundations for discipleship and ministry

111. A man should not be admitted to diaconal formation unless it is demonstrated that he is already living a life of mature Christian spirituality.[13] The spiritual dimension of formation should "affirm and strengthen" this spirituality, and it should emphasize "specific traits of diaconal spirituality."[14]

A mature spirituality in imitation of Jesus

112. Configured sacramentally to Christ the Servant, a deacon's spirituality must be grounded in the attitudes of Christ. These include "simplicity of heart, total giving of self and disinterest for self, humble and helpful love for the brothers and sisters, especially the poorest, the suffering and the most needy, the choice of a lifestyle of sharing and poverty."[15] This diaconal spirituality is nourished by the Eucharist, which, "not by chance, characterizes the ministry of the deacon."[16] A diaconal spirituality is conditioned by participation in the apostolic ministry and should be marked by

openness to God's word, to the Church, and to the world.[17] The fundamental spiritual attitude should be one of openness to this word contained in revelation, as preached by the Church, celebrated in the liturgy and lived out in the lives of God's People. To herald the Gospel requires missionary zeal—a new evangelization—to bring God's love and salvation to all in word and action. The preaching of the word is always connected, therefore, with prayer, the celebration of the Eucharist, and the building of community. The earliest community of Christ's disciples was a model of this.[18] To attain an interior spiritual maturity requires an intense sacramental and prayer life.

Goals of the spiritual dimension

Objectives

113. The objectives of the spiritual dimension in formation are (a) to deepen his prayer life—personal, familial, communal, and liturgical—with special emphasis upon participation in Eucharist, daily if possible; daily celebration of the Liturgy of the Hours, especially morning and evening prayer; *lectio divina*, devotion to the Blessed Virgin Mary and the saints; and regular reception of the Sacrament of Reconciliation; (b) to assist the participant, with the help of his spiritual director and those responsible for formation, to deepen and cultivate a service commitment to God's word, the Church, and the world; (c) to acquaint him with the Catholic spiritual tradition reflected in classic spiritual writings and in the lives of the saints, and with contemporary developments in spirituality—a faith seeking to be expressed and celebrated; (d) to affirm the Christian witness of matrimonial and celibate spirituality; (e) to incarnate his spirituality in the real life and history of the people whom he encounters each day in places where he lives, works, and serves.[19]

Discernment in spiritual formation

114. Discernment is an essential spiritual process in determining the presence of a vocation to the diaconate, as well as the capacity to live it fully after ordination. The spiritual dimension of formation, therefore, should assist the participant in assessing the depth and quality of his integration of personal, family, employment, and ministerial responsibilities. Further, it should assist his growth in self-knowledge, in his commitment to Christ and his Church, and in his dedication to service, especially to the poor and those most suffering.[20] A strong spiritual life and a realistic commitment to serve people converge in the continual transformation of the participant's mind and heart in harmony with Christ.

115. Spiritual formation helps the participant to develop the virtue of penance, which includes mortification, sacrifice, and generosity toward others. The participant must be open to conversion of heart about issues of justice, peace, and respect for life. He needs to be instructed on how his prayer, simplicity of life, and commitment to the poor add credibility to his capacity to witness and, as a deacon, to preach effectively the Word of God.[21]

Credibility in one's lifestyle

116. Each person in formation is called to a mature relationship with those in authority that includes a spirit of trust, mutual respect, and obedience. Accountability in formation is an invitation to a deeper conversion. A spirit of service to others is finally an imitation of Christ himself, who came not to do his own will but the will of his Father.[22] Formation personnel, especially the spiritual director, should give instructions on the meaning of authentic obedience and help each participant to appreciate and practice it in his life.

Obedience and respect

117. The role of the spiritual director, who must always be a priest,[23] is critical to the formation process, particularly in assisting the participant to discern and affirm the signs of his vocation.[24] An individual's spiritual director may be chosen directly by the participant with the approval of the bishop, or from a list of spiritual directors similarly approved. The distinction between internal and external forums must always be clearly maintained. A participant may also consult (or be requested to do so) with an advisor whom he may select with the approval of the director of formation. The advisor, however, does not substitute for the unique role of the spiritual director in formation and discernment.[25]

Spiritual director

Intellectual Dimension

118. Intellectual formation offers the participant "substantial nourishment" for the pastoral, human, and spiritual dimensions of his life. Intellectual formation is a "precious instrument" for effective discernment and ministry. An increasingly educated society and the new roles of leadership in diaconal ministry require that a deacon be a knowledgeable and reliable witness to the faith and a spokesman for the Church's teaching. Therefore, the intellectual dimension of formation must be designed to communicate a knowledge of the faith and church tradition that is "complete and serious," so that each participant will be prepared to carry out his vital ministry.[26]

Knowledge of faith and Church

> The commitment to study, which takes up no small part of the time of those preparing for the [diaconate], is not in fact an external and secondary dimension of their human, Christian, spiritual and vocational growth. In reality, through study, especially the study of theology, the future [deacon] assents to the Word of God, grows in his spiritual life and prepares himself to fulfill his pastoral ministry.[27]

Goals of the intellectual dimension

OBJECTIVES

119. Deacons must first understand and practice the essentials of Christian doctrine and life before they can communicate them to others in a clear way in their ministries of word, liturgy, and charity. Sacred Scripture is the soul of the program. Around it are structured the other branches of theology. Liturgical studies are to be given prominence, as the participants are prepared to lead the faith community in prayer and sacramental life. Preaching, with its preparation and practice, requires a significant segment of time in the program of study. Attention should also be given to topics reflecting the specific needs of the Church in the United States: (1) a family life perspective; (2) respect for and understanding of our national multicultural diversity and the incorporation of the Gospel into all aspects of society; (3) the social dimension of the Gospel as taught by the Church, especially in the social encyclicals of the Popes, and the significant documents promulgated by the United States Conference of Catholic Bishops, with special reference to concerns surrounding immigration as experienced within the Church in America;[28] (4) the study of the beliefs and practices of other religions and Christian denominations—deepening a spirit of ecumenism and interreligious dialogue. Ample opportunities also need to be given to the study and practice of missiology—learning how to evangelize—so as to form deacons who will be actively present in society, offering true diaconal witness, entering into sincere dialogue with others, and cooperating in charity and justice to resolve common concerns.[29]

The intellectual content should be oriented toward a pastoral context

120. The intellectual content should be organized, presented, and directed fundamentally to prepare participants for the pastoral context of service.[30] It should provide the participant with the knowledge, skills, and appreciation of the faith that he needs to effectively fulfill his ministry of word, liturgy, and charity. It should, therefore,

be authentic and complete. In spite of the diversity of subjects, the intellectual dimension should offer an overall vision of faith that brings unity and harmony to the educational process.[31] The theological formation of the participants needs to be presented as originating from within the Church's life of faith, worship, and pastoral care.[32] In this way, intellectual formation will be perceived as crucial to the deacon's responsible exercise of his ministry.

Cultural analysis

121. The intellectual dimension should also be constructed to help the participant "to evaluate his society and culture in light of the Gospel and to understand the Gospel in the light of the particular features of the society and culture in which he will be serving."[33] Of equal importance is the discernment and understanding of what is shared in common, as well as the cultural and ethnic expressions of the faith.

Adult educational methodology

122. Since participants enter formation as mature men, the intellectual dimension of formation "should make use of the methods and processes of adult education. . . . [The participants] should be invited to draw and reflect upon their adult life and faith experiences."[34]

Integration of learning and life

123. Theology is traditionally described as "faith seeking understanding." Therefore, the formation faculty and staff should structure an intellectual process that includes an invitation to each participant to reflect on his adult life and experience in the light of the Gospel and the Church's teaching. The intellectual dimension in each path in the formation program should be designed and presented in such a way as to integrate doctrine, morality, and spirituality.

Academic content

124. The following criteria focus the preparation and presentation of a systematic, comprehensive, and integrated intellectual formation, faithful to the Magisterium of the Church. Based on Scripture and Tradition, the documents of the Second Vatican Council, the *Catechism of the Catholic Church*, and the *General Directory for Catechesis*,[35] this formation must take into account the following theological content:

a. Introduction to sacred Scripture and its authentic interpretation; the theology of the Old and New Testaments; the interrelation between Scripture, Tradition, and the Magisterium; the use of Scripture in spiritual formation, preaching, evangelization, catechesis, and pastoral activity in general
b. Introduction to the study of the Fathers of the Church and an elementary knowledge of the history of the Church
c. Fundamental theology, with illustration of the sources; topics and methods of theology; presentation of the questions relating to revelation and the formulation of the relationship between faith and reason, which will enable the participant to explain the reasonableness of the faith[36]
d. Dogmatic theology, with its trinitarian, christological, pneumatological, and ecclesial dimensions, including the Church as a communion of churches—Latin and Eastern Catholic Churches;[37] Christian anthropology; sacraments; eschatology; Mariology
e. Christian morality in its personal, familial, and social dimensions, including the social doctrine of the Church
f. Spiritual theology, the spiritual traditions of the Church as applied to one's own spiritual journey, and the spiritual life of the faithful
g. Liturgy and its historical, spiritual, and juridical aspects, with particular attention to the Rite of Christian Initiation of Adults and to the liturgical rites the deacon will celebrate
h. Canon Law, especially canonical considerations of the rights and obligations of the clergy, and the canons applicable to Baptism, marriage, and Christian burial
i. Ecumenism and interreligious dialogue principles, norms, and dimensions in pastoral ministry;[38]
j. Theology of Catholic evangelization: "evangelization of cultures and the inculturation of the message of faith," multicultural expressions of the faith, and missiology[39]

125. This content is structured further in Norms 5-12 at the end of Chapter Six. Those responsible for the preparation of the academic component in the candidate and post-ordination paths of formation should determine a course of study that complies with this content prior to ordination, as well as a course of study that will further develop this content after ordination as part of a structured

post-ordination program for continuing education and formation. Before ordination, the deacon candidate must demonstrate competence in all these areas.

Pastoral Dimension

Integrating role of pastoral formation

126. An integral formation must relate the human, spiritual, and intellectual dimensions to pastoral practice. "The whole formation imparted to [the participants] . . . aims at preparing them to enter into communion with the charity of Christ. . . . Hence their formation in its different aspects must have a fundamentally pastoral character."[40] Within that context, the pastoral dimension in formation is not merely an apprenticeship to familiarize the participant in diaconal formation with some pastoral techniques. Its aim, however, is to initiate the aspirant and candidate into the sensitivity of what it means to be a disciple of Jesus, who came to serve and not be served. Pastoral field education embodies this orientation, promoting learning through active engagement in a pastoral situation. Pastoral field education fosters a general integration in the formational process forging a close link between the human, spiritual, and intellectual dimensions in formation. Evangelization; Catholic schools; catechetics; religious education; youth ministry, social justice outreach opportunities; rural ministry; ecumenism; the care of the sick, elderly, and dying; as well as service opportunities in varied cultural settings indicate the breadth of experiences to which an aspirant and candidates may be exposed in the course of his pastoral field-education program.

Objectives

Objectives of the pastoral dimension

127. The pastoral dimension in diaconal formation should strengthen and enhance the exercise of the prophetic, priestly, and servant-leadership functions—deriving from his baptismal consecration—already lived and exercised by the participant in diaconal formation. In each path in formation, they must be taught how to proclaim the Christian message and teach it, how to lead others in communal celebrations of liturgical prayer, and how to witness to the Church in a Christian service marked by charity and justice. The demonstration of pastoral skills is a crucial element in the assessment of fitness for ordination. Therefore, the qualities to be developed for these tasks are as follows: a spirit of pastoral responsibility and servant-leadership; generosity and perseverance; creativity; respect for ecclesial communion; and filial obedience to

the bishop. Through his participation in pastoral field education, the participant should have a genuine confidence in his abilities and a realistic sense of his limitations.

Pastoral formation content

128. Pastoral formation should take into account that those preparing for the diaconate have already been involved in the mission of the Church. The pastoral field education program should be designed, therefore, to build upon previous experiences and talents already displayed. In addition to identifying and developing the gifts already at work, the pastoral dimension of formation should aim at helping the participant to discover talents, perhaps unrecognized, and to develop the skills necessary for exercising the threefold diaconal ministry. A participant needs to demonstrate a genuine confidence in his own ability—a realistic sense of achieving the knowledge and skills required for an effective diaconal ministry—and a strong desire to serve in a broad range of ministerial circumstances.

Pastoral formation interfaces with spiritual formation

129. Pastoral formation interfaces with spiritual formation. It is a formation for an ever-greater identification with the *diakonia* entrusted to the Church by Christ. Care is to be taken to introduce the participant actively into the pastoral life of the diocesan Church and to ensure periodic meetings with the diocesan bishop, priests, other deacons, religious, and laity serving in official ministry, to ensure a coordinated unity for different pastoral activities.[41] Supervised pastoral formation placements should be designed and adapted to the needs of the individual participant, helping him to gradually and appropriately experience in his pastoral placement what he has learned in his study.[42] He should also be given ample opportunities to share experiences with deacons already in ministry.

Pastoral theology

130. Pastoral formation develops by means of a specific theological discipline and a practical internship. This theological discipline, traditionally called "pastoral theology," is "a scientific reflection on the Church as she is built up daily."[43] The pastoral dimension of formation needs to pay particular attention to the following elements.

a. **The Church's Ministry of the Word**—Proclamation of the word in the varied contexts of ministerial service: *kerygma*, catechesis, preparation for the sacraments, homiletics—both in theory and practice, evangelization and missiology
b. **The Church's Ministry of Liturgy**—Liturgical praxis: celebration of the sacraments and sacramentals, service at the altar
c. **The Church's Ministry of Charity and Justice**—Preaching, educating the Christian community on the social dimensions of the Gospel; fostering by facilitation, motivation, and organization the Church's ministry of charity and justice, and the preferential option for the poor.

The *diakonia* of word, liturgy, and charity

131. As part of his pastoral field education formation, the candidate should acquire an appropriate multicultural awareness, exposure, and sensitivity, suitable to the needs of the diocese, including the possibility of learning a second language and studying its cultural context.

The life of the community, in particular the guidance of family teams, small communities, groups, and movements

132.

a. Certain technical subjects that prepare the participant for specific pastoral care can be useful, such as pastoral counseling, with particular emphasis on appropriate referral, especially as applied to family ministry; catechetical pedagogy; sacred music; ecclesiastical administration
b. A practical internship that permits the participant to encounter and respond in ministry to that which he has learned in his study
c. Progressive involvement in the pastoral activity of the diocese
d. The developing of the participant's commitment to ecumenism and interreligious dialogue; appropriate shared pastoral experiences should be considered[44]
e. A maturing in the participant of "a strong missionary sensitivity"[45]
f. According to particular situations and needs, an appropriate integration with other disciplines, such as philosophy, economics and politics, psychology, and sociology[46]
g. Information technology, distance learning, and the use of the Internet in pastoral ministry

Other recommended elements of the participant's pastoral formation

Theological reflection

133. Pastoral formation must include theological reflection so the participant may integrate his ministerial activity with the broad scope of diaconal studies. This process should lead him to a lifelong effort in reflecting on his ministry in the light of faith.

III. Additional Considerations

Topics of value in the United States

134. Attention should be given to the following topics which represent a value central to the life of the Catholic Church in the United States and, therefore, in the formation, ministry, and life of candidates and deacons.

A Family Life Perspective

INTRODUCTION

A family-centered formation

135. A family life perspective is rooted in the challenge of Pope John Paul II as stated in *Familiaris Consortio*: "No plan for organized pastoral work at any level must ever fail to take into consideration the pastoral area of the family."[47] Refocusing one's thinking from an individual-centered approach to a family-centered approach now represents an important component in organizing diaconal formation, ministry, and life.[48]

The family is the primary formation community

136. Individuals do not enter into formation alone. Those who participate in diaconal formation, married or unmarried, come with their families. They come as members of a family known as the "domestic Church" where life is shared and nurtured. They come from that primary community, where God is first discovered and known, into a new and wider community that can expand their love and deepen their faith. They come with their experiences of faith and personal life.

Family life requires a proper balance

137. Each participant must explore ways to keep his family life a priority in the face of the growing demands of formation and ministry, which include issues of age, faith, health, economics, employment, and relationships.

The role of the wife

THE MARRIED PARTICIPANT

138. In deciding to pursue a possible diaconal vocation, a married man must comply with the wishes of his wife, in a spirit of mutual commitment and love. A wife is an equal partner in the Sacrament

of Matrimony and is an individual person with her own gifts, talents, and call from God. A candidate's diaconal formation can be a unique and challenging situation and opportunity for his wife. She should be involved in the program in appropriate ways, remembering, however, that it is the husband who is responding to a call to the diaconate. The Church has determined that a married man cannot be considered for the diaconate without the consent of his wife.[49] After ordination, a deacon's wife needs to "be duly informed of [her] husband's activities in order to arrive at a harmonious balance between family, professional and ecclesial responsibilities."[50]

Appropriate inclusion

139. The participation of a wife in her husband's formation program strengthens an awareness of the husband's diaconal vocation and helps the wife to accept the challenges and changes that will take place, should her husband be ordained. It also provides an opportunity for those responsible for diaconal formation to assess whether she has "the Christian moral character and attributes which will neither hinder [her] husband's ministry nor be out of keeping with it."[51] To help the candidate's wife to give an informed consent to her husband's request for ordination, it is necessary to include specific resources and programming addressed to her. When workshops and spiritual exercises for wives are planned, wives should be consulted to ascertain their questions and concerns. While every effort ought to be made to provide scheduling and material assistance to make wives' participation possible, care must simultaneously be taken to keep clear the essential distinction between ordained and familial life and the clear independence of diaconal ministry.[52]

The role of children

140. Children of participants also need to be included in the formation process in "appropriate ways."[53] This will depend, among other considerations, on their ages, circumstances, and interests. These occasions provide opportunities for parents and their children to support and assist each other in keeping communication open and expectations clear. Younger children and teens especially need to be encouraged to express their concerns about the public role of this ministry and how it affects their lives both within the family and among their peers. They need to express honestly their concerns over the commitment of time and energy by their parents and what this means to the life of the family and to each member. This is not only a family concern; it is a formation concern.

Formation and family life

141. A man's diaconal formation can be a gift in the life of his family, providing it with an opportunity to explore together the meaning of discipleship, Church, and church vocations. It can strengthen the bonds between parents and their children through prayer, communication, and shared virtue. It can also be a powerful experience of community, service, and compassion.

The Unmarried Participant

Support and encourage his vocation

142. What has been described regarding the role of the family in the formation of a married man also applies to the family of the unmarried participant (i.e., one who never married, one now widowed, or one now divorced[54]). His family should likewise be invited to share appropriately in the formation community. His parents, siblings, children, and extended family need similar grounding in understanding the ministry of the deacon so they can be supportive and encouraging of his vocation.

143. The unmarried participant must grow in clear and realistic understanding of the value of celibate chastity and its connection to diaconal ministry.[55] To be lived fruitfully, the value of celibacy must be internalized. To achieve these formation goals, the unmarried participant should be incorporated into a mentoring group composed of priests and celibate deacons from whom he can receive support and encouragement, a group where a dialogue on the challenges and a faith-filled response to a celibate lifestyle can be fostered.

Multicultural Diversity

Formation for ministry in a multicultural Church

144. Deacons are called to serve a multiracial, multiethnic, multicultural Church. Immigration will only increase the challenge. This changing face of the Catholic Church in the United States should have a significant effect on diaconal formation. The cultures and traditions of those in diaconal formation—mirroring as they do the rich diversity of gifts and unity in faith—need to be respected, valued, and understood. Formation must be sensitive and responsive to the circumstances of different cultures,[56] especially in their unique patterns of learning and expressing their understanding. There should be formal instruction regarding the developmental role and function of culture in the life of the individual and community. Recognizing the cultural diversity of the Catholic Church in the United States and incorporating experiences and an appreciation

of it enhances the present and future ministerial effectiveness of each participant.

145. Formation objectives and methods should accommodate an appropriate inculturation of each participant for his effective service within a multicultural community. Given the ethnic and racial diversity of our national population and the mobility that is so characteristic of our society, a participant in diaconal formation ought to have meaningful cross-cultural experiences and specific training for ministry in his own cultural context. This would include reasonable levels of language study in areas where large numbers of Catholics are not proficient in English. As an ordained servant-leader in a Church called to welcome and embrace all people, the deacon should be a living example of that spirit, particularly conscious of the potential for misunderstanding and alienation that can occur when cultural, ethnic, or racial diversity occasions discrimination rather than social harmony.[57]

Appropriate inculturation of each participant

Practical Aspects of Charity

146. The social encyclicals of the Popes, and the significant documents promulgated by the United States Conference of Catholic Bishops on the integrity of human life from conception to death, on the economy, on racism, on immigration, on peace have focused attention on the social dimension of the Gospel. In a world that seeks to privatize religious commitment, diaconal formation should appropriately emphasize the social dimension of the Gospel, its concern for human life, for justice in the marketplace, and for peace in the world. A major resource in meeting this essential challenge is the *Guidelines for the Study and Teaching of the Church's Social Doctrine in the Formation of Priests,* from the Congregation for Catholic Education.

Social dimension of the Gospel

147. The ministry of charity is "most characteristic of the deacon."[58] "In fact, with sacred ordination, [the deacon] is constituted a living icon of Christ the servant within the Church."[59] Therefore, as he conforms his life to Christ the Servant, making himself a generous and faithful servant of God and of those in need, especially among the poorest and those most suffering,[60] he helps to shape the vitality and genuineness of the exercise of the corporal and spiritual works of charity in the life of the believing community. His

Deacon: A living icon of Jesus, the servant

attentiveness to the manifold physical, emotional, social, and spiritual needs of people in his immediate environment and throughout the world reminds the Church that it is a servant-people sent into a needy world.[61] Within this commitment to a strong social consciousness, an essential emphasis emerges: "The practice and the commandment of love and mercy in everything which, in the spirit of the Gospel, gives priority to the poor."[62]

The spirit of the Gospel

148. From its beginnings, the ministry of the deacon encompassed stewardship of the Church's material goods, making evident the claim of the poor on the resources of the community. Deacons helped to ensure that the allocation of those resources made provision for meaningful assistance to those who suffered from poverty, hunger, homelessness, and disease. Today, the restored diaconate maintains this traditional stewardship through its commitment to the poor. The deacon's service encompasses a witness to charity that may assume different forms, depending on what responsibilities the bishop assigns to the deacon.[63]

Catholic social teaching

149. Although all those in sacred orders have a responsibility to preach justice, the deacon may have a particular advantage in bringing this message to the laity because he lives and works in the secular world. The deacon, because of his familiarity with the day-to-day realities and rhythms of the family, neighborhood, and workplace, can relate the rich tradition of Catholic social teaching to the practical problems experienced by people. He also may serve to link the Catholic Church to other Christian communities, other faith traditions, and civic organizations to address pressing social needs and to foster a collaborative sharing of material resources and personnel in response to those needs.[64]

150. The deacon, as a servant of the Church's ministry of charity and justice, helps the faith community to understand and carry out its baptismal responsibilities. Formation programs, therefore, can help the participant to grow in an understanding of the Church's teaching and tradition of social justice. They also can impart the skills needed for promoting that teaching in the marketplace, parish, and diocese. Formation programming needs to provide opportunities to include an ever-deepening reflection upon the participant's experience and his growing commitment to the Church's social teaching.[65]

A Spirit of Ecumenism and Interreligious Dialogue

151. The Second Vatican Council taught that the restoration of full visible communion among all Christians is the will of Christ and essential to the life of the Catholic Church.[66] An ecumenical spirit should be integrated into all aspects of formation. Those who are or will be engaged in pastoral ministry must acquire "an authentically ecumenical disposition"[67] in their lives and ministry. The purpose of formation in ecumenism is to educate hearts and minds in the necessary human and religious dispositions that will favor the search for Christian unity. A genuine ecumenism should be thoroughly incorporated into all aspects of diaconal formation,[68] remembering that "genuine ecumenical formation must not remain solely academic; it should also include ecumenical experience."[69]

Ecumenism and dialogue

152. The Second Vatican Council also urged "its sons and daughters to enter with prudence and charity into discussion and collaboration with members of other religions."[70] Such a spirit must imbue a desire for ecumenical and interreligious cooperation with Jews, Muslims, and members of other religions. The formation program must assist the participant in achieving a spirit of welcome, respect, and collaboration among people of good will. "The concerns of justice, peace, and the integrity of human life join together all churches and all religions."[71] Diaconal formation should model and facilitate this collaborative cooperation.

Interreligious cooperation

IV. Assessment: Integrating the Four Dimensions in Formation Programming

153. "To each individual the manifestation of the Spirit is given for some benefit."[72] All ministry flows out of the gifts of the Holy Spirit. These gifts are given to the People of God not for the benefit of the individual minister but for the benefit of the Church. As a result, any discernment of gifts and charisms must involve the ecclesial community. Since the charisms are ecclesial, any discernment process must also be ecclesial in nature. This is especially true for the ordained ministries of the Church. An individual who presents himself for ordination to the diaconate is accountable to the Church, who mediates—confirms—his vocation.

Discernment must be ecclesial in nature

Consultation in discernment

154. It is essential, therefore, that those who are responsible for selection and formation, including pastoral placement, discern whether the participant has integrated the various dimensions in formation that are needed for an effective diaconal ministry. Further, consultation with the participant's pastor, the faculty, other pastoral field education supervisors, mentors, those whom the participant serves, and, if married, his wife is crucial to the discernment process. The surest indicator, however, is the participant's previous and present effectiveness in Church service.

Assessments should be communicated on a regular basis

155. If conducted seriously and communicated frankly, assessments can be valuable occasions for the discernment, affirmation, and development of a vocation. Assessments should be made and communicated on a regular basis. There are multiple ways of assessing, including self-assessment, faculty and mentor assessment, and peer and pastoral supervisory assessment, to name but a few. Different situations will require different forms and levels of assessment.

Each assessment has a dual purpose

156. Every assessment, however, has a dual purpose. It affirms the participant in identifying his gifts and capabilities, exhibits areas for his further growth and development, and indicates his limitations. It concurrently provides a similar assessment of the formation program itself. The assessment outcome of an individual participant can demonstrate the program's achievement in integrating the various dimensions of formation, that is, the effectiveness of its structures and scheduling, and the competency of its faculty, staff, and administrators. Simply stated, the assessment of the individual participant also points out the strength, potential, and limitation of the formation program.

Some criteria to evaluate the effectiveness of a formation program

157. The following are some indicators that a formation program is successful, measured by the participant's ability to manifest

1. An increase in holiness of life
2. An ability to clearly articulate the Catholic faith
3. The capacity to apply church teaching and practice to concrete societal issues and pastoral concerns
4. A sensitivity to inculturate the Gospel within the communities in which he lives, works, and ministers

5. His embrace of the universal nature of the Church and its missionary-evangelical spirit
6. A balanced capacity for and commitment to the ministries of word, liturgy, and charity, demonstrated in his words and deeds
7. A commitment to ongoing growth in the human, spiritual, intellectual, and pastoral dimensions of formation
8. A capacity to foster the communion and mission of the lay faithful, in collaboration with the bishop and diocesan priests
9. An obedient and humble service to all in the name of the Church
10. His ability to celebrate, in accordance with the Church's legislation and with due reverence and devotion, those liturgical and sacramental acts that the Church entrusts to the deacon.

158. A well-conceived diocesan formation program will comply fully with the Congregation for Catholic Education's document *Basic Norms for the Formation of Permanent Deacons*, as well as this *Directory*.

NORMS

1. There are three separate but integral paths that constitute a unified diocesan formation program for deacons: aspirant, candidate and post-ordination. (104)
2. Each path should include the four dimensions for a complete formation process: human, spiritual, intellectual, and pastoral. (104)
3. The role of the spiritual director, who must always be a priest, is critical to the formation process, particularly in assisting the participant in discerning and affirming the signs of his vocation. (117)
4. Intellectual formation must introduce the diaconal candidate and the ordained deacon to the fundamental teachings of the Church covering the areas delineated by the document *Basic Norms for the Formation of Permanent Deacons,* as well as in this *Directory*. It is essential that before ordination the candidate have a thorough knowledge of the Catholic faith and be able to communicate it effectively. (124)
5. During formation, the aspirant and candidate should have ample opportunities to participate appropriately in pastoral experience. (128-132)

6. Pastoral formation must include theological reflection so the participant may integrate his ministerial activity with the broad scope of diaconal studies. (133)
7. A married man cannot be considered for the diaconate without the consent of his wife. (138)
8. While every effort ought to be made to involve the wife of a married candidate and deacon in an appropriate level of participation in her husband's formation, care must simultaneously be taken to keep clear the essential distinction between ordained and familial life and the clear independence of diaconal ministry. (139)
9. The cultures and traditions of those in diaconal formation—mirroring as they do the rich diversity of gifts in the Church—need to be respected and valued. Formation, therefore, must be sensitive and adapted to the circumstances of different cultures. (144)
10. Assessments are valuable occasions for the discernment, affirmation, and development of a participant's vocation. Assessments should be made and communicated on a regular basis. (155)
11. A well conceived diocesan formation program will comply fully with the document of the Congregation for Catholic Education *Basic Norms for the Formation of Permanent Deacons,* as well as this *Directory*. (158)

NOTES

1 PDV, no. 42.
2 BNFPD, nos. 66-88.
3 PDV, no. 43.
4 Congregation for the Clergy, General Directory for Catechesis (GDC) (August 15, 1997) (Washington, D.C.: United States Catholic Conference-Libreria Editrice Vaticana, 1998), nos. 222-223.
5 Congregation for the Evangelization of Peoples, Guide for Catechists (December 3, 1993) (Washington, D.C.: United States Catholic Conference, 1993), no. 21.
6 BNFPD, no. 66-70.
7 Ibid., no. 67.
8 Ibid., no. 68.
9 Ibid., no. 69; cf. PDV, no. 44.
10 Ibid., no. 66, citing PDV, no. 43.
11 Ibid., no. 66.
12 Ibid., no. 71.
13 Ibid., nos. 32-33.
14 Ibid., no. 71.
15 Ibid., no. 72.
16 Ibid., no. 73.
17 PDV, nos. 47-49.
18 Cf. Acts 2-4; 1:14.
19 DMLPD, nos. 50-62; cf. BNFPD, no. 12.
20 BNFPD, no. 11.
21 Ibid., no. 72; cf. PDV, no. 30.
22 Jn 5:30.
23 BNFPD, no. 23.
24 Ibid.
25 Ibid., nos. 70, 76; cf. PDV, no. 66.
26 Ibid., no. 79.
27 PDV, no. 51.
28 Pope John Paul II, Post-Synodal Exhortation, The Church in America (Ecclesia in America) (Washington, D.C.: United States Catholic Conference, 1999).
29 PDV, nos. 51-56.
30 Ibid., no. 57.
31 BNFPD, no. 85.
32 PDV, no. 53.
33 PDG (1984), no. 76.
34 Ibid., no. 77.
35 GDC, no. 120.

36 Cf. Pope John Paul II, Encyclical Letter, On the Relationship Between Faith and Reason (Fides et Ratio) (Washington, D.C.: United States Catholic Conference, 1998).

37 Committee on the Relationship between Eastern and Latin Catholic Church, National Conference of Catholic Bishops, Eastern Catholics in the United States of America (Washington, D.C.: United States Catholic Conference, 1999).

38 Pontifical Council for Promoting Christian Unity, The Ecumenical Dimension in the Formation of Pastoral Workers (March 9, 1998), in Ecumenical Formation of Pastoral Workers (Washington, D.C.: United States Catholic Conference, 1998); cf. BNFPD, no. 88.

39 PDV, no. 55.

40 Ibid., no. 57; cf. BNFPD, no. 85.

41 DMLPD, no. 78.

42 BNFPD, no. 87.

43 PDV, no. 57.

44 Pontifical Council for Promoting Christian Unity, op. cit.

45 BNFPD, no. 88.

46 Ibid., nos. 81, 86.

47 Pope John Paul II, Apostolic Exhortation, On the Family (Familiaris Consortio) (Washington, D.C.: United States Catholic Conference, 1981). no. 70.

48 Aspirants, candidates and deacons will be required to participate in classes, pastoral ministries and services, and spiritual exercises. It is necessary, therefore, to focus this injunction proposed by the Holy Father in his encyclical letter, Familiaris Consortio, in its application to the specific pastoral work of organizing the formation, ministry, and life of aspirants, candidates and deacons—"No plan for organized pastoral work at any level must ever fail to take into consideration the pastoral area of the family." To assist the director of formation and the director of deacon personnel to comply with this injunction in preparing and implementing a diocesan plan, organization, and schedule for the formation, ministry and life of aspirants, candidates, and deacons, A Family Perspective in Church and Society, published by the United States Conference of Catholic Bishops' Committee on Marriage and Family (Tenth Anniversary Edition, September, 1998) will prove useful. In reflecting upon the experience of the Synod of Bishops convoked in 1980 by John Paul II on the topic of family life in the modern world, as well as his apostolic exhortation in 1981 on the family, the committee authored this document with the intent "to elicit continuing pastoral action in support of family life" (p. v). The entire document needs to be read, studied, and reflected upon "so that the concept of a family perspective will have practical implications"(p. vi) in the formation, ministry, and life of aspirants, candidates, and deacons. It will be helpful in the scheduling of formation events to include the formation participants. Therefore, "to develop a family perspective in policies, programs, ministries, and services," those responsible for formation need to:

- Keep up-to-date with family changes and trends in the nation and in their locale, and then examine their policies, programs, ministries, and service in light of this information.
- Be sensitive to the fact that many kinds of families participate in programs.
- Be sensitive to the special needs families experience and the pressures and stress these needs create. Leaders need to help families identify these pressures and [in partnership help families] deal with them.
- Be sensitive, in planning, to the time and energy commitments of families where both parents—or the only parent—are employed.
- Be sensitive to the economic pressures families experience today.
- Understand that all programs affect families, even programs aimed at individuals. All social institutions, including the Church, make a direct or indirect impact on the unity, well-being, health, and stability of families. There is a tendency to replace family responsibilities, in part or in their entirety, by social institutions or to marginalize families' participation in the various programs and services provided by these institutions because these services are designed primarily for individuals.
- Help families manage their coordinating and mediating responsibility, rather than complicate it. For example, parish leaders often tell family members that their participation in parish programs is imperative. But families need to be active participants in determining parish priorities, and they have a responsibility to determine their participation . . . based on a realistic assessment of their energy, family time, and resources.
- What the Church does and how it does it affect the unity, well-being, health, and stability of families. Church leaders need to be more aware of how the Church's policies, programs, ministries, and services can either help or hinder families in fulfilling their own basic responsibilities. Church leaders need to see themselves as partners with families.

FP, pp. 10-11, 46-47 (Cf., also, DMLPD, no. 61; BNFPD, no. 27).

49 CIC, c. 1031: 2; cf. BNFPD, no. 37.

50 DMLPD, no. 61.

51 BNFPD, no. 37.

52 DMLPD, no. 81.

53 BNFPD, no. 56; cf. DMLPD, nos. 61, 81.

54 "While the decision to accept such a [divorced] man remains with the bishop, it must be exercised with the highest caution and prudence. This is particularly so if the candidate has had his marriage declared null by a Church tribunal on psychological grounds (cf. Letter of the Sacred Congregation for Catholic Education, dated 8 July 1983, Prot. N. 657/83 & 982/80/136, to His Excellency the Most Rev. John Roach, Archbishop of St. Paul and Minneapolis, President of the Episcopal Conference of the USA, concerning the admission to seminary of men whose marriages have been declared null by ecclesiastical tribunals)."

Congregation for Catholic Education and the Congregation for the Clergy, Joint Study of the US Draft Document—National Directory for the Formation, Ministry and Life of Permanent Deacons in the United States, Prot. No. 78/2000 (March 4, 2002).

55 PDV, no. 29.

56 BNFPD, no. 10.

57 Bishops' Committee on Migration, National Conference of Catholic Bishops, One Family Under God, Revised Edition (Washington, D.C.: United States Catholic Conference, 1998), p. 20.

58 BNFPD, no. 9.

59 Ibid., no. 11.

60 DMLPD, no. 38.

61 PDV, nos. 10, 27, 32; Second Vatican Council, Decree on the Missionary Activity of the Church (Ad Gentes Divinitus) (December 7, 1965) (Washington, D.C.: United States Catholic Conference, 1965), nos. 11-12.

62 Congregation for Catholic Education, Guidelines for the Study and Teaching of the Church's Social Doctrine in the Formation of Priests (Washington, D.C.: United States Catholic Conference, 1988), no. 61.

63 DMLPD, nos. 37-38, 42.

64 Pontifical Council for Promoting Christian Unity, The Ecumenical Dimension in the Formation of Pastoral Workers, op. cit.; cf. Pontifical Council for Promoting Christian Unity, Ecumenical Formation: Ecumenical Reflections and Suggestions (May 20, 1993), III, nos. 17-25, in Ecumenical Formation of Pastoral Workers (Washington, D.C.: United States Catholic Conference, 1998).

65 Committee on Domestic Social Policy and Committee on International Policy, National Conference of Catholic Bishops, Communities of Salt and Light: Reflections on the Social Mission of the Parish (Washington, D.C.: United States Catholic Conference, 1994).

66 Cf. Second Vatican Council, Decree on Ecumenism (Unitatis Redintegratio) (November 21, 1964) (Washington, D.C.: United States Catholic Conference, 1964), nos. 1-4.

67 Pontifical Council for Promoting Christian Unity, Directory for the Application of Principles and Norms on Ecumenism (March 25, 1993), no. 70.

68 Pontifical Council for Promoting Christian Unity, The Ecumenical Dimension in the Formation of Pastoral Workers, op. cit., nos. 2-4; cf. nos. 16-29.

69 Ibid., no. 28.

70 Second Vatican Council, Declaration on the Relation of the Church to Non-Christian Religions (Nostra Aetate) (October 28, 1965) (Washington, D.C.: United States Catholic Conference, 1965), no. 2.

71 National Conference of Catholic Bishops, Program of Priestly Formation, Fourth Edition (Washington, D.C.: United States Catholic Conference, 1993), no. 21.

72 1 Cor 12:7.

CHAPTER FOUR

VOCATION, DISCERNMENT, AND SELECTION

I. Promotion and Recruitment

Grace builds on nature

159. The First Letter of St. Paul to Timothy provides the first principle for the selection of deacons: "They should be tested first; then, if there is nothing against them, let them serve as deacons."[1] St. Thomas Aquinas offers an additional insight: Grace builds on nature. Those who have worked closely with the reestablishment of the diaconate conclude that the diaconate is a particular vocation called forth by the Holy Spirit, that a successful process of training and development can only cooperate with fundamental preexisting traits and dispositions that point to a diaconal vocation and build upon them, and that the process of training and development can be successful only in supportive life circumstances.

160. The promotion and recruitment of qualified men for the diaconate should be a collaborative ministry between the staffs of the diocesan vocations office and the diaconate office, as well as the diocesan bishop and pastors. If the diocesan Church wishes to nominate appropriate men, it may be helpful for the diocesan diaconate office to prepare guidelines, approved by the bishop, that provide specific information about recruitment, as well as the selection and formation processes. If the reestablishment of the diaconate is made part of a coherent diocesan pastoral plan for ministry in which deacons will have an important role, then the diocese and parishes can more easily identify and recruit potential candidates, describe to them the challenges and opportunities of diaconal ministry in the diocese, and urge them to consider it as a service to which they can commit themselves.

Cultural, racial, and ethnic involvement in promoting church vocations

161. The Church in the United States is enriched by the diversity of its cultural, racial, and ethnic communities. Since these communities share in the responsibility for promoting Church vocations, their leaders ought to be formally invited and included in the planning and implementation of vocation programs directed to their

communities. Their support and encouragement will effectively assist in the recruitment of qualified nominees from their communities. Representatives of U.S. ethnic and cultural communities—such as Americans of African, Pacific Asian, Native American, and Hispanic heritage—who participate as consultants to the diaconate office, can provide significant insight on cultural subtleties and their effect upon discernment and formation programming, including pastoral placement.

Hispanic Americans

162. Of particular importance in the United States is the large Hispanic Catholic population. Knowledge of Spanish and of Hispanic cultures is important in both recruiting and retaining Hispanic candidates. In each path in formation, essential resources—e.g., translators, textbooks, mentors, community support—should be provided to ensure the inclusion of each participant.

Study of language and culture

163. Care ought to be taken, especially in the post-ordination path in formation, to provide opportunities for English-speaking deacons to learn Spanish, or other appropriate languages used in the diocese, on a conversational level. The opportunity for formal study of Hispanic and other cultures also should be provided. Further, the study of English and the historical development of a multicultural society within the United States should be provided to those whose primary language is not English.

Multicultural sensitivity

164. The above discussion regarding the recruitment and retention of Hispanic candidates applies to each cultural, racial, and ethnic community. Those responsible for recruitment, discernment, and formation have a responsibility to exercise multicultural sensitivity. They need to appreciate cultural subtleties and differences, acknowledging the historical constrictions experienced within these communities. Further, familiarity with family structures and traditions is important. This cultural/racial/ethnic orientation and sensitivity enables recruiters and those involved in formation to competently discern and foster diaconal vocations within these diverse faith communities.

II. The Mystery of Vocation

Personal and public call

165. "The history . . . of every Christian vocation, is the history of an *inexpressible dialogue between God and human beings*, between the love of God who calls and the freedom of individuals who respond lovingly to him."[2] This calling-forth from God is marked first in the reception of the sacraments of Christian initiation. From out of this body of believers Christ then calls some of his disciples, and the Church, discerning their vocational charism, asks the bishop to ordain them to a service of the whole Church.

Diaconal call

166. From the experience of the restored diaconate in the United States, certain behavioral patterns have been discerned among exemplary deacons: a "natural inclination of service to the . . . Christian community,"[3] and to all in need; psychological integrity; a capacity for dialogue, which implies a sense of docility and openness; the ability to share one's faith yet listen respectfully to other points of view; the capacity to listen carefully and without prejudices—respecting people in the context of their religion, race, gender, ethnicity, and culture; good communication skills; a sense of responsibility that includes the fulfilling of one's word and completing one's work; self-directed and collaborative accountability; balanced and prudent judgment; generosity in service; and the ability to lead, motivate, facilitate, and animate others into appropriate action and service.[4]

167. The profile is completed with certain spiritual and evangelical qualities. Among these are a sound faith; good Christian reputation; active involvement in the Church's apostolate; personal integrity, maturity, and holiness; regular participation in the Church's sacramental life; evidence of recognized, ongoing commitment to the Church's life and service; participation in faith enrichment opportunities (e.g., retreats, days of recollection, adult education programming); a positive and stable marriage, if married, or a mature celibate state of life, if single; active membership in a Christian community; capacity for obedience and fraternal communion; and a deep spirituality and prayer life. The presence of these qualities, experienced in kindness and humility, may demonstrate a call to the Order of Deacons.[5]

Element of readiness

168. Additional considerations that need to be stressed are the element of readiness and the timeliness of one's response to a vocation. Since inquirers to the diaconate have many commitments to family, career, employment, community, and church service, it is a matter of prudential judgment to explore not only whether the call to the diaconate is from the Holy Spirit, but also whether the inquirer is ready and able to respond to that call at the present time.

III. The Discernment of the Call

Personal discernment

169. The first stirrings of a vocation to the diaconate are often explored at a personal level and usually begin with seeking information about the diaconate and formation. Here, an individual initially reflects upon the nature of his perceived call. Primacy must be given at this time to the spiritual dimension, and central to this is spiritual guidance. "Because every spiritual journey is personal and individual, it requires personal guidance."[6] The pastor and others on the parish staff are particular resources at this time.

Family discernment

170. As the majority of those who inquire about the diaconate are married, they should be directed to pay particular attention to discussing their possible vocation with their wives and families. The initial information and conversations with their pastor and others should assist and encourage these discussions. For a married man, the support and consent of his wife is required. Therefore, both spouses need to make sure that support and consent, even at this early stage of discernment, arise from an informed understanding. Many regions and cultures also place emphasis on the participation of the extended family. This, too, is an important resource for discernment.

Communal discernment

171. An inquiry and eventual application for entrance into diaconal formation is not just a personal and family journey. The Church must accompany it. The parish is the primary experience of Church for most inquirers. It is the responsibility of this community and, in particular, its pastor to invite from among its members those who may be qualified to serve as ordained ministers of the Church.[7] Similarly, those church and community agencies that have often carried out the Church's mission of charity and justice have a unique opportunity to call forth appropriate nominees from among their personnel.

Ecclesial discernment

172. An inquiry about the diaconate and the formation process eventually includes the diocesan Church. Information sessions, the exploration of the criteria for a diaconal vocation, and particular counsel presented by the diocesan diaconate office can aid an individual in his decision to move forward to a formal application.

Careful scrutiny

173. When the inquirer is presented by his pastor and submits an application, the formal process for admission begins. This initial discernment is continued with particular focus on the applicant's abilities and potential for ordained ministry. Both the applicant and the diocesan Church enter into an intensive screening process.

IV. Admission and Selection Procedures

The Role of the Pastor and Parish Community

Community recommendation

174. The inquirer who seeks consideration for ordination to the diaconate needs to enter into dialogue with his parish community. It is the pastor who initially presents him for consideration into diaconal formation through a letter that confirms he is a practicing Catholic of good repute and in good standing.[8]

The Role of the Diocese

Admission interview

175. The director of formation, who coordinates the selection process, arranges an interview with the diocese's committee on admission and scrutinies.[9] The purpose of the interview is to assess the applicant's level of awareness of a diaconal vocation, as well as to obtain information and background on his family life, employment stability, and general aptitude for diaconal ministry. The interview must include his wife, if he is married, and any children living at home.

Impediments to ordination

176. As part of the application process, those charged with admission must—with appropriate care for confidentiality and manifestation of conscience—explore for the presence of impediments to ordination.[10] If canonical dispensations are required, these must be obtained before admission to aspirant formation.

Psychological consultation

177. Appropriate psychological consultation may be included as part of the application process, but always with the written consent of the applicant.[11] Those selected as psychological consultants must

use psychological methods in harmony with Christian anthropology and Catholic teaching, particularly with respect to the theology of the diaconal vocation, the various states of life of the deacon, and the basic human qualities expected of a mature deacon. They also should obtain any pertinent and helpful information received in the admission process regarding the applicant. Care also must be taken in the selection of psychological consultants who will be assigned to applicants whose primary language is not English.

Required Application Documents

Required forms

178. Required application documents include the following:

a. A church certificate of Baptism, Confirmation, and, if relevant, marriage, issued within the past six months[12]
b. Proof of age: In accord with Canon Law,[13] the United States Conference of Catholic Bishops has established the minimum age of ordination at thirty-five years
c. A completed application form, and, as appropriate, a consent form regarding psychological consultation and the confidentiality of consultative reports[14]
d. A recent photograph of the nominee[15] and, if married, of his wife, for administrative and faculty identification
e. A personal handwritten statement from the wife of a married applicant indicating her initial consent for his application and entrance into aspirant formation[16]
f. Letters of recommendation[17]
g. A recent medical certificate[18]
h. An official transcript of past or present academic studies, if applicable[19]
i. "A written report of the rector of any previous house in which the candidate has spent time in formation,"[20] including "explicit reference to the evaluations of the candidate and the votes he received"[21]
j. A background check of each nominee under the auspices of the diocesan diaconate office
k. Proof of legal residency in the diocese[22]
l. A letter of recommendation from the applicant's employer[23]

Discernment of Readiness for the Aspirant Path in Formation

179. Assessment of readiness at the application level is accomplished in a variety of ways. Common resources are letters of recommendation by those who know the applicant; a self-assessment prepared by the applicant, usually as an autobiographical statement; an interview with the committee on admission and scrutinies; and a review of his pastoral experience, especially noting any experience with the poor and the marginalized. Intellectual readiness is often assessed on the basis of prior experience through academic transcripts from schools attended and through evidence of participation in a lay ecclesial ministry formation program, parish adult education programs, or similar adult religious training.

Assessment of readiness

V. Admission into the Aspirant Path in Formation

180. The diocese's committee on admission and scrutinies should develop a procedural process to review the application dossier of each applicant. Since admission into formation occurs through two distinct but unified processes—(1) acceptance into the aspirant path; (2) admittance into the candidate path in diaconal formation[24]—the committee should nominate to the bishop only those applicants whom they have judged as possessing the necessary qualities for entrance and successful completion of the aspirant path. Upon reviewing the recommendation, vote, and rationale of the committee, the bishop is the one who decides whether to admit the applicant into the aspirant path. If an applicant is judged not to be ready but to be a suitable aspirant in the future, the director of formation should convey to the applicant various options for how he might prepare himself to achieve the basic entrance requirements. It is also essential for the director of formation to keep frequent contact with these potential candidates.

Committee on admission and scrutinies

181. With the acceptance of the applicant into aspirant formation, the admission process continues with an assessment of readiness for entrance into the candidate path in formation. This phase of discernment extends throughout the entire aspirant formation process, thereby allowing ample opportunity for personal observations, dialogue, interviews, and additional assessments of each aspirant.

NORMS

1. The inquirer who seeks consideration for ordination to the permanent diaconate needs to enter into dialogue with his parish since it is the pastor who is required to initially present him for diaconal formation. (174)
2. A formal application process, as well as a committee on admission and scrutinies, should be in place to review and nominate applicants. (175, 284)
3. As part of the application process, those charged with admission must—with appropriate care for confidentiality and manifestation of conscience—explore for the presence of canonical impediments to ordination. If canonical dispensations are required, these must be obtained before admission to aspirant formation. (176)
4. Required application documents are listed in paragraph 178.
5. With acceptance into aspirant formation, the admission process continues with an assessment of readiness for entrance into the candidate path in formation. (181)

NOTES

1 1 Tm 3:10.

2 BNFPD, no. 29, citing PDV, no. 36.

3 DMLPD, no. 49, citing Pope Paul VI, Apostolic Letter, *Sacrum Diaconatus Ordinem* (June 18, 1967), no. 8.

4 BNFPD, no. 32.

5 Ibid., nos. 31-33.

6 National Conference of Catholic Bishops, *Program for Priestly Formation, Fourth Edition* (Washington, D.C.: United States Catholic Conference, 1993), no. 280.

7 BNFPD, no. 40.

8 Ibid. This letter should attest that the man shows evidence of the qualities, attitudes, experience, and spirituality deemed necessary for admission into formation, namely, that he is

a) Actively involved in parish and other community service

b) In full communion with the Church (At least two or three years should elapse between a convert's or returning Catholic's entry into the Church and his acceptance into formation; care must be given to someone in whom a sudden conversion experience seems to precipitate a diaconal vocation.)

c) In a positive and stable marriage, if married, or in a mature celibate state of life, if single

d) If married, has the consent of his wife (An applicant whose marriage has been annulled should be screened carefully to ascertain if and how previous obstacles to a marriage commitment might affect his viability as a candidate for the diaconate. Care also should be extended to those who are recently widowed—normally, at least two years should elapse *prior* to acceptance; those recently married should live their married vocation for three years prior to requesting admittance.)

e) Properly motivated and gives evidence of an overall personal balance and moral character

f) A frequent participant in adult faith enrichment opportunities (e.g., retreats, days of reflection, spiritual direction, study of Scripture and church teachings)

g) Free of canonical impediments or irregularities (CIC, cc. 1040-1042)

9 Cf. this *Directory*, Chapter Eight, no. 284, on committee on admission and scrutinies.

10 BNFPD, no. 35; cf. Footnote 39 of BNFPD, no. 35.

11 Ibid., no. 70.

12 If the information regarding Confirmation or marriage, if relevant, is not recorded on the baptismal record, separate certificates for Confirmation and marriage are to be obtained (cf. CIC, cc. 1033; 1050:3; 241:2); annulment documents should also be obtained, if applicable.

13 CIC, c. 1031:3.

14 The application form should provide information on his family, as well as his religious, academic, employment, and service history, and a personal handwritten statement requesting admission into aspirant formation, indicating his motivation for seeking ordination to the

diaconate, his willingness to pledge his service to the diocesan Church, *and* his ability to fulfill the requirements of aspirant formation, if accepted (cf. CL, Enclosure I, 9; Enclosure II, 1): "It is necessary that this request be composed by the candidate personally and written out in his own hand and may not be a copied formulary, or worse, a photocopied text (cf. CIC, c. 1034:1)." (CL, Enclosure II, 1)

15 CL, Enclosure I, 5.

16 Cf. Note 14 above. This letter also should indicate her willingness to participate in the formation program as required.

17 CL, Enclosures I, 11. Letters should be requested from priests, deacons, parishioners, and colleagues.

18 Ibid., 7.

19 Ibid., 3 and 4.

20 Ibid., 10.

21 Ibid., 4; cf. CL, 8.

22 Cf. CIC, c. 265.

23 The contact with the employer provides a way to inform him of the applicant's possible participation in a program of education that may require occasional time alterations in his work schedule.

24 BNFPD, nos. 40, 45.

CHAPTER FIVE
ASPIRANT PATH IN DIACONAL FORMATION

I. Introduction

182. Upon completion of the initial inquiry process, the bishop may accept some inquirers into aspirancy. This aspirant path in diaconal formation, as described in this *Directory*, corresponds to the "propaedeutic period" required by the *Basic Norms for the Formation of Permanent Deacons* of the Congregation for Catholic Education.[1] The aspirant path is primarily a time to discern the capability and readiness of an aspirant to be nominated to the bishop for acceptance as a candidate for diaconal ordination.[2]

Propaedeutic period

183. Those responsible for the aspirant path in formation should be thoroughly familiar with the doctrinal understanding of the diaconate: including its ministry and life and the dimensions of formation, as described in the *Basic Norms for the Formation of Permanent Deacons* and this *Directory*. These components converge on a common goal: to enable the aspirant to demonstrate the possibility of a diaconal vocation and an appropriate level of readiness for eventual selection into candidate formation.[3]

The goal of aspirant formation

184. To create an environment conducive to adult Christian formation, the director of formation should prepare an aspirant handbook that details the components of the program, provides a rationale and guidance for assessment, and clearly delineates the expectations and responsibilities of the aspirant, including those regarding the wife of a married aspirant. This handbook is to be approved by the bishop.[4]

Aspirant handbook

185. Because of the aspirant's secular employment and personal and family commitments, appropriate attention is to be given to the implementation of a family life perspective in organizing the aspirant path. In this regard, the most common formation models that have emerged in the United States organize formation meetings on various evenings, weekends, holidays, or a combination of such times. Different ways of organizing the aspirant formation path

Aspirant path: Ordinarily one year in duration

are possible.[5] Since the director of formation, in collaboration with those who share in the responsibility for formation,[6] is expected to prepare a declaration of readiness for the bishop that profiles the aspirant's personality and provides a judgment of suitability for candidate formation and ultimately ordination, the aspirant path of formation must be of an appropriate length.[7] In the diocesan churches of the United States, the aspirant path of formation will ordinarily last one year.

A distinctive program

186. Although some aspects of the aspirant path may be linked with other lay apostolate formation programs in a diocese, the aspirant path must be a distinctive program that provides for a thorough discernment of a diaconal vocation. Therefore, it must provide an appropriate initiation into diaconal spirituality; supervised pastoral experiences, especially among the poor and marginalized; and an adequate assessment of the aspirant's potential to be promoted to candidate formation, and ultimately to ordination. The aspirant path also must enable the formation personnel to create an environment in which a wife of a married aspirant can be appropriately prepared to give her consent to his continuation, and more essentially, to ascertain her compatibility with her husband's diaconal vocation and eventual ministry.[8]

The components of the aspirant path of formation

187. During this period of discernment, the aspirant is to be introduced to the study of theology, to a deeper knowledge of the spirituality and ministry of the deacon, and to a more attentive discernment of his call. This period is also a time to form an aspirant community with its own cycle of meetings and prayer. Finally, this period is to ensure the aspirant's regular participation in spiritual direction, to introduce him to the pastoral ministries of the diocesan Church, and to assist his family in their support of his formation.[9]

II. The Dimensions of Formation in the Aspirant Path

188. At the aspirant level in formation, the following objectives are to be highlighted. These are presented in greater detail in Chapter Three, "Dimensions in the Formation of Deacons."

Human Dimension

Goal of human dimension

189. In his post-Synodal Apostolic Exhortation *Pastores Dabo Vobis*, Pope John Paul II quoted Proposition 21 of the 1990 Extraordinary Synod of Bishops: "The whole work of priestly formation would be deprived of its necessary foundation if it lacked a suitable human formation."[10] In a similar way, the same may be said about the human dimension of diaconal formation. The goal of a "suitable human dimension" is to help the deacon develop "his human personality in such a way that it becomes a bridge and not an obstacle for others in their meeting with Jesus Christ."[11]

A family perspective

190. The aspirant path in formation is also a time for a married aspirant and his wife to assess the quality of their relationship and consider the ramifications of his possible ordination to the diaconate for their married life. For the single aspirant, it is a time to discern his capacity and receptivity for celibacy.

Spiritual Dimension

Goal of spiritual dimension

191. The aspirant path of formation must create an environment in which the individual is encouraged to grow in his personal relationship with Christ and in his commitment to the Church and its mission in the world. The goal of spiritual formation is "putting on the mind of Christ," thereby establishing and nurturing attitudes, habits, and practices that provide a foundation for the development of an authentic and ongoing spiritual life.

192. Although the fact that the wife of the married aspirant is not seeking ordination is clearly understood, nevertheless, their marriage and family are involved in the discernment of his diaconal vocation. The aspirant and his wife need to realistically assess how her own life, Church service, and family are affected and respected. The enrichment and deepening of the reciprocal and sacrificial love between husband and wife constitutes perhaps the most meaningful way the wife of the aspirant is involved in the discernment of her husband's vocation.[12]

Content of spiritual dimension

193. The aspirant formation community plays a significant role in spiritual formation. The aspirant path should include the following:

a. Regular celebration of the Eucharist, Liturgy of the Hours, and the Sacrament of Reconciliation
b. Time scheduled for private prayer, meditation, and *lectio divina*
c. Devotions to the Virgin Mary and saints
d. Conferences and workshops on the meaning of authentic obedience, celibacy, and simplicity of life
e. Conferences on a Christian witness in both matrimonial and celibate life to the Church and world
f. An understanding and appreciation of the diaconal vocation, with an ability to articulate this call through the primary ministries of word, liturgy, and charity
g. An introduction and experience of the spiritual writings of our Catholic tradition

Spiritual direction

194. The aspirant's spiritual director is critical to the formation process. This priest, who is to be approved by the bishop, must be well trained and knowledgeable about the diaconate. The spiritual director accompanies, supports, and challenges the aspirant in his ongoing conversion. The spiritual director assists the aspirant in his relationship with God and his understanding that it is Christ who "calls," the Church that affirms his diaconal vocation, and the bishop who responds to that affirmation by the imposition of hands.

Parish and pastor

195. As collaborators in discerning the readiness of the aspirant to move into candidate formation, the parish and its pastor also should accompany the aspirant and his family through their prayers, support, and presence. In the aspirant path in formation, the parish is the primary place to observe the aspirant's relational skills and his practice in pastoral service. The pastor, therefore, is to provide an assessment of the aspirant and his family. This assessment will further enable the formation staff to support and challenge the aspirant's discernment of his readiness to move into candidate formation.

Intellectual Dimension

Academic objectives and content

196. The objectives and content for intellectual formation at the aspirant level should communicate a deeper knowledge of the faith and church tradition than the aspirant has already attained. It would be appropriate to promote an in-depth and systematic study of the *Catechism of the Catholic Church*, and to introduce the traditions of Catholic philosophy, spirituality, and doctrine, especially

the doctrinal understanding of the diaconate, and the threefold ministry of the deacon. The aspirant also should be taught how to participate in a theological reflection group and how to develop his ability to apply the Church's teaching on moral matters, including her social teaching, to the pressing moral questions that emerge in pastoral ministry. Such intellectual pursuits assist those responsible for formation in assessing the aspirant's readiness for the academic rigors of candidate formation. Further, he should be made aware of the needs of the people of the diocesan Church, as well as of his own parish, and be made to understand *diakonia* as a descriptive word for the mission of the Church in the world. Workshops on family issues, personal health, time management, caregiving skills, and married and celibate spirituality all contribute to an aspirant's human, spiritual, and intellectual formation.

Pastoral Dimension

Discernment: The ultimate focus of the pastoral dimension in formation

197. The focus of the pastoral dimension in the aspirant path in formation is ultimately the discernment of the aspirant's gifts for the threefold ministry of word, liturgy, and charity, and of his capacity to make a lifelong commitment to these ministries. It also enables an assessment of his wife and family in their readiness to give consent and support to his vocation and ministry. Pastoral formation should introduce the aspirant to the practical services provided by the diocesan Church. Pastoral placements, matched to the aspirant's experience and need, allow an exploration of core issues regarding charity and the social dimension of the Gospel as confronted by the diocesan Church. Exemplary deacons, approved by the bishop, should serve as mentors inviting the aspirant to accompany, observe, co-minister, and reflect upon the specific diaconal ministries experienced.[13] Appropriate ecumenical pastoral experiences should be considered and implemented as opportunities emerge. Opportunities should also be provided, when possible, for involvement with the Jewish community and with representatives of other religions.

III. Assessment for Nomination into the Candidate Path in Formation

198. The conclusion of the aspirant path of formation is determined through a formal assessment conducted by the committee on admission and scrutinies. This occurs when the aspirant (with the

consent of his wife, if married), with the express permission of those responsible for his formation, makes a written petition to the bishop for admission to candidacy.

Required documentation

199. When the decision to petition for candidacy is determined, the following documents are to be prepared:

a. A personal, handwritten, and signed letter prepared for the diocesan bishop by the aspirant requesting admission to the candidate path of formation, as well as the reception of the Rite of Admission to Candidacy[14]
b. A personal, handwritten, and signed letter of consent prepared by the married aspirant's wife[15]

Interviews

200. Each petitioner will be interviewed by the committee on admission and scrutinies to appraise his readiness for nomination into the candidate path of formation. The committee will also meet with the wife of a married aspirant to ascertain her level of consent and support for her husband's promotion into candidate formation. Finally, the committee will review all pertinent data on the aspirant.[16] The vote of each member and the rationale for the vote is to be recorded. The director of formation, on behalf of the committee, will prepare "a declaration which outlines the profile of the [aspirant's personality] . . . and a judgment of suitability."[17] This declaration, accompanied by the individual vote and rationale of each member of the committee, is prepared for the bishop, who selects those to be admitted to candidate formation. A copy of both the declaration and the bishop's letter to the aspirant regarding his acceptance into candidacy is placed in the petitioner's personal file.[18]

IV. The Rite of Admission to Candidacy

201. Since entrance into the clerical state is deferred until ordination to the diaconate, the Rite of Admission to Candidacy is to be celebrated as soon as possible after the aspirant is admitted. In this rite, the one who aspires to ordination publicly manifests his will to offer himself to God and the Church to exercise a sacred order. In this way, he is admitted into the ranks of candidates for the diaconate.[19] "Enrollment among the candidates for the diaconate does not constitute any right necessarily to receive diaconal ordination. It

is a first official recognition of the positive signs of the vocation to the diaconate, which must be confirmed in the subsequent years of formation."[20]

202. Because of its public character and its ecclesial significance, this rite should be celebrated in a proper manner, preferably on a Sunday or feast day. Special consideration should be given to the inclusion of the candidate's wife and children, as well as to the cultural traditions represented.

203. Those accepted for candidacy—and, if married, their wives—should prepare themselves for the reception of the rite through a spiritual retreat.[21] It will usually be helpful for wives to participate in the retreat, although during portions of the retreat it will usually be helpful to provide the opportunity for separate treatment of the respective roles of each in the vocation of the husband to the diaconate. After the celebration of the Rite of Admission to Candidacy, a certificate indicating the reception, date, place, and the name of the presiding prelate must be prepared and signed by the chancellor and officially sealed. This document is to be maintained carefully in the candidate's personal file and recorded in the diocesan book on ministries and ordinations.[22]

NORMS

1. The aspirant path is primarily a time to discern the readiness of the aspirant to be nominated to the diocesan bishop for acceptance into the candidate path in diaconal formation. (182)
2. A handbook should be available to aspirants detailing the components of the program, rationale and guidance for assessment, and the expectations and responsibilities of the aspirants, including the wife of a married aspirant. (184)
3. The aspirant phase, which will ordinarily last one year, involves discernment with emphasis on spiritual readiness, intellectual capacity, and pastoral abilities. (185)
4. The aspirant path must create an environment in which the wife of a married aspirant can give her consent to her husband's continuance in formation. More essentially, it must ascertain her compatibility with her husband's diaconal vocation and eventual ministry. (186)

5. The objectives and content for intellectual formation at the aspirant level should communicate a deeper knowledge of the faith and church tradition, as well as diaconal theology and spirituality, and should include meetings for prayer, instructions, and moments of reflection that will ensure the objective nature of vocational discernment. (196)
6. The conclusion of the aspirant path in formation is determined through a formal assessment conducted by the committee on admission and scrutinies. (198)
7. After the aspirant path is completed, the aspirant is selected by the diocesan bishop. The aspirant then begins the candidate path in formation with the Rite of Admission to Candidacy, which is to be celebrated as soon as possible and in a proper manner. (201)
8. A retreat should precede the Rite of Admission to Candidacy. (203)
9. A certificate indicating the reception, date, place, and the name of the presiding prelate must be prepared and signed by the chancellor and officially sealed. This document is to be maintained carefully in the candidate's personal file and recorded in the diocesan book on ministries and ordinations. (203)

NOTES

1 BNFPD, nos. 41-44. "With admission among the aspirants to diaconate there begins a propaedeutic period . . . [in which] the aspirants will be introduced to a deeper knowledge of theology, of spirituality and of the ministry of deacon and they will be led to a more attentive discernment of their call." The propaedeutic period may be compared to the pre-seminary program in priestly formation or postulancy in religious life.

2 Ibid.

3 Cf. CL, 1-2.

4 BNFPD, no. 16.

5 BNFPD, no. 51.

6 Ibid., no. 44 (formation team, supervisors, and pastor).

7 Ibid., nos. 41, 44.

8 Ibid., no. 37.

9 Ibid., nos. 41-44.

10 PDV, no. 43.

11 Ibid.

12 ADUS.

13 Ibid., no. 22.

14 The aspirant should state his motivation and reasons for the requests; if he is married, he should indicate his awareness of the impact of diaconal ordination and ministry on his marriage and family; he also must state that he has received the consent of his wife; if he is not married, he should indicate his awareness of the meaning of diaconal ordination and ministry, as well as his understanding of and ability to live the requirement of perpetual celibacy.

15 CL, Enclosure I, 14. The wife must declare her consent for his petition to enter into candidacy formation; she also should clearly state her understanding of the meaning of diaconal ordination and ministry and its impact on their marriage and family.

16 The following assessments are to be conducted, some annually, and maintained in the aspirant's and candidate's permanent file:

   a. Written pastoral supervisors' assessments and reports
   b. Written parochial assessments prepared by the pastor and parish staff
   c. If applicable, a written assessment of the rector of any previous house of formation, or a similar report from the director of diaconal formation in which the aspirant or candidate previously participated
   d. In a case where an aspirant comes from another diocesan church, a letter of recommendation from his previous pastor is to be obtained, as well as consultation with that church's vocation and diaconate offices
   e. An assessment of the aspirant's or candidate's aptitude for preaching, catechizing, and evangelization

f. A personal assessment from the director of formation is to be prepared for the committee on admission and scrutinies, making use of the model prescribed by the Congregation for Divine Worship and the Discipline of the Sacraments (CL, Enclosure V).

17 BNFPD, no. 44.

18 CL, Enclosure III, especially 4, 6, and 8.

19 Pope Paul VI, Apostolic Letter, *Ministeria Quaedam* (August 15, 1972).

20 BNFPD, no. 48.

21 Ibid., no. 47.

22 CL, Enclosure I.

CHAPTER SIX

CANDIDATE PATH IN DIACONAL FORMATION

I. Introduction

204. The candidate path in diaconal formation is the occasion for continued discernment of a diaconal vocation and immediate preparation for ordination. Throughout this path in formation, the candidate himself assumes the primary responsibility for his discernment and development.[1]

> Self-formation does not imply isolation . . . or independence from formators, but responsibility and dynamism in responding with generosity to God's call, valuing to the highest the people and tools which Providence puts at one's disposition. Self-formation has its roots in a firm determination to grow in life according to the Spirit and in conformity with the vocation received. . . .[2]

II. The Length of the Candidate Path in Formation

"Do not be hasty in the laying-on of hands."

205. In accord with the Code of Canon Law, the *Basic Norms for the Formation of Permanent Deacons* by the Congregation for Catholic Education specifies that the candidate path in diaconal formation "must last at least three years, in addition to the *propaedeutic period*, for all candidates."[3] Readiness for ordination is assessed annually by both the candidate and formation personnel to ascertain what level of achievement the candidate has reached in his understanding of the diaconal vocation, its responsibilities, and its obligations; his growth in the spiritual life; his competency in required diaconal knowledge and skills; his practical experience in pastoral ministry; and his witness of human and affective maturity. If he is married, an appraisal of his wife's readiness and consent is also to be made. In a Circular Letter directed to diocesan ordinaries on assessing the readiness of candidates for ordination, the Congregation for Divine Worship and the Discipline of the Sacraments recalls that

"St. Paul's admonition remains true for the Church today, as it did in his own time: '*Do not be hasty in the laying-on of hands*.'"[4]

Candidate path in formation: An integral and substantive program

206. Regarding the precise number of hours for lectures, seminars, and related educational activities specified in the *Basic Norms for the Formation of Permanent Deacons*,[5] the objective is to guarantee the planning and implementation of an integral and substantive program of formation that adequately prepares a candidate to represent the Church as a deacon. A substantive program includes not only class preparation, participation, and attendance, but also seminars, workshops, field education projects, theological reflection, shared opportunities for spiritual growth (e.g., liturgical celebrations and prayer, spiritual conferences, retreats), individual spiritual direction, and other formation experiences. Diocesan compliance with this requirement and others as specified in the *Basic Norms for the Formation of Permanent Deacons* and in this *Directory* may be verified by the review of its formation program by the Bishops' Committee on the Diaconate (see Appendix I).

III. Formation Environments

207. The communities in which the candidate participates influence the formation process.[6] Those entrusted with formation must take care to assess these environments as resources for discerning, supporting, and nurturing a diaconal vocation.

Candidate Formation Community

Adult experience

208. The candidate community should become primarily an integrating experience where dialogue and collaborative activity provide a unique opportunity for adults to discern the activity of the Holy Spirit in their lives and experiences.

Candidate handbook

209. To create an environment conducive to adult Christian formation, the director of formation should prepare a candidate handbook that details the components of the program; provides the rationale, criteria, and guidance for assessments, especially regarding readiness for institution into the ministries of lector and acolyte, and ultimately, for ordination to the diaconate; and clearly delineates the expectations and responsibilities of the candidate, including the wife of a married candidate. This handbook is to be approved by the bishop.[7]

The Community of Deacons

210. The community of deacons can be a "precious support in the discernment of vocation, in human growth, in the initiation to the spiritual life, in theological study and pastoral experience."[8] Scheduled opportunities for conversation and shared pastoral experiences between a candidate and deacon, as well as meetings between the wife of a candidate and the wife of a deacon can mutually sustain their enthusiasm and realism about the diaconate. Some deacons should be appointed by the bishop to serve as mentors to individual candidates or a small group of candidates.[9]

The role of the ordained community

The Parish Community

211. The parish community is an essential extension of the formation community. Through its prayer and support, the parish "makes the faithful aware of this ministry, [and] gives to the candidate a strong aid to his vocational discernment."[10]

The parish community

The Family Community

212. The family is the primary community accompanying the candidate on the formative journey. For married candidates, the communion of life and love, established by the marriage covenant and consecrated by the Sacrament of Matrimony, offers a singular contribution to the formation process.[11] The single candidate's family also contributes to his formation; those responsible for implementing the formation process should consult with the single candidate to ascertain the strength of his support from his family and friends to ensure that his vocation is also encouraged and fostered.

The family formation community

The Marketplace Community

213. Those responsible for implementing the formation process are to thoroughly determine the impact of the candidate's employment situation—his *marketplace* formation community—on his preparation, discernment, and readiness for ordination to the diaconate. Pope John Paul II stressed the importance of this particular formation environment at the plenary assembly of the Congregation for the Clergy: "It is the circumstances of his life—prudently evaluated by the candidate himself and by the bishop, before ordination—which should, if necessary, be adapted to the exercise of his ministry by facilitating it in every way."[12]

Circumstances of life prudently evaluated

IV. The Dimensions of Formation in the Candidate Path

214. Those responsible for the candidate path in formation should be thoroughly familiar with the doctrinal understanding of the diaconate, the ministry and life of deacons, the dimensions of formation, and the discernment of a diaconal vocation described earlier in this *Directory*. These components have a common goal: to enable the candidate to demonstrate an appropriate level of preparedness for nomination to the diocesan bishop for ordination to the diaconate. The following descriptions highlight specific components to be emphasized.

Human Dimension

Development of human qualities

215. The aim of the human dimension of the candidate path in formation is to continue to build on the human qualities already discerned during the aspirancy period (see paragraphs 189 and 190 above), developing them and adding necessary skills for an effective and responsible diaconal ministry. Emphasis needs to be placed upon his relational and collaborative qualities and skills, especially his strengths and limitations in this regard. During the candidate path, the candidate also needs to acknowledge his giftedness and to develop the habit of authentic self-criticism in light of the Gospel. He must learn how to balance his personal, familial, work, and ministerial responsibilities.

Spiritual Dimension

216. One of the primary objectives of the spiritual dimension of the candidate path in formation is "to assist the candidate in achieving a spiritual integration" of his life, family, work, and apostolic service.[13] The candidate, therefore, should be thoroughly introduced to the theology and spirituality of work as both a vocation and an apostolate, as well as a profession. The spiritual goal is for the candidate to increase in holiness by "equipping and motivating" him to lay a foundation upon which he may "continue [his] spiritual growth after ordination." Throughout his formation, the candidate is "to secure the assistance of a . . . [priest spiritual director], to cultivate regular patterns of prayer and sacramental participation, and . . . to reflect spiritually on [his] ministry."[14] It would also be useful for small groups of candidates to engage together in theological reflection "on the challenges and opportunities of their

ministries" in relationship to the Gospel and magisterial teaching.[15] Further, throughout the formation process, it is expedient that the candidate's spiritual director and those responsible for his formation ascertain the candidate's understanding, willingness, and capacity to accept the Church's discipline regarding perpetual celibacy not merely among those who are not married but, also, among married men who will be required to embrace this ecclesiastical discipline in widowhood or divorce (even with a subsequent annulment). Dispensations from the requirement of celibacy cannot be presumed. Continuation in ministry cannot be presumed even with the reception of the requested dispensation.

217. The goals of the spiritual dimension during the candidate path in formation include the following:

Spiritual goals

a. To help each candidate to increase in holiness by deepening and cultivating his commitment to Christ and the Church
b. To assist the candidate in discerning whether he has a vocation to the diaconate
c. To help him deepen his prayer life, personal, familial, communal, and liturgical; and to instill in the candidate a commitment to pray daily for the Church, especially through the Liturgy of the Hours
d. To strengthen the personal charisms he has already demonstrated in his life
e. To help him integrate his new commitment to prepare for the diaconate with his previous commitments to his family and professional employment
f. To acquaint him with the relationship between spirituality and his commitment to the Church's ministry of charity and justice
g. To acquaint him with Catholic classical and contemporary spiritual writings and the witness of the saints
h. To prepare him for the challenges of spiritual leadership that his ministry will entail

Intellectual Dimension

218. The intellectual dimension of the candidate path in formation should be carefully designed. A description of the core content for the candidate can be found in Norms 5-12 at the end of this chapter. The intellectual dimension is "oriented toward ministry,

Intellectual goals

providing the candidate with the knowledge and appreciation of the faith that he needs in order to carry out his ministry"[16] of word, liturgy, and charity. The course of study should be complete and must be in harmony with the magisterial teaching of the Church so that the future deacon is a "reliable witn[ess] of the faith and spokes[man] for the Church's teaching."[17] It should also take into account the specific diaconal services the candidate will provide in the communities that he will be appointed to serve, as well as topics that reflect the specific concerns of the Church in the United States. The intellectual dimension must equip the candidate for his leadership and participation in the new evangelization and for his effective heralding of the Gospel in today's society. The study of sacred Scripture, liturgy, evangelization, and missiology are to be given prominence.

Pastoral Dimension

Pastoral placement and supervision

219. "During formation, engagement in a wide diversity of" pastoral field education placements, "at least on a limited basis, will not only give the candidate a greater awareness of the needs and mission of the [diocesan] Church, but will assist in the discernment and development of his own . . . talents and gifts."[18] These pastoral field education experiences "should provide an opportunity for theological reflection, as well as occasions to translate" intellectual knowledge into pastoral service.[19] A description of the core content for the formation of candidates can be found in Norms 13-15 at the end of this chapter. "Competent, objective, and" supportive supervisors will be required in order to achieve these goals.[20] The diocesan Church "must be committed to the [selection and] preparation of skillful . . . supervisors who possess pastoral experience, [training] . . . in the art of supervision, and . . . [the ability to assist] mature men with [diverse] life experiences. . . ."[21] During candidacy, emphasis also should be given to the study of the role of culture in human, spiritual, and pastoral formation. Further, the pastoral dimension should provide a significant grounding in the social justice teaching of the Church.

V. The Assessment of Candidates

Measurement of achievement in a pastoral setting

Academic Assessment

220. A primary opportunity for assessment of the candidate would be within an actual pastoral setting. Can the candidate do that which his training is preparing him to do? Does the way in which

he presents himself in pastoral ministry show, for example, an integrated and balanced sense of the ecclesiology of the Second Vatican Council and an understanding of his role within the Church and in its mission of service? Does the way he participates in and leads prayerful gatherings of his community give evidence of liturgical knowledge and cultural sensitivity? Can he demonstrate a properly formed conscience and moral sensitivity? Can he form others in a convincing, sound manner?

Theological reflection

221. Another assessment option is theological reflection on his pastoral practice. Here the role of the peer community is of utmost importance. The candidate reports on his field education experience and the community enables him to reflect upon the human, spiritual, intellectual, and pastoral dimensions of his actions. This format greatly fosters the sense of partnership in assessment.

Pastoral simulation

222. Another opportunity for assessment lies in the classroom imitation of pastoral practice, whether through case study, role playing, or some form of pastoral problem solving. Although not empowered by the sense of immediacy or by connection to a real incident, such simulations can be designed to explore any number of competencies in a structured and progressive program.

Traditional examinations

223. For the assessment of the candidate's intellectual formation, traditional examinations or academic papers are necessary, as prescribed by the *Basic Norms for the Formation of Permanent Deacons* of the Congregation for Catholic Education.

Independent study

224. A sense of partnership can be fostered by allowing the candidate to present a portfolio of his accomplishments, to design a variety of ways in which he may demonstrate his readiness, or to engage in a collaborative study venture with those charged with his formation.

Comprehensive and integrative seminar at the conclusion of the course of study

225. A comprehensive and integrative seminar, such as those used in professional education, is recommended as a model to determine the level of assimilation and achievement of the candidate at the completion of his theological course of study. This model fulfills the requirement of a comprehensive review as required by the *Basic Norms for the Formation of Permanent Deacons*.[22] The faculty facilitators of the seminar evaluate how effectively the individual candidate

is "able to explain his faith and bring to maturity a lively ecclesial conscience,"[23] how he has acquired "the capacity to read a situation and an adequate inculturation of the Gospel,"[24] and how successfully he has used "communication techniques and group dynamics, the ability to speak in public, and [the ability] to give guidance and counsel."[25] In such seminars, typically formatted around case studies of a pastoral nature, the candidate has an opportunity to explore pastoral solutions in the presence of his peers, formation faculty, and pastoral supervisors. In the seminar, he is called upon not only to demonstrate an intellectual understanding of theology, but also its application in pastoral practice. He gives and receives feedback, thus demonstrating his competency in such areas as communication and his ability to work constructively within a group. In addition, his pastoral world view is exposed and assessed and his "pastoral intuition" is honored and challenged. The goal of this comprehensive and integrative seminar is always to project how the candidate will live a diaconal lifestyle and ministry.

Vocational Assessment

Regular evaluation meetings

226. Interviews should be scheduled regularly with the candidates and their families, their pastors and pastoral supervisors, members of the faculty, and mentors. The director of formation and those who collaborate with him should gather at regularly scheduled times to stay informed about a candidate's progress. They should address concerns and become collectively aware of their common collaborative role in assisting, counseling, and assessing the candidate. This responsibility should be regarded as their most important task. Due care must be taken, however, to preserve the confidentiality of spiritual direction in these proceedings.

Annual written report for the bishop

227. The responsibility of formation personnel culminates in the preparation of a yearly written report on each candidate. This report, which is to be presented to the diocesan bishop, provides a synthesis of the candidate's achievements and limitations, particularly in reference to his human, spiritual, intellectual, and pastoral readiness for continuation in the formation process and, ultimately, for nomination to ordination.[26] The written report is to be maintained in the candidate's personal file, where accumulated reports can be compared to ascertain patterns of growth or regression, as well as new areas for affirmation or concern.

Other recipients of the report

228. The director of formation must transmit this report verbally to the candidate. It should be made available to the candidate's spiritual director, whose "task is that of discerning the workings of the Spirit in the soul of those called and, at that same time, of accompanying and supporting their ongoing conversion."[27] It may be helpful to share the report with the candidate's pastor, if he did not participate in the formal review. Finally, the director of formation also will share this report with the committee on admission and scrutinies, especially in its deliberations regarding admittance to the ministries of lector and acolyte, and ordination to the diaconate.

Dismissal from formation

229. If a candidate does not possess the necessary human, spiritual, intellectual, or pastoral qualities that will allow him to minister as a deacon in a collaborative and effective way, it is only just to the individual and to the Church to communicate this to him as early as possible and in a constructive manner. Sometimes the evaluation consensus clearly indicates termination of formation or a refusal of recommendation for ordination. Candidates who lack positive qualities for continuing in the formation process should not nourish false hopes and illusions that could damage themselves and their families, their peers, or the Church. Therefore, with the approval of the diocesan bishop, the candidate should be advised to leave formation. Although no one has a right to continue in formation or a right to be ordained, in justice and with pastoral sensitivity the reasons for this decision should be shared with the candidate, and a fair hearing should be given to his own assessment of the situation, as well as to that of others who may wish to speak on his behalf.

Leave of absence

230. In situations of doubt about the readiness of a candidate to be called to ordination or about his progress in achieving appropriate levels of adult formation, the diocesan bishop may consider a period of probation. This time, however, should be specifically limited, not left open-ended. Likewise, appropriate supervision is absolutely necessary during this period to bring about needed growth and provide suitable information on which to base a judgment. It will be helpful, therefore, to prepare a written plan of action indicating the goals to be achieved, the actions that will be followed to meet the goals, and the means of evaluating and verifying the achievement of the goals. This written plan should further specify the supervisor who will accompany the candidate through the process. It must be understood that in such situations, the burden of proof of readiness

for ordination rests with the candidate, and doubt is resolved in favor of the Church.

231. Paralleling the process indicated for the external forum, spiritual direction is similarly crucial to the candidate's discernment. The individual's spiritual director should receive the information regarding this period of probation, and through internal forum, he should assist the individual through regularly scheduled meetings.

VI. Scrutinies for Installation into the Ministries of Lector and Acolyte and Ordination to the Diaconate

Canonical requirements prior to ordination

232. In accord with the Circular Letter from the Congregation for Divine Worship and the Discipline of the Sacraments, scrutinies are to take place prior to installation into the ministries of lector and acolyte[28] and prior to ordination to the diaconate.[29]

233. A collegial session of the committee on admission and scrutinies is to be scheduled for these assessments.[30] Having consulted the committee, the bishop will select those to be admitted to the specific ministry and those to be called to ordination.

Rite of Installation into the Ministry of Lector and Ministry of Acolyte

Retreat and celebration of the liturgical rite

234. It is appropriate for a retreat or a day for reflection to precede the reception of the specific ministry. It will usually be helpful to wives to participate in the retreat, although during portions of the retreat it will usually be helpful to provide the opportunity for separate treatment of the respective roles of each in the vocation of the husband to the diaconate. The conferral of the ministry should be celebrated on a Sunday or feast day, according to the rite of *The Roman Pontifical*. These rites are public celebrations with ecclesial significance.[31] Special attention should be given to the participation of the wives and children of married candidates. The ministry of lector is to be conferred first. "It is appropriate that a certain period of time elapse between the conferring of the lectorate [rite of lector[and acolytate [rite of acolyte] in such a way that the candidate may exercise the ministry he has received."[32]

Documentation of the installation

235. After the reception of the ministry, a certificate indicating the ministry received, date, place, and conferring prelate should be

prepared and signed by the chancellor of the diocese and officially sealed. This document is to be kept in the candidate's personal file and noted in the diocesan book of ministries and ordinations.

The Rite of Ordination to the Diaconate

236. An interval of at least six months must elapse between the conferring of the ministry of acolyte and ordination to the diaconate.[33] Further, a canonical retreat must precede the ordination.[34] It will usually be helpful to wives to participate in the retreat, although during portions of the retreat it will usually be helpful to provide the opportunity for separate treatment of the respective roles of each in the vocation of the husband to the diaconate. Prior to ordination to the diaconate, the ordinand must make the Profession of the Faith in the presence of the bishop or his delegate and must sign it by his own hand. He must take the Oath of Fidelity and make a personal declaration concerning his freedom to receive sacred ordination, as well as his own clear awareness of the obligations and commitments implied by that ordination. An unmarried candidate must make a declaration regarding the obligation of sacred celibacy; this declaration must be written in the candidate's own handwriting and expressed in his own words. All of these documents are to be carefully preserved in the candidate's personal file.[35]

Six-month interval between installation and ordination

237. It is preferable to celebrate the ordination in the cathedral church on a Sunday or feast day, according to the rite of *The Roman Pontifical*, inviting the diocesan Church's full participation. "During the rite special attention should be given to the participation of the wives and children of the married ordinands."[36]

238. After the ordination, a certificate should be prepared containing the date, place, and name of the ordaining prelate. It should be signed and sealed by the chancellor. This information also should be recorded in the diocesan book of ministries and ordinations. The certificate, together with the letter of petition and the bishop's letter of call to ordination, should be enclosed in the newly ordained's personal and permanent file. This file should be transferred as soon after the ordination as is convenient from the formation office to a permanent location among the curia records in the diocesan chancery. The director of formation or someone designated by the bishop should also notify the church in which the newly ordained

Curia and parish records

was baptized so that the information regarding the ordination may be included in that church's baptismal-sacramental records. The parish of Baptism should notify the director of formation when the information has been recorded.[37]

NORMS

1. The candidate path in formation must last at least three years in addition to the aspirant path. (205)
2. Regarding the number of hours of lectures, seminars, and related educational activities specified in the *Basic Norms for the Formation of Permanent Deacons*, the objective of this requirement is to guarantee the planning and implementation of an integral and substantive program of formation that adequately prepares a candidate to represent the Church as an ordained minister. (206)
3. The human dimension of this path in formation continues to develop the human qualities already discerned during the aspirant path, adding necessary skills for an effective and responsible diaconal ministry. (215)
4. The spiritual dimension of this path happens through the candidate's meeting regularly with his spiritual director and those responsible for formation. The goals are for the candidate to increase in holiness; to deepen his prayer life through the Eucharist, the Sacrament of Reconciliation, the Liturgy of the Hours, and devotions; and to acquaint himself with the Catholic spiritual tradition reflected in classic and modern spiritual writings. (216, 217)
5. The intellectual dimension of this path in formation introduces the candidate to the essentials of Christian doctrine and practice, including the core areas of theology faithful to the Magisterium of the Church and based on Scripture and Tradition, the documents of the Second Vatican Council, the *Catechism of the Catholic Church*, and the *General Directory for Catechesis*. (218, 124)
6. From Scripture, the core studies should include the major themes and content of the Old and New Testaments: Christian Scriptures, their stages of formation, and their place at the heart of Scripture. Attention should be given to the biblical

themes of justice and peace that root and foster Catholic social teaching. (124)

7. From dogmatic theology, the core studies should include fundamental theology, God as trinity, christology, creation and the nature of sin, redemption, grace and the human person, ecclesiology (both the Latin and Eastern Catholic Churches), ecumenism and interreligious dialogue, sacraments (especially the Sacrament of Holy Orders and the theology and the relationship of the diaconate to the episcopate, the presbyterate, and the laity), eschatology, Mariology, missiology, and Catholic evangelization. (124)
8. From moral theology, the core studies should include fundamental moral theology, medical-moral ethics, sexuality, and social-ministerial ethics. The social teaching of the Church should be presented substantially. (124)
9. From historical studies, the candidate should be introduced to the history of the Church through the ages with an emphasis on patristics. The candidates should be familiar with the multicultural origins of the Church in the United States. (124)
10. From Canon Law, the core studies should include a general introduction and those canons specific to the exercise of the diaconate, in particular, marriage legislation, as well as the obligations and rights of clerics. (124)
11. From spirituality, the core studies should include an introduction to spirituality, to spiritual direction, and to a selection of classic spiritual writers. (124)
12. From liturgy, the core studies should include an introduction to liturgy and to the historical, spiritual, and juridical aspects of liturgy. (124)
13. Practica for the ministry of liturgy should include specific training in the functions of the deacon during the Eucharist, Baptism, RCIA, marriage, the rites of Christian burial, and other liturgical ministries of the diaconate. (130)
14. From homiletics, deacons should have courses specifically aimed at preparing and delivering homilies. (130)
15. Pastoral formation must include a wide diversity of pastoral services, including opportunities for theological reflection. Attention should be given to the study of the role of culture in human and spiritual formation. (219)

16. A comprehensive seminar should be conducted at the end of the candidate path of formation to enhance the candidates' integration of learning and to assess their readiness for ordination. (225)
17. The responsibility of formation personnel culminates in the preparation of a yearly written report on each aspirant and candidate that will be presented to the diocesan bishop through the director of formation. (227)
18. The director of formation must verbally transmit a yearly report to each candidate. (228)
19. Scrutinies are to take place prior to installation into the ministries of lector and acolyte and prior to ordination to the diaconate. (232)
20. A retreat or day of reflection should precede the reception of the ministries of lector and acolyte. (234)
21. An interval of at least six months must elapse between the conferring of the ministry of acolyte and ordination to the diaconate. (236)
22. A canonical retreat must precede ordination. (236)
23. After the installation into each ministry and after ordination, a certificate should be prepared containing the date, place, and name of the installing/ordaining prelate. It should be signed and sealed by the chancellor. This information also should be recorded in the diocesan book of ministries and ordinations. The director of formation should also notify the church in which the newly ordained was baptized so that the information regarding the ordination may be included in that church's baptismal-sacramental records. The parish of Baptism should notify the director of formation when the information has been recorded. All of these canonical documents should be transferred as soon after the ordination as is convenient from the formation office to a permanent location among the curia records in the diocesan chancery.

NOTES

1 BNFPD, no. 28.
2 Ibid.
3 Ibid., nos. 49-50, italics added; cf. CIC, c. 236.
4 CL, 9, citing 1 Tm 5:22.
5 BNFPD, no. 82.
6 Ibid., no. 26.
7 Ibid., no. 16.
8 Ibid., no. 26.
9 Ibid., no. 22.
10 BNFPD, no. 27.
11 Ibid.
12 PDO, no. 4.
13 PDG (1984), no. 94.
14 Ibid., no. 99.
15 Ibid., no. 99.
16 Ibid., no. 75.
17 Ibid., no. 78.
18 Ibid., no. 84.
19 Ibid.
20 Ibid.
21 Ibid., no. 85.
22 BNFPD, no. 82.
23 Ibid., no. 80.
24 Ibid.
25 Ibid.
26 This written assessment should include an estimation of an unmarried candidate's capacity to lead a perpetual chaste and celibate life. For a married candidate, it should present an appraisal of his family's stability and capacity to support his vocation, especially addressing the status of his wife's consent and her own integrity. Each year, the number of affirmative and negative votes of the formation team and faculty regarding the continuance or separation of the candidate from formation is to be recorded. If there are abstentions, they are to be explained (CL, Enclosure III, 7, 8). The diocesan bishop expects the objective and critical judgment of those who collaborate with him in formation. This report should reflect a clear consensus among those who have been involved with the candidate's training and formation.
27 BNFPD, no. 23.
28 CL, Enclosures II, III. Required documentation and procedures for institution into the ministries of lector and acolyte include the following (these are to be followed when

petitioning for institution into the ministry of lector and repeated when petitioning for the ministry of acolyte):

a. The candidate handwrites his request to be admitted to the specific ministry. This request must be composed by the candidate personally, written out in his own hand; it "may not be copied formulary, or worse, a photocopied text" (CL, Enclosure II, 1)
b. The director of formation prepares a personal report, which should be detailed, making use of the model found in CL, Enclosure V, and which should include the candidate's annual self and peer assessments
c. The candidate's pastor is consulted, and he writes a letter of recommendation
d. The committee on admission and scrutinies interviews the candidate's wife, if he is married, to ascertain her understanding of her husband's institution into these ministries as part of the formation discernment process
e. Faculty and pastoral field supervisors provide assessments of the candidate
f. A smaller team from the committee on admission and scrutinies interviews the candidate to ascertain his knowledge of the ministry to be received and his capacity to fulfill its responsibilities
g. Other documentation is provided, as requested by the committee (CL, Enclosure II)

29 Required documentation and procedures for ordination to the diaconate include the following (these are to be followed when petitioning for ordination to the diaconate):

a. Before petitioning for ordination, the candidate keeps in mind that there must be an interval of at least six months between the conferring of the ministry of acolyte and ordination to the diaconate (CIC, c. 1035:2)
b. The candidate submits a written request to be admitted to the Order of Deacons. This request must be composed by the candidate personally, written out in his own hand; it "may not be copied formulary, or worse, a photocopied text" (CL, Enclosure II, 1)
c. The candidate's wife writes and signs a statement in which she declares her consent to the ordination petition of her husband and makes clear her own understanding of the meaning of diaconal ministry (CL, Enclosure II, 8)
d. The director of formation prepares a personal report, which should be detailed, making use of the model proposed in CL, Enclosure V, and which should include the annual Vocational Assessment Report
e. The director, in compliance with CIC c. 1032, must present a certificate verifying the candidate's completion of all required studies
f. The candidate's pastor is consulted, and he writes a letter of recommendation
g. The committee on admission and scrutinies interviews the candidate to ascertain his knowledge of the Order of Deacons to be received and its obligations and rights; his understanding and willingness, if single or widowed, to accept the Church's discipline regarding perpetual celibate chastity; his understanding and willingness, if married, to embrace the magisterial teaching on marriage and sexuality, as well as

its ecclesiastical discipline in widowhood; and his understanding of the rights and obligations of a cleric and his capacity to fulfill these responsibilities

h. The committee interviews the wife of a married candidate to ascertain her willingness to support his petition and to live as a wife of a deacon

i. The canonical banns are published within a sufficiently extended period of time in advance of ordination in the parishes where the candidate has had an extended residence or presence in his formation ministries (CL, Enclosure II, 8; CIC, c. 1051:2)

j. The candidate provides a recent photograph and biographical information for use in the publicizing of his ordination

k. Other documentation is provided, as requested by the committee (CL, Enclosure IV)

"It should not be permitted that the candidate's family or the parish community presume his future Ordination" before the call of the competent authority, especially by mailing invitations or making other preparations for the ordination celebration. "Behavior of this kind can constitute a form of psychological pressure that must be avoided in every way possible (CL, Enclosure IV:3)." The bishop will select those to be ordained to the diaconate and will set the date and other specifications for the ordination. It is assumed that this will be done in consultation with the ordinand and his family.

30 The recommendation and vote on each request is to be recorded and attached to the written report submitted to the diocesan bishop. All documentation generated by the committee should be maintained. (CL)

31 BNFPD, nos. 57-59.

32 Ibid., no. 59.

33 Ibid., quoting CIC, c. 1035:2.

34 Ibid., no. 65; cf. CIC, c. 1039.

35 CL, Enclosure IV.

36 BNFPD, no. 65.

37 Cf. CIC, c. 1054.

CHAPTER SEVEN

POST-ORDINATION PATH IN DIACONAL FORMATION

I. Introduction

Goals for post-ordination formation

239. The post-ordination path in diaconal formation "is first and foremost a process of continual conversion."[1]

> [It] requires that ongoing formation strengthen in [each deacon] the consciousness and willingness to live in intelligent, active and mature communion with their bishops and priests of their diocese, and with the Supreme Pontiff who is the visible foundation of the entire Church's unity. When formed in this way, they can become in their ministry effective promoters of communion. . . . The continuing formation of deacons is a human necessity which must be seen in continuity with the divine call to serve the Church in the ministry and with the initial formation given to deacons, to the extent that these are considered two initial moments in a single, living, process of Christian and diaconal life.[2]

The goal for this path in formation is to responsibly address the various aspects of a deacon's ministry, the development of his personality and, above all, his commitment to spiritual growth. "Ongoing formation must include and harmonize all dimensions of the life and ministry of the deacon. Thus . . . it should be complete, systematic and personalized in its diverse aspects whether human, spiritual, intellectual or pastoral."[3] The primary source for post-ordination formation is the ministry itself.

> The deacon matures in its exercise and by focusing his own call to holiness on the fulfillment of his social and ecclesial duties, in particular, of his ministerial functions and responsibilities. The formation of deacons should, therefore, concentrate in a special way on awareness of their ministerial character.[4]

"Do not neglect the gift you have [received]."

240. The post-ordination path in formation is motivated by the same dynamism as the holy order received:

> Do not neglect the gift you have, which was conferred on you through the prophetic word with the imposition of hands. . . . Be diligent in these matters, be absorbed in them, so that your progress may be evident to everyone. Attend to yourself and to your teaching; persevere in both tasks, for by doing so you will save both yourself and those who listen to you.[5]

II. The Dimensions of Formation in the Post-Ordination Path

241. The post-ordination path should provide the deacon with ample opportunities to continue to develop and integrate the dimensions of formation into his life and ministry.[6] In this way, the quality of his life and ministry will be ensured, avoiding the risk of ministerial burnout. In certain cases of difficulty, such as discouragement or a change in ministry, post-ordination formation can entail a process of renewal and revitalization.

Two distinct levels of formation

242. In designing the content for an ongoing formation program, those responsible "should take into consideration two distinct but closely related levels of formation: the diocesan level, in reference to the bishop. . . . and the community level in which the deacon exercises his own ministry, in reference to the parish priest."[7] The deacon is ordained for service to the diocesan Church, even though the focus of that service will usually be within a particular parochial community. Keeping a balance in this dual relationship is essential to his effectiveness as a deacon.

Wife and family ongoing formation

243. Just as the role of the wife and children needed to be carefully discerned throughout the aspirant and candidate paths in formation, this discernment is equally important in the post-ordination path. It is appropriate to recognize the importance of the ongoing formation of the wives and families of deacons and to provide formation resources and opportunities for them. A family life perspective remains an essential point of reference. Care must, however, be exercised so that "the essential distinction of roles and the clear independence of the ministry" are maintained.[8]

244. Some deacons, because of a strong desire to function in their diaconal ministries, may dismiss valid areas of concern and conflict with their spouse and family. This dismissal is to be avoided. A married deacon and his family must be instructed on how to request help early when they experience a need. "Unfortunately, our society still focuses almost exclusively on a remedial approach; families [usually] seek help [only] after a crisis has occurred and other problems develop. An alternative is a preventive strategy."[9]

Preventive strategy

Human Dimension:
Developing "Human Qualities as Valuable Instruments for Ministry"[10]

245. To effectively carry out his diaconal ministry, the deacon must extend himself generously in various forms of human relations without discrimination so that he is perceived by others as a credible witness to the sanctity and preciousness of human life. Post-ordination formation should enable the deacon to pursue this witness to the faith with greater effectiveness.

Spiritual Dimension: "Diaconal Spirituality"[11]

246. In Baptism, each disciple receives the universal call to holiness. In the reception of the Sacrament of Holy Orders, the deacon receives a "new consecration to God" through which he is configured to Christ the Servant and sent to serve God's people.[12] Growth into holiness, therefore, is "a duty binding all the faithful." But "for the deacon it is has a further basis in the special consecration received. It includes the practice of the Christian virtues and the various evangelical precepts and counsels according to [his] own state of life."[13] The celibate deacon should, therefore, "be especially careful to give witness to [his] brothers and sisters by [his] fidelity to the celibate life the better to move them to seek those values consonant with man's transcendent vocation."[14] He also must be "faithful to the spiritual life and duties of [his] ministry in a spirit of prudence and vigilance, remembering that 'the spirit is willing but the flesh is weak.'"[15] For the married deacon, the Sacrament of Matrimony

> is a gift from God and should be a source of nourishment for [his] spiritual life. . . . it will be necessary to integrate these various elements [i.e., family life and professional responsibilities] in a unitary fashion, especially by means of shared prayer.

> In marriage, love becomes an interpersonal giving of self, a mutual fidelity, a source of new life, a support in times of joy and sorrow: in short, love becomes service. When lived in faith, this family service is for the rest of the faithful an example of the love of Christ. The married deacon must use it as a stimulus of his diakonia in the Church.[16]

To foster and nurture his diaconal ministry and lifestyle according to his state in life, each deacon must be rooted in a spirit of service that verifies "a genuine personal encounter with Jesus, a trusting dialogue with the Father, and a deep experience of the Spirit."[17]

247. Some recommended spiritual exercises to assist the deacon in developing and promoting his spiritual life include the following:

a. Daily or frequent participation in the Eucharist, the source and summit of the Christian life, as well as daily or frequent eucharistic adoration, as often as his secular employment and family requirements permit
b. Regular reception of the Sacrament of Reconciliation
c. Daily celebration of the Liturgy of the Hours, especially morning and evening prayer
d. Shared prayer with his family
e. Meditative prayer on the holy Scriptures—*lectio divina*
f. Devotion to Mary, the Mother God
g. Prayerful preparation of oneself prior to the celebration of the sacraments, preaching, or beginning one's ministry of charity
h. Theological reflection
i. Regular spiritual direction
j. Participation in an annual retreat
k. Authentic living of one's state of life
l. Time for personal and familial growth

Intellectual Dimension: Theological Renewal[18]

248. The intellectual dimension of diaconate formation does not end with ordination but is an ongoing requirement of the vocation. The theological demands of their call to a singular ministry of ecclesial service and pastoral servant-leadership require of deacons a growing love for the Church—for God's Holy People—shown by their faithful and competent carrying out of their proper functions

and responsibilities. The intellectual dimension of post-ordination formation must be systematic and substantive, deepening the intellectual content initially studied during the candidate path of formation. Study days, renewal courses and participation in academic institutes are appropriate formats to achieve this goal. In particular,

> it is of the greatest use and relevance to study, appropriate and diffuse the social doctrine of the Church. A good knowledge of that teaching will permit many deacons to mediate it in their different professions, at work and in their families. [It may also be useful to] the diocesan bishop [to] invite those who are capable to specialize in a theological discipline and obtain the necessary academic qualifications at those pontifical academies or institutes recognized by the Apostolic See which guarantee doctrinally correct information. . . . Ongoing formation cannot be confined simply to updating, but should seek to facilitate a practical configuration of the deacon's entire life to Christ who loves all and serves all.[19]

Pastoral Dimension:
"Pastoral Methodology for an Effective Ministry"[20]

249. Pastoral formation constantly encourages the deacon "to perfect the effectiveness of his ministry of making the love and service of Christ present in the Church and in society without distinction, especially to the poor and to those most in need. Indeed, it is from the pastoral love of Christ that the ministry of deacons draws its model and inspiration."[21]

"For an adequate pastoral formation, it is necessary to organize encounters in which the principal objective is the reflection upon the pastoral plan of the Diocese."[22] When the diaconate is conceived from the start as an integral part of an overall pastoral plan, deacons will have a richer and firmer sense of their own identity and purpose. Thus, an ongoing pastoral formation program responds to the concerns and issues pertinent to the deacon's life and ministry, in keeping with the pastoral plan of the diocesan Church and in loyal and firm communion with the Supreme Pontiff and with his own bishop.

III. Additional Considerations

Specialization Programming

Personalizing ongoing formation

250. "The ministry of the word leads to ministry at the altar, which in turn prompts the transformation of life by the liturgy, resulting in charity."[23] As a deacon eventually focuses on more specific ministries through his responsiveness to the growing needs of the people he serves, it will be necessary to provide more specific programming designed to address his personal needs, talents, and ministry.[24] Initially, however, consideration should be given to deepening his understanding and skills in the ministries of the word, liturgy, and charity.

Program for the Newly Ordained

First three years of diaconate ministry

251. There are particular matters relevant to the newly ordained. It is important, therefore, that the newly ordained begin their diaconate ministry in a positive and supportive manner. A program should be planned for the first three years of their diaconate ministry[25] and coordinated by the director of deacon personnel. In the early phase of their ministry, ongoing formation will largely reinforce the basic training and its application in ministerial practice. Later formation will entail a more in-depth study of the various components proposed in the dimensions in diaconal formation. Consideration also should be given to introducing the newly ordained to a conversational study of a second language used within the diocese and the study of its cultural environment. Deacons, as ministers of Christ the Servant, should be prepared to link people of diverse languages and cultures into the local faith community of the diocese and parish. Deacons in their initial pastoral assignments should be carefully supervised by an exemplary pastor especially appointed to this task by the bishop.[26]

Urgent missionary and pastoral work

New Evangelization: The Deacon in the Third Christian Millennium

252. "The vocation of the permanent deacon is a great gift of God to the Church and for this reason is 'an important enrichment for the Church's mission.'"[27] Being called and sent by the Lord have always been important, but in contemporary historical circumstances they acquire a particular urgency. "The mission of Christ the Redeemer, which is entrusted to the Church, is still very far from

completion. . . . An overall view of the human race shows that this mission is still only beginning and that we must commit ourselves wholeheartedly to its service."[28] To this end, the ministry of the deacon holds great promise, especially for the urgent missionary and pastoral work of the new evangelization. The post-ordination path in diaconal formation should give priority to this task. Pope John Paul II stresses this urgency: "Heralds of the Gospel are needed who are experts in humanity, profoundly knowing the heart of contemporary man, who share his hopes and joys, his fears and sorrow and, at the same time, who are contemplatives in love with God."[29]

IV. Diocesan Organization for Post-Ordination Path Formation

A Diocesan Post-Ordination Program

253. With the approval of the diocesan bishop, a program for the ongoing formation of deacons should be designed annually. It must take into consideration the demands made upon the deacons by their pastoral ministry, distances to be traveled, the frequency of gatherings, their time commitments to their families and secular employment, as well as the differing ages and needs of the deacons. In some places, regional or interdiocesan collaboration should be given serious consideration.[30] The use of distance-learning modules also should be explored, especially when travel is a hardship.[31]

Diocesan Policy

254. Each diocesan Church is to establish a basic minimum of continuing education hours to be fulfilled on an annual basis by all diocesan deacons in active service.[32] This would be in addition to time allocated for the annual diaconal community retreat.

Models for Post-Ordination Formation

255. At times, the post-ordination path in diaconal formation may be accomplished in common with priests, religious, and laity of the diocese to enhance collaborative ministerial formation in the diocese. This would use the resources of the diocese in a prudent manner.[33] However, sensitivity to the timing of such events is important, especially for deacons who are engaged in secular employment. On other occasions, ongoing formation programs should be specifically designed for deacons and particularly address the threefold ministry of word, liturgy, and charity.

256. The models presented earlier in aspirant and candidate formation all lend themselves to a post-ordination formation methodology. Some additional possibilities might include the following:

a. Diocesan, regional, or national conferences
b. Workshops and seminars
c. Educational and developmental themes for retreats and days of recollection
d. Self-guided study
e. Distance learning
f. Ministry reflection groups
g. Mentoring groups among deacons that meet to discuss ministry, exchange experiences, advance formation, and encourage each other in fidelity

NORMS

1. A program should be planned for the first three years of their diaconal ministry. They should be supervised by a pastor appointed to this ministry by the diocesan bishop. The program should be coordinated by the director for deacon personnel. (251)
2. Each diocesan Church should establish a basic minimum of continuing education hours to be fulfilled on an annual basis by all diocesan deacons in active service. (254)

NOTES

1 DMLPD, no. 65.

2 Ibid., no. 71, 63.

3 Ibid., no. 68; cf. Footnote 204 of DMLPD, no. 68.

4 Ibid., no. 75.

5 1 Tm 4:14-16.

6 DMLPD, no. 68.

7 Ibid., no. 76.

8 Ibid., no. 81.

9 FP, p. 33.

10 DMLPD, no. 69.

11 Ibid., no. 70.

12 Ibid., no. 44, citing Second Vatican Council, Decree *Presbyterorum Ordinis*, no. 12a.

13 Ibid., no. 45.

14 Ibid., no. 60.

15 Ibid., no. 60; Mt. 26:41.

16 Ibid., no. 61.

17 PDV, no. 72.

18 DMLPD, no. 72; cf. also nos. 65 and 71.

19 Ibid., no. 67.

20 Ibid., no. 73.

21 Ibid.

22 Congregation for the Clergy, *Directory on the Ministry and Life of Priests* (January 31, 1994) (Washington, D.C.: United States Catholic Conference, 1994), no. 78. (This is analogous for diaconal formation.)

23 DMLPD, no. 39.

24 Ibid., no. 66.

25 Ibid., no. 77.

26 Ibid.

27 PDO, no. 2.

28 Pope John Paul II, Encyclical Letter, *On the Permanent Validity of the Church's Missionary Mandate* (*Redemptoris Missio*) (December 7, 1990) (Washington, D.C.: United States Catholic Conference, 1990), no. 1.

29 Pope John Paul II, Allocution to the Sixth Symposium of European Bishops (November 11, 1985).

30 DMLPD, no. 79.

31 Cf. this *Directory*, Chapter Eight, nos. 262-265, on distance learning.

32 Ibid., no. 76.

33 Ibid., no. 78.

CHAPTER EIGHT

ORGANIZATION, STRUCTURE, AND PERSONNEL FOR DIACONAL FORMATION

I. Organization

Diocesan Plan for Diaconal Ministry

257. The establishment or renewal of diaconal ministry within a diocesan Church needs to be conceived and established within an overall diocesan plan for ministry in which the diaconate is seen as an integral component in addressing pastoral needs. In this way, deacons, who are ordained for service to the diocesan Church, will have a richer and firmer sense of their identity and purpose, as will those who collaborate in ministry with them.

The importance of a diocesan plan for ministry

Resources for Organization

258. Primary resources to guide a diocese in its discernment and readiness for the reestablishment or renewal of the diaconate are the documents of the Holy See: *Basic Norms for the Formation of Permanent Deacons* and *Directory for the Ministry and Life of Permanent Deacons,* as well as this *National Directory for the Formation, Ministry, and Life of Permanent Deacons in the United States.* These resources establish norms and directives that each diocese is to follow in the formation, ministry, and life of their deacons. Those responsible for the planning and implementation of the diaconal program should be thoroughly familiar with the intent and content of these documents.

Primary resources for norms and directives

259. The Secretariat for the Diaconate of the United States Conference of Catholic Bishops is also at the service of the diocesan bishop, especially regarding procedures for planning, requesting review of a formation proposal, and implementing the diaconate. Formal review of existing programs by a visiting team organized by the Bishops' Committee on the Diaconate is another resource available through the secretariat.

USCCB Secretariat for the Diaconate

II. Structures

Diocesan program for diacronal formation

Diocesan Program for Diaconal Formation

260. "The diocese should provide appropriate structures for the formation,"[1] ministry, and life of deacons. Possible structures include an office, a policy board, admissions and evaluation committees, and so forth. Some practical functions of a diocesan diaconate structure include collaboration, formation planning, policy development, and post-ordination activities.[2]

Models for Diaconal Formation

261. Various models for diaconal formation have developed in the United States. They provide the essential components for diaconal formation independently or in affiliation with other institutions.

1. The **freestanding** structure is the most common model for diaconal formation in the United States. Within this diocesan structure, diaconal formation takes place in its entirety, usually with personnel drawn from the various academic, spiritual and formational resources of the diocese.

2. The **college/university**-related model incorporates one or more parts of formation from diocesan staff and resources, while one or several parts of formation, such as the intellectual and/or pastoral, are provided and supervised by a Catholic college or university, usually located within the diocese. In these situations, diocesan coordinators carefully and comprehensively integrate the components of formation. Similar to the college/university model is the model that involves a **graduate school of theology**.

3. A **diocesan or religious seminary** may offer valuable resources for the formation of deacons. The unique and dedicated role of the seminary for priestly formation and the distinction between priestly and diaconal identities must be maintained. "Prudent, limited" use of seminary facilities may be a useful resource available to the bishop in the formation of deacon candidates.[3]

4. In a **collaborative** model, several specific groups, such as religious institutes or dioceses of a province, may choose to unite

their resources. Each group maintains separate formation directors and selection processes, but join together for one or more parts of formation. Care should be taken to ensure that the various components of formation are integrated in a comprehensive manner so that each participating group has a clear understanding of its specific responsibilities.

Distance Learning

262. Regional provinces, as well as large individual dioceses, may consider employing distance learning as an alternative model for achieving part of the intellectual and pastoral dimensions of diaconal formation. The flexibility that distance learning offers can be a desirable feature in diaconal formation, as it honors a family life perspective in formation and ministry and recognizes the multiple demands on the participants that can make it difficult to be present at one location.[4]

Distance learning

263. In the United States, a significant number of educational institutions, such as a local community colleges or universities, have the capacity to conduct video interactive conferencing with multiple sites in a state, county, and city. This technology provides one format for distance learning and is usually available to organizations and institutions as a public service. Some dioceses in the United States make good use of this technology.

264. Another rapidly developing distance-learning format is the online seminar. Through the accessibility of the World Wide Web, Internet seminars and courses in theological, pastoral, and religious studies are being expanded at a reasonable cost to the participant. These courses are offered on undergraduate, graduate, and adult extension levels through Catholic colleges and universities in the United States and throughout the world. If a distance-learning format is incorporated into the diocesan program for part of the intellectual and pastoral dimensions in formation, it is the responsibility of the diocesan bishop to verify that the course of study offered fulfills the requirements of the *Basic Norms for the Formation of Permanent Deacons*, the *Directory for the Ministry and Life of Permanent Deacons*, and this *Directory*. The course must be complete, be in harmony with magisterial teaching, and be taught by a competent instructor. Of particular interest in distance learning

Verification of the course of study

is the availability on the Internet of major theological libraries and research centers throughout the world. A valuable resource in this regard is the web site of the Congregation for the Clergy, *www.clerus.org*.[5]

265. Distance learning alone cannot build a diaconal formation community. However, it is a powerful instrument that supports a family perspective in diaconal formation, as well as an adult's capacity for self-formation with professional guidance.

III. The Role of the Diocesan Bishop in Diaconate Formation

The bishop: Primary formator

266. In the formation of deacons, "the first *sign and instrument* of the Spirit of Christ is the proper Bishop. . . . He is the one ultimately responsible for the discernment and formation" of aspirants and candidates, as well as the pastoral care of deacons.[6] He discharges this responsibility personally, as well as through "suitable associates" who assist him—the director of deacon formation and the director of deacon personnel. Both directors are accountable directly to the bishop or, in his absence, to a priest whom the bishop has appointed as his delegate: e.g., vicar general, vicar for clergy.[7] While the bishop may exercise his responsibility through his formation associates, nevertheless "he will commit himself, as far as is possible, to knowing personally those who are preparing for the diaconate."[8]

IV. Recruitment and Preparation of Formation Personnel

Competent staffing

267. Because of the specialized nature of deacon formation and in order to ensure continuity among program personnel, the diocesan bishop or religious ordinary should encourage experienced and qualified priests and deacons to consider preparing themselves for the apostolate of deacon formation. Religious and lay persons may assist in suitable capacities in deacon formation; those selected by the bishop to do so should receive appropriate preparation for their role.

Climate of stability

Continuity

268. Continuity in staffing and programming, as well as a planned transition in personnel, ought to receive the highest priority. The

administrative staff and formation faculty should comply with the personnel policies established by the diocesan Church for its clergy and lay staff, policies that may include term limits. Such compliance will help in planning for an orderly transition among formation personnel.

269. Opportunities for sabbaticals, training, and internships for priests, deacons, and professional lay employees in preparation for eventual placements on the diaconal formation staff should be anticipated and scheduled as far in advance as possible.

V. Aspirant/Candidate Formation Personnel

270. For the administration of the aspirant and candidate paths in diaconate formation, the following personnel have a special responsibility.

Director of Formation

Responsibilities of the formation director

271. The director of formation, who should be either a priest or a deacon,[9] is appointed by the diocesan bishop to be head of the deacon formation program. He reports directly to the bishop and should have regular communication with him. The director is ultimately responsible for both aspirant and candidate formation. However, the number of participants in either path may require the additional appointment of an associate. The director oversees the implementation of the formation program. He conducts regularly scheduled assessments; makes home and parish visitations; supervises the formation team, faculty, and mentors; and maintains contact with the aspirants' and candidates' pastors.

Qualities of an effective director

272. The director should be familiar with the diaconate—its history, theology, and practice. He should have parish experience, as well as practical skills and experience in formation, curriculum development, adult educational methodology, vocational discernment, supervision, and administration. He should be capable of providing spiritual leadership to the formation community. In most dioceses, the director of formation fulfills several administrative functions, except the spiritual direction of aspirants and candidates.[10]

Director of Spiritual Formation[11]

Responsibilities of the director of spiritual formation

273. The director of spiritual formation assists the director of formation by coordinating the entire spiritual formation program, giving

it unity and direction. He makes provision for the individual spiritual direction of each aspirant and candidate. He also may serve as a spiritual director for an aspirant and/or candidate. He provides an orientation to the spiritual dimension in aspirant and candidate formation to other priest spiritual directors, who have been chosen by the aspirants or candidates with the approval of the bishop.[12] The director of spiritual formation provides for the liturgical life and prayer of the aspirant and candidate communities, making appropriate provision for the celebration of the Eucharist, the Liturgy of the Hours, and opportunities for celebration of the sacrament of penance in formation gatherings. He is also responsible for retreats and days of recollection, assuring that they are well planned and carefully executed. The director of spiritual formation, who must be a priest,[13] is nominated by the director of formation and approved and appointed by the bishop.

Qualifications of the director of spiritual formation

274. The director of spiritual formation must be dedicated to the Church's *diakonia* and particularly knowledgeable of the diaconate and its mission within the Church. He should possess formal training in spirituality and related areas, including ascetical and spiritual theology, pastoral counseling, and referral skills.

Coordinator of Pastoral Field Education

Responsibilities of the coordinator of pastoral field education

275. An integral formation must relate the human, spiritual, and intellectual dimensions to pastoral practice. "The whole formation imparted [to aspirants and candidates for the diaconate] . . . aims at preparing them to enter into communion with the charity of Christ. . . . Hence their formation in its different aspects must have a fundamentally pastoral character."[14] To ensure that all pastoral field education experiences are closely integrated with the human, spiritual, and intellectual dimensions of formation, the coordinator of pastoral field education assists the director of formation in the apostolic formation of aspirants and candidates. He systematically introduces the aspirants and candidates into suitable pastoral experiences, equipping them with practical skills for pastoral and, eventual, diaconal ministry. The coordinator for pastoral field formation, who must be either a priest or a deacon, is nominated by the director of formation and is approved and appointed by the bishop. The coordinator for pastoral field formation corresponds to the office of the "pastor (or other minister)" required by the *Basic Norms for the*

Formation of Permanent Deacons of the Congregation for Catholic Education. He administers and coordinates the program of field education for the aspirant and candidate paths of formation. In consultation with the director of formation and others responsible for formation, he arranges for the pastoral field placement of each participant, including an orientation and training of those who assist him in the field placement. Supervisory skills cannot be presumed, and teaching them is a high priority. Good supervision guarantees that the pastoral field experience remains systematically educative and formational. The coordinator for pastoral field formation also provides a written assessment of the participant's pastoral field education experience. The coordinator for pastoral field formation has faculty status, thereby ensuring that all pastoral field experiences are carefully coordinated with the other dimensions in formation.

Qualifications of the coordinator for pastoral formation

276. It is important that the coordinator for pastoral field formation have parish experience, be familiar with pastoral education, be knowledgeable in theology and supervisory techniques, be familiar with the value and practice of theological reflection—its goals, objectives, and methods. He should possess formal training in supervision and counseling. Since the pastoral service of the diocesan Church extends to all individuals and groups, including all social classes, with special concern for the poor and those alienated from society, the coordinator for pastoral field formation also should have knowledge of the needs and resources within the diocesan Church and be familiar with deacon placements within the diocese and their effectiveness in the local Church.

Faculty

SELECTION

Vatican directives for educators

277. Faculty members are nominated by the director of formation and approved and appointed by the bishop. The faculty contributes in a significant way to the formation of future deacons. The quality and expertise of the faculty determine the qualities and abilities of the future deacon. The Congregation for Catholic Education has formulated, in its *Directives Concerning the Preparation of Seminary Educators*, specific criteria to guide the selection of faculty that apply to the selection of diaconal faculty members as well.[15] The criteria established by the Congregation are highlighted in the notes of this chapter.[16]

EXPECTATIONS

Mutual expectations: Administration & faculty

278. Each member of the faculty is expected to do the following:

a. Submit a course outline and list of required textbooks[17]
b. Participate in the assessment of aspirants or candidates for their continuance in the formation process and eventual readiness for ordination to the diaconate
c. Be available for student consultation, providing feedback to them on their achievements as well as further development needed
d. Submit a written assessment of the student's level of achievement in the course, as well as any area that may require further growth
e. Participate whenever possible in the formation community's life and prayer, faculty discussions, and in-service programming
f. Be familiar with and experienced in adult learning processes and a family perspective in class preparation, presentation, and assignment

279. The faculty should expect assistance from the director of formation in the following areas:

a. An **orientation** to
   i. The dimension in diaconal formation: the formation process, including philosophy, mission, formation goals, and doctrinal understanding of the identity and mission of deacons
   ii. The personal, ministerial, and academic background of current aspirants, candidates, and deacons
b. **In-service programming** that includes the following:
   i. Vatican documents on deacon formation, such as *Basic Norms for the Formation of Permanent Deacons* and *Directory for the Ministry and Life of Permanent Deacons*; the *Instruction on Certain Questions Regarding the Collaboration of the Non-Ordained Faithful in the Sacred Ministry of Priests*
   ii. *National Directory for the Formation, Ministry, and Life of Permanent Deacons in the United States*
   iii. The role of field education in the academic curriculum and assessment
c. **Equitable compensation/stipend** based on travel to and from the formation site, course preparation and grading, and participation in evaluation sessions and faculty meetings, student conferences, and in-service programming. The basic criteria to be used

in determining a just stipend are the level of a faculty member's academic credentials and experience, together with the time commitment in preparing, teaching, and counseling participants

d. An **educational environment** that includes proper equipment, classroom space, and materials
e. **Feedback** from the administrators and students regarding the faculty member's presentations and response
f. A **formal service agreement** between the director of formation and the individual faculty member that incorporates the above expectations and that makes as explicit as possible mutual services and obligations

Service agreement

Mentors

280. The director of formation, with the approval and appointment of the bishop, should designate mentors from among deacons or priests who are knowledgeable and competent to assist him in assessing the potential and qualifications of those in formation. The mentor is equivalent to the "tutor" described in the *Basic Norms for the Formation of Permanent Deacons*. The mentor is charged with following the formation of those committed to his care, offering support and encouragement. Depending upon the size of the formation community, a mentor will be responsible for one aspirant or candidate, or he may be invited to minister to a small group of aspirants or candidates. Mentors receive their orientation and supervision from the director of formation. They also help the director for pastoral formation facilitate theological reflection among those assigned to them. Mentors are members of the formation team and are invited "to collaborate with the director of formation in the programming of the different formational activities and in the preparation of the judgment of suitability."[18]

VI. Advisory Structures for Aspirant and Candidate Paths of Formation

281. Members of advisory structures should be representative of the pastors, deacons, deacons' wives, religious, and laity. Whenever possible they ought to reflect the variety of cultures and diverse ethnic and racial groups in the diocese. Members may be nominated by the director of formation and be approved and appointed by the bishop. The director of formation serves as an *ex officio*, non-voting member.

Diocesan support structures for the formation program

282. Some possible advisory structures include the following.

Formation Policy Board

283. The bishop may constitute a formation policy board to assist him and the director of formation in matters of formation. The functions of this board are to advise on the planning, implementation, and evaluation of the formation program. Practical skills and experience in curriculum development, formation work, discernment and supervision, spiritual direction, counseling, finances, planning, and organizational development would be some of the essential criteria in selecting appropriate board members. The board might also be set up in such a way that not all the members' specific terms of service conclude together, allowing for continuity in the board's deliberations. The membership and procedures of the board should be determined in accordance with its statutes, as approved by the bishop.

Committee on Admission and Scrutinies

284. As prescribed by the Congregation for Divine Worship and the Discipline of the Sacraments, the diocesan bishop is to establish a committee on admission and scrutinies, unless another structure exists. The formation policy board might include this responsibility among its tasks. The committee on admission and scrutinies could, thereby, be constituted as a subcommittee of the formation policy board with its members selected from the board. The specific responsibilities of this committee are to review and recommend applicants for admission to aspirant and candidate formation, nominate aspirants for the Rite of Admission to Candidacy, and review and nominate candidates for installation into the ministries of lector and acolyte, and eventually, for ordination to the diaconate.[19]

VII. Post-Ordination Formation Personnel

Pastoral care of deacons and the diaconal community

285. It is a particular responsibility of the bishop to provide for the pastoral care of the deacons and the diaconal community in his diocese. This care is discharged both personally and through the director of deacon personnel. Special care should always be shown to those deacons experiencing difficulties because of personal circumstances. Whenever possible the bishop should attend the deacons' community meetings, as well as those of the deacon

community board or the deacon personnel board, if these structures have been authorized and constituted. If the bishop is unable to attend, he may designate a priest—e.g., his vicar general or vicar for the clergy—to represent him in his absence.[20]

The Director of Deacon Personnel

Director of deacon personnel

286. The diocesan bishop appoints the director of deacon personnel. He is directly responsible to the bishop. The director, who is to be either a priest or a deacon, should have regular and comprehensive communications with the bishop on matters regarding individual deacons, as well as their families.[21] In fulfilling his responsibilities, the director of deacon personnel should be thoroughly familiar with the intent and context of the *Directory for the Ministry and Life of Permanent Deacons* of the Congregation for the Clergy, and this *Directory*, especially the post-ordination components.

Formation and post-ordination administration should be distinct

287. The director serves as the bishop's representative in the implementation of the post-ordination path in diaconate formation. He assists the bishop in his supervision of the spiritual and personal welfare of deacons and their families. The duties of the director of deacon personnel, although separate, parallel those of the director of formation. He is not, however, responsible for those in aspirant and candidate formation.[22]

Responsibilities for the director of deacon personnel

288. In most dioceses, the director of deacon personnel fulfills several administrative functions, except that of the spiritual direction of deacons.[23] The director of deacon personnel, together with the deacon's designated pastor or priest supervisor (if the deacon is assigned to an office or agency not directed by a priest), as well as a representative of that office or agency, and the deacon are to be involved in the preparation of the text of the bishop's *decree of appointment*. Further, the director oversees the program for the newly ordained. He also ministers, as delegated by the bishop, to the other deacons in their assigned ministries, conducting regularly scheduled visits with the deacons and their families, reviewing and evaluating diaconal assignments, and making appropriate recommendations to the bishop. He assists the bishop and the deacons' designated pastors in planning and implementing an annual program for diaconate continuing formation. He further assists the bishop and the designated pastors in their pastoral care of deacons

and their families, especially monitoring those living and ministering outside the diocese, or deacons who may be ill or on a ministerial leave of absence. The director of deacon personnel also complements the bishop's presence to and care for retired deacons and their families, as well as to deacon widowers and widows and their families.

289. At the discretion of the diocesan bishop, the director of deacon personnel may be appointed as a liaison to diocesan departments and public agencies, as well as parishes, on diaconal matters.

VIII. Post-Ordination Advisory Structures

Deacon Community Board

290. The bishop may constitute a deacon community board to represent the deacons and their spouses. Members of such an organization would include a suitable number of deacons and wives elected by the diaconal community and others appointed by the bishop, in accordance with the organization's statutes, as approved by the ordinary. The statutes should govern everything that relates to the purposes and operation of the organization. A responsibility of the community board could be the preparation of a deacon personnel handbook, specifying appropriate norms or policies—rights, obligations, and responsibilities—for deacons serving the diocesan Church. The bishop must authorize this text. This board also could assist the bishop in planning, coordinating, and evaluating the post-ordination educational and spiritual formation program. The bishop or a priest designated as the bishop's delegate in his absence serves as the board's president.[24]

Deacon Personnel Board

291. It may be desirable for the diocesan bishop to establish a deacon personnel board to assist him in assigning and evaluating deacons. Its role would be analogous to that of the priests' personnel board, which assists the diocesan bishop in ascertaining appropriate and suitable assignments based on the needs of the particular Church and the capabilities of the individual. The establishment of a deacon personnel board could be a valuable resource to the bishop and director of deacon personnel. If constituted, the bishop or, in his absence, a priest designated by the bishop (e.g., his vicar general, vicar for the clergy) chairs this board. This board should maintain

appropriate links to other diocesan entities to ensure a collaborative and integrative approach to the understanding and use of deacons and diaconal ministry throughout the diocese.

NORMS

1. The diocesan bishop is the one ultimately responsible for the discernment and formation of aspirants and candidates, as well as the pastoral care of deacons. He exercises his responsibility personally, as well as through his director of diaconal formation and the director of deacon personnel whom he has appointed and who are responsible directly to him or, in his absence, to a priest whom he has appointed as his delegate. (267)
2. The director of formation, who must be either a priest or a deacon, is appointed by the diocesan bishop to be head of the diaconate office. He is directly responsible to the bishop. (272)
3. The bishop may set up a formation policy board to assist him and the director of formation in matters of diaconal formation. (283)
4. The director of spiritual formation, who must be a priest, is nominated by the director of formation. He is approved and appointed by the bishop. He personally oversees the spiritual formation of each participant and provides an orientation to other spiritual directors, who must also be priests and who may be chosen by the aspirants or candidates with the approval of the bishop. (274)
5. The coordinator for pastoral formation, who corresponds to "the pastor (or other minister)" required by the *Basic Norms for the Formation of Permanent Deacons* of the Congregation for Catholic Education, is nominated by the director of formation.[25] He is approved and appointed by the bishop. (276)
6. Faculty members are nominated by the director of formation and then approved and appointed by the bishop. (278)
7. Mentors for aspirants and candidates, who are to be knowledgeable and competent to assist the director of formation, are nominated from among priests and deacons by the director of formation. They also are approved and appointed by the bishop. Mentors are charged with closely following the formation of those committed to their care, offering support and encouragement. (281)

8. If a distance-learning model is incorporated into the diocesan formation program, it is the responsibility of the diocesan bishop to verify that the course of study offered fulfills the requirements of this *Directory*. It must be complete, be in harmony with magisterial teaching, and be taught by a competent instructor. (265)
9. The diocesan bishop should appoint a director of deacon personnel, who should be either a priest or a deacon. At the discretion of the diocesan bishop, the director of deacon personnel serves as the bishop's representative in directing the post-ordination path of formation and assists the bishop in the supervision of diocesan deacons. This director also coordinates the program for the newly ordained deacons. (286-289)

NOTES

1 PDG (1984), no. 52.

2 Some of the specific responsibilities would include the following:

Collaboration

i Involvement of and accountability to the diocesan bishop

ii Relationship with diocesan offices, departments, and agencies; linkage with other ministry preparation programs in the diocese

iii Liaison with pastors, priests, religious, and laity

iv Relationship with regional and national diaconate associations and organizations

Planning

i Appointment, readiness, and supervision of appropriate personnel to carry out the diaconal formation plan/activities

ii Initial and ongoing catechesis of the diaconate

iii Integrate diaconal ministry into the local Church

Policy Development

i Development of policies and procedures for recruitment, screening, and admissions

ii Development of policies and procedures for evaluation of those in formation

iii Development of the program, taking account of concrete needs and local circumstances

Post-Ordination Activities

i Development of policies and procedures for diocesan diaconal life

ii Support structures for deacons, deacon spouses, and families

iii Policies/procedures for assignment and review of deacons

iv Continuing formation and spiritual formation policies and program opportunities

v Regular assessment of diaconal ministry in the diocese

3 Congregation for Catholic Education and the Congregation for the Clergy, *Joint Study of the U.S. Draft Document—National Directory for the Formation, Ministry and Life of Permanent Deacons in the United States*, Prot. No. 78/2000 (March 4, 2002).

4 Cf. Congregation for the Clergy, *General Directory for Catechesis* (August 15, 1998) (Washington, D.C.: United States Conference of Catholic Bishops-Libreria Editrice Vaticana, 1998), no. 160.

5 The Congregation for the Clergy offers its web site to assist in the continuing formation of priests, deacons, and catechists. The web site provides a library on the magisterial teachings of the Sovereign Pontiffs, with recent documentation from the Holy Father, Church Fathers, Sacred Writings; it provides links to several theological libraries; live teleconferences or documentation from the teleconferences on Christology, Ecclesiology, Sacramental and Moral Theology, Mariology, Pneumatology; Statistical information on diocesan, religious priests, and deacons; as well as an e-mail option for updated information on future offerings.

6 BNFPD, no. 19.

7 Ibid., no. 16; cf. also nos. 21, 42, 44, 62; cf. DMLPD, nos. 3, 78, 80.

8 Ibid., no. 19.

9 Ibid., no. 21.

10 Ibid.

11 Ibid., no. 23.

12 PDV, no. 57; cf. BNFPD, no. 85.

13 "It is the intention of our Dicasteries that the variety of offices in diaconal formation and post-ordination ministry: the Director of the Formation Program, the Coordinator for Pastoral Formation, Mentors, the Director of Deacon Personnel should be reserved to clerics —and in the case of the Director of Spiritual Formation (an office not mentioned in the *Ratio fundamentalis*), Pastors and Priest Pastoral Supervisors, they must be a priest." Congregation for Catholic Education and the Congregation for the Clergy, *Joint Study of the US Draft Document—National Directory for the Formation, Ministry and Life of Permanent Deacons in the United States*, Prot. No. 78/2000 (March 4, 2002).

14 Ibid., no. 24.

15 Congregation for Catholic Education, *Directives Concerning the Preparation of Seminary Educators* (November 4, 1993) (Washington, D.C.: United States Catholic Conference, 1994), pp. 5-6.

16 The following considerations are this *Directory*'s commentaries on the criteria for faculty selections as established by the Congregation for Catholic Education:

i A *spirit of faith*: A lived commitment to the Church, its Magisterium, and the deposit of faith accompanied and sustained by a love of prayer—the educator who lives by faith teaches more by what he is than by what he says

ii A *pastoral sense*: A commitment to the pastoral-theological vision of the Second Vatican Council and to the identity and mission of diaconal ministry that the council and post-conciliar documents promote in the contemporary Church; a sensitivity also from their own participation in the pastoral charity of Christ

iii A *spirit of communion*: Collaboration and understanding of their role in the vocational discernment for admission to candidacy and ordination to the diaconate

iv *Human maturity and psychological equilibrium*: A right consciousness of oneself, of one's own values and limits, honestly recognized and accepted

v A *clear and mature capacity to love*: An ability to be an example and model of the primacy of love in service—a capacity and inclination to self-giving attention to the other person, to an understanding of his concerns, and to a clear perception of his real good

vi *Listening, dialogue, and the capacity for communication*: The success of the formational relationship depends in great part on these three capacities

vii *Positive and critical attention to modern culture*: Inspired by the cultural richness of Christianity (i.e., rooted in biblical, liturgical, and patristic sources), a broad knowledge of contemporary culture—a positive and critical awareness of the transmission of contemporary culture, making it easier to enable students to form an interior synthesis in the light of faith.

Following are some additional criteria:

i *Academic qualifications*: An advanced degree in theology, religious studies, or a related field; a demonstrated ability as a competent teacher

ii *Multicultural sensitivity*: Experience with multicultural, gender, economic, and educational diversity

iii *Adult formation*: Ability to teach adults in theory and practice; knowledge and experience in adult developmental theory and methodologies

iv *Diversity*: Represent the ethnicity, racial, and cultural diversity of the diocesan Church

v *Knowledge and experience of the diaconate*: Knowledge of the identity and ministry of deacons in the Church

17 Regarding the selection of textbooks, faculty presenters should be familiar with the USCCB's *Guidelines for Doctrinally Sound Catechetical Materials* (Washington, D.C.: United States Catholic Conference, 1990). The following excerpts from that document are provided here for easier accessibility to several highlights of the text:

The first principle of doctrinal soundness is that the Christian message be *authentic* and *complete*. For expressions of faith and moral teachings to be authentic, they must be in harmony with the doctrine and traditions of the Catholic Church, which are safeguarded by the bishops who teach with a unique authority. For completeness, the message of salvation, which is made up of several parts that are closely interrelated, must, in due course, be presented in its entirety, with an eye to leading individuals and communities to maturity of faith. Completeness also implies that individual parts be presented in a balanced way, according to the capacity of the learners and in the context of a particular doctrine. (p. 7)

The second principle in determining the doctrinal soundness of catechetical materials is the recognition that the mystery of faith is *incarnate* and *dynamic* [and that the discourse of faith with adults must take serious account of their experience, of their conditioning, and of the challenges which they encounter in life]. The mystery of the divine plan for human salvation, revealed in the person of Jesus Christ and made known in the Sacred Scriptures, continues as a dynamic force in the world through the power of the Holy Spirit until finally all things are made subject to Christ and the kingdom is handed over to the Father "so that God may be all in all" (1 Cor 15:28). God's creative power is mediated in the concrete experiences of life, in personal development, in human relationships, in culture, in social life, in science and technology, and in "signs of the times." The *National Catechetical Directory* refers to the Scriptures, the teaching life and witness of the Church, the Church's liturgical life, and life experiences of various kinds as "signs of God's saving activity" in the world (NCD [*Sharing the Light of Faith: National Catechetical Directory for Catholics in the United States* (1979)], 42). These biblical, ecclesial, liturgical, and natural signs should inform the content and spirit of all catechetical materials. (p. 7)

A second set of guidelines—no less important than the first if catechesis is to be effective—are based on pastoral principles and practical concerns. They are reminders that catechetical materials must take into account the community for whom they are intended, the conditions in which they live, and the ways in which they learn (cf. GCD [*General Catechetical Directory* (1971)], Foreword). . . . Catechetical materials [must] take into consideration the needs of the Hispanic community and other ethnic and culturally diverse groups that comprise the Church in the United States. No single text or program can address the many cultures and groups that make up society in the United States, but all catechetical materials must take this diversity into account. Effective catechesis, as we have noted above, requires that the Church's teaching be presented correctly and in its entirety, and it is equally important to present it in ways that are attractive, appealing, and understandable by the individuals and communities to whom it is directed. (p. 23)

18 BNFPD, no. 22.

19 CL, Enclosure III.

20 DMLPD, no. 80.

21 Cf. BNFPD, no. 21: "could be either a priest or a deacon" is applied equivalently in this *Directory* to that of the director of deacon personnel. Cf., also, footnote no. 12, above.

22 Ibid.

23 Ibid.

24 DMLPD, no. 80.

25 BNFPD, no. 24.

CONCLUSION

292. It is the desire of the United States Conference of Catholic Bishops that, as implemented in accord with local or regional resources, this *Directory* will provide a sure directive for promoting harmony and unity in diaconal formation and ministry throughout the United States and its territorial sees. In so doing, this *Directory* will ensure a certain uniformity in the identity, selection, and formation of deacons, as well as provide for more clearly defined pastoral objectives in diaconal ministries.

293. This *Directory* is presented to the diaconal communities in the United States as a tangible expression of the Conference's gratitude to them for their dedicated ministry to God's People. It is also intended to challenge and encourage them to be, with greater dedication and clarity, the sacrament of Jesus—the Servant Christ to a servant Church.